With Perfect Faith

The Foundations of Jewish Belief

With Perfect Faith

The Foundations of Jewish Belief

Edited with Introductions by
J. David Bleich

Ktav Publishing House, Inc.
New York, New York

Library of Congress Cataloging in Publication Data

Main entry under title:

With perfect faith.

Selections from works originally published in Hebrew, translated into English.
Includes bibliographical references.
1. Thirteen articles of faith (Judaism)—History of doctrines—Sources. 2. Philosophy, Jewish—History—Sources. 3. Philosophy, Medieval—History—Sources.
I. Bleich, J. David.
BM607.W53 1982 296.1'7 82-21156
ISBN 0-87068-891-X
ISBN 0-87068-452-3 (pbk.)

MANUFACTURED IN THE UNITED STATES OF AMERICA

Dedicated
to the memory of
my wife's revered grandfather
ר׳ שמואל יצחק ב״ר צבי מרדכי רייך ז״ל
whose life was an expression
of perfect faith

How great is faith before He who spoke and the world came to be! . . . The dispersed are ingathered solely in the merit of faith; similarly, our fathers were redeemed from Egypt solely in the merit of faith; even Abraham inherited this world and the world-to-come solely in the merit of the faith which he professed. What does Scripture say of masters of faith? "Open ye the gates, that the righteous nation which keeps the faith may enter" (Isaiah 26:2).

Yalkut Hosea, 519

Table of Contents

Preface

This work is a direct outgrowth of a course in Jewish philosophy which I taught at Yeshiva University over a period of years. The syllabus was structured thematically around Maimonides' Thirteen Principles. I found myself greatly hampered by the lack of a suitable textbook and the unavailability in English translation of many of the required readings. I also discovered quite rapidly how unrealistic it was to assign material in as many as a dozen or so different works, some of which were out of print.

The present endeavor is an attempt to bring together in one volume representative selections from the writings of major medieval Jewish philosophers as they relate to crucial areas of Jewish belief. To this end I prevailed upon a number of colleagues to translate materials which heretofore were unavailable in English. I am particularly grateful to Professor Menachem Marc Kellner for his translation of a section of Abravanel's *Rosh Amanah*; to Professor Norbert Max Samuelson for his translation of a section of Ibn Daud's *Emunah Ramah*; to Professor Seymour Feldman for his translation of a portion of Crescas' *Or ha-Shem*; to Rabbi Ephraim Kanarfogel for his translation of a responsum of R. Isaac ben Sheshet; and to Dr. Eugene Korn for his translation of a section of Naḥmanides' *Sha'ar ha-Gemul.* I am also grateful to Professor David Wolf Silverman and to Professor Warren Zev Harvey for permission to use material from their respective unpublished works on Gersonides and Crescas. I also wish to express my personal thanks to Professor Alexander Altmann, Rabbi Charles B. Chavel, Dr. Fred Rosner, and Professor Norbert M. Samuelson for permission to reprint selections from their published works.

Professor Kellner undertook the translation of the herein included selection from Abravanel's *Rosh Amanah* at my invitation and made it available for publication in this volume. It is gratifying to note that Professor Kellner has now completed the translation of *Rosh Amanah* and that this work has been published by Associated Universities Press (London, 1981) under the title *Principles of Faith (Rosh Amanah).*

I am particularly gratified to be able to include large sections of Isaac Husik's *Sefer ha-Ikkarim* which has long been out of print. Morais' translation of Maimonides' *Ma'amar Teḥiyat ha-Metim* is reprinted with mixed feelings. This material was originally serialized in *The Jewish Messenger*, 1859, nos. 11–15. As a translation it leaves much to be desired, but as yet no other English version is available. The notes, which are few in number, were omitted because, in the editor's opinion, they are not particularly helpful.

In a number of cases other translations were available which are clearly superior to those here presented. Professor Shlomo Pines' translation of Maimonides' *Moreh Nevukhim* is an obvious example. Regrettably, I was unable to use this translation because of copyright considerations. The footnotes to the Friedlander translation have been omitted. Should the reader be prompted to pursue a difficult point he would be well advised to consult the Pines translation. There is additional valuable material in Samuel Rosenblatt's translation of Saadia's *Emunot ve-De'ot* and in the Yale Judaica translation of Maimonides' *Mishneh Torah*, which would have been included but for the same considerations. I would also have been pleased to include selections from Professor Seymour Feldman's forthcoming translation of Gersonides' *Milḥamot ha-Shem*. The publisher was understandably reluctant to authorize use of material from a work still in press.

I wish to express my appreciation to my esteemed friend and colleague, Rabbi Joseph Grunblatt, for his valuable comments and suggestions. I owe a special debt of gratitude to David M. L. Olivestone for his painstaking and arduous work in every stage of the preparation of the manuscript. My appreciation also to Mr. Bernard Scharfstein of Ktav Publishing House for the cooperative spirit with which he assumed the particular difficulties associated with the publication of this volume and to Mr. Irving Ruderman for his painstaking efforts in shepherding the manuscript through the various stages of publication.

Note on the Use of This Book

In order to preserve the editorial integrity of each individual selection, no attempt has been made to make either the transliteration or the bibliographical citations uniform. Footnotes have been renumbered where necessary in order to avoid confusion. Page references and references to previously cited works are pages and citations in the translator's published volume rather than in the present work. Occasionally, footnotes have been added by the editor. These appear within square brackets and bear the editor's initials.

The usual indices have been omitted due to the nature of this book. The interested reader will readily find further bibliographical information in the works from which these readings were selected and in standard histories of Jewish philosophy.

Acknowledgments

Grateful acknowledgment is made for permission to reprint selections from the following:

Albo, Joseph, *Book of Principles,* trans. by Isaac Husik, Philadelphia: Jewish Publication Society, 1946.

Baḥya ibn Pakuda, *Duties of the Heart,* trans. by Moses Hyamson, Jerusalem: Boys Town Jerusalem Publishers, 1965. Reprinted by permission of Feldheim Publishers Ltd., Jerusalem—New York.

Bleich, J. David, *Providence in the Philosophy of Gersonides,* New York: Yeshiva University Press, 1973.

Gersonides, *The Wars of the Lord, Treatise Three; On God's Knowledge,* trans. by Norbert M. Samuelson, Toronto: Pontifical Institute of Mediaeval Studies, 1977. Reprinted by permission of the translator.

Halevi, Judah, *The Kuzari,* trans. by Hartwig Hirschfeld, and with an introduction by Henry Slonimsky, © 1964 by Schocken Books Inc., New York: Schocken Books Inc., 1964.

Maimonides, Moses, *Commentary on the Mishnah, Introduction to Ḥelek,* trans. by J. Abelson, *Jewish Quarterly Review,* o.s. XIX (1907), reprinted by Ktav, 1966, pp. 28–58.

Maimonides, Moses, *Commentary on the Mishnah: Introduction to Seder Zeraim,* trans. by Fred Rosner, New York: Feldheim Publishers Ltd., 1975.

Maimonides, Moses, *A Discourse on the Resurrection of the Dead,* trans. by Sabato Morais, *The Jewish Messenger,* 1859, nos. 11–15.

Maimonides, Moses, *The Guide of the Perplexed,* trans. by M. Friedländer, New York: Hebrew Publishing Co., n.d.

Maimonides, Moses, *Mishneh Torah, The Book of Judges,* trans. by Abraham M. Hershman, New Haven: Yale University Press, 1949.

Maimonides, Moses, *Mishneh Torah, The Book of Knowledge,* trans. by Moses Hyamson, Jerusalem: Boys Town Jerusalem Publishers, 1965. Reprinted by permission of Feldheim Publishers, Ltd., Jerusalem—New York.

Naḥmanides, Moses, *Ramban, Commentary on the Torah, Book of Genesis,* trans. by Charles Chavel, New York: Shilo Publishing House, Inc., 1971. We acknowledge the kind permission of Shilo Publishing House, Inc. to include pp. 226–230 of *Ramban, Commentary on the Torah, Book of Genesis,* translated and annotated by Rabbi Dr. Charles B. Chavel.

Saadia, *Book of Doctrines and Beliefs,* trans. by Alexander A. Altmann, Oxford: East and West Library, 1946. Reprinted by permission of Hebrew Publishing Co.

General Introduction

Faith and Dogma in Judaism

One widespread misconception concerning Judaism is the notion that Judaism is a religion which is not rooted in dogma. The view that Judaism has no dogmas originated with Moses Mendelssohn[1] and subsequently gained wide currency. In some circles this idea has been maintained with such vigor that it has been somewhat jocularly described as itself constituting the "dogma of dogmalessness." Nevertheless, even a superficial acquaintance with the classical works of Jewish philosophy is sufficient to dispel this misconceived notion. To be sure, membership in the community of Israel is not contingent upon a formal creedal affirmation. This, however, does not imply that members of the community of Israel are free to accept or to reject specific articles of faith. Birth as a Jew carries with it unrenounceable obligations and responsibilities, intellectual as well as ritual.

While great stress is placed upon fulfillment of commandments and performance of good deeds, it is a gross error to assume that this stress is accompanied by a diminution of obligations with regard to belief. It is certainly true that lessened concern with explication of the dogmas of Judaism was evidenced during certain periods of Jewish history. This, however, was the result of an unquestioning acceptance of basic principles of faith rather than of disparagement of the role of dogma. In some epochs formulations of essential beliefs were composed by foremost thinkers as a corrective measure designed to rectify this lack of attention; in other ages endeavors designed to explicate the dogmas of Judaism constituted a reaction to creedal formulations on the part of other religions.

The importance of correct belief as a religious obligation is stressed in particular in the writings of Baḥya ibn Pakuda. In the introduction to his widely acclaimed *Ḥovot ha-Levavot* (properly translated as *Duties of*

[1] See his "Betrachtungen über Bonnets Palingenesie," *Gesammelte Schriften*, III (Berlin, 1843), 159–166.

the Intellect rather than *Duties of the Heart*[2]), Baḥya wrote that the Torah demands of man that he acquire the knowledge requisite for fulfillment of the obligations of the intellect, just as it makes demands of him with regard to fulfillment of the obligations of the physical organs. Nevertheless, he found that his predecessors had devoted themselves in their writings to the discussion and detailed clarification of "duties of the organs" but had neglected to set forth systematically the principles pertaining to the "duties of the intellect" and their ramifications. *Ḥovot Ha-Levavot* was composed to fill this lacuna.

The role of dogma as the fulcrum of Judaism was most dramatically highlighted by Maimonides. His *magnum opus,* the *Mishneh Torah,* is devoted to a codification of Jewish law. Yet the opening section of this work is entitled *Hilkhot Yesodei ha-Torah* ("Laws of the Foundations of the Torah") and includes a detailed presentation of Jewish belief together with unequivocal statements declaring acceptance of those beliefs to be binding upon all Jews. Dogma, then, does not stand apart from the normative demands of Judaism but is the *sine qua non* without which other values and practices are bereft of meaning. By incorporating this material in his *Mishneh Torah,* Maimonides demonstrated that basic philosophical beliefs are not simply matters of intellectual curiosity but constitute a branch of *Halakhah.* By placing them at the very beginning of this monumental work he demonstrated that they constitute the most fundamental area of Jewish law. In Judaism, profession of faith is certainly no less significant than overt actions. Contrary to the dictum of Moses Mendelssohn, Judaism imposes obligations not only with regard to action but with regard to religious belief as well.

Baḥya demonstrates the existence and the binding nature of obligations incumbent upon the intellect, not simply on the basis of Scripture and tradition, but on the basis of reason as well. Reason dictates that the heart and mind, the choicest and most unique elements of human existence, should not be exempt from obligations imposed in the service of God. The manifold references in Scripture to man's duty to love God and, moreover, the very existence of a biblical code establishing rules of conduct for mankind implies the existence of a divine lawgiver. While in his *Sefer ha-Miẓvot* Maimonides cites the verse "I am the Lord your God who has brought you out of the land of Egypt" (Exodus 20:2) as constituting the first in his list of 613 commandments, i.e., belief in the existence of a Deity, others among his predecessors failed to do so, not

[2] In medieval usage the heart is frequently spoken of as the seat of knowledge and the word *lev* is used as a synonym for "intellect."

because they did not feel belief in God to be incumbent upon each Jew, but because they viewed such belief to be already assumed by, and hence outside of, a system of commandments. There can be no commandment without one who commands. As Baḥya puts it, there can be no fulfillment of physical duties without assent of the mind. Accordingly, acceptance of obligatory commandments presumes antecedent acceptance of the existence and authority of God.

Naḥmanides pursues this argument to its logical conclusion by declaring that a heretic need not anticipate reward even for meritorious deeds which he has performed. In the introduction to his commentary on the Book of Job, Naḥmanides writes, "There is no merit in the actions of the evil persons who deny God . . . even if they comport themselves in accordance with beautiful and good traits all their days," and proceeds to query how it is possible for them to be the recipients of any form of beneficence. A noted talmudic scholar, the late Rabbi Elchanan Wasserman, although apparently unaware of Naḥmanides' comments, categorizes the fulfillment of a commandment on the part of an unbeliever as *mitasek*, an unmeditated, thoughtless performance devoid of religious significance.[3] Commandments, regardless of their intrinsic rationality, are binding and significant in the theological sense only because they constitute the fulfillment of a divine command. Thus, not only the existence of God but also the authenticity of revelation as a historical event and the divinity of the entire corpus of Torah are inherent even in those moments of Judaism which concern themselves with action and conduct rather than belief.

To be sure, the formal promulgation of a creed of faith is unknown in Judaism. By the same token, official synods for the comprehensive codification of the laws and regulations governing ceremonial obligations or other areas of human conduct are also virtually unknown to Judaism. Within Judaism, *Halakhah* is hardly monolithic in nature. "Judges and bailiffs shall you appoint for yourselves in all your gates" (Deut. 16:18), commands the Torah. Each community possesses not only the authority but also the obligation to appoint ecclesiastical authorities. In all matters of doubt or dispute their decisions are binding upon all who are subject to their authority. Only when local authorities were unable to resolve a complex question was the question referred to the Great Court sitting in Jerusalem, whose decision was binding upon all of Israel. Inevitably, divergent practices arose in different locales. With the redaction of the Mishnah, and later of the Gemara, binding decisions were

[3] *Kovez̧ Ma'amarim* (Jerusalem, 1963), no. 11, sec. 14.

promulgated with regard to many matters of *Halakhah* which served to establish normative practices in areas which previously had been marked by diversity born of dispute. This, of course, did not preclude subsequent disagreement with regard to other questions which had not been expressly resolved.

Since matters of belief are inherently matters of *Halakhah*, it is not at all surprising that disagreements exist with regard to substantive matters of belief just as is the case in other areas of Jewish law. Thus, while there is unanimity among all rabbinic authorities with regard to the existence of a body of Jewish law which is binding in nature with respect to matters of faith, there is considerable disagreement of opinion with regard to precisely which beliefs are binding and which are not, as well as, in some instances, substantive matters of faith.

The concept of the Messiah is one example of a fundamental principle of belief concerning which, at one point in Jewish history, there existed a legitimate divergence of opinion, since resolved normatively. The Gemara, *Sanhedrin* 99a, cites the opinion of the Amora, Rav Hillel, who asserted, "There is no Messiah for Israel." Rashi modifies the literal reading of this dictum by explaining that Rav Hillel did not deny the ultimate redemption of Israel but asserted, rather, that the redemption will be the product of direct divine intervention without the intermediacy of a human agent. Nevertheless, Rav Hillel certainly denied that reestablishment of the monarchy and restoration of the Davidic dynasty are essential components of the process of redemption. Rabbi Moses Sofer quite cogently points out that were such views to be held by a contemporary Jew he would be branded a heretic.[4] Yet, the advancement of this opinion by one of the sages of the Talmud carried with it no theological odium. The explanation is quite simple. Before the authoritative formulation of the *Halakhah* with regard to this belief, Rav Hillel's opinion could be entertained. Following the resolution of the conflict in a manner which negates this theory, normative *Halakhah* demands acceptance of the belief that the redemption will be effected through the agency of a mortal messiah. As is true with regard to other aspects of Jewish law, the Torah "is not in Heaven" (Deut. 30:12) and hence halakhic disputes are resolved in accordance with canons of law which are themselves part of the Oral Law.

Certainly, there remain many points regarding various articles of faith which have not been formally resolved by the sages of the Talmud. Indeed, in subsequent periods controversies did arise with regard to sig-

[4] *Teshuvot Ḥatam Sofer, Yoreh De'ah,* no. 356.

nificant theological issues, such as, for example, the nature of providence and freedom of the will. In the absence of a definitive ruling, the question which presents itself is, would the exponent of a certain view with regard to any of these matters consider an opponent and his followers simply to be in error, or would he view them as heretics as well? The answer is itself a matter of *Halakhah* having many ramifications, and, as proves to be the case, is the subject of considerable dispute.

The Mishnah which forms the opening section of the last chapter of *Sanhedrin* posits that all Jews enjoy a share in the world-to-come, but proceeds to exclude from this ultimate reward those who espouse certain heretical doctrines which are then enumerated in the text of the Mishnah. Maimonides' understanding of the underlying principle expressed in the Mishnah is that denial of a share in the world-to-come is not in the nature of punishment for failure to discharge a religious duty, but rather that profession of certain creeds is a necessary condition of immortality. The reason which prompts an individual to deny any specific article of faith is irrelevant. The person who has been misled or who, through error in the syllogistic process, reaches false conclusions, fails to affirm the basic propositions of Jewish faith and hence cannot aspire to the ultimate intellectual reward. This is entirely consistent with Maimonides' view, as will be explained below, that development of the intellect in recognition of fundamental metaphysical truths culminates in the perfection of the intellect and leads naturally to the ability of the soul to participate in the intellectual pleasures of the world-to-come. The nature of these pleasures is such that they simply cannot be apprehended by the totally undeveloped intellect. Thus, attainment of a share in the world-to-come is more in the nature of development of potential than of reward and punishment. Accordingly, the causes and motivating forces which lead either to belief or to nonbelief are irrelevant.

Simeon ben Zemaḥ Duran, who was followed in this matter, by his pupil, Joseph Albo, adopted an opposing view. Duran asserts that intellectual rejection of any doctrine of revelation constitutes heresy. Scripture must be accepted as divinely revealed and the contents of Scripture in their entirety must be acknowledged as absolute truth. Conscious denial of the veracity of any biblical statement constitutes heresy. Nevertheless, for Duran, one who is ignorant or fails to interpret the details of a revealed doctrine correctly may be an unwitting transgressor, but is not to be considered a heretic. For example, it is possible to interpret the biblical narrative concerning the creation of the universe in a manner which assumes the existence of a primordial hylic substance and thus contradicts the doctrine of *creatio ex nihilo*. In fact, there are midrashic statements which, at least on the basis of a superficial reading, seem to support this view; Albo declares that some sages did indeed subscribe to a view akin to the Platonic doctrine of primordial substance.[5] Such an interpretation, while in error, is not heretical, so long as it is not advanced as a knowing contradiction of the biblical account. Thus, man is free to engage in philosophical speculation and is not held culpable if as a result of such endeavors he espouses a false doctrine. False beliefs, if sincerely held as the result of honest error, do not occasion loss of eternal bliss. This position is also assumed by Abraham ben David of Posquières (Rabad) in a gloss to Maimonides' *Mishneh Torah*[6] and received wide circulation through Albo's exposition in his *Sefer ha-Ikkarim.*[7]

In his introduction to *Ḥovot ha-Levavot,* Baḥya seeks to establish, on the basis of reason, that it is entirely logical that God should impose duties upon the intellect. Man is a composite of body and soul, i.e., corporeal substance and intellect. As was to be stressed by later thinkers, it is the intellectual component which is uniquely human and which constitutes the essence of man. The corporeal aspect of man is consecrated to the service of God by virtue of commandments imposed upon, and fulfilled by means of, the physical organs of man. It is to be anticipated that the intellect should also be impressed into the service of God in a like manner through imposition of commandments specifically binding upon the mind.

It is axiomatic that God does not impose obligations which cannot be fulfilled. Quite apart from questions of theodicy which would arise from the imposition of such obligations, it simply does not make sense to speak of an obligation which cannot under any circumstances be discharged. Jewish philosophers have repeatedly stressed that God cannot command man to accept the illogical or the irrational. The human intellect, no matter how much it may desire to do so, cannot affirm the absurd. Man may, if prompted by a sufficiently compelling reason, postulate the existence of unicorns or mermaids, but he cannot affirm the existence of a geometric object which is at one and the same time endowed with the properties of both a square and a circle. He cannot fathom the concept of a square circle, much less affirm the ontological existence of such an object.

Propositions which constitute objects of belief must, then, first and

[5] *Sefer ha-Ikkarim,* Book I, chap. 2.
[6] *Hilkhot Teshuvah* 3:7.
[7] Book I, chap. 2.

foremost do no violence to human credulity. They must be readily apprehended and accepted by human thought. Yet belief implies more than hypothesization. Belief connotes unequivocal affirmation of that which is regarded as certain, rather than speculative postulation of the contingent. The latter is compatible with a state of doubt; the former is not. And herein lies a dilemma: the intellect need not be commanded to recognize the possible. An open, honest, and inquiring mind must of necessity recognize the ontological contingency of that which is affirmed by any proposition which does not violate the canons of logic. Recognition of the contingent nature of such propositions need not at all be commanded and does not constitute belief. Belief, by virtue of its very nature, entails positive affirmation of the veracity of a proposition. But how can intellectual certainty be commanded? Certainty is a psychological state of mind. It would appear that such certainty is either present or it is absent. If present, the commandment to believe is superfluous; if absent, the commandment to believe poses an obligation which cannot be fulfilled.

This paradox is presented and discussed forthrightly in the essay by Rabbi Elchanan Wasserman cited above.[8] Rabbi Wasserman's thesis is that an unbiased and unimpeded mind cannot escape an awareness and affirmation of the existence of a Creator. The Midrash presents what is probably the oldest, and certainly one of the most eloquent, formulations of the argument from design. A heretic approached Rabbi Akiva and asked him, "Who created the universe?" R. Akiva answered, "The Holy One, blessed be He." Thereupon, the heretic demanded a demonstrative proof that this was indeed so. R. Akiva responded by posing a question of his own: "Who wove your coat?" he inquired of the heretic. "A weaver," replied the latter. "Present me a demonstrative proof!" demanded Rabbi Akiva. The exchange concludes with R. Akiva's simple but forceful formulation of the teleological argument. Addressing his students, he declared: "Just as the garment testifies to [the existence of] the weaver, just as the door testifies to [the existence of] the carpenter, and just as the house testifies to [the existence of] the builder, so does the universe testify to [the existence of] the Holy One, blessed be He, who created it."[9]

A different version of the teleological argument is recorded by Baḥya with the comment that experience teaches that intelligent writing never

[8] *Loc. cit.*, secs. 1–7.

[9] *Midrash Temurah*, chap. 3, published in *Bet ha-Midrash*, ed. Adolf Jellinek, I (Leipzig, 1853), 114, and in *Oẓar ha-Midrashim*, ed. J. D. Eisenstein (New York, 1915), II, 583.

results from overturning an inkwell onto a piece of paper.[10] To put it in a different idiom, the mathematical odds militating against the probability that a chimpanzee seated at a typewriter might peck at the keys in a random manner and in the process produce the collected works of Shakespeare are so great as to render the prospect preposterous. Baḥya categorizes one who seriously entertains such a belief as either a simpleton or a lunatic. Yet, on the cosmic level, there are many who find it possible to dismiss evidence of intelligence and design and to attribute the ordered nature of the universe to random causes.

Rabbi Wasserman endeavors to explain this denial by pointing to the stated consideration underlying the prohibition against bribery. This prohibition is not limited to accepting a bribe for purposes of favoring one litigant over another. Such conduct is independently forbidden by the injunction "Thou shalt not bend judgment" (Deut. 16:19). The prohibition against bribe-taking encompasses even instances in which the gift is presented on the express condition that a lawful and just verdict be issued. It also applies to situations in which both the plaintiff and the defendant present the judge with gifts of equal value. And the prohibition stands no matter how upright and incorruptible the judge might be. The reason for this extreme and all-encompassing ban is spelled out clearly in Scripture: "For a bribe blinds those who have sight and perverts the words of the righteous" (Exodus 23:8).

A judge, if he is to be entirely objective, must remain detached and emotionally uninvolved in the controversy between the litigants who appear before him. Justice is assured only when evidence can be examined in a cool and dispassionate manner. Human emotions cloud judgment. No matter how honest and objective a person may strive to be, once personal interests are introduced, objectivity is compromised. Receipt of a favor creates a bond of friendship. When a judge receives a gift from a litigant, the litigant's concern becomes, in a measure, that of the judge himself. When he accepts gifts from both parties, the concerns of both become his concerns, and he can no longer dispassionately adjudicate between competing claims solely on the basis of evidence and applicable law. The Torah testifies that all men are affected in this way at least to some extent.

All of mankind, points out Rabbi Wasserman, is subject to a subtle form of bribery. With the pleasure experienced in imbibing mother's milk, we begin to enjoy sensual gratification. Pleasure is addictive in nature; our desire for pleasure is, in a very real sense, insatiable. The

[10] *Ḥovot ha-Levavot, Sha'ar ha-Yiḥud*, chap. 6.

need for gratification is very real, very human, and very constant.

Recognition of the existence of the Deity entails acknowledgment of His authority over us. Acceptance of other cardinal beliefs entails an awareness that our freedom to seek pleasure may be drastically curtailed. As beneficiaries of the gift of sensual gratification even before attaining the age of reason, human beings are never capable of entirely dispassionate analysis of the evidence substantiating basic religious beliefs. The sages put it succinctly in their statement, "Israel engaged in idol worship solely in order to permit themselves public licentiousness."[11] Worship of pagan gods surely involves an ideological commitment. Yet, psychologically speaking, the sages testify, intellectual conviction did not serve as the impetus for idolatry. Rather, the acknowledgment of pagan gods on the part of the worshippers of the golden calf was born of a desire for unbridled sexual gratification. Passion prevented a reasoned adjudication between the claims of idolatrous cults and monotheistic belief. Man is a logical animal; he finds it difficult to lead a life of self-contradiction. It is hard for him to accept certain concepts intellectually and then to act in a manner inconsistent with those affirmed principles. Denial of basic theological principles prevents such contradictions from arising. Certainly man has strong, albeit unconscious, motives for such denial. It is Rabbi Wasserman's thesis that many non-believers close themselves off from faith-commitments in order to avoid tension between a desire for untrammeled sensual gratification and ackowledgment of divinely imposed restraints.

The notion of a commandment concerning belief can be understood in a different manner on the basis of a statement of Hananiah Kazis, contained in his *Kinat Soferim,* one of the classic commentaries on Maimonides' *Sefer ha-Mizvot.*[12] *Kinat Soferim* understands the commandment affirming the existence of God as bidding us to disseminate knowledge of God's existence and to impart the knowledge upon which this belief is predicated to future generations. His argument is both conceptual and textual. The community of Israel which experienced a beatific vision of God at Mount Sinai did not need to be commanded to believe in Him; they *knew* Him. Moreover, the preamble to the Decalogue, "And God spoke all these words, *saying*" (Exodus 20:1), employs the Hebrew term *leimor.* In rabbinic exegesis, this term is customarily understood as meaning not simply "saying," but connoting that the person addressed is bidden "to say," that is, to convey to others the information which fol-

[11] *Sanhedrin* 63b.

[12] *Miẓvot aseh,* no. 1.

lows. Most frequently, this formula is employed in reporting that God addressed Moses bidding him to convey divine commandments to the Children of Israel. In light of the tradition which teaches that the first two commandments of the Decalogue were not transmitted to the assembled populace by Moses but were received by them directly from God,[13] the use of the term *leimor* in this context seems incongruous. *Kinat Soferim* argues that the connotation of the phrase in this instance is that those to whom the commandment was addressed were instructed to convey this information to succeeding generations for all of eternity. The commandment, then, is to *teach* in order that belief be possible.

Extending this concept, it certainly seems feasible to understand that the commandment as formulated delineates the *telos,* or goal, to which man is commanded to aspire. Although belief itself, while obligatory, cannot be commanded, nevertheless, activities through which belief is acquired may properly constitute the object of divine commandment. Thus, in defining the commandment, "And you shall love the Lord, your God" (Deut. 6:5), Maimonides writes: "One only loves God with the knowledge with which one knows Him. According to the knowledge will be the love. If the former be little, the latter will be little; if the former be much, the latter will be much. Therefore, a person must devote himself to the understanding and comprehension of those sciences and studies which will inform him concerning his Master, as far as is the power within man to understand and comprehend, as indeed we have explained in the Laws of the Foundations of the Torah."[14]

Baḥya also posits an obligation to engage in philosophical investigation directed to the rational demonstration of the objects of belief: ". . . Scripture expressly bids you to reflect and exercise your intellect on such themes. After you have attained knowledge of them by the method of tradition which covers all the precepts of the law, their principles and details, you should investigate them with your reason, understanding, and judgment, till the truth becomes clear to you and false notions dispelled; as it is written, 'Know this day and lay it to your heart that the Lord, He is God' (Deut. 4:39)."

Man is endowed with the capacity for knowledge and, hence, for belief. To state this is not at all to assume that the task is a facile one or that faith is immediately within the grasp of man. The hasidic sage, Rabbi Menaḥem Mendel of Kotzk, explained the matter by means of an allegory. God prepares a ladder by means of which souls descend from

[13] *Makkot* 24a.
[14] *Hilkhot Teshuvah* 10:6.

heaven to earth. The soul alights from the ladder and steps upon the ground. The ladder is immediately withdrawn and a voice calls out to the soul bidding it to return. Some souls do not even attempt what appears to be an impossible task. Some jump and fall; becoming disillusioned, they make no further attempt. Others try and try again, leaping time after time, refusing to become discouraged, until God Himself draws them nigh to Him. "You must understand," concluded the Rabbi of Kotzk, "that God does not extend mercy on the basis of a single leap!"[15] Judaism does not teach that God requires of man a "leap of faith" in the Kierkegaardian sense, i.e., blind faith to the extent of acceptance of the absurd. It teaches, rather, that God's beneficence assures man that his diligence and perseverance will ultimately lead to understanding and intellectual satisfaction.

Every age has witnessed the presence of both believers and doubters. Intellectual doubt and the questioning of fundamental beliefs have always been present in one form or another. It is nevertheless axiomatic that man has the ability to rise above such inner conflict and to experience faith. A just and beneficent God could not demand belief without bestowing upon man the capacity for faith. Abiding belief must, however, be firmly rooted in knowledge. Study has the unique effect of dispelling doubt. There is a story of a group of Jewish students in Berlin during the *Haskalah* period who, as a result of their encounter with secular society, began to experience religious doubts. Questioning the faith claims of Judaism, they were on the verge of rejecting fundamental theological beliefs. But before making a final break with Judaism they resolved to send one of their company to the Yeshiva of Volozhin, which at the time was the foremost Torah center of the world, to determine whether or not there existed satisfactory answers to the questions which troubled them. The young man to whom they delegated this task spent a period of time as a student in the Yeshiva and immersed himself completely in that institution's program of studies. Upon his return to Berlin he was met by his friends, who eagerly awaited his report. The young man described his experiences and related that he had never before experienced such intellectual delight. "But," they demanded, "have you brought answers to the questions which we formulated?" "No," he replied. "I have brought no answers—but the questions no longer plague me."

Centuries ago the sages provided an explanation for this phenomenon. They depict the Almighty as declaring, "I have created an evil incli-

[15] See Yehudah Leib Lewin, *Bet Koẓk: Ha-Saraf* (Jerusalem, 1958), p. 98.

nation but I have created the Torah as its antidote."[16] With acquisition of Torah knowledge doubt recedes and ultimately dissipates. This is the essence of Jewish belief with regard to the dilemma of faith. "*Ve'idakh perusha; zil gemor*—the rest is explanation; go and study!"

[16] *Kiddushin* 30b; *Sifre, Parshat Eikev* 11:18; see also *Baba Batra* 16a.

Introduction

The Thirteen Principles

INTRODUCTION

Maimonides' Thirteen Principles of Faith are widely regarded as a creedal formulation of Jewish belief. Widespread familiarity with the Thirteen Principles is due, in large measure, to their adaptation and inclusion in the daily prayerbook in two separate forms. Neither of these was composed by Maimonides himself. The *Yigdal* hymn, usually ascribed to Daniel ben Judah of Rome, who lived during the early part of the fourteenth century, occupies a position of prominence near the very beginning of the prayerbook. A second prose form of unknown authorship, composed in the early sixteenth century, is appended at the conclusion of the morning service in many prayerbooks. This addendum, expressed as a first-person affirmation, "I believe with perfect faith . . ." is designed as a personal confession of faith. Both formulations, designed for daily recitation, are necessarily briefer than Maimonides' original version. As abridged versions they not only lack in comprehensiveness but are, at times, inaccurate, insofar as felicity to the original is concerned.[1] Maimonides' own formulation forms an integral part of his *Commentary on the Mishnah,* serving as an introduction to the final chapter of the tractate *Sanhedrin.* The initial Mishnah of this chapter lists the various classes of nonbelievers or heretics who are excluded from everlasting life.

Despite popular acceptance of the Thirteen Principles over the ages as *the* definitive creed of Judaism, Maimonides' endeavor remains a source of perplexity to philosophers and theologians.[2] Some, arguing that all teachings of the Torah are equally binding, contested the very notion of labeling certain specific propositions as "principles" of faith. This was

[1] For an enumeration of the disparities between the *Ani Ma'amin* and Maimonides' own formulation see R. Eleazar Meir Preil, *Ha-Ma'or* (Jerusalem, 5689), p. 13–15.

[2] The notion that the creedal principles of faith are thirteen in number may well be an ancient tradition. R. Avraham ha-Levi Horowitz, *Shnei Luḥot ha-Brit, Sha'ar ha-Otiyyot,* sec. 1, p. 60a, cites a certain prayer ascribed to Rav Tavyomi, one of the talmudic sages, which contains a reference to thirteen principles. R. Avraham Horowitz himself sees an intrinsic connection between Maimonides' Thirteen Principles and the Thirteen Divine Attributes. He maintains that each of these principles may be derived from the corresponding Divine Attribute.

Abravanel's objection as well as that of the kabbalists. Indeed, Maimonides himself, in discussing the divine nature of Torah, the eighth of his Thirteen Principles, stresses that there is no difference between verses such as 'And the sons of Ham were Cush and Miẓrayim and Put and Canaan' (Gen. 10:6), 'And his wife's name was Mehetabel, daughter of Matred' (Gen. 36:39), or 'And Timna was a concubine to Eliphaz' (Gen. 36:12) and verses such as 'I am the Lord thy God' (Exodus 20:2) and 'Hear O Israel the Lord our God the Lord is one' (Deut. 6:4). Each is divinely revealed and incorporated in the Torah at the divine behest. Hence, denial of any of these truths is tantamount to rejection of the Torah itself. In his *Mishneh Torah, Hilkhot Teshuvah* 3:8, Maimonides declares that one who denies divine authorship of even a single word of the Torah or of its explanation and amplification in the Oral Law is a heretic. Thus every proposition embodied in either the Written or Oral Law is, in effect, a principle of faith. In positing the Thirteen Principles Maimonides could not conceivably have intended to convey the impression that Judaism mandates affirmation of only those enumerated articles of faith but permits denial or doubt with regard to others.

Others took exception to Maimonides' enumeration because they found his list to be too detailed and because it contains propositions which they did not regard as fundamental. Both Ḥasdai Crescas and Simeon ben Zemaḥ Duran criticized Maimonides' formulation on this account. Crescas asserted that the list should be limited to six fundamentals, or beliefs, without which Judaism as a religious faith is inconceivable: (1) Cod's knowledge of all created things; (2) divine providence; (3) divine omnipotence; (4) prophecy; (5) freedom of the will; (6) the Torah leads man to his true goal and ultimate happiness. Crescas declared that the existence of God, a concept which includes the notion of unity and incorporeality as well, is in a class by itself and need not be included in this listing because it is logically prior to any enumeration of the fundamentals of Jewish belief.

Simeon ben Zemaḥ Duran maintained that the list can be reduced still further. According to Duran, whose views were adapted and popularized by Joseph Albo in the latter's widely known *Sefer ha-Ikkarim*, the principles of belief are three in number: (1) the existence of God; (2) revelation; (3) reward and punishment. Duran and Albo both maintained that each of these dogmas entails a series of corollaries which can be derived from these three basic principles. The concept of revelation, for example, also includes God's knowledge of particulars; reward and punishment entails individual providence. One cannot deny the conclusion of a valid syllogism without denying the premise upon which it is based. Hence, denial of any of the corollaries implies a denial of the basic principle from which it is derived and is no less heretical than a denial of one of the three enumerated fundamental principles. Thus most of Maimonides' Thirteen Principles may be derived from the three principles to which they are reduced by Duran and Albo. Albo recognized still other beliefs which are a necessary and integral part of Jewish belief and binding upon its adherents. Although these beliefs, which include among others the doctrine of creation, resurrection of the dead and the coming of the Messiah, cannot be derived from the basic principles in a vigorous and demonstrable fashion, they are included within the general framework of these principles. Albo's demonstration that most of the principles enumerated by Maimonides are reducible to three basic fundamental concepts makes it even more difficult to comprehend the purpose underlying Maimonides' formulation and enumeration.

The usual and most facile explanation of the considerations which prompted Maimonides' enumeration of these particular propositions is that he sought to delineate and emphasize those articles of faith which were most frequently subject to question and challenge in the historical period in which he lived. Thus, the doctrine of the unity of God had to be reiterated to counteract the polemics of Christians seeking to establish a scriptural basis for the doctrine of the Trinity; the supremacy of the prophecy of Moses needed to be underscored in order to emphasize the essential point of difference between Judaism and Islam. Formulation of the Thirteen Principles as a creed of faith served both a pedagogic and supportive function. It served to delineate and to teach beliefs which could not be renounced by a professing Jew. Publicization of the Thirteen Principles and their widespread acceptance as the *sine qua non* of Jewish faith meant that no believing Jew might be led astray by ignorance or confusion. Furthermore, their formulation in the nature of a creed served as reinforcement of faith for those finding themselves under relentless pressure to renounce the tenets of Judaism and to adopt the faith of the dominant culture. The Thirteen Principles, when placed against the professions of faith of other religious denominations, is an eloquent denial of religious and theological universalism. The oft-professed thesis that all men serve the same God and that differences of belief pale into insignificance against the backdrop of this underlying truism could no longer function as the opiate dulling the pain of apostasy. Widespread familiarity with the contents of the Thirteen Principles served to reinforce the simple faith of the Jewish populace and became a source of spiritual strength in deflecting theological assault.

Yet another thesis has been propounded which serves to explain

Maimonides' motivation. This explanation has been offered independently by two such disparate personalities as Julius Guttmann, in his *Philosophies of Judaism,*[3] and the late Rabbi Isaac Ze'ev Soloveichik, a prominent Talmudist popularly known as the *Brisker Rav,* in his unpublished lectures as recorded by his students.[4] For Maimonides, knowledge—but knowledge of a very special nature—is man's highest perfection and bliss. This knowledge, or at least a measure or approximation of this knowledge, is also a necessary condition for achieving immortality of the soul. Maimonides (*Guide,* I, 70 and III, 27) accepts the doctrine which teaches that immortality can be achieved only by virtue of actualization of man's intellectual power. Not only is achievement of this knowledge the human *telos,* contemplation of this knowledge in its supreme form is the exclusive activity of the soul in the world-to-come. The statement that "the righteous sit with crowns upon their heads and enjoy the splendor of the *Shekhinah*" (*Berakhot* 17a) is understood by Maimonides as a poetic description of the intellectual bliss associated with ultimate comprehension of the nature of God. Those in the requisite state of perfection savor this intellectual contemplation. Those who in their lifetime do not develop the requisite intellectual powers for such perception are not denied a share in the world-to-come as a stern punishment; they are simply incapable of its enjoyment.

This intellectualization of Judaism does not, however, serve to restrict immortality to a select few. There are certain simple and basic theological truths which in their simple formulation are not at all esoteric in nature. These truths can be recognized and comprehended by all, and, when affirmed, provide a degree of intellectual achievement sufficient to guarantee immortality.[5] The Thirteen Principles, then, constitute the minimum degree of knowledge sufficient to assure a portion in the world-to-come. The profession, or better, the awareness without which profession is impossible, of these Thirteen Principles thus serves, so to speak, as the minimum entrance requirements for admission to the Heavenly Academy.

Moreover, although the quality of bliss enjoyed in the world-to-come is commensurate with the degree to which the individual has perfected his intellectual perception of the nature of God, this is by no means the sole criterion of reward. In addition to compensation for fulfillment of the commandments and performance of meritorious deeds, man is

[3] Translated by David W. Silverman (Garden City, N.Y., 1966), pp. 202–203.

[4] Undated typescript in the possession of this writer, p. 61.

[5] See Maimonides, *Mishneh Torah, Hilkhot Yesodei ha-Torah* 4:13.

rewarded in the hereafter for yet another type of intellectual pursuit, namely, Torah study, which is not at all theological or philosophical in nature. Thus, in *Hilkhot Yesodei ha-Torah* 4:13, Maimonides cautions the uninitiated against delving into divine mysteries and points out that even among the great scholars of the Mishnah there were those who could not properly comprehend such matters. He points out that "bread and meat" to the extent of satiation are necessary prerequisites for engaging in these esoteric studies. Maimonides defines "bread and meat" as the talmudic discussions of Abbaye and Rava, i.e., Torah study dealing with ritual obligations and the like. These studies must be given priority, declares Maimonides, not only because they are intellectual prerequisites for the study of theology but because these studies are, in themselves, the greatest beneficence bestowed upon man, for it is such study which enables man to inherit the world-to-come. Perfection of the intellect achieved through study of Torah is within the reach of all, "young and old, men and women, those gifted with great intellectual capacity as well as those whose intelligence is limited."

The *Brisker Rav* acknowledges that Albo is correct in pointing to the essential redundancy inherent in Maimonides' list of principles. Albo, indeed with great acumen, formulates the philosophical arguments necessary for deriving additional propositions from the basic postulates. But not everyone has the intellectual prowess to examine these basic truths and to construct for himself the arguments, proofs, and conclusions which they entail. In order to guarantee that even those lacking contemplative power, as well as the intellectually lazy, may remain eligible for a portion in the world-to-come, an enumeration of the Thirteen Principles must be provided so that they may be affirmed by all. Once these principles have been formulated and presented in the form of a creed, it is no longer necessary for every individual to undertake an arduous and intellectually taxing process of derivation in order to arrive at truths which serve as a guarantee of immortality. The *Brisker Rav* points to Maimonides' use of the verbs "to know" (*leida*) and "to believe" (*le-ha'amin*) rather than "to understand" (*le-havin*) as indicating that what is required is only simple knowledge or awareness rather than comprehensive understanding. The requirement as set forth by Maimonides is awareness rather than formal demonstration, affirmation of the conclusion rather than reconstruction of the argument form, acknowledgment rather than erudite analysis. In acquiring knowledge of the Principles of Faith, the individual attains a threshold of intellectual development sufficient to make the contemplative existence of the world-to-come meaningful and blissful. Although S. Urbach (*The*

Philosophical Teachings of Crescas, p. 26, note 29) dismisses this analysis as formulated by Guttmann as an exercise in "philosophical homiletics," it is an exposition which is thoroughly congruous with Maimonides' philosophical system.

This analysis also serves to illuminate an otherwise puzzling statement contained in the *Mishneh Torah, Hilkhot Melakhim* 8:11. Maimonides codifies the talmudic statement which declares that the righteous of all nations possess a share in the world-to-come. He defines righteousness as scrupulous adherence to the seven Noachide commandments but then proceeds to add the stipulation that fulfillment of these precepts guarantees a share in the world-to-come only if they are accepted and carried out because "God commanded them in the Torah and made them known to us through our teacher, Moses, that the children of Noah had already been commanded with regard to them." He excludes from this category those who observe these commandments on the basis of their own subjective decision. Commentators on the *Mishneh Torah* were puzzled by this qualification appended by Maimonides since no explicit talmudic sources exist requiring Noachides to accept the obligations of the Noachide code on the basis of revelation. However, it appears that Maimonides is simply extending his thesis to its logical conclusion. Participation in the delights of the world-to-come is not essentially a reward but is the culmination of an intellectual process. If non-Jews as well are to share in the world-to-come, it can also be only on the basis of the confession of certain basic principles of faith which in their acceptance create at least a minimal level of intellectual attainment. Hence, observance of the Noachide laws alone cannot be sufficient to guarantee a share in the world-to-come. Immortality is assured only on the basis of an intellectual affirmation which must accompany observance of the Noachide commandments. It is this ideological commitment which Maimonides spells out: affirmation of revelation and the divinity of Torah which, of course, entails belief in the existence of God.

It appears that in compiling divergent lists of principles Maimonides, Crescas, and Albo are not so much in disagreement with regard to substantive teachings or the need to accept these teachings as divinely revealed truths (although there do exist disagreements with regard to the nature and status of some of these principles), as they are with regard to what it is that they are endeavoring to formulate. Albo is intent upon formulating a system of axioms consiting of the *sine qua non* of *any* system of religious belief. Every theological system must, by definition, posit the existence of a Deity. Any such system must embody the concept of revelation, else religion can make no demands upon man. And the concept of reward and punishment must be established in order to provide a basis for compliance with the demands of revelation. Crescas, on the other hand, is not concerned with the premises of religious belief in general but with the unique claims of faith set forth by Judaism. Crescas presents the distinctive demands which Judaism makes upon faith and formulates the beliefs which are unique to Judaism. Finally, Maimonides, depending upon which explanation is accepted, either presents the particular beliefs which require bolstering and reinforcement or enumerates the minimum content of the theological knowledge necessary for development of the "acquired intellect" which, in turn, makes possible the reality of immortality.

MAIMONIDES, *COMMENTARY ON THE MISHNAH*

Translation by J. Abelson

INTRODUCTION TO *ḤELEK*

All Israel have a portion in the world to come, as it is said (Isa. lx. 21), "And thy people shall be all righteous; they shall inherit the land for ever." The following have no portion in the world to come:—

(a) He who denies the resurrection of the dead[1].

(b) He who denies the divine origin of the Torah.

(c) The unbeliever[2].

Rabbi Akiba would include among these the following two:—

(a) He who reads heretical books[3].

(b) He who whispers a charm over a wound.

As it is said, "I will put none of those diseases upon thee which I have brought upon the Egyptians; for I am the Lord that healeth thee" (Exod. xv. 26).

Abba Saul would include also:—

(a) He who utters the letter of the Tetragrammaton.

I have thought fit to speak here concerning many principles belonging to fundamental articles of faith which are of very great importance. Know that the theologians are divided in opinion as to the good which man reaps from the performance of those precepts which God enjoined upon us by the hand of Moses our teacher; and that they also differ among themselves with regard to the evil which will overtake us if we transgress them. Their differences on these questions are very great and in proportion to the differences between their respective intellects. As a consequence, people's opinions have fallen into such great confusion that you can scarcely in any way find any one possessing clear and certain ideas on this subject; neither can you alight upon any portion of it which has been transmitted to any person without abundant error.

One class of thinkers holds that the hoped-for good will be the Garden of Eden, a place where people eat and drink without bodily toil or faintness. Houses of costly stones are there, couches of silk and rivers flowing with wine and perfumed oils, and many other things of this kind. But the evil, they think, will be Gehinnom, a place flaming with fire where bodies are burned, and where human beings suffer varied tortures which it would take too long to describe. This set of thinkers on this principle of faith bring their proofs from many statements of the Sages (peace to them) whose literal interpretation forsooth accords with their contention, or with the greater part of it.

The second class of thinkers firmly believes and imagines that the hoped-for good will be the Days of the Messiah (may he soon appear!). They think that when that time comes all men will be kings forever. Their bodily frames will be mighty and they will inhabit the whole earth unto eternity. According to their imagination that Messiah will live as long as the Creator (greatly be He praised!), and at that epoch the earth will bring forth garments ready woven, and bread ready baked, and many other impossible things like these. But the evil will consist in the fact that mankind will not exist at that epoch and will be unworthy to witness it. They also bring proofs for their statements from many remarks of the Sages, and from scriptural texts which in their outward interpretation agree with their claim, or a portion of it.

The third class is of opinion that the desired good will consist in the resurrection of the dead. This implies that man will live after his death; that in the company of his family and relatives he will once again eat and drink, and never more die. But the evil will mean that he will not again come to life. These thinkers also point for proof to the remarks of the Sages, and to certain verses[4] of the Bible, whose literal sense tallies with their view.

The fourth class is of opinion that the good which we shall reap from obedience to the Law will consist in the repose of the body and the attainment in this world of all worldly wishes, as, for example, the fertility of lands, abundant wealth, abundance of children, long life, bodily health and security, enjoying the sway of a king, and prevailing over the oppressor. The evil which will overtake us when we act in opposition [to the Torah] will mean the reversal of the aforementioned conditions, a state of things such as we now have in this the time of our exile. The holders of this view point for proof to all the texts of Scripture which speak of blessings and curses and other matters, and to the whole body of narratives existing in Holy Writ.

The fifth set of thinkers is the largest. Its members combine all the aforegone opinions, and declare the objects hoped for are the coming of the Messiah, the resurrection of the dead, their entry into the Garden of Eden, their eating and drinking and living in health there so long as heaven and earth endure.

But with regard to this strange point—I mean the world to come—you will find very few who will in any way take the matter to heart, or meditate on it, or adopt this or that principle, or ask to what these names[5] (the world to come) refer, whether the last-mentioned view constitutes the object to be aimed after, or whether one of the preceding opinions rightly expresses it. And you will rarely come across any one who will distinguish between the end desired and the means which lead to it. You will not by any means find any one to ask about this, or speak of it. What, however, all people ask, both the common folk and the educated classes is this:—In what condition will the dead rise to life, naked or clothed? Will they stand up in those very garments in which they were buried, in their embroideries and brocades, and beautiful needlework, or in a robe that will merely cover the body? And when the Messiah comes will rich and poor be alike, or will the distinctions between weak and strong still exist—and many similar questions from time to time.

Now, O reader, understand the following simile of mine[5a], and then you will make it your aim to grasp my meaning throughout. Figure to yourself a child young in years brought to a teacher to be instructed by him in the Torah. This is the greatest good he can derive in respect of his attainment of perfection. But the child, on account of the fewness of his years and the weakness of his intellect, does not grasp the measure of that benefit, or the extent to which it leads him towards the attainment of perfection. The teacher (who is nearer perfection than the pupil) must therefore necessarily stimulate him to learning by means of things in which he delights by reason of his youth. Thus he says to him, "Read, and I shall give you nuts or figs[6], or a bit of sugar." The child yields to this. He learns diligently, not indeed for the sake of the knowledge itself, as he does not know the importance of it, but merely to obtain that particular dainty (the eating of that dainty being more relished by him than study, and regarded as an unquestionably greater boon). And consequently he considers learning as a labour and a weariness to which he gives himself up in order by its means to gain his desired object, which consists of a nut, or a piece of sugar. When he grows older and his intelligence strengthens, he thinks lightly of the trifle in which he formerly found joy and begins to desire something new. He longs for this newly-chosen object of his, and his teacher now says to him, "Read, and I shall buy you pretty shoes, or a coat of this kind!" Accordingly he again exerts himself to learn, not for the sake of the knowledge, but to acquire that coat; for the garment ranks higher in his estimation than the learning and constitutes the final aim of his studies. When, however, he reaches a higher stage of mental perfection, this prize also ranks little with him, and he sets his heart upon something of greater moment. So that when his teacher bids him "learn this פרשה 'section,' or that פרק 'chapter,' and I shall give you a dinar or two," he learns with zest in order to obtain that money which to him is of more value than the learning, seeing that it constitutes the final aim of his studies. When, further, he reaches the age of greater discretion, this prize also loses its worth for him. He recognizes its paltry nature and sets his heart upon something more desirable. His teacher then says to him, "Learn, in order that you may become a Rabbi, or a Judge; the people will honour you, and rise before you; they will be obedient to your authority, and your name will be great, both in life and after death, as in the case of so and so." The pupil throws himself into ardent study, striving all the time to reach this stage of eminence. His aim is that of obtaining the honour of men, their esteem and commendation.

But all these methods are blameworthy. For in truth it is incumbent upon man, considering the weakness of the human mind, to make his aim in his acquisition of learning something which is extraneous to learning. And he should say of anything which is studied for the sake of gaining reward, "Of a truth this is a silly business." This is what the Sages meant when they used the expression שלא לשמה "not for its own sake." They meant to tell us that men obey the laws of the Torah, perform its precepts, and study and strive, not to obtain the thing itself, but for a further object. The Sages prohibited this to us in their remark[7], "Make not of the Torah a crown wherewith to aggrandize thyself, nor a spade wherewith to dig." They allude to that which I have made clear to you, viz. not to make the be-all and end-all of learning either the glorification of men or the acquisition of wealth. Also not to adopt the Law of God as the means of a livelihood, but to make the goal of one's study the acquisition of knowledge for its own sake. Similarly, the aim of one's study of truth ought to be the knowing of truth. The laws of the Torah are truth, and the purport of their study is obedience to them. The perfect man must not say, "If I perform these virtues and refrain from these vices which God forbade, what reward shall I receive?" For this would resemble the case of the lad who says, "If I read, what present will be given me?" and he receives the reply that he will get such and such a thing. This is only because when we notice the poverty of his intelligence, which fails to grasp this stage of things and aims at getting something other than what ought to be its real aim, we answer him according to his folly. "Answer a fool according to his folly[8]." The Sages warned us against this also, viz. against a man making the attainment of some worldly object the end of his service to God, and his obedience to his precepts. And this is the meaning of the dictum of that distinguished and perfect man who understood the fundamental truth of things—Antigonus of Socho—"Be not like servants who minister to their master upon the condition of receiving a reward; but be like servants who minister to their master without the condition of receiving a reward[9]." They really meant to tell us by this that a man should believe in truth for truth's sake[10]. And this is the sense they wished to convey by their expression עובד מאהבה "serving from motives of love," and by their comment on the phrase במצותיו חפץ מאוד[11] "that delighteth in his commandments." R. Eliezer said במצותיו "in his commandments," and *not* בשכר מצותיו= "in the reward for performance of his commandments." How strong a proof we have here of the truth of our argument, and how decisive! It is a clear confirmation of the text we have previously quoted. And we possess a stronger proof still in their remark in Sifre: שמא תאמר הריני למד תורה בשביל שאהיה עשיר בשביל שאקרא רבי שאקבל שכר בעולם הבא תלמוד לומר לאהבה[12] את ה׳ כל שאתם עושין לא תעשון אלא מאהבה. "Peradventure thou mayest say, Verily I will learn the Torah in order that I may become rich or that I may be called 'Rabbi,' or that I may receive a recompense in the future world. Therefore does Holy Writ say 'to love the Lord thy God.' Let everything that thou doest be done out of pure love for him."

The significance of this matter is now clear, and it is evident that what we have here stated is really the aim of the Torah, and the basis of the theological principles laid down by the Sages. No one can be blind to it except the imbecile boor who has fallen a prey to the whisperings of inane thoughts and defective imaginings. It was in this that the preeminence of Abraham our father consisted. He was עובד מאהבה "a server from motives of pure love[13]." And it is in this direction that effort should be put forward.

But our Sages knew how difficult a thing this was and that not every one could act up to it. They knew that even the man who reached it would not at once accord with it and think it a true article of faith. For man only does those actions which will either bring him advantage or ward off loss. All other action he holds vain and worthless. Accordingly, how could it be said to one who is learned in the Law—"Do these things, but do them not out of fear of God's punishment, nor out of hope for His reward"? This would be exceedingly hard, because it is not every one that comprehends truth, and becomes like Abraham our father. Therefore, in order that the common folk might be established in their convictions, the Sages permitted them to perform meritorious actions with the hope of reward, and to avoid the doing of evil out of fear of punishment. They encourage them to these conceptions and their opinions become firmly rooted, until eventually the intelligent among them come to comprehend and know what truth is and what is the most perfect mode of conduct. It is exactly the way in which we deal with the lad in his studies, as we have explained in our foregoing simile. Antigonus of Socho was blamed by them for the particular exposition he gave to the multitude and they applied to him the words[14], "Oh, wise men, be cautious of your words," as we shall explain in our remarks on "The ethics of the Fathers." The people at large are not one jot the worse off through their performance of the precepts of the Torah by reason of their fear of punishment and expectation of reward; for they are in a state of imperfection. On the contrary, they are by this means drawn to cultivate the necessary habits and training for acting in loyalty to the Torah. They bring themselves over to an understanding of truth and become עובדים מאהבה "servers out of pure love." And this is what the Sages meant by their remark:[15] לעולם יעסוק אדם בתורה אפילו שלא לשמה, שמתוך שלא לשמה בא לשמה "Man should ever engage himself in the Torah, even though it be not for the Torah's sake. Action regardless of the Torah's sake will lead on to action regardful of it."

We must now come to the point which it is necessary for you to know, viz., that men are divided into three different classes in respect of their notions regarding the words of the Sages. The first class is, as far as I have seen, the largest in point of their numbers and of the numbers of their compositions; and it is of them that I have heard most. The members of this class adopt the words of the Sages literally, and give no kind of interpretation whatsoever. With them all impossibilities are necessary occurrences. This is owing to their being ignorant of science and far away from knowledge. They do not possess that perfection which would spur them on of their own accord, neither have they found any means for rousing their attention. They think that in all their emphatic and precise remarks the Sages only wished to convey the ideas which they themselves comprehend, and that they intended them to be taken in their literalness. And this, in spite of the fact that in their literal significance some of the words of the Sages would savour of absurdity. And so much so that were they manifested to the ordinary folk (leave alone the educated) in their literalness, they would reflect upon them with amazement and would exclaim: "How can there exist any one who would seriously think in this way and regard such statements as the correct view of things, much less approve of them." This class of men are poor, and their folly deserves our pity. For in their own opinions they are honouring the Sages, whereas in reality they are all the time degrading them to the lower depths—and this all unconsciously. As God lives, it is this class of thinkers that robs our religion of its beauties, darkens its brilliance, and makes the Law of God convey meanings quite contrary to those it was intended to convey. For God says in the perfect book of his revelation: "For this is your wisdom and your understanding in the sight of the nations which shall hear all these statutes and say, Surely this great nation is a wise and understanding people."[16] But this class strings together the literal interpretations of the remarks of the Sages, so that when the nations hear them they exclaim, "Surely this small nation is a foolish and untutored people." And as for the many things that are done by those preachers[17] who explain to the people what they do not themselves understand, would that their ignorance caused them to be silent, even as Job says, "Would that ye were silent, and this would be unto you for wisdom."[18] Or would that they were to say, "We do not know what the wise men intended by this assertion, nor how it is to be interpreted." But, of a truth, they imagine that they do understand, and devote themselves to inculcating among the people that which they themselves think, and not what the Sages said. And they expound sermons before the leaders of the people on such themes as The Talmud Treatise "Berachoth" and the "10th chap. of Mishna Sanhedrin," &c., in their literal senses word by word.

The second class of reasoners is also numerous. They see and hear the words of the Sages and accept them in their literal significations, thinking that the Sages meant nothing but what the literal interpretation indicates. They consequently apply themselves to showing the weakness of the Rabbinical statements, their objectionable character, and to calumniate that which is free from reproach. They make sport of the words of the Sages from time to time, and imagine themselves more intellectually gifted and possessed of more penetrating minds, whereas they (peace to them!) are deceived, shortsighted, ignorant of all existing things, and consequently unable to comprehend anything. The majority of those who fall into these beliefs consists of those who pretend to a knowledge of medicine, and of those who rant about the decrees of the stars. For these are men who in their own estimation are sages and philosophers. But how far removed are they from humanity when placed side by side with the true philosophers! They are more stupid than the first class (of which we have spoken), and more steeped in folly! They are an accursed class, because they put themselves in opposition to men of great worth, whose learning is manifest to scholars. If only they trained themselves in knowledge so as to know how necessary it is to use the appropriate speech in theology and in like subjects which are common to both the uneducated and the cultured, and to understand also the practical portion of philosophy, it would then be clear to them whether the Sages were really men of wisdom or no, and the significance of their assertions would be comprehensible to them.

The third class of thinkers is (as God liveth!) so very small in numbers that one would only call it a class in the sense that the sun is termed a species (although it is a single object). They are the men who accept as established facts the greatness of the Sages and the excellence of their thoughts, as found in the generality of their remarks, where each word points to a very true theme. Although the number of these discourses is small and scattered about in different portions of their writings, they nevertheless indicate the perfection of their authors and the fact that they attained truth. The members of this class are convinced also of the impossibility of the impossible and the necessary existence of what must exist. For they know that they (peace to them!) would not talk absurdities to one another. And they are convinced beyond doubt that their words have both an outer and an inner meaning, and that in all that they said of things impossible their discourses were in the form of riddle and parable. For this was the method of the great savants, and for this reason did the wisest of men open his book with the words,[19] להבין משל ומליצה דברי חכמים וחידותם "To understand parable and saying, the words of the wise and their riddles." Those who study philosophy know that חידה is a mode of speech whose meaning is inward not outward, as in the verse[20] אחודה נא לכם חידה "I will now put forth a riddle unto you." For the theme of the speech of men of learning consists entirely in matters of the highest import. But they are put in the form of riddle and parable. And how can we disapprove of their literary productions being in the manner of proverb and simile of a lowly and popular kind, seeing that the wisest of men did the same ברוח הקודש "by holy inspiration," viz. Solomon, in the Book of Proverbs, the Song of Songs, and part of Ecclesiastes? How can we disapprove of the method of placing interpretations on the words of the Sages, and drawing them out of their literalness to adjust them to reason and make them accord with truth and the books of Scripture, seeing that the Sages themselves place their interpretations on the words of the text and by bringing them out of their literal meaning present them as parable? And that this is true can be seen from what we find in their interpretation of the verse (2 Sam. xxiii. 20), "He slew two lion-like men of Moab," &c.[21] All of which they regard as allegory. And similarly the verse (2 Sam. xxiii. 20), "he slew the lion in the midst of the pit," they treat as allegory. And likewise (2 Sam. xxiii. 15),[22] "Oh that one would give me drink of the water of the well of Bethlehem!" and all that follows they interpret figuratively. And so it is with the whole Book of Job, of which one of the Rabbins says,[23] משל היה "it is an allegory," but he does not explain what meaning the allegory is intended to convey. And so again in the case of the dry bones of Ezekiel, which one Rabbi declares to have been allegorically meant.[24] And we could quote many similar instances.

If, O Reader, you belong to one of the first-named classes, do not pay any attention to any of my remarks on this subject, because not a word of it will suit you. On the contrary, it will harm you and you will dislike it. For how can food of light weight and temperate character suit a person accustomed to partaking of bad and gross fare? It would really injure him, and he would loathe it. Do you not see what we said concerning the manna by those who had grown accustomed to eating onions and garlic, and fish? ונפשנו קצה בלחם הקלוקל[25] "and our soul loatheth this light bread." If, however, you are of those who constitute the third class, and when you come across any of the Sages' remarks which reason rejects, you pause and learn that it is a dark saying and an allegory. And if you then pass the night wrapped up in thought and dwelling in anxious reflection over its interpretation, mentally striving to find the truth and the correct point of view, as it is said, למצוא דברי חפץ וכתוב יושר דברי אמת[26] "To find out acceptable words, and the writing of uprightness, even words of truth," you will then consider this discourse of mine, and it will profit you, if God wills it.

I shall now begin to treat the subject which I originally intended. Know that just as a blind man can form no idea of colours, nor a deaf man comprehend sounds, nor a eunuch feel the desire for sexual intercourse, so the bodies cannot comprehend the delights of the soul. And even as fish do not know the element[27] fire because they exist ever in its opposite, so are the delights of the world of spirit unknown to this world of flesh. Indeed, we have no pleasure in any way except what is bodily, and what the senses can comprehend of eating, drinking, and sexual intercourse. Whatever is outside these is non-existent to us. We do not discern it, neither do we grasp it at first thought, but only after deep penetration. And truly this must necessarily be the case. For we live in a material world and the only pleasure we can comprehend must be material. But the delights of the spirit are everlasting and uninterrupted, and there is no resemblance in any possible way between spiritual and bodily enjoyments. We are not sanctioned either by the Torah or by the divine philosophers to assert that the angels, the stars, and the spheres enjoy no delights. In truth they have exceeding great delight in respect of what they comprehend of the Creator (glorified be He!). This to them is an everlasting felicity without a break. They have no bodily pleasures, neither do they comprehend them, because they have no senses like ours, enabling them to have our sense experiences. And likewise will it be with us too. When after death the worthy from among us will reach that exalted stage he will experience no bodily pleasures, neither will he have any wish for them, any more than would a king of sovereign power wish to divest himself of his imperial sway and return to his boyhood's games with a ball in the street, although at one time he would without doubt have set a higher worth upon a game with a ball than on kingly dominion, such being the case only when his years were few and he was totally ignorant of the real significance of either pursuit, just as we to-day rank the delights of the body above those of the soul.

And when you will give your consideration to the subject of these two pleasures, you will discover the meanness of the one and the high worth of the other. And this applies even to this world. For we find in the case of the majority of men that they all burden their souls and bodies with the greatest possible labour and fatigue in order to attain distinction or a great position in men's esteem. This pleasure is not that of eating or drinking. Similarly, many a man prefers the obtaining of revenge over his enemies to many of the pleasures of the body. And many a man, again, shuns the greatest among all physical delights out of fear that it should bring him shame and the reproach of men, or because he seeks a good reputation. If such then is our condition in this world of matter, how much more will it be our case in the world of the spirit, viz. the world to come, where our souls will attain to a knowledge of the Creator as do the higher bodies, or more. This pleasure cannot be divided into parts. It cannot be described, neither can anything be found to compare with it. It is as the prophet exclaimed, when admiring its great glories[28]: "How great is thy goodness which thou hast laid up for them that fear thee, which thou hast wrought for them that trust in thee before the children of men." And in a similar sense the Sages remarked[29]: "In the world to come there will be no eating and no drinking, no washing and no anointing and no marriage; but only the righteous sitting with crowns on their heads enjoying the splendour of the Shechinah." By their remark, "their crowns on their heads," is meant the preservation of the soul in the intellectual sphere[30], and the merging of the two into one as has been described by the illustrious philosophers in ways whose exposition would take too long here. By their remark, "enjoying the splendour of the Shechinah," is meant that those souls will reap bliss in what they comprehend of the Creator, just as the Holy Chayoth and the other ranks of angels enjoy felicity in what they understand of His existence. And so the felicity and the final goal consist in reaching to this exalted company and attaining to this high pitch[31]. The continuation of the soul, as we have stated, is endless, like the continuation of the Creator (praised be He!) who is the cause of its continuation in that it comprehends Him, as is explained in elementary philosophy. This is the great bliss with which no bliss is comparable and to which no pleasure can be likened. For how can the enduring and infinite be likened to a thing which has a break and an end? This is the meaning of the scriptural phrase[32] למען ייטב לך והארכת ימים "In order that it may well with thee and that thou mayest prolong thy days"; for which we possess the traditional interpretation, which is[33]: למען ייטב לך לעולם שכלו טוב "In order that it may be well with thee in the world which is all good": והארכת ימים לעולם שכלו ארוך "and that thou mayest prolong thy days in a world which is of unending length."

The consummate evil (of punishment) consists in the cutting off of the soul, its perishing and its failure to attain durability. This is the meaning of כרת "cutting off," mentioned in the Torah. The meaning of כרת is the cutting off of the soul, as the Torah manifestly declares[34] הכרת תכרת הנפש ההיא "That soul shall surely be cut off." And the Sages remarked (peace to them!): הכרת "cutting off in this world[35]," תכרת "cutting off in the world to come." Scripture also contains the verse[36], והיתה נפש אדוני צרורה בצרור החיים "And the soul of my lord shall be bound in the bond of life."All those who devote themselves to bodily pleasures, rejecting truth and choosing falsehood, are cut off from participation in that exalted state of things and remain as detached matter merely. And in this connection the prophet in his remark[37], עין לא ראתה אל' זולתך יעשה למחכה לו "The eye hath not seen, O God, beside thee, what He hath prepared for him that waiteth for Him," has made it clear that the world to come cannot be comprehended by the bodily senses. The Sages, in interpretation of this phrase, said[38]: כל הנביאים כולן לא נתנבאו אלא לימות המשיח אבל לעולם הבא עין לא ראתה אל' זולתך "All prophets prophesy only concerning the days of the Messiah, but the world to come no eye hath seen save God."

As regards the promises and threats alluded to in the Torah, their interpretation is that which I shall now tell you. It says to you, "If you obey these precepts, I will help you to a further obedience of them and perfection in the performance of them. And I shall remove all hindrances from you." For it is impossible for man to do the service of God when sick or hungry or thirsty or in trouble, and this is why the Torah promises the removal of all these disabilities and gives man also the promise of health and quietude until such a time as he shall have attained perfection of knowledge and be worthy of the life of the world to come. The final aim of the Torah is not that the earth should be fertile, that people should live long, and that bodies should be healthy. It simply helps us to the performance of its precepts by holding out the promise of all these things. Similarly, if men transgress, their punishment will be that of all these hindrances will come into being, rendering them powerless to do righteousness, as we read: תחת אשר לא עבדת את ה׳[39], "Because thou servedst not the Lord thy God with joyfulness . . . Therefore shalt thou serve thine enemies which the Lord shall send against thee. . . ." If you give this matter more than ordinary consideration, you will find it to be equivalent to being told, "If you carry out a portion of these laws with love and diligence, we shall help you to a performance of all of them by removing from you all difficulties and obstacles; but if you abandon any of them out of disdain we shall bring hindrances into your path that will prevent you from doing any of them, so that you will gain neither perfection nor eternity." This is what is meant by the assertion of the Rabbins[40]: שכר מצוה מצוה ושכר עברה עברה "The recompense of a precept is a precept, and the recompense of transgression, transgression."

As for the Garden of Eden[41], it is a fertile spot on the earth's sphere rich in streams and fruits. God will of a certainty disclose it to man one day, and will show him the path leading to it. Man will reap enjoyment within it, and there may possibly be found therein plants of a very extraordinary sort, great in usefulness and rich in pleasure-giving properties, in addition to those which are renowned with us. All this is not impossible nor far-fetched. On the contrary, it is quite near possibility, and would be so even if the Torah failed to allude to it. How much more is it the case seeing that it has a clear and conspicuous place in the Torah!

Gehinnom is an expression for the suffering that will befall the wicked. The nature of this suffering is not expounded in the Talmud. One authority there states that the sun will draw near them [the wicked] and burn them[42]. He gets his proof from the verse כי הנה היום בא בוער כתנור[43], "For behold the day cometh, burning as an oven." Another asserts that a strange heat will arise in their bodies, and consume them. He derives proof for this from the phrase רוחכם אש תאכלכם[44] "Your breath as fire shall devour you."

The Resurrection of the Dead is one of the cardinal doctrines of the Law of Moses. He who does not believe in this has no religion, and no bond with the Jewish faith. But it is the reward of the righteous only, as is shown by the statement in *Bereshith Rabba*, גבורת גשמים לצדיקים

ולרשעים ותחיית המתים לצדיקים בלבד "The great benefits of the rain are for both the righteous and the wicked, but the resurrection of the dead applies to the righteous only." And forsooth how shall the evil-doers live after death, seeing that they were dead even in life, as the Sages said, רשעים אפילו בחייהם קרויים מתים צדיקים אפילו במיתתם קרויים חיים[45] "The wicked are called dead even during their lives, but the good are called living even after their death." And know that man is bound to die and become dissolved into his component parts.

The days of the Messiah will be the time when the kingdom will return to Israel who will return to the Holy Land[46]. The king who will then reign will have Zion as the capital of his realm. His name will be great and fill the earth to its uttermost bounds[47]. It will be a greater name than that of King Solomon and mightier. The nations will make peace with him, and lands will obey him by reason of his great rectitude and the wonders that will come to light by his means. Any one that rises up against him God will destroy and make him fall into his hand. All verses of scripture testify to his prosperity and our prosperity in him. So far as existing things are concerned there will be no difference whatever between now and then, except that Israel will possess the kingdom. And this is the sense of the Rabbins' statement, אין בין העולם הזה לימות המשיח אלא שעבוד מלכיות בלבד[48] "There is no difference between this world and the Days of the Messiah except the subjugation of the kingdoms alone." In his days there will be both the strong and the weak in their relations to others. But verily in those days the gaining of their livelihood will be so very easy to men that they will do the lightest possible labour and reap great benefit. It is this that is meant by the remark of the Rabbins, עתידה ארץ ישראל להוציא גלוסקאות וכלי מילת[49] "The land of Israel will one day produce cakes ready baked, and garments of fine silk." For when one finds a thing easily and without labour, people are in the habit of saying, "So and So found bread ready baked, and a meal ready cooked." And you have a proof of this in the scriptural statement ובני נכר אכריכם וכורמיכם[50] "And the sons of the stranger shall be your husbandmen, and the tillers of your vineyards." This is an indication that seed-time and harvest will exist there [in the land of Israel at the time of the Messiah]. And it was for this reason that the particular Rabbi who made the aforementioned assertion blamed his pupil for not understanding the drift of his remarks, and thinking them to be intended literally. And consequently the reply he gave him was commensurate with the latter's power of comprehension; but it was not the real answer. And the proof that he did not intend it for the truth is seen in the fact that he corroborates his attitude by quoting the verse אל תען כסיל כאולתו[51]

"Answer not a fool according to his folly." The great benefits that will accrue to us at that epoch will consist in our enjoying rest from the work of subjagating the kingdoms of wickedness, a work which prevents us from the full performance of righteous action. Knowledge will increase, as it is said, כי מלאה הארץ דעה את ה׳[52] "For the earth shall be full of the knowledge of God." Discords[53] and wars will cease, as it is said, לא ישאו גוי אל גוי חרב[54] "Nation shall no more lift up sword against nation." Great perfection will appertain to him that lives in those days, and he will be elevated[55] through it to the חיי העולם הבא "the life of the world to come." But the Messiah will die, and his son and son's son will reign in his stead. God has clearly declared his death in the words, לא יכהה ולא ירוץ עד ישים בארץ משפט[56] "He shall not fail nor be discouraged, till he have set judgment in the earth." His kingdom will endure a very long time and the lives of men will be long also, because longevity is a consequence of the removal of sorrows and cares. Let not the fact of the duration of his kingdom for thousands of years seem strange to you, for the Sages have said that when a number of good things come together it is not an easy thing for them to separate again. The days of the Messiah are not ardently longed for on account of the plentiful vegetation, and the riches which they will bring in their train, nor in order that we may ride on horses, nor that we may drink to the accompaniment of various kinds of musical instruments, as is thought by those people who are confused in their ideas on such things. No! the prophets and saints wished and ardently desired [the days of the Messiah] because it implies the coming together of the virtuous, with choice deeds of goodness and knowledge, and the justice of the King[57], the greatness of his wisdom and his nearness to his Creator, as it is said: "The Lord said unto me, thou art my son; this day have I begotten thee[58]." And because it implies obedience to all the Laws of Moses, without ennui or disquietude[59] or constraint, as it is promised[60] in the words, ולא ילמדו עוד איש את רעהו... כי כולם ידעו אותי[61]... ונתתי תורתי בלבם[62] והסירותי לב האבן מבשרכם[63] "And they shall teach no more every man his neighbour and every man his brother saying, Know the Lord; for they shall all know me from the least of them unto the greatest of them." "And I will take away the stony heart from your flesh." And there are many more similar verses on like themes.

It is under conditions like these that one will obtain a firm hold upon the world to come. The final goal is the attaining to the world to come, and it is to it that the effort must be directed. And it is in this sense that the particular sage, gifted with truth looked towards the final goal and omitting what was extraneous to it, declared כל ישראל יש להם חלק לעולם הבא "All Israel have a portion in the world to come." Although the "world to come" constitutes the final object of desire, it is not meet that he who wishes to be עובד מאהבה should work to attain "the world to come," as we have explained in the foregoing remarks. Rather must he serve God in the way that I shall prescribe. This is as follows: when he firmly believes that the Torah contains knowledge which reached the prophets from before God, who through it taught them that virtuous deeds are of such and such a kind and ignoble deeds of such and such a kind, it is obligatory for him, in so far as he is a man of well balanced temperament, to bring forth meritorious deeds and shun vice. When he acts like this, the significance of man has in him reached the point of perfection and he is divided off from the brute. And when a man arrives at the point of being perfect he belongs to that order[64] of a man whom no obstacle hinders from making the intellectual element in his soul live on after death. This is "the world to come" as we have made clear, and herein lies the significance of the Psalmist's remark, אל תהיו כסוס כפרד אין הבין במתג ורסן עדיו לבלום[65] "Be ye not as the horse or as the mule which have no understanding; whose mouth must be held with bit and bridle . . ." This means that what restrains beasts from doing harm is something external, as a bridle or a bit. But not so with man. His restraining agency lies in his very self, I mean in his human framework. When the latter becomes perfected it is exactly that which keeps him away from those things which perfection withholds from him and which are termed vices; and it is that which spurs him on to what will bring about perfection in him, viz. virtue.

These are the ideas which I have acquired from the generality of the Sages' remarks upon this exalted and most prominent theme. I hope to compose a work in which I shall collect all the maxims that are found in the Talmud and other works. I shall throw light upon them and give them an interpretation suiting the truth. And I shall bring proof for all of it from the Sages' own words also. I shall make clear which of their statements have to be taken literally and which are figures of speech; and also which of them were only incidents of sleep but spoken of in express terms as if they happened during the waking state. In that work I shall explain to you many principles of faith, and in these explanations I will make clear all the things of which I have given you a few rudimentary facts in this treatise of mine. You can compare them with others. Let no one blame me for the freedom with which I have used certain expressions and assertions in this my treatise, and which provokes the criticism of the learned. For I have enlarged freely upon this section in order to give understanding to him who has previously had no training in this exalted subject which is not comprehended by every man.

The expression אפיקורס.—This is an Aramaic word. It signifies disdain of and contempt for the Torah or the traditional[66] explanation of the Torah. For this reason they give this name to those who do not believe in the fundamental principles of the Torah, or to those who make light of the Sages or any disciple of the Sages, or harm them[67].

The expression ספרים החיצונים "Heretical Books." They called these ספרי מינים[68] "Books of the Minim." The books of Ben Sira belong to this class. He was a man who composed books of idle talk on the subjects of the art of physiognomy. They contain no knowledge and serve no useful purpose, but are a mere wasting of time in vain amusement. And of such a kind are e.g. those books existing among the Arabs dealing with chronologies, legends of kings, the genealogies of the Arabs, the books of songs[69], and similar books, which contain no knowledge and are of no practical use, but mere waste of time.

The expression והלוחש על המכה "He who whispers a charm over a wound" has no portion in the world to come. But this is only the case if there is any spitting[70], because this would be indecent before God.

The expression וההוגה את השם באותיותיו "He who pronounces the letters of the Tetragrammaton." This means that he utters the letters יהוה, which constitute the שם המפורש[71] lit. the proper name, i.e. the name exclusively applied to one Being. It is used repeatedly in the Mishnah and Gemara *Yoma.* See Commentary of Shemtob on chapter 62 of *Moreh Nebuchim.* They also mentioned other things besides these, the doer of which will have no portion in the world to come. Thus they said, "He that publicly puts the face of his neighbour to the blush shall have no portion in the world to come[72]." "He that calls his neighbour by his nicknames[73]." "He that takes honour to himself in the disgrace of his neighbour[74]." Although these may seem small offences to the ordinary thinker, actions of this kind will only emanate from a soul defective, without perfection, and not fitted for the life of the world to come.

What I have to mention now (and this is the most correct place for alluding to it) is that the roots of our Law and its fundamental principles are thirteen.

The first Principle of Faith.

The existence of the Creator (praised be He!), i.e. that there is an existent Being invested with the highest perfection of existence. He is the cause of the existence of all existent things. In Him they exist and from Him emanates their continued existence. If we could suppose[75] the removal of His existence then the existence of all things would entirely cease and there would not be left any independent existence whatsoever[76]. But if on the other hand we could suppose the removal of all existent things but He, His existence (blessed be He!) would not cease to be, neither would it suffer any diminution. For He (exalted be He!) is self-sufficient, and His existence needs the aid of no existence outside His. Whatsoever is outside Him, the intelligences (i.e. the angels) and the bodies of the spheres, and things below these[77], all of them need Him for their existence. This is the first cardinal doctrine of faith, which is indicated by the commandment, "I am the Lord thy God" אנכי ה׳ אלהיך.[78]

The second Principle of Faith.

The Unity of God. This implies that this cause of all is one; not one of a genus nor of a species, and not as one human being who is a compound divisible into many unities; not a unity like the ordinary material body which is one in number but takes on endless divisions and parts. But He, the exalted one, is a unity in the sense that there is no unity like His in any way. This is the second cardinal doctrine of faith which is indicated by the assertion, "Hear, O Israel, the Lord our God the Lord is one" שמע ישראל ה׳ אלוהינו ה׳ אחד.[79]

The third Principle of Faith.

The removal of materiality from God. This signifies that this unity is not a body nor the power of a body, nor can the accidents of bodies overtake Him, as e.g. motion and rest, whether in the essential or accidental sense. It was for this reason that the Sages (peace to them!) denied to Him both cohesion and separation of parts, when they remarked לא ישיבה ולא עמידה ולא עורף ולא עפוי[80], i.e. "no sitting and no standing, no division[81] (עורף) and no cohesion[82]" (עפוי) [according to the verse ועפו בכתף פלשתים, i.e. they will push them with the shoulder in order to join themselves to them]. The prophet again said[83], "And unto whom will ye liken God," &c., "and[84] unto whom will ye liken me that I may be like, saith the Holy One." If God were a body He would be like a body. Wherever in the scriptures God is spoken of with the attributes of material bodies, like motion, standing, sitting, speaking, and such like, all these figures of speech, as the Sages said, דברה תורה כלשון בני אדם[85] "The Torah speaks in the language of men." People[86] have said a great deal on this point. This third fundamental article of faith is indicated by the scriptural expression, כי לא ראיתם כל תמונה[87] "for ye have seen no likeness," i.e. you have not comprehended him as one who possesses a likeness, for, as we have remarked, he is not a body nor a bodily power.

The fourth Principle of Faith.

The priority of God. This means that the unity whom we have described is first in the absolute sense. No existent thing outside Him is primary in relation to Him. The proofs of this in the Scriptures are numerous. This fourth principle is indicated by the phrase מעונה אל' קדם[88] "The eternal God is a refuge."

The fifth Principle of Faith.

That it is He (be He exalted!) who must be worshipped, aggrandized, and made known by His greatness and the obedience shown to Him. This must not be done to any existing beings lower than He—not to the angels nor the spheres nor the elements, or the things which are compounded from them. For these are all fashioned in accordance with the works they are intended to perform. They have no judgement or freewill, but only a love for Him (be He exalted!). Let us adopt no mediators to enable ourselves to draw near unto God, but let the thoughts be directed to Him, and turned away from whatsoever is below Him. This fifth principle is a prohibition of idolatry. The greater part of the Torah is taken up with the prohibition of idol-worship.

The sixth Principle of Faith.

Prophecy. This implies that it should be known that among this human species there exist persons of very intellectual natures and possessing much perfection. Their souls are predisposed for receiving the form of the intellect. Then this human intellect joins itself with the active intellect, and an exalted emanation[89] is shed upon them. These are the prophets. This is prophecy, and this is its meaning. The complete elucidation of this principle of faith would be very long, and it is not our purpose to bring proofs for every principle or to elucidate the means of comprehending them, for this affair includes the totality of the sciences. We shall give them a passing mention only. The verses of the Torah which testify concerning the prophecy of prophets are many.

The seventh Principle of Faith.

The prophecy of Moses our Teacher. This implies that we must believe that he was the father of all the prophets before him and that those who came after him were all beneath him in rank. He (Moses) was chosen by God from the whole human kind. He comprehended more of God than any man in the past or future ever comprehended or will comprehend. And we must believe that he reached a state of exaltedness beyond the sphere of humanity, so that he attained to the angelic rank and became included in the order of the angels. There was no veil which he did not pierce. No material hindrance stood in his way, and no defect whether small or great mingled itself with him. The imaginative and sensual powers of his perceptive faculty were stripped from him. His desiderative power was stilled and he remained pure intellect only. It is in this significance that it is remarked of him that he discoursed with God without any angelic intermediary.

We had it in our mind to explain this strange subject here and to unlock the secrets firmly enclosed in scriptural verses; to expound the meaning of פה אל פה "mouth to mouth"; and the whole of this verse and other things belonging to the same theme. But I see that this theme is very subtle; it would need abundant development and introductions and illustrations. The existence of angels would first have to be made clear and the distinction between their ranks and that of the Creator. The soul would have to be explained and all its powers. The circle would then grow wider until we should have to say a word about the forms which the prophets attribute to the Creator and the angels. The שעור קומה and its meaning would consequently have to enter into our survey. And even if this one subject were shortened into the narrowest compass it could not receive sufficient justice, even in a hundred pages. For this reason I shall leave it to its place, either in the book of the interpretation of the דרשות[90] "discourses," which I have promised, or in the book on prophecy which I have begun, or in the book which I shall compose for explaining these fundamental articles of faith.

I shall now come back to the purpose of this seventh principle and say that the prophecy of Moses differs from that of all other prophets in four respects:—

(1) Whosoever the prophet, God spake not with him but by an intermediary. But Moses had no intermediary, as it is said, פה אל פה אדבר בו[91] "mouth to mouth did I speak with him."

(2) Every other prophet received his inspiration only when in a state of sleep, as it is asserted in various parts of scripture, [92]בחלום הלילה "in a

dream of the night." בחלום חזיון לילה[93] "in a dream of a vision of a night," and many other phrases with similar significance; or in the day when deep sleep has fallen upon the prophet and his condition is that in which there is a removal of his sense-perceptions, and his mind is a blank like a sleep. This state is styled מחזה and מראה, and is alluded to in the expression במראות אלהים= "in visions of God." But to Moses the word came in the day-time when "he was standing between the two cherubim," as God had promised him in the words ונועדתי לך שם ודברתי אתך[94] "And there I will meet with thee and I will commune with thee." And God further said, אם יהיה נביאכם ה׳ במראה אליו אתודע בחלום אדבר בו לא כן עבדי משה . . . פה אל פה אדבר בו[95] "If there be a prophet among you, I the Lord will make myself known unto him in a vision and will speak unto him in a dream. My servant Moses is not so, who is faithful in all mine house. With him I will speak mouth to mouth . . . ."

(3) When the inspiration comes to the prophet, although it is in a vision and by means of an angel, his strength becomes enfeebled, his physique becomes deranged. And very great terror falls upon him so that he is almost broken through it, as is illustrated in the case of Daniel. When Gabriel speaks to him in a vision, Daniel says: ולא נשאר בי כח והודי נהפך עלי למשחית ולא עצרתי כח[96] "And there remained no strength in me; for my comeliness was turned in me into corruption and I retained no strength." And he further says: ואני הייתי נרדם על פני ופני ארצה[97] "Then was I in a deep sleep on my face, and my face towards the ground." And further: במראה נהפכו צירי עלי[98] "By the vision my sorrows are turned upon me." But not so with Moses. The word came unto him and no confusion in any way overtook him, as we are told in the verse ודבר ה׳ אל משה פנים אל פנים כאשר ידבר איש אל רעהו[99] "And the Lord spake unto Moses face unto face as a man speaketh unto his neighbour." This means that just as no man feels disquieted when his neighbour talks with him, so he (peace to him!) had no fright at the discourse of God, although it was face to face; this being the case by reason of the strong bond uniting him with the intellect, as we have described.

(4) To all the prophets the inspiration came not at their own choice but by the will of God. The prophet at times waits a number of years without an inspiration reaching him. And it is sometimes asked of the prophet that he should communicate a message [he has received], but the prophet waits some days or months before doing so or does not make it known at all. We have seen cases where the prophet prepares himself[100] by enlivening his soul and purifying his spirit[101], as did Elisha in the

incident when he declared ועתה קחו לי מנגן[102] "But now bring me a minstrel!" and then the inspiration came to him. He does not necessarily receive the inspiration at the time that he is ready for it. But Moses our teacher was able to say at whatsoever time he wished, עמדו ואשמעה מה יצוה ה׳ לכם[103] "Stand, and I shall hear what God shall command concerning you." It is again said, דבר אל אהרן אחיך ואל יבא בכל עת אל הקדש[104] "Speak unto Aaron thy brother that he come not at all times into the sanctuary;" with reference to which verse the Talmud remarks "that only Aaron is בכל יבא, but Moses is not בכל יבא. The prohibition ("That he come not at all times") applies only to Aaron. But Moses may enter the sanctuary at all times.

The eighth Principle of Faith.

That the Torah has been revealed from heaven. This implies our belief that the whole of this Torah found in our hands this day is the Torah that was handed down by Moses and that it is all of divine origin. By this I mean that the whole of the Torah came unto him from before God in a manner which is metaphorically called "speaking"; but the real nature of that communication is unknown to everybody except to Moses (peace to him!) to whom it came. In handing down the Torah, Moses was like a scribe writing from dictation the whole of it, its chronicles, its narratives, and its precepts. It is in this sense that he is termed מחוקק = "lawgiver." And there is no difference between verses like ובני חם כוש ומצרים ופוט וכנען[105] "And the sons of Ham were Cush and Mizraim, Phut and Canaan," or ושם אשתו מהיטבאל בת מטרד[106] "And his wife's name was Mehatabel, the daughter of Matred," or ותמנע היתה פילגש[107] "And Timna was concubine," and verses like אנכי ה׳ אלהיך[108] "I am the Lord thy God," and שמע ישראל[109] "Hear, O Israel." They are all equally of divine origin and all belong to the תורת ה׳ תמימה טהורה וקדושה אמת "The Law of God which is perfect, pure, holy, and true." In the opinion of the Rabbins, Manasseh was the most renegade and the greatest of all infidels because he thought that in the Torah there were a kernel and a husk, and that these histories and anecdotes have no value and emanate from Moses. This is the significance of the expression אין תורה מן השמים "The Torah does not come from heaven," which, say the Rabbins[110], is the remark of one who believes that all the Torah is of divine origin save a certain verse which (says he) was not spoken by God but by Moses himself. And of such a one the verse says כי דבר ה׳ בזה[111] "For he hath despised the word of the Lord." May God be exalted far above and beyond the speech of the infidels! For truly in every letter of the Torah there reside wise maxims and admirable truths for him to whom God has given understanding. You cannot grasp the uttermost bounds of its wisdom. "It is larger in measure than the earth, and wider than the sea[112]." Man has but to follow in the footsteps of the anointed one of the God of Jacob, who prayed גל עיני ואביטה נפלאות מתורתך[113] "Open my eyes and I shall behold wonderful things from thy Law." The interpretation of traditional law is in like manner of divine origin. And that which we know today of the nature of Succah, Lulab, Shofar, Fringes, and Phylacteries (סוכה, לולב, שופר, ציצית, תפילין) is essentially the same as that which God commanded Moses, and which the latter told us. In the success of his mission Moses realized the mission of a נאמן[114] (a faithful servant of God). The text in which the eighth principle of faith is indicated is: בזאת תדעון כי ה׳ שלחני לעשות את כל המעשים האלה כי לא מלבי[115] "Hereby ye shall know that the Lord hath sent me to do all these works; for I have not done them of mine own mind."

The ninth Principle of Faith.

The abrogation of the Torah. This implies that this Law of Moses will not be abrogated and that no other law will come from before God. Nothing is to be added to it nor taken away from it, neither in the written nor oral law, as it is said לא תוסף עליו ולא תגרע ממנו[116] "Thou shalt not add to it nor diminish from it." In the beginning of this treatise we have already explained that which requires explanation in this principle of faith.

The tenth Principle of Faith.

That He, the exalted one, knows the works of men and is not unmindful of them. Not as they thought who said, עזב ה׳ את הארץ[117] "The Lord hath forsaken the earth," but as he declared who exclaimed גדל העצה ורב העליליה אשר עיניך פקוחות על כל דרכי בני אדם[118] "Great in counsel, and mighty in work; for thine eyes are open upon all the ways of the sons of men." It is further said, וירא ה׳ כי רבה רעת האדם בארץ[119] "And the Lord saw that the wickedness of man was great in the earth." And again, זעקת סדום ועמורה כי רבה[120] "the cry of Sodom and Gomorrah is great." This indicates our tenth principle of faith.

The eleventh Principle of Faith.

That He, the exalted one, rewards him who obeys the commands of the

Torah, and punishes him who transgresses its prohibitions. That God's greatest reward to man is עולם הבא "the future world," and that his strongest punishment is כרת "cutting off." We have already said sufficient upon this theme. The scriptural verses in which the principle is pointed out are. אם תשא חטאתם ואם אין מחני נא מספרך[121] "Yet now if Thou wilt forgive their sin —; but if not, blot me out of Thy book." And God replied to him, מי אשר חטא לי אמחנו מספרי[122] "Whosoever hath sinned against Me, him will I blot out of My book." This is a proof of which the obedient and the rebellious each obtain[123]. God rewards the one and punishes other.

The twelfth Principle of Faith.

The days of the Messiah. This involves the belief and firm faith in his coming, and that we should not find him slow in coming. אם יתמהמה חכה לו[124] "Though he tarry, wait for him." No date must be fixed for his appearance[125], neither may the scriptures be interpreted with the view of deducing the time of his coming. The Sages said, תפח רוחן של מחשבי קצין[126] "A plague on those who calculate periods" (for Messiah's appearance). We must have faith in him, honouring and loving him, and praying for him according to the degree of importance with which he is spoken of by every prophet, from Moses unto Malachi. He that has any doubt about him or holds his authority in light esteem imputes falsehood to the Torah, which clearly promises his coming in פרשת בלעם[127] "the chapter of Balaam," and in אתם נצבים[128] "Ye stand this day all of you before the Lord your God." From the general nature of this principle of faith we gather that there will be no king of Israel but from David and the descendants of Solomon exclusively. Every one who disputes the authority of this family denies God and the words of his prophets.

The thirteenth Principle of Faith.

The resurrection of the dead[129]. We have already explained this.

When all these principles of faith are in the safe keeping of man, and his conviction of them is well established, he then enters בכלל ישראל "into the general body of Israel," and it is incumbent upon us to love him, to care for him, and to do for him all that God commanded us to do for one another in the way of affection and brotherly sympathy. And this, even though he were to be guilty of every transgression possible, by reason of the power of desire or the mastery of the base natural passions. He will receive punishment according to the measure of his perversity, but he will have a portion in the world to come, even though he be of the פושעי ישראל "transgressors in Israel." When, however, a man breaks away from any one of these fundamental principles of belief, then of him is it that יצא מן הכלל "he has gone out of the general body of Israel," and כפר בעיקר "he denies the root-truths of Judaism." And he is then termed מין, and אפיקורס, and קוצץ בנטיעות[130] "hewer of the small plants," and it is obligatory upon us to hate him and cause him to perish, and it is concerning him that the scriptural verse says:— הלוא משנאיך ה׳ אשנא[131] "Shall I not hate those who hate Thee, O Lord?"

I find that I have prolonged my remarks very much and have departed from the main thread of my thesis. But I have been obliged to do so because I consider it advantageous to religious belief. For I have brought together for you many useful things scattered about in many collections of books. Therefore find happiness in them, and repeat this my discourse many times over, and ponder it well. And if your power of desire make you wish that you grasped its purport after going through it once, or even after reading it ten times, verily God knows that you have been made to desire an absurd thing. And so do not go through it hurriedly, for, of a truth, I have not composed it in random fashion but after reflection and conviction and the attentive examination of correct and incorrect views; and after getting to know what things out of all of them it is incumbent upon us to believe, and bringing to my assistance arguments and proofs for every individual section of the subject. I shall now ask God's assistance to what is right and true, and return to the main theme of the chapter (X of *Sanhedrin*).

NOTES

1. Holzer adopts the reading of אין תחיית המתים, and not the fuller reading אין תחיית המתים מן תורה, which is the usual one found in the ordinary editions of the Talmud and adopted by Rashi. According to the longer reading, a man has no portion in the world to come even if he believes in the resurrection but denies that it is alluded to in the Torah. Holzer believes this to be a later addition, because it is not found in the MSS. he used, neither does it occur in the הלכות תשובה of the Mishna Torah. He also instances the commentary to Sanhedrin of Meir Halevi, entitled יד רמה, where the reading is simply הכופר בתחיית המתים. The shorter reading is also found in the Mishnah of the *Palestinian Talmud,* ed. Lowe. It is interesting to note how much turns upon this point in the elaborate discussion of the matter in Sanhedrin. Rashi ingeniously shows why a man forfeits the world to come even if he admits the fact of the resurrection but refuses to admit the existence of any Biblical hint to the fact.

2. The translation "unbeliever" seems the usually accepted one. In the אבות we get דע מה שתשיב לאפיקורוס "Know what answer to give to the unbeliever." Maimonides, however, seems to use it in quite a new sense. He regards it as an Aramaic word from the root פקר "to treat as of little importance," "to despise." Hence, says he, its original meaning is, "He who holds the Torah in light esteem." From this, it has come to be applied to him who does not believe in the fundamental principles of the Torah, or to him who despises the old Jewish Sages, or any Jewish Sage or teacher. Maimonides uses the word in this comprehensive significance (see Schechter, *Studies in Judaism,* p.192).

3. "Heretical books." According to *Sanhedrin* (99b) these are ספרי צדוקים, and the works of Ben Sira. For ספרי צדוקים Maimonides has ספרי מינים. The low estimate at which he held Ben Sira is astonishing. It was a mere waste of time to read him. His aversion went much further than that of the Talmud, which finds parallels to many of Ben Sira's sayings in many a biblical verse or Rabbinic aphorism, and finally declares מילי מעלייתא דאית ביה דרשינן "We may study and give public utterance to the useful remarks found in it" (i.e. in Ben Sira). This is a further proof of Maimonides' dislike of poetry.

4. פואסק. The Arabicized plural form of the Hebrew word פסוק. Maimonides often uses these Arabic forms.

5. אסמיה̈. As Holzer points out, this form of the word אסם (a name) is not to be found in the Arabic dictionaries. He thinks it an incorrect form of the plural אסמיאת (names).

5a. Bachya makes use of the same figure of speech in the section שער הבטחון of his חובות הלבבות.

6. The Arabic has the plural "we shall give," whereas the Hebrew keeps to the singular, as it refers to the teacher. A similar usage occurs a few lines later, where we get the Arabic ונשתרי "and we shall buy," with the Hebrew singular ואקח.

7. *Ethics of the Fathers,* IV, 7.

8. Prov. xxvi. 5.

9. Ethics of the Fathers, I, 3.

10. Maimonides develops the idea in his Mishna Torah הלכות תשובה, I, 2, 4, 5.

11. *Aboda Zara,* 19a, and Ps. cxii. I.

12. Deut. xi. 13.

13. *Sota,* 31a, מה ירא אלקים האמור באברהם מאהבה וכו׳.

14. *Ethics of the Fathers,* I, 11.

15. *Pesachim,* 50b.

16. Deut. iv. 6.

17. It is not at all certain to whom Maimonides is here alluding as אלה הדרשנים. He is

evidently referring to contemporary preachers. Holzer suggests that it is a blow directed against the contemporary French school of exegetists who opposed Maimonides' rationalist method of interpretation with great bitterness.

18. Job xiii. 5.
19. Prov. i. 6.
20. Judges xiv. 12.
21. *Berachoth*, 18b.
22. *Baba Kama*, 60b.
23. *Baba Bathra*, 15a. The Hebrew קצתם is hardly as accurate as the Arabic בעצ̇הם. The later means "a certain one of them," the former signifies "some of them," which is not correct, because it is an individual that holds this view about איוב משל היה. The same applies to the next statement about the מתי יחזקאל, which is the individual view of R. Jehuda.
24. *Sanhedrin*, 92b.
25. Num. xxi. 5.
26. Eccles. xii. 10.
27. אסטקם=Greek *στοιχεῖον*= element.
28. Ps. xxxi. 19.
29. *Berachoth*, 17a.
30. Cp. *Moreh Nebuchim*, I, 41, where Maimonides distinguishes three kinds of soul: (1) "that which constitutes animal life in general; (2) that which constitutes human life in particular; (3) that part of man's individuality which exists independently of his body—i.e., the soul" (Dr. Friedlander's note to his translation). This third kind of soul is the intellect, and it is the only one that is immortal. According to Maimonides it would seem that it is only the souls of men of exemplary intellectual and moral standing that are immortal.
31. The Hebrew literally means "to be included in this glory" (להיות בכבוד הזה). But this is too free a translation of the Arabic ואלחצול פי הד̇א אלחד, which literally means "attaining to (or arriving at') this limit."
32. Deut. xxii. 7.
33. *Kiduschin*, 39b, and *Chulin*, 142a.
34. Num. xv. 31.
35. *Sanhedrin*, 64b and 90b.
36. I Sam. xxv. 29. Maimonides quotes the same verse in *Moreh Nebuchim*, I, 41, where he speaks of the intellectual soul which lives on after death of the body.
37. Isa. lxiv. 3.
38. *Berachoth*, 34b.
39. Deut. xxviii. 47.
40. *Ethics of the Fathers*, IV, 2.
41. It is noteworthy that Maimonides places גן עדן and גיהנום on this side of the grave, and gives them no connection whatsoever with the life hereafter. He holds the view consistently with the Talmudic dictum, "In the world to come there will be no eating and no drinking," &c. But it seems in direct opposition to the average Jewish view expressed in our liturgy in such terms as בגן עדן תהא מנוחתו and to prevailing Jewish conceptions about גיהנום, which it always included in the paraphernalia of the hereafter, and not of the mundane existence. [Abelson's comment is not substantive. The incorporeal nature of reward in the world to come is not challenged by any authority. References to physical activity or sensual pleasure are entirely allegorical in nature. — J.D.B.]
42. *Aboda Zara*, 3b, and *Nedarim*, 8b.
43. Malachi iii. 19.
44. Isa. xxxiii. 12.
45. Berachoth, 18a.
46. אלשאם is used here to denote Palestine. Cf. Prof. Bacher's note, *J.Q.R.*, XVIII, 564.

47. The Arabic is וימלא אפאק אלארץ֗ which is freely translated by the Hebrew וזכרו יהיה מלא הגוים. The translator may possibly have been anxious to imitate the verse (Gen. xlviii. 19) וזרעו יהיה מלא הגוים.

48. *Berachoth*, 34b, *Sabbath*, 63a.

49. *Sabbath*, 30b.

50. Isa. lxi. 5.

51. Prov. xxvi. 4.

52. Isa. xi. 9.

53. The Hebrew renders the Arabic אלפתן ואלחרוב by the one word המלחמות "wars," which seems barely sufficient. The Arabic פתנה̈ is most probably here in the sense of civil war. This goes well with מלחמות which is mostly used for political war. The cessation of both will be a prominent feature in the Messianic time.

54. Micah iv. 3.

55. The Arabic ירתקי= to be elevated [to holy orders]. This is barely done justice to by the Hebrew ונזכה. Besides, the Arabic is third person singular, whereas the Hebrew is first person plural.

56. Isa. xlii. 4.

57. The Hebrew here has ורוב ישרו "the greatest of his rectitude," which is not found in the Arabic version.

58. Ps. ii. 7. It is interesting to note the smoothness with which Maimonides glides over this passage which is the *pièce de résistance* of Christological interpreters. He takes "sonship" in the sense of kinship, nearness, i.e. in the moral and spiritual senses. The Messiah is the "son" of God in so far as he is, humanly speaking, as near God as possible in the possession of the highest of virtues.

59. The Arabic קלק=disquietude, agitation. I cannot find in it a correspondence of meaning with the Hebrew עצלה which=sloth, laziness.

60. The Hebrew has the ordinary expression כמו שנאמר "as it is said."

61. Jer. xxxi. 34.

62. Jer. xxxi. 33. This is a portion of the verse, but incorrectly quoted. It is נתתי את תורתי בקרבם.

63. Ezek. xxxvi. 26.

64. The meaning varies according as you read פצ̇ול or פצול. Holzer in the Arabic test before me adopts the latter reading, but the Hebrew version seems to be a translation of the former.

65. Ps. xxxii. 9.

66. "The traditional explanation of the Torah." This seems to be the meaning of חמלה̈ אלשריעה̈—from the verb חמל to carry. חמלה̈=a carrying from one place to another. Such was the case with the oral law which was handed down to successive generations in all climes. The Hebrew renders the words חמלה̈ אלשריעה̈ by לומדיה "its learners, students"—possibly because it is they who carry about and disseminate its teachings.

67. אסתאד̇ה. This seems to be the X. form of אד̇י= to injure, damage. The Hebrew has רבו= his master. This is obviously another reading. Or it may be that the word המבזה "he who despises" (which Holzer repudiates) should stand, and then the Arabic word would be equivalent to המבזה רבו "he who injures him," viz. his master.

68. *Sanhedrin*, 99b. As to the exact significance of the *Minim* see Travers Herford, *Christianity in the Talmud.* [The term *Minim* has a distinct halakhic connotation. See *Mishneh Torah, Hilkhot Teshuvah* 3:7.—J.D.B.]

69. כתב אלאג̇אני "Books of songs." It is surprising that Maimonides dismisses these with contempt although they occupy a great and distinguished place on the Parnassus of Arabic literature. The Mu'allaqat, the Mufaddaliyyat, the Jamharat Ash'ar al-'Arab, the

Hamasa of Abu Tammam are all great collections of Bedouin poems of the greatest importance in Arabic literature, both from a poetical and historical point of view. Then there is the great כתאב אלאגׄאני (Book of Songs), published at the Bulaq printing press in twenty volumes, to which Brünnow has added a twenty-first from MSS. discovered in European libraries. In his *History of Arabic Literature* Prof. Clément Huart says "This huge literary compilation is our most valuable source as to everything regarding the circumstances amidst which the poets of the first centuries of Arab literature lived their lives and composed their works." That any one should say of all this that it is a mere "waste of time" is really extraordinary. Maimonides evidently loathed poetry. [Abelson fails to understand the thrust of Maimonides' comment. Maimonides, in keeping with his general denigration of esthetics, denies that poetry is condusive to intellectual or spiritual perfection. The place of poetry in Arabic literature has no bearing whatsoever on this judgment.—J.D.B.]

70. ברקיקה. The Arabic verb רקי= to use magic or incantation, and has therefore a striking resemblance in the lettering to this Hebrew word and it fits in well with the theme. But there is no such grammatical form of the Arabic word and the resemblance is merely accidental.

71. For the full discussion of the שם המפורש, see *Moreh Nebuchim,* chap. 61–64. Dr. Friedlander has an interesting note there explaining the literal meaning of the phrase שם המפורש.

72. *Baba Mezia,* 58b.

73. *Baba Mezia,* 58b. The wording, however, is not as here, but המכנה שם רע לחברו.

74. *Baba Mezia,* 58b.

75. To accord with the Arabic קדרנא we should expect נעלה על הלב, and not the third pers. sing. יעלה.

76. The Arabic מסתקל בוגודה "that which is independent, absolute, in its existence," is rather loosely and inaccurately rendered by נמצא שיתקיים מציאותי.

77. The Hebrew has ומה שיש בתוכם "and what is inside them," which is not represented in the Arabic, unless the translator understood דון (دُون) to contain this meaning among the many others which it possesses in Arabic. I cannot, however, find this meaning indicated in the dictionaries.

78. Exod. xx. 2.

79. Deut. vi. 4.

80. *Hagiga,* 15a.

81. עורף. The Arabic ערף means "to divide." In Hebrew we get this meaning in וערפתו (Exod. xiii. 13) "and thou shall break its neck," i.e. separate, divide the head from the trunk. In Hosea x. 2 we get the phrase הוא יערף מזבחותם "he shall break down their altars," i.e. take them to pieces, separate stone from stone.

82. This translation is in accord with the Targum of Jonathan which renders the verse Isa. xi. 14 ויתחברון כתף חד.

83. Isa. xl. 18.

84. Isa. xl. 25.

85. *Berachoth,* 31b.

86. For the Arabic אלנאס "people" the Hebrew has החכמים "the sages." The reason for this change is not clear.

87. Deut. iv. 15.

88. Deut. xxxiii. 27.

89. The Arabic פאץׄ literally signifies "to flow" (of water, blood, & c.), and is usually represented in Hebrew by שפע which has an exactly similar significance. This whole subject is thoroughly discussed in the *Moreh,* II, 12. Everything that happens in the world is influenced by the פיץ of the Divine Creator. It is that that is shed upon the prophets, enabling them to prophesy. נאמר שהעולם נתחדש משפע הבורא ושהוא המשפיע עליו כל מה שיתחדש בו וכן יאמר שהוא השפיע חכמתו על הנביאים. "It is said that the universe renews

itself by the emanation of the Creator, and that it is He who is the cause of the emanation of everything that renews itself in it. Similarly, it is said that He causes His wisdom to emanate to the prophets." Maimonides instances the usage of this idea in the prophetical books of the Bible by quoting Jeremiah xvii, 13 אותי עזבו מקור מים חיים "They have forsaken me, the fountain of living waters."

90. This promised work was left undone by Maimonides. His son Abraham wittily alluded to the fact in the words ויירא משה מגשת אליו "And Moses was afraid to draw near to it" (a slight alteration of Exod. xxxiv. 30).

91. Num. xii. 8.

92. Gen. xx. 3.

93. Job xxxiii. 15.

94. Exod. xxv. 22.

95. Num. xii. 6–8.

96. Dan. x. 8.

97. Dan. x. 9.

98. Dan. x. 16.

99. Exod xxxiii. 11. For the full discussion of all the meanings of פנים, see *Moreh*, I, 37. He there explains פנים בפנים as שמיעת הקול מבלתי אמצעיות מלאך "the perception of the Divine voice without the intervention of an angel."

100. The Arabic word פאטר is only found in the sense of "Creator," which cannot possibly fit in here. Holzer suggests that it may be meant by Maimonides for פטרה̈, which means "religious sentiment," "natural disposition." As an instance of the necessity for previous self-preparation on the part of a prophet one would have thought that Maimonides would have mentioned the case of the severe ordeal of Isaiah (chap. vi) which is far more striking than the instance he quotes in the life of Elisha.

101. The Arabic יבסט נפסה does not seem to be rendered in the Hebrew version.

102. 2 Kings iii. 15.

103. Num. ix. 8.

104. Lev. xvi. 2.

105. Gen. x. 6.

106. Gen. xxxvi. 39.

107. Gen. xxxvi. 12.

108. Exod. xx. 2.

109. Deut. vi. 4.

110. *Sanhedrin,* 99a.

111. Num. xv. 31.

112. Job xi. 9.

113. Ps. cxix. 18.

114. Num. xii. 7.

115. Num. xvi. 28.

116. Deut. xiii. 1.

117. Ezek. viii. 12; ix. 9.

118. Jer. xxxii. 19.

119. Gen. vi. 5.

120. Gen. xviii. 20.

121. Exod. xxxii. 32.

122. Exod. xxxii. 33.

123. For the Arabic תחציל (II. infin. of חצל) the Hebrew has שיודע "that he knows." The word חצל signifies "to obtain," either in the material sense or figuratively in the sense of grasping or comprehending some scientific idea. The Hebrew gives the second signification. I have translated, however, in its first meaning.

124. Hab. ii. 3.

125. Many computations were made by Jews in the middle ages with regard to the time

of the Messiah's appearance. It was one such computation by a Jewish enthusiast in Yemen (about 1172) that caused Maimonides to compose his famous **איגרת תימן** in which he says: "It is wrong to calculate the Messianic period, as the Yemen enthusiast thinks he has succeeded in doing; for it can never be exactly determined, it having been purposely concealed, as a deep secret, by the prophets" (Graetz, *History of the Jews*, English transl., vol. III, p. 478).

126. *Sanhedrin*, 97b.

127. Num. xxiii-xxiv. In the **איגרת תימן** Maimonides derives the exact date of the coming of the Messiah from the verse **כעת יאמר ליעקב וכו'** (Num. xxiii. 23). This is most strangely inconsistent with the advice given in this essay, and in the *Iggereth Teman*, against calculating the date of the Messiah's appearance. (See Dr. Friedlander's Introduction to Translation of *Moreh*, vol. I.)

128. Deut. xxx. 1–10.

129. From the briefness with which Maimonides dismisses this thirteenth article concerning the Resurrection of the Dead, it has been inferred by many that he was really opposed to classing it among the fundamental dogmas of Judaism, and only did so as an unwilling concession to the current orthodox views of his day. His *Moreh Nebuchim* is quite silent on the point. Maimonides was attacked on this very question by his opponents during his lifetime. They complained that whereas he had made an exhaustive examination of the question of immortality, he had passed over the doctrine of Resurrection with little notice. Maimonides vindicated himself by writing his famous **מאמר תחיית המתים** in Arabic in the year 1191. He says there that he "firmly believes in the Resurrection as a miracle whose possibility is granted with the assumption of a temporal Creation" (Graetz, English transl., vol. III, p.503). Maimonides seems to have looked on the Resurrection as a secondary consideration. [See the General Introduction to this book in which I have attempted to place Maimonides' views on resurrection in proper perspective. — J.D.B.]

130. קוצץ בנטיעות. The phrase is taken from the famous Midrash commencing ארבעה נכנסו לפרדס בן עזאי ובן זומא אלישע בן אבויה ורבי עקיבא. It is Elisha ben Abuya who is קוצץ בנטיעות "the hewer of the small plants," because he used to enter synagogues and schools in which children were receiving religious instruction, and would endeavour to lead them away from the paths of the Torah by telling them his heretical views (היה אומר עליהון מיליא ומסתתמין). See Midrash *Rabbah Shir Ha-Shirim*, chapter הביאני המלך חדריו; also Talmud *Jerushalmi* on Chagiga in Perek אין דורשין.

131. Ps. cxxxix. 21.

MAIMONIDES, *MISHNEH TORAH*

Translation by Moses Hyamson

BOOK OF KNOWLEDGE, LAWS OF REPENTANCE, CHAPTER 3

6. XIV. The following have no portion in the world to come, but are cut off and perish, and for their great wickedness and sinfulness are condemned for ever and ever. Heretics and Epicureans; those who deny the Torah, the resurrection of the dead or the coming of the Redeemer; apostates; those who cause a multitude to sin, and those who secede from the ways of the community; any one who commits transgressions like Jehoiakim, in high-handed fashion and openly; informers; those who terrorise a community, not for a religious purpose; murderers and slanderers, and one who obliterates the physical mark of his Jewish origin.

7. XV. Five Classes are termed Heretics; he who says that there is no God and the world has no ruler; he who says that there is a ruling power but that it is vested in two or more persons; he who says there is one ruler, but that He is a body and has form; he who denies that He alone is the First Cause and Rock of the Universe; likewise, he who renders worship to any one beside Him, to serve as a mediator between the human being and the Lord of the Universe. Whoever belongs to any of these five classes is termed a heretic.

8. XVI. Three Classes are called Epicureans:[1] he who denies the reality of prophecy and maintains that there is no knowledge which emanates from the Creator and directly reaches the human mind; he who denies the prophecy of Moses, our teacher; and he who asserts that the Creator has no cognizance of the deeds of the children of men. Each of these classes consists of Epicureans. XVII. Three Classes are deniers of the Torah; he who says that the Torah is not of divine origin—even if he says of one verse, or of a single word, that Moses said it, of himself,[2]—is a denier of the Torah; likewise, he who denies its interpretation, that is, the Oral Law, and repudiates its reporters, as Zadok and Boethus did; he who says that the Creator changed one commandment for another, and that this Torah, although of divine origin, is now obsolete, as the

Nazarenes and Moslems assert. Everyone belonging to any of these classes is a denier of the Torah.

9. XVIII. There are two classes of apostates—an apostate with respect to the violation of a single precept, and an apostate with respect to the whole Torah. The former is a person who has determined to violate a certain precept, commits the transgression habitually and has become notorious for it. Even if it is one of the lighter sins, as, for instance, if a person wears garments "of diverse sorts" (a mixture of wool and flax) (Deut. 22:11) or "rounds the corner of his head" (Lev. 19:27), doing so habitually, so that it appears that the precept is regarded by him as no longer binding, he is an apostate in regard to that particular observance, provided that he acted in a provocative spirit. An apostate with respect to the whole Torah is one, for example, who at a time of religious persecution becomes converted to the idolaters' religion, clings to them, saying "what advantage is it to me to adhere to the people of Israel, who are of low estate and persecuted. Better for me to join these nations who are powerful." A person who acts thus is an apostate in respect to the whole Torah.

10. XIX. Those who cause the multitude to sin, include one who induces others to sin, whether in a great matter, like Jeroboam, Zadok and Boethus, or in a light matter even if he only induces them to nullify the observance of an affirmative precept; and any one who coerces others to sin, like Manasseh who put Israelites to death and so forced the people into idolatry; or deceives others and leads them astray.

11. XX. One who separates himself from the Community, even if he does not commit a transgression but only holds aloof from the congregation of Israel, does not fulfill religious precepts in common with his people, shows himself indifferent when they are in distress, does not observe their fast, but goes his own way, as if were one of the gentiles and did not belong to the Jewish people—such a person has no portion in the world to come. XXI. He, who, like Jehoiakim, commits transgressions arrogantly, whether these are light or grave offences, has no portion in the world to come. Such a one is called a shameless transgressor, because he exhibits effrontery and shamelessness and is unabashed by the words of the Torah.

12. XXII. There are two classes of informers: one who delivers a coreligionist into the power of a heathen, who will put him to death or assault him; and one who delivers the property of a coreligionist to a heathen or to a despot, who is like a heathen. Both classes of informers have no portion in the world to come.

13. XXIII. The terrorisers of a community, not for the sake of God,

are those who rule a congregation arbitrarily so that all fear and are afraid of them—their aim, like that of the heathen kings, being to advance their own glory and interests but not to promote the glory of God.

14. XXIV. All these twenty-four classes which we have enumerated, even if they are Israelites, have no portion in the world to come. There are transgressions less grave than those mentioned, concerning which, however, the sages said that whoever habitually commits them will have no portion in the world to come. One should therefore avoid, and beware of such transgressors. . .

NOTES

1. אפיקורוס, literally a follower of the freethinking school of Epicurus; extended scoffing sceptics.
2. Without divine authority.

ALBO, *IKKARIM*

Translation by Isaac Husik

BOOK I, CHAPTER 2[1]

Every Israelite is obliged to believe that everything that is found in the Torah is absolutely true, and any one who denies anything that is found in the Torah, knowing that it is the opinion of the Torah, is an unbeliever; as the Rabbis say in chapter "Ḥelek,"[2] that anyone who says, the whole Torah emanates from the divine Being except one verse, which Moses said on his own authority, is liable to the imputation charged in the biblical expression, "Because he hath despised the word of the Lord,"[3] and is classed among those who deny the divine inspiration of the Torah. But a person who upholds the law of Moses and believes in its principles, but when he undertakes to investigate these matters with his reason and scrutinizes the texts, is misled by his speculation and interprets a given principle otherwise than it is taken to mean at first sight; or denies the principle because he thinks that it does not represent a sound theory which the Torah obliges us to believe; or erroneously denies that a given belief is a fundamental principle, which however he believes as he believes the other dogmas of the Torah which are not fundamental principles; or entertains a certain notion in relation to one of the miracles of the Torah because he thinks that he is not thereby denying any of the doctrines which it is obligatory upon us to believe by the authority of the Torah,—a person of this sort is not an unbeliever. He is classed with the sages and pious men of Israel, though he holds erroneous theories. His sin is due to error and requires atonement.

We find such opinions expressed by some of the ancient sages of Israel. Thus we find a statement[4] that temporal sequence existed before creation. What the author of this opinion meant to say is that the Torah does not oblige us to believe that time was itself created. Similarly Rabbi Eliezer the Great, in chapter three of his treatise,[5] endeavors to name the material out of which the heavens and the earth were made. Now even if we should understand his words in their literal sense, as indicating, namely, that the world was not created out of nothing, but out of something, namely out of a primitive matter, we should have no reason for bringing a charge against him. For his idea is that the Torah does not oblige us to believe in creation *ex nihilo.* He has no intention to deny anything that is in the Torah, Heaven forbid!

Maimonides also, the author of the *Guide of the Perplexed,* in chapter twenty-five of the second part, says that his belief in creation *ex nihilo* was not due to the authority of scriptural texts—texts can be interpreted—but to the fact that it is a true doctrine, and therefore the texts must be interpreted so as to harmonize with this doctrine. His meaning is that anything which is opposed to the texts must not be believed at all, provided the texts do not give expression to an absurd idea which the reason can not conceive. For the Torah does not oblige us to believe absurdities, which are opposed to first principles, or any imaginary notions which the reason can not conceive. But a thing which can be conceived by the mind, we are obliged to believe, though it is opposed to nature, for example, resurrection of the dead and the miracles of the Torah. An absurd idea, however, which can not be conceived by the mind need not be believed even if it is plainly expressed in the Torah. Thus the expression, "Circumcise, therefore, the foreskin of your heart,"[6] must not be taken in its literal sense, but should be explained in accordance with the truth.

This is the method of Onkelos the proselyte,[7] of Jonathan ben Uziel,[8] and the other sages of Israel. They interpret all the expressions in the Torah and the Prophets which signify corporeality of the deity so as to harmonize with the truth. They reject the literal meaning because it expresses an absurdity. Their maxim is that "the Torah speaks in the language of man" and "in order to quiet the ear."

The method we have been describing is precisely that which is used by some of the modern scholars, who interpret the speech of Balaam's ass in a manner different from the interpretation of the Rabbis of the Talmud.[9] Their idea is that the Torah does not intend us to believe that miracle except in the manner in which they understand it. We say, therefore, that a person whose speculative ability is not sufficient to enable him to reach the true meaning of scriptural texts, with the result that he believes in the literal meaning and entertains absurd ideas because he thinks they represent the view of the Torah, is not thereby excluded from the community of those who believe in the Torah, Heaven forbid! Nor is it permitted to speak disrespectfully of him and accuse him of perverting the teaching of the Torah and class him among unbelievers and heretics.

Rabbi Abraham ben David[10] has gone even further than this. He says that even if a person understands a fundamental principle of the Torah in an erroneous manner because of a speculative error, he must not be called a heretic. We find this idea of his in his *Book of Criticisms* on Maimonides.[11] Commenting on the latter's statement that one who believes God is corporeal is a heretic, Rabbi Abraham ben David says: "It is true that God is not corporeal; nevertheless a person who believes He is corporeal by reason of biblical and midrashic expressions which he understands literally, must not be called a heretic."

This seems to be the correct view as held by the Rabbis of the Talmud. For in speaking of Elisha ben Abuya[12] they quote the biblical expression, "Return, ye rebellious children,"[13] and add by way of comment, "except Elisha Aher, who knows his Creator and deliberately rebels against Him."[14] They thus indicate clearly that that man alone who knows the truth and deliberately denies it, belongs to the class of the wicked whose repentance is rejected. But the man whose intention is not to rebel, nor to depart from the truth, nor to deny what is in the Torah, nor reject tradition, but whose sole intention is to interpret the texts according to his opinion, though he interprets them erroneously, is neither a heretic nor an unbeliever.

Accordingly a person who believes that those who are resurrected will not live forever in the resurrected state of body and soul, but will return to dust, as is the opinion of Maimonides in his letter *On the Resurrection of the Dead,* can not be regarded as rejecting the dogma of resurrection, though, according to Rabbi Moses ben Nahman,[15] this is not the true belief. Similarly one who believes that the real retribution in the future world is imposed upon body and soul jointly, and that the soul alone has no retribution apart from the body, this being the opinion of Rabbi Moses ben Nahman and some of the wise men of the Cabala, is not a denier of the dogma of spiritual reward and punishment, though according to Maimonides this is not the true belief.

I had to write all this because I have seen insignificant men, who think they are wise, open their mouths wide in lengthy and unintelligent discourses against great men. It is clear now that every intelligent person is permitted to investigate the fundamental principles of religion and to interpret the biblical texts in accordance with the truth as it seems to him. And though he believe concerning certain things which the ancients regarded as principles, like the dogma of the Messiah and of the creation, that they are not fundamental principles, but merely true doctrines, which the believer in the Torah is obliged to believe in the same way as he believes in the earth's opening its mouth on the occasion of Korah's rebellion, or the coming down of fire from heaven, and similar miracles and promises mentioned in the Torah, which are true without being fundamental principles of the Torah,—he is not a denier of the Torah or of its principles. For if he were, it would follow that there are as many fundamental principles in the Law of Moses as there are miracles and promises in the Torah, an idea which has never occurred to any one.

NOTES

1. The discussion in this chapter is also parallelled in the Magen Abot of Duran, chs. 8 and 9, as Jaulus l.c., [MGWJ, 23 (1874), pp. 457–63.]

2. Eleventh chapter of the talmudic treatise *Sanhedrin*, p. 99a.

3. Num. 15, 31.

4. Bereshit Rabbah 3.

5. "Pirke de-Rabbi Eliezer," though attributed here to R. Eliezer ben Hyrcanus, surnamed the Great, a tannaitic scholar of the first and second centuries, is in reality of more recent date, having been composed in Italy(?) shortly after 833. See J. E., X, 58; also G. Friedlander, Pirke de Rabbi Eliezer, London, 1916, Introduction, §1.

6. Deut. 10, 16.

7. The reference here is to the Babylonian Targum or the official Aramaic translation of the Pentateuch, which is erroneously ascribed in the Talmud to the proselyte Onkelos, a tannaitic scholar of the end of the first century. See J. E., s. vv. Onkelos and Targum.

8. The reference to the Targum, i.e. Aramaic translation, of the Prophets, doubtfully ascribed to Jonathan ben Uzziel, Hillel's most distinguished pupil. See J. E., s. v. Jonathan ben Uzziel.

9. Cf. Gersonides, Commentary on the Pentateuch, who says it was a dream.

10. Abraham ben David of Posquières, French talmudic commentator; born in Provence about 1125; died at Posquières, Nov. 27, 1198. See J. E., s. v., I, 103.

11. Yad ha-Hazakah, Hilkot Teshubah, III, 7. Albo does not quote the exact words of Abraham ben David, which are more caustic than polite, and read as follows: ולמה קרא לזה מין וכמה גדולים וטובים ממנו הלכו בזו המחשבה לפי מה שראו במקראות ויותר ממה שראו בדברי האגדות המשבשות את הדעות. Many greater and better men than Maimonides, says Abraham ben David, have had this opinion [viz. that God is corporeal] by reason of biblical texts and more especially by reason of the words of certain haggadic passages which are apt to confuse one in his ideas.

Joseph Caro, in his commentary, "Kesef Mishneh," ad loc., takes Abraham ben David to task for speaking of the anthropomorphists as greater and better men than Maimonides, and suggests that Albo's quotation may be a more correct version of Abraham ben David's stricture.

12. The bête noire of the Talmud. He was born in Jerusalem before 70. See J. E., s. v., V, 138.

13. Jer. 3, 22.

14. Ḥagigah, 15a.

15. Spanish talmudist, exegete and physician; born at Gerona in 1195, died in Palestine about 1270. See J. E. IX, 87; S. Schechter, Studies in Judaism, First Series, 99 ff.

BOOK I, CHAPTER 4[1]

It seems to me that the general and essential principles of divine law are three: existence of God, providence in reward and punishment, and divine revelation. These three embrace all the principles of the various divine laws, such as the law of Adam, the law of Noah, the law of Abraham, the law of Moses, and any other divine laws, if there be such, at the same time or in succession. Implicit in every one of these are subordinate and derivative principles coming from that principle as a branch issues from a tree. Thus from the existence of God is derived God's eternity, perpetuity, and so on. In revelation is implied God's knowledge, prophecy, and so on. And from providence follows physical reward and punishment in this world, and spiritual in the next.

From these three general principles issue special dogmas peculiar to the various divine laws, genuine or spurious, as follows: From the existence of God is derived His incorporeality, which is a special principle of the law of Moses, and likewise His unity. Under revelation comes the prophecy and mission of Moses. Under providence and reward and punishment comes the belief in the advent of the Messiah, which is a special principle of the law of Moses according to the opinion of Maimonides. But according to our opinion the belief in the Messiah is not a principle. And if it is, it is not special to the law of Moses, for the Christians too regard it as a principle, and that too in order to abrogate the law of Moses. It is indeed a special principle for them for their law can not be conceived without it. All these and similar dogmas which are special to certain religions are included in the three principles which we have mentioned. The question whether there can be more than one divine law at the same time or at different times, will be discussed later with the help of God.[2]

That these three principles are the basis of the faith by which man attains true happiness is proved by the fact that the Men of the Great Synagogue[3] composed three blessings which they incorporated in the Additional Service for New Year, going by the name of "Kingdoms," "Memorials" and "Trumpets."[4] These three blessings correspond to the three principles and are intended to call our attention to the fact that by properly believing in these principles together with the dogmas derived from them we shall win a favorable verdict in the divine judgment.

The blessing known as "Kingdoms" corresponds to the principle of the existence of God. This is proved by the words of the benediction, "Therefore do we wait for Thee, O Lord our God, that we may quickly see Thy glorious strength, when the images will be removed from the earth and the idols will be completely cut off, when the world will be established under the Kingdom of the Almighty . . . when all the inhabitants of the world will recognize and know that to Thee shall every knee bend, by Thee every tongue swear . . . and all shall accept the yoke of Thy Kingdom."

The benediction called "Memorials" points to providence and reward and punishment, as is indicated by its contents: "Thou rememberest the works of the universe, and visitest all the creatures from the beginning; before Thee are all hidden things revealed . . ."

The benediction called "Trumpets" alludes to the third principle, revelation. Therefore it begins, "Thou didst reveal Thyself in the cloud of Thy glory to Thy holy people and didst speak unto them. From Heaven didst Thou cause them to hear Thy voice. . . ." This benediction is called "Trumpets" because at the time of the giving of the Law there was a very loud sound of the trumpet, such as never had been heard before in the world. Thunders and lightning like those seen at Sinai or of the same nature had been heard and seen before, but the sound of a trumpet without a trumpet had never been heard before, and will not be heard again until the time of the redemption. At that time the true law will be made known before the whole world. This is the time that is referred to in the words of the prophet, "And the Lord God will blow the horn,"[5] according to some authorities.

I have seen a statement that the benediction "Trumpets" bears an allusion to the sacrifice of Isaac. But this is not correct, for if that were the case, we should expect the sacrifice of Isaac to be mentioned in this blessing, whereas mention is made of it in the benediction "Memorials." The origin of this opinion is to be sought in the statement of the Rabbis[6] that the ceremony of blowing the ram's horn on New Year is in memory of the ram which was substituted for Isaac. But this does not justify the opinion. For what the Rabbis mean is that the requirement of a ram's horn is to commemorate the ram of Isaac, not that the command itself to blow an instrument has that meaning, much less does it follow that the benediction "Trumpets" alludes to that event.

Isaiah refers to these three principles, which are the cause of happiness, in a single sentence: "For the Lord is our judge, the Lord is our lawgiver, the Lord is our king, He will save us."[7] "The Lord is our judge," alludes to the dogma of providence, denoting the same idea that is contained in the expression, "He is near that justifieth me; who will contend with me?

Let us stand up together . . .,"[8] namely that we may win a favorable verdict. "The Lord is our lawgiver (*meḥokek*)," refers to the dogma of revelation, which is the second principle. For the word *meḥokek* applies to a lawgiver, as we see in Deuteronomy,[9] "For there a portion of the *meḥokek* was reserved," a reference to Moses through whom the law was given. The meaning is similar to that expressed in the words of the prophet, "Hearken unto Me, ye that know righteousness, the people in whose heart is My law; fear ye not the taunt of men . . .,"[10] namely that though the verdict may not be favorable to us in so far as He is our judge, seeing that a judge can not go against the law that is laid down by another, nevertheless we ought to win because He is also the legislator who lays down the statutes. "The Lord is our king," alludes to the third principle, the existence of God, who is the king of the whole world, and is especially called "the King of Israel and their Redeemer." The thought here is that even if in His capacity of legislator He may refuse to transgress His own law, nevertheless as being our king, He must save us, for a king has the power to go against the law and to do whatever he desires in order to save his people. That is why the above text concludes with the words, "He will save us." The meaning is that inasmuch as we have an advantage over the whole world in the possession of these three principles, upon belief in which depends man's true happiness, it is fitting that God should save us above all others.

It may be that Maimonides has the same idea concerning the number of fundamental principles as the one we have just indicated, and that his list consists of the three chief principles that we have mentioned, plus the derivative dogmas issuing from them, being all called by him principles. Thus he lays down the existence of God, a fundamental doctrine, as the first principle. Then he enumerates along with it as principles four other dogmas which are derived from it, viz., unity, incorporeality, eternity, and exclusive worship. Then he lists as principles revelation, another fundamental doctrine, together with three other dogmas derived from it, viz., prophecy, superiority of Moses, and immutability of the law. Then comes divine omniscience and providence in reward and punishment, the third fundamental doctrine, together with three other dogmas implied in it and derived therefrom, viz., spiritual retribution, Messiah, and resurrection.

According to this explanation it is clear why he did not include the doctrine of creation, for it does not come under any of the three which we mentioned. He did not include freedom and purpose because, though they are essential to divine law, they are not essential to it *qua* divine, as will appear later.[11] The question still remains, however, why he did not include under existence of God life and power and other attributes, seeing that he included eternity and other attributes. The same criticism applies to the dogmas he derives from the other fundamental principles. All this will be made clear as we go on. We must now resume our discussion of the fundamental principles, which in our opinion consist of three chief dogmas. We must, however, first explain the principles of conventional laws, and then we will treat of the principles of divine law, with the help of God.

NOTES

1. J. Guttmann, l. c., p.60, finds the source of this in Duran's commentary on Job, introduction, ch. 8.
2. I, 25; III, 13.
3. J. E. XI, 640; G.F. Moore, Judaism, I, 31 ff.
4. Dembitz, L.N., Jewish Services in Synagogue and Home, pp. 155–162, 170.
5. Zech. 9, 14.
6. Rosh Hashanah, 16a.
7. Is. 33, 22.
8. Is. 50, 8.
9. Deut. 33, 21.
10. Is. 51, 7.
11. Ch. 9.

BOOK I, CHAPTER 23

There are six dogmas which every one professing the law of Moses is obliged to believe. They are connected with the three fundamental principles that we laid down, but they are not derivative principles.

1. Creation of the world in time out of nothing. It is clear from its nature that it is a dogma common to divine law generally and belonging especially to the Law of Moses, though it is neither a fundamental nor a derivative principle, because we can conceive a divine law in general and the Law of Moses in particular without the idea of creation *ex nihilo,* as we explained in chapter twelve of this book. But it may be likened to a branch issuing from the first principle, which is the existence of God. We explained above that God is free from defects. Now if He can not create out of nothing, this would be a defect in His nature. We can not say that creation *ex nihilo* is *ipso facto* an impossibility, that creation must be out of something. For since the mind can conceive it, it may be believed, and comes within the power of the Omnipotent Being. Even those who believe in the eternity of the world, admit that God, though a simple intellect, is the cause of all things. Therefore matter is caused by God through the instrumentality of the Separate Intelligence which is also caused by God. But how can a Separate Intelligence be a cause of matter if there can be no coming into being *ex nihilo*? There can be no greater creation *ex nihilo* than this. If you say that the reason they maintain the eternity of the world is because they can not conceive that He should create or produce at one time rather than at another, our answer is that this difficulty is valid only in the case of an agent who acts by necessity, but not in an agent who acts by will, for it is the nature of the will to act at one time rather than at another, as Maimonides explains in the *Guide of the Perplexed,* Book II, chapter 18. Now since God, being the best of agents, must act voluntarily and not through necessity, as will be explained in the Second Book,[1] it follows that He must produce the world at a particular time; since this follows necessarily from the nature of will.

2. The second dogma is the superiority of Moses' prophecy to that of all other prophets who ever were or will be. Though this dogma is not essential to divine law in general nor the Law of Moses in particular, nevertheless since the Torah says explicitly, "And there hath not arisen a prophet since in Israel like unto Moses"[2] (the meaning is that there has not arisen and there will not arise, indicating the high value of the law

that was given through him, as we will explain in the Third Book),[3] every one who professes the Law of Moses is obliged to believe it as a dogma issuing like a branch from the principle of revelation.

3. The third dogma is that the Law of Moses will not be repealed nor changed nor exchanged for another by any prophet. This dogma, too, though it is not essential to divine law in general or the Law of Moses in particular, as we explained above,[4] nevertheless it is like a branch issuing from the dogma of the authenticity of the messenger, and therefore it is incumbent upon every one who professes the Law of Moses to believe it, as we will explain in the Third Book.[5]

4. The fourth dogma is that human perfection may be attained by fulfilling even a single one of the commandments in the Law of Moses. If this were not so, it would follow that the Law of Moses hinders man from attaining human perfection, which the Rabbis call "the life of the world to come." For mankind attained some degree of future life through the Noachian law, as the Rabbis say, "The pious men of the Gentiles have a share in the world to come."[6] This means that those who observe the seven Noachian commandments have a share in the world to come. Now if every one professing the Law of Moses must fulfill all the many commandments mentioned therein before he can attain any degree of future life, then the Law of Moses would hinder man from the acquisition of perfection rather than help him. But this can not be the purpose of the Law, as the Rabbis say, "God desired to bestow merit upon Israel, therefore He gave them many laws and commandments."[7] Therefore it seems that this dogma is a special principle of the Law of Moses, as we shall explain in the twenty-ninth chapter of the Third Book.

5. The fifth dogma is the resurrection of the dead. Some of our Rabbis say that only those who are perfect will have this privilege. According to this opinion, since it is not a species of reward promised to all mankind, since all mankind cannot be perfect, one who disbelieves this dogma is like one who denies some one of the great miracles performed for righteous men, which are within the limits of logical possibility. This dogma would then come under the first principle. But if resurrection embraces all persons, as some of the authorities hold, then a person who disbelieves it is like one who denies a part of reward and punishment which is promised to all mankind or to the whole nation. In that case the dogma comes under the third principle. But it is not itself either a fundamental or a derivative principle of divine law in general or of the Law of Moses in particular, for they can be conceived without it. As long as one believes in reward and punishment generally, whether corporeal, in this world, or spiritual, in the world to come, he does not deny a prin-

ciple of the Law of Moses if he disbelieves in resurrection. Nevertheless it is a dogma accepted by our nation, and every one professing the Law of Moses is obliged to believe it, as will be explained in the Fourth Book.[8]

6. The dogma of the coming of the Messiah is of the same nature as the one before. It comes under the third principle, reward, and is an accepted dogma, which every one professing the Law of Moses is obliged to believe, as will be explained in the Fourth Book.[9] But it is not a principle, fundamental or derived, of the Law of Moses, because the latter with its principles, fundamental and derivative, can be conceived without it.

We did not include among these dogmas, beliefs which are based upon specific commandments, like repentance, prayer, etc., for example the dogma that God hears the prayer of those who supplicate Him, or that He receives those who turn to Him in repentance, and other such dogmas based upon specific commandments, because no one commandment should be counted as a dogma rather than another. Nor did we include such beliefs as that the Shekinah dwelt in Israel, that fire came down from heaven upon the altar of the burnt-offering, that the priests received answers from God through the Urim and the Thumim, and so on, because they are included in the belief in the biblical miracles generally, and there is no reason for naming these rather than others, such as the dividing of the Red Sea, the opening of the earth and the swallowing of Korah and his congregation, their going into Sheol alive, and the still more wonderful phenomenon of the earth closing up again after they went down, as we read, "And the earth closed upon them,"[10] so different from an opening made by an earthquake, which remains that way forever,—all these are included in a belief in the Torah and in the miracles told therein. We did enumerate specially the six beliefs above mentioned, because they are accepted dogmas among our people necessary for the maintenance of the fundamental and derivative principles of the Torah. The fulfillment of the Torah is dependent upon them, though they are not essential principles, since the Law can exist without them, as we explained above. He who denies them is called a heretic, though he does not deny the Torah, and has no share in the world to come.

NOTES

1. Ch. 3.
2. Deut. 34, 10.
3. Ch. 20.
4. Ch. 15.
5. Chs. 19 and 20.
6. See Maimonides, Yad ha-Hazakah, Hilkot Teshubah, III, 5, and Kesef Mishneh ad loc.; also Hilkot 'Edut, XI, 10: Hilkot Melakim VIII, 11. The source is Tosefta Sanhedrin 13, 2, where our texts read: יש צדיקים באומות שיש להם חלק לעולם הבא; see G.F. Moore, Judaism, II, 386, note 3.
7. Makkot 23b.
8. Chs. 29–31.
9. Ch. 42.
10. Num. 16, 33.

BOOK I, CHAPTER 26

The result of our discussion in this Book is that the number of fundamental principles of a divine law is three, existence of God, revelation, and reward and punishment. Without these we can not conceive of a divine law.

Subordinate to these three are other secondary principles derived from them and related to them as species are to their genera, namely that if you remove one of the derivative principles you do not remove thereby the fundamental principle, but if you remove the fundamental principle, the derivative principles disappear also, as we have explained.

The derivative principles coming under the existence of God, as demanded by reason and by the Law of Moses, are: unity, incorporeality, independence of time, freedom from defects. Under revelation we have prophecy and authenticity of the messenger. Under reward and punishment are: God's knowledge and providence in reward and punishment, in this world or in the next, spiritual or corporeal.

There is no need of laying down any other principle of the Law of Moses, fundamental or derived from these, except those mentioned. We have already explained that the duty to worship God exclusively is a commandment, and that a commandment is not a principle, either fundamental or derived. The irrepealability of the Torah and the superiority of Moses as a prophet come under the authenticity of the messenger, as will be explained in Book Three.[1] The coming of the Messiah and the resurrection of the dead are implied in the belief in reward and punishment, such as every one professing the Law of Moses should believe.

This is also the opinion of my teacher Rabbi Hasdai Crescas,[2] that all these as well as creation are true doctrines which every one professing the Law of Moses should believe, but they are not principles of this law, derivative or primary, general or special. One special principle of the Law of Moses is that one single commandment is sufficient to enable one to acquire perfection and some degree of future life, as we explained in the twenty-third chapter of this Book.[3]

The other laws, called divine, lay down other derivative principles under the fundamental ones, the removal of one of which makes the law fall. Thus the Christians put under the existence of God trinity and corporeality. But it is clear that this is opposed to the derivative principles which follow from the existence of God. Under reward and punishment they place the coming of the Messiah and resurrection of the dead. Without these it is clear that their religion can not exist. Similarly the Mohammedans place fate and predestination, called in Arabic *al kada*[4] and *al kadr*,[5] under providence. But it is clear that if this were true, there would be an end to freedom of choice, and there would be no room at all for reward and punishment. The reason we did not include freedom of choice among the fundamental principles of divine law, though it is essential to it, is because it is not a principle of divine law *qua* divine, but it is necessarily presupposed in any code of law, whether human or divine.

Accordingly the number of principles, fundamental and derived, is eleven: existence of God, unity, incorporeality, independence of time, freedom from defect, prophecy, authenticity of the messenger, revelation, God's knowledge, providence, reward and punishment. If we count God's knowledge and providence as one, as Maimonides does, the number of principles will be ten. And if we count freedom among the principles of divine law, since it is necessarily presupposed by it, though it is not essential to it as divine, the number of principles will be twelve or eleven. We did not include purpose in general as a principle of divine law, although it is presupposed in any system or code of law, human or divine, like freedom, because the special purpose of divine law is the reward that is promised, and that has already been included as a principle.

NOTES

1. Chs. 19 and 20.
2. See Husik, A History of Mediaeval Jewish Philosophy, p. 388ff.
3. P. 183, 4.
4. See p. 122, note 3.
5. P. 123, note 1.

ABRAVANEL, *ROSH AMANAH*

Translation by Menachem Marc Kellner

CHAPTER 23. AN EXPLANATION OF THE CORRECT OPINION IN THIS MATTER

That which I believe to be true, certain, and established in this matter is that these men —Maimonides and those who follow after him— "are peaceable with us."[1] They were brought to postulate principles in the divine Torah only because of their having been drawn after the custom of gentile scientists [as described] in their books. For they saw in every science, whether *a priori* or *a posteriori*, roots and principles which ought not to be denied or argued against. They [further saw] how the master of any science is obliged to explain [these roots and principles] and demonstrate them to the extent that he is [indeed] a master of that science. [These principles] are the accepted axioms [of the science in question] which have already been explained in [terms of] another science, more general than and prior to this [science], or [have been explained] through metaphysics, which precedes and is the first of all the sciences, the first principles of which are self-evident.

Thus, when one doubts one of the assumptions of a science and contradicts it, it can be clarified and proved with these general first principles, since they are the root principles on which that entire science is based. It is not fit for the student [of a science] to disagree with it[s principles], nor is it proper to dispute them, since they are matters generally accepted in it, which have already been explained in [terms of] a different science, more general than it, or are self-evident. In this way physics takes its first principles from metaphysics and the science of music [takes its first principles] from mathematics.

Our wise men, after having been intermingled with the gentiles, [and after having] studied their books and learned their sciences, learned from their deeds and copied their ways and approaches with respect to the divine Torah. [This is evident] in their saying, "How do these gentiles pursue their sciences?[2] By laying down first principles and roots upon which the science is based. I will do so also, in postulating principles and foundations for the divine Torah."

But to my eyes, "the conclusion is not similar to the premise,"[3] for the sciences of the gentiles and their books, in that they [are pursued] by way of investigation and speculation, and so that their speculations need not become confused with the explanation of their premises, were forced to postulate accepted first principles, which would be accepted by the student of that science, without the demand for demonstration and evidence. Those first principles [in turn] would be explained by a different, more general, science, or they would be self-evident, like the primary intelligibles. God, however, understands the way of the divine Torah and He gave it to His people, to be accepted in faith, according to what He saw as necessary for their perfection. For this reason He did not have to set down in it some beliefs as more fundamental than others, or some as more acceptable than others; nor did He establish the relative importance of the commandments, since they were all given by one Shepherd. Nor is there any other Torah, or any science or divine understanding more general than or prior to our Torah, such that we could derive first principles [for the Torah] from it, or explain or validate them through it.

Therefore, I said "this I recall to my mind,"[4] that the divine Torah, with all its beliefs, is completely true. All of its commandments were ordained from Heaven. The validation and substantiation of all the beliefs and commandments, minor as well as major, is the same. The validation of one is like the validation of another. I therefore believe that it is not proper to postulate principles for the divine Torah, nor foundations in the matter of beliefs. This is so because we are obliged to believe everything that is written in the Torah. We do not have the right to doubt even the smallest thing in it, in order to establish its truth with those principles and roots. For he who denies or doubts a belief or story [of the Torah], be it small or great, is a sectarian and heretic. For, since the Torah is true, no belief or story in it has any advantage over any other.

So it is said in *Perek Ḥelek:*

> Our Rabbis taught: "Because he hath despised the word of the Lord," [Nu. 15: 31] this refers to him who maintains that the Torah is not from Heaven. . . Another interpretation: "Because he hath despised the word of the Lord" — Even if he asserts that the whole Torah is from Heaven, excepting a particular verse, which he maintains was not uttered by God but by Moses himself, he is included in "because he hath despised the word of the Lord." And even if he admits that the whole Torah is from Heaven, excepting a single point . . . or a [law derived from a] comparison of similar expressions, he is still included in "because he hath despised the word of the Lord."[5]

[The Rabbis] made it clear by saying this that there is nothing in the divine Torah which a man can either deny or be obliged to believe along the lines of the first principles of a science and its postulates. Rather, every Israelite is obliged to accept every single part of the Torah, the small as well as the great. There is no difference between denying the whole Torah, saying it is not from Heaven, and denying part of it, be it a verse, a derivation, or a [law derived from the] comparison of similar expressions. Therefore [the Rabbis] said there that

> Manasseh ben Hezekiah examined [Biblical] narratives to prove them worthless. Thus, he jeered, had Moses nothing [better] to write but "And Lotan's sister was Timna" [Gen. 36: 22].[6]

Because of this they thought him to be a heretic and *apikoros.*

Maimonides wrote in his commentary to the Mishnah, in his list of principles, in the eighth principle [which asserts] that the Torah is from Heaven, that

> There is no distinction between "The sons of Ham were Cush and Mizraim," [Gen. 10: 6] and "I am the Lord your God," [Ex. 20: 2] and "Hear, O Israel, the Lord, your God, the Lord is One" [Deut. 6: 4]. All came from God, and all are the Torah of God, perfect, holy and true.[7]

He thus admitted with his mouth and lips that in the matter of beliefs, from the point of view of the truth, it is not proper that we postulate in the Torah of God [some] beliefs as roots and first principles which every religionist must accept and other beliefs which may be doubted, for all of them must be accepted and believed since they are divine truth and one may not doubt or object to any one of them.

If the matter is like this in the matter of beliefs, that we may not postulate principles and foundations among them, so it is in the matter of commandments. We may not take some of them as being fundamental, having greater importance than others. For we find very general commandments of great significance relating [both] to man's relations with God and with his fellow man. For example, [the commandment] to remember the great day of the Assembly at Sinai,[8] [the commandment] to remember the Exodus from Egypt,[9] [the commandment,] "you shall do the right and the good,"[10] and [the commandment,] "you shall love your neighbor as yourself."[11] These authors did not mention [even] one of these among their principles. How can we [presume to] examine the commandments, choosing some from others? Did they not say in the Mishnah, "Be careful in the case of a light commandment as in that of a weighty one, since you do not know how the rewards of commandments are given"?[12] How then can we make distinctions among [the commandments], postulating some of them to be at the level of roots and some to be at the level of branches?

We may say in defense of Maimonides that he did not intend to make principles and foundations of any of the commandments of the Torah, for he did not number among [his principles] any actual commandment, as I have noted. With regard to beliefs also [we may say] that he did not choose principles among them in order to say that we are obliged to believe these principles but no others. His intention was, rather, correctly to guide those men who did not study Torah deeply, and did not study or serve [their teachers] enough. Since they could not encompass or conceive all the beliefs and opinions which are included in the divine Torah, Maimonides selected the thirteen most general beliefs, briefly to teach them things which have among them the sciences which I discussed in the fifth proposition [above], in such a way that all men, even the ignorant, could become perfected through their acceptance. From this point of view he called them principles and foundations, adapting it to the thinking of the student while it is not so according to the truth itself.

This will be confirmed by what Maimonides wrote after his principles, which I cited at the beginning of this treatise. This is the reason why he did not mention these principles in his book, the *Guide,* in which he investigated deeply into the Torah faith, but mentioned them [rather] in his commentary to the Mishnah, which he wrote in his youth. He postulated the principles for the masses, and for beginners in the study of Mishnah, but not for those individuals who plumbed the knowledge of truth, for whom he wrote the *Guide.* If this was his opinion, then his intentions were acceptable and his actions for the sake of heaven.

However, R. Ḥasdai, and the author of the *Ikkarim,* "and those after them who approve their sayings, selah,"[13] took these things literally and put those beliefs at the level of roots and principles, like the first principles of the sciences, as I have discussed.

This, in my eyes, is a great mistake and error. [For,] even if we admit that there is a great difference among beliefs, some being of a higher degree than others, according to the importance of their subject matter, since some of them deal with the essence of the Creator, some deal with the separate intellects, some with the spheres, and some with the rest of things, we still ought not to think because of this that the belief about any one of them is a principle and a foundation while another belief is neither a principle nor a foundation, for all of them are true beliefs. From the point of view of the truth they are all principles upon which the divine Torah is based. [This is so] to the extent that if a man denies or contradicts any one of them, even the smallest, it is as if he said that the Torah is not from Heaven. That being so, and since the divine Torah would collapse with the denial of any story, opinion, or belief in it, it follows necessarily that all the stories, beliefs, opinions, and commandments in the Torah are, without exception, principles and foundations of it; [it is not the case] that we should believe this of some of them but not of others.

Among those things which teach the truth of this opinion are, [first], that if there were roots and principles in the Torah, it would have been appropriate that they be included in the Ten Commandments which God told to His people at Sinai, so that everyone could have heard them and so that all Jews could ordain and accept them upon themselves and upon their descendants.[14] From those thirteen principles which Maimonides listed, only one of them—or two, according to Maimonides' opinion—is included in the Ten Commandments.

[Second], if there were principles and roots in the divine Torah, they would have been mentioned in the beginning of the Torah, just as the axioms and roots of a science are postulated at its beginning. I remarked in [my commentary to] Genesis that [the creation account] might be interpreted as a principle and foundation of the Torah, [teaching] the creation of the world at the beginning of the Torah. But inasmuch as we have seen that these first principles and roots were mentioned neither at the beginning of the Torah, nor in [the account of] Sinai, nor in the Ten Commandments, it is clear that there are no principles or foundations [in the Torah].

[Third], if there were roots and principles in the Torah, it would be proper that the punishment for denying them be graver [than the punishment for] denying the other things in the Torah. Inasmuch as this is not the case, since the punishment of he who denies the lightest of the commandments, or the smallest of the verses, is equal to that of he who denies "I am the Lord your God,"[15] or the commandment of monotheism, it is [thus] clearly explained that there is nothing in [the Torah] having the level of principles and roots.

Therefore, they said there in *Perek Ḥelek*, about he who denies that the Torah is from Heaven, that

> R. Eliezer of Modi'im taught: "He who defiles the sacred food, despises the festivals, abolishes the covenant of our Father Abraham, gives an interpretation of the Torah not according to the *halakhah* . . . even if he has Torah and good deeds to his credit, has no portion in the world to come.[16]

Therefore the Talmud mentioned other things there, in addition to the foregoing, such as shaming one's fellow in public, calling one's fellow by a [demeaning] nickname, and one who glories in his fellow's shame. The reason for this is not as was thought by Maimonides in his commentary to the Mishnah, viz., that one who does one of these things has a deficient soul, lacking in perfection, [and] not worthy of the world to come. For what is the deficiency in these things that is worse than that found in other things?

But the reason for this is as follows: all the commandments of the Torah, [as well as] the attributes and opinions taught therein are divine. He who denies the smallest of them all, in that he uproots something from the Torah and denies it, is not worthy to be in the world to come.

[Fourth], if there were principles and roots in the Torah, why were they never mentioned by the sages? It would have been more appropriate that they mention these and explain them in some special place than what they did with the commandments of the Torah and the ethical teachings of the Fathers. Now, in that they directed us correctly beforehand, and did not feel the need to mention principles and foundations which a man ought to believe and live by, it is clearly evident that in their wisdom the sages did not assent to the postulating of principles and roots in the divine Torah. [This is so] because all of it is true and divine, and there are no beliefs in it more fundamental than others.

NOTES

1. Gen. 34: 21.
2. Cf. Deut. 12: 30.
3. *Pesahim* 15a.
4. Lam. 3: 21.
5. *Sanhedrin* 99a.
6. *Sanhedrin* 99b.
7. *Commentary to the Mishnah, Sanhedrin,* Chapter 10.
8. Deut. 4: 9.
9. Deut. 16: 3.
10. Deut. 6: 18.
11. Lev. 19: 18.
12. *Aboth* II: 1.
13. Ps. 49: 14.
14. Cf. Esther 9: 27.
15. Ex. 20: 2.
16. *Sanhedrin* 99a.

The First Principle

Existence of God

INTRODUCTION

The arguments for the existence of God most frequently encountered in Jewish literature are various formulations of the cosmological and teleological arguments. The oldest of these arguments is the teleological argument, or the argument from design. The essence of the argument, which has been expressed in a variety of different ways, is that the universe gives evidence of an orderliness or design which is the antithesis of accident or random occurrence. There are indications that the component parts of the universe have been assembled in order to achieve a specific purpose. Life, indeed the continued existence of the universe itself, would be impossible if not for the unique manner in which the universe is constructed. The design which is manifest in the universe is evidence of intelligence, foresight and planning. This leads to the conclusion that the universe must be subject to the dominion of a Supreme Being. The teleological argument not only demonstrates the existence of a Deity but at the same time demonstrates that reason and intelligence of the highest order must, in some sense, be attributed to God.

There is evidence that the teleological argument was viewed not only as the oldest but also as the most fundamental and readily perceivable demonstration of the existence of the Deity. The Midrash reports that Abraham became aware of the existence of God by means of a simple teleological argument based upon an analogy drawn from common experience. *Bereshit Rabbah* 39:1 states:

> It is like unto a man who was traveling from place to place when he saw a mansion all lighted up. He wondered, "Is it conceivable that the mansion is without a caretaker?" Thereupon, the master of the mansion looked out and said to him, "I am the master of the mansion and the caretaker." Similarly, because Abraham, our father, wondered, "Is it conceivable that the world be without a caretaker?" Therefore, the Holy One, blessed be He, looked at him and said, "I am the master of the universe and its caretaker."

Another midrashic narrative, which has been cited earlier, is even more explicit in underscoring the absurdity of denying the existence of God as the guiding power governing the universe. The Midrash records an exchange between a nonbeliever and R. Akiva and the latter's formulation of the teleological argument. In advancing this argument R. Akiva asserts that every rational mind, if but capable of functioning without prejudice or self-serving motivation, would readily and of its own accord recognize the existence of a Creator. Evidence of design and purpose is ubiquitous and readily perceivable by an unbiased mind seeking truth.

Judah Halevi predicates belief in God upon an argument from tradition. Belief in God is rooted in the collective experience of the Jewish people. God's presence was manifest in the miracles which occurred in conjunction with the Exodus from Egypt, the wandering in the desert, and most especially in the phenomenon of revelation at Mount Sinai, at which time the entire community of Israel were recipients of divine revelation and achieved direct cognitive knowledge of the existence of God. This phenomenon was experienced by an entire nation numbering several million persons and a report of this experience was passed on to subsequent generations. The scriptural account of events still fresh in the memory of the community was accepted as accurate without a dissonant voice being raised. Revelation, which is predicated upon and which confirms [that] the existence of God, is thus a historical phenomenon accepted on the basis of an uninterrupted tradition affirmed by an entire faith-community.

Much has been made of the fact that Maimonides does not enumerate the doctrine of *creatio ex nihilo* among his fundamentals of faith. Indeed, Maimonides goes so far as to state that had philosophical investigation convinced him that the universe was not created *ex nihilo* he would have had no difficulty in interpreting the scriptural passages which ostensibly teach the principle of *creatio ex nihilo* in a manner compatible with Aristotle's doctrine of the eternity of the universe. [Although Maimonides does not indicate how these passages might be understood, he presumably had in mind an explanation similar to that advanced by Ibn Ezra, Genesis 1:1.] Because he maintained that this question could not be resolved on the basis of philosophical investigation, Maimonides felt constrained to develop proofs for the existence of God which are not in any way predicated upon the concept of God as the Creator of the universe. Thus the proofs which he advances demonstrating the existence of God are designed to convince even an Aristotelian who accepts the notion of the eternity of the universe. It is only after the existence of God has been demonstrated that Maimonides turns to the question of the eternity of the universe and, on the basis of what he has already shown with regard to the existence and nature of God, develops the arguments which support the thesis that the universe must be created rather than eternal.

There is, nevertheless, no question that for Maimonides belief in the created nature of that universe is incumbent upon all Jews. This is stated by Maimonides with utmost clarity in his *Sefer ha-Mizvot,* a work in which he enumerates each of the 613 commandments contained in the Torah. The very first of the *mizvot* enumerated is the commandment to believe in the existence of God. Maimonides carefully spells out that this entails not simply belief in God as a transcendent being, but belief in God, the Creator of the universe. As Maimonides puts it: "The first precept is the commandment which He has commanded us with regard to belief in the Deity. That is, that we believe that there exists a Source and a Cause *who creates all existing things.* This is the meaning of His saying, may He be exalted, 'I am the Lord thy God.'" The very same concept is incorporated by Maimonides in his compendium of Jewish law, the *Mishneh Torah.* In the very opening statement of this work, *Hilkhot Yesodei ha-Torah* 1:1, Maimonides states: "The foundation of all foundations and the pillar of wisdom is to know that there is a First Being and it is He *who has brought every existing thing into being* and [that] all existing things of heaven and earth and what is between them do not exist other than through His true existence."

A careful examination of the Thirteen Principles reveals that the doctrine of *creatio ex nihilo* is subsumed by principles one and four. The First Principle, although it does not explicitly state that God created all things out of nothing, not only asserts the existence of God, but posits God as Creator. Moreover, the First Principle affirms the truth of a concept which, in philosophical terminology, is known as the doctrine of constant conservation. This doctrine states that creation is a continuous dynamic process rather than a single act which requires no repetition. It is not the case that the world exists solely by virtue of an act of creation which took place "in the beginning" and continues to remain in existence on the basis of this primordial act. Rather, the act of creation must be repeated each and every moment, otherwise the created universe would revert to nothingness. Existence is constantly infused into created entities by the Creator. This creation is an ongoing process of which God is the author. That the creation takes place *ex nihilo* is readily apparent from the Fourth Principle. The Fourth Principle does not simply state that God is eternal, which would conceivably allow for the co-eternity of the universe or of matter, but states that God "is first in the absolute sense." The Fourth Principle thus explicitly denies the possibility of the eternity of any being or substance other than God. Thus, the Thirteen

Principles themselves assert that God is Creator of the universe and, since nothing else is eternal, God of necessity must be viewed as having created the universe out of nothing.

Selections from Baḥya, Judah Halevi, Maimonides and Albo, seminal thinkers in Jewish philosophy, have been included in this section, as well as in most of the other sections.

Baḥya demonstrates the existence of God on the basis of the created nature of the universe. In view of the evidence of harmony and wisdom which is manifest in nature, it is absurd to assume that the world came into being by accident. There must, then, exist a First Cause who brought the world into existence.

Judah Halevi does not find it necessary to formulate complex philosophical proofs for the existence of God. The existence of the Jewish people and their wondrous history, particularly the incidents associated with the Exodus from Egypt, constitute eloquent testimony to the existence of God. The beatific experience at Mount Sinai, in which the entire community of Israel participated, constitutes irrefutable experiential proof of the existence of God.

Maimonides advances four separate proofs for the existence of God based upon a number of propositions whose validity had already been demonstrated by Aristotle and his followers. The first proof is based upon an analysis of motion. No motion can take place without an agent or mover. Since the series of such movers is finite, there must exist a Prime Mover who is responsible for all motion. The second proof is based upon the principle that elements of a compound may also exist independently of the compound. If one of the two elements of a compound exists separately, the second must exist separately as well. There exist objects which possess both the characteristic of being in motion and also the characteristic of causing other objects to move. Some objects possess only the first characteristic, i.e., they are in motion but do not cause other objects to move. Therefore, there must exist a being which causes motion without itself being moved. The third proof demonstrates that an eternal being must exist. If the existence of all things in the universe were temporary in nature, the universe would cease to exist. Only the existence of an eternal being explains the continued existence of beings and objects which are merely transitory in nature. The fourth proof parallels the line of argumentation employed in the first, but bases itself upon the ubiquitous phenomenon of transition from potentiality to actuality, rather than upon motion. This argument serves to establish the existence of God as the First Cause.

The selfsame proofs are presented by Albo, but formulated in a manner which the reader may find more readily understandable. Albo accepts the validity of the third and fourth arguments but rejects the first two. The principle which forms the basis of the second argument, namely, that if one of the two elements of a compound exists separately the second must exist separately as well, is rejected by Albo as being untrue. Albo dismisses the first argument as being predicated upon the notion of the eternity of motion and hence as being incompatible with acceptance of the doctrine of creation. It should be remembered, however, that Maimonides sought to establish the existence of God even according to the belief of those who accepted the eternity of the universe.

BAḤYA, *ḤOVOT HA-LEVAVOT*

Translation by Moses Hyamson

FIRST TREATISE, CHAPTER 5

The Premises which clearly lead to the inference that the world has a Creator who created it *ex nihilo* are three: 1. that a thing does not make itself; 2. that causes are limited in number; and since their number is limited, they must have a First Cause unpreceded by a previous Cause; 3. that every thing that is a compound must have been brought into existence. When these premises will have been established, the inference from them will be clear to everyone who knows how to combine and apply them that the world has a Creator who created it *ex nihilo*, as will, with God's help, appear from our exposition.

The demonstration of these three propositions is as follows:

Concerning anything which now exists and which (at one time) had not existed, one of two things must be predicated. Either it brought itself into existence, or another brought it into existence. If we assume that it made itself, one of two things must be predicated of it: Either it made itself before it existed or after it was already in existence. Both are impossible. For if we say that it made itself after it already existed, it did nothing. There was no need for it to make itself; it already existed. Consequently it did nothing. If, on the other hand, we say that it made itself before it existed—at that time it was nothing. And out of nothing neither action nor remission can proceed; since that which is nothing cannot do aught. Hence it is impossible that a thing can make itself. The first proposition has accordingly been demonstrated.

The second proposition is demonstrated as follows: Whatever is finite must have a beginning. (*i.e.*, what appears as the definite effect of a cause must have a First Cause.) For it is evident that what has no beginning is not finite. Since, where a thing has no beginning, there is no point where one could stop. (*i.e.*, in an endless series of causes stretching back to infinity, an effect observable at the present time is inconceivable. The present would never be reached.) Consequently, everything that has an end had, we know, a beginning unpreceded by another beginning, a First Cause unpreceded by any other Cause. When we realize the finite character of the Causes existing in the world (*i.e.*, that all phenomena that we observe are definite effects of causes) we must conclude that they had a Beginning unpreceded by any other beginning, a First Cause unpreceded by any other Cause; since there are no causes unlimited in number (*i.e.*, a series of causes of a definite effect cannot conceivably be infinite).

Furthermore, it is obvious that anything which has parts has a whole. For the whole is nothing else than the sum of its parts. That the infinite should have parts is inconceivable. For a part is defined as one quantity separated from another, the lesser being the measure of the greater, as Euclid has set forth at the beginning of the Fifth Book of his Geometry.

Let us assume a thing actually infinite; and that we take a part from it. The remainder will undoubtedly be less than it was before. If this remainder is infinite, one infinite will be greater than another infinite, which is impossible. If the remainder is finite, and we put back the part that we took away, the whole will be finite. But *ex hypothesi* the whole was infinite. So the same thing would be finite and infinite, which is self-contradictory and impossible. Accordingly it is impossible to take away a part from that which is infinite; since whatever has parts is undoubtedly finite.

Now of all individuals that have ever existed in the world, let us suppose a part abstracted, say those who lived from the days of Noah to the days of Moses. They would form a part of all the individuals in the world. Their number is limited. Hence the whole is also a limited number. Since the whole of this world is finite in the number of its individuals, it necessarily follows that the number of its causes is finite. Hence the inference that this world must have a First Cause unpreceded by another cause (*i.e.*, the series of causes must come to a stop with their First Cause), as we have stated.

The Proof of the Third Proposition is as follows:

Every compound consists necessarily of more than one constituent and those constituents must, in their very nature, precede it. Likewise, the one who made the compound must have preceded it in order of time and by necessary implication. Now what is eternal has no cause. What has no cause has no beginning. What has no beginning is infinite. Consequently what has a beginning is not eternal. And what is not eternal has been brought into existence, since between that which is eternal and that which has been brought into existence, there is no third term that can be said to be neither eternal nor called into existence. Hence every compound is not eternal (for it had a beginning) and therefore must have been brought into existence. The third proposition having been demonstrated, all three premises are now established.

FIRST TREATISE, CHAPTER 6

The application of the above premises; to demonstrate the Creator's existence, is as follows:

When we contemplate this world, we find that it is synthetic and composite. There is no part of it that has not the character of composition and coordination. For to our senses and intellect it appears as a house built and furnished with all needful appointments—the heaven above like a roof, the earth, spread out beneath, like a carpet, the stars in their array like lamps, all objects accumulated in it like treasures—everything with a definite use; man, like the master of a house, disposing of all that is therein. The various plants are provided for his benefit; the different species of animals serve his pleasure, as David said: (Ps. 8:7–9) "Thou hast made him to have dominion over the work of Thy hands; everything hast Thou set beneath his feet, sheep and oxen, all of them, yea, and also the beasts of the field, the fowl of the air and the fish of the sea; whatsoever passeth through the paths of the seas." The regular rising and setting of the sun, which determine the hours of day and night; its ascension and declension which produce cold and heat, summer and winter—the seasons, with their advantages and uniform amd unbroken succession—as it is said (Job 9:7) "Who commandeth the sun and it riseth not, and sealeth up the stars," (Ps. 104:20) "Thou makest darkness and it is night"; the courses of the spheres with their various movements, the fixed stars and planets which proceed in a measured, balanced, unvarying order—all these have, as their purpose, the benefit and improvement of human beings, as Solomon said (Eccles. 3:11) "He hath made everything beautiful in its time; also hath He set the world in their heart"; (ib. 3:1) "To everything there is a season, and a time to every purpose under the heaven." This Universe, as a whole and in each of its parts, exhibits throughout combination and synthesis.

If we study plants and animals, we find that they are composed of the four elements—Fire, Air, Water and Earth—elements that are distinct and separate; which we cannot join in a natural combination, because they are diverse and even mutually repellent; and if we artificially effect a combination of any of them, the constituents rapidly change and assume other forms. The synthesis, however, wrought by Nature, is complete and endures for an indefinite period.

Some philosophers were of the opinion that the heavenly spheres, stars and higher beings, were of the element of fire. This is similar to what David said (Ps. 104:4) "Who makest winds Thy messengers, the flaming fire Thy ministers"—which would support the view just enunciated and not that of Aristotle who held that the heavens consist of a fifth element (Quintessence).

As all existing things come from the Elements and are composed of them, and since we know that, because of their heterogeneity, the Elements did not coalesce of themselves or combine through their essential character, it occurs to us, yea, we are convinced, that a Being other than these Elements joined, bound and combined them against their nature and will. This Being is the Creator who ordained and established their union. If we investigate the four Elements, we find that they consist of Matter and Form, Substance and Accident. Their Matter is that primal matter, which is the root of the elements, their original substance, their *hyle.* Their form is that universal primal form, which is the root of all forms—whether essential or accidental—heat, cold, humidity, dryness, heaviness, lightness, motion, rest, etc. Combination and union are apparent throughout the world, as a whole, and in all its parts, in its roots and in its ramifications, in that which is simple as well as in that which is complex, in that which is above and in that which is below. Hence it follows from what we have already premised that the world must have been brought into existence, since it has been demonstrated that what is composite must have been brought into existence. This being so, and as a thing cannot make itself, it necessarily follows that this Universe had a Maker to whom it owes its beginning and its existence. It having been demonstrated that a series of beginnings (causes) cannot be infinite, it consequently follows that the world must have a beginning unpreceded by any other beginning, a First Cause without a cause before it. This First Cause it is that formed it and brought it into being out of nought, with the aid of nought, and with nought as a foundation, as Scripture saith (Is. 44:24) "I am the Lord that maketh all things, that stretched forth the heavens alone, that spread abroad the earth by myself"; again (Job 26:7) "He stretcheth out the North over empty space, and hangeth the earth over nothing." This is the Creator, exalted be He, Whom we seek, and to Whom we direct our minds and hearts. He is the First—before Whom there was no predecessor—Whose Eternity is endless as Scripture saith, (Is. 44:6) "I am the first, and I am the last"; again, (Ibid. 41:4) "I, the Lord, who am the first, and with the last am the same."

There are men who say that the world came into existence by chance, without a Creator who caused and formed it. I wonder how any rational person in a normal state of mind can entertain such a notion. If one holding such an opinion would hear a person expressing a similar view in regard to a water-wheel that revolves, in order to irrigate a portion of a field or garden, and were to say that he thinks it had been set up without any intention on the part of a mechanic who labored to put it together and adjust it, using all his tools so as to obtain this useful result, the hearer would wonder, be exceedingly astonished, and think the man who made such a statement extremely foolish. He would promptly charge him with lying and would reject his assertion. Now, if such a statement is rejected in regard to a small, and insignificant wheel, the fashioning of which requires but little contrivance and which serves for the improvement of but a small portion of the earth, how can anyone permit himself to harbor such a thought concerning the immense sphere that encompasses the whole earth with all the creatures on it; which exhibits a wisdom so great that the minds of all living creatures, the intellects of all rational mortals, cannot comprehend it; which is appointed for the benefit of the whole earth and all its inhabitants—how can one say that it all came into existence without a wise and mighty designer purposing and conceiving it. Whatever takes place without purpose shows, as is well known, no trace of wisdom or power. Do you not realize that if ink were poured out accidentally on a blank sheet of paper, it would be impossible that proper writing should result, legible lines such as are written with a pen? If a person brought us a fair copy of script that could only have been written with a pen, and said that ink had been spilt on paper and these written characters had come of themselves, we would charge him to his face with falsehood, for we would feel certain that this result could not have happened without an intelligent person's purpose. Since this appears to us an impossibility in the case of characters the form of which is conventional, how can one assert that something far finer in its art and which manifests in its fashioning a subtlety infinite beyond our comprehension could have happened without the purpose, power, and wisdom of a wise and mighty designer? What we have adduced from His works to demonstrate the existence of a Creator, will suffice to convince anyone intelligent and candid enough to admit the truth, and will serve to refute those who maintain that the Universe is eternal, and to disprove their contentions. Note it well.

HALEVI, *KUZARI*

Translation by Hartwig Hirschfeld

PART I

10. Al Khazari: Indeed, I see myself compelled to ask the Jews, because they are the relic of the Children of Israel. For I see that they constitute in themselves the evidence for the divine law on earth.

He then invited a Jewish Rabbi, and asked him about his belief.

11. The Rabbi replied: I believe in the God of Abraham, Isaac and Israel, who led the children of Israel out of Egypt with signs and miracles; who fed them in the desert and gave them the land, after having made them traverse the sea and the Jordan in a miraculous way; who sent Moses with His law, and subsequently thousands of prophets, who confirmed His law by promises to the observant, and threats to the disobedient. Our belief is comprised in the Torah—a very large domain.

12. I had not intended to ask any Jew, because I am aware of their reduced condition and narrow-minded views, as their misery left them nothing commendable. Now shouldst thou, O Jew, not have said that thou believest in the Creator of the world, its Governor and Guide, and in Him who created and keeps thee, and such attributes which serve as evidence for every believer, and for the sake of which He pursues justice in order to resemble the Creator in His wisdom and justice?

13. The Rabbi: That which thou dost express is religion based on speculation and system, the research of thought, but open to many doubts. Now ask the philosophers, and thou wilt find that they do not agree on one action or one principle, since some doctrines can be established by arguments, which are only partially satisfactory, and still much less capable of being proved.

14. Al Khazari: That which thou sayest now, O Jew, seems to be more to the point than the beginning, and I should like to hear more.

15. The Rabbi: Surely the beginning of my speech was just the proof, and so evident that it requires no other argument.

16. Al Khazari: How so?

17. The Rabbi: Allow me to make a few preliminary remarks, for I see thee disregarding and depreciating my words.

18. Al Khazari: Let me hear thy remarks.

19. The Rabbi: If thou wert told that the King of India was an excellent man, commanding admiration, and deserving his high reputation, one whose actions were reflected in the justice which rules his country and the virtuous ways of his subjects, would this bind thee to revere him?

20. Al Khazari: How could this bind me, whilst I am not sure if the justice of the Indian people is natural, and not dependent on their king, or due to the king or both?

21. The Rabbi: But if his messenger came to thee bringing presents which thou knowest to be only procurable in India, and in the royal palace, accompanied by a letter in which it is distinctly stated from whom it comes, and to which are added drugs to cure thy diseases, to preserve thy health, poisons for thy enemies, and other means to fight and kill them without battle, would this make thee beholden to him?

22. Al Khazari: Certainly. For this would remove my former doubt that the Indians have a king. I should also acknowledge that a proof of his power and dominion has reached me.

23. The Rabbi: How wouldst thou, then, if asked, describe him?

24. Al Khazari: In terms about which I am quite clear, and to these I could add others which were at first rather doubtful, but are no longer so.

25. The Rabbi: In this way I answered thy first question. In the same strain spoke Moses to Pharaoh, when he told him: 'The God of the Hebrews sent me to thee,' viz. the God of Abraham, Isaac and Jacob. For Abraham was well known to the nations, who also knew that the divine spirit was in contact with the patriarchs, cared for them, and performed miracles for them. He did not say: 'The God of heaven and earth,' nor 'my Creator and thine sent me.' In the same way God commenced His speech to the assembled people of Israel: 'I am the God whom you worship, who has led you out of the land of Egypt,' but He did not say: 'I am the Creator of the world and your Creator.' Now in the same style I spoke to thee, a Prince of the Khazars, when thou didst ask me about my creed. I answered thee as was fitting, and is fitting for the whole of Israel who knew these things, first from personal experience, and afterwards through *uninterrupted* tradition, which is equal to the former.

MAIMONIDES, *MOREH NEVUKHIM*

Translation by Michael Friedlander

PART II, INTRODUCTION

Twenty-five of the propositions which are employed in the proof for the existence of God, or in the arguments demonstrating that God is neither corporeal nor a force connected with a material being, or that He is One, have been fully established, and their correctness is beyond doubt. Aristotle and the Peripatetics who followed him have proved each of these propositions. There is, however, one proposition which we do not accept—namely, the proposition which affirms the Eternity of the Universe, but we will admit it for the present, because by doing so we shall be enabled clearly to demonstrate our own theory.

Proposition I.

The existence of an infinite magnitude is impossible.

Proposition II.

The co-existence of an infinite number of finite magnitudes is impossible.

Proposition III.

The existence of an infinite number of causes and effects is impossible, even if these were not magnitudes; if, *e.g.*, one Intelligence were the cause of a second, the second the cause of a third, the third the cause of a fourth, and so on, the series could not be continued *ad infinitum*.

Proposition IV.

Four categories are subject to change:—

(*a.*) *Substance.*—Changes which affect the substance of a thing are called genesis and destruction.

(*b.*) *Quantity.*—Changes in reference to quantity are increase and decrease.

(*c.*) *Quality.*—Changes in the qualities of things are transformations.

(*d.*) *Place.*—Change of place is called motion.

The term "motion" is properly applied to change of place, but is also used in a general sense of all kinds of changes.

Proposition V.

Motion implies change and transition from potentiality to actuality.

Proposition VI.

The motion of a thing is either essential or accidental; or it is due to an external force, or to the participation of the thing in the motion of another thing. This latter kind of motion is similar to the accidental one. An instance of essential motion may be found in the translation of a thing from one place to another. The accident of a thing, as, *e.g.*, its black colour, is said to move when the thing itself changes its place. The upward motion of a stone, owing to a force applied to it in that direction, is an instance of a motion due to an external force. The motion of a nail in a boat may serve to illustrate motion due to the participation of a thing in the motion of another thing; for when the boat moves, the nail is said to move likewise. The same is the case with everything composed of several parts: when the thing itself moves, every part of it is likewise said to move.

Proposition VII.

Things which are changeable, are, at the same time, divisible. Hence everything that moves is divisible, and consequently corporeal; but that which is indivisible cannot move, and cannot therefore be corporeal.

Proposition VIII.

A thing that moves accidentally must come to rest, because it does not move of its own accord; hence accidental motion cannot continue for ever.

Proposition IX.

A corporeal thing that sets another corporeal thing in motion can only effect this by setting itself in motion at the time it causes the other thing to move.

Proposition X.

A thing which is said to be contained in a corporeal object must satisfy either of the two following conditions: it either exists through that object, as is the case with accidents, or it is the cause of the existence of that object; such as, *e.g.*, its essential property. In both cases it is a force existing in a corporeal object.

Proposition XI.

Among the things which exist through a material object, there are some which participate in the division of that object, and are therefore accidentally divisible, as, *e.g.*, its colour, and all other qualities that spread throughout its parts. On the other hand, among the things which form the essential elements of an object, there are some which cannot be divided in any way, as, *e.g.*, the soul and the intellect.

Proposition XII.

A force which occupies all parts of a corporeal object is finite, that object itself being finite.

Proposition XIII.

None of the several kinds of change can be continuous, except motion from place to place, provided it be circular.

Proposition XIV.

Locomotion is in the natural order of the several kinds of motion the first and foremost. For genesis and corruption are preceded by transformation, which, in its turn, is preceded by the approach of the transforming agent to the object which is to be transformed. Also, increase and decrease are impossible without previous genesis and corruption.

Proposition XV.

Time is an accident that is related and joined to motion in such a manner that the one is never found without the other. Motion is only possible in time, and the idea of time cannot be conceived otherwise than in connection with motion; things which do not move have no relation to time.

Proposition XVI.

Incorporeal bodies can only be numbered when they are forces situated in a body; the several forces must then be counted together with substances or objects in which they exist. Hence purely spiritual beings, which are neither corporeal nor forces situated in corporeal objects, cannot be counted, except when considered as causes and effects.

Proposition XVII.

When an object moves, there must be some agent that moves it, either without that object, as, *e.g.*, in the case of a stone set in motion by the hand; or within, *e.g.*, when the body of a living being moves. Living beings include in themselves, at the same time, the moving agent and the thing moved; when, therefore, a living being dies, and the moving agent, the soul, has left the body, *i.e.*, the thing moved, the body remains for some time in the same condition as before, and yet cannot move in the manner it has moved previously. The moving agent, when included in the thing moved, is hidden from, and imperceptible to, the senses. This circumstance gave rise to the belief that the body of an animal moves without the aid of a moving agent. When we therefore affirm, concerning a thing in motion, that it is its own moving agent, or, as is generally said, that it moves of its own accord, we mean to say that the force which really sets the body in motion exists in that body itself.

Proposition XVIII.

Everything that passes over from a state of potentiality to that of actuality, is caused to do so by some external agent; because if that agent existed in the thing itself, and no obstacle prevented the transition, the thing would never be in a state of potentiality, but always in that of actuality. If, on the other hand, while the thing itself contained that agent, some obstacle existed, and at a certain time that obstacle was removed, the same cause which removed the obstacle would undoubtedly be described as the cause of the transition from potentiality to actuality, [and not the force situated within the body]. Note this.

Proposition XIX.

A thing which owes its existence to certain causes, has in itself merely the possibility of existence; for only if these causes exist, the thing likewise exists. It does not exist if the causes do not exist at all, or if they have ceased to exist, or if there has been a change in the relation which implies the existence of that thing as a necessary consequence of those causes.

Proposition XX.

A thing which has in itself the necessity of existence cannot have for its existence any cause whatever.

Proposition XXI.

A thing composed of two elements has necessarily their composition as the cause of its present existence. Its existence is therefore not necessitated by its own essence; it depends on the existence of its two component parts and their combination.

Proposition XXII.

Material objects are always composed of two elements [at least], and are without exception subject to accidents. The two component elements of all bodies are substance and form. The accidents attributed to material objects are quantity, geometrical form, and position.

Proposition XXIII.

Everything that exists potentially, and whose essence includes a certain state of possibility, may at some time be without actual existence.

Proposition XXIV.

That which is potentially a certain thing is necessarily material, for the state of possibility is always connected with matter.

Proposition XXV.

Each compound substance consists of matter and form, and requires an agent for its existence, viz., a force which sets the substance in motion, and thereby enables it to receive a certain form. The force which thus prepares the substance of a certain individual being, is called the immediate motor.

Here the necessity arises of investigating into the properties of motion, the moving agent and the thing moved. But this has already been explained sufficiently; and the opinion of Aristotle may be expressed in the following proposition: Matter does not move of its own accord—an important proposition that led to the investigation of the Prime Motor (the first moving agent).

Of these foregoing twenty-five propositions some may be verified by means of a little reflection and the application of a few propositions capable of proof, or of axioms or theorems of almost the same force, such as have been explained by me. Others require many arguments and propositions, all of which, however, have been established by conclusive proofs partly in the Physics and its commentaries, and partly in the Metaphysics and its commentary. I have already stated that in this work it is not my intention to copy the books of the philosophers or to explain difficult problems, but simply to mention those propositions which are closely connected with our subject, and which we want for our purpose.

To the above propositions one must be added which enunciates that the universe is eternal, and which is held by Aristotle to be true, and even more acceptable than any other theory. For the present we admit it, as a hypothesis, only for the purpose of demonstrating our theory. It is the following proposition:—

Proposition XXVI.

Time and motion are eternal, constant, and in actual existence.

In accordance with this proposition, Aristotle is compelled to assume that there exists actually a body with constant motion, viz., the fifth element. He therefore says that the heavens are not subject to genesis or destruction, because motion cannot be generated nor destroyed. He also holds that every motion must necessarily be preceded by another motion, either of the same or of a different kind. The belief that the locomotion of an animal is not preceded by another motion, is not true; for the animal is caused to move, after it had been in rest, by the intention to obtain those very things which bring about that locomotion. A change in its state of health, or some image, or some new idea can produce a desire to seek that which is conducive to its welfare and to avoid that which is contrary. Each of these three causes sets the living being in motion, and each of them is produced by various kinds of motion. Aristotle likewise asserts that everything which is created, must, before its actual creation, have existed *in potentia.* By inferences drawn from this assertion he seeks to establish his proposition, viz., The thing that moves is finite, and its path finite; but it repeats the motion in its path an infinite number of times. This can only take place when the motion is circular, as has been stated in Proposition XIII. Hence follows also the existence of an infinite number of things which do not co-exist but follow one after the other.

Aristotle frequently attempts to establish this proposition; but I believe that he did not consider his proofs to be conclusive. It appeared to him to be the most probable and acceptable proposition. His followers, however, and the commentators of his books, contend that it contains not only a probable but a demonstrative proof, and that it has, in fact, been fully established. On the other hand, the Mutakallemim try to prove that the proposition cannot be true, as, according to their opinion, it is impossible to conceive how an infinite number of things could even come into existence successively. They assume this impossibility as an axiom. I, however, think that this proposition is admissible, but neither demonstrative, as the commentators of Aristotle assert, nor, on the other hand, impossible, as the Mutakallemim say. We have no intention to explain here the proofs given by Aristotle, or to show our doubts concerning them, or to set forth our opinions on the Creation of the universe. I here simply desire to mention those propositions which we shall require for the proof of the three principles stated above. Having thus quoted and admitted these propositions, I will now proceed to explain what may be inferred from them.

PART II, CHAPTER 1

According to Proposition XXV., a moving agent must exist which has moved the substance of all existing transient things and enabled it to receive Form. The cause of the motion of that agent is found in the existence of another motor of the same or of a different class, the term "motion," in a general sense, being common to four categories (Prop. IV.). This series of motions is not infinite (Prop. III.); we find that it can only be continued till the motion of the fifth element is arrived at, and then it ends. The motion of the fifth element is the source of every force that moves and prepares any substance on earth for its combination with a certain form, and is connected with that force by a chain of intermediate motions. The celestial sphere [or the fifth element] performs the act of locomotion which is the first of the several kinds of motion (Prop. XIV.), and all locomotion is found to be the indirect effect of the motion of this sphere; *e.g.*, a stone is set in motion by a stick, the stick by a man's hand, the hand by the sinews, the sinews by the muscles, the muscles by the nerves, the nerves by the natural heat of the body, and the heat of the body by its form. This is undoubtedly the immediate motive cause, but the action of this immediate motive cause is due to a certain design, *e.g.*, to bring a stone into a hole by striking against it with a stick in order to prevent the draught from coming through the crevice. The motion of the air that causes the draught is the effect of the motion of the celestial sphere. Similarly it may be shown that the ultimate cause of all genesis and destruction can be traced to the motion of the sphere. But the motion of the sphere must likewise have been effected by an agent (Prop. XVII.) residing either without the sphere or within it; a third case being impossible. In the first case, if the motor is without the sphere, it must either be corporeal or incorporeal; if incorporeal, it cannot be said that the agent is *without* the sphere; it can only be described as *separate* from it; because an incorporeal object can only be said metaphorically to reside without a certain corporeal object. In the second case, if the agent resides within the sphere, it must be either a force distributed throughout the whole sphere so that each part of the sphere includes a part of the force, as is the case with the heat of fire; or it is an indivisible force, *e.g.*, the soul and the intellect (Props. X. and XI.). The agent which sets the sphere in motion must consequently be one of the following four things: a corporeal object without the sphere; an incorporeal object separate from it; a force spread throughout the whole of the sphere; or an indivisible force [within the sphere].

The first case, viz., that the moving agent of the sphere is a corporeal object without the sphere, is impossible, as will be explained. Since the moving agent is corporeal, it must itself move while setting another object in motion (Prop. IX.), and as the sixth element would likewise move when imparting motion to another body, it would be set in motion by a seventh element, which must also move. An infinite number of bodies would thus be required before the sphere could be set in motion. This is contrary to Proposition II.

The third case, viz., that the moving object be a force distributed throughout the whole body, is likewise impossible. For the sphere is corporeal, and must therefore be finite (Prop. I.); also the force it contains must be finite (Prop. XII.), since each part of the sphere contains part of the force (Prop. XI.): the latter can consequently not produce an infinite motion, such as we assumed according to Proposition XXVI., which we admitted for the present.

The fourth case is likewise impossible, viz., that the sphere is set in motion by an indivisible force residing in the sphere in the same manner as the soul resides in the body of man. For this force, though indivisible, could not be the cause of infinite motion by itself alone; because if that were the case the prime motor would have an accidental motion. (Prop. VI.) But things that move accidentally must come to rest (Prop. VIII.), and then the thing comes also to rest which is set in motion. (The following may serve as a further illustration of the nature of accidental motion. When man is moved by the soul, *i.e.*, by his form, to go from the basement of the house to the upper story, his body moves directly, while the soul, the really efficient cause of that motion, participates in it accidentally. For through the translation of the body from the basement to the upper story, the soul has likewise changed its place, and when no fresh impulse for the motion of the body is given by the soul, the body which has been set in motion by such impulse comes to rest, and the accidental motion of the soul is discontinued.) Consequently the motion of that supposed first motor must be due to some cause which does not form part of things composed of two elements, viz., a moving agent and an object moved; if such a cause is present the motor in that compound sets the other element in motion; in the absence of such a cause no motion takes place. Living beings do therefore not move continually, although each of them possesses an indivisible motive element; because this element is not constantly in motion, as it would be if it produced motion of its own accord. On the contrary, the things to which the action is due are separate from the motor. The action is caused either by desire for that which is agreeable, or by aversion to that which is disagreeable, or by some image, or by some ideal when the moving being has the capacity of conceiving it. When any of these causes are present then the motor acts; its motion is accidental, and must therefore come to an end (Prop. VIII.). If the motor of the sphere were of this kind the sphere could not move *ad infinitum*. Our opponent, however, holds that the spheres move continually *ad infinitum*; if this were the case, and it is in fact possible (Prop. XIII.), the efficient cause of the motion of the sphere must, according the the above division, be of the second kind, viz., something incorporeal and separate from the sphere.

It may thus be considered as proved that the efficient cause of the motion of the sphere, if that motion be eternal, is neither itself corporeal nor does it reside in a corporeal object; it must move neither of its own accord nor accidentally; it must be indivisible and unchangeable (Prop. VII. and Prop. V.). This Prime Motor of the sphere is God, praised be His name!

The hypothesis that there exist two Gods is inadmissible, because absolutely incorporeal beings cannot be counted (Prop. XVI.), except as cause and effect; the relation of time is not applicable to God (Prop. XV.), because motion cannot be predicated of Him.

The result of the above argument is consequently this, the sphere cannot move *ad infinitum* of its own accord; the Prime Motor is not corporeal, nor a force residing within a body; it is One, unchangeable, and in its existence independent of time; three of our postulates are thus proved by the principal philosophers.

The philosophers employ besides another argument, based on the following proposition of Aristotle. If there be a thing composed of two elements, and the one of them is known to exist also by itself, apart from that thing, then the other element is likewise found in existence by itself separate from that compound. For if the nature of the two elements were such that they could only exist together—as, *e.g.*, matter and form—then neither of them could in any way exist separate from the other. The fact that the one component is found also in separate existence proves that the two elements are not indissolubly connected, and that the same must therefore be the case with the other component. Thus we infer from the existence of honey-vinegar and of honey by itself, that there exists also vinegar by itself. After having explained this Proposition, Aristotle continues thus: We notice many objects consisting of a *motor* and a *motum*, *i.e.*, objects which set other things in motion, and whilst doing so are themselves set in motion by other things; such is clearly the case as regards all the middle members of a series in motion. We also see a thing that is moved, but does not itself move anything, viz., the last member of the series; consequently a *motor* must exist without being at the same time a *motum*, and that is the Prime Motor, which, not being subject to motion, is indivisible, incorporeal, and independent of time, as has been shown in the preceding argument.

Third Philosophical Argument.—This is taken from the words of Aristotle, though he gives it in a different form. It runs as follows: There is no doubt that many things actually exist, as, *e.g.*, things perceived with the senses. Now there are only three cases conceivable, viz., either all these things are without beginning and without end, or all of them have beginning and end, or some are with and some without beginning and end. The first of these three cases is altogether inadmissible, since we clearly perceive objects which come into existence and are subsequently destroyed. The second case is likewise inadmissible, for if everything had but a temporary existence all things might be destroyed, and that which is enunciated of a whole class of things as possible is necessarily actual. All things must therefore come to an end, and then nothing would ever be in existence, for there would not exist any being to produce anything. Consequently nothing whatever would exist [if all things were transient]; but as we see things existing, and find ourselves in existence, we conclude as follows:—Since there are undoubtedly beings of a temporary existence, there must also be an eternal being that is not subject to destruction, and whose existence is real, not merely possible.

It has been further argued that the existence of this being is necessary, either on account of itself alone or on account of some external force. In the latter case its existence and non-existence would be equally possible, because of its own properties, but its existence would be necessary on account of the external force. That force would then be the being that possesses absolute existence (Prop. XIX.). It is therefore certain that there must be a being which has absolutely independent existence, and is the source of the existence of all things, whether transient or permanent, if as Aristotle assumes, there be in existence such a thing, which is the effect of an eternal cause, and must therefore itself be eternal. This is a proof the correctness of which is not doubted, disputed, or rejected, except by those who have no knowledge of the method of proof. We further say that the existence of anything that has independent existence is not due to any cause (Prop. XX.), and that such a being does not include any plurality whatever (Prop. XXI.); consequently it cannot be a body, nor a force residing in a body (Prop. XXII.). It is now clear that there must be a being with absolutely independent existence, a being whose existence cannot be attributed to any external cause, and which does not include different elements; it cannot therefore be corporeal, or a force residing in a corporeal object; this being is God.

It can easily be proved that absolutely independent existence cannot be attributed to two beings. For, if that were the case, absolutely independent existence would be a property added to the substance of both; neither of them would be absolutely independent on account of their essence, but only through a certain property, viz., that of this independent existence, which is common to both. It can besides be shown in many ways that independent existence cannot be reconciled with the principle of dualism by any means. It would make no difference, whether we imagine two beings of similar or of different properties. The reason for all this is to be sought in the absolute simplicity and in the utmost perfection of the essence of this being, which is the only member of its species, and does not depend on any cause whatever; this being has therefore nothing in common with other beings.

Fourth Argument.—This is likewise a well-known philosophical argument. We constantly see things passing from a state of potentiality to that of actuality, but in every such case there is for that transition of a thing an agent separable from it (Prop. XVIII.). It is likewise clear that the agent has also passed from potentiality to actuality. It has at first been potential, because it could not be actual, owing to some obstacle contained in itself, or on account of the absence of a certain relation between itself and the object of its action; it became an actual agent as soon as that relation was present. Whichever cause be assumed, an agent is again necessary to remove the obstacle or to create the relation. The same can be argued respecting this last-mentioned agent that creates the relation or removes the obstacle. This series of causes cannot go on *ad infinitum;* we must at last arrive at a cause of the transition of an object from the state of potentiality to that of actuality, which is constant, and admits of no potentiality whatever. In the essence of this cause nothing exists potentially, for if its essence included any possibility of existence it would not exist at all (Prop. XXIII.); it cannot be corporeal, but it must be spiritual (Prop. XXIV.); and the immaterial being that includes no possibility whatever, but exists actually by its own essence, is God. Since He is incorporeal, as has been demonstrated, it follows that He is One (Prop. XVI.).

Even if we were to admit the Eternity of the Universe, we could by any of these methods prove the existence of God; that He is One and incorporeal, and that He does not reside as a force in a corporeal object.

The following is likewise a correct method to prove the Incorporeality and the Unity of God: If there were two Gods, they would necessarily have one element in common by virtue of which they were Gods, and another element by which they were distinguished from each other and existed as two Gods; the distinguishing element would either be in both different from the property common to both—in that case both of them would consist of different elements, and neither of them would be the First Cause, or have absolutely independent existence; but their existence would depend on certain causes (Prop. XIX.)—or the distinguishing element would only in one of them be different from the element common to both: then this being could not have absolute independence.

Another proof of the Unity of God.—It has been demonstrated by proof that the whole existing world is one organic body, all parts of which are connected together; also, that the influences of the spheres above pervade the earthly substance and prepare it for its forms. Hence it is impossible to assume that one deity be engaged in forming one part, and another deity in forming another part of that organic body of which all parts are closely connected together. A duality could only be imagined in this way, either that at one time the one deity is active, the other at another time, or that both act simultaneously, nothing being done except by both together. The first hypothesis is certainly absurd for many reasons; if at the time the one deity be active the other *could* also be active, there is no reason why the one deity should then act and the other not; if, on the other hand, it be impossible for the one deity to act when the other is at work, there must be some other cause [besides these deities], which [at a certain time] enables the one to act and disables the other. [Such difference would not be caused by time], since time is without change, and the object of the action likewise remains one and the same organic whole. Besides, if two deities existed in this way, both would be subject to the relations of time, since their actions would depend on time; they would also in the moment of acting pass from potentiality to actuality, and require an agent for such transition; their essence would besides include possibility [of existence]. It is equally absurd to assume that both together produce everything in existence, and that neither of them does anything alone; for when a number of forces must be united for a certain result, none of these forces acts of its own accord, and none is by itself the immediate cause of that result, but their union is the immediate cause. It has, furthermore, been proved that the action of the absolute cannot be due to an [external] cause. The union is also an act which presupposes a cause effecting that union, and if that cause be one, it is undoubtedly God; but if it also consists of a number of separate forces, a cause is required for the combination of these forces, as in the first case. Finally, one simple being must be arrived at, that is the cause of the existence of the Universe, which is one whole; it would make no difference whether we assumed that the First Cause had produced the Universe by *creatio ex nihilo*, or whether the Universe co-existed with the

First Cause. It is thus clear how we can prove the Unity of God from the fact that this Universe is one whole.

Another argument concerning the Incorporeality of God.—Every corporeal object is composed of matter and form (Prop. XXII.); every compound of these two elements requires an agent for effecting their combination. Besides, it is evident that a body is divisible and has dimensions; a body is thus undoubtedly subject to accidents. Consequently nothing corporeal can be a unity, either because everything corporeal is divisible or because it is a compound; that is to say, it can logically be analysed into two elements; because a body can only be said to be a certain body when the distinguishing element is added to the corporeal substratum, and must therefore include two elements; but it has been proved that the Absolute admits of no dualism whatever.

Now that we have discussed these proofs, we will expound our own method in accordance with our promise.

ALBO, *IKKARIM*

Translation by Isaac Husik

BOOK II, CHAPTER 4

We have already explained in the First Book[1] that the Torah begins with the story of creation to prove the existence of the Maker. The account of the way in which the things passed from potentiality to actuality proves the existence of an agent who brought them into actuality. And the fact that they passed into actuality at different times, namely in the six days of creation, shows that the agent is one who acts with intention and will, and does things at different times as His wisdom dictates, though they could have all come into being at the same time. The reason they were produced at different times is to indicate intention and will. For these are at the basis of the Torah as a whole and of the reward and punishment mentioned therein, as we said before. And the Rabbis say also, "The world could have been created with one word. And the reason there were ten is in order to exact punishment from the wicked . . . and to give reward to the righteous."[2] The order in which the different things came into being denotes the natural priority of some creatures over others, and shows that every one of them came into being at the time that was suitable and appropriate to its nature, so that it may realize the utmost perfection of which it is capable, as the wisdom and will of the Maker had decreed. The expression, "And God saw that it was good,"[3] which concludes the account of every work of creation points to the idea just mentioned.

From the testimony of the senses in regard to the passing of things from potentiality to actuality, we can find a rational proof of the existence of God, as follows: We see things which are potential and then become actual. Now every thing that passes from potentiality to actuality must have a cause outside of it. For if the cause were within and there is no obstacle, the thing would never be potential at all, but always actual. And if, the cause being within, there was an obstacle preventing its actualization, which was removed, then that which removed the obstacle is the cause of the thing's passing from potentiality to actuality. Now that cause which was itself potential before it became actual, was in this condition either because of an obstacle in itself, or because of the absence of a certain relation between the agent and the thing acted upon;

and as soon as the relation appeared, the cause became actual. Whichever of these alternatives we adopt, there must be something that removes the obstacle, or that produces the required relation. But the same thing applies to this thing that removed the obstacle or brought about the relation, and this can not go on ad infinitum. We must therefore finally reach a cause actualizing the potential, which has no potentiality at all. For if it had, it would be subject to possibility. This means to have the possibility of existing or not existing. But if so it would need another actualizing cause which would determine one of the alternative possibilities in preference to the other. This other therefore would be an actualizing cause without potentiality or obstacles, but one that does whatever it desires with its simple will, and it is a necessary existent.

It can not be material, for a material thing is subject to possibility and can not be a necessary existent. It is clear also from this that it is abstract or separate. But an abstract cause without possibility that causes things to pass from potentiality to actuality is God. It is clear that He is not body, and it is also clear that He is one, for the abstract is not susceptible of numerical quantity, except in so far as the one may be the cause and the other the effect. But the abstract without possibility is necessarily a cause and not an effect, for the effect is a possible existent, since its existence is dependent on another. It follows therefore that He is one. It is also clear that He is independent of time, for if He were dependent upon time, He would exist at a particular time and not at another, and then He would be subject to possibility. It is also clear that He is free from defects, for if He were defective, His work could not be absolutely perfect, whereas we see that all His works are as perfect as they can be, as the Bible says, "The Rock, His work is perfect."[4] It is clear therefore that He is free from defect.

This proof of the existence of God is equivalent to the fourth proof mentioned by Maimonides in the *Guide*, where he treats of the existence of God and the principles which follow from it.[5] It is a biblical proof which is in agreement with philosophy, and is alluded to in the creation story in Genesis, as we have seen.

NOTES

1. Ch. 11, p. 101.
2. Mishnah Abot, 5, 1.
3. Gen. 1, 4, 10, 12, 18, 21, 25, 31.
4. Deut. 32, 5.
5. Guide, II, 1, fourth proof.

BOOK II, CHAPTER 5

There are other philosophical proofs of the existence of God mentioned by Maimonides in the beginning of the second part of the *Guide*, which I will mention briefly to call the attention of the reader to those which are valid and those which are not. The first proof of Maimonides is based upon the existence of continuous and eternal motion, as is assumed by the Philosopher.[1] But this is not admitted by any of those who profess a divine law and believe in creation. Nor can our senses testify to such a doctrine. We did not therefore trouble to mention that proof.

But the second proof given by Maimonides is very weak, because it is based on a premise cited in the name of Aristotle which is not proven to be true. The proposition is that if of a thing composed of two elements one element is found to exist also by itself apart from the composite thing, then it follows that the other element must also be found to exist by itself apart from the compound. For if their nature compelled them to exist in combination only, like matter and natural form, neither could exist without the other. The fact therefore that one element does exist by itself shows that there is no such necessity, and therefore the other too must exist by itself. An example of this is *sakanjabin*,[2] a drink composed of vinegar and honey. Since honey is found by itself also, it follows necessarily that vinegar also is found by itself.

Then the argument proceeds as follows: We find many things composed of a mover and a moved. That is, they both move others and are themselves moved by others while they move the others. We also find a thing which is moved, but does not move another, viz. the last moved thing. It follows therefore that there must be a thing that moves another, but is not itself moved by another. This is the First Mover.

This proof is based upon the proposition above mentioned, which Maimonides cites in the name of Aristotle, but it is not true. For it does not follow that because one of the two elements of a composite thing exists alone, the other must exist alone also. Thus man is composed of animal and rational, and animal also exists by itself without rational. But rational does not exist by itself without animal, unless we say that angel is rational alone, i.e. actually intelligent without being body, nutritive and sentient, which is the definition of animal. To be sure, it is possible to object to this example by saying that animal does not exist alone, but in combination with some specific form, thus neighing animal, braying animal, roaring animal, but animal in the abstract does not exist by itself. And therefore it is not necessary that rational should exist by itself without any other form. But this is not the case in mover and moved.

Still, inasmuch as the opponent may dispute the proposition in a way by citing animal or plant which is composed of body and soul, and yet body exists alone, whereas animality or the vegetative force does not exist alone, Maimonides did not rely on this proof and cited a third philosophical proof which is very strong and can not be disputed, as Maimonides says.

The argument is as follows: Existences must belong to one of three classes. (1) They are all without origination and destruction, (2) they are all subject to origination and destruction, (3) some are subject to origination and destruction and some are not. There is no escape from this classification.

Now they can not all be without genesis and destruction, for we see with our senses many things coming into being and ceasing to be. They can not all be subject to generation and destruction, because if all existing things were subject to generation and destruction, all existing things would be possible existents, and they would all have been destroyed,[3] and there would be no cause to compel their existence in preference to their non-existence. Nothing would therefore exist, since there is no cause to produce or maintain them or to compel their existence in preference to their non-existence. And yet we see that they exist. It follows therefore that there is an existent, not subject to generation and destruction, one that has not the possibility of being destroyed, and that this being compels the existence of those things which are subject to generation and destruction, in preference to their non-existence. This being is a necessary existent, not a possible existent. For this being is determined to exist either by virtue of itself or by virtue of its cause. If by virtue of itself, then it is God. And if by virtue of its cause, then its cause is a necessary existent by virtue of itself, and it is God, who produces all things that are subject to generation and decay. Without Him a thing can not exist, and He is not subject to generation and decay.

This is a very strong proof of the matter, because it shows the existence of God through a necessary classification, and not because existing things require a Maker, which is the essence of the first proof, as we have seen. Therefore Maimonides says that it can not be rejected or disputed except by one who does not know the methods of proof. He points out also that it follows from this that He is not corporeal. For we have made clear that God is a necessary existent by virtue of Himself, and such a being is incorporeal. For all body is composed of two things, and the composition is the cause of its existence. Hence it can not be a necessary existent through itself, because its existence is dependent upon the existence of its parts and their composition. It is clear therefore that He is not body, nor a force residing in a body. It is easily proved also that He is one. For it is impossible that there should be two necessary existents equally, without any composition. For there must necessarily be in each one of them the element of necessary existence and another element by which it is differentiated from the other. The necessary existent would therefore be composed of two elements. But we have seen that the necessary existent can not have any composition in it at all. It is also clear that He is not subject to time. For everything that is subject to time is subject to change, and everything that is subject to change has a cause that makes it change. But the necessary existent through itself has no cause which makes it change. Nor can He be the cause and the subject of the change at the same time, for then He would consist of two elements, the element which causes the change and the element which undergoes the change, and He would be composite. It is also clear that He is free from defects. For if He had a defect He would have need of another to make good the defect, and He would not be a necessary existent through Himself but through another.

Though this proof is valid and reliable, as we have seen, nevertheless Maimonides cites a fourth proof, which is the first one that we mentioned in the preceding chapter, because it agrees with the statements of the Torah in the account of creation. We gave it here first because it is biblical and at the same time is in agreement with philosophy. We find also that Ibn Roshd[4] relies upon this proof in the fourth question of his book, *Destructio Destructionis*. We followed it by this second proof, because it is a philosophical proof which Maimonides believes in, saying that it can not be objected to or disputed. We have proved therefore the principle of the existence of God by means of two valid demonstrations.

NOTES

1. Aristotle was known as *the* Philosopher (par excellence).

2. Ar. سكنجبين from Persian سكنڭبين.

3. The argument requires ראוי, which I adopted with S in preference to איפשר of A. The point is that a possibility which is never realized is not a possibility. However, this is true only if we assume the eternity of the world. The reading ראוי is confirmed by the original of Maimonides, Guide, II, 1, 3d proof. Cf. Munk, Le Guide des Egarés, II, 39, note 2. [S designates the edition princeps of the *Ikkarim*, Soncino, 1485. A designates the manuscript written by Abraham Benieto, dated 1454, in the possession of the National Library of Paris and listed as 740 in Zotenberg's catalogue. — J.D.B.]

4. Ibn Roshd is the Arab philosopher, who is called by the Christian Scholastics Averroes. He was an older contemporary of Maimonides, and was much studied by the Post-Maimonidean Jewish philosophers. See Renan, "Averroes et l'Averroisme."

The Second Principle

Unity

INTRODUCTION

The Second Principle, which affirms the oneness and unity of God, is most often perceived as a negation of polytheism or trinitarianism. It is thus seen simply as a statement negating the existence of a plurality of deities. Actually, Maimonides makes no reference in his formulation of the Second Principle to the question of the possible existence of multiple gods. Indeed, there is no reason for him to do so. His discussion of the unity of God, a concept which is much more profound than mere negation of the existence of more than one God, renders consideration of the possibility of a plurality of deities superfluous and hence unnecessary of explicit rejection.

God is a unity, and His unity is unique in nature. The Second Principle not only affirms the unity of God, but also serves to negate a number of possible misconceptions concerning the nature of this unity:

(1) Mankind, for example, is a single species, a unity composed of all individual men. God, however, is not such a collective unity; He is not to be construed as a genus composed of distinct beings or powers. The unity of God is not the unity of collectivity.

(2) The unity of God is not the unity of an aggregate. God is not a compound divisible into parts. His unity is not the unity of a composite divisible into its component parts.

(3) It is not sufficient to state that the unity of God is not similar to the unity of a compound of other elements or unities. This does not exclude the logical possibility of a nature analogous to that of an atom which may itself be further divided or broken down. God's unity is not the unity of magnitude. God's unity is unique and unparalleled. His unity is such that it cannot admit of any division whatsoever. It follows that God cannot die or be destroyed. No "simple substance," i.e., a substance not composed of parts, can be broken down. Since destruction involves the breaking down or division of an entity into component parts, it follows that God, who is a perfect unity, is not susceptible to destruction.

This concept of unity gives rise to a formidable problem with regard to the proper understanding of the nature of divine attributes. It is impossible to ascribe any attribute to the Deity without doing violence to the "simple" nature of God. The mere ascription of an attribute in subject-predicate form implies that there is a subject in whom the attribute is inherent. The attribute is thus superimposed upon the subject, and conversely, the subject is one which can be conceived without the attribute. Subject and attribute, since they are logically divisible are no longer a unity. To take a simple example, the proposition "John is good" implies the existence of John, who, logically speaking, may or may not be good. Goodness is thus a quality distinct from the concept or nature of John and is merely cojoined with John. John and his goodness are clearly not one and the same. Yet God can be conceived as a unity only if God and His attributes are one and the same or, more precisely, only if God possesses no attributes whatsoever.

Saadia's primary proof for the unity of God is predicated upon acceptance of His incorporeality. The attribute of number applies only to corporeal substances, since it is matter which is the principle of individualization. At the same time, Saadia is willing to attribute to God the attributes of Life, Power and Wisdom, but only because these attributes do not involve multiplicity in His nature. They are encompassed in the very meaning of the concept God and are immediately perceived as such by reason. Separate words are used only because human language does not have a single word through which to convey the unitary nature of God.

Baḥya ibn Pakuda distinguishes between what he terms "essential" and "active" attributes. The first are three in number: Existing, One and Eternal. These essential attributes do not imply multiplicity in God because each one implies the other two. The quality denoted is the essence of God, which is single in nature, but which, when expressed in human language, requires different terms for adequate expression. Moreover, fundamentally, these attributes are to be understood as denying their opposites; i.e., they are used to convey to us the notion that God is not nonexistent, not more than one, nor was there a time when He did not exist. The "active" attributes are ascribed by us to God not as an attempt to describe His essence, but as a description of His actions or of their effect upon us. In doing so, we describe how God appears to us, but do not attempt to describe the objective nature of God.

Baḥya ascribes a certain instrumental value to anthropomorphic descriptions of God. Scripture could not convey a concept of God in terms and concepts appropriate to His nature because, in the absence of any frame of reference, such descriptions would have no cognitive meaning to us. It was therefore necessary to employ anthropomorphic terms having corporeal connotations which are readily understandable in order to present basic information about God. The properly attuned mind will then be able to develop a more sophisticated understanding of the nature of God even while lacking language for proper verbalization.

Judah Halevi adopts essentially the same explanation but classifies the attributes in a somewhat different manner. Halevi regards divine attributes as being divisible into three classes: actional, relative and negative. Actional attributes are appellations which are suggested to us by God's acts. A human being alleviates misery because he feels pity; accordingly, when misery is removed as a result of a divine act, we (erroneously) ascribe a comparable feeling to God and call Him merciful. Relative attributes reflect the attitude of man toward God. God is blessed because man blesses Him, not because of a quality inherent in God. Negative attributes are simply ways of excluding their opposites. To speak of God as living is not to ascribe life to God as distinct from His essence, but simply to deny that He is dead.

It remained for Maimonides to assert the complete denial of all attributes. For Maimonides, all attributes, insofar as they purport to describe God, rather than His effects, involve a plurality. The only attributes which may be ascribed to God are negative ones. They do not tell us what God is, but what He is not. Hence, any number of negative attributes may be employed without implying plurality. Whenever attributes are applied to God, they must be understood as a type of verbal shorthand; they are intended not to ascribe the quality expressed but to deny its opposite. Maimonides espouses the doctrine of negative attributes both because he believes that any other explanation does violence to the notion of the unity of God and also because he believes that the human mind cannot fathom the essence of the Deity. Man cannot possibly describe the nature of God since God's essence is beyond human comprehension. He can only say what God's essence is not. Thus "powerful" means "not weak," "wise" means "not ignorant," "eternal" means "not caused," etc. The doctrine of negative attributes is one of the most significant elements in Maimonides' analysis of the nature of God.

Albo struggles with the problem of how multiplicity can be generated from unity. Although God is absolutely one, He is the cause of plurality. Albo argues that many different acts may be performed for the sake of a single purpose. God orders the universal order, which contains a plurality of elements, in order to unite all parts of existence.

Albo is particularly desirous of negating the notion that it is possible to attribute location to God. Just as God cannot be described as occupying a place, so also He cannot be described as being located above or below a place. When God is described in Scripture as occupying a heavenly abode, the description is to be understood only metaphorically.

God is portrayed as being in the heavens in the sense that divine power is perceived more clearly in the motion of the spheres by virtue of the intensity and continuity of their motion. The movements of the spheres are, of course, proximately related to a divine cause.

SAADIA, *EMUNOT VE-DE'OT*

Translation by Alexander Altmann

SECOND TREATISE
THE UNITY OF THE CREATOR

1. *The Abstract Character of the Knowledge of God*

...I further remarked that man progresses from knowledge to knowledge until he reaches a point beyond which no further knowledge is possible. There are three reasons for this. (1) Since the body of man is limited and finite, it necessarily follows that all his faculties, including the faculty of knowledge, are also finite just as with regard to the heaven, as I have already stated, the time of its duration must necessarily be assumed to be finite.[1] (2) Knowledge can be acquired by man only because it is of a finite nature. If thought were to entail an infinite process, it would be impossible to master it, and if this were impossible, man would not know anything. (3) Since the root from which all knowledge springs, i.e., sense perception, is undoubtedly finite in character, it is impossible that its offspring should be infinite, and the branch different from the root.

I further said that man in his pursuit of knowledge progresses from one stage to another. This point is based on the fact that all knowledge has a root from which it springs, whereas ignorance has no root from which to spring, but is merely the absence (privation)[2] of knowledge in the same way as we have explained with reference to darkness that it is the absence of light, not its opposite.[3] One of our arguments also was that if darkness were the opposite of light, the dark atmosphere (of the night) could not change into the brightness (of daylight). In the same way we contend here that if ignorance had a root like knowledge, it would be impossible for the ignorant to become knowing; for knowledge and ignorance, if combined in the same person,[4] would destroy each other. On these grounds I said that man progresses in knowledge from stage to stage, seeing that knowledge springs from a root and branches out, whereas it is impossible to suppose that one progresses in ignorance from one stage to another, because in ignorance there are no conclusions towards which one could travel, ignorance being merely the abandoning, step by step, of knowledge, and its disappearance.

I further said that the ultimate conclusion reached is more abstract and subtle than all previous discoveries. This can be shown from a physical example: Snow, as it drops from the air, has the appearance of a solid crystal.[5] If we examine it more closely, we shall find that it originates from water. If we probe still more deeply, we shall learn that this water could not have been lifted up except in the form of rising vapour. Thus we conclude that snow originates from vapour.[6] Then we go still deeper into the matter and assert that there must be some cause for the rising of vapour. It should already be clear that the final cause which we shall discover will be more subtle than vapour, which, in turn, is more subtle than water, which, in turn, is again more subtle than snow. It is this subtle cause which formed the real object and the goal of our inquiries. For this reason I said that one who desires this final knowledge to be similar to his initial knowledge does violence to the very nature of knowledge, as I have made clear from my description of its laws and methods.

Having completed these explanations, it is desirable that I should now state the reason which prompted me to enunciate them here at the beginning of this chapter. It is that, when I came to deal with the subject of the Creator,[7] I found that people rejected this whole inquiry, some because they could not see God; others on account of the profundity and extrēme subtleness of His nature; still others claim that beyond the knowledge of God there is some other knowledge; others again go so far as to picture Him as a body; others, while not explicitly describing Him as a body, assign to Him quantity or quality or space or time, or similar things, and by looking for these qualities they do in fact assign to Him a body, since these attributes belong only to a body. The purpose of my introductory remarks is to remove their false ideas, to take a load from their minds, and to point out that the extreme subtleness which we have assigned to the nature of the Creator is, so to speak, its own warrant, and the fact that, in our reasoning, we find the notion of God to be more abstract than other knowledge shows that reasoning to be correct. Those who declare that they only hold true what they perceive with their own eyes, and deny all knowledge (of Reason), I refuted already when discussing the theories of the Sensualists,[8] the Subjectivists,[9] and the Sceptics.[10] Those who reject the conception of God on account of its subtleness and profundity fail to proceed to their second objective after attaining the first,[11] for the reader will remember what I have already explained in regard to the Creation of the world, namely, that our aim in this respect was something deep, subtle, fine and profound the like of which cannot be met in our experience. I noted that Scripture says with reference to such a thing, 'That which is far off, and exceeding deep; who can find it out?' (Eccl. 7.24).[12] I have met some thinkers who are not of our Faith and who imagined this object to be something subtle like dust and hair, or like the indivisible atom.[13] But we have arrived at the result that the world was created from nothing, and this being the character of the object investigated at that stage, it is necessary that the character of the objective investigated at the next stage, namely, the Creator (be He exalted and glorified) should be more abstract than anything abstract, more profound than anything profound, more subtle than anything subtle, deeper than anything deep, more powerful than anything powerful, and higher than anything high, so that it becomes impossible to probe His quality.[14] With regard to this, Scripture has said, 'Canst thou find out the deep things of God? Canst thou attain unto the purpose of the Almighty? It is high as heaven; what canst thou do? Deeper than the nether-world; what canst thou know? The measure thereof is longer than the earth, and broader than the sea' (Job II.7–9).

As to those who wish us to imagine God as a body, they should wake up from their illusions. Is not the conception of the body the first stage arrived at in our pursuit of knowledge? As to the characteristics[15] which apply to the body, did we not proceed in our examination and investigation until we reached the conception of the Maker of the body? How, then, do these people go back to the A B C and seek to conceive God as a body? Was the body whose Maker we endeavoured to find some person known to us so that it would have been proper that his Maker should be some person other than himself? No, what we endeavoured to find was the Creator of all bodies which we can perceive and imagine, and every body which can be grasped in our thought must be the work of that Maker who is external to all the bodies.

In regard to those who seek to find something beyond God, we have already declared such a desire to be inadmissible from the point of view of the person who knows, seeing that his knowledge is necessarily limited by his faculties; of the object of knowledge, for that which does not reach a limit and stop cannot be comprehended by the soul; and finally of the root from which all knowledge is derived.[16]

2. *The Attributes of God*

Our Lord (be He exalted and glorified) has informed us through the words of His prophets that He is One, Living, Powerful and Wise, and that nothing can be compared unto Him or unto His works. They established this by signs and miracles, and we accepted it immediately.

Later, speculation led us to the same result. In regard to His Unity, it is said, 'Hear O Israel, the Lord our God, the Lord is One' (Deut. 6.4); furthermore, 'See now that I, even I, am He, and that there is no god with Me' (Deut. 32.39), and also, 'The Lord alone did lead him, and there was no strange god with Him' (Deut. 32.12). In regard to His Life, it is said, 'For who is there of all flesh, that hath heard the voice of the living God speaking out of the midst of the fire, as we have, and lived?' (Deut. 5.23); furthermore, 'But the Lord God is a true God, He is the living God, and the everlasting King' (Jer. 10.10). As to His Power, it is said, 'I know that Thou canst do everything, and that no purpose can be withholden from Thee' (Job 42.2); and furthermore, 'Thine, O Lord, is the greatness, and the power, and the glory, and the victory, and the majesty' (I Chron. 29.11). As to His Wisdom, it is said, 'He is wise in heart, and mighty in strength; who hath hardened himself against Him, and prospered?' (Job 9.4); and furthermore, 'His discernment is past searching out' (Isa. 40.28). In regard to the incomparability of God and His works, it is said, 'There is none like unto Thee among the gods, O Lord; and there are no works like Thine' (Ps. 86.8).

Having accepted these six attributes[17] from the Books of the Prophets, we endeavoured to confirm them by way of speculation, and found them in agreement with Reason. At the same time, we discovered the arguments with which to refute the attacks of our opponents who disagree with us in regard to some of these attributes. Their attacks arise from two sources only: (1) from their practice of drawing analogies[18] between God and His creatures; (2) from their tendency to blame us on account of the terms by which we express His attributes,[19] because they take the anthropomorphic expressions which occur in Scripture not in a metaphorical[20] sense, but literally. We hope to make all this clear in our exposition of this doctrine.[21]

(a) *The Unity of God.*—My first argument for the Unity of God is based on the proofs which I have given before, to the effect that God is the Maker of the physical world. As the Maker of corporeal bodies, He cannot be of their kind.[22] Since there exist many bodies, he must necessarily be One. For if He were more than One, the category of number would apply to Him, and He would enter the realm of the physical world.[23]

My second argument is: Reason decides that a Maker exists only because it cannot avoid this assumption. But what it cannot avoid is only the assumption of one Maker. If, however, anything is added to Him, this further assumption is not an unavoidable, but an unnecessary, one.[24]

My third argument is: The existence of the One Maker has been established by the first proof, i.e. the proof for Creation.[25] Anything added to Him requires a second proof in addition to this one in order to demonstrate it. But no further proofs can be brought beyond those given for Creation.

(b) *The three attributes of God.*—Considering the subject further I found that the conception of God as Creator, which we established, implies the attributes of Life, Power, and Wisdom. By means of our faculty of ratiocination[26] it becomes clear to us that creation is impossible without power, and that power is impossible without life, and that a well-ordered creation presupposes an intelligence which knows in advance the result of its activities. Our Reason discovers these three aspects of the notion of a Creator in a single flash of intuition,[27] as one reality. For the very idea that God is the Creator involves the attribution to Him of Life, Power, and Wisdom, as I explained. Reason can in no way find one of these three aspects prior to the other, but arrives at all of them at one stroke, since it cannot possibly conceive of God as Creator without conceiving of Him as endowed with Life and Power, and it cannot think of a complete and well-ordered creation otherwise than as the product of an intelligence capable of knowing in advance the result of its activities. For the work of a mind lacking in such knowledge cannot be well-ordered and skillfully designed. Now these three aspects of God, which occur to our Reason in combination, cannot be expressed by one single word in our language. For we do not find a word in language which covers all these three aspects. We must needs express them by three different words, but it should be well understood that Reason conceived them as one single idea. Let nobody assume that the Eternal (blessed be He) contains a plurality of attributes. For all the attributes which we assign to Him are implied in the one attribute of Creator, and it is merely the deficiency of our language which makes it necessary for us to express our notion of God in three different words, since there exists no word in our vocabulary which covers all the three aspects. Nor would it be advisable to create a special term for this conception, because that new term would convey no meaning by itself, and it would still be necessary to explain it, so that it would lead us back to a plurality of words in place of one term. If someone imagines that these attributes imply a diversity[28] within God, i.e. some difference between the various attributes, I will show him his mistake by pointing out the real truth of the matter, viz. that diversity and change can take place in bodies and their accidents only, but the Creator of all bodies and accidents is above diversity and change.[29] Nor should I be satisfied until I had made the matter perfectly clear to him by saying that in the same way as the attribute of 'Creator' does not imply something in addition to the essence[30] of God, but merely implies that there exists a world created by Him, so the attributes of Life, Power and Wisdom, which explain the term Creator—it being understood that there can be no Creator unless He possesses these aspects simultaneously—add nothing to His essence but merely denote the existence of a world created by Him.[31]

Having thus established this conception by force of reason, I turned to Scripture and found that it precludes any notion of plurality within God: 'There is none else beside Him' (Deut. 4.35); furthermore, 'Lo, these are but the outskirts of His ways; and how small a whisper is heard of Him' (Job. 26.14); furthermore, 'In that day shall the Lord be One, and His name One' (Zech. 14.9).

NOTES

1. Cf. above, p. 52.
2. Cf. above, p. 72, n. 3.
3. Cf. Saadya's argument against Dualism, pp. 72-3.
4. Lit. 'part,' 'element.'
5. Lit. 'Like the stone.'
6. The above explanation of the origin of snow is borrowed from Aristotle, *Meteorologica,* I, 10-12; the 'Faithful Brethren of Basra' also accepted it. Cf. Dieterici, *Naturanschauung,* p. 80.
7. I.e. the doctrine of the Divine attributes, having proved the existence of the Creator in Chapter I.
8. Lit. 'Those who profess the eternity of the world' (*dahriyya*). Cf. above, p. 62, n. 4.
9. Lit. 'The people of obstinacy' (*'anūd*), according to whom the reality of things depends on subjective opinion. This group, also called *indiyya,* follows the Sophistic view (Protagoras), which makes man the measure of all things. Cf. M. Ventura, La Philosophie de Saadia Gaon, 1934, pp. 154-7.
10. Lit. 'The people of abstention' (*wuḳūf*), who insist on the suspension of judgment (Ἐποχή) on all matters which involve reasoning. Cf. Ventura, pp. 157–9.—The three above-mentioned views figure as No. 10, 11 and 12 in Saadya's list of cosmological theories and are not included in the Selection presented in Chapter 1.
11. They have reached the first objective, namely, the doctrine of Creation which implies the existence of the Creator, but they are reluctant to pursue the second objective, namely, the doctrine of the Divine attributes.
12. Cf. above, p. 49.
13. Saadya obviously refers to the theories of the Greek and Islamic atomists.
14. The crescendo of epithets describing the absolute transcendence and unfathomable depth of the *Deus Absconditus* bears eloquent testimony to Saadya's religious fervour.
15. Arab, *āṯār*; traces, signs. The reference is to the Aristotelian categories.
16. I.e. Sense perception, which is finite in character.
17. In the course of his later exposition, Saadya omits the last-mentioned attribute (that of God's incomparability) since it expresses only a formal aspect of God's essence.
18. Arab. *ḳiyās*; deduction by analogy. Cf. *EI,* Vol. II, p. 1051 ff.—Tibbon translates it by *haḳashah.*
19. Arab. *ṣifa.*

20. Arab. *majāz.*

21. I.e. the doctrine of the Divine attributes.

22. Saadya follows the Mutakallimūn whose arguments for the incorporeality of God included one which was based on the principle of the 'impossibility of comparison,' i.e. the belief that God cannot be compared to any of His creatures, and that He would be comparable to other corporeal objects if He were conceived of as corporeal. The anthropomorphists, however, believed that the substance of God differed from the substances of all bodies created by Him, but that it was none the less of a corporeal nature. It was sublime, perfect, simple, constant and immutable. Cf. *Moreh*, I, 76, 2.

23. Saadya obviously accepts Aristotle's statement that 'all things that are many in number have matter.' Cf. *Metaphysica*, XII, 8, 1074a, 33-4. Maimonides also accepted this view. Cf. *Moreh*, II, Introd., XVI. See J. Guttmann, Die Religions philosophie des Saadia, 1882, p. 95; H.A. Wolfson, Crescas' Critique of Aristotle, 1929, p. 666.

24. Cf. the Mu'tazilite argument quoted by Maimonides, *Moreh*, I, 75, 4, 'The existence of an action is necessarily positive evidence of the existence of an *agens*, but does not prove the existence of more than one *agens*'. Baḥya, *Ḥoḇōt Hal-leḇaḇōt* 7, III, elaborates this argument, which is of Aristotelian origin. Cf. *Physica*, I, 6, 189 b, 17-20; cf. also Spinoza, *Cog. met.*, II, 2; Guttmann, p. 95; Ventura, pp. 177-8.

25. Saadya refers to the set of Four Proofs for Creation in Chapter I, which demonstrate the existence of a Creator.

26. Arab. *fī-fiṭari 'aḵlinā*; Tibbon: *be-ḵoaḥ siḵlenū.* The Arabic term *fiṭra* denotes 'man's natural gifts, his mental equipment by birth.' Cf. H. Malter, 'Mediaeval Hebrew Terms for Nature,' in *Judaica*, p. 253; A. J. Wensinck, *The Muslim Creed*, 1932, pp. 214–5, 261.

27. Arab. *badīhā*, which is insufficiently rendered by Tibbon's Hebr. *pit'om*, suddenly.

28. Arab. *taghayyur*, change, diversity.

29. In a subsequent passage not included in the present Selection (*Amānāt*, 86-7; Hebr. 45–6). [References are to S. Landauer's edition of the Arabic text (*Amānāt*), Leiden, 1880, and to D. Slucki's edition of Ibn Tibbon's Hebrew translation, Leipzig, 1864.] Saadya elaborates this argument by pointing out that in the case of man life and wisdom are distinct and separate from his self (essence) seeing that he dies and is liable to ignorance. Unless we witnessed the changes which take place in regard to man—the changes from life to death and from ignorance to wisdom—we should have assumed that he is living and wise by virture of his essence. God in whom no change takes place is living, wise and powerful by virtue of His essence. In other words, these three attributes are identical with His essence. Saadya stresses this point in his treatment of the Christian doctrine of Trinity, which, in his opinion (cf. also al-Sharastānī I, 260, 266, who mentions particularly the Nestorians), interpreted the three attributes of Existence, Wisdom and Life in the sense of the three separate persons of Father, Son *(Logos)* and Holy Spirit. Saadya's view that the three attributes are not separate aspects of God follows in the footsteps of Mu'tazilite theology, particularly Abū-l-Huḏail's school of thought, who insisted that the three attributes of Life, Wisdom and Power are identical with the essence of God. Cf. Kaufmann, *loc. cit.*, pp. 33 ff. The Mu'tazilites combated the orthodox Islamic doctrine of *Sifa Dhātīyya* (Attributes of Essence) because of its christological implications. Cf. the Translator's article, 'Saadya's Theory of Revelation' in *Saadya Studies* (ed. E.I.J. Rosenthal), p. 12 ff.

30. Arab. *ḏāt.*

31. Having refuted the idea that the three attributes describe separate aspects of God's essence, Saadya now goes further in suggesting that all that is really implied in these attributes is the notion of God as Creator. In other words, they are not 'attributes of essence' at all, but merely state the relation of God to the world, i.e. the implications of the notion of Creator. They are, in Yehudah Hallevi's and Maimonides' terminology, 'attributes of action,' and leave the essence and nature of God untouched. This view amounts to the thesis of 'negative theology' and is not quite consistent with the idea previously expressed (see above p. 83, n. 2) that the three attributes are identical with God's essence. Cf. Julius Guttmann, *Die Philosophie d. Judentums*, pp. 79–80. Saadya's prime concern is to safeguard the principle of the Unity of God against any misconception.

BAḤYA, *ḤOVOT HA-LEVAVOT*

Translation by Moses Hyamson

FIRST TREATISE, INTRODUCTION

Which treats of the grounds for the whole-hearted acceptance of the Unity of God.

Preliminary

When we inquired as to what is the most necessary among the fundamental principles of our religion, we found that the wholehearted acceptance of the Unity of God—the root and foundation of Judaism—is the first of the gates of the Torah. By the acceptance of the Unity of God, the believer is distinguished from the infidel. It is the head and front of religious truth. Whoever has deviated from it will neither practise any duty properly nor retain any creed permanently. Hence, God's first words to us on Mount Sinai were (Exodus 20:2) "I am the Lord thy God. . .Thou shalt have no other gods before Me." And later on, He exhorted us through His prophet (Deut. 6:4) "Hear, O Israel, The Lord our God, the Lord is One." You should study this section (of the Shema) to its close, and you will observe how its contents proceed from topic to topic, comprising in all ten topics, that number corresponding to the Ten Commandments. First there is the command to believe in the Creator, when it says, "Hear, O Israel, The Lord." In using the word *Shema* (Hear), the text refers not to hearing with the ear, but to inward belief, as in the passages (Ex. 24:7) "We will do and we will hear"; (Deut. 6:3) "Hear therefore O Israel, and observe to do it." Whenever the term "hear" is used in this way, it is intended to express nothing else but believing and accepting.

Having thus been placed under the obligation of believing in the reality of the Creator's existence, we are enjoined to believe that He is our God, as indicated in the word *Elohenu* "our God." Then we are commanded to believe that He is the true Unity, as it is said, "The Lord is One." Having been bidden to believe and accept the three principles just mentioned, Scripture proceeds to a duty which we are bound to add to the foregoing, namely, to love God whole-heartedly, in private and in public, with our soul and with our might, as it is said, (Deut. 6:5) "And thou shalt love the Lord thy God, with all thine heart, with all thy soul, and with all thy might." This theme, I will, with God's help, expound in the last part, entitled The Love of God. The section then goes on to inculcate duties of the heart, when it says, "And these words which I command thee this day shall be upon thy heart"; that is to say: Impress them upon your heart and believe in them inwardly.

FIRST TREATISE, CHAPTER 7

The demonstration of God's Unity is as follows: It having been logically demonstrated that the World has a Creator, it becomes now our duty to institute an enquiry as to whether He is One or more than One. We deem it requisite to prove His Unity in seven arguments.

The first is drawn from our observation of the causes of existing things. When we consider them, we find that causes are always fewer than their effects. The causes of these causes are still fewer. The higher the series of causes ascends, the smaller their number. And so at last, one Cause is reached, who is the Cause of all causes.

To explain this more fully. Individual things are innumerable. But when we consider the species which comprise them, they are found to be fewer than the individuals included in them, for each of the species comprehends many individuals, and the species are definite in number. Arranging the species again under their respective genera, the latter are found to be fewer than the former, for every genus includes several species. The higher the classes the fewer they are, till the most comprehensive divisions are reached. These, according to the philosopher, Aristotle, are ten; namely, Substance, Quantity, Quality, Relation, Place, Time, Position, Possession, Action, Passion. The causes of these categories are five: Motion and the four elements—Fire, Air, Water, Earth. The causes of these four elements are, on investigation, found to be Matter and Form. As they are two, their cause again should accordingly be less than two. This cause is the Will of the Creator. There is no number less than two but One. The Creator is therefore One. So David, peace be upon him, said (I Chron. 29:11) "Thine is the Kingdom, O Lord, and Thou art exalted as head above all"; that is to say, God is exalted above all that are exalted; He is the Supreme, the First of all beginnings, the Cause of all causes and effects.

The second argument for the Unity of God is drawn from the marks of wisdom manifested in the Universe, in every part of it, above and below, in its mineral, vegetable and animal kingdoms. If we observe it intelligently, we will be convinced that the entire Universe is the design of One Designer, the work of One Maker. For we find that, with all the differences in causes and original elements, it shows a similarity in effects, a uniformity in its parts. The marks of divine wisdom, evident in the smallest as in the largest creatures, testify that they all have one wise Creator. If the Universe had more than one Creator, the creative wisdom would exhibit different forms in the different parts of the world, and would vary both in its larger and smaller divisions.

Moreover we find that for the existence and perfection of the universe its parts are necessary to each other. No portion of it can be completed without the help of some other portion; just as links in chain armour, the sections of a couch, the limbs of the human body, or the parts of other things that are put together are mutually necessary for their efficiency and completeness. Do you not perceive that the moon and the other planets need the light of the sun; that the earth needs the sky and the water; that animals need each other, since some species, birds of prey, fish and wild beasts, for example, feed on others? Man needs the Universe. And for its perfection the Universe needs Man. Countries, towns, sciences and arts are interdependent. Divine wisdom is manifested in the smallest animals and in the largest. The wisdom displayed in the creation of the huge elephant is not more marvelous than that shown in the creation of the tiny ant. On the contrary, the minuter the creature, the more evidence does it furnish of the Creator's wisdom and power, and the more wondrous and striking does the work of God appear. This proves that all things are the design of One Designer and Creator; for all things show similarity and uniformity and contribute to the completeness of the world and the maintenance of all its parts.

If this world had more than one Creator, its different parts would exhibit different forms of wisdom; and these parts would not be necessary to each other. Since, however, despite difference in its roots and foundations (original constituent elements), the world exhibits uniformity in its products and combinations, it is clear that its Creator who put it together, its Governor and Designer is One. A philosopher once said: No one part of the creation is more wonderful than any other part; that is to say, equal and identical wisdom is shown in the smallest as in the largest of God's creatures. So, David, describing the Earth and its inhabitants, exclaims (Ps. 104:24) "How manifold are thy works, O Lord. In wisdom hast Thou made them all. The earth is full of Thy possessions." (Ps. 92:6) "How great are Thy works, O Lord. Thy thoughts are very deep."

The third argument is drawn from the fact of Creation which applies to the entire Universe. It has been demonstrated that the World is created. It must therefore have had a Creator; since nothing can come into existence of itself. When we find that a thing exists and we are certain that at one time it had not existed, we know, by the testimony of our sound reason, that some one other than itself created it, brought it into being and formed it. We need not inquire whether He is One or more than one, since the world could not have come into existence without at least one Creator. If we could possibly conceive that the world could have come into existence with a Creator less than one, we would so conceive Him. But as we cannot conceive that something less than one can bring anything into existence, we conclude that the Creator is One. For in the case of things which are established by adducing proofs, as soon as the existence of those things is proved beyond dispute, we need not assume more than is necessary to account for the entire phenomenon, which constitutes the proof.[1] The following will serve as an illustration: When we see a manuscript, uniform in composition and handwriting, it will at once occur to us that one individual wrote and composed it. For it could not conceivably have been written by less than one person, and if that were possible, we would assume such to be the case. It might indeed have had more than one writer. Still, in the absence of evidence, such as variety of handwriting, etc., we are not warranted in making this assumption. The conditions being as stated, there is no need for us to know the author personally, if it is impossible to arrive at the truth in this way. The inference drawn from his work—the style of the handwriting—takes the place of his personal acquaintance, and we feel certain that there exists a writer, knowing how to write and able to write, who wrote it. The style and uniformity of the script indicates that no one cooperated with him, since the work of two persons varies, is not uniform, is irregular and differs in quality and character.

Similarly we may reason concerning the Creator. Since the marks of wisdom manifested in His creatures are of a similar and uniform character, we are bound to believe that one Creator created them, and that without Him they could not have come into existence, though He is not something that can be perceived either in essence or accident. As He is invisible, we cannot find Him or know Him except by reasoning and by use of intelligent observation, which point to Him when we direct our attention to His creatures. And so our faith will be confirmed that He exists, that He is One, that He is Eternal who was and will be, the First and the Last, Mighty, Wise, Living. Since He does not belong to the class of things that can be seen, logical demonstrations have to take the place of direct intuition and visible apprehension of Him. We are bound to believe in One God, because without Him the Existence of created things is inconceivable. The assumption of more than one God is superfluous and unnecessary. Hence, if any one maintains that God is more than One, his contention will not stand unless he brings a proof other than that which I have adduced. It is however impossible to establish such a view, for rational proofs do not contradict each other. All demonstrations thus bear witness to God's Unity and negative the attribution to Him of any plurality, association or similarity; as the Creator himself declares (Is. 44:8) "Is there a god beside Me? Yea, there is no Rock; I know not any"; further (Is. 44:6) "I am the First, and I am the Last"; (Is. 48:13) "Yea, My hand hath laid the foundations of the earth, and My right hand hath spread out the heavens. When I call unto them, they stand up together"; (Is. 45:21) "A just God and a Saviour. There is none beside Me."

Fourth Argument. To anyone who thinks that the Creator is more than one, we say that the essence of all these (supposed creators) cannot but be either one or not one. If it be assumed that in essence they are one, then they are identical and the Creator is not more than One. But if one assumes that each of them is, in essence, different from the other, it necessarily follows that there is a distinction between them, due to their difference and dissimilarity. Whatever is distinct is limited. Whatever is limited is finite. Whatever is finite is compound. Whatever is compound has been brought into existence. Whatever has been brought into existence was brought into existence by a Being. He who thinks that the Creator is more than one must necessarily then assume that this Creator was brought into existence. We have however already demonstrated that the Creator is Eternal, Cause of all causes, Beginning of all beginnings. He is therefore One, as Scripture saith (Nehem. 9:6) "Thou art the Lord, even Thou alone."

The fifth argument is drawn from the concepts of Unity and Plurality. Euclid, in his book, defined Unity as follows: "Unity is that property which is predicated of any thing that is one." Unity, accordingly, in its nature, precedes the individual thing, just as heat precedes anything hot.[2] If there were no unity, we could not predicate of any thing that it is one. The idea that we have to form in our mind of unity, is of oneness that is complete, a uniqueness, that is absolutely devoid of composition or resemblance; free, in every respect, of plurality or number; that is neither associated with aught, nor dissociated from aught. The idea of plurality is that of a sum of unities. Plurality therefore cannot precede unity of which it has been formed. When we conceive a plurality with our intellects, or apprehend it with our senses, we know of a certainty that unity preceded it, just as the numeral one precedes the remaining numbers. Whoever thinks that the Creator is more than one must, in any case, concede that there was a preceding unity, just as the numeral one precedes the other numbers, and just as the notion of unity precedes that of plurality. Consequently, the Creator is absolutely One, and Eternal, and none is Eternal but He, as it is said, (Isaiah 43:10) "Before Me there was no God formed; neither shall any be after Me."

The sixth argument is drawn from a consideration of the accidental properties that attach to everything that is plural. Plurality is an accidental property superadded to the substance of a thing, and comes under the category of quantity. As the Deity is the Creator of substance and accident, none of these attributes can be ascribed to His glorious Being. For, it having been clearly demonstrated from Scripture and Reason, that God is above all comparison with, and similarity to, any of His creatures, and seeing that plurality which adheres to the substance of anything that is plural is an accidental property, any such quality cannot be fittingly ascribed to the Creator's glorious essence. And if He cannot be described as plural, He must certainly be One, since between unity and plurality there is no middle term. Hence, God is not more than one; and He is therefore One; as Hannah said (I Sam. 2:2) "There is none holy as the Lord, for there is none beside Thee."

Seventh argument: If we were to grant that the Creator is more than one, then each of these hypothetical creators could have created the universe by himself or could not have done so except with the help of the other. If any one of these creators was able to do so, any other creator is superfluous; since the former did not need the assistance of the latter. If, on the other hand, the work of Creation could not have been completed unless the deities cooperated, then no single one of them had full and complete strength and capacity. Each of them lacked the necessary power and ability and was weak. What is weak is finite in strength and essence. The finite is compound. Everything that is compound has been brought into existence. Whatever has been brought into existence must have some one who brought it into existence. Consequently what is weak cannot possibly be eternal, since what is eternal does not fall short in any respect nor stands in need of another's help. The Creator accordingly is not more than One.

If there were a possibility that the Creator was more than one, it might have happened that at the Creation discord would have broken out among the assumed deities, and the Creation would never have been accomplished by them. Since we find that the whole of this world exhibits one order, and a uniform movement is manifested in all its parts, which is unchanged throughout the generations, we know that its Creator and Ruler is One; and that none beside Him alters His work or changes His rule; as Scripture saith (Is. 44:7) "And who, as I, can proclaim, declare it and set it in order for Me?"; (Ps. 119:89-90) "Forever, O Lord, Thy Word standeth fast in Heaven; Thy faithfulness is unto all generations; Thou hast established the earth and it standeth." The Creator's perfect government which we observe in His creatures (also indicates God's Unity). For Government can be perfect and abidingly consistent only when counsel and management are vested in one individual, as in a King ruling the state or in the soul controlling the body. Thus Aristotle states in his book in reference to Unity: "It is not good when there are many heads, but only when there is one head." So too Solomon says (Prov. 28:2) "For the transgression of a land, many are the princes thereof." What we have adduced on this theme will suffice to convince the intelligent and refute the assumption of the plurality of the Deity. For when we establish the Unity of the Creator, the contention of anyone who says that He is more than One is refuted. Note this well.

NOTES

1. The Law of Parsimony.
2. This reasoning is in harmony with Plato's doctrine of Realism that Universals, that is, general ideas are independent of and exist prior to individual objects. Aristotle's view, nominalism, is that Concepts are only names and have no objective reality.

FIRST TREATISE, CHAPTER 10

Of the attributes of God ascribed to Him by Reason, as well as those ascribed to Him in Scripture, and the modes in which these should be affirmed of Him or denied to Him:

In regard to the Divine attributes, both those derived from Reason and those set forth in Holy Writ, it has to be observed that the senses in which they are understood are exceedingly numerous, in correspondence with the large number of God's creatures and the benefits bestowed upon them all.

These attributes fall into two classes: Essential and active. The reason why we call the attributes in the one class essential, is because they belonged to God before the existence of any creatures; and after all creatures shall have ceased to exist, these attributes will continue to apply to Him and to His glorious essence. These attributes are three: That He is; that He is One; and that He is eternal without predecessor.

We ascribe to Him these attributes, to indicate His being and true Existence, to call attention to His glory, to make human beings understand that they have a Creator whom they are under an obligation to serve. Existence we must necessarily ascribe to Him; for His existence is demonstrated by proofs based on the evidence of His works, as it is said: (Is. 40:26) "Lift up your eyes on high, and see: who hath created these? He that bringeth out their host by number, He calleth them all by name. By the greatness of His might, and for that He is strong in power, not one faileth." We must necessarily, ascribe Existence to Him; for it is a principle accepted by our Reason that from that which is nonexistent, no action or result can come. Since His works and creations are manifest, His existence is equally manifest to our intellect.

We ascribe to Him Eternity, because rational arguments have demonstrated that the world has a beginning unpreceded by another beginning, a commencement without an antecedent. It has been demonstrated that the number of antecedents cannot be infinite. It logically follows that the Creator is the First Beginning before whom there is no Beginning. And this is what is meant by His Eternity, as it is said (Ps. 90:2) "Even from everlasting to everlasting, Thou are God." (Is. 43:10) "Before Me there was no god formed, neither shall any be after Me."

As to our declaring concerning Him that He is One: We have already sufficiently demonstrated this by well known arguments; and it has been established by clear evidence, that true Unity is inseparable from His glorious essence. This Unity implies the absence of plurality in His Being, the absence of change, transformation, accident, origin or extinction, combination or any other properties of objects that are plural.

You are however to understand that these attributes do not imply change or alteration in the Creator's Essence, but only signify a denial of their contradictories. What the attribution of them should convey to our minds is that the Creator of the world is neither plural, nor nonexistent, nor created.

You are further to note that each of the three attributes we have mentioned necessarily implies the other two. This will now be demonstrated.

When true (absolute) Unity is the inseparable and permanent property of anything, that object must necessarily have been eternally existing.

It must be existing. For that which is non-existent cannot, as has been demonstrated, be described as one or many. If true (absolute) Unity is the attribute of any thing and essentially belongs to it, it logically follows that the attribute of Existence with its implication also belongs to it.

It must also be eternal. For absolute Unity neither comes into existence nor passes out of existence; neither changes nor is transformed. It must accordingly be eternal, for it has no beginning.[1] Hence, that to which absolute Unity belongs, has also the attributes of Existence and Eternity.

So too, we say that permanent Existence, attributed to a thing, implies the attribution to it of absolute Unity and Eternity.

It implies absolute Unity. For that which permanently exists could not have come into existence out of nought, and cannot pass from the state of existence into that of non-existence. An object of which this can be predicated is not plural. For that which is plural is not permanently existent, being preceded by Unity. What exists permanently is therefore not plural, and is accordingly One.

The attribute of Eternity also belongs to it. For that which exists permanently has neither beginning nor end. The attribute of Eternity therefore belongs to it.

So too, we assert that the attribute of Eternity, belonging to any Being, implies also, in that Being, the attributes of Unity and permanent existence.

It implies Unity. For that which is eternal has neither beginning nor end, and is accordingly not plural; since all things that are plural have a beginning, namely, an antecedent Unity. Hence, that which is plural is not Eternal; and that which is Eternal cannot but be One. Therefore the attribute of Unity is implied in that of Eternity.

So too, the attribute of Existence is implied in that of Eternity. For the non-existent cannot be described as either eternal or created.

These three attributes, as has already been explained, are one in meaning and are so to be regarded. They do not imply any change in the Creator's glorious essence, nor the intrusion of any accidental properties of plurality into His being, because all that we are to understand by them is that the Creator is neither non-existent, nor created, nor plural. If we could express the conception of His Being in a single word that would at once denote these attributes even as they are comprehended by the Reason, so that the thought of these three attributes would arise in our mind when the one word was used, we would employ that word to express the conception. But as we do not find in any of the spoken languages a word that would designate the true conception of God, we express it in more than one word.

This plurality in the Creator's attributes does not, however, exist in His glorious essence but is due to inadequacy of language on the part of the speaker to express the conception in one term. In regard to the Creator, you are to understand that there is none like Him. Whatever attributes you ascribe to the Creator, you are to infer from them the denial of their contraries. As Aristotle said "negatives give a truer conception of God's attributes than affirmatives." For all affirmative attributes ascribed to God cannot but have the character of substantial or accidental properties. And the Creator of substance and accident has not the qualities of His creatures. The denial, however, of such qualities to Him is undoubtedly true, and appropriate to Him. For He is above all quality and form, similarity or comparison. These attributes are accordingly to be understood as the negation of their opposites.

The active attributes of the Deity are those ascribed to the Creator, with reference to His works. It is possible that in attributing these qualities to Him, He is made an associate of some of his creatures. We are permitted, however, to ascribe these qualities to Him, because of the urgent need of acquainting ourselves with, and realizing His existence, so that we may assume the obligation of His service. . .

HALEVI, *KUZARI*

Translation by Hartwig Hirschfeld

PART II

1. . . . While the king studied the Torah and the books of the prophets, he employed the Rabbi as his teacher, and put many questions to him on Hebrew matters. The first of these questions referred to the names and attributes ascribed to God and their anthropomorphistic forms, which are unmistakably objectionable alike both to reason and to law.

2. Said the Rabbi: All names of God, save the Tetragrammaton, are predicates and attributive descriptions, derived from the way His creatures are affected by His decrees and measures. He is called *merciful*, if he improves the condition of any man whom people pity for his sorry plight. They attribute to Him mercy and compassion, although this is, in our conception, surely nothing but a weakness of the soul and a quick movement of nature. This cannot be applied to God, who is a just Judge, ordaining the poverty of one individual and the wealth of another. His nature remains quite unaffected by it. He has no sympathy with one, nor anger against another. We see the same in human judges to whom questions are put. They decide according to law, making some people happy, and others miserable. He appears to us, as we observe His doings, sometimes a 'merciful and compassionate God,' (Exod. xxxiv. 6), sometimes 'a jealous and revengeful God' (Nahum i. 2), whilst He never changes from one attribute to the other. All attributes (excepting the Tetragrammaton) are divided into three classes, viz. *creative, relative* and *negative*. As regards the *creative* attributes, they are derived from acts emanating from Him by ways of natural medium, e.g. *making poor and rich, exalting or casting down, 'merciful and compassionate,' 'jealous and revengeful,' 'strong and almighty,'* and the like. As regards the *relative attributes*, viz. 'Blessed, praised, glorified, holy, exalted, and extolled,' they are borrowed from the reverence given to Him by mankind. However numerous these may be, they produce no plurality, as far as He is concerned, nor do they affect His Unity. As regards the *negative* attributes, such as 'Living, Only, First and Last,' they are given to Him in order to negative their contrasts, but not to establish them in

the sense we understand them. For we cannot understand life except accompanied by sensibility and movement. God, however, is above them. We describe Him as living in order to negative the idea of the rigid and dead, since it would be an *a priori* conclusion that that which does not live is dead. This cannot, however, be applied to the intellect. One cannot, e.g. speak of time as being endowed with life, yet it does not follow that it is dead, since its nature has nothing to do with either life or death. In the same way one cannot call a stone ignorant, although we may say that it is not learned. Just as a stone is too low to be brought into connection with learning or ignorance, thus the essence of God is too exalted to have anything to do with life or death, nor can the terms light or darkness be applied to it. If we were asked whether this essence is light or darkness, we should say light by way of metaphor, for fear one might conclude that that which is not light must be darkness. As a matter of fact we must say that only material bodies are subject to light and darkness, but the divine essence is no body, and can consequently only receive the attributes of light or darkness by way of simile, or in order to negative an attribute hinting at a deficiency. Life and death are, therefore, only applicable to material bodies, whilst the divine essence is as much exempt from both as it is highly extolled above them. The 'life' of which we speak in this connection is not like ours, and this is what I wish to state, since we cannot think of any other kind of life but ours. It is as if one would say: We know not what it is. If we say 'living God' and 'God of life' (Ps. cvi. 28), it is but a relative expression placed in opposition to the gods of the Gentiles, which are 'dead gods' from which no action emanates. In the same way we take the term *One*, viz. to negative plurality, but not to establish unity as we understand it. For we call a thing one, when the component parts are coherent and of the same materials, e.g. *one* bone, *one* sinew, one water, one air. In a similar way time is compared to a compact body, and we speak of one day, and one year. The divine essence is exempt from complexity and divisibility, and 'one' only stands to exclude plurality. In the same way [we style Him] 'First' in order to exclude the notion of any later origin, but not to assert that He has a beginning; thus also 'Last' stands to repudiate the idea that His existence has no end, but not to fix a term for Him. All these attributes neither touch on the divine essence, nor do they lead us to assume a multiplicity. The attributes which are connected with the Tetragrammaton are those which describe His power of creating without any natural intermediaries, viz. Creator, Producer, Maker, 'To Him who alone doeth great wonders' (Ps. cxxxvi. 4), which means that [He creates] by His bare intention and will, to the exclusion of any assisting cause.

This is perhaps meant in the word of the Bible: 'And I appeared unto Abraham. . .as *El Shaddāi'* (Exod. vi. 3), viz. in the way of power and dominion, as is said: 'He suffered no man to do them wrong; yea, He reproved kings for their sake' (Ps. cv. 14). He did not, however, perform any miracle for the patriarchs as He did for Moses, saying: 'but my name J H W H was I not known to them' (Exod. 1. c). This means by My name J H W H, since the *bēth* in *beēl shaddāi* refers to the former. The wonders done for Moses and the Israelites left no manner of doubt in their souls that the Creator of the world also created these things which He brought into existence immediately by His will, as the plagues of Egypt, the dividing of the Red Sea, the manna, the pillar of a cloud, and the like. The reason of this was not because they were higher than the Patriarchs, but because they were a multitude, and had nourished doubt in their souls, whilst the patriarchs had fostered the utmost faith and purity of mind. If they had all their lives been pursued by misfortune, their faith in God would not have suffered. Therefore they required no signs. We also style Him wise of heart, because He is the essence of intelligence, and intelligence itself; but this is no attribute. As to 'Almighty,' this belongs to the creative attributes.

3. Al Khazari: 'How dost thou explain those attributes which are even of a more corporeal nature than those, viz. seeing, hearing, speaking, writing the tablets, descending on Mount Sinai, rejoicing in His works, grieved in His heart.'

4. The Rabbi: Did I not compare Him with a just judge in whose qualities no change exists, and from whose decrees result the prosperity and good fortune of people, so that they say that He loves them and takes pleasure in them? Others, whose fate it is to have their houses destroyed and themselves be annihilated, would describe Him as filled with hate and wrath. Nothing, however, that is done or spoken escapes Him, 'He sees and hears'; the air and all bodies came into existence by His will, and assumed shape by His command, as did heaven and earth. He is also described as 'speaking and writing.' Similarly from the aethereal and spiritual substance, which is called 'holy spirit,' arose the spiritual forms called 'glory of God' (Exod. xix. 20). Metaphorically He is called J H W H (ibid.) who descended on the Mount Sinai. We shall discuss this more minutely when treating on metaphysics.

5. Al Khazari: Granting that thou hast justified the use of these attributes, so that no idea of plurality need of necessity follow, yet a difficulty remains as regards the attribute of Will with which thou dost invest Him, but which the philosopher denies.

6. The Rabbi: If no other objection is raised, except the Will, we will

soon vindicate ourselves. We say: O philosopher, what is it which in thy opinion made the heavens revolve continually, the uppermost sphere carrying the whole, without place or inclination in its movement, the earth firmly fixed in the centre without support or prop; which fashioned the order of the universe in quantity, quality, and the forms we perceive? Thou canst not help admitting this, for things did neither create themselves nor each other. Now the same adapted the air to giving the sound of the Ten Commandments, and formed the writing engraved in the tables, call it will, or thing, or what thou wilt.

7. Al Khazari: The secret of the attributes is now clear, and I understand the meaning of 'The Glory of God,' 'Angel of God,' and Shekhinah. They are names applied by the prophets to things perceptible, as 'Pillar of Cloud,' 'Consuming Fire,' 'Cloud,' 'Mist, Fire, Splendour,' as it is said of the light in the morning, in the evening, and on cloudy days that the rays of light go forth from the sun, although it is not visible. Yet we say that the rays of light are inseparable from the sun, although in reality this is not so. It is the terrestrial bodies which, being opposite to it, are affected by it, and reflect its light.

8. The Rabbi: Even so does the glory of God, which is only a ray of the divine light, benefit His people in His country.

MAIMONIDES, *MOREH NEVUKHIM*

Translation by Michael Friedlander

PART I, CHAPTER 51

On the necessity of proving the inadmissibility of attributes in reference to God.

There are many things whose existence is manifest and obvious; some of these are innate notions or objects of sensation, others are nearly so; and in fact they would require no proof if man had been left in his primitive state. Such are the existence of motion, of man's free will, of phases of production and destruction, and of the natural properties of things perceived by the senses, *e.g.*, the heat of fire, the coldness of water, and many other similar things. False notions, however, may be spread either by a person labouring under error, or by one who has some particular end in view, and who establishes theories contrary to the real nature of things, by denying the existence of things perceived by the senses, or by affirming the existence of what does not exist. Philosophers are thus required to establish by proof things which are self-evident, and to disprove the existence of things which only exist in man's imagination. Thus Aristotle gives a proof for the existence of motion, because it had been denied; he disproves the reality of atoms, because it had been asserted.

To the same class belongs the rejection of essential attributes in reference to God. For it is a self-evident truth that the attribute is not inherent in the object to which it is ascribed, but it is superadded to its essence, and is consequently an *accident*; if the attribute denoted the essence [τὸ τί ἦν εἶναι] of the object, it would be either mere tautology, as if, *e.g.*, one would say "man is man," or the explanation of a name, as, *e.g.*, "man is a speaking animal"; for the words "speaking animal" include the true essence of man, and there is no third element besides life and speech that constitutes man; when he, therefore, is described by the attributes of life and speech, these are nothing but an explanation of the name "man," that is to say, that the thing which is called man, consists of life and speech. It will now be clear that the attribute must be one of two things, either the essence of the object described—in that case it is a mere explanation of a name, and on that account we might admit the attribute in reference to God, but we reject it from another cause as will be shown—or the attribute is something different from the object described, some extraneous superadded element; in that case the attribute would be an accident, and he who merely rejects the appellation "accidents" in reference to the attributes of God, does not thereby alter their character; for everything superadded to the essence of an object joins it without forming part of its essential properties, and that constitutes an accident. Add to this the logical consequence of admitting many attributes, *viz.*, the existence of many eternal beings. There cannot be any belief in the unity of God except by admitting that He is one simple substance, without any composition or plurality of elements; one from whatever side you view it, and by whatever test you examine it; not divisible into two parts in any way and by any cause, nor capable of any form of plurality either objectively or subjectively, as will be proved in this treatise.

Some thinkers have gone so far as to say that the attributes of God are neither His essence nor anything extraneous to His essence. This is like the assertion of some theorists, that the ideals, *i.e.*, the *universalia*, are neither existing nor non-existent, and like the views of others, that the atom does not fill a definite place, but keeps an atom of space occupied; that man has no freedom at all, but has acquirement. Such things are only said; they exist only in words, not in thought, much less in reality. But as you know, and as all know who do not delude themselves, these theories are preserved by a multitude of words, by misleading similes sustained by declamation and invective, and by numerous methods borrowed both from dialectics and sophistry. If after uttering them and supporting them by such words a man were to examine for himself his own belief on this subject, he would see nothing but confusion and stupidity in an endeavour to prove the existence of things which do not exist, or to find a mean between two opposites that have no mean. Or is there a mean between existence and non-existence, or between the identity and non-identity of two things? But, as we said, to such absurdities men were forced by the great licence given to the imagination, and by the fact that every existing material thing is necessarily imagined as a certain substance possessing several attributes; for nothing has ever been found that consists of one simple substance without any attribute. Guided by such imaginations, men thought that God was also composed of many different elements, *viz.*, of His essence and of the attributes superadded to His essence. Following up this comparison, some believed that God was corporeal, and that He possessed attributes; others abandoning this theory, denied the corporeality, but retained the attributes. The adherence to the literal sense of the text of Holy Writ is the source of all this error, as I shall show in some chapters devoted to this theme.

PART I, CHAPTER 52

Classification of Attributes.

Every description of an object by an affirmative attribute, which includes the assertion that an object is of a certain kind, must be made in one of the following five ways:—

First. The object is described by its *definition*, as *e.g.*, man is described as a being that lives and has reason; such a description, containing the true essence of the object, is, as we have already shown, nothing else but the explanation of a name. All agree that this kind of description cannot be given of God; for there are no previous causes to His existence, by which He could be defined: and on that account it is a well-known principle, received by all the philosophers who are precise in their statements, that no definition can be given of God.

Secondly. An object is described by *part of its definition*, as when, *e.g.*, man is described as a living being or as a rational being. This kind of description includes the necessary connection [of the two ideas]; for when we say that every man is rational, we mean by it that every being which has the characteristics of man must also have reason. All agree that this kind of description is inappropriate in reference to God; for if we were to speak of a portion of His essence, we should consider His essence to be a compound. The inappropriateness of this kind of description in reference to God is the same as that of the preceding kind.

Thirdly. An object is described by something different from its true essence, by something that does not complement or establish the essence of the object. The description, therefore, relates to a *quality;* but quality, in its most general sense, is an accident. If God could be described in this way, He would be the substratum of accidents: a sufficient reason for rejecting the idea that He possesses quality, since it diverges from the true conception of His essence. It is surprising how those who admit the application of attributes to God can reject, in reference to Him, comparison and qualification. For when they say "He cannot be qualified," they can only mean that He possesses no quality; and yet every positive essential attribute of an object either constitutes its essence,—and in that case it is identical with the essence—or it contains a quality of the object.

There are, as you know, four kinds of quality; I will give you instances of attributes of each kind, in order to show you that this class of attributes cannot possibly be applied to God. *(a.)* A man is described by any of his intellectual or moral qualities, or by any of the dispositions appertaining to him as an animate being, when, *e.g.*, we speak of a person who is a carpenter, or who shrinks from sin, or who is ill. It makes no difference whether we say, a carpenter, or a sage, or a physician; by all these we represent certain physical dispositions; nor does it make any difference whether we say "sin-fearing" or "merciful." Every trade, every profession, and every settled habit of man are certain physical dispositions. All this is clear to those who have occupied themselves with the study of Logic. *(b.)* A thing is described by some physical quality it possesses, or by the absence of the same, *e.g.*, as being soft or hard. It makes no difference whether we say "soft or hard," or "strong or weak;" in both cases we speak of physical conditions. *(c.)* A man is described by his passive qualities, or by his emotions; we speak, *e.g.*, of a person who is passionate, irritable, timid, merciful, without implying that these conditions have become permanent. The description of a thing by its colour, taste, heat, cold, dryness, and moisture, belongs also to this class of attributes. *(d.)* A thing is described by any of its qualities resulting from quantity as such; we speak, *e.g.*, of a thing which is long, short, curved, straight, etc.

Consider all these and similar attributes, and you will find that they cannot be employed in reference to God. He is not a magnitude that any quality resulting from quantity as such could be possessed by Him; He is not affected by external influences, and therefore does not possess any quality resulting from emotion. He is not subject to physical conditions, and therefore does not possess strength or similar qualities; He is not an animate being, that He should have a certain disposition of the soul, or acquire certain properties, as meekness, modesty, etc., or be in a state to which animate beings as such are subject, as, *e.g.*, in that of health or of illness. Hence it follows that no attribute coming under the head of quality in its widest sense, can be predicated of God. Consequently, these three classes of attributes, describing the essence of a thing, or part of the essence, or a quality of it, are clearly inadmissible in reference to God, for they imply composition, which, as we shall prove, is out of question as regards the Creator. We say, with regard to this latter point, that He is absolutely One.

Fourthly. A thing is described by its *relation* to another thing, *e.g.*, to time, to space, or to a different individual; thus we say, Zaid, the father of A, or the partner of B, or who dwells at a certain place, or who lived at a stated time. This kind of attribute does not necessarily imply plurality or change in the essence of the object described; for the same Zaid, to whom reference is made, is the partner of Amru, the father of Becr, the master of Khalid, the friend of Zaid, dwells in a certain house, and was born in a certain year. Such relations are not the essence of a thing, nor are they so intimately connected with it as qualities. At first thought, it would seem that they may be employed in reference to God, but after careful and thorough consideration we are convinced of their inadmissibility. It is quite clear that there is no relation between God and time or space. For time is an accident connected with motion, in so far as the latter includes the relation of anteriority and posteriority, and is expressed by number, as is explained in books devoted to this subject; and since motion is one of the conditions to which only material bodies are subject, and God is immaterial, there can be no relation between Him and time. Similarly there is no relation between Him and space. But what we have to investigate and to examine is this: whether some real relation exists between God and any of the substances created by Him, by which He could be described? That there is no correlation between Him and any of His creatures can easily be seen; for the characteristic of two objects correlative to each other is the equality of their reciprocal relation. Now, as God has absolute existence, while all other beings have only possible existence, as we shall show, there consequently cannot be any correlation [between God and His creatures]. That a certain kind of relation does exist between them is by some considered possible, but wrongly. It is impossible to imagine a relation between intellect and sight, although, as we believe, the same kind of existence is common to both; how, then, could a relation be imagined between any creature and God, who has nothing in common with any other being; for even the term existence is applied to Him and other things, according to our opinion, only by way of pure homonymity. Consequently there is no relation whatever between Him and any other being. For whenever we speak of a relation between two things, these belong to the same species; but when two things belong to different species though of the same class, there is no relation between them. We therefore do not say, this red compared with that green, is more, or less, or equally intense, although both belong to the same class—colour; when they belong to two different classes, there does not appear to exist any relation between them, not even to a man of ordinary intellect, although the two things belong to the same category; *e.g.*, between a hundred cubits and the heat of pepper there is no relation, the one being a quality, the other a quantity; or between wisdom and sweetness, between meekness and bitterness, although all these come under the head of quality in its more general signification. How, then, could there be any relation between God and His creatures, considering the important difference between them in respect to true existence, the greatest of all differences. Besides, if any relation existed between them, God would be subject to the accident of relation; and although that would not be an accident to the essence of God, it would still be, to some extent, a kind of accident. You would, therefore, be wrong if you applied affirmative attributes in their literal sense to God, though they contained only relations; these, however, are the most appropriate of all attributes, to be employed, in a less strict sense, in reference to God, because they do not imply that a plurality of eternal things exists, or that any change takes place in the essence of God, when those things change to which God is in relation.

Fifthly. A thing is described by its *actions;* I do not mean by "its actions" the inherent capacity for a certain work, as is expressed in "carpenter," "painter," or "smith"—for these belong to the class of qualities which have been mentioned above—but I mean the action the latter has performed; we speak, *e.g.*, of Zaid, who made this door, built that wall, wove that garment. This kind of attributes is separate from the essence of the thing described, and, therefore, the most appropriate to be employed in describing the Creator, especially since we know that these different actions do not imply that different elements must be contained in the substance of the agent, by which the different actions are produced, as will be explained. On the contrary, all the actions of God emanate from His essence, not from any extraneous thing superadded to His essence, as we have shown.

What we have explained in the present chapter is this: that God is one in every respect, containing no plurality or any element superadded to His essence: and that the many attributes of different significations applied in Scripture to God, originate in the multitude of His actions, not in a plurality existing in His essence, and are partly employed with the object of conveying to us some notion of His perfection, in accordance with what we consider perfection, as has been explained by us. The possibility of one simple substance excluding plurality, though accomplishing different actions, will be illustrated by examples in the next chapter.

PART I, CHAPTER 53

The arguments on which the Attributists found their theory.

The circumstance which caused men to believe in the existence of divine attributes is similar to that which caused others to believe in the corporeality of God. The latter have not arrived at that belief by speculation, but by following the literal sense of certain passages in the Bible. The same is the case with the attributes; when in the books of the Prophets and of the Law, God is described by attributes, such passages are taken in their literal sense, and it is then believed that God possesses attributes; as if He were to be exalted above corporeality, and not above things connected with corporeality, *i.e.*, the accidents, I mean psychical dispositions, all of which are qualities [and connected with corporeality]. Every attribute which the followers of this doctrine assume to be essential to the Creator, you will find to express, although they do not distinctly say it, a quality similar to those which they are accustomed to notice in the bodies of all living beings. We apply to all such passages the principle, "The Torah speaketh in the language of man," and say that the object of all these terms is to describe God as the most perfect being, not as possessing those qualities which are only perfections in relation to created living beings. Many of the attributes express different acts of God, but that difference does not necessitate any difference as regards Him from whom the acts proceed. This fact, *viz.*, that from one agency different effects may result, although that agency has not free will, and much more so if it has free will, I will illustrate by an instance taken from our own sphere. Fire melts certain things and makes others hard, it boils and consumes, it bleaches and blackens. If we described the fire as bleaching, blackening, consuming, boiling, hardening and melting, we should be correct, and yet he who does not know the nature of fire, would think that it included six different elements, one by which it blackens, another by which it bleaches, a third by which it boils, a fourth by which it consumes, a fifth by which it melts, a sixth by which it hardens things—actions which are opposed to one another, and of which each has its peculiar property. He, however, who knows the nature of fire, will know that by virtue of one quality in action, namely, by heat, it produces all these effects. If this is the case with that which is done by nature, how much more is it the case with regard to those who act by free will, and still more with regard to God, who is above all description. If we, therefore, perceive in God certain relations of various characters—for wisdom in us is different from power, and power from will—it does by no means follow that different elements are really contained in Him, that He contains one element by which He knows, another by which He wills, and another by which He exercises power, as is, in fact, the signification of the attributes [of God] according to the Mutakallemim. Some of them express it plainly, and enumerate the attributes as elements added to the essence. Others, however, are more reserved with regard to this matter, but indicate their opinion, though they do not express it in distinct and intelligible words. Thus, *e.g.*, some of them say: "God is omnipotent by His essence, wise by His essence, living by His essence, and endowed with a will by His essence." (I will mention to you, as an instance, man's reason, which being one faculty and implying no plurality, enables him to know many arts and sciences; by the same faculty man is able to sow, to do carpenter's work, to weave, to build, to study, to acquire a knowledge of geometry, and to govern a state. These various acts resulting from one simple faculty, which involves no plurality, are very numerous; their number, that is, the number of the actions originating in man's reason, is almost infinite. It is therefore intelligible how in reference to God, those different actions can be caused by one simple substance, that does not include any plurality or any additional element. The attributes found in Holy Scripture are either qualifications of His actions, without any reference to His essence, or indicate absolute perfection, but do not imply that the essence of God is a compound of various elements.) For in not admitting the *term* "compound," they do not reject the *idea* of a compound when they admit a substance with attributes.

There still remains one difficulty which led them to that error, and which I am now going to mention. Those who assert the existence of the attributes do not found their opinion on the variety of God's actions; they say it is true that one substance can be the source of various effects, but His essential attributes cannot be qualifications of His actions, because it is impossible to imagine that the Creator created Himself. They vary with regard to the so-called essential attributes—I mean as regards their number—according to the text of the Scripture which each of them follows. I will enumerate those on which all agree, and the knowledge of which they believe that they have derived from reasoning, not from some words of the Prophets, namely, the following four:—life, power, wisdom, and will. They believe that these are four different things, and such perfections as cannot possibly be absent in the Creator, and that these cannot be qualifications of His actions. This is their opinion. But you must know that wisdom and life in reference to God are not different from each other; for in every being that is conscious of itself, life and wisdom are the same thing, that is to say, if by wisdom we understand the consciousness of self. Besides, the subject and the object of that consciousness are undoubtedly identical [as regards God]; for according to our opinion, He is not composed of an element that apprehends, and another that does not apprehend; He is not like man, who is a combination of a conscious soul and an unconscious body. If, therefore, by "wisdom" we mean the faculty of self-consciousness, wisdom and life are one and the same thing. They, however, do not speak of wisdom in this sense, but of His power to apprehend His creatures. There is also no doubt that power and will do not exist in God in reference to Himself; for He cannot have power or will as regards Himself; we cannot imagine such a thing. They take these attributes as different relations between God and His creatures, signifying that He has power in creating things, will in giving to things existence as He desires, and wisdom in knowing what He created. Consequently, these attributes do not refer to the essence of God, but express relations between Him and His creatures.

Therefore we, who truly believe in the Unity of God, declare that as we do not believe that some element is included in His essence by which He created the heavens, another by which He created the [four] elements, a third by which He created the ideals, in the same way we reject the idea that His essence contains an element by which He has power, another element by which He has will, and a third by which He has a knowledge of His creatures. On the contrary, He is a simple essence, without any additional element whatever; He created the universe, and knows it, but not by any extraneous force. There is no difference whether these various attributes refer to His actions or to relations between Him and His works; in fact, these relations, as we have also shown, exist only in the thoughts of men. This is what we must believe concerning the attributes occurring in the books of the Prophets; some may also be taken as expressive of the perfection of God by way of comparison with what we consider as perfections in us, as we shall explain.

PART I, CHAPTER 54

On Exodus xxxiii. 13, to xxxiv. 7.

The wisest man, our Teacher Moses, asked two things of God, and received a reply respecting both. The one thing he asked was, that God should let him know His true essence; the other, which in fact he asked first, that God should let him know His attributes. In answer to both these petitions God promised that He would let him know all His attributes, and that these were nothing but His actions. He also told him that His true essence could not be perceived, and pointed out a method by which he could obtain the utmost knowledge of God possible for man to acquire. The knowledge obtained by Moses has not been possessed by any human being before him or after him. His petition to know the attributes of God is contained in the following words: "Show me now Thy way, that I may know Thee, that I may find grace in Thy sight" (Exod. xxxiii. 13). Consider how many excellent ideas found expression in the words, "Show me Thy way, that I may know Thee." We learn from them that God is known by His attributes, for Moses believed that he knew Him, when he was shown the way of God. The words "That I may know Thee," imply that He who knows God will find grace in His eyes. Not only is he acceptable and welcome to God, who fasts and prays, but everyone who acquires a knowledge of Him. He who has no knowledge of God is the object of His wrath and displeasure. The pleasure and the displeasure of God, the approach to Him and the withdrawal from Him are proportional to the amount of man's knowledge or ignorance concerning the Creator. . .

Whenever any one of His actions is perceived by us, we ascribe to God that emotion which is the source of the act when performed by ourselves, and call Him by an epithet which is formed from the verb expressing that action. We see, *e.g.*, how well He provides for the life of the embryo of living beings; how He endows with certain faculties both the embryo itself and those who have to rear it after its birth, in order that it may be protected from death and destruction, guarded against all harm, and assisted in the performance of all that is required [for its development]. Similar acts, when performed by us, are due to a certain emotion and tenderness called mercy (רחמנות and חמלה). God is therefore, said to be merciful (רחום); *e.g.*, "Like as a father is merciful (כרחם) to his children, so the Lord is merciful (רחם) to them that fear Him" (Ps. ciii. 13); "And I will spare (וחמלתי) them, as a man spareth (יחמל) his own son that serveth him" (Mal. iii. 17). Such instances do not imply that

God is influenced by a feeling of mercy, but that acts similar to those which a father performs for his son, out of pity, mercy and real affection, emanate from God solely for the benefit of His pious men, and are by no means the result of any impression or change [produced in God].—When we give something to a person who has no claim upon us, we perform an act of grace (חנינה); *e.g.*, חנונו אותם, "Grant them graciously unto us" (Judges xxi. 22). [The same term is used in reference to God, *e.g.*,] אשר חנן אלהים, "which God hath graciously given" (Gen. xxxiii. 5); כי חנני אלהים, "Because God hath dealt graciously with me" (*ib.* 11). Instances of this kind are numerous. God creates and guides beings who have no claim upon Him to be created and guided by Him; He is therefore called gracious (חנון).—His actions toward mankind also include great calamities, which overtake individuals and bring death to them, or affect whole families and even entire regions, spread death, destroy generation after generation, and spare nothing whatsoever. Hence there occur inundations, earthquakes, destructive storms, expeditions of one nation against the other for the sake of destroying it with the sword and blotting out its memory, and many other evils of the same kind. Whenever such evils are caused by us to any person, they originate in great anger, violent jealousy, or a desire for revenge. God is therefore called, because of these acts, "jealous" (קנוא), "revengeful" (נוקם), "wrathful" (בעל חמה), and "keeping anger" (נוטר, Nah. i. 2); that is to say, He performs acts similar to those which, when performed by us, originate in certain psychical dispositions, in jealousy, desire for retaliation, revenge, or anger; they are in accordance with the guilt of those who are to be punished, and not the result of any emotion; for He is above all defect! The same is the case with all divine acts; though resembling those acts which emanate from our passions and psychical dispositions, they are not due to anything superadded to His essence.—The governor of a country, if he is a prophet, should conform to these attributes. Acts [of punishment] must be performed by him moderately and in accordance with justice, not merely as an outlet of his passion. He must not let loose his anger, nor allow his passion to overcome him; for all passions are bad, and they must be guarded against as far as it lies in man's power. At times and towards some persons he must be merciful and gracious, not only from motives of mercy and compassion, but according to their merits; at other times and towards other persons he must evince anger, revenge, and wrath in proportion to their guilt, but not from motives of passion. He must be able to condemn a person to death by fire without anger, passion, or loathing against him, and must exclusively be guided by what he perceives of the guilt of the person, and by a sense of the great benefit which a large number will derive from such a sentence. You have, no doubt, noticed in the Torah how the commandment to annihilate the seven nations, and "to save alive nothing that breatheth" (Deut. xx. 16) is followed immediately by the words "That they teach you not to do after all their abominations, which they have done unto their gods; so should you sin against the Lord your God" (*ib.* 18); that is to say, you shall not think that this commandment implies an act of cruelty or of retaliation; it is an act demanded by the tendency of man to remove everything that might turn him away from the right path, and to clear away all obstacles in the road to perfection, that is, to the knowledge of God. Nevertheless, acts of mercy, pardon, pity, and grace should more frequently be performed by the governor of a country than acts of punishment. . .

The principal object of this chapter was to show that all attributes ascribed to God are attributes of His acts, and do not imply that God has any qualities.

PART I, CHAPTER 55

On Attributes implying Corporeality, Emotion, Non-existence, and Comparison.

We have already, on several occasions, shown in this treatise that everything that implies corporeality or passiveness, is to be negatived in reference to God, for all passiveness implies change; and the agent producing that state is undoubtedly different from the object affected by it; and if God could be affected in any way whatever, another being beside Him would act on Him and cause change in Him. All kinds of non-existence must likewise be negatived in reference to Him; no perfection whatever can therefore be imagined to be at one time absent from Him, and at another present in Him: for if this were the case, He would [at a certain time] only be potentially perfect. Potentiality always implies non-existence, and when anything has to pass from potentiality into reality, another thing that exists in reality is required to effect that transition. Hence it follows that all perfections must really exist in God, and none of them must in any way be a mere potentiality. Another thing likewise to be denied in reference to God, is similarity to any existing being. This has been generally accepted, and is also mentioned in the books of the Prophets; *e.g.*, "To whom, then, will you liken me?" (Is. xl. 25); "To whom, then, will you liken God?" (*ib.* 18); "There is none like unto Thee" (Jer. x. 6). Instances of this kind are frequent. In short, it is necessary to demonstrate by proof that nothing can be predicated of God that implies any of the following four things: corporeality, emotion or change, non-existence,—*e.g.*, that something would be potential at one time and real at another—and similarity with any of His creatures. In this respect our knowledge of God is aided by the study of Natural Science. For he who is ignorant of the latter cannot understand the defect implied in emotions, the difference between potentiality and reality, the non-existence implied in all potentiality, the inferiority of a thing that exists *in potentia* to that which moves in order to cause its transition from potentiality into reality, and the inferiority of that which moves to that for the sake of whose realisation it moves. He who knows these things, but without their proofs, does not know the details which logically result from these general propositions; he will not be able to prove that God exists, or that the [four] things mentioned above are inadmissible in reference to God.

Having premised these remarks, I shall explain in the next chapter the error of those who believe that God has essential attributes; those who have some knowledge of Logic and Natural Science will understand it.

PART I, CHAPTER 56

Existence, Life, Power, Wisdom, and Will are homonymously ascribed to God and His Creatures.

Similarity is based on a certain relation between two things; if between two things no relation can be found, there can be no similarity between them, and there is no relation between two things that have no similarity to each other; *e.g.*, we do not say this heat is similar to that colour, or this voice is similar to that sweetness. This is self-evident. Since the existence of a relation between God and man, or between Him and other beings has been denied, similarity must likewise be denied. You must know that two things of the same kind—*i.e.*, whose essential properties are the same, distinguished from each other by greatness and smallness, strength and weakness, etc.—are necessarily similar, though different in a certain particular point; *e.g.*, a grain of mustard and the sphere of the fixed stars are similar as regards the three dimensions, although the one is exceedingly great, the other exceedingly small, the property of having [three] dimensions is the same in both; or wax melted by the heat of the sun and wax melted by the heat of fire, are similar as regards heat; although the heat is exceedingly great in the one case, and exceedingly small in the other, the existence of that quality is the same in both. Thus those who believe in the existence of essential attributes in reference to God, *viz.*, Existence, Life, Power, Wisdom, and Will, should know that these attributes, when applied to God, have not the same meaning as when applied to us, and that the difference does not only consist in magnitude, or in the degree of perfection, stability, and durability. It cannot be said, as they practically believe, that His existence is only more stable, His life more permanent, His power greater, His wisdom more perfect, and His will more general than ours, and that the same definition applies to both. This is in no way admissible, for the expression "more than" is used in comparing two things as regards a certain attribute predicated of both of them in exactly the same sense, and consequently implies similarity [between God and His creatures]. When they ascribe to God essential attributes, these so-called essential attributes should not have any similarity to the attributes of other things, and should according to their own opinion, not be included in one and the same definition, in the same manner as there is no similarity between the essence of God and that of other beings. They do not follow this principle, for they hold that one definition may include them, and that, nevertheless, there is no similarity between them. Those who are familiar with the meaning of similarity will certainly understand that the term existence, when applied to God and to other beings, is perfectly homonymous. In like manner, the terms Wisdom, Power, Will, and Life are applied to God and to other beings by way of perfect homonymity, admitting of no comparison whatever. Nor must you think that the homonymity of these terms is doubtful. For an expression, the homonymity of which is uncertain, is applied to two things which have a similarity to each other in respect to a certain relation which is in both of them an accident, not an essential, constituent element. The attributes of God, however, are not considered as accidental by any intelligent person, while all attributes applied to man are accidents, according to the Mutakallemim. I am therefore at a loss to see how they can find any similarity [between the attributes of God and those of man]; how their definitions can be identical, and their significations the same! This is a decisive proof that there is, in no way or sense, anything common to the attributes predicated of God, and those used in reference to ourselves; they have only the same names, and nothing else is common to them. Such being the case, it is not proper to believe, on account of the identity in those names, that there is in God something additional to His essence, similar to the properties which are joined to our essence. This is most important for those who understand it. Keep it in memory, and study it thoroughly, in order to be well prepared for that which I am going to explain to you.

PART I, CHAPTER 57

The Essence of God and His Attributes are Identical.

On attributes; remarks more recondite than the preceding. It is known that existence is an accident appertaining to all things, and therefore an element superadded to their essence. This must evidently be the case as regards everything the existence of which is due to some cause; its existence is an element superadded to its essence. But as regards a being whose existence is not due to any cause—God alone is that being, for His existence, as we have said, is absolute—existence and essence are perfectly identical; He is not a substance to which existence is joined as an accident, as an additional element. His existence is always absolute, and has never been a new element or an accident in Him. Consequently God exists without possessing the attribute of existence. Similarly He lives, without possessing the attribute of life; knows, without possessing the attribute of knowledge; is omnipotent without possessing the attribute of omnipotence; is wise, without possessing the attribute of wisdom; all this reduces itself to one and the same entity; there is no plurality in Him, as will be shown. It is further necessary to consider that unity and plurality are accidents supervening to an object according as it consists of many elements or of one. This is fully explained in the book called *Metaphysics.* In the same way as number is not the substance of the things numbered, so is unity not the substance of the thing which has the attribute of unity, for unity and plurality are accidents belonging to the category of discrete quantity, and supervening to such objects as are capable of receiving them.

To that being, however, which has truly simple, absolute existence, and in which composition is inconceivable, the accident of unity is as inadmissible as the accident of plurality; that is to say, God's unity is not an element superadded, but He is One without possessing the attribute of unity. The investigation of this subject, which is almost too subtle for our understanding, must not be based on current expressions employed in describing it, for these are the great source of error. It would be extremely difficult for us to find, in any language whatsoever, words adequate to this subject, and we can only employ inadequate language. In our endeavour to show that God does not include a plurality, we can only say "He is one," although "one" and "many" are both terms which serve to distinguish quantity. We therefore make the subject clearer, and show to the understanding the way of truth by saying He is one but does not possess the attribute of unity.

The same is the case when we say God is the First, (קדמון), to express that He has not been created; the term קדמון, "First," is decidedly inaccurate, for it can in its true sense only be applied to a being that is subject to the relation of time; the latter, however, is an accident to motion which again is connected with a body. Besides the attribute קדמון ("first" or "eternal") is a relative term, being in regard to time the same as the terms "long" and "short" are in regard to a line. Both expressions, "created" and "eternal" (or "first"), are equally inadmissible in reference to any being to which the attribute of time is not applicable, just as we do not say "crooked" or "straight" in reference to taste, "salted" or "insipid" in reference to the voice. These subjects are not unknown to those who have accustomed themselves to seek a true understanding of the things, and to establish their properties in accordance with the abstract notions which the mind has formed of them, and who are not misled by the inaccuracy of the words employed. All attributes, such as "the First," "the Last," occurring in the Scriptures in reference to God, are as metaphorical as the expressions "ear" and "eye." They simply signify that God is not subject to any change or innovation whatever; they do not imply that God can be described by time, or that there is any comparison between Him and any other being as regards time, and that He is called on that account "the first" and "the last." In short, all similar expressions are borrowed from the language commonly used among the people. In the same way we use "One" (אחד), in reference to God, to express that there is nothing similar to Him, but we do not mean to say that an attribute of unity is added to His essence.

PART I, CHAPTER 58

The True Attributes of God Have a Negative Sense.

This chapter is even more recondite than the preceding. Know that the negative attributes of God are the true attributes: they do not include any incorrect notions or any deficiency whatever in reference to God, while positive attributes imply polytheism, and are inadequate, as we have already shown. It is now necessary to explain how negative expressions can in a certain sense be employed as attributes, and how they are distinguished from positive attributes. Then I shall show that we cannot describe the Creator by any means except by negative attributes. An attribute does not exclusively belong to the one object to which it is related; while qualifying one thing, it can also be employed to qualify other things, and is in that case not peculiar to that one thing. *E.g.*, if you see an object from a distance, and on enquiring what it is, are told that it is a living being, you have certainly learnt an attribute of the object seen, and although that attribute does not exclusively belong to the object perceived, it expresses that the object is not a plant or a mineral. Again, if a man is in a certain house, and you know that something is in the house, but not exactly what, you ask what is in that house, and you are told, not a plant nor a mineral. You have thereby obtained some special knowledge of the thing; you have learnt that it is a living being, although you do not yet know what kind of living being it is. The negative attributes have this in common with the positive, that they necessarily circumscribe the object to some extent, although such circumscription consists only in the exclusion of what otherwise would not be excluded. In the following point, however, the negative attributes are distinguished from the positive. The positive attributes, although not peculiar to one thing, describe a portion of what we desire to know, either some part of its essence or some of its accidents; the negative attributes, on the other hand, do not, as regards the essence of the thing which we desire to know, in any way tell us what it is, except it be indirectly, as has been shown in the instance given by us.

After this introduction, I would observe that—as has already been shown—God's existence is absolute, that it includes no composition, as will be proved, and that we comprehend only the fact that He exists, not His essence. Consequently it is a false assumption to hold that He has any positive attribute; for He does not possess existence in addition to His essence; it therefore cannot be said that the one may be described as an attribute [of the other]; much less has He [in addition to His existence] a compound essence, consisting of two constituent elements to which the attribute could refer; still less has He accidents, which could be described by an attribute. Hence it is clear that He has no positive attribute whatever. The negative attributes, however, are those which are necessary to direct the mind to the truths which we must believe concerning God; for, on the one hand, they do not imply any plurality, and, on the other, they convey to man the highest possible knowledge of God; *e.g.*, it has been established by proof that some being must exist besides those things which can be perceived by the senses, or apprehended by the mind; when we say of this being, that it exists, we mean that its non-existence is impossible. We thus perceive that such a being is not, for instance, like the four elements, which are inanimate, and we therefore say it is living, expressing thereby that it is not dead. We call such a being incorporeal, because we notice that it is unlike the heavens, which are living, but material. Seeing that it is also different from the intellect, which, though incorporeal and living, owes its existence to some cause, we say it is the first (קדמון), expressing thereby that its existence is not due to any cause. We further notice, that the existence, that is, the essence, of this being is not limited to its own existence; many existences emanate from it, and its influence is not like that of the fire in producing heat, or that of the sun in sending forth light, but consists in constantly giving them stability and order by well-established rule, as we shall show: we say, on that account, it has power, wisdom, and will, *i.e.*, it is not feeble or ignorant, or hasty, and does not abandon its creatures; when we say that it is not feeble, we mean that its existence is capable of producing the existence of many other things; by saying it is not ignorant, we mean "it perceives" or "it lives,"—for everything that perceives is alive—by saying "it is not hasty, and does not abandon its creatures," we mean that all these creatures preserve a certain order and arrangement; they are not left to themselves, or produced aimlessly, but whatever condition they receive from that being is given them with design and intention. We thus learn that there is no other being like unto God, and we say that He is One, *i.e.*, there are not more Gods than one.

It has thus been shown that every attribute predicated of God either denotes the quality of an action, or—when the attribute is intended to convey some idea of the Divine Being itself, and not of His actions—the negation of the opposite. Even these negative attributes must not be formed and applied to God, except in the way in which, as you know, sometimes an attribute is negatived in reference to a thing, although that attribute can naturally never be applied to it in the same sense, as, *e.g.*, we say, "This wall does not see." Those who read the present work, are aware that, notwithstanding all the efforts of the mind, we can obtain no knowledge of the essence of the heavens,—a revolving substance which has been measured by us in spans and cubits, and examined even as regards the proportions of the several spheres to each other and respecting most of their motions—although we know that they must consist of matter and form; but the matter not being the same as sublunary matter, we can only describe the heavens in terms expressing negative properties, but not in terms denoting positive qualities. Thus we say that the heavens are not light, not heavy, not passive and therefore not subject to impressions, and that they do not possess the sensations of taste or smell; or we use similar negative attributes. All this we do, because we do not know their substance. What, then, can be the result of our efforts, when we try to obtain a knowledge of a Being that is free from substance, that is most simple, whose existence is absolute, and not due to any cause, to whose perfect essence nothing can be superadded, and whose perfection consists, as we have shown, in the absence of all defects. All we understand, is the fact that He exists, that He is a Being to whom none of all His creatures is similar, who has nothing in common with them, who does not include plurality, who is never too feeble to produce other beings, and whose relation to the universe is that of a steersman to a boat; and even this is not a real relation, a real simile, but serves only to convey to us the idea that God rules the universe; that is, that He gives it duration, and preserves its necessary arrangement. This subject will be treated more fully. Praised be He! In the contemplation of His essence, our comprehension and knowledge prove insufficient; in the examination of His works, how they necessarily result from His will, our knowledge proves to be ignorance, and in the endeavour to extol Him in words, all our efforts in speech are mere weakness and failure!

PART I, CHAPTER 60

On the Difference between Positive and Negative Attributes.

I will give you in this chapter some illustrations, in order that you may better understand the propriety of forming as many negative attributes as possible, and the impropriety of ascribing to God any positive attributes. A person may know for certain that a "ship" is in existence, but he may not know to what object that name is applied, whether to a substance or to an accident; a second person then learns that the ship is not an accident; a third, that it is not a mineral; a fourth, that it is not a plant growing in the earth; a fifth, that it is not a body whose parts are joined together by nature; a sixth, that it is not a flat object like boards or doors; a seventh, that it is not a sphere; an eighth, that it is not pointed; a ninth, that it is not round-shaped, nor equilateral; a tenth, that it is not solid. It is clear that this tenth person has almost arrived at the correct notion of a "ship" by the foregoing negative attributes, as if he had exactly the same notion as those have who imagine it to be a wooden substance which is hollow, long, and composed of many pieces of wood, that is to say, who know it by positive attributes. Of the other persons in our illustration, each one is more remote from the correct notion of the ship than the next mentioned, so that the first knows nothing about it but the name. In the same manner you will come nearer to the knowledge and comprehension of God by the negative attributes. But you must be careful, in what you negative, to negative by proof, not by mere words, for each time you ascertain by proof that a certain thing, believed to exist in the Creator, must be negatived, you have undoubtedly come one step nearer to the knowledge of God. . .

I do not merely declare that he who affirms attributes of God has not sufficient knowledge concerning the Creator, admits some association with God, or conceives Him to be different from what He is; but I say that he unconsciously loses his belief in God. For he whose knowledge concerning a thing is insufficient, understands one part of it while he is ignorant of the other, as, *e.g.*, a person who knows that man possesses life, but does not know that man possesses understanding; but in reference to God, in whose real existence there is no plurality, it is impossible that one thing should be known, and another unknown. Similarly he who associates an object with [the properties of] another object, conceives a true and correct notion of the one object, and applies that notion also to the other; while those who admit the attributes of God, do not consider them as identical with His essence, but as extraneous elements. Again, he who conceives an incorrect notion of an object, must necessarily have a correct idea of the object to some extent; he, however, who says that taste belongs to the category of quantity has not, according to my opinion, an incorrect notion of taste, but is entirely ignorant of its nature, for he does not know to what object the term "taste" is to be applied.—This is a very difficult subject; consider it well.

According to this explanation you will understand, that those who do not recognise, in reference to God, the negation of things, which others negative by clear proof, are deficient in the knowledge of God, and are remote from comprehending Him. Consequently, the smaller the number of things is which a person can negative in relation to God, the less he knows of Him, as has been explained in the beginning of this chapter; but the man who affirms an attribute of God, knows nothing but the name; for the object to which, in his imagination, he applies that name, does not exist; it is a mere fiction and invention, as if he applied that name to a non-existing being, for there is, in reality, no such object. *E.g.*, some one has heard of the elephant, and knows that it is an animal, and wishes to know its form and nature. A person, who is either misled or misleading, tells him it is an animal with one leg, three wings, lives in the depth of the sea, has a transparent body; its face is wide like that of a man, has the same form and shape, speaks like a man, flies sometimes in the air, and sometimes swims like a fish. I should not say, that he described the elephant incorrectly, or that he has an insufficient knowledge of the elephant, but I would say that the thing thus described is an invention and fiction, and that in reality there exists nothing like it; it is a non-existing being, called by the name of a really existing being, and like the griffin, the centaur, and similar imaginary combinations for which simple and compound names have been borrowed from real things. The present case is analogous; namely, God, praised be His name, exists, and His existence has been proved to be absolute and perfectly simple, as I shall explain. If such a simple, absolutely existing essence were said to have attributes, as has been contended, and were combined with extraneous elements, it would in no way be an existing thing, as has been proved by us; and when we say that that essence, which is called "God," is a substance with many properties by which it can be described, we apply that name to an object which does not at all exist. Consider, therefore, what are the consequences of affirming attributes of God! As to those attributes of God which occur in the Pentateuch, or in the books of the Prophets, we must assume that they are exclusively employed, as has been stated by us, to convey to us some notion of the perfections of the Creator, or to express qualities of actions emanating from Him.

ALBO, *IKKARIM*

Translation by Isaac Husik

BOOK II, CHAPTER 1

The term "existence" which is applied to all existing things is a subject of dispute among philosophers, whether it denotes an accident of the existing thing or whether it is something essential. However, the term existence as applied to God can not denote an accident, because God is not receptive of accidents, as we shall explain.[1] Nor can it be an essential element added to God's quiddity. For then God's essence would be composed of two things, which is impossible, as we shall see.[2] It follows therefore that the term existence when applied to God denotes nothing else but His quiddity. But His quiddity is absolutely unknown, as Maimonides explains.[3] For he says that this is what Moses desired to know when he said to God, "Show me, I pray Thee, Thy glory." [4] And the answer came to him, "Thou canst not see My face, for man shall not see Me and live."[5] The Rabbis in Sifre,[6] commenting on this, say, "Not even the angels, who are living beings." The meaning is that His quiddity is known to none beside Him. It follows, therefore, that His existence also is absolutely unknown, even to the angels. This being so, one may ask, How can that be a principle of divine law which no one can comprehend except God Himself?

The answer is that the existence of God is not a principle of the Torah from that side which is impossible of comprehension, namely from the side of God's quiddity, but from the side which is possible of comprehension, namely from a consideration that all existing things are due to His influence, that He is their cause and their maker. From this point of view we can estimate God's excellence as the one who made existing things to be with extreme perfection and splendor. From this aspect one may speak of God and estimate His excellence. But we can not speak of God's essence because it is altogether ineffable. David alludes to this in the Psalm beginning, "Bless the Lord, O my soul."[7] Alluding to the first aspect, he says, "O Lord my God, Thou are very great," i.e. from the side of Thy quiddity Thou art very great, so that man can not speak about Thee, and with all this, "Thou art clothed with glory and majesty," i.e. from the side concerning which it is possible to speak about Thee, namely from the visible activities which come from Thee. They show Thy glory and Thy majesty. Therefore he describes in the sequel the creations which come from God, and which point to God's excellence and perfection by the perfection which is visible in them. . .

NOTES

1. II, 9, p. 52 f.
2. II, 5, p. 33 f.
3. Guide, I, 57.
4. Ex. 33, 18.
5. Ibid. 20.
6. A tannaite Midrash to Numbers and Deuteronomy. The citation is found §103, ed. Friedman, 27b.
7. 104.

BOOK II, CHAPTER 8

It is clear without much reflection that an attribute ascribed to a thing to denote its activities does not imply plurality in the essence of the active thing. For many different acts may proceed from one agent. And this is true of both kinds of agents, the natural as well as the voluntary.

Thus take a natural agent, like fire. Fire melts certain things, while it hardens others. It boils and it burns, and it makes black and it makes white. One who does not know the nature of fire might think that it has six different forces, from which the six different results follow, which we have mentioned. He might think that there is an element by which it boils, an element by which it burns, an element by which it makes black, an element by which it causes the opposite of blackness, namely it makes white, an element by which it melts, and another element by which it does the opposite, viz. it hardens. For he would say, it is not possible that one and the same agent should produce opposite effects. But he who knows the nature of fire, understands that with one and the same force which it has, namely heat, it does all those things, and that the results are different because of the difference in the recipients, without there being any multiplicity in the essence of fire.

The very same thing applies to a voluntary agent. Thus the rational faculty in man, who is a voluntary agent, does many different things though the agent is one. He acquires the sciences and the arts, he governs states, he rips and he sews, he destroys and he builds, and does a great many different and opposite acts, though he is one and simple. For there is no one who holds that the rational faculty in man is composite. Similarly the human soul as a whole is the author of many different natural activities, like nutrition, growth, sensation, and of voluntary acts, like the activities of the conative and the rational faculties. And yet there is no philosopher who maintains that the human soul is composite.[1] But since we find the function of growth by itself in plants, the function of sensation in animals, and the function of ratiocination by itself in the Separate Intelligences, some have been led to think that the human soul is composite, as some physicians[2] have written that man has three souls. But it is not so. The various functions and activities come from one and the same human soul.

Maimonides has explained this matter in the introduction to his commentary on the treatise *Abot.*[2a] He cites as an example three dark places, one of which is illuminated by the lighting of a lamp, the second by the rising of the moon, and the third by the rising of the sun. Every one of these three places has in it light, a substance which causes sight to pass from potentiality to actuality. . .and yet since the causes are not the same, they are different with respect to their causes. Similarly the faculties of growth and sensation in man are not the same as the faculties of growth and sensation in animals and plants, but the activities come from the human soul as they come from the souls of the ass and the eagle, though their causes are different. He also says there that they have nothing in common except the name. In conclusion he says: This is a matter of great importance and deserving of notice. Many of those who philosophize go astray in relation to it and derive theories and opinions which are far-fetched and untrue.

From these words of his it appears that from one existent there may come many different acts, some natural, some voluntary. He who does not understand the nature of the human soul will think that the many acts must come from so many different powers or faculties. But he who reflects upon the rational faculty and considers that though it is one and simple and without multiplicity, yet we say about a person, he built that house or that city, he destroyed it, he conquered a certain land, he invented a certain science, without all this necessitating multiplicity in the essence of the rational power, will understand that many acts may come from one agent. And if we find this to be the case in the sensible and inferior agents of our experience, how much more is this likely to be true in the First Agent, who is the cause of all acts, natural and voluntary. This is why we say that though we perceive that many different acts come from God, they do not necessitate any plurality in Him.

This is the reason why philosophers are permitted to ascribe attributes to God, different because of different acts, whether in different recipients, like the power of growth in the plant and the power of animality in the animal, or in one recipient, as for example that He is now gracious and merciful and now bearing grudge against one and the same person or one and the same people, and other attributes of the same kind which denote acts coming from Him. For this reason we say that even though we characterize Him essentially by a given attribute because of a certain act we perceive to come from Him, this does not necessitate plurality in Him. Thus if we characterize Him as living, by reason of an act which comes from Him, namely life for all living beings, this does not necessitate multiplicity in His essence. For our meaning is that since we see life coming from Him, we judge that He is the source of life which He bestows upon all living things. This is why we describe Him as living, in the words of Scripture, "For with Thee is the fountain of life."[3]

In the same way we judge that light is with Him, because we see that "in His light we see light,"[4] that He it is who gives us the power to see light, and causes sight to pass from potentiality to actuality. Similarly we judge that all perfections are found in Him, because they come from Him. In the words of the Psalmist, "He that planted the ear, shall He not hear? He that formed the eye, shall He not see?"[5]

In the same way we describe Him as wise, by reason of the acts which we see coming from Him with wonderful wisdom and admirable order, indicating that He has wisdom. He may therefore be characterized by different attributes by reason of all the various acts which we see emanating from Him, without this necessitating any plurality in Him. In the same way He may be characterized by different attributes by reason of various relations, reciprocal and otherwise.[6] For example, we say God is near to man or far from him, or in the words of the Bible, "The Lord is nigh unto them that are of a broken heart,"[7] "The Lord is far from the wicked."[8] The nearness and the farness are on man's side, according as he comes near to God or keeps far away from Him, as the Rabbis say,[9] in commenting on the expression, "The Lord, the Lord,"[10] "I am He before man sins, and I am the same after he has sinned," i.e. the change is not in God, but in man. Before he sins, he stands in a certain relation to God, after he has sinned, he stands in a different relation, he departs from Him, like a tree, which is now near to Reuben, now far from him, now east of Reuben, now west of him, not because of any change in the tree, but because of a change in Reuben. Or when the Bible speaks of God as Creator, and Maker, and King, and Lord, and uses other similar appellations. This does not necessitate any plurality or change in God, as it does not necessitate any plurality in Reuben when we say of him that he is the son of Jacob and the brother of Simon and the father of Enoch and the partner of Naphtali and the owner of an ox and of a pit. All these attributes do not by any means necessitate any plurality in Reuben, for the plurality is not in the essence of Reuben, but the attributes are due to the things with which he stands in various relations.

In the same way God may be characterized by different attributes from different aspects. Thus when we say of God that He is possessed of will, or is wise, or powerful, we do not mean that He has one attribute by which He has power to create, another attribute with which He exercises will, another with which He creates, another with which He knows that which He has created, any more than we say that He has one attribute with which He created the elements, another with which He created the spheres, another with which He created the angels, and another with which He created man, all of which are different acts emanating from one agent, as we said before. But since a perfect agent can not do anything without having the power, the knowledge and the desire to do it, we say that God has will and power and knowledge, these being different aspects of the agent which do not necessitate plurality in Him.

In these various ways God is characterized by various attributes by reason of acts different because of the recipients, or differing in their essence, or by reason of the relations and connections between Him and them, or because of difference in aspect. All these things do not necessitate any plurality in God, and are all permissible. This is the method of the Torah and the Prophets in relation to the attributes which are ascribed to God. The question whether God can be characterized by different attributes in respect to His own essence, will be left for later discussion.

NOTES

1. Plato, as is well known, held that the human soul is composed of three parts. Either Albo did not know this fact, or he did not include Plato in the term "philosophers," which in its strict use by the Arabs denotes the Aristotelians. Both are unlikely. But the fact is that Aristotle himself divided the soul into the rational and the irrational, and so does Albo himself. The explanation no doubt is, that Albo thought the classification is based upon the different modes of the soul's activity and was purely logical and not intended to signify a division or composition in the soul itself. In the sequel, however, he ascribes the tripartite division of the soul to "some physicians." See Duran, Magen Abot, p. 35a: אבל הרופאים אומרים כי כל אחד מאלו הכחות הוא נפש אחת וזהו דעת גאלינים וכן היה דעת אבוקרט ואפלטון. See M. Wolff, Musa Maimuni's Acht Kapitel, Leiden, 1903, p. 1, note 2.

2. See preceding note.

2a. In his commentary on the Mishnah. The introduction to Abot is known as the "Eight Chapters." The passage cited is in chapter 1.

3. Ps. 36, 10.

4. Ibid.

5. Ibid. 94, 9.

6. The difference between יחס and הצטרפות, both of which are translated "relation," is that the former is used in the loose sense in which we use the word relation to denote various degrees of resemblance or dependence, as when we speak of the relation between mathematics and astronomy, or the relation between law and economics. הצטרפות is used in the strict technical sense of the Aristotelian category of relation, *πρός τι*. Cf. Munk, Le Guide des Egarés, I, 200 note 1; Efros, Philosophical Terms in the Moreh Nebukim, s. vv; Klatzkin, op. cit., s. vv. J. Klatzkin, Thesaurus Philosophicus Linguae Hebraicae, s. vv.

7. Ps. 34, 19.

8. Prov. 15, 29.

9. Rosh Hashanah, 17b.

10. Ex. 34, 6.

BOOK II, CHAPTER 9

An attribute by which a thing is characterized is not the essence of the thing characterized, but something attaching to the essence. For an attribute must be either something essential or something accidental. If it is something essential, as when we say man is *rational animal*, it is not an attribute added to the essence, but it is like saying man is *man*, for man is nothing else except animality and rationality. It is merely an explanation of the name, since [by hypothesis] the attribute is the essence of the thing characterized and not something pertaining to the essence. There is no objection to ascribing to God an attribute of this sort, since it is not something added to the essence. For a plurality of words does not necessarily represent a plurality of things, but is merely used to explain the nature of the essence. Thus if we say, body nutritive sensitive,[1] these words do not add any plurality to the meaning of the word animal.

But we must know that God can not be characterized by two things as denoting His essence, in the way in which animality and rationality denote the essence of man. Nor can God be characterized by one word as denoting a part of His essence, for in either case God would be composed of two things. But we have already proved that God is absolutely simple.[2] But He may be characterized by an attribute which is an explanation of the name by which He is called. This can be the case only if the attribute is something essential which explains the essence of the thing characterized. For example, if we say that the First Cause is a necessary existent and the absolute truth. Here the words are an explanation of the term necessary existent, as we shall see when we deal with the word truth.[3]

If an attribute is something accidental, it is clear that it can not be ascribed to God. For an accident requires a subject, an accident not being able to exist by itself. God would therefore be a subs bearing accidents. Now if the existence of the substance and the necessity of its essence are independent of the accidents, then the accident may exist or not exist, whereas the substance exists by necessity. God would therefore be composed of two things, necessary existence and possible existence. As necessary existent He would be cause, as possible existent, effect. He would therefore be cause and effect at the same time, while being a substance depending upon itself. This is a contradiction, which is impossible. On the other hand if His existence and the necessity of His essence are not independent of the accident, then the accident is a necessary existent, and the substance bearing the accident a necessary existent likewise, and there would be two necessary existents, or else one that is composed of two elements, substance and accident. But all this has been shown to be absurd. It is clear therefore that God can not be characterized by any attribute, essential or accidental. This would make it necessary to reject all divine attributes except those which are explanatory of God's necessary existence, as we said before.

On the other hand it can be shown that God must have attributes, as follows: It follows from the above mentioned proofs that if God is a necessary existent, He must be one, else He would not be a necessary existent. It is clear, on the other hand, that unity is in every thing an attribute added to the essence. For if Reuben were one *qua* man, a horse and a tree could not have unity, since unity is [by hypothesis] the quiddity of Reuben. Nor could whiteness or wisdom be characterized as one. Without doubt, then, unity is something added to the essence. Now since unity is something added to the essence, and God, as we have seen,[4] can not be characterized by any attribute except such as is explanatory of His name, we must explain in what way it can be said that God is one. For unity is not, like the other attributes ascribed to God, named after God's acts. Having explained the meaning of unity, we will then discuss the same question concerning the other attributes, viz. in what way they can be ascribed to God.

NOTES

1. "Body nutritive sensitive," is taken as the definition of animal.
2. Above, p. 33 f.
3. II, 27 p. 165.
4. P. 52.

BOOK II, CHAPTER 10

The term one applies to that which gives specialization and separation to an existing thing by which it is distinguished from another. Thus, the term one is applied to a collection of many different individuals, because they agree in a certain matter which singles them out and distinguishes them from others. This common element may be an accidental thing, as in the expression, "One people and one language."[1] Because they have one accidental element in common, such as religion among the Ishmaelites (Arabs, Mohammedans), or blackness among Ethiopians, which separates them from others, we say that they are one people. Or the common element may be an essential thing, as when we say that Reuben and Simeon are one in humanity, or that man and horse are one in animality. These are called one because they have in common one essential thing which separates them from others. And the more this specializing thing singles them out from others, the more truly does the term one apply. Thus the term one applies more truly to an individual, say Reuben, though he is composed of many visible members different in kind, than to a people.

A still more proper use of the term one is when it is applied to flesh, bone or a member composed of homogeneous parts. For though it is composed of different elements, the term one is applicable because it is hard to separate them and they are not perceptible to the senses.

Still more proper is the application of the term one to a simple element, which can not be divided into the matter and form of which it is composed except mentally, and neither of them is perceptible to the senses by itself. A surface is one in a truer sense still, and a line even more so, since it has only one dimension, and is not composed of elements into which it may be resolved, actually or mentally, as a simple element is resolved into matter and form and a surface into length and breadth. A line is one simple dimension, by which attribute it is distinguished from all other existing things, and does not share it with any other thing. And yet the unity of a line is not perfect, because it may be divided into curved and straight. Moreover every line you can point to may be divided into small parts, each one of which is a line. A point is more truly one than a line. For a point can not be divided actually or mentally; it is different from all other existing things, with which it has nothing in common except position. But the unity of point is not perfect because it has position in common with other things. A truer unity is the numerical one, which has no position and has nothing in common with other things. But it has no real actual existence, only a mental one. And for this reason the mind may conceive of a large aggregation of numerical units, constituting number, which may be defined as an aggregation of units. Therefore it is clear that the numerical one is not a perfect unit either, since it does not single out and separate an actual existent from other existents, seeing that we can conceive many ones of the same kind.

Absolute unity is that which singles out and separates from others a thing existing actually, which can not be conceived as having others like it. Now since there is not among existing things any thing which has nothing in common with others, and to which there is nothing equal, except God, it follows that there is nothing in the world to which the term one applies in the sense that it is really different from every thing else, except God. For He alone is a necessary existent, while all other things are possible existents, and share this attribute in common. But there is no one that shares with God in the attribute of necessary existence or in anything else, including the word existent. For we have explained that there can not be two necessary existents, since the mind can not conceive of them as being equal in all respects, and that the term existence as applied to God and to other things is used in a purely homonymous[2] sense. God's unity, therefore, is absolute, for no existing thing has anything in common with Him, or is like unto Him in any respect.[3]

We have now shown that one in the true sense is applied to an existent to which there is nothing equal or similar. We have also shown that the Necessary Existent, whose existence has been proved demonstratively, has no like, nor anything in common with any existing thing. Hence it is clear that the term one which is applied to God is, as it were, a negative concept and not a positive, and therefore does not necessitate multiplicity in God's essence. The Torah expresses this idea clearly in the words, "Hear O Israel, the Lord our God, the Lord is one." [4] The meaning is as follows: As being "our God," i.e. as the cause of all existing things—in allusion to our first proof—He must be a necessary existent, being alone the cause of all things and having none like Him, as the Bible says, "To whom then will ye liken Me, that I should be equal?"[5] for all things outside of Him are effects. Similarly in Himself[6] he is "one," having no second similar to Him, and there is no other necessary existent—this being an allusion to our second proof above. This explains, so to speak, that the concept of unity which is predicated of God is negative and not positive, and therefore does not require plurality in God's essence, since it is not an attribute added to the essence.

NOTES

1. Gen. 11, 6.
2. See above, p. 45, note 3 end.
3. This discussion of unity is modelled upon the Hobot ha-Lebabot of Bahya, I, 8.
4. Deut. 6, 4.
5. Isa. 40, 25.
6. Jhvh (=Lord) denotes God's essence or self. Cf. above, I, 11, p. 105, note 1.

BOOK II, CHAPTER 13

Difference and number of functions are due to one of three causes. They may be due to a difference in the active faculties. Thus the activity of the faculty of desire is different from that of the faculty of anger. The difference may be due to a difference in the matter. Thus fire melts pitch and hardens salt. Finally the difference may be due to a difference in the instruments. Thus a tailor sews with a needle, and cuts with scissors. But the activity of God can not be multiplied through any one of these causes, because He is one and simple, in whom there is no plurality of faculties or difference of matters or variety of instruments. The multiplicity can therefore only be due to something else beside these things, namely the intermediate. That is, there emanates from Him first a single being; from this one there emanates another, from this other a third, as we explained in chapter eleven, so that the intermediate beings increase and plurality arises through them. Outside of this way, they say, it is impossible to conceive real plurality coming from God, who is absolutely one, for from the one only one thing can come. . .

The truth is that the conceptions mentioned do not induce plurality either in the First Principle or in the beings which emanate from it, so as to account for the different existences which are caused by them. And if so, we ask again, how does plurality come from simple unity? This is the reason why among the ancients there were some who thought that there are two original principles, one good and one evil. For they said, "Out of the mouth of the Most High proceedeth not evil and good,"[1] meaning that it is impossible that the contradictory principles should be combined in one. And seeing that the most general contradictories, including all the species of contradiction, are good and evil, they said that there were two principles, one the principle of good, the other, the principle of evil. This was the opinion of a person whose name was Mani.[2] His followers are called Manichaeans[3] in the same way as those who follow the opinions of the philosopher Epicurus, who thought that the world has no ruler and denied the existence of God, are called Epicureans.

The philosophers have disputed this view in many ways. The best and clearest of the arguments against this dualism, so far as concerns the purpose of this book, is this: If we reflect upon the existing things of the world, we find that they all together tend to one end, namely the order which exists in the world, like the order existing in a camp, which emanates from the military commander, and the order existing in states, which emanates from the rulers. Now in these cases though there is multiplicity of various kinds, namely many different arts and activities and different offices, nevertheless we regard the state or the camp as one[4] because the end to which they all tend is one, namely the stability and order of the state or camp, so we say that the world has in it good and evil so that existence as a whole may be good. Evil is not intended for its own sake,[5] it arises by accident, like punishment or chastisement inflicted by the father upon the son, which is evil for the sake of good and not intended for its own sake. For since good things exist, it is imperative that a little evil should be mixed with the good. Thus man is composed of a rational and an animal soul, which are the good and the evil inclinations. The good inclination was placed in man to secure the survival of the individual, so far as possible, in the immortality of the soul, while the evil inclination was implanted in him to secure the survival of the species without which man can not exist. The wisdom of the Most High decreed that it is fitting there should be great good even though a little evil must be mixed with it, for it stands to reason that it is better to have a great good plus a little evil than to lose the great good in order to avoid the little evil.

It does not follow therefore from the existence of good and evil that they come from different principles. For it is quite possible that from one principle good comes for its own sake and evil *per accidens.* Thus fire is the cause of good to all sublunar existence in the genesis of all things, and yet evil comes from it sometimes when by accident it burns the garment of a good man.

In the same way there are things which, though in themselves bad, are tolerated for the sake of the good which may come from them, like penalties enacted by the founders of good codes of law which, though bad in themselves, are enacted for the sake of the general good which will follow for the nation or state as a whole, that men may be guided to happiness by uniting with one another in a perfect manner, and establish a perfect society, consisting of different kinds of people; like the human body, which has different members and different controlling organs and qualities opposed to one another, and yet all of them are intended for one purpose, namely the duration and unity of the body. It has also things injurious to the body which are due to the matter and can not be avoided.

The ancient philosophers were therefore all agreed, as Ibn Roshd says, that there is one principle in the absolute sense of the word one, and that by it all the various things of existence were ordered first for one purpose, viz. the permanence of all existence and the complete union of its parts so that existence may be unified into a complete unit; as the head of a state assigns certain people to do a given work and no other, that it may be done in a perfect manner, and assigns other people to do another kind of work exclusively, and so on with the different kinds of work. Thus he makes some to be tailors, some to be weavers, some to be builders, and in this way are completed all the arts needed in the state, and the order of the state is perfected.[6] And yet all the many arts come from the one first head, though he is absolutely one.

In the same way though God is absolutely one, He is the cause of plurality, without this necessitating plurality in His essence. They say that the proposition, "from one can come only one," is a dialectical judgment,[7] which is applicable indeed to a particular and concrete[8] agent, whereas in the case of God who is the universal and general agent—the term agent as applied to Him and to others is a homonym—(for He can not be identified with one act rather than another, seeing that His relation is the same to all acts) we say that He does many different specific acts for the sake of perfect unity, i.e. in order that all the parts of nature may be combined into one, and that all the many existences may tend to one purpose, viz. the permanence of existence, in the same way as the rational soul in man, though one, does different acts for one purpose, the permanent existence of man. In this way God orders only one act, viz. the universal order, which contains a plurality of elements so as to unite all the parts of existence together. . .

The result we have reached. . .is that the plurality of things existing in the world is due to the series of intermediate beings and not to a plurality existing in the First Principle, whose unity is simple in the absolute sense of the word. This is the reason we are told in the Bible, "Hear, O Israel, the Lord our God, the Lord is one."[9] The meaning is that we should believe that though He is our God, i.e. the cause of plurality, He is nevertheless one in the absolute meaning of the word. This will suffice in explanation of the dogma of unity and the other matters depending upon it, so as not to induce plurality in the essence of God. We will now begin to treat of the second dogma, incorporeality.

NOTES

1. Lam. 3, 38.

2. Mani, the founder of Manichaeism, was a high-born Persian of Ecbatana, having been born in 215-216 A.C.E. Cf. Encyclopaedia Britannica, 11th ed., s.v. Manichaeism.

3. The Hebrew text of the first edition and four of the five MSS. consulted by the present editor read מינים, the term frequently used in the Talmud to denote a heretic, not necessarily, however, a Manichaean. Apparently, however, Albo identifies מינים with Manichaeans. The reading מאמנים of the Warsaw edition has no authority, though MS.D has מנים.

4. The Hebrew text means to express this thought, but is defective in construction, though there are no variants.

5. Cf. Thomas Aquinas, Summa Contra Gentiles, III, ch. 4, "quod malum est praeter intentionem in rebus."

6. This seems a reminiscence of the regulations in Plato's Republic that every one should do that for which he is best fitted and nothing but that.

7. A dialectical proposition or premise is contrasted by Aristotle with an apodictic. The latter is true, the former is probable or generally accepted, without being necessarily true: *ὥστε ἔσται . . . . πρότασις ἀποδεικτικὴ . . ἐὰν ἀληθὴς ᾖ . . . διαλεκτικὴ δὲ . . . λῆψις τοῦ φαινομένου καὶ ἐνδόξου*. Prior Analytics I, 1, p. 24a 28 ff.

8. מעוין is opposed to משולח. Cf. I. Klatzkin, Thesaurus, II, 234, s. v. מְעֻיָּן ב׳. The criticism of Diesendruck, Kirjath Sefer, V. p. 342, is not well taken.

9. Deut. 6, 4.

BOOK II, CHAPTER 21

We will now explain the fourth dogma mentioned above, that God is free from defects. If we reflect very carefully and deeply upon the matter of attributes, we shall find that God must necessarily be characterized by many attributes, and not merely from the point of view of His acts alone and for the reason mentioned in chapter eight of this Book, [1] but from the point of view of Himself.

The affirmative and the negative always divide between them the true and the false in all modes of predication, the necessary, the impossible and the possible. Taking the possible mode as an instance, it is clear that we can not escape the disjunction that God is either wise or not wise, possessing power or not possessing power, having a will or not having a will. But it can not be true that God is not wise, or does not possess power, for there can not be any defect in God. It follows therefore that the other part of the disjunction is true, namely that He is wise, possesses power, a will, is kind, upright, reliable. The same thing holds of all perfections, viz. that He must have the perfection because He can not have the defect. This is a necessary conclusion without regard to the acts which emanate from God, as when we say He is living because life emanates from Him, or He is wise because wisdom emanates from Him, and so with the other attributes. No, He is living and wise because He can not be dead or ignorant. But since perfections are of different kinds, knowledge being different from power, power different from life, life different from will and from wisdom, it follows that He has many different attributes. Approaching the problem in this way, therefore, we come to the conclusion that God has many attributes, while from the discussion in the tenth chapter of this book we concluded that He has no attribute except Himself. The problem therefore is how God can have many attributes without introducing plurality in His essence.

Our solution is this: The attributes ascribed to God are of two kinds. There is one class of attributes which we ascribe to Him because He is a necessary existent and the cause of all existing things, neither of which He can be conceived to be unless He has the attributes in question. Such attributes are, one, eternal, perpetual, wise, having will, possessing power, and others besides, which God must have in order to be the author of all existing things. There is another class of attributes which we ascribe to Him because we imagine that they constitute perfection. Thus we ascribe to Him riches because we imagine that riches constitute perfection in God as they constitute perfection in us, the opposite being a defect. We also ascribe hearing and seeing to God, because they are perfections in us, though we can exercise those powers only by means of corporeal organs.

Now every attribute ascribed to any subject has in it two aspects. One aspect is that of the perfection inherent in the attribute. The other is the defect which supervenes as a result of the attribute. Accordingly the attribute is, so to speak, composed mentally of two elements, one being a perfection, the other a defect. Thus if we attribute wisdom to a subject, the attribute is in itself a mark of perfection in the subject. But on the other hand, from the fact that it is acquired by the subject and accidental in him, there results a defect in the subject, because the attribute is not essential in him, and thus induces plurality.

Now when we attribute wisdom to God we do so only with a view to the perfection that is involved and not the defect. The defect involved in the perfection exists only if we view wisdom in relation to ourselves who acquire it gradually through one conclusion after another as each is derived from its premises. It is therefore something that originates in us from a state of not being, and is an attribute added to our essence. But when we attribute knowledge to God we do not think of it as derived from premises or as coming into being in Him as it comes into being in us. We rather think of it as inherent in God Himself, in the same way as the axioms exist in man, requiring neither learning nor teaching, except that knowledge is in God in a more perfect manner. When we attribute wisdom to God, therefore, our purpose is to indicate that He has this perfection without any defect, though the only way we can conceive of attaining wisdom is that in which man acquires it. Similarly we say concerning power, will and the other attributes, that they are ascribed to God with a view to the perfection attaching to the attribute in question and not with a view to the defect.[2]

In this way we can ascribe to Him attributes of the second class also, which involve corporeal perceptions. Thus we attribute to Him the sense of smell, which is a sensuous perception, as we read, "And the Lord smelled the sweet savour."[3] But we do not attribute it to God as being a corporeal perception, but with a view to the perfection which it involves, namely that God accepts favorably the offering of a person who brings it with a worthy purpose; we do not think of God as deriving pleasure from the offering, which would be a defect. . . .

We have thus made it clear that the attributes are ascribed to God with a view to the perfection they involve and not the defect, for God is free from defects. Our fourth dogma, therefore, that God is free from defects, signifies that all attributes of imperfection, such as ignorance, poverty, sleep, fatigue, and so on, must be rejected, and also that all attributes of perfection which are ascribed to God are conceived as being in Him so far as they involve perfection, but not so far as they involve or are the source of a defect, such as plurality or change, which are defects in God, since He endures forever in the same manner and without any change. . .

NOTES

1. P. 47.
2. Cf. Thomas Aquinas, Summa Contra Gentiles, I, 30.
3. Gen. 8, 21.
4. Jer. 7, 22 f.
5. Ps. 50, 13 f.
6. Ibid. 130, 2.
7. Ibid. 33, 18.
8. Zech. 4, 10.

BOOK II, CHAPTER 23

Those attributes which are ascribed to God and are not based upon His acts, like one, eternal, true, and so on, can not, according to the philosophic view, be ascribed to Him except in a negative way, as we have explained in relation to the attributes one and eternal. The same thing applies to the attribute true. The meaning of this attribute is, as we shall see, one whose existence does not depend upon anything not himself. But these attributes can not be applied to God in a positive sense, because those attributes which are predicated of God as He is in Himself, if taken in a positive sense, far from being appreciative are rather derogatory in relation to God, and are not of the class of attributes which are becoming to Him, as Maimonides says.[1]

He cites in this connection the words of Rabbi Hanina who, hearing a person employ many attributes in his prayer, used the following comparison. A king who had thousands upon thousands of gold denars was praised for his wealth, which was estimated at thousands upon thousands of silver denars. This praise was surely, in the king's estimation, derogatory.[2]

It will be noticed that he does not say that they estimated his wealth at a thousand gold denars. In that case the derogation would be due to the fact that the amount attributed to him was less than the actual amount. But he says that they attributed to the king silver denars, indicating that the difference between the praise and the reality was not one of degree but of kind, as silver, though valuable, does not belong to the same species as gold.

This is the reason why Maimonides says that all those attributes which are not derived from God's acts must be understood as negative and not positive, as we explained in chapter ten of this Book in relation to the attribute one. For this reason we must refrain from using attributes of our own invention, not employed by Moses and the prophets. And even those that are used by them, we must understand, are merely metaphorical when used positively, in reality they can only have a negative sense.

Accordingly the attributes applied to God are of two kinds. First, those which describe His own nature, which is absolutely unknown even to the wise. These can not be understood in a positive sense, not to speak of being expatiated upon. The other kind are those attributes which are derived from the acts of God. This meaning of the attributes is known to all, even to fools and ignoramuses, as the Psalmist says, "Consider, ye brutish among the people; and ye fools, when will ye understand? He that planted the ear, shall He not hear? He that formed the eye, shall He not see?. . ."[3] The same is true of the manner in which God governs His creatures. These aspects of God we may expatiate upon. . . .

In reality, however, it is impossible to ascribe any attribute to Him, even one that is based upon His acts, in the manner in which we ascribe it to a human being, "For He is highly exalted."[4] The meaning is, I speak of Him in poetic style, but in reality He is highly exalted above all kinds of praise. The most fitting praise, therefore, in the case of God is silence, as David says, "For Thee silence is praise."[5] The Rabbis understand it in the same way, when they say, the most wholesome recipe of all is silence, as is said, "For Thee silence is praise,"[6] and therefore Moses called Him, "Fearful in praises."[7]

NOTES

1. Guide I, 59.
2. Berakot 33b; Megillah 25a.
3. Ps. 94, 8-9.
4. Ibid. 1.
5. Ps. 65, 2. Note the peculiar interpretation; cf. p. 131, note 1 and p. 133, note 2.
6. Megillah 18a.
7. Ex. 15, 11.

BOOK II, CHAPTER 24

We have seen that there are two kinds of attributes by which God is characterized, attributes which describe Himself and attributes which are derived from His activities. In each of these classes there are attributes in respect to which it is perfectly clear that they describe God in respect to His activities or that they describe Himself, as the case may be. Thus the attributes, "Merciful and gracious, long-suffering and abundant in goodness," are obviously drawn from God's activities, while such attributes as "one" and "eternal" clearly describe God Himself, and, as we have seen, must be understood in a negative sense and not as really characterizing God's essence.

But there are certain attributes as to which it is doubtful whether they describe God's essence or the activities which come from Him. We must therefore explain the manner of understanding these attributes. We will explain a few as an example of the rest.

When we say that God is good, the attribute must be understood in both of the ways mentioned above. God is good because of His actions, for all good things come from Him, and the good can only come from the good, as we read in the Psalms, "The Lord is good to all."[1] But when the same attribute is applied to God to describe His essence, it must be understood in a negative sense. God is called good because His essence is free from defect, since there is no potentiality in Him, as we explained before. Therefore no change or privation attaches to Him, for all privation is evil.[2]

We find that the Bible too has these two modes of characterizing God as good: "Thou art good, and doest good; Teach me Thy statutes."[3] "Thou art good" is intended as a description of God's essence, while "doest good" has reference to the good things which come from God.

Similarly when we say that God is wise, the attribute may be understood as referring to God's acts. Since God is the author of existence, which is perfect and wonderful in its order and arrangement, it follows that He is wise and understands all the things of which He is the author, as is said in the Bible, "He that planted the ear, shall He not hear?. . . He that instructeth nations, shall not He correct, even He that teacheth man knowledge?"[4] Here we see the Psalmist inferring God's understanding and knowledge from the fact that all understanding and knowledge come from God. But when the attribute wise is applied to God to describe His essence, it must be understood in a negative sense, meaning that nothing is concealed from Him. For since God is pure intellect and separate from matter, as we proved before, nothing can be hidden from Him.

It is matter that obstructs and prevents us from apprehending the sensible and intelligible things. Thus water flowing from the eye or other diseases of the eye prevent it from seeing what it desires to see. The same is true of diseases of the nose and the ear. In general it is true that matter prevents us from apprehending sensible things as they really are. In the same way the vapors rising from the stomach confuse the powers of the brain, preventing them from apprehending their objects, as is the case with persons who are drunk. Similarly excessive moisture hinders one from apprehending intelligible things, as we see in young people. During the period of growth, when the moisture is abundant, they do not attain the degree of comprehension which their intellect is able to attain. It is clear therefore that one who is pure intellect is called wise because nothing is hidden from Him, and He is not ignorant of anything which it is in His nature to understand, because there are no causes in Him which obstruct understanding.

When we say that God has will, the statement may have reference to God's activities. Then the meaning is that all things which exist in heaven and earth were made by His simple will, as we read, "Whatever the Lord pleased, that hath He done, in heaven and in earth." [5] This expression is constantly used in relation to God. When we see a certain act coming from God, being realized and completed like the act of a voluntary agent, we say that the agent no doubt willed the act, else it would not have been realized. So we read, "Be pleased, O Lord, to deliver me";[6] "For the Lord taketh pleasure in His people; He adorneth the humble with salvation."[7] The coming of salvation indicates will, as the prophet says, "That he understandeth, and knoweth Me, that I am the Lord who exercise mercy, justice and righteousness, in the earth; for these things I desire, saith the Lord."[8] Here we see that the prophet infers God's desire from His doings, for in a person of intellect and reason the doing of a thing is an indication of the will and desire to do it.

It is clear therefore that since we see acts emanating from God which are similar to those acts which emanate from a voluntary agent, we speak of God as desiring and willing; though we can not understand how will and desire reside in God without causing change and affection. This is unknown to us, as the nature of His knowledge is unknown to us. We ascribe knowledge to Him because it is a perfection which it is inconceivable that God should be without. The same is true of will, as we explained in chapter three of this Book.[9]

If we wish to explain this attribute in a negative sense, the meaning is that God does not reject or abandon or forget to bestow goodness and perfection, as we read in the Bible, "Lord, Thou hast shown good will unto Thy land, Thou hast turned the captivity of Jacob."[10] "Good will" in this case means that God did not reject or abandon them, and did not forget to show them mercy, unlike the sentiment expressed in the passage, "Then My anger shall be kindled against them in that day, and I will forsake them, and I will hide My face from them, and they shall be devoured."[11] Hence the Psalmist adds, "Thou hast withdrawn all Thy wrath; Thou hast turned from the fierceness of Thine anger."[12]

When we say that God is powerful or strong, we may likewise have reference to God's acts, in which case the meaning is that He can carry out His wish in relation to all existing things without any hindrance, as a strong man does whatever he desires. And if we use the word to describe God's essence, we must understand it in a negative sense as indicating that God is not infirm and unable to do what He desires. It follows therefore that He has infinite power. For if His power were finite, there would be some infirmity. But the meaning of the attribute powerful is that He has no infirmity.

The attribute living if applied to God with reference to His acts, means that life flows from Him. He must therefore necessarily be living, else life could not issue from Him. If applied to describe God's essence, it must be understood in a negative sense. In this sense our meaning is that the influences which emanate from Him do not come in the manner of light from a lamp or heat from fire, both of which flow from their sources without any knowledge or will on the part of the latter. Not so with God, for He exerts His influence in the best manner possible, namely with knowledge and will, like a living being. He knows what He bestows, He has the power to bestow, and He desires to bestow, else the object would not receive His influence. The meaning is that the influence which comes from God is accompanied by knowledge, will and power, like the influence which comes from a living being.

The matter is very subtle and difficult to expatiate upon. The important thing is to understand what is meant, namely that God has infinite power, i.e. is not unable to bestow, and is willing to bestow, viz. does not reject or abandon or forget the idea of bestowing. And He knows what He bestows, i.e. He is not ignorant and not unaware of the content of His bestowal or of the object which receives favors from Him. This is why we say that He is living, for a living being understands what it does and wills it, i.e. it does not act by nature like the radiation of heat from fire.

Thus the four attributes, living, wise, willing, powerful, all come to one negative idea, as we have explained. All the attributes applied to describe God's essence must be understood in this way, namely in a negative sense, no matter how many there are, for all negative attributes can be truly predicated of God. And there is no harm if one enumerates more than those we mentioned, or if one says that there is an infinite number of them, as long as they are understood in a negative sense, so that no defect is implied in the nature of God. This is the reason why we lay down, as a fourth derivative principle, that God is free from defects, following the opinion of Maimonides, that positive attributes can not be ascribed to the nature of God, and must be excluded because they would imply a defect.

NOTES

1. Ps. 145, 9.
2. Privation is a technical term corresponding to the Aristotelian *στὲρησις*, as to which see Zeller, Aristotle and the Earlier Peripatetics, I, 344 note 1.
3. Ps. 119, 68.
4. Ibid. 94, 9 f.
5. Ps. 135, 6.
6. Ibid. 40, 14.
7. Ibid. 149, 4.
8. Jer. 9, 23.
9. P. 16.
10. Ps. 85, 2.
11. Deut. 31, 17.
12. Ps. 85, 4.

The Third Principle

Incorporeality

INTRODUCTION

The incorporeality of God is so clearly implied by the notion of the unity of God that it is difficult to understand why Maimonides found it necessary to formulate a separate principle in order to give expression to this doctrine. The Second Principle clearly states that the notion of God's unity excludes the concept of a being subject to division. Every corporeal substance is subject to division. Moreover, the very concept of corporeality implies substance and form; substance and form constitute a dualism which is excluded by the doctrine of unity. It may be assumed that Maimonides formulated a special principle expressing the incorporeality of God because this principle required special emphasis. The many anthropomorphisms employed by Scripture and the manifold prosaic descriptions of the Deity in aggadic literature certainly convey an image of corporeality. It was this image, so firmly rooted in Scripture and rabbinic statements, which pietists, particularly those lacking a philosophical orientation, were apt to accept in a literal manner, and it was this error which Maimonides sought to dispel.

In the *Mishneh Torah, Hilkhot Teshuvah* 3:7, Maimonides reaffirms the incorporeality of God and declares that one who accepts the notion of a corporeal God is a heretic who has forfeited his share in the world-to-come. To that statement is appended the oft-quoted gloss of Abraham ben David, or Rabad, as he is usually known, who exclaims: "Why does he call such a person a heretic? Greater and better [men] than he have accepted this view of the basis of scriptural verses, and even more so on the basis of aggadic statements which confuse the mind." There is, of course, no substantive disagreement between Abraham ben David and Maimonides with regard to the incorporeal nature of the Deity. Their disagreement is limited to the question of whether one who errs as a result of deficient understanding of Scripture and rabbinic teaching is to be deemed a heretic or whether a person is not culpable for sincerely held but incorrect beliefs which result from honest error. Abraham ben David's position is identical to that of Duran and Albo, whose views have been presented earlier. Maimonides' view was succinctly paraphrased by R. Chaim Soloveichik of Brisk in the pithy Yiddish comment, "*Nebach an apikores iz ober oich an apikores*—a heretic by misadventure is a heretic nonetheless." The position that extenuating factors do not mitigate the onus of heresy can best be understood in light of the comments made in the introductory section with regard to Maimonides' view of the world-to-come. The eternal bliss associated with the world-to-come is not bestowed as a reward or withheld as a form of punishment but is the culmination of a process of intellectual perfection. The heretic has failed in this task and, regardless of his degree of culpability, has not attained the perfection required to enjoy "the splendor of the *Shekhinah.*" The situation is crudely analogous to that of the student who fails to master algebra through no fault of his own and must then be refused permission to enroll in a calculus course. Such denial is not by way of punishment, but an assessment of the fact that one who has not mastered the rudiments of a subject cannot profit from advanced instruction in that discipline.

Although it is not astonishing that untutored persons may conceive of God in anthropomorphic terms and view Him as a corporeal being, Abraham ben David's retort that individuals "greater and better" (i.e., more erudite and more pious) than Maimonides have fallen into this error is rather surprising, to say the least. Anthropomorphic views of God were certainly not held by any major or authoritative Jewish thinker. One relatively obscure contemporary of Abraham ben David, the thirteenth-century Tosafist and liturgical poet Moses Taku, is, however, known to have expressed such views. The manuscript of Taku's work in which these views are expressed, *Ketav Tamim,* was published by Raphael Kirchheim in *Oẓar Neḥmad,* vol. III (Vienna, 1860), 54–99.

The idea that God's essence cannot be fathomed by the human intellect and that anthropomorphic language is necessary to describe the Deity, as developed at length by Maimonides, was, in fact, discussed earlier by Baḥya. Baḥya asserts that the foolish and simple will indeed conceive of God in accordance with the literal sense of Scripture. Although incorrect, this conception is necessary and fostered by Scripture because otherwise "the majority of mankind, because of their intellectual deficiency and weak perception of things spiritual, would have been left without religion." Given a choice between a corporeal perception of God and no knowledge of God, the first is viewed by Baḥya as the lesser of the two evils since it serves to impress upon the heart and mind of such a person that "he has a Creator whom he is bound to serve."

Baḥya is consistent in maintaining, as do Abraham ben David, Duran and Albo, that persons lacking in intellectual acumen are not held accountable for maintaining a corporeal view of the Deity. A person is accountable for his thoughts and intellectual perceptions "only according to his powers of apprehension and comprehension." Nevertheless, asserts Baḥya, a person who is able to acquire a correct understanding of God's nature but fails to do so will be held accountable for his failure to do so.

As did his predecessors, Albo endeavors to elucidate the underlying concept contained in many of the biblical verses which are couched in anthropomorphic language. Albo is particularly concerned with scriptural passages which appear to attribute place or location to God. Following a discussion of Aristotle's view of place as a limit which bounds a body on the outside, and his own definition of place as a vacuum into which a body enters, Albo rejects the possibility of attributing either locality or place to the Deity.

BAḤYA, *HOVOT HA-LEVAVOT*

Translation by Moses Hyamson

FIRST TREATISE, CHAPTER 10

. . .Attributes are ascribed to God, connoting bodily movements and actions, as in the following passages (Gen. 8:21) "And the Lord smelt" (Gen 6:5), "And the Lord saw" (ib. 6:6), "It repented the Lord "And it grieved the Lord in His heart" (ib. 11:5), "The Lord came down" (ib. 8:1), "And God remembered" (Num. 11:1), "And the Lord heard" (Ps. 78:65), "And the Lord awoke as one asleep." Many similar activities of human beings are attributed to Him.

Our Rabbis, when expounding the Scriptures, paraphrased the expressions used for this class of attributes, and were careful to interpret them as well as they could in a dignified way, and ascribed them all to the Glory of the Creator.[2] For example (Gen. 28:13) "And the Lord stood beside him," is paraphrased in the Targum "The glory of God was present with him"; (Gen 6:5) "And the Lord saw"—"It was revealed before the Lord"; (Gen. 11:5; Num. 12:5), "And the Lord came down—the glory of the Lord was revealed"; (Gen. 35:13) "And God went up from him"—"The glory of God departed from him." These expressions were translated in a reverential manner and were not applied to the Creator himself, so as to avoid imputing to him any corporeality or accidental property. In his work *Emunoth Vedeoth,* in his commentary on *Sidra Bereshith* (Gen. 1:6) and on *Sidra Vaera* (Ex. 6:9) and on the book *Yetzirah,* R. Saadiah has dilated on this theme at sufficient length, so that there is no need for us to repeat his explanations here. What we are all agreed upon is that necessity forced us to ascribe corporeal attributes to God, and to describe Him by attributes properly belonging to His creatures, so as to obtain some conception by which the thought of God's existence should be fixed in the minds of men. The books of the prophets expressed this in corporeal terms which were more easily understood by their contemporaries. Had they limited themselves to abstract terms and concepts appropriate to God, we would have understood neither the terms nor the concepts; and it would have been impossible for us to worship a Being whom we did not know, since the worship of that which is unknown is impossible. The words and ideas used had accordingly to be such as were adapted to the hearer's mental capacity, so that the subject would first sink into his mind in the corporeal sense in which the concrete terms are understood. We will then deal discreetly with him and strive to make him understand that this presentation is only approximate and metaphorical, and that the reality is too fine, too exalted and remote for us to comprehend its subtlety. The wise thinker will endeavor to strip the husk of the terms—their materialistic meaning—from the kernel, and will raise his conception, step by step, till he will at last attain to as much knowledge of the truth as his intellect is capable of apprehending.

The foolish and simple person will conceive the Creator in accordance with the literal sense of the Scriptural phrase. And if he assumes the obligation of serving his God and strives to labor for His glory, he has in his simplicity and lack of understanding, a great excuse for his erroneous conception. For man is accountable for his thoughts and deeds only according to his powers of apprehension and comprehension, physical strength and material means. Only if a man is able to acquire wisdom, and foolishly neglects to do so, will he be called to account and punished for his failure to learn.

Had Scripture, when expounding this theme, employed a terminology, appropriate in its exactness but only intelligible to the profound thinker, the majority of mankind, because of their intellectual deficiency and weak perception in things spiritual, would have been left without a religion. But the word which may be understood in a material sense will not hurt the intelligent person, since he recognizes its real meaning. And it will help the simple, as its use will result in fixing in his heart and mind the conception that he has a Creator whom he is bound to serve.

This may be compared to the case of a man who visited one of his friends, belonging to the wealthy classes. The host had the duty of supplying the visitor with meals and also providing provender for the cattle which the latter had brought with him. He sent the guest a quantity of barley for his cattle, but of food for his own sustenance the host only furnished a small amount, enough for the guest's needs. So too, the Hebrew language as well as all the books of the Prophets and the writings of the pious, when referring to the attributes of the Creator, make liberal use of the concrete expressions (anthropomorphisms and anthropopathisms) we have mentioned, which are such as people easily understand and employ in their current vocabulary, when conversing with each other. In a similar connection, our Rabbis have said: "The Torah speaks in the language of men." On the other hand, Scripture furnished but a few hints of f the spiritual subtleties that are only intelligible to the intellectual. And thus all people are on the same level with regard to the knowledge of the Creator's existence, even though the truth of His real glorious essence is variously apprehended by them. This too, we assert, is the case with every abstruse topic referred to in Holy Writ; e.g., Reward and Punishment in the life hereafter. Thus also, in regard to the elucidation of the Science of Inward Duties which it is our aim to treat in this work, we say that the Torah is very brief in its exposition, relying on our using our intellect; it only gives a few hints, such as are mentioned in the Introduction, which are calculated to call attention to these inward duties so that any competent person will be stimulated to enquire into and investigate the subject, till he has fully comprehended and mastered it, as it is said, (Prov. 28:5) "But they that seek the Lord will understand all things.". . .

As it is impossible to form a representation of Him with the intellect or picture Him in the imagination, Scripture, we find, ascribes most of God's praises to the Creator's name. Thus it is said (Nehem. 9:5) "And they shall bless Thy glorious name." (Deut. 28:58) "That thou mayest fear this glorious and revered name." (Ps. 99:3) "Let them praise Thy name, great and revered." (Mal. 2:5) "And of My name he was afraid." (ib. 3:20) "But unto you that fear My name, shall the sun of righteousness arise." (Ps. 68:5) "Sing unto God. Sing praises to His name. Extol Him that rideth upon the skies; Jah is His name."

The purpose in these texts is to magnify and exalt His glorious essence. For beyond the fact of His existence, there is no clear knowledge in our minds of God's Being but His Name. His essence and real nature we cannot picture or imagine. Hence, His Name is frequently repeated in the Pentateuch and also in the Prophets, since we comprehend nothing of Him but His Name and His existence. . . .

If we could have conceived God's true nature, there would have been no need of His becoming known to us in any other way. But since it is impossible for our intellect to apprehend His real Being, His glorious essence declared that He is the God of the choicest of His creatures, rational and otherwise. Thus when Moses asked Him (Ex. 3:13) "If they shall say unto me What is His name, what shall I say unto them," God replied (ibid.) "Thus shalt thou say unto the children of Israel, I AM hath sent me unto you." And as God knew that under this name, the people would not understand His real nature, He added, in further explanation, (Ex. 3:15) "Thus shalt thou say unto the children of Israel: The Lord, the God of your fathers, the God of Abraham, the God of Isaac, and the God of Jacob, hath sent me unto you: this is My name forever, and this is My memorial unto all generations";—by which He meant to say: if the people will not understand these terms and their contents by the exercise of their intellects, tell them that I am He who is known to them through the tradition that they received from their fathers. For the Creator appointed no other way of knowing Him but these two; namely, that which the intellect points out in the evidences of His activity exhibited in His creatures, and that of ancestral tradition, as Scripture saith (Job 15:18) "Which wise men have told from their fathers and have not hid it."

Since our apprehension of all existing things takes place in three ways, first, through our physical senses—Sight, Hearing, Taste, Smell, Touch—; secondly, through our Reason, by which the existence of an object is demonstrated from its indications and effects, so that the reality of its existence and nature are impressed upon us with the same certainty as that resulting from direct apprehension with the senses,— this is termed in Scripture Rational Knowledge and Intellectual Discipline — and thirdly through true reports and faithful tradition; and since it is an impossibility to apprehend Him with our senses, we can only know Him through true reports (traditions) or through the proof of His existence drawn from the evidences of His works. . . .

If we institute investigation on this subject with our intellect and perception, we will weary in the effort to apprehend the smallest part of His attributes and glories, as David said (Ps. 40:6) "Many things hast Thou done, O Lord my God; even Thy wondrous works and Thy thoughts towards us—there is none to be compared unto Thee." And further (Ps. 106:2) "Who can express the mighty acts of the Lord, or make all His praises to be heard?" Likewise it is said (Nehem. 9:5) "And let men bless Thy glorious name that is exalted above all blessing and praise."

Our sages relate that the reader of a congregation once conducted the service in the presence of Rabbi Chanina and began:— "O God, Great, Mighty, Awe-inspiring, Strong, Powerful, Puissant." "Have you," asked the Rabbi, "come to the end of the praises of thy Lord? Even the epithets—Great, Mighty, Awe-inspiring,—. . . would not have been used by us, had not Moses uttered them and the men of the Great Synagogue instituted them as part of the Liturgy. And you utter so many terms of eulogy! It is as if a human king had thousands upon thousands of gold *dinars*, and one would praise him for his silver. Would this not be an affront to him?" The Scripture also saith (Ps. 65:2) "To Thee silence is praise," on which our ancient teachers comment: "The best medicament is Silence. The more you praise a flawless pearl, the more you depreciate it.". . .

A sage once said "The further one advances in the knowledge of God the more awe-stricken one becomes with regard to His nature." Another remarked ["The man who is wisest in the knowledge of the Creator is aware that he is most ignorant of His reality." But one who does not know Him, fancies that he knows His glorious Being.]. . . The reason why we ascribe certain attributes to God is because otherwise it would be impossible for us to know Him. . . . The ultimate result of your knowledge of God should be the confession and conviction that of His real glorious essence you are completely ignorant. If you form in your mind or imagination a picture or representation of the Creator, strive to investigate His Being; and then you will be convinced of His existence, and all likeness of Him will be rejected by you, so that you will find Him through reasoning alone.

Take the following as an approximate analogy. We realize the reality of the Soul's existence. But we receive from it no apprehension of form, appearance or odor, though its activities and effects are visible to us, and cognizable by us. So with the intellect, whose activities and marks are cognizable and evident; we do not obtain from it any impression of form or likeness; nor do we form any representation of it in our imagination. How much less then can we thus apprehend the Creator of all, Who has none like Him. A philosopher said: "If our efforts to know the soul are vain, how much more futile must all attempts be to know the Creator." Having reached this point, there is no need to expatiate on this theme any further. Awe, reverence and reserve should restrain us, as a sage once said "Into that which is too wonderful for thee, do not enquire. That which has been hidden from thee, do not investigate. Reflect on that which is permitted. Have nought to do with mysteries." Our wise men also say "Whoever shows no regard for the honor of his master—better that he had never been born.". . .

It is impossible to apprehend any object of sensation without the appropriate sense. Whoever should attempt to do so will fail; as for example, if a person were to seek to recognize a melody with his sense of sight, or colors with his sense of hearing, or tastes with his sense of touch, he will be unable to apprehend them even when they are present, because he seeks them by means of organs other than those with which they can be apprehended. The same we assert of the mental faculties which we mentioned. Each of them has a special capacity to grasp its definite class of apprehensions that cannot be grasped with any other faculty. Like the physical senses, every mental faculty has its limits where its activity stops. It realizes things directly and through evidences. That which is near, it apprehends in its reality. That which is remote and hidden from it, it apprehends through evidences that point to it. Since the Creator is, in His glorious essence, unknown to, and infinitely remote from us, the intellect can apprehend nothing of Him except the fact of His existence. And if the intellect should endeavor to appreciate the reality of His glorious essence, or form some representation of it, it will miss that which it had already attained; namely, the realization of God's existence, because it strove for something outside its power; as we have already remarked in reference to the failure to perceive objects of sensation, if the attempt is made with the inappropriate sense. We should therefore seek to realize the existence of the Creator through the evidences of His activities afforded by His creatures,—which should serve us as proofs of Him.

When we have in this way become convinced of His existence, we should stop, and not try to make comparisons of Him in our minds, or represent and figure Him in our imaginations, or attempt to apprehend the nature of His glorious essence. For if we do this, thinking that we will thus bring Him nearer to our understanding, the realization of His existence will disappear from our consciousness. For any representation of Him forming itself in our minds applies to something other than the Creator. As Scripture saith (Prov. 25:16) "Hast thou found honey? Eat so much as is sufficient for thee, lest thou be filled therewith and vomit it."

I have deemed it fit to bring the subject nearer to you by means of two familiar illustrations. The first will show you that a sense apprehends its special class of sensation to a limited extent, and then stops; another sense then begins to be active and also ceases to function; and so with all the senses. When the activity of all of them has ceased, the intellect commences to function. This will be demonstrated by means of one object. Imagine that a stone is thrown a considerable distance, makes a whistling noise and strikes a man. With his sense of sight, the man perceives the shape and color of the stone; with his sense of hearing, the whistling sound it made; with his sense of touch, he becomes aware of its coldness and hardness. The bodily senses now stop and apprehend nothing more of the nature of the stone. And then the intellect comprehends that some person must have cast the stone, since it is evident that it had not been thrust from its place of itself. For that which it is the function of the senses to apprehend cannot possibly be apprehended by the intellect without them, and *a fortiori*, the senses cannot possibly apprehend that which it is the function of the intellect to apprehend. Now, since our intellect cannot possibly apprehend the essence of God's glory, how can we permit ourselves to form a representation of Him, limit Him, or liken Him to anything that is perceived by our physical senses. This is an impossibility.

The second illustration will show you that, in regard to spiritual things, once we are convinced of their existence, it is not proper to investigate them minutely. Such a course will only injure our intellect. The analogy is the case of a person who desires to inform himself concerning the sun. [If he endeavors to do so] by observing its light and radiance and its power of dissipating darkness, he will realize its existence, enjoy it, make use of its light, and attain all that he seeks from it. If one, however, should strive to know it in reference to its roundness and should fix his gaze intently on the dazzling orb, his sight will become dim and ultimately fail completely, when he will be unable to enjoy its light.

Similarly will it happen to us. If we study the existence of the Creator in the evidences pointing to Him, in His wisdom manifested by those evidences, in His power shown in all His creatures, we will understand and comprehend the matter; our intellects will become luminous with the knowledge of Him; and we will attain all that it is possible for our intellect to attain, as it is said (Isaiah 48:17), "I am the Lord thy God, who teacheth thee for thy profit, who leadeth thee by the way thou shouldst go." But if we strain our intellect, trying to realize the essence of His glory, and represent Him in our minds under a form or likeness, our powers of reasoning and apprehension will fail, and we will no longer grasp aught of what had already been known to us, just as will happen to our eyesight when we gaze at the sun. We should be heedful in this regard and bear it in mind when we investigate the subject of the existence of the Creator.

So too we must be careful in regard to God's attributes — whether those by which His glorious essence is described or those the prophets ascribed to Him—not to take them literally or in a material sense. We should clearly understand that they are to be regarded as metaphorical and literary expressions adapted to our powers of perception, comprehension and intelligence, and which we use, because of our urgent need to know and exalt Him; while God Himself, blessed be He, is infinitely exalted above all this, as Scripture saith (Nehemiah 9:5) "Exalted above all blessings and praise."

A philosopher once said: He whose mind is incapable of grasping the abstract, fastens on the terms used in the Divinely given Scriptures, and is unaware that the style of the Biblical books is adapted to the intelligence of those to whom they were addressed, but does not express the real nature of Him who addressed them and concerning Whom these terms are used. It is like the whistling call, when cattle are to be watered, which is more effective in making the beast drink, than clear and intelligent speech would be. When with your mind and reason you have reached this stage of knowledge of the Divine Unity, devote your soul wholly to the Creator. Strive to realize Him in His wisdom, might, mercy, grace and abounding providence, vouchsafed to His creatures. Make yourself acceptable to Him by doing His will. Then will you be of those who seek the Lord. And then you will obtain from Him aid and strength to know Him and apprehend His reality; as David said (Ps. 25:14) "The counsel of the Lord is with them that fear Him; and His covenant, to make them know it."

NOTES

1. And no end, for what has no beginning is endless.
2. That is, not to God Himself; but to His Glory.

MAIMONIDES, *MOREH NEVUKHIM*

Translation by Michael Friedlander

PART I, CHAPTER 1

Some have been of opinion that by צלם in Hebrew, the shape and figure of a thing is to be understood, and this explanation led men to believe in the corporeality [of the Divine Being]: for they thought that the words נעשה אדם בצלמנו, "Let us make man in our form" (Gen. i. 26), implied that God had the form of a human being, *i.e.*, that He had figure and shape, and that, consequently, He was corporeal. They adhered faithfully to this view, and thought that if they were to relinquish it they would *eo ipso* reject the truth of the Bible: and further, if they did not conceive God as having a body possessed of face and limbs, similar to their own in appearance, they would have to deny even the existence of God. The sole difference which they admitted, was that He excelled in greatness and splendour, and that His substance was not flesh and blood. Thus far went their conception of the greatness and glory of God. The incorporeality of the Divine Being, and His unity, in the true sense of the word—for there is no real unity without incorporeality—will be fully proved in the course of the present treatise. (Part II., ch. i.) In this chapter it is our sole intention to explain the meaning of the words צלם and דמות.[1] I hold that the Hebrew equivalent of "form" in the ordinary acceptation of the word, *viz.*, the figure and shape of a thing, is תאר. Thus we find יפה תאר ויפה מראה "(And Joseph was) beautiful in form and beautiful in appearance" (Gen. xxxix. 6): מה תארו, "What form is he of?" (1 Sam. xxviii. 14): כתאר בני המלך, "As the form of the children of a king" (Judges viii. 18). It is also applied to form produced by human labour, as יתארהו בשרד and ובמחוגה יתארהו, "He marketh its form with a line," "and he marketh its form with the compass" (Is. xliv. 13). This term is not at all applicable to God. The term צלם, on the other hand, signifies the specific form, *viz.*, that which constitutes the essence of a thing, whereby the thing is what it is; the reality of a thing in so far as it is that particular being. In man the "form" is that constituent which gives him human perception: and on account of this intellectual perception the term צלם is employed in the phrase בצלם אלהים ברא אותו, "In the form of God He created him"

(Gen. i. 27). It is therefore rightly said, צלמם תבזה, "Thou despisest their form" (Ps. lxxiii. 20); the "contempt" can only concern the soul—the specific form of man, not the bodily properties and shape. I am also of opinion that the reason why "idols" are called צלמים, may be found in the circumstance that they are worshipped on account of some idea conveyed by them, not on account of their figure and shape. In the same way is used the expression צלמי טחוריכם, "the forms of your emerods" (1 Sam. vi. 5), for the chief object was the removal of the injury caused by the emerods, not a change of their shape. If, however, it must be assumed that the images of the emerods and the idols are called צלמים on account of their external shape, the term צלם would be either a real or an apparent homonym, and would denote both the specific form and the artificial shape, or similar properties relating to the dimensions and the figure of material bodies; and in the phrase נעשה אדם בצלמנו, "Let us make man in our form" (Gen. i.26), the term צלם would then signify "the specific form," *viz.*, intellectual preception, not "figure" or "shape." Thus we have shown the difference between צלם and תאר, and explained the meaning of צלם.

דמות is derived from the verb דמה, "to be similar." This term likewise denotes agreement with regard to some abstract relation: comp. דמיתי לקאת מדבר, "I am like a pelican of the wilderness" (Ps. cii. 7); the author does not compare himself to the pelican in point of wings and feathers, but in point of sadness. כל עץ בגן אלהים לא דמה אליו ביפיו "nor any tree in the garden of God was like unto him in beauty" (Ez. xxxi. 8); the comparison refers to the idea of beauty. חמת למו כדמות חמת נחש, "Their poison is like the poison of a serpent" (Ps. lviii.5); דמיונו כאריה, "He is like unto a lion" (Ps. xvii. 12); the resemblance indicated in these passages does not refer to the figure and shape, but to some abstract idea. In the same manner is used דמות הכסא, "the likeness of the throne" (Ez. i. 26); the comparison is made with regard to greatness and glory, not, as many believe, with regard to its square form, its breadth, or the length of its legs: this explanation applies also to the phrase דמות החיות, "the likeness of the living creatures" (Ez. i. 13).

As man's distinction consists in a property which no other creature on earth possesses, *viz.*, intellectual perception, in the exercise of which he does not employ his senses, nor move his hand or his foot, it has been compared—though only apparently, not in truth—to the Divine excellency, which requires no instrument whatever. On this account, *i.e.*, on account of the Divine intellect with which man has been endowed, he is said to have been made in the form and likeness of the Almighty, but far from it be the notion that the Supreme Being is corporeal, having a material form.

ALBO, *IKKARIM*

Translation by Isaac Husik

BOOK II, CHAPTER 14

It has already been proved demonstratively that God is neither body nor a force residing in body. It follows that we must deny God all bodily accidents and corporeal affections. It is necessary therefore to give a reason for the expressions found in all the Prophets that God is jealous, wrathful, vengeful and bearing grudge. Thus Nahum says, "The Lord is a jealous and avenging God. The Lord avengeth and is full of wrath, The Lord taketh vengeance on His adversaries, and He reserveth wrath for His enemies."[1] All these descriptions denote corporeal affections. Moreover, they are ignoble qualities which should not be attributed to any excellent person, not to speak of God. The Bible also attributes to Him pride, "The Lord reigneth; He is clothed in majesty"; [2] also the emotion of pity, "My compassions are kindled together,"[3] as well as sorrow, "And it grieved Him at His heart";[4] and grief, "And His soul was grieved for the misery of Israel."[5]

The explanation is this. The purpose of the prophets is to lead all mankind to worship God and to love Him. But the masses of the people can not be made to humble themselves for service except from fear of punishment. Therefore it was necessary for the prophets to speak in a language understood by the generality of the people. Now since, in human phraseology, when a king punishes those who have rebelled against him and given his kingdom to another, he is said to be jealous and revengeful and full of wrath, so the prophets say of God when He punishes those who violate His will that He is a jealous and avenging God and is full of wrath, because the act which emanates from Him against those who transgress His will is the act of a revengeful, grudging and jealous person.

The attribution of sorrow to God must be explained in the same way. Just as human beings feel sorrow when necessity compels their works to be destroyed, so the Bible says, "And it grieved Him at His heart," and in the immediate sequel we read, "And the Lord said, 'I will blot out man whom I have created. . .for it repenteth Me that I have made them.' "[6] God is said to repent because He does the act of a person who repents of what he has made and desires to destroy it. And just as when a human being finds himself compelled by the requirements of justice to destroy what he has made, he looks about for a way which will enable him to save some of it from destruction, so God sought a way to prevent the destruction of all things. Therefore the narrative concludes, "But Noah found grace in the eyes of the Lord."[7] The meaning is that God brought it about that the world should be continued through Noah and his sons.

The expression, "And His soul was grieved for the misery of Israel,"[8] is to be explained in the same way. God did the act of a person who is in sorrow, whose soul grieves for the misery of his neighbor, and who puts himself to inconvenience in order to help him. So here, though Israel had sinned and were not deserving at that time of such great deliverance, nevertheless God saved them of His own accord as if He was affected by their trouble and misery, as we read, "I have surely seen the affliction of My people that are in Egypt. . .and I am come down to deliver them out of the hand of the Egyptians."[9] Similarly is to be explained the expression, "My compassions are kindled together."[10]

The other expressions of corporeal affections must be understood in the same way, as a mode of bringing to the human understanding the nature of the act which emanates from Him, in a manner consonant with human habits of perception. Thus the Bible says expressly, "Take ye therefore good heed unto yourselves, for ye saw no manner of form,"[11] and yet it attributes corporeal members to God, speaking of the Tables of Stone, as "written with the finger of God";[12] and in the following expressions, "When I behold Thy heavens, the work of Thy fingers";[13] "Thy right hand, O Lord, glorious in power";[14] "Thy hands have made me and fashioned me";[15] and many others of the same kind. The explanation is that as a human person writes with the finger, finger is attributed to God; as strength in man comes from the right hand, right hand is ascribed to Him; as human acts are done with hands and fingers, hands and fingers are attributed to God; and as the acceptation of words in man is attributed to the hearing of the ears, the Bible says, "Let thine ears be attentive."[16]

In the same way must be explained the saying of God in relation to the Temple, "And Mine eyes and Mine heart shall be there perpetually."[17] The meaning is, My providence and My good will, indicating that God desires its permanent existence. Similarly when the prophets picture God as a king sitting on a throne, as in Isaiah, "And I saw the Lord sitting on a throne";[18] "For mine eyes have seen the King, the Lord of hosts";[19] or when they describe Him as a strong man, "The Lord will go forth as a mighty man";[20] "The Lord mighty in battle";[21]—all this is done in order to bring before human understanding a picture of His mighty glory and majesty. Thus David says, "They shall speak of the glory of Thy kingdom . . . To make known to the sons of men His mighty acts, and the glory of the majesty of His kingdom."[22] The meaning is that the only reason why they speak of Thee thus is in order to make known to the sons of men, but not in order tocompare Thy kingdom with a human kingdom, for Thy kingdom is eternal, "a kingdom for all ages."[23] It is done merely to bring the matter before the human understanding and for no other reason.

When the Bible attributes to Him pride, which is an ignoble quality in man, as is said, "Every one that is proud in heart is an abomination to the Lord,"[24] the meaning is that man should not boast of any excellence or good quality, for all comes from God, and a man should not boast of that which does not belong to him. As regards wisdom, the Bible says, "For the Lord giveth wisdom";[25] also, "That turneth wise men backward, and maketh their knowledge foolish."[26] This explains that human wisdom is worth nothing, and that wisdom comes from God and from no one else. Nor should a man boast of wealth, for that is not his either, as David says, "For all things come of Thee, and of Thine own have we given Thee."[27]

Similarly kingdom and all exalted station and excellence come from God, as the Bible says, "Thine is the kingdom, O Lord, and Thou art exalted as head above all."[28] And the Rabbis say, "Even the overseer of wells is appointed from heaven."[29] The blessing concludes, "Both riches and honour come of Thee, and Thou rulest over all."[30] That is, since everything comes from God, and man alone has nothing which is not due to the will of God, for in His "hand it is to make great, and to give strength unto all,"[31] he should not boast of that which does not belong to him and is not in his power. Therefore pride is becoming only to God from whom everything comes. Hence the Bible attributes pride to God when it says, "The Lord reigneth; He is clothed in majesty,"[32] and in the words of Moses, "I will sing unto the Lord, for He is highly exalted";[33] which Onkelos[34] translates, "Because He is exalted above the proud, and pride is His."

Therefore if a person boasts of some quality which is not his, it is proper that the quality should be taken away from him, as an indication that the honor and the excellence which he enjoys do not come to him from himself, but from God and by the divine will. Thus we find in the case of Nebuchadnezzar who boasted of glory and royal status, that the Bible expresses itself as follows: "But when his heart was lifted up, and his spirit was hardened that he dealt proudly, he was deposed from his kingly throne and his glory was taken from him . . . till thou know that the Most High ruleth in the kingdom of men, and giveth it to whomsoever He will . . . and setteth up over it the lowest of men."[35]. . .

The majesty of the king is dependent upon the multitude of the people, the more people the greater the glory. But God, being king over glory, is not exalted because of any one else nor does His kingship change or diminish as those subject to Him are diminished or changed. Thus the Psalmist says, "The voice of the Lord maketh the hinds to calve, and strippeth the forests bare, and in His temple all say: 'Glory.'"[36] The meaning is that even when God executes judgment and destroys the forests and the animals, His royalty and His glory are not diminished thereby, for in His palace, i.e. in His degree of existence, all is glory. And the proof of this is that "The Lord sat enthroned at the flood; Yea, the Lord sitteth as King forever."[37] That is, God existed in the time of the flood, and though of the world before the flood, which was full of men and animals, all things were destroyed, Noah alone and those with him in the ark remaining, nevertheless God's kingdom did not change in extent, hence "the Lord sitteth as King forever." The reason it says "sitteth" and not "is," is because sitting better expresses the idea of permanence, as Maimonides says where he discusses the scriptural homonym *yashab* (=to sit).[38] For this reason the prophet, too, ascribes to God the attribute of sitting more frequently than other attributes. Thus he says, "I saw the Lord sitting upon a throne high and lifted up,"[39] and not simply: "I saw the Lord upon a throne high and lifted up." The explanation is that since sitting implies permanence, without change, it is attributed to God, though neither standing nor sitting applies to Him, as the Rabbis say in the treatise Hagigah,[40] that up above there is neither sitting nor standing, etc. A similar interpretation must be given to all the expressions of corporeal affections ascribed to God in the Bible. They are used in order to bring the matter before human understanding, but not to indicate that it is so in reality. The Rabbis have a general maxim in this connection, "The Torah uses human expressions."[41]

NOTES

1. Nah. 1, 2.
2. Ps. 93, 1.
3. Hos. 11, 8.
4. Gen. 6, 6.
5. Judg. 10, 16.
6. Gen. 6, 7.
7. Ibid. 6, 8.
8. Judg. 10, 16.
9. Ex. 3, 7-8.
10. Hos. 11, 8.
11. Deut. 4, 15.
12. Ex. 31, 18.
13. Ps. 8, 4.
14. Ex. 15, 6.
15. Ps. 119, 73.
16. Ibid. 130, 2.
17. I Kings 9, 3.
18. Isa. 6, 1.
19. Ibid. 5.
20. Ibid. 42, 13.
21. Ps. 24, 8.
22. Ibid. 145, 11-12.
23. Ibid. 13.
24. Prov. 16, 5.
25. Prov. 2, 6.
26. Isa. 44, 25.
27. I Chron. 29, 14.
28. Ibid. 11.
29. Baba Batra 91b.
30. I Chron. 29, 12.
31. Ibid.
32. Ps. 93, 1.
33. Ex. 15, 1.
34. The Aramaic translation of the Pentateuch Cf. I, 52, note 1.
35. The text, somewhat inaccurate, is a combination of Dan. 5, 20, and 4, 22 and 14.
36. Ps. 29, 9.
37. Ibid. 10.
38. Guide I, 11.
39. Isa. 6, 1.
40. 15a. The quotation is not exact.
41. Sanhedrin 64b, 90b; 'Arakin 3a.

BOOK II, CHAPTER 17

"Place" (Heb. *makom*) is a term applied to the thing which surrounds bodies and bounds them. An incorporeal thing can not be said to be in place, because the name place applies only to a thing which is filled by another body having dimensions, which enters place and is surrounded by it. Hence it can not be said of God or of the separate intellects that they are in place, for they are not bodies having dimensions which place can surround.

The Bible says in reference to this, "Behold, the heaven and the heaven of heavens can not contain Thee,"[1] meaning that God does not need place to stand in. Such expressions as, "And I will dwell among the children of Israel";[2] "Then it shall come to pass that the place which the Lord your God shall choose to cause His name to dwell there";[3] do not mean that God needs a place to dwell in. The explanation is this. The revelation of God's glory takes place by means of a body that is visible to the senses, like a fire or a pillar of cloud. Thus we read: "And the appearance of the glory of the Lord was like devouring fire on the top of the mount";[4] "And behold, the glory of the Lord appeared in the cloud";[5] "And the angel of the Lord appeared unto him in a flame of fire out of the midst of a bush." [6] The sudden appearance of the pillar of cloud or of a flame of fire out of the midst of a bush, the bush not being consumed, was an indication that the glory of the Lord, which could not be seen with the senses, was there. This is why the Bible assigns a particular place to the presence of the divine glory, not that the glory has need of a place or of a body to stay in. And inasmuch as place holds a thing in permanency, God is called "dwelling-place" (Heb. *ma'on*), as Moses says, "Thou hast been our dwelling-place,"[7] meaning that God contains the world and holds it in permanency as a place holds an object. For this reason the Rabbis call Him "place," as in "Blessed be the Place (God) who gave the Torah to Israel,"[8] also, "And wave his hand to the Place (God), that He remove the leper."[9]

The substance of a thing is also called place, as the Rabbis say, "From its own place the matter is proved,"[10] also, "Blessed be the glory of the Lord from His place."[11] The last expression means that the glory of the Lord which appeared to the prophets emanated from God's own essence without a mediator, and not that the glory has a place.

There is a question, however, worth noting, whether it is possible to attribute to God location. For though God is not in place, a specific location may be applied to Him, like above, as we read in the Bible, "For God is in heaven, and thou upon earth";[12] and all authorities agree that heaven is the dwelling of the spiritual beings, though they have no need of place. It would appear, therefore, from this that even though He is not corporeal, it is possible to attribute to Him location, without this necessitating corporeality in Him. The same is true of the soul; though she is incorporeal, nevertheless she has a certain location, viz. in the body. For since she is not outside of the body, she is identified with a certain locality, though she is not in place. Similarly we say that the soul of the wicked is judged in Gehenna. Here again though she is not body so as to be in place, place nevertheless bounds her, and she is there to receive her punishment, in the same way as she was in the body when she sinned, though she is not corporeal. In this way it is possible to say of God that though He is not in place, He is in a certain locality, above or below or some special locality.

On the other hand one may argue against it and say that locality necessarily implies place, for locality is either above or below, and these are without doubt place. To this, however, it may be said that above in the absolute sense is not a place, for the uppermost sphere is above absolutely, and it is clear that it is not in place, since there is no other body outside of it that can surround it.[13] Therefore we may attribute to Him location above, since it is not place. But this is based upon the opinion of Aristotle that place is the limit which bounds a body on the outside, and hence he says that the world as a whole is not in place because there is nothing outside of it to surround it.

But this opinion is clearly unsound, for according to him it would follow that the part has a different place from the whole.[14] For the parts of fire have no other external surrounding limit except other parts of fire or air, whereas the natural place of the element fire is the concavity of the lunar sphere, which is different from the place of the parts of fire. The same thing applies to the other elements. Moreover, it would follow according to him that the elements remain in their places by force. For the natural place of the element fire is the concave surface of the lunar sphere, which is above. Hence all the parts of fire outside of those which are adjacent to the inner surface of the sphere remain where they are by force;[15] and similarly in the case of the other elements. Again, if the place of the element earth is the surface of the element water which bounds it on the outside, the place of earth would not be below in the absolute sense, as he maintains, since below in the absolute sense is the center.[16] Furthermore, it follows according to him that the place of the part is greater than the place of the whole. For if you remove part of the inside of a sphere, it will require a greater surface to bound it outside and inside than when it is solid. Besides, it would follow according to him that one and the same body will have many places differing in magnitude. For if you divide a body into parts, each of the latter will require a greater place than before the division, and the same is true if you divide the parts into other parts, and those again into parts. But this is contrary to the statement of Euclid in his book *Concerning the Heavy and the Light,*[17] where he says that equal bodies occupy equal places. But according to the Aristotelian hypothesis this is not true. For of two equal bodies the one that is divided will require a greater place than the other.

All these difficulties follow from the opinion that place is an external bounding surface. But if place is defined as being the vacuum into which the body enters, none of the difficulties results.[18] Aristotle objects to this definition on the ground that if there are such things as self-existent distances, and these distances are place,[19] two absurdities will follow. One is that one and the same thing will have an infinite number of places all at once. The other is that places would be subject to motion, and that place, which is in the basin of water,[20] would in turn require a place. This absurd result, however, follows only if the distances are subject to motion, but if we say that they are not subject to motion, and that it is the body and its parts that move from distances to other distances, no absurdity will follow at all.[21] For the basin and the water have each special distances which they fill and which are not changed when they move. According to this opinion the uppermost sphere and the world as a whole are in place.[22] And therefore it is impossible to attribute to God locality any more than place.

And as to the fact that the Bible does attribute to God location above, in the expressions, "O Thou that art enthroned in the heavens,"[23] "He that sitteth in heaven laugheth,"[24] and others, it may be that because the divine power appears more clearly in the motion of the spheres by reason of the intensity and continuity of their motions, and because they are made of a nobler material than the other bodies,[25] and because location above is superior, it says that the heavens are the dwelling-place of the spiritual beings. And it may be that the Bible attributes to God location as it attributes place and the other corporeal attributes, because, as the Rabbis say, "The Torah speaks in human language."[26] We shall now conclude the discussion of the dogma of incorporeality. What we have said on this topic, may be used to throw light on analogous topics.

NOTES

1. I Kings 8, 27.
2. Ex. 29, 45.
3. Deut. 12, 11.
4. Ex. 24, 17.
5. Ibid. 16, 10.
6. Ibid. 3, 2.
7. Ps. 90, 1.
8. The statement occurs in the Passover Haggadah. The nearest rabbinic parallel is found in Midrash Tanhuma, 'Ekeb, §1; יתברך שמו של הקב״ה שנתן תורה לישראל.
9. II Kings, 5, 11.
10. Shebu'ot, 7b.
11. Ezek. 3, 12.
12. Ecc. 5, 1.
13. Cf. Wolfson, Crescas' Critique of Aristotle, 1929, p. 432, note 54.
14. Cf. id., p. 447, note 66.
15. The natural place of a thing is contrasted with the place which a thing may occupy because it is held there by force against the natural tendency of the thing. Now since according to Aristotle the natural place of fire is the inner surface of the lunar sphere and place means according to him the bounding limit, it follows that all the lower layers of fire do not occupy their natural place, but are kept down out of their natural place by force.
16. See Wolfson, loc. cit., p. 445, note 64.
17. A spurious work. Cf. Steinschneider, Die Hebräischen Uebersetzungen, p. 503, note 20.
18. See Wolfson, op. cit., p. 455, note 75.
19. The Hebrew word רחַק may be translated distance, interval or dimension. Here the word is an abbreviation of the definition of space expressed by Hasdai Crescas (Or Adonai, ed. Ferrara 7b, end): הרחק אשר בין תכליות המקיף = *τὸ διάστημα τὸ μεταξὺ τῶν ἐσχάτων τοῦ περιέχοντος*, the interval or distance between the limits of the surrounding body. See Efros, The Problem of Space in Jewish Mediaeval Philosophy, p. 69, note 87.
20. The translation of this passage is based upon the reading בספל of the Warsaw edition. MSS. A, B, C, D and first edition read הספל, but this cannot be correct, for according to Albo's definition of space, which is here assumed, the vessel is not the place of the water. I read therefore בספל with the Warsaw edition and translate: "place, which is in the basin of the water," i.e. the distance or interval between the limits of the water in the basin.
21. See H.A. Wolfson, Crescas' Critique of Aristotle, 1929, loc. cit., pp. 441-443, note 57.
22. The entire discussion of place in this chapter is taken from the Or Adonai of Hasdai Crescas, who criticizes Aristotle's definition of place. The Aristotelian argument against identifying place (*τόπος*) with the distance between the limits of the surrounding body (*διάστημα τὸ μεταξὺ τῶν ἐσχάτων*) is found in the Physics, IV, ch. 4, p. 211b 19–25: *εἰ δ'ἦν τι τὸ διάστημα τὸ πεφυκὸς καὶ μένον ἐν τῷ αὐτῷ τόπῳ, ἄπειροι ἂν ἦσαν τόποι. μεθισταμένου γὰρ τοῦ ὕδατος καὶ τοῦ ἀέρος ταὐτὸ ποιήσει τὰ μόρια πάντα ἐν τῷ ὅλῳ ὅπερ ἅπαν τὸ ὕδωρ ἐν τῷ ἀγγείῳ. ἅμα δὲ καὶ ὁ τόπος ἔσται μεταβάλλων. ὥστ' ἔσται τοῦ τόπου τ' ἄλλος τόπος, καὶ πολλοὶ τόποι ἅμα ἔσονται.* The passage is somewhat obscure, but as Simplicius interprets it, Aristotle says that three absurdities follow from the definition of place as interval or distance: 1, that there are an infinite number of places. 2,that place is in place. 3, that a given body has many places at the same time. Crescas, whom Albo follows, combines 1 with 3.

The relevant passages in the Or Adonai of Crescas are p. 8a and p. 22a (ed. Ferrara). The first is as follows:

וארסטו יאמר בזה המאמר בשיש הנה רחקים עומדים בעצמם יתחייבו ממנו ב׳ שקרים שא׳ (הא׳ read) שיהיה לדבר הא׳ בעצמו מקומות רבים יחד בב״ת והב׳ שיהיו המקומות מתנועעים ושיהיה המקום במקום, והנה איך יחוייב זה, כפי מה שאומר. וזה שאם היה הרחק אשר בין תכליות הגשם הוא המקום חוייב שיהיו חלקי הגשם במקום בעצם. וזה כי כמו שהגשם בכללו הוא במקום להיותו ברוחק שוה לו הנה כל אחד מחלקיו במקום להיותו ברחק השוה לו. וכאשר הנחנו כלי מים יתנועע ממקום אל מקום הנה כמו שהמים יעתקו בכלי עם הרחק השוה לו אשר יטרידהו ויהיה ברחק אחד (אחר?) כאשר המיר הכלי בכללו מקומו כן יעשו חלקי המים, רצו׳ שהם יעתקו עם הרחקים המיוחדים להם אל הרחקים אחרים אשר הם מקומות להם וכאש׳ חלקנו החלקים אל חלקים אחרים תמיד הנה יתחייבו הב׳ שקרים אם שיהיו להם מקומות בב״ת ואם שיהיו המקומות מתנועעים ושיהיה המקום במקום.

In this passage Crescas states the Aristotelian arguments against the conception of place as distance.

The second passage contains Crescas' answer to these arguments and reads as follows:

והשקרים אשר חייב ארסטו לזה הדעת אין ענין להם שהוא מיוסד על שהרחקים אשר בתוך הכלי מים נעתקים בהעתק הכלי ואז היו מתחייבים השקרים ההם והוא בדיו ואינו אמת, שהרחקים לאומרים כפנוי ורקות בלתי מתנועעים, ולזה לא יתחייבו הבטולים ההם.

Cf. Wolfson, loc. cit., pp. 421 ff., notes 36, 54, 57, 64, 66, 75, 78, 80.

23. Ps. 123, 1.

24. Ibid. 2, 4.

25. According to Aristotle, whose opinion the mediaeval philosophers adopted, the sublunar bodies are composed of fire, air, water, earth, whereas the heavenly spheres and bodies are made of a fifth element, ether, which is not subject to change or to destruction.

26. Sanhedrin 64b, 90b.

The Fourth Principle

Eternity

INTRODUCTION

The Fourth Principle embodies the concept of the eternity of God. God, as an infinite being, has no beginning in time; since He is the uncaused First Cause, God must always have existed. As an infinite being, God's existence is subject to no limitations; He will, therefore, not cease to exist. Since He is not subject to destruction, He must always exist. Stated in this manner, the Fourth Principle expresses nothing novel with regard to the eternal nature of the Deity. However, in his *Guide,* Maimonides presents an analysis of time which serves to demonstrate the eternity of God in an entirely different way. According to Maimonides, time is an object of creation. If this is so, it follows that God cannot conceivably exist in time. God, the Creator of time, is transcendental; He stands above the processes of time. We should not, properly speaking, speak of God as eternal, because the very term "eternity" connotes an infinite expanse of time. To say that God's existence spans the infinite expanse of time is inaccurate. God is neither eternal nor noneternal; He is totally removed from all time processes and all time concepts. Eternity, like all other attributes, can be attributed to God only in a negative sense. In ascribing eternity to God one can only intend to convey the idea that God is not limited by time.

Grammatically, the term "time" is treated as a noun. Since a noun is defined as the name of a person, place or thing, we tend to think of time as an entity or "thing" which possesses ontological existence in its own right. This view is rejected by Maimonides in favor of a view which regards time not as an independent entity but as a relationship which exists between objects in motion.

For Maimonides, as for Plato (*Timaeus* 37c–39e) and Aristotle (*Physics* IV, 11), time is an accident of motion. Time depends upon motion because it is a measure of the relative motion of different objects. Motion itself is quite obviously an accident of matter. There can be no motion unless there exist material objects which are the subjects of motion. Since time is a measure of motion, and motion is an accident of matter, it follows that time cannot precede the creation of matter. Time must be regarded as itself having been created, in the sense that it is an epiphenomenon, or by-product, of matter. Hence God is eternal, not in the sense that His existence is coextensive with time, but in the sense that His existence precedes the creation of time.

Saadia's proof of the eternity of God is closely related to his exposition of *creatio ex nihilo.* In rejecting the eternity of the universe, Saadia argues that acceptance of an eternal universe involves postulation of an infinite regress. The concept of an infinite regress, Saadia believes, involves a logical contradiction. The argument is similar to one of Zeno's paradoxes. The infinite cannot be completely traversed. Hence, if the universe were eternal, it would not have reached the present and we could not exist. Since we do exist, it follows, therefore, that the universe has existed for a finite length of time and is not eternal. God, as Creator of the universe, must be eternal.

For Judah Halevi there is no more reason to adduce rigorous proofs for the eternity of God than there was to demonstrate the existence of God. The doctrine of creation is derived from the prophetic tradition of Adam, Noah, and Moses. This is true also of the concomitant notion of the eternity of God.

Albo is willing to accept a notion of time which is not contingent upon motion. This type of time is of unmeasured duration conceived only in thought. Nevertheless, God is independent of all time. A being which is dependent upon time is limited in power. God, who is omnipotent, is eternal.

SAADIA, *EMUNOT VE-DE'OT*

Translation by Alexander Altmann

FIRST TREATISE
CREATIO EX NIHILO

2. *Four Arguments for Creation*[1]

From these introductory remarks I go on to affirm that our Lord (be He exalted) has informed us that all things were created in time, and that He created them *ex nihilo*, as it is said, 'In the beginning God created[2] the heaven and the earth' (Gen. 1.1), and as it is further said, 'I am the Lord that maketh all things; that stretched forth the heavens alone; that spread abroad the earth by Myself' (Isa. 44.24). He verified this truth for us by signs and miracles, and we have accepted it. I probed further into this matter with the object of finding out whether it could be verified by speculation as it had been verified by prophecy. I found that this was the case for a number of reasons, from which, for the sake of brevity, I select the following four.[2a]

(1) The first proof is based on the finite character of the universe. It is clear that heaven and earth are finite in magnitude,[3] since the earth occupies the centre and the heaven revolves round it. From this it follows that the force residing in them is finite in magnitude.[4] For it is impossible for an infinite force to reside in a body which is finite in magnitude. This would be contradictory to the dictates of Reason. Since, therefore, the force which preserves[5] heaven and earth is finite, it necessarily follows that the world has a beginning and an end.[6] Being struck by the force of this argument, I subjected it to a close examination, taking good care not to be hasty in drawing definite conclusions before having scrutinized it. I, therefore, asked myself: Perhaps the earth is infinite in length, breadth and depth? I answered: If this were the case, the sun could not encompass it and complete his revolution once every day and night, rising again in the place in which he rose the day before, and setting again in the place in which he set the day before; and so with the moon and the stars. Then I asked myself: Perhaps the heaven is infinite? To this I answered: How could this be the case seeing that all celestial bodies are moving and

continually revolving round the earth?[7] For it cannot be supposed that only the sphere that is next to us performs this rotation, whereas the others are too large to perform any movement. For by 'heaven' we understand the body which revolves, and we are not aware of anything else beyond it, far less do we believe it to be the heaven and not revolving. Then I explored further and asked: Perhaps there exists a plurality of earths and heavens, each heaven revolving round its earth? This would involve the assumption of the co-existence of an infinite number of worlds,[8] a thing in its nature[9] impossible. For it is inconceivable that, nature being what it is, some earth should exist above the fire, or that air should be found beneath the water. For both fire and air are light, and both earth and water are heavy. I cannot doubt that if there were a clod of earth outside our earth, it would break through all air and fire until it reached the dust of our earth. The same would happen if there were a mass of water outside the waters of our oceans. It would cut through air and fire until it met our waters. It is, therefore, perfectly clear to me that there exists no heaven apart from our heaven, and no earth except our earth; moreover, that this heaven and this earth are finite, and that in the same way as their bodies are limited, their respective force, too, is limited and ceases to exist once it reaches its limit. It is impossible that heaven and earth should continue to exist after their force is spent, and that they should have existed before their force came into being. I found that Scripture testifies to the finite character of the world by saying, 'From the one end of the earth, even unto the other end of the earth' (Deut. 13.8), and, 'From the one end of heaven unto the other' (Deut. 4.32). It further testifies that the sun revolves round the earth and completes its circle every day by saying, 'The sun also ariseth, and the sun goeth down, and hasteneth to his place where he ariseth' (Eccl. 1.5).

(2) The second proof is derived from the union of parts and the composition of segments. I saw that bodies consist of combined parts and segments fitted together. This clearly indicated to me that they are the skilful work of a skilful artisan and creator.[10] Then I asked myself: Perhaps these unions and combinations are peculiar to the small bodies only, that is to say the bodies of the animals and plants? I, therefore, extended my observation to the earth, and found the same was true of her. For she is a union of soil and stone and sand, and the like.[11] Then I turned my mental gaze to the heavens and found that in them there are many layers of spheres,[12] one within another, and that there are in them also groups of luminaries called stars which are distinguished from one another by being great or small, and by being more luminous or less

luminous, and these luminaries are set in those spheres.[13] Having noted these clear signs of the union and composition which has been created in the body of the heaven and the other bodies, I believe also, on the strength of this proof, that the heaven and all it contains are created. I found that Scripture also declares that the separateness of the parts of the organisms and their combination prove that they are created. In regard to man it is said, 'Thy hands have made me and fashioned me' (Ps. 119.73); in regard to the earth it is said, 'He is God, that formed the earth and made it, He established it' (Isa. 45.18); in regard to the heaven it is said, 'When I behold Thy heavens, the work of Thy fingers, the moon and the stars, which Thou hast established' (Ps. 8.4).

(3) The third proof[14] is based on the nature of the accidents.[15] I found that no bodies are devoid of accidents which affect them either directly or indirectly.[16] Animals, e.g. are generated, grow until they reach their maturity, then waste away and decompose. I then said to myself: Perhaps the earth as a whole is free from these accidents? On reflection, however, I found that the earth is inseparable from plants and animals which themselves are created, and it is well known that whatsoever is inseparable from things created must likewise be created.[17] Then I asked myself: Perhaps the heavens are free from such accidents?[18] But, going into the matter, I found that this was not the case. The first and principal accident affecting them is their intrinsic movement which goes on without pause. There are, however, many different kinds of movement. If you compare them, you will find that some planets move slowly, others quickly. And another kind of accident is the transmission of light from one celestial body to another one, which becomes illumined by it, like the moon. The colours of the various stars also differ. Some are whitish, some reddish, others yellowish and greenish.[19] Having thus established that these bodies are affected by accidents which are coeval with them, I firmly believe that everything which has accidents coeval with it must be created like the accident, since the accident enters into its definition.[20] Scripture also uses the accidents of heaven and earth as argument for their beginning in time by saying, 'I, even I, have made the earth and created man upon it; I, even My hands, have stretched out the heavens, and all their hosts have I commanded' (Isa. 45.12).

(4) The fourth proof is based on the nature of Time.[21] I know that time is threefold: past, present and future. Although the present is smaller than any instant, I take the instant as one takes a point[22] and say: If a man should try in his thought to ascend from that point in time to the uppermost point, it would be impossible for him to do so, inasmuch as time is now assumed to be infinite and it is impossible for thought to

penetrate to the furthest point of that which is infinite.[23] The same reason will also make it impossible that the process of generation should traverse an infinite period down to the lowest point so as ultimately to reach us. Yet if the process of generation did not reach us, we would not be generated, from which it necessarily follows that we, the multitude of generated beings, would not be generated and the beings now existent would not be existent. And since I find myself existent, I know that the process of generation has traversed time until it has reached us, and that if time were not finite, the process of generation would not have traversed it. I profess unhesitatingly the same belief with regard to future time as with regard to past time.[24] I find that Scripture speaks in similar terms of the far distant time by saying, 'All men have looked thereon; man beholdeth it afar off' (Job 36.25); and the faithful one says, 'I will fetch my knowledge from afar' (Job. 36.3).

It has come to my notice that a certain heretic in conversation with one of the Believers in the Unity (of God) objected to this proof. He said: 'It is possible for a man to traverse that which has an infinite number of parts by walking. For if we consider any distance which a man walks, be it a mile, or an ell, we shall find that it can be divided into an infinite number of parts.'[25] To answer this argument some thinkers resorted to the doctrine of the indivisible atom.[26] Others spoke of *tafra* (the leap).[27] Others again asserted that all the parts (in space) are covered by corresponding parts (in time).[28] Having carefully examined the objection raised I found it to be a sophism for this reason: the infinite divisibility of a thing is only a matter of imagination,[29] but not a matter of reality.[30] It is too subtle to be a matter of reality, and no such division occurs. Now if the process of generation had traversed the past in the imagination, and not in reality, then, by my life, the objection raised would be valid. But seeing that the process of generation has traversed the real time and reached us, the argument cannot invalidate our proof, because infinite divisibility exists only in the imagination.

In addition to these four proofs, there are some more, part of which I have adduced in my Commentary on Genesis,[31] others in my Commentary on Hilk̲ōt Yesīrah,[32] and in my Refutation of Ḥiwi al-Balkhi,[33] in addition to more details which the reader will find in other books of mine. Moreover, the arguments employed by me in the present chapter in refutation of the various opponents of our belief, are all sources[34] of this belief, and strengthen and confirm it.

NOTES

1. For an analysis of the following exposition cf. in particular H.A. Wolfson, 'The Kalam Arguments for Creation in Saadya, Averroes, Maimonides and St. Thomas,' in *Saadya Anniversary Volume*, New York, 1943, pp. 197 ff.

2. The verb *bara'*, by which Gen. 1.1 denotes the act of creation, is used only with reference to God. It implies the totally new and unprecedented. Cf. B. Jacob, *Genesis* (1934), pp. 20–2. Doubt has been expressed as to whether *bara'* necessarily implies the idea of a *creatio ex nihilo*. Cf. S.R. Driver, *The Book of Genesis*, p. 3. Saadya asserts that this is the case. Cf. his *Comm. Isaiah*, p. 123; *La Philosophie de Saadia Gaon*, 1934, Ventura, p. 110. He is followed by Naḥmanides (*Comm. Gen.* 1.21), Maimonides (*Moreh* II.30; III.10), and others, whereas Abraham ibn Ezra holds that *bara'* does not necessarily convey this meaning. Cf. A. Schmiedl, *Studien* (1869), p. 94.

2a. All the four proofs are borrowed from the Kalam. Maimonides' list of seven Kalam proofs includes three of Saadya's four. Cf. Wolfson, *loc. cit.*, pp. 197–8.

3. Cf. Aristotle, *De caelo* I, 5–7.

4. Cf. Aristotle, *Physica* VIII, 10.

5. Aristotle speaks of the force which causes the *motion* of the world. Saadya, who describes the force in question as one which *preserves* the world, i.e. keeps it from corruption, follows a line of argument reported in the name of John Philoponos, who argued that the force which keeps the world from corruption must be finite. Cf. Wolfson, *loc. cit.*, pp. 201–3.

6. John Philoponos concluded from the corruptibility of the world its createdness on the basis of the Aristotelian principle that 'Whatever is corruptible must be generated.' Cf. *De caelo* I, 12, 282b, 2. Saadya's argument must be interpreted in the light of this original version of the idea. Aristotle's own view is that beyond the finite force which is within the body of the world there must be an external bodiless force which causes motion to continue during an *infinite* time. Cf. *Physica* VIII, 10, 266a, 10–11; 267b, 17–26. John Philoponos rejects this assumption on the grounds of Aristotle's own principle, 'That it is impossible that that which is capable of corruption should not at some time be corrupted.' Cf. *De caelo* 283a, 24–5. Saadya omits this essential proposition. See Wolfson, *loc. cit.*

7. Cf. Aristotle, *De caelo* I, 5, 271b, 26: 'The body which moves in a circle must necessarily be finite in every respect.'

8. Cf. Aristotle, *De caelo* I, 6, 274a, 26–8; II, 13, 293a, 24–5; Plato, *Tim.* 31 A, B. Saadya mentions this view also in his *Comm. Yes.*, p. 5 (19). Crescas discusses it in connection with his criticism of Maimonides' proofs of the existence of God. Cf. H.A. Wolfson, *Crescas' Critique of Aristotle* (1929), p. 472.

9. Lit. 'in a natural way.' This does not mean 'according to the laws of Nature,' as Fürst translates, but 'in its natural place.' Every body has its natural place towards which it tends and moves unless impeded by force. Cf. Aristotle, *Physica* IV, 5, 212b, 29; Ventura, p. 97.

10. As Wolfson has shown, Saadya's argument is from design, not from the mere fact of composition. Aristotle proved the existence of God from the composite nature of the world, but held that the world was eternal and determined by an immutable order. Cf. *Physica* I, 7; *Metaphysica* I, 3, 984a, 21–5; XII, 3, 1096b, 35–1070a, 2. Saadya's argument is directed against Aristotle in that it emphasizes not the immutable order of the world, but the fact that the composition of heaven and earth exhibits a certain degree of arbitrariness and deviation from order, which can only be explained by reference to the design of a creator. Cf. Wolfson, *loc. cit.*, pp. 204–8.

11. Saadya makes no mention of the world being composed of matter and form, according to Aristotle, or of atoms and accidents, according to the Kalam, since he wishes to emphasize the aspect of arbitrary design, not the one of order, as explained in the preceding note. Cf. Wolfson, *loc. cit.* Apart from this motive, he adopts neither the Aristotelian distinction between matter and form, nor the Kalam notion of the atom. Cf. Ventura, p. 102.

12. The spheres of the planets were considered to be set one within another like the 'coats of an onion.' Cf. Maimonides, *Yes. ha-Torah* 3.2; Dieterici, *Philosophie der Araber*, vol. I, p. 179; M. Sachs, *Die religiöse Poesie der Juden in Spanien* (1845), p. 230.

13. Since Saadya shares the Aristotelian view that the heavens consist of a subtle ether which is wholly homogenous (cf. below, pp. 145–6), he speaks of the composite nature of the heavens only with reference to their size, form and movements. Cf. *Amānāt*, Landauer, p. 282, (Slucki 144); p. 282; *Comm. Yes.*, p. 33 (53–54); Guttmann, *Die Religionsphilosophie des Saadia*, 1882, p. 38; Ventura, p. 99, n. 29. By stressing the difference of the stars in size and degree of light, Saadya clearly shows that his argument is one from design.

14. Averroes ascribes this argument to the Ash'arites. There exist two versions of it, an earlier and a later one. Saadya uses the earlier version. Cf. Wolfson, *loc. cit.*, pp. 211–4.

15. Arab. *'arad*; Hebr. *miḳreh*. The Arabic philosophers restrict the use of the term to the 2–10 Aristotelian categories, whereas the Mutakallimūn use it in a very wide sense for everything that is not substance (*ḏjawhar*). Cf. *EI*, I, 417. According to some Mu'tazilites, the term includes movement and rest, standing and sitting, composition and separation, length and breadth, colours, tastes, and smells, speech and silence, etc. Ibn al-Murtaba compiled a list of 19 accidents. Cf. Pines, *Beitrage zur Islamischen Atomenlehre*, 1936, pp. 19–20. Saadya employs the term in this wide sense, but he does not follow the Mu'tazilite view, which combines the doctrine of the accidents with the doctrine of the atoms.

16. Directly, like generation and corruption; indirectly, like reflected light, or animals and plants as they affect the earth. Cf. Ventura, p. 103.

17. Cf. *Kuzari*, V, 18; *Moreh*, I, 74.5.

18. According to Aristotle, the celestial bodies are not affected by accidents; their circular motion being eternal, the spheres which perform those motions are likewise eternal. Cf. *Metaphysica*, XII, 7; *Moreh*, I, 74.4; Guttmann, p. 39.

19. As to the coloration of the stars, cf. Plato, *Rep.* 616 e–617 b; Plotinus, *En.* II, 1.7.

20. The definition of the celestial bodies includes both their substance and their accidents, such as motion, colour, etc.

21. Cf. Aristotle, *Metaphysica*, I, 2, 944a, 18–19; *Physica*, VIII, 5, 256a, 11–12; Themistius, *De caelo*, I, 1; Baḥya, *Hoḇōt hal-Leḇaḇōt*, I, 5; *Kuzari*, V, 18; *Moreh*, I, 73(2); 74(2); Spinoza, *Cogitata metaphysica*, II.10; Wolfson, *Crescas' Critique of Aristotle*, pp. 492–3; Z. Diesendruck, 'Saadya's Formulation of the Time-Argument for Creation,' in *Jewish Studies in Memory of George A. Kohut* (1935), pp. 145–58; Wolfson, *Kalam Arguments*, etc., pp. 214–29.

22. The present is a mere geometrical point. Cf. Klatzkin-Zobel, *Thesaurus Philosophicus. . .*, 1928, Vol. III, p. 65.

23. The first part of the argument is based on Aristotle's definition of the infinite as 'that which cannot be traversed.' Saadya paraphrases Aristotle's statement that 'It is impossible to traverse infinites by thought; consequently there are infinites neither upwards nor downwards' (*Anal. Post.*, I, 22, 83b, 6–7). The term 'Uppermost point' (*ṣu'd*) used by Saadya corresponds to the 'Beginning' (ἀρχή) and 'First' (πρῶτον) in Aristotle. Like Aristotle, Saadya holds that in an infinite series there is no beginning and no first which thought could reach. Cf. Wolfson, *Kalam Arguments*, etc., p. 215.

24. The basis of this argument is the principle that 'If there is no first there is no cause at all.' Cf. Aristotle, *Metaphysica*, II, 2, 994a, 18–19. Aristotle himself, however, combines the principle of the impossibility of an infinite series with the principle of the eternity of the world by distinguishing between an essential causal series and an accidental causal series. An infinite causal series is possible, according to him, when the causes and effects exist in succession to each other, which is the case with the relation of the successive revolutions of the spheres and with the successive generations of man. This 'accidental' series can go on to infinity. On the difference between Aristotle and the Kalam, which Saadya does not discuss, see Maimonides, *Moreh*, I, 73 (11); Wolfson, *loc. cit.*, pp. 222 ff.

25. The well-known argument of Zeno.

26. Ibn Ḥazm in the first of his five proofs for the existence of the atom argues: If there were no indivisible atom one would traverse an infinite space by walking any distance. Cf. Pines, p. 11.

27. According to Naẓẓām, a moving body does not touch all the parts of the space in which it moves, but leaps over some of them. Cf. Pines, ibid.; Guttmann, p. 43, n. 1.

28. Cf. Aristotle, *Physica,* Vi, 1, 233a, 21–3.

29. Arab. *wahm;* Tibbon translates it by *maḥshabah.* The Arabic philosophers sometimes use the term *bi'-l-wahm* in the sense of 'potentially.' Cf. Pines, p. 12.

30. Arab. *fi'l;* hebr. *pō'al;* actuality, reality. Naẓẓām seems to have assumed the actual existence of infinite parts. Ibn Sinna rejects this view. Cf. Pines, *ibid.* In admitting an infinite divisibility *in potentia,* Saadya follows Aristotle, *Physica,* III, 6, 206b, 12–13; Ventura, p. 108.

31. In an extract from Saadya's lost Commentary on Genesis, which is extant in R. Yehudah b. Barzillai's Commentary on the *Sefer Yeṣirah* (ed. S.J. Halberstam, Berlin, 1885), p. 89, reference is made to the argument for Creation from the fact that the created beings require time, space and a preserving force.

32. Cf. *Comm. Yeṣ.,* pp. 3–4 (16–17); 11–12 (27–8).

33. Cf. I. Davidson, *Saadia's Polemic against Ḥiwi al-Balkhi,* New York (1913), pp. 74–5, where it is said, 'Through them (i.e. the accidents) we learn that it (the world) is new (i.e. *creata ex nihilo*).' See note 241 by Davidson.

34. Arab. *mawādd.* Cf. above, p. 36, n. 1.

3. *The Transcendence of the Creator: Arguments for the* Creatio ex Nihilo

Having made it perfectly clear to myself that all things are created, I considered the question whether it was possible that they had created themselves, or whether the only possible assumption is that they were created by someone external to them. In my view it is impossible that they should have created themselves, for a number of reasons of which I shall mention three. The first reason is this: Let us assume that an existing body has produced itself. It stands to reason that after having brought itself into existence that particular body should be stronger and more capable of producing its like than before. For if it was able to produce itself when it was in a relatively weak state, it should all the more be able to produce its like now that it is relatively strong. But seeing that it is incapable of creating its like now when it is relatively strong, it is absurd to think that it created itself when it was relatively weak. The second reason is: If we imagine that a thing has created itself, we shall find that the question of the time when it did so presents an insuperable difficulty. For if we say that the thing created itself before it came into being, then we assume that it was non-existent at the time when it created itself, and obviously something non-existent cannot create a thing. If, on the other hand, we say that it created itself after it had come into being, the obvious comment is that after a thing has come into existence there is no need for it to create itself. There is no third instant between 'before' and 'after' except the present which, however, has no duration in which an action can take place.[1] The third reason is: If we assume that a body is able to create itself, we must necessarily admit that at the same time it is likewise capable of abstaining from the act of self-creation.[2] Under this assumption we shall find that the body is both existent and non-existent at the same time. For in speaking of the body as *capable*, we take it to be existent, but in going on to speak of it as being capable of abstaining from the act of self-creation, we assume it to be non-existent. Obviously, to attribute existence and non-existence to the same thing at the same time is utterly absurd. I found that Scripture had already anticipated the refutation of this belief, namely, that things created themselves, by saying, 'It is He that hath made us, not we' (Ps. 100.3),[3] and by rebuking the one who said, 'My river is mine own, and I have made it for myself' (Ez. 39.3).[4]

Having proved by these arguments that things can on no account have created themselves, and that they must necessarily be regarded as created by a Creator who is external to them, I tried to reason out an answer to the question whether the Creator made them from something (*prima materia*) or from nothing (*ex nihilo*) as revealed in the Scriptures.[5] I found that it is wrong to assume that things were created from something already existent. Such a view is self-contradictory, because the term *creation* implies that the substance[6] of the thing is created and has a beginning in time, whilst the qualifying statement, 'From something' implies that its substance was eternal, uncreated and without beginning in time. If we assume that things were created *ex nihilo*, there is no self-contradiction.

Someone may raise the following objection: 'You have affirmed as a conclusion acceptable to Reason that things have a Creator because in the realm of sense perception you have witnessed that nothing is made without a maker. But you likewise find in the realm of sense perception that nothing comes from nothing.[7] Why, then, have you made use of the proposition that nothing is made except by a maker, and have ignored the proposition that everything comes from something already existent,[8] seeing that the two propositions are equally valid? My answer is: The problem which forms the object of my inquiry, and to the solution of which my arguments are directed, is the question whether or not the world is created *ex nihilo*. Obviously it is inadmissible that a proposition which is under examination should be adduced as evidence in favour of itself against an alternative proposition.[9] We must seek evidence on its behalf from elsewhere; and since the principle that nothing is made except by a maker has a bearing on the subject-matter of our inquiry, I applied this to the solution of our problem, and it led to the conclusion that the world is created *ex nihilo*. I followed this procedure although I found that in certain cases it is permissible to use a proposition in this way as evidence;[10] but this is a subtle matter which lies outside the province of this book.[11] I, therefore, decided to leave it alone and to follow the plain course.

Another point which I made clear to myself is this: Whatever we imagine to be the thing from which the existent beings were created, it must necessarily be assumed to have existed from all eternity.[12] But if it were pre-existent, it would be equal to the Creator in regard to its eternity. From this it follows that God would not have had the power to create things out of it, since it would not have accepted His command, nor allowed itself to be affected according to His wish and shaped accordingly to His design,[13] except if we were to imagine, in addition to these two, the existence of a third cause which intervened between the two with the result that the one of the two became the Maker, and the other the thing made. But such a view would postulate the existence of something which does not exist; for we have never found anything except a maker and the thing made.

I remembered further that the principal object of our inquiry was to find out who created the substance of things. Now it is well known to us that the maker must necessarily be prior to the thing made by him, and that, by virtue of his being prior to the substance of the thing, the thing becomes one that is created in time. Should we, however, believe the substance to be eternal, the maker would not be prior to the thing created by him, and neither of the two could claim priority so as to be the cause of the other's existence, which is completely absurd.

There is another point which I remembered: The assertion that God created the world from something already existent must inevitably lead to the conclusion that He created nothing at all. For the reason which causes us to think that the world originated from something (*prima materia*) is the fact that such is the way we find the objects of sense perception come into being. Now it is common ground that the objects of sense perception are also found to exist in Space and Time, in shape and form, in measured quantity, in a fixed position and mutual relation, and other similar conditions.[14] All of these experiences are on the same footing[15] as the experience that everything comes from something. Now if we are going to allow all these experiences their full weight and say that things were created from something which existed in Time, Space, form, quantity, position, relation, etc., all this would have to be considered as eternal, and nothing would remain to be created. Creation would become meaningless altogether.[16]

I went still further, arguing that if we fail to admit the existence of something which has nothing prior to it, it is impossible for us to accept the fact that there exists anything at all. For if we consider in our mind that one thing comes from another thing, we have to predicate the same thing of the second as of the first, and say that it could only have come into being from a third thing; the same predicate again must be made of the third thing, namely that it could only have come into being from a fourth thing, and so *ad infinitum.* Since, however, an infinite series cannot be completed, it follows that we are not in existence. But, behold, we are in existence, and unless the things which preceded us were finite (in number), they could not have been completed so as to reach us.[17]

What we have deduced from the postulates of Reason, has also been intimated in the Books of the Prophets, namely, that material bodies originate from the design of the Creator, as is said, 'Before the mountains were brought forth, or ever Thou hadst formed the earth and the world, even from everlasting to everlasting, Thou art God' (Ps. 90.2).

NOTES

1. Cf. above, p. 56 n. 3.
2. 'Capability' as distinct from necessity implies freedom of choice. Necessity of creation is incompatible with creation in time. Cf. *Moreh*, II, Prop. 18.
3. Cf. the passage *Gen. R.* 100.1, which, after quoting Ps. 100.3, continues, 'R. Yehudah b. Simon said, "Ye shall know that the Lord God hath made us, and that we have not made ourselves".'
4. Referring to Pharaoh and the Nile.
5. Cf. above, p. 51, n. 2.
6. Arab. *'ayn;* Hebr. *eṣem.*
7. Lit. 'That everything comes into being from something.'
8. Cf. D. Kaufmann, *Geschichte der AttributenLehre in der jüdischen Religionsphilosophie des Mitelalters von Saadja bis Maimûni*, 1877, p. 6, and Ventura, *loc. cit.*, p. 110, both of whom explain the sentence in the sense of 'Why did you accept as decisive the one sense experience and not the other?'
9. Arab. *manzila;* Hebr. *ma'alah;* degree, rank, here used in the sense of proposition, conclusion. Cf. also *Amānāt*, p. 73 (39); Ventura, p. 111, n. 77.—Saadya's answer is that his aim is the solution of the problem whether or not the world is created *ex nihilo*. It would, therefore, have been a *petitio principii*, had he allowed the sense experience which testifies that nothing comes from nothing, to influence his rational argument.
10. In the interpretation of this obscure sentence we follow Ventura (p. 111) against Kaufmann (Attrib.-Lehre, p. 7), although we admit that even Ventura's suggestion is not wholly satisfactory. According to Ventura, Saadya refers to the logical possibility of using the proposition as a premise on condition that the sense of the term is more comprehensive in the premise than in the conclusion.
11. A distinction of this kind, Saadya means to say, is out of place in a book which is not a treatise on logic.
12. Arab. *ḳadīm.*
13. Saadya advances the same argument in *Comm. Yeṣ.*, p. 4 (18). Cf. al-Sharastānī, *Religionspartheien und Philosophen-Schulen*, trans. by T. Haarbrucker, 1850–51, I, p. 135; Guttmann, p. 44, n.1.
14. A reference to the ten Aristotelian Categories.
15. Lit. 'have the same title'; Arab. *ḥaḳ.*
16. The same argument is found in *Comm. Yeṣ.*, p. 4 (18).
17. Cf. above, p. 56.

HALEVI, *KUZARI*

Translation by Hartwig Hirschfeld

PART I

44. Al Khazari: It is strange that you should possess authentic chronology of the creation of the world.

45. The Rabbi: Surely we reckon according to it, and there is no difference between the Jews of Khazar and Ethiopia in this respect.

46. Al Khazari: What date do you consider it at present?

47. The Rabbi: Four thousand and nine hundred years. The details can be demonstrated from the lives of Adam, Seth and Enōsh to Noah; then Shem and Eber to Abraham; then Isaac and Jacob to Moses. All of them represented the essence and purity of Adam on account of their intimacy with God. Each of them had children only to be compared to them outwardly, but not really like them, and, therefore, without direct union with the divine influence. The chronology was established through the medium of those sainted persons who were only single individuals, and not a crowd, until Jacob begat the Twelve Tribes, who were all under this divine influence. Thus the divine element reached a multitude of persons who carried the records further. The chronology of those who lived before these has been handed down to us by Moses.

48. Al Khazari: An arrangement of this kind removes any suspicion of untruth or common plot. Not ten people could discuss such a thing without disagreeing, and disclosing their secret understanding; nor could they refute any one who tried to establish the truth of a matter like this. How is it possible where such a mass of people is concerned? Finally, the period involved is not large enough to admit untruth and fiction.

49. The Rabbi: That is so. Abraham himself lived during the period of the separation of languages. He and his relatives retained the language of his grandfather Eber, which for that reason is called Hebrew. Four hundred years after him appeared Moses at a time when the world was rich in information concerning the heavens and earth. He approached Pharaoh and the Doctors of Egypt, as well as those of the Israelites. Whilst agreeing with him they questioned him, and completely refused to believe that God spoke with man, until he caused them to hear the Ten

Words. In the same way the people were on his side, not from ignorance, but on account of the knowledge they possessed. They feared magic and astrological arts, and similar snares, things which, like deceit, do not bear close examination, whereas the divine might is like pure gold, ever increasing in brilliancy. How could one imagine that an attempt had been made to show that a language spoken five hundred years previously was none but Eber's own language split up in Babel during the days of Peleg; also to trace the origin of this or that nation back to Shem or Ham, and the same with their countries? Is it likely that any one could to-day invent false statements concerning the origin, history, and languages of well-known nations, the latter being less than five hundred years old?

50. Al Khazari: This is not possible. How could it be, since we possess books in the handwriting of their authors written five hundred years ago? No false interpolation could enter the contents of a book which is not above five hundred years of age, such as genealogical tables, linguistic and other works.

51. The Rabbi: Now why should Moses' speeches remain uncontradicted? Did not his own people raise objections, not to speak of others?

52. Al Khazari: These things are handed down well founded and firmly established.

53. The Rabbi: Dost thou think that the languages are eternal and without beginning?

54. Al Khazari: No; they undoubtedly had a beginning, which originated in a conventional manner. Evidence of this is found in their composition of nouns, verbs, and particles. They originated from sounds derived from the organs of speech.

[55. The Rabbi: Didst thou ever see any one who contrived a language, or didst thou hear of him?]

56. Al Khazari: Neither the one nor the other. There is no doubt that it appeared at some time, but prior to this there was no language concerning which one nation, to the exclusion of another, could come to any agreement.

57. The Rabbi: Didst thou ever hear of a nation which possessed different traditions with regard to the generally acknowledged week which begins with the Sunday and ends with the Sabbath? How is it possible that the people of China could agree with those of the western islands without common beginning, agreement and convention?

58. Al Khazari: Such a thing would only have been possible if they had all come to an agreement. This, however, is improbable, unless all men are the descendants of Adam, of Noah, or of some other ancestor from whom they received the hebdomadal calculation.

59. The Rabbi: That is what I meant. East and West agree on the decimal system. What instinct induced them to keep to the number *ten*, unless it was a tradition handed down by the first one who did so?

60. Al Khazari: Does it not weaken thy belief if thou art told that the Indians have antiquities and buildings which they consider to be millions of years old?

61. The Rabbi: It would, indeed, weaken my belief had they a fixed form of religion, or a book concerning which a multitude of people held the same opinion, and in which no historical discrepancy could be found. Such a book, however, does not exist. Apart from this, they are a dissolute, unreliable people, and arouse the indignation of the followers of religions through their talk, whilst they anger them with their idols, talismans, and witchcraft. To such things they pin their faith, and deride those who boast of the possession of a divine book. Yet they only possess a few books, and these were written to mislead the weak-minded. To this class belong astrological writings, in which they speak of ten thousands of years, as the book on the Nabataean Agriculture, in which are mentioned the names of Janbūshār, Sagrīt and Roanai. It is believed that they lived before Adam, who was the disciple of Janbūshār, and such like.

62. Al Khazari: If I had supported my arguments by reference to a negro people, i.e. a people not united upon a common law, thy answer would have been correct. Now what is thy opinion of the philosophers who, as the result of their careful researches, agree that the world is without beginning, and here it does not concern tens of thousands, and not millions, but unlimited numbers of years?

63. The Rabbi: There is an excuse for the Philosophers. Being Grecians, science and religion did not come to them as inheritances. They belong to the descendants of Japheth, who inhabited the north, whilst that knowledge coming from Adam, and supported by the divine influence, is only to be found among the progeny of Shem, who represented the successors of Noah and constituted, as it were, his essence. This knowledge has always been connected with this essence, and will always remain so. The Greeks only received it when they became powerful, from Persia. The Persians had it from the Chaldaeans. It was only then that the famous [Greek] Philosophers arose, but as soon as Rome assumed political leadership they produced no philosopher worthy the name.

64. Al Khazari: Does this mean that Aristotle's philosophy is not deserving of credence?

65. The Rabbi: Certainly. He exerted his mind, because he had no

tradition from any reliable source at his disposal. He meditated on the beginning and end of the world, but found as much difficulty in the theory of a beginning as in that of eternity. Finally, these abstract speculations which made for eternity, prevailed, and he found no reason to inquire into the chronology or derivation of those who lived before him. Had he lived among a people with well authenticated and generally acknowledged traditions, he would have applied his deductions and arguments to establish the theory of creation, however difficult, instead of eternity, which is even much more difficult to accept.

66. Al Khazari: Is there any decisive proof?

67. The Rabbi: Where could we find one for such a question? Heaven forbid that there should be anything in the Bible to contradict that which is manifest or proved! On the other hand it tells of miracles and the changes of ordinary, things newly arising, or changing one into the other. This proves that the Creator of the world is able to accomplish what He will, and whenever He will. The question of eternity and creation is obscure, whilst the arguments are evenly balanced. The theory of creation derives greater weight from the prophetic tradition of Adam, Noah, and Moses, which is more deserving of credence than mere speculation. If, after all, a believer in the Law finds himself compelled to admit an eternal matter and the existence of many worlds prior to this one, this would not impair his belief that *this* world was created at a certain epoch, and that Adam and Noah were the first human beings.

MAIMONIDES, *MOREH NEVUKHIM*

Translation by Michael Friedlander

PART II, CHAPTER 13

Among those who believe in the existence of God, there are found three different theories as regards the question whether the Universe is eternal or not.

First Theory—Those who follow the Law of Moses, our Teacher, hold that the whole Universe, *i.e.*, everything except God, has been brought by Him into existence out of non-existence. In the beginning God alone existed, and nothing else; neither angels, nor spheres, nor the things that are contained within the spheres existed. He then produced from nothing all existing things such as they are by His will and desire. Even time itself is among the things created; for time depends on motion, *i.e.*, on an accident in things which move, and the things upon whose motion time depends are themselves created beings, which have passed from non-existence into existence. We say that God *existed* before the creation of the Universe, although the verb *existed* appears to imply the notion of time; we also believe that He existed an infinite space of time before the Universe was created; but in these cases we do not mean time in its true sense. We only use the term to signify something analogous or similar to time. For time is undoubtedly an accident, and, according to our opinion, one of the created accidents, like blackness and whiteness; it is not a quality, but an accident connected with motion. This must be clear to all who understand what Aristotle has said on time and its real existence.

(The following remark does not form an essential part of our present research; it will nevertheless be found useful in the course of this discussion. Many scholars do not know what time really is, and men like Galen were so perplexed about it as to ask whether time has a real existence or not; the reason for this uncertainty is to be found in the circumstance that time is an accident of an accident. Accidents which are directly connected with material bodies, *e.g.*, colour and taste, are easily understood, and correct notions are formed of them. There are, however, accidents which are connected with other accidents, *e.g.*, the splendour of colour, or the inclination and the curvature of a line; of these it is very difficult to form a correct notion, especially when the accident which forms the substratum for the other accident is not constant but variable. Both difficulties are present in the notion of time: it is an accident of motion, which is itself an accident of a moving object; besides, it is not a fixed property; on the contrary, its true and essential condition is, not to remain in the same state for two consecutive moments. This is the source of ignorance about the nature of time.

We consider time a thing created; it comes into existence in the same manner as other accidents, and the substances which form the substratum for the accidents. For this reason, viz., because time belongs to the things created, it cannot be said that God produced the Universe *in the beginning*. Consider this well; for he who does not understand it, is unable to refute forcible objections raised against the theory of *Creatio ex nihilo*. If you admit the existence of time before the Creation, you will be compelled to accept the theory of the Eternity of the Universe. For time is an accident and requires a substratum. You will therefore have to assume that something [beside God] existed before this Universe was created, an assumption which it is our duty to oppose.)

This is the first theory, and it is undoubtedly a fundamental principle of the Law of our teacher Moses; it is next in importance to the principle of God's unity. Do not follow any other theory. Abraham, our father, was the first that taught it, after he had established it by philosophical research. He proclaimed, therefore, "the name of the Lord the God of the Universe" (Gen. xxi. 33); and he had previously expressed this theory in the words, "The possessor of heaven and earth" (ibid. xiv. 22).

Second Theory—The theory of all philosophers whose opinions and works are known to us is this: It is impossible to assume that God produced anything from nothing, or that He reduces anything to nothing; that is to say, it is impossible that an object consisting of matter and form should be produced when that matter is absolutely absent, or that it should be destroyed in such a manner that that matter be absolutely no longer in existence. To say of God that He can produce a thing from nothing or reduce a thing to nothing is, according to the opinion of these philosophers, the same as if we were to say that He could cause one substance to have at the same time two opposite properties, or produce another being like Himself, or change Himself into a body, or produce a square the diagonal of which be equal to its side, or similar impossibilities. The philosophers thus believe that it is no defect in the Supreme Being that He does not produce impossibilities, for the nature of what which is impossible is constant—it does not depend on the action of an agent, and for this reason it cannot be changed. Similarly there is, according to them, no defect in the greatness of God, when He is unable to produce a thing from nothing, because they consider this as one of the impossibilities. They therefore assume that a certain substance has co-existed with God from eternity in such a manner that neither God existed without that substance nor the latter without God. But they do not hold that the existence of that substance equals in rank that of God; for God is the cause of that existence, and the substance is in the same relation to God as the clay is to the potter, or the iron to the smith; God can do with it what He pleases: at one time He forms of it heaven and earth, at another time He forms some other thing. Those who hold this view also assume that the heavens are transient, that they came into existence, though not from nothing, and may cease to exist, although they cannot be reduced to nothing. They are transient in the same manner as the individuals among living beings which are produced from some existing substance, and are again reduced to some substance that remains in existence. The process of genesis and destruction is, in the case of the heavens, the same as in that of earthly beings.

The followers of this theory are divided into different schools, whose opinions and principles it is useless to discuss here; but what I have mentioned is common to all of them. Plato holds the same opinion. Aristotle says in his book *Physics,* that according to Plato the heavens are transient. This view is also stated in Plato's *Timaeus.* His opinion, however, does not agree with our belief; only superficial and careless persons wrongly assume that Plato has the same belief as we have. For whilst we hold that the heavens have been created from absolutely nothing, Plato believes that they have been formed out of something.—This is the second theory.

Third Theory—viz., that of Aristotle, his followers, and commentators. Aristotle maintains, like the adherents of the second theory, that a corporeal object cannot be produced without a corporeal substance. He goes, however, farther, and contends that the heavens are indestructible. For he holds that the Universe in its totality has never been different, nor will it ever change: the heavens, which form the permanent element in the Universe, and are not subject to genesis and destruction, have always been so; time and motion are eternal, permanent, and have neither beginning nor end; the sublunary world, which includes the transient elements, has always been the same, because the *materia prima* is itself eternal, and merely combines successively with different forms; when one form is removed, another is assumed. This whole arrangement, therefore, both above and here below, is never disturbed or interrupted, and nothing is produced contrary to the laws or the ordinary course of Nature. He further says—though not in the same terms—that he considers it impossible for God to change His will or conceive a new desire; that God produced this Universe in its totality by His will, but not from nothing. Aristotle finds it as impossible to assume that God changes His will or conceives a new desire, as to believe that He is non-existing, or that His essence is changeable. Hence it follows that this Universe has always been the same in the past, and will be the same eternally.

This is a full account of the opinions of those who consider that the existence of God, the First Cause of the Universe, has been established by proof. But it would be quite useless to mention the opinions of those who do not recognize the existence of God, but believe that the existing state of things is the result of accidental combination and separation of the elements, and that the Universe has no Ruler or Governor. Such is the theory of Epicurus and his school, and similar philosophers, as stated by Alexander [Aphrodisiensis]; it would be superfluous to repeat their views, since the existence of God has been demonstrated, whilst their theory is built upon a basis proved to be untenable. It is likewise useless to prove the correctness of the followers of the second theory in asserting that the heavens are transient, because they at the same time believe in the Eternity of the Universe, and so long as this theory is adopted, it makes no difference to us whether it is believed that the heavens are transient, and that only their substance is eternal, or the heavens are held to be indestructible, in accordance with the view of Aristotle. All who follow the Law of Moses, our Teacher, and Abraham, our Father, and all who adopt similar theories, assume that nothing is eternal except God, and that the theory of *Creatio ex nihilo* includes nothing that is impossible, whilst some thinkers even regard it as an established truth.

PART II, CHAPTER 25

We do not reject the Eternity of the Universe, because certain passages in Scripture confirm the Creation; for such passages are not more numerous than those in which God is represented as a corporeal being; nor is it impossible or difficult to find for them a suitable interpretation. We might have explained them in the same manner as we did in respect to the Incorporeality of God. We should perhaps have had an easier task in showing that the Scriptural passages referred to are in harmony with the theory of the Eternity of the Universe if we accepted the latter, than we had in explaining the anthropomorphisms in the Bible when we rejected the idea that God is corporeal. For two reasons, however, we have not done so, and have not accepted the Eternity of the Universe. First, the Incorporeality of God has been demonstrated by proof; those passages in the Bible, which in their literal sense contain statements that can be refuted by proof, must and can be interpreted otherwise. But the Eternity of the Universe has not been proved; a mere argument in favour of a certain theory is not sufficient reason for rejecting the literal meaning of a Biblical text, and explaining it figuratively, when the opposite theory can be supported by an equally good argument.

Secondly, our belief in the Incorporeality of God is not contrary to any of the fundamental principles of our religion; it is not contrary to the words of any prophet. Only ignorant people believe that it is contrary to the teaching of Scripture; but we have shown that this is not the case; on the contrary, Scripture teaches the Incorporeality of God. If we were to accept the Eternity of the Universe as taught by Aristotle, that everything in the Universe is the result of fixed laws, that Nature does not change, and that there is nothing supernatural, we should necessarily be in opposition to the foundation of our religion, we should disbelieve all miracles and signs, and certainly reject all hopes and fears derived from Scripture, unless the miracles are also explained figuratively. The Allegorists amongst the Mahometans have done this, and have thereby arrived at absurd conclusions. If, however, we accepted the Eternity of the Universe in accordance with the second of the theories which we have expounded above, and assumed, with Plato, that the heavens are likewise transient, we should not be in opposition to the fundamental principles of our religion; this theory would not imply the rejection of miracles, but, on the contrary, would admit them as possible. The Scriptural text might have been explained accordingly, and many expressions might have been found in the Bible and in other writings that would confirm and support this theory. But there is no necessity for this expedient, so long as the theory has not been proved. As there is no proof sufficient to convince us, this theory need not be taken into consideration, nor the other one; we take the text of the Bible literally, and say that it teaches us a truth which we cannot prove; and the miracles are evidence for the correctness of our view.

Accepting the Creation, we find that miracles are possible, that Revelation is possible, and that every difficulty in this question is removed. We might be asked, Why has God inspired a certain person and not another? why has He revealed the Law to one particular nation, and at one particular time? why has He commanded this, and forbidden that? why has He shown through a prophet certain particular miracles? what is the object of these laws? and why has He not made the commandments and the prohibitions part of our nature, if it was His object that we should live in accordance with them? We answer to all these questions: He willed it so; or, His wisdom decided so. Just as He created the world according to His will, at a certain time, in a certain form, and as we do not understand why His will or His wisdom decided upon that peculiar form, and upon that peculiar time, so we do not know why His will or wisdom determined any of the things mentioned in the preceding questions. But if we assume that the Universe has the present form as the result of fixed laws, there is occasion for the above questions; and these could only be answered in an objectionable way, implying denial and rejection of the Biblical texts, the correctness of which no intelligent person doubts. Owing to the absence of all proof, we reject the theory of the Eternity of the Universe; and it is for this very reason that the noblest minds spent and will spend their days in research. For if the Creation had been demonstrated by proof, even if only according to the Platonic hypothesis, all arguments of the philosophers against us would be of no avail. If, on the other hand, Aristotle had a proof for his theory, the whole teaching of Scripture would be rejected, and we should be forced to other opinions. I have thus shown that all depends on this question. Note it.

PART II, CHAPTER 27

We have already stated that the belief in the Creation is a fundamental principle of our religion; but we do not consider it a principle of our faith that the Universe will again be reduced to nothing. It is not contrary to the tenets of our religion to assume that the Universe will continue to exist for ever. It might be objected that everything produced is subject to destruction, as has been shown; consequently the Universe, having had a beginning, must come to an end. This axiom cannot be applied according to our views. We do not hold that the Universe came into existence, like all things in Nature, as the result of the laws of Nature. For whatever owes its existence to the action of physical laws is, according to the same laws, subject to destruction: the same law which caused the existence of a thing after a period of non-existence, is also the cause that the thing is not permanent; since the previous non-existence proves that the nature of that thing does not necessitate its permanent existence. According to our theory, taught in Scripture, the existence or non-existence of things depends solely on the will of God and not on fixed laws, and, therefore, it does not follow that God must destroy the Universe after having created it from nothing. It depends on His will. He may, according to His desire, or according to the decree of His wisdom, either destroy it, or allow it to exist, and it is therefore possible that he will preserve the Universe for ever, and let it exist permanently as He Himself exists. It is well known that our Sages never said that the throne of glory will perish, although they assumed that it has been created. No prophet or sage ever maintained that the throne of glory will be destroyed or annihilated; but, on the contrary, the Scriptural passages speak of its permanent existence. We are of opinion that the souls of the pious have been created, and at the same time we believe that they are immortal. Some hold, in accordance with the literal meaning of the Midrashim, that the bodies of the pious will also enjoy everlasting happiness. Their notion is like the well-known belief of certain people, that there are bodily enjoyments in Paradise. In short, reasoning leads to the conclusion that the destruction of the Universe is not a certain fact. There remains only the question as to which the prophets and our Sages say on this point; whether they affirm that the world will certainly come to an end, or not. Most people amongst us believe that such statements have been made, and that the world will at one time be destroyed. I will show you that this is not the case; and that, on the contrary, many passages in the Bible speak of the permanent existence of the Universe. Those passages which, in the literal sense, would indicate the destruction of the Universe, are undoubtedly to be understood in a figurative sense, as will be shown. If, however, those who follow the literal sense of the Scriptural texts reject our view, and assume that the ultimate certain destruction of the Universe is part of their faith, they are at liberty to do so. But we must tell them that the belief in the destruction is not necessarily implied in the belief in the Creation; they believe it because they trust the writer, who used a figurative expression, which they take literally. Their faith, however, does not suffer by it.

PART II, CHAPTER 30

There is a difference between *first* and *beginning* (or principle). The latter exists in the thing of which it is the beginning, or co-exists with it; it need not precede it; *e.g.*, the heart is the beginning of the living being; the element is the beginning of that of which it is the basis. The term "*first*" is likewise applied to things of this kind; but is also employed in cases where precedence in time alone is to be expressed, and the thing which precedes is not the beginning (or the cause) of the thing that follows. *E.g.*, we say A. was the first inhabitant of this house, after him came B.; this does not imply that A. is the cause of B. inhabiting the house. In Hebrew, *techillah* is used in the sense of "first"; *e.g.*, when God first (*techillath*) spake to Hosea (Hos. i. 1), and the "beginning" is expressed by *reshith*, derived from *rosh*, "head," the principal part of the living being as regards position. The Universe has not been created out of an element that preceded it in time, since time itself formed a part of the Creation. For this reason Scripture employs the term "*bereshith*" (in a principle), in which the *beth* is a preposition denoting "in." The true explanation of the first verse of Genesis is as follows: "In [creating] a principle God created the beings above and the things below." This explanation is in accordance with the theory of the Creation. We find that some of our Sages are reported to have held the opinion that time existed before the Creation. But this report is very doubtful, because the theory that time cannot be imagined with a beginning, has been taught by Aristotle, as I showed you, and is objectionable. Those who have made this assertion have been led to it by a saying of one of our Sages in reference to the terms "one day," "a second day." Taking these terms literally, the author of that saying asked, What determined "the first day," since there was no rotating sphere, and no sun? and continues as follows: Scripture uses the term "one day"; R. Jehudah, son of R. Simon, said: "Hence we learn that the divisions of time have existed previously." R. Abahu said, "Hence we learn that God built worlds and again destroyed them." This latter exposition is still worse than the former. Consider the difficulty which these two Rabbis found in the statement that time existed before the creation of the sun. We shall undoubtedly soon remove this difficulty, unless these two Rabbis intended to infer from the Scriptural text that the divisions of time must have existed before the Creation, and thus adopted the theory of the Eternity of the Universe. But every religious man rejects this. The above saying is, in my opinion, certainly of the same character as that of R. Eliezer, "Whence were the heavens created," &c. (chap. xxvi.) In short, in these questions, do not take notice of the utterances of any person. I told you that the foundation of our faith is the belief that God created the Universe from nothing; that time did not exist previously, but was created; for it depends on the motion of the sphere, and the sphere has been created.

You must know that the particle *eth* in the phrase *eth ha-shamayim ve-eth ha-arez* ("the heavens and the earth") signifies "together with"; our Sages have explained the word in the same sense in many instances. Accordingly they assume that God created with the heavens everything the heavens contain, and with the earth everything the earth includes. They further say that the simultaneous Creation of the heavens and the earth is implied in the words, "I call unto them, they stand up together" (Ps. xlviii). Consequently, all things were created together, but were separated from each other successively. Our Sages illustrated this by the following simile: We sow various seeds at the same time; some spring forth after one day, some after two, and some after three days, although all have been sown at the same time. According to this interpretation, which is undoubtedly correct, the difficulty is removed, which led R. Jehudah, son of R. Simon, to utter the above saying, and consisted in the doubt as to the thing by which the first day, the second, and the third were determined. In Bereshith Rabbah, our Sages, speaking of the light created on the first day according to the Scriptural account, say as follows: these lights [of the luminaries mentioned in the Creation of the fourth day] are the same that were created on the first day, but were only fixed in their places on the fourth day. The meaning [of the first verse] has thus been clearly stated. . .

ALBO, *IKKARIM*

Translation by Isaac Husik

BOOK I, CHAPTER 12

Creation *ex nihilo* is a dogma which every one who professes a divine law is obliged to believe, in the same way as he who professes the Law of Moses is obliged to believe that the earth opened her mouth and swallowed up Korah and his congregation, because they rebelled against Moses. But it is not one of the fundamental principles of divine law, whose existence can not be conceived without it.[1] The story of creation at the beginning of the Torah is not intended to teach that creation *ex nihilo* is a fundamental principle of the Torah, as many authorities have thought. It is true that if one believes in the eternity of the world after the manner of Aristotle, it follows that God can not lengthen the wing of a fly, nor create an ant having only four legs. Moreover, he who entertains such belief must deny all the miracles of the Torah. For he can not believe that God has the power to change a rod into a serpent momentarily, or water into blood, or dust into vermin. More than that, he would have to deny the existence of Moses and the Messiah, because an individual whose existence must be preceded by the existence of an infinite number of individuals can never exist, for the infinite can never be completed. Thus the whole Torah falls to the ground. But one may believe that there is a primary eternal matter, from which the world was created when and as God willed. Such an opinion as this does not contradict the miracles and wonders of the Torah. For all those miracles, which consist in a change of natural law and custom, are instances of something coming from something and not something from nothing, for example the rod turning into a serpent, or water, though a simple substance, changing instantaneously into blood. A simple substance can not change into blood. This is the reason why water is not nourishing to an animal. Yet God through Moses gave to one portion of the water the form of fire, to another portion the form of air, to a third the form of earth. Then these portions were mixed together, so that they combined and were transubstantiated instantaneously into blood. The change was not merely apparent, for if it had been only in appearance and not in substance, the fish would not have died, nor the river become foul. Similarly all the transubstantiatory miracles of the Torah and the Prophets are instances of something coming from something and not of something coming from nothing. Much more is this true of those miracles in which there is no transubstantiation but merely a change in quality or accident, like the instance of Moses' hand turning leprous and as white as snow.[2]

It follows therefore that though a person who believes in the eternity of the world as Aristotle conceives the doctrine, is a denier of the Torah and its miracles, one who conceives the doctrine of eternity in the manner mentioned before, does not deny the Teorah or its miracles, for belief in the Torah and the miracles does not imply belief in creation *ex nihilo*. This is why we said in the preceding chapter that the purpose of the first section of Genesis is merely to teach the existence of the Maker, which is the first essential principle of the existence of a divine law, without which it can not be conceived. As to creation *ex nihilo*, it is indeed a dogma which every one professing the Torah is obliged to believe, as he is obliged to believe that Moses split the rock so that the water flowed, that he caused the quails to fly and the manna to descend, but it is not one of the fundamental principles of divine law. For this reason Maimonides did not include it among the fundamental dogmas of the Torah. This becomes even more significant if we observe that in "Madda',"[3] in the third chapter of the treatise *On Repentance*, he enumerates five classes of heretics, one of them being the person who denies that God alone is the first and the Creator of all. For it is clear that one who believes in a primary eternal matter, by implication denies that God alone is the first, for primary matter is coeval with God according to this notion. We see then that though Maimonides calls that one a heretic who does not believe in creation *ex nihilo*, yet he does not include this doctrine among the fundamental principles, because it is not a principle without which divine law can not be conceived. It follows therefore that the purpose of beginning the Torah with the creation story is to teach the existence of the Maker, which is the first fundamental and essential principle of divine law, as we said before.

NOTES

1. This distinction between a fundamental principle and a true belief is also taken from Crescas. See Or Adonai, III, beg.: באמונות האמתיות . . . והנה לא ראינו לשומם מכלל פנות התורה למה שאם היות האמונה בהם מחוייבת . . . הנה כבר יצוייר מציאות התורה זולתם.

2. Ex. 4, 6.

3. See above, p. 44, note 1.

BOOK II, CHAPTER 18[1]

The third dogma is that God is independent of time. This means that God existed before time and will exist after time ceases, therefore His power is infinite. For every one who is dependent upon time is necessarily limited in power, which ends with time. Since therefore God is not dependent upon time, His power is infinite. It must be understood therefore that when we say, God is prior,[2] the expression is used figuratively and loosely. For the word prior is predicated of a thing in relation to something else, thus we say, Noah was prior to David, Enoch was prior to Elijah, because the one existed at a time which was prior to the time at which the other existed. But it is clear that the term prior as applied to God is not predicated in relation to anything else, as if to say that He existed a certain length of time before something else. If this were the case, time would limit His existence; and if so, time would necessarily be prior to Him, and He would exist at a certain time and not at another, and would be preceded by privation or non-existence. But whatever is preceded by non-existence is a possible and not a necessary existent, as we explained before. Moreover, the Bible, too, says, "Who hath preceded Me, that I should repay Him?"[3] which means that He is prior to all existing things, and nothing is prior to Him. Therefore the term priority[4] which is predicated of God must be understood in a negative manner, in the sense that nothing was prior to Him, not even non-existence, but that He always existed in the same way without change.

Similarly the term perpetual, applied to God, means that nothing is posterior to Him. For just as time can not be prior to Him, as we have explained,[5] so nothing can come after Him, nor can time outlast Him in the direction of the end, as it can not be prior to Him in the direction of the beginning. For if time could outlast Him in the direction of the end, He would exist at one time and not at another, and would not be a necessary existent, as we explained in relation to the term prior. Therefore the concepts of priority and perpetuity predicated of God are negative in meaning, they deny non-existence *a parte ante* as well as *a parte post.*

That time is not prior or posterior to God is true even if by time we mean unmeasured duration conceived only in thought, existing always, both before the creation of the world and after its cessation, but without the order apparent from the motion of the sphere, since the sphere was then neither in motion nor existent. Our Rabbis are of the opinion that time in the abstract is such a duration. Time measured or numbered through the motion of the sphere they call "order of times," not simply time. According to this there are two species of time, the one is numbered and measured by the motion of the sphere, to which are applicable the terms prior and posterior, equal and unequal. The other is not numbered or measured, but is a duration existing prior to the sphere, to which the words equal and unequal do not apply. This is what Maimonides calls imagination of time.[6] This latter kind may be perpetual. The kind that has an origin is the "order of time," not time simply. In this way all the doubts and difficulties disappear, which are raised concerning the quiddity of time, namely whether time originates in time or not. The solution is that though time has no origin, the order of time originates in time.

We can also answer the other question in relation to the now. The now, it is said, divides the past from the future. There is therefore a time before the first now, and hence time and the sphere are eternal.[7] The answer to this on the basis of our analysis is not difficult. Time in which there is motion has in it the elements prior and posterior, but time in which there is no motion has not the elements prior and posterior, and it is not subject to measure because measure can not apply to time without motion. The terms prior and posterior apply to it only figuratively and loosely. The same thing is illustrated in the saying that outside of the world there is neither a plenum nor a vacuum.[8] To the objection that if there is an outside there must necessarily be a plenum or a vacuum, the answer is that the word outside is used figuratively and loosely. The same is true of the words prior and posterior as applying to the imaginary duration before the creation of the world.

The difficulty of understanding how the world can end with something which is neither a plenum nor a vacuum, or how there can be a duration before the creation of the world which has in it neither prior nor posterior, such as are contained in the order of time as it exists at present, accounts for the statement of the Rabbis that one must not ask what is above, what is below, what is before and what is behind.[9] Above and below refer to what is outside of the world, before and behind refer to the duration which is prior to the creation of the world and posterior to its cessation, in reference to which the Rabbis say that one must not ask whether the words prior and posterior apply to it or not.

One may object here on the basis of a statement of Rabbi Judah son of Rabbi Simon. From the expression in Genesis, "and there was evening and there was morning, one day,"[10] he infers that the order of time existed before creation.[11] From this statement it would seem that his opinion was either that the sphere is eternal, as Aristotle thought, or that the unmeasured duration is called order of time. The answer is that this is not the meaning of Rabbi Judah. The purpose of his statement is to obviate the notion suggested at first sight that the order of day and night did not begin until the fourth day when the luminaries were suspended in the sky. Having this in view, he says that from the first day when the sphere was created it was in motion, resulting in the order of day and night before the fourth day. Thus the appearance of evening and morning mentioned at the beginning is true. The reason why the Bible mentions the suspension of the luminaries and the stars on the fourth day is to show that their different motions by which they serve "for signs and for seasons, and for days and years,"[12] are for the purpose of exerting an influence upon the lower world by the different position of their light in relation to the earth. This is explained in the statement, "And God set them in the firmament of the heaven to give light upon the earth."[13] It is clear therefore from the words of Rabbi Judah son of Rabbi Simon that the time that is measured by the motion of the sphere is called order of time and not time simply, and that time simply is the duration which has no prior and posterior, nor order of time, since there is no motion in it.

If, however, time is not a conceptual duration but one that is measured by the motion of the sphere, according to Aristotle's view,[14] the meaning of divine priority and perpetuity would be that God is prior to all existing things and to time which is numbered by the motion of the sphere. The essential meaning of priority and perpetuity, though they are different, would thus be the same, namely that God always exists in the same way before time and after time will cease.

Therefore we make independence of time one dogma, in order to include priority and perpetuity, whether time is a conceptual duration, as the Rabbis maintain, or one that is numbered by the motion of the sphere, according to the opinion of Aristotle. Thus we find that wherever the Bible describes God as first it also characterizes Him as last, to indicate that He has one attribute, independence of time, which embraces both. Isaiah says, "Thus saith the Lord, the King of Israel, and his Redeemer, the Lord of hosts: I am the first, and I am the last, and beside Me there is no God."[15] The meaning is, there is no existing thing outside of Me that can be characterized as first and last, for all other existing things have time before them or after them and therefore are possible existents, whereas I, being independent of time, am not a possible but a necessary existent. This is why Isaiah concludes, "And beside Me there is no God," i.e. among all existing things there is no necessary existent, i.e. one who is all-powerful, outside of Me, for there is no one to whom the names first and last apply outside of Me, and therefore it is clear that I alone am God, i.e. a necessary existent.

NOTES

1. The discussion of time in this chapter is also taken from Crescas, Or Adonai, I, 2, 11.

2. The Hebrew word קדמון, used by the philosophers in the sense of eternal, means literally prior.

3. Job 41, 3.

4. The Hebrew word קדמות is the abstract of קדמון,for which see note 2.

5. P. 108 f.

6. Guide, II, 13. On this discussion of the meaning of time, see Wolfson, in Jewish Quarterly Review, N.S., vol. X, pp. 1–17; id., "Solomon Pappenheim on Time and Space," in Israel Abrahams Memorial Volume, p. 428.

7. Aristotle, Physics VIII, 1, p. 251b 19: *εἰ οὖν ἀδύνατόν ἐστι καὶ εἶναι καὶ νοῆσαι χρόνον ἄνευ τοῦ νῦν, τὸ δὲ νῦν ἐστὶ μεσότης τις, καὶ ἀρχὴν καὶ τελευτὴν ἔχον ἅμα, ἀρχήν μὲν τοῦ ἐσομένου χρόνου, τελευτὴν δὲ τοῦ παρελθόντος, ἀνάγκη ἀεὶ εἶναι χρόνον.*

8. Cf. Wolfson, Crescas' Critique of Aristotle, 1929, p. 421, note 36.

9. Hagigah 11b.

10. Gen. 1, 5.

11. Gen. Rab. 2.

12. Gen. 1, 14.

13. Ibid. 17.

14. Physics IV, 14, p. 223b 22, *διὸ καὶ δοκεῖ ὁ χρόνος εἶναι ἡ τῆς σφαίρας κίνησις.*

15. Isa. 44, 6.

BOOK II, CHAPTER 19

From our discussion proving that God is not subject to time, it follows that every attribute applied to God, whether it be positive or negative, must be prior and perpetual like Him, i.e. must be infinite on both sides, *a parte ante* and *a parte post*. For it is impossible that any of His attributes should come into being, not having been before, else God would be composed of things having origin. But whatever is composed of things having origin, itself has origin and is not prior in the general sense of the term. Similarly it is impossible that any attribute should be in Him at one time and not at another, for then God would be subject to change, which is impossible. For change is motion and the realization of the potential.[1] Moreover all motion takes place in time.[2] God would therefore have need of time to change in, and if He is subject to change He would be subject to genesis and would not be eternal, but we have already proved that He is absolutely eternal. It is clear therefore that no change can apply to Him.

The other existing things, however, are subject to time, therefore time causes them to change. Even the Separate Intelligences, which are not composed of opposites, and thus are not subject to qualitative or quantitative change which are due to the presence of opposites, may nevertheless be subject to change in time. Thus the first effect, having come into being in time, was, let us say, two thousand years old in the time of Abraham, whereas now it is five thousand years old or more. Similarly everything that was created is necessarily older to-day than it was in the time of David, and hence is subject to time. But we can not say of God that He is older to-day than He was in the time of David, or when He created the world, because He has always existed in the same way before the world was created, will continue the same after the world comes to an end, and time will not change Him. . . Therefore the Bible says, "See now that I, even I, am He,"[3] "I, even I, am the Lord; and beside Me there is no saviour."[4] The meaning of the latter expression is, I can save because I exist always in the same way without change, but no other being can save, because he is subject to change.

NOTES

1. Aristotle, Physics III, 1, p. 201a 11, *ἡ τοῦ δυνάμει ὄντος ἐντελέχεια, ᾗ τοιοῦτον, κίνησίς ἐστιν.*
2. Ibid. IV, 11, p. 219b 16, *ἀκολουθεῖ τῇ κινήσει ὁ χρόνος.*
3. Deut. 32, 29.
4. Isa. 43, 11.

The Fifth Principle

Prayer

INTRODUCTION

It may appear that the Fifth Principle concerns itself with matters of religious practice rather than belief. This principle is indeed first stated in the positive and expressed in language which is directed to action. Maimonides states that God "must be worshippped, aggrandized and made known by His greatness and the obedience shown to Him"—all of which are matters of specific performance. Similarly, the corollary which immediately follows in Maimonides' formulation of this principle, "This must not be done to any existing being other than Him . . ." also addresses itself to matters of religious expression. An exhortation regarding practice, whether positive or negative, would appear to be incongruous in an exposition of principles of belief.

Actually, this principle must be understood as an expression of monotheistic belief which goes beyond the mere exclusion of other divinities. Profession of monotheism and the denial of other gods is already asserted in the Second Principle. The Fifth Principle goes beyond this. It forbids the worship not only of other gods but of intermediaries as well. Such worship is forbidden not merely because it constitutes a violation of divine law, but for another reason entirely—and it is the underlying rationale which demands a commitment of faith. Such worship is essentially purposeless: These intermediaries "have no judgment or freedom." Angels, the spheres, the elements, etc., lack an autonomous will; their actions are determined rather than voluntary, and are performed only in accordance with divine direction. A petition addressed to a being or entity which is powerless either to grant or to withhold a response is not merely an exercise in futility, it is absurd. Prayer addressed to such beings is, then, a tacit affirmation of their ability to engage in volitional activity in an independent manner. The belief that God has endowed intermediaries with this power, even if it be recognized that this volitional discretion exists only because God so permits, compromises the principle of monotheism and constitutes a form of idolatry. It is the *belief* that angels or other beings are endowed with this power which is abjured by the Fifth Principle. This belief is heretical in and of itself; the act of worship is merely the concretization of a false belief.

The belief which is excluded by the Fifth Principle is one which, it might otherwise be supposed, could readily be affirmed by a religionist without doing violence to monotheistic belief. A king appoints ministers to administer various departments and delegates to them the authority to act in accordance with their judgment. The king may even retain the prerogative of reviewing the decisions of his ministers and may indeed overrule them on occasion. However, in making decisions and in performing their executive duties, the ministers function not as programmed robots, but as rational creatures exercising free will. There are passages in rabbinic writings, and indeed occasionally in the liturgy itself, which might be understood as indicating that God delegates authority to inferior beings as well. Any such interpretation is denied by Maimonides. In formulating the Fifth Principle, Maimonides stresses that even the voluntary delegation of authority constitutes a dilution of divine power and is antithetical to the belief in the one God.

Although it is the most fundamental and most universal form of religious expression, prayer is fraught with theological difficulties. Ostensibly, prayer is an attempt on the part of man to effect a change in God's conduct vis-à-vis man. God has afflicted man with, or allowed man to be afflicted by, sickness; man wishes God to restore him to good health. God has placed man, or allowed man to be placed, in a situation of poverty; man aspires to good fortune. He pleads with God to grant that which heretofore has been withheld. Is it not the height of audacity and unseemliness for man to presume to "pressure" God with prayer and argument in an attempt to dictate to God how He shall act! Moreover, the very act of prayer, unless it be completely futile, assumes that prayer is efficacious. The apparent implication is that the will of God is subject to change. Yet God and His will are one. Hence, God's will, which is identical with His essence, is itself eternal and immutable. Thus any change in the divine will is an impossibility. What, then, is the purpose of prayer?

The kabbalists take the position that all human actions are endowed with cosmic significance. Prayer is necessary because it is part of the causal process which brings divine beneficence upon man. According to kabbalistic teaching, God revealed Himself and governs the universe through a series of manifestations called *sefirot*. Man, through prayer and good deeds, causes the divine influence to produce a state of harmony and balance within the *sefirot* which, in turn, enables divine grace to flow throughout creation by providing the necessary channels for the manifestation of divine goodness and beneficence.

Maimonides, in his *Guide*, regards prayer essentially as an exercise designed to enable man to achieve spiritual perfection rather than as an attempt to elicit a specific response on the part of God. Indeed, in his formulation of this principle, Maimonides carefully avoids any comment with regard to the efficacy of prayer. The notion that an individual who prays fervently, and with faith that the prayer will be answered, will necessarily receive a favorable response to his petition is not explicitly formulated in classical Jewish sources. Maimonides views prayer as an opportunity to contemplate the nature and grandeur of the Deity. This contemplation leads to intellectual perfection and the establishment of a bond or contact between the human intellect and the Active Intellect. In its highest degree this state of perfection is identical with prophecy. A person who has attained a high state of spiritual perfection, and who, through contemplation, has achieved a state of intense communication with God, is immune from misfortune.

For Judah Halevi prayer is also a self-fulfilling activity. Its function is to enable man to transcend the mundane and to establish a connection with the Divine Spirit. In enabling man to rise above his corporeal nature and to purge himself, in part, of sensuality, prayer provides periodic spiritual sustenance. Man is thereby assured of a measure of spirituality which sustains him even in the intervals between periods of prayer.[1]

The responsum of R. Isaac ben Sheshet is included for the purpose of presenting both the kabbalistic view of the function of the *sefirot* and their relationship to prayer as well as R. Isaac ben Sheshet's own rejection of the mode of prayer adopted by the kabbalists.

The kabbalist Joseph ibn Shoshan is quoted as stating that petitions are not directly addressed to the *sefirot*. As Maimonides has stated, this

[1] Later scholars, whose works are not represented in this anthology, stressed the contemplative and introspective nature of prayer and its effect upon man. The nineteenth-century writer, Rabbi Samson Raphael Hirsch, viewed prayer primarily as an occasion for introspection rather than as an attempt to communicate with the Active Intellect. Hirsch's explanation of the effect of prayer on the worshipper is based upon his philological interpretation of the Hebrew word for "prayer," *tefillah*. Hirsch regards this term as being derived from the verb *pallel*, meaning "to judge," forms of which occur twice in I Samuel 2:23. Grammatically, the Hebrew word for the verb "to pray"—*le-hitpallel*—is in the reflexive form. Prayer, then, for Hirsch, is a form of self-judgment. Prayer becomes the occasion for man to bring himself to trial, to engage in self-examination with a view to determining whether his conduct conforms to the norms required of a true servant of God, and to reflect upon the ways in which his conduct may be improved and brought into conformity with these ideals. A similar description of prayer as an act of self-judgment in the ongoing conflict between man's good and evil inclinations, as well as a similar philological analysis of the term *tefillah*, is found in the preface of Rabbi Jacob Zebi Meklenburg's commentary on the prayerbook, *Iyun Tefillah*. The author of this work was a contemporary of Rabbi Samson Raphael Hirsch.

would be tantamount to idolatry. Rather, concentration upon different *sefirot* is comparable to presentation of a petition to a king with the request that the appropriate minister be directed to fulfill the suppliant's desire. Similarly, prayer is addressed to God beseeching Him to cause His influence to be directed through the appropriate *sefirah.*

R. Isaac ben Sheshet does not reject the kabbalistic cosmogony. He professes never to have been instructed in the kabbalistic system and hence to be unable either to accept or to reject its teachings. However, he accepts without hesitation that God does not require instruction in order to discover the proper means of responding to man's petition. Accordingly, R. Isaac ben Sheshet advises simple supplication directed to God alone as the object of prayer.

In his resolution of the philosophical difficulties associated with prayer, Albo simultaneously upholds both the efficacy of prayer as this concept is usually understood and the principle of the immutability of the divine will. God eternally wills certain benefits for man, but such benefits correspond to the degree of preparation and perfection which each person has achieved. Such benefits are commensurate with, and proportional to, the individual's state of preparation. Prayer effects a positive change in the worshipper's state of spiritual perfection, thereby preparing the individual to receive beneficence and to avert evil. Prayer is thus efficacious in the sense that it effects a changed state of human preparation without effecting a change in divine will since the benefits associated with this state were always willed by God, but are willed by Him to be contingent upon man achieving the requisite state of preparation.

HALEVI, *KUZARI*

Translation by Hartwig Hirschfeld

PART III

2. Al Khazari: Give me a discription of the doings of one of your pious men at the present time.

3. The Rabbi: A pious man is, so to speak, the guardian of his country, who gives to its inhabitants provisions and all they need. He is so just that he wrongs no one, nor does he grant anyone more than his due. Then, when he requires them, he finds them obedient to his call. He orders, they execute; he forbids, they abstain.

4. Al Khazari: I asked thee concerning a pious man, not a prince.

5. The Rabbi: The pious man is nothing but a prince who is obeyed by his senses, and by his mental as well as his physical faculties, which he governs corporeally, as it is written: 'He that ruleth his spirit [is better] than he that taketh a city' (Prov. xvi. 32). He is fit to rule, because if he were the prince of a country he would be as just as he is to his body and soul. He subdues his passions, keeping them in bonds, but giving them their share in order to satisfy them as regards food, drink, cleanliness, etc. He further subdues the desire for power, but allows them as much expansion as avails them for the discussion of scientific or mundane views, as well as to warn the evil-minded. He allows the senses their share according as he requires them for the use of hands, feet, and tongue, as necessity or desire arise. The same is the case with hearing, seeing, and the kindred sensations which succeed them; imagination, conception, thought, memory, and will power, which commands all these; but is, in its turn, subservient to the will of intellect. He does not allow any of these limbs or faculties to go beyond their special task, or encroach upon another. If he, then, has satisfied each of them (giving to the vital organs the necessary amount of rest and sleep, and to the physical ones waking, movements, and worldly occupation), he calls upon his community as a respected prince calls his disciplined army, to assist him in reaching the higher or divine degree which is to be found above the degree of the intellect. He arranges his community in the same manner as Moses arranged his people round Mount Sinai. He orders his

will power to receive every command issued by him obediently, and to carry it out forthwith. He makes faculties and limbs do his bidding without contradiction, forbids them evil inclinations of mind and fancy, forbids them to listen to, or believe in them, until he has taken counsel with the intellect. If he permits they can obey him, but not otherwise. In this way his will power receives its orders from him, carrying them out accordingly. He directs the organs of thought and imagination, relieving them of all worldly ideas mentioned above, charges his imagination to produce, with the assistance of memory, the most splendid pictures possible, in order to resemble the divine things sought after. Such pictures are the scenes of Sinai, Abraham and Isaac on Moriah, the Tabernacle of Moses, the Temple service, the presence of God in the Temple, and the like. He, then, orders his memory to retain all these, and not to forget them; he warns his fancy and its sinful prompters not to confuse the truth or to trouble it by doubts; he warns his irascibility and greed not to influence or lead astray, not to take hold of his will, nor subdue it to wrath and lust. As soon as harmony is restored, his will power stimulates all his organs to obey it with alertness, pleasure, and joy. They stand without fatigue when occasion demands, they bow down when he bids them to do so, and sit at the proper moment. The eyes look as a servant looks at his master, the hands drop their play and do not meet, the feet stand straight, and all limbs are as frightened and anxious to obey their master, paying no heed to pain or injury. The tongue agrees with the thought, and does not overstep its bounds, does not speak in prayer in a mere mechanical way as the starling and the parrot, but every word is uttered thoughtfully and attentively. This moment forms the heart and fruit of his time, whilst the other hours represent the way which leads to it. He looks forward to its approach, because while it lasts he resembles the spiritual beings, and is removed from merely animal existence. Those three times of daily prayer are the fruit of his day and night, and the Sabbath is the fruit of the week, because it has been appointed to establish the connection with the Divine Spirit and to serve God in joy, not in sadness, as has been explained before. All this stands in the same relation to the soul as food to the human body. Prayer is for his soul what nourishment is for his body. The blessing of one prayer lasts till the time of the next, just as the strength derived from the morning meal lasts till supper. The further his soul is removed from the time of prayer, the more it is darkened by coming in contact with worldly matters. The more so, as necessity brings it into the company of youths, women, or wicked people; when one hears unbecoming and soul-darkening words and songs which exercise an attraction for his soul which he is unable to master. During prayer he purges his soul from all that passed over it, and prepares it for the future. According to this arrangement there elapses not a single week in which both his soul and body do not receive preparation. Darkening elements having increased during the week, they cannot be cleansed except by consecrating one day to service and to physical rest. The body repairs on the Sabbath the waste suffered during the six days, and prepares itself for the work to come, whilst the soul remembers its own loss through the body's companionship. He cures himself, so to speak, from a past illness, and provides himself with a remedy to ward off any future sickness. This is almost the same as Job did with his children every week, as it is written: 'It may be that my sons have sinned' (Job i. 5). He, then, provides himself with a monthly cure, which is 'the season of atonement for all that happened during this period,' viz. the duration of the month, and the daily events, as it is written: 'Thou knowest not what a day may bring forth' (Prov. xxvii. 1). He further attends the Three Festivals and the great Fast Day, on which some of his sins are atoned for, and on which he endeavours to make up for what he may have missed on the days of those weekly and monthly circles. His soul frees itself from the whisperings of imagination, wrath, and lust, and neither in thought or deed gives them any attention. Although his soul is unable to atone for sinful thoughts—the result of songs, tales, etc., heard in youth, and which cling to memory—it cleanses itself from real sins, confesses repentance for the former, and undertakes to allow them no more to escape his tongue, much less to put them into practice, as it is written: 'I am purposed that my mouth shall not transgress' (Ps. xvii. 3). The fast of this day is such as brings one near to the angels, because it is spent in humility and contrition, standing, kneeling, praising and singing. All his physical faculties are denied their natural requirements, being entirely abandoned to religious service, as if the animal element had disappeared. The fast of a pious man is such that eye, ear, and tongue share in it, that he regards nothing except that which brings him near to God. This also refers to his innermost faculties, such as mind and imagination. To this he adds pious works.

MAIMONIDES, *MISHNEH TORAH*

Translation by Moses Hyamson

BOOK OF KNOWLEDGE, LAWS CONCERNING IDOLATRY, CHAPTER 1

1. In the days of Enosh, the people fell into gross error, and the counsel of the wise men of the generation became foolish. Enosh himself was among those who erred. Their error was as follows: "Since God," they said, "created these stars and spheres to guide the world, set them on high and allotted unto them honour, and since they are ministers who minister before Him, they deserve to be praised and glorified, and honour should be rendered them; and it is the will of God, blessed be He, that men should aggrandise and honour those whom He aggrandised and honoured—just as a king desires that respect should be shown to the officers who stand before Him, and thus honour is shown to the king." When this idea arose in their minds, they began to erect temples to the stars, offered up sacrifices to them, praised and glorified them in speech, and prostrated themselves before them—their purpose, according to their perverse notions, being to obtain the Creator's favour. This was the root of idolatry, and this was what the idolaters, wyo knew its fundamentals, said. They did not however maintain that there was no God except the particular star (which was the object of their worship). Thus Jeremiah said "Who would not fear thee, O king of nations? For it befitteth Thee; for as much as among all the wise men of the nations and in all their kingdom, there is none like unto Thee. But in one thing they are brutish and foolish. The vanities by which they are instructed are but a stock" (Jerem. 10:7–8). This means that all know that Thou alone art God; their error and folly consists in imagining that this vain worship is Thy desire.

2. In course of time, there arose among men false prophets who asserted that God had commanded and expressly told them, "Worship that particular star, or worship all the stars. Offer up to it such and such sacrifices. Pour out to it such and such libations. Erect a temple to it. Make a figure of it, to which all the people—the women, children, and the rest of the folk—shall bow down." The false prophet pointed out to them the figure which he had invented out of his own mind, and asserted that it is the figure of that particular star, which had been shown him in

his prophetic vision. And then, they began to make figures in temples, under the trees, on the mountain-tops and the hills. There they would assemble, bow down to the figures, and tell all the people that this particular figure conferred benefits and inflicted injuries, and that it was proper to worship and fear it. Their priests would say to them, "Through this worship, shall ye increase and prosper. Do this, and do not do that." Other imposters then sprang up, who declared that the star, celestial sphere or angel, had communed with them, and said to them "Worship me in such and such fashion," had taught them a definite ritual and said to them "Do this, and do not do that." So gradually the custom spread throughout the world of worshipping figures with various modes of worship, such as offering up sacrifices to them, and bowing down to them. As time passed, the honoured and revered Name of God was forgotten by mankind, vanished from their lips and hearts, and was no longer known to them. All the common people and the women and children knew only the figure of wood and stone, and the temple edifice in which they had, from their childhood, been trained to prostrate themselves to the figure, worship it and swear by its name. Even their wise men, such as priests and men of similar standing, also fancied that there was no other god but the stars and spheres, for whose sake and in whose similitude these figures had been made. But The Creator of the Universe was known to none, and recognized by none, save a few solitary individuals, such as Enosh, Methuselah, Noah, Shem and Eber. The world moved on in this fashion, till that Pillar of the World, the Patriarch Abraham, was born. After he was weaned, while still an infant, his mind began to reflect. By day and by night he was thinking and wondering: 'How is it possible that this (celestial) sphere should continuously be guiding the world and have no one to guide it and cause it to turn round; for it cannot be that it turns round of itself.' He had no teacher, no one to instruct him in aught. He was submerged, in Ur of the Chaldees, among silly idolaters. His father and mother and the entire population worshipped idols, and he worshipped with them. But his mind was busily working and reflecting till he had attained the way of truth, apprehended the correct line of thought and knew that there is One God, that He guides the celestial Sphere and created everything, and that among all that exist, there is no god beside Him. He realized that the whole world was in error, and that what had occasioned their error was that they worshipped the stars and the images, so that the truth perished from their minds. Abraham was forty years old when he recognised his Creator. Having attained this knowledge, he began to refute the inhabitants of Ur of the Chaldees, arguing with them and saying to them, "The course you are following is not the way of truth." He broke the images and commenced to instruct the people that it was not right to serve any one but the God of the Universe, to Whom alone it was proper to bow down, offer up sacrifices and make libations, so that all human creatures might, in the future, know Him; and that it was proper to destroy and shatter all the images, so that the people might not err like these who thought that there was no god but these images. When he had prevailed over them with his arguments, the king (of the country) sought to slay him. He was miraculously saved, and emigrated to Haran. He then began to proclaim to the whole world with great power and to instruct the people that the entire Universe had but one Creator and that Him it was right to worship. He went from city to city and from kingdom to kingdom, calling and gathering together the inhabitants till he arrived in the land of Canaan. There too, he proclaimed his message, as it is said "And he called there on the name of the Lord, God of the Universe" (Gen. 21:33). When the people flocked to him and questioned him regarding his assertions, he would instruct each one according to his capacity till he had brought him to the way of truth, and thus thousands and tens of thousands joined him. These were the persons referred to in the phrase, "men of the house of Abraham." He implanted in their hearts this great doctrine, composed books on it, and taught it to Isaac, his son. Isaac settled down, instructing and exhorting. He imparted the doctrine to Jacob and ordained him to teach it. He, too, settled down, taught and morally strengthened all who joined him. The patriarch Jacob instructed all his sons, set apart Levi, appointed him head (teacher) and placed him in a college to teach the way of God and keep the charge of Abraham. He charged his sons to appoint from the tribe of Levi, one instructor after another, in uninterrupted succession, so that the doctrine might never be forgotten. And so it went on with ever increasing vigour among Jacob's children and their adherents till they became a people that knew God. When the Israelites had stayed a long while in Egypt, they relapsed, learnt the practices of their neighbours, and, like them, worshipped idols, with the exception of the tribe of Levi, which steadfastly kept the charge of the Patriarch. This tribe of Levi never practiced idolatry. The doctrine implanted by Abraham would, in a very short time, have been uprooted, and Jacob's descendants would have relapsed into the error and perversities universally prevalent. But because of God's love for us and because He kept the oath made to our ancestor Abraham, He appointed Moses to be our teacher and the teacher of all the prophets, and charged him with his mission. After Moses had begun to exercise his prophetic functions and Israel had been chosen by the Almighty as His heritage, he crowned them with precepts, and showed them the way to worship Him and how to deal with idolatry and with those who go astray after it.

MAIMONIDES, *MOREH NEVUKHIM*

Translation by Michael Friedlander

PART III, CHAPTER 51

The present chapter does not contain any additional matter that has not been treated in the [previous] chapters of this treatise. It is a kind of conclusion, and at the same time it will explain in what manner those worship God who have obtained a true knowledge concerning God; it will direct them how to come to that worship, which is the highest aim man can attain, and show how God protects them in this world till they are removed to eternal life.

I will begin the subject of this chapter with a simile. A king is in his palace, and all his subjects are partly in the country, and partly abroad. Of the former, some have their backs turned towards the king's palace, and their faces in another direction; and some are desirous and zealous to go to the palace, seeking "to inquire in his temple," and to minister before him, but have not yet seen even the face of the wall of the house. Of those that desire to go to the palace, some reach it, and go round about in search of the entrance gate; others have passed through the gate, and walk about in the ante-chamber; and others have succeeded in entering into the inner part of the palace, and being in the same room with the king in the royal palace. But even the latter do not immediately on entering the palace see the king, or speak to him; for, after having entered the inner part of the palace, another effort is required before they can stand before the king—at a distance, or close by—hear his words, or speak to him. I will now explain the simile which I have made. The people who are abroad are all those that have no religion, neither one based on speculation nor one received by tradition. Such are the extreme Turks that wander about in the north, the Kushites who live in the south, amd those in our country who are like these. I consider these as irrational beings, and not as human beings; they are below mankind, but above monkeys, since they have the form and shape of man, and a mental faculty above that of the monkey.

Those who are in the country, but have their backs turned towards the king's palace, are those who possess religion, belief, and thought, but happen to hold false doctrines, which they either adopted in consequence of great mistakes made in their own speculations, or received from others who misled them. Because of these doctrines they recede more and more from the royal palace the more they seem to proceed. These are worse than the first class, and under certain circumstances it may become necessary to slay them, and to extirpate their doctrines, in order that others should not be misled.

Those who desire to arrive at the palace, and to enter it, but have never yet seen it, are the mass of religious people; the multitude that observe the divine commandments, but are ignorant. Those who arrive at the palace, but go round about it, are those who devote themselves exclusively to the study of the practical law; they believe traditionally in true principles of faith, and learn the practical worship of God, but are not trained in philosophical treatment of the principles of the Law, and do not endeavour to establish the truth of their faith by proof. Those who undertake to investigate the principles of religion, have come into the ante-chamber; and there is no doubt that these can also be divided into different grades. But those who have succeeded in finding a proof for everything that can be proved, who have a true knowledge of God, so far as a true knowledge can be attained, and are near the truth, wherever an approach to the truth is possible, they have reached the goal, and are in the palace in which the king lives.

My son, so long as you are engaged in studying the Mathematical Sciences and Logic, you belong to those who go round about the palace in search of the gate. Thus our Sages figuratively use the phrase: "Ben-zoma is still outside." When you understand Physics, you have entered the hall; and when, after completing the study of Natural Philosophy, you master Metaphysics, you have entered the innermost court, and are with the king in the same palace. You have attained the degree of the wise men, who include men of different grades of perfection. There are some who direct all their mind toward the attainment of perfection in Metaphysics, devote themselves entirely to God, exclude from their thought every other thing, and employ all their intellectual faculties in the study of the Universe, in order to derive therefrom a proof for the existence of God, and to learn in every possible way how God rules all things; they form the class of those who have entered the palace, namely, the class of prophets. One of these has attained so much knowledge, and has concentrated his thoughts to such an extent in the idea of God, that it could be said of him, "And he was with the Lord forty days," &c. (Exod. xxxiv. 28); during that holy communion he could ask Him, answer Him, speak to Him, and be addressed by Him, enjoying beatitude in that which he had obtained to such a degree that "he did neither eat bread nor drink water" (ibid.); his intellectual energy was so predominant that all coarser functions of the body, especially those connected with the sense of touch, were in abeyance. Some prophets are only able to see, and of these some approach near and see, whilst others see from a distance: comp. "The Lord hath appeared from far unto me" (Jer. xxxi. 3). We have already spoken of the various degrees of prophets; we will therefore return to the subject of this chapter, and exhort those who have attained a knowledge of God, to concentrate all their thoughts in God. This is the worship peculiar to those who have acquired a knowledge of the highest truths; and the more they reflect on Him, and think of Him, the more are they engaged in His worship. Those, however, who think of God, and frequently mention His name, without any correct notion of Him, but merely following some imagination, or some creed received from another person, are, in my opinion, like those who remain outside the palace and distant from it. They do not mention the name of God in truth, nor do they reflect on it. That which they imagine and mention does not correspond to any being in existence; it is a thing invented by their imagination, as has been shown by us in our discussion on the Divine Attributes (Part I. ch. 1.). The true worship of God is only possible when correct notions of Him have previously been conceived. When you have arrived by way of intellectual research at a knowledge of God and His works, then commence to devote yourself to Him, try to approach Him amd strengthen the intellect, which is the link that joins you to Him. Thus Scripture says, "Unto thee it was showed, that thou mightest know that the Lord He is God" (Deut. iv. 35); "Know therefore this day, and consider it in thine heart, that the Lord He is God" (ibid. 36); "Know ye that the Lord is God" (Ps. c. 3). Thus the Law distinctly states that the highest kind of worship, to which we refer in this chapter, is only possible after the acquisition of the knowledge of God. For it is said, "To love the Lord your God, and to serve Him with all your heart and with all your soul" (Deut. xi. 13), and, as we have shown several times, man's love of God is identical with his knowledge of Him. The Divine Service enjoined in these words must, accordingly, be preceded by the love of God. Our Sages have pointed out to us that it is a service in the heart, which explanation I understand to mean this: man concentrates all his thoughts on the First Intellect, and is absorbed in these thoughts as much as possible. David therefore commands his son Solomon these two things, and exhorts him earnestly to do them: to acquire a true knowledge of God, and to be earnest in His service after that knowledge has been acquired. For He says, "And thou, Solomon my son, know thou the God of thy father, and serve Him with a perfect heart . . . if thou seek Him, He will be found of thee; but if thou forsake Him,

He will cast thee off for ever" (1 Chron. xxviii. 9). The exhortation refers to the intellectual conceptions, not to the imaginations; for the latter are not called "knowledge," but "that which cometh into your mind" (Ez. xx. 32). It has thus been shown that it must be man's aim, after having acquired the knowledge of God, to deliver himself up to Him, and to have his heart constantly filled with longing after Him. He accomplishes this generally by seclusion and retirement. Every pious man should therefore seek retirement and seclusion, and should only in case of necessity associate with others.

Note—I have shown you that the intellect which emanates from God unto us is the link that joins us to God. You have it in your power to strengthen that bond, if you choose to do so, or to weaken it gradually till it breaks, if you prefer this. It will only become strong when you employ it in the love of God, and seek that love; it will be weakened when you direct your thoughts to other things. You must know that even if you were the wisest man in respect to the true knowledge of God, you break the bond between you and God whenever you turn entirely your thoughts to the necessary food or any necessary business; you are then not with God, and He is not with you; for that relation between you and Him is actually interrupted in those moments. The pious were therefore particular to restrict the time in which they could not meditate upon the name of God, and cautioned others about it, saying, "Let not your minds be vacant from reflections upon God." In the same sense did David say, "I have set the Lord always before me; because He is at my right hand, I shall not be moved" (Ps. xvi. 8); *i.e.*, I do not turn my thoughts away from God; He is like my right hand, which I do not forget even for a moment on account of the ease of its motions, and therefore I shall not be moved, I shall not fall.

We must bear in mind that all such religious acts as reading the Law, praying, and the performance of other precepts, serve exclusively as the means of causing us to occupy and fill our mind with the precepts of God, and free it from worldly business; for we are thus, as it were, in communication with God, and undisturbed by any other thing. If we, however, pray with the motion of our lips, and our face toward the wall, but at the same time think of our business; if we read the Law with our tongue, whilst our heart is occupied with the building of our house, and we do not think of what we are reading; if we perform the commandments only with our limbs, we are like those who are engaged in digging in the ground, or hewing wood in the forest, without reflecting on the nature of those acts, or by whom they are commanded, or what is their object. We must not imagine that [in this way] we attain the highest perfection; on the contrary, we are then like those in reference to whom Scripture says, "Thou art near in their mouth, and far from their reins" (Jer. xii. 2).

I will now commence to show you the way how to educate and train yourselves in order to attain that great perfection.

The first thing you must do is this: Turn your thoughts away from everything while you read *Shema* or during the *Tefillah*, and do not content yourself with being devout when you read the first verse of Shema, or the first paragraph of the prayer. When you have successfully practised this for many years, try in reading the Law or listening to it, to have all your heart and all your thought occupied with understanding what you read or hear. After some time when you have mastered this, accustom yourself to have your mind free from all other thoughts when you read any portion of the other books of the prophets, or when you say any blessing; and to have your attention directed exclusively to the perception and the understanding of what you utter. When you have succeeded in properly performing these acts of divine service, and you have your thought, during their performance, entirely abstracted from worldly affairs, take then care that your thought be not disturbed by cares for your wants or for superfluous food. In short, think of worldly matters when you eat, drink, bathe, talk with your wife and little children, or when you converse with other people. These times, which are frequent and long, I think, must suffice to you for reflecting on everything that is necessary as regards business, household, and health. But when you are engaged in the performance of religious duties, have your mind exclusively directed to what you are doing.

When you are alone by yourself, when you are awake on your couch, be careful to meditate in such precious moments on nothing but the intellectual worship of God, viz., to approach Him and to minister before Him in the true manner which I have described to you—not in hollow emotions. This I consider as the highest perfection wise men can attain by the above training.

When we have acquired a true knowledge of God, and rejoice in that knowledge in such a manner, that whilst speaking with others, or attending to our bodily wants, our mind is all that time with God; when we are with our heart constantly near God, even whilst our body is in the society of men; when we are in that state which the Song on the relation between God and man poetically describes in the following words: "I sleep, but my heart waketh; it is the voice of my beloved that knocketh" (Song v. 2):—then we have attained not only the height of ordinary prophets, but of Moses, our Teacher, of whom Scripture relates: "And

Moses alone shall come near before the Lord" (ibid. xxxiv. 28); "But as for thee, stand thou here by Me" (Deut. v. 28). The meaning of these verses has been explained by us.

The Patriarchs likewise attained this degree of perfection; they approached God in such a manner that with them the name of God became known in the world. Thus we read in Scripture: "The God of Abraham, the God of Isaac, and the God of Jacob. . . .This is My name for ever" (Ex. iii. 15). Their mind was so identified with the knowledge of God, that He made a lasting covenant with each of them: "Then will I remember my covenant with Jacob," &c. (Lev. xxvi. 42). For it is known from statements made in Scripture that these four, viz., the Patriarchs and Moses, had their minds exclusively filled with the name of God, that is, with His knowledge and love; and that in the same measure was Divine Providence attached to them and their descendants. When we therefore find them also, engaged in ruling others, in increasing their property, and endeavouring to obtain possession of wealth and honour, we see in this fact a proof that when they were occupied in these things, only their bodily limbs were at work, whilst their heart and mind never moved away from the name of God. I think these four reached that high degree of perfection in their relation to God, and enjoyed the continual presence of Divine Providence, even in their endeavours to increase their property, feeding the flock, toiling in the field, or managing the house, only because in all these things their end and aim was to approach God as much as possible. It was the chief aim of their whole life to create a people that should know and worship God. Comp. "For I know him, that he will command his children and his household after him" (Gen. xviii. 19). The object of all their labours was to publish the Unity of God in the world, and to induce people to love Him; and it was on this account that they succeeded in reaching that high degree; for even those [worldly] affairs were for them a perfect worship of God. But a person like myself must not imagine that he is able to lead men up to this degree of perfection. It is only the next degree of it that can be attained by means of the above-mentioned training. And let us pray to God and beseech Him that He clear and remove from our way everything that forms an obstruction and a partition between us and Him, although most of these obstacles are our own creation, as has several times been shown in this treatise. Comp. "Your iniquities have separated between you and your God" (Is. lix. 2).

An excellent idea presents itself here to me, which may serve to remove many doubts, and may help to solve many difficult problems in metaphysics. We have already stated in the chapters which treat of

Divine Providence, that Providence watches over every rational being according to the amount of intellect which that being possesses. Those who are perfect in their perception of God, whose mind is never separated from Him, enjoy always the influence of Providence. But those who, perfect in their knowledge of God, turn their mind sometimes away from God, enjoy the presence of Divine Providence only when they meditate on God; when their thoughts are engaged in other matters Divine Providence departs from them. The absence of Providence in this case is not like its absence in the case of those who do not reflect on God at all; it is in this case less intense, because when a person perfect in his knowledge [of God] is busy with wordly matters, he has not knowledge in actuality, but only knowledge in potentiality [though ready to become actual]. This person is then like a trained scribe when he is not writing. Those who have no knowledge of God are like those who are in constant darkness and have never seen light. We have explained in this sense the words: "The wicked shall be silent in darkness" (1 Sam. ii. 9), whilst those who possess the knowledge of God, and have their thoughts entirely directed to that knowledge, are, as it were, always in bright sunshine; and those who have the knowledge, but are at times engaged in other themes, have then as it were a cloudy day: the sun does not shine for them on account of the cloud that intervenes between them and God.

Hence it appears to me that it is only in times of such neglect that some of the ordinary evils befall a prophet or a perfect and pious man; and the intensity of the evil is proportional to the duration of those moments, or to the character of the things that thus occupy their mind. Such being the case, the great difficulty is removed that led philosophers to assert that providence does not extend to every individual, and that man is like any other living being in this respect, viz., the argument based on the fact that good and pious men are afflicted with great evils. We have thus explained this difficult question even in accordance with the philosophers' own principles. Divine Providence is constantly watching over those who have obtained that blessing which is prepared for those who endeavor to obtain it. If man frees his thoughts from worldly matters, obtains a knowledge of God in the right way, and rejoices in that knowledge, it is impossible that any kind of evil should befall him while he is with God, and God with him. When he does not meditate on God, when he is separated from God, then God is also separated from him; then he is exposed to any evil that might befall him; for it is only that intellectual link with God that secures the presence of Providence and protection from evil accidents. Hence it may occur that the perfect man is at times not happy, whilst no evil befalls those who are imperfect;

in these cases what happens to them is due to chance. This principle I find also expressed in the Law. Comp. "And I will hide my face from them, and they shall be devoured, and many evils and troubles shall befall them; so that they will say in that day, Are not these evils come upon us, because our God is not among us?" (Deut. xxxi. 17). It is clear that we ourselves are the cause of this hiding of the face, and that the screen that separates us from God is of our own creation. This is the meaning of the words: "And I will surely hide My face in that day, for all the evils which they shall have wrought" (ibid. ver. 18). There is undoubtedly no difference in this regard between one single person and a whole community. It is now clearly established that the cause of our being exposed to chance, and abandoned to destruction like cattle, is to be found in our separation from God. Those who have their God dwelling in their hearts, are not touched by any evil whatever. For God says: "Fear thou not, for I am with thee; be not dismayed, for I am thy God" (Isa. xli. 10). "When thou passest through the waters, I will be with thee; and through the rivers, they shall not overflow thee" (ibid. xliii. 2). For if we prepare ourselves, and attain the influence of the Divine Intellect, Providence is joined to us, and we are guarded against all evils. Comp. "The Lord is on my side; I will not fear; what can man do unto me?" (Ps. cxviii. 6). "Acquaint now thyself with Him, and be at peace" (Job xxii. 21); *i.e.*, turn unto Him, and you will be safe from all evil.

Consider the Psalm on mishaps, and see how the author describes that great Providence, the protection and defence from all mishaps that concern the body, both from those that are common to all people, and those that concern only one certain individual; from those that are due to the laws of Nature, and those that are caused by our fellow-men. The Psalmist says: "Surely He will deliver thee from the snare of the fowler, and from the noisome pestilence. He shall cover thee with His feathers, and under His wings shalt thou trust: His truth shall be thy shield and buckler. Thou shalt not be afraid for the terror by night; nor for the arrow that flieth by day" (Ps. xci. 3–5). The author then relates how God protects us from the troubles caused by men, saying, If you happen to meet on your way with an army fighting with drawn swords, killing thousands at your left hand and myriads at your right hand, you will not suffer any harm; you will behold and see how God judges and punishes the wicked that are being slain, whilst you remain unhurt. "A thousand shall fall at thy side, and ten thousand at thy right hand; but it shall not come nigh thee. Only with thine eyes shalt thou behold and see the reward of the wicked" (ibid. vers. 7, 8). The author then continues his description of the divine defence and shelter, and shows the cause of this great protection, saying that such a man is well guarded, "Because he hath set his love upon Me, therefore will I deliver him: I will set him on high, because he hath known My name" (ibid. ver. 14). We have shown in previous chapters that by the "knowledge of God's name," the knowledge of God is meant. The above passage may therefore be paraphrased as follows: "This man is well guarded, because he hath known Me, and then (*bi chashak*) loved Me." You know the difference between the two Hebrew terms that signify "to love," *ahab* and *chashak*. When a man's love is so intense that his thought is exclusively engaged with the object of his love, it is expressed in Hebrew by the term *chashak*.

The philosophers have already explained how the bodily forces of man in his youth prevent the development of moral principles. In a greater measure this is the case as regards the purity of thought which man attains through the perfection of those ideas that lead him to an intense love of God. Man can by no means attain this so long as his bodily humours are hot. The more the forces of his body are weakened, and the fire of passion quenched, in the same measure does man's intellect increase in strength and light; his knowledge becomes purer, and he is happy with his knowledge. When this perfect man is stricken in age and is near death, his knowledge mightily increases, his joy in that knowledge grows greater, and his love for the object of his knowledge more intense, and it is in this great delight that the soul separates from the body. To this state our Sages referred, when in reference to the death of Moses, Aaron, and Miriam, they said that death was in these three cases nothing but a kiss. They say thus: We learn from the words, "And Moses the servant of the Lord died there in the land of Moab by the mouth of the Lord" (Deut. xxxiv. 5), that his death was a kiss. The same expression is used of Aaron: "And Aaron the priest went up into Mount Hor . . . by the mouth of the Lord, and died there" (Num. xxxiii. 38). Our Sages said that the same was the case with Miriam; but the phrase "by the mouth of the Lord" is not employed, because it was not considered appropriate to use these words in the description of her death as she was a female. The meaning of this saying is that these three died in the midst of the pleasure derived from the knowledge of God and their great love for Him. When our Sages figuratively call the knowledge of God united with intense love for Him a kiss they follow the well-known poetical diction, "Let Him kiss me with the kisses of His mouth" (Song i. 2). This kind of death, which in truth is deliverance from death, has been ascribed by our Sages to none but to Moses, Aaron, and Miriam. The other prophets and pious men are beneath that degree; but their knowledge of God is strengthened when death approaches. Of them

Scripture says, "Thy righteousness shall go before thee; the glory of the Lord shall be thy reward" (Isa. lviii. 8). The intellect of these men remains then constantly in the same condition, since the obstacle is removed that at times has intervened between the intellect and the object of its action; it continues for ever in that great delight, which is not like bodily pleasure. We have explained this in our work, and others have explained it before us.

Try to understand this chapter, endeavour with all your might to spend more and more time in communion with God, or in the attempt to approach Him; and to reduce the hours which you spend in other occupations, and during which you are not striving to come nearer unto Him. This instruction suffices for the object of this treatise.

ISAAC BEN SHESHET, *RESPONSA*

Translation by Ephraim Kanarfogel

RESPONSUM NO. 157

Oran — To R. Amram b. Mervam

Most exalted brother, may the guardian of His pious ones watch over you. Your letters have reached me, the first via the Jew from Seville. There further reached me a second letter via ben Bitash. With regard to both of them, the community did what was proper. I signed ben Bitash's document in your honor since he was going to Bougie and Constantinople. There further reached me a third letter on the intermediate days of Tabernacles via my dear brother-in-law. To all these letters, I had no time or opportunity to answer, except for the first one to which I returned an answer via that Jew; and I informed you that I wrote to you by way of [the city of] Honein via an honored merchant from Tlemcen, an acquaintance of the revered R. Abraham b. Sasportas, and with his documents I sent you a copy of my responsum to Malaga. . . . I have no doubt that it reached or will reach you; if it does not reach you, inform me and I will write it to you again.

I also informed you that my teacher, R. Pereẓ ha-Kohen of blessed memory, did not speak of or recognize such *sefirot* (Divine emanations). I also heard from him that R. Samson of Chinon, who was a greater master than all of his contemporaries, and of whom I also have memories even though I did not actually see him, was wont to say, "I pray with the knowledge of a child," to distinguish himself from the Kabbalists who sometimes pray to one *sefirah* and sometimes to a different one, according to the content of the prayer. They claim that this is the meaning of the statement by the Rabbis of blessed memory (*Baba Batra* 25b) "One who wishes to become wise [should turn] to the south; to become rich, one [should turn] to the north." That is to say, one should direct himself to the attribute of the right or to the attribute of the left. Also, in the *shemoneh esreh* prayer, they direct each blessing to a particular *sefirah*. All this is extremely bizarre in the eyes of one who is not a Kabbalist as they. They consider this to be a secondary belief. I have heard one of the philosophers speak disparagingly of the Kabbalists and remark that the Christians believe in a Trinity while the Kabbalists believe in a Decem-Unity (ten *sefirot*). It happened to me while I was in Saragosa that there came to the city the venerable scholar Don Joseph ibn Shushan of blessed memory, whom I had already seen in Valencia. He was knowledgeable in the Talmud and had seen philosophical works; he was a Kabbalist and a very saintly man, meticulous in [observing] the commandments. There was a great love between us. I once asked him, "How is it that you Kabbalists direct one blessing to one *sefirah* and another blessing to a different one? Furthermore, are the *sefirot* so endowed with divinity so that one should pray to them?" He answered me, "Far be it that prayers be other than to God, blessed be He, the Cause of all causes. The matter is comparable to [the situation] of a person engaged in a quarrel [who] asks for judgment, petitioning [the king] to command the person sitting in judgment to judge the case. He does not [petition the king] to command the official appointed over the treasury [to judge the case] for that would be an erroneous request. Similarly, should he ask the king to give him a gift, he does not ask the king to command the judge but rather to command the finance minister. Similarly, should he ask [the king] for wine, he petitions the king to give the command to the wine steward and should he ask for bread, [the king] will tell the baker, and not the reverse. Such is the case with regard to prayer—which is always [addressed] to the Cause of causes. But, one directs his thought . . . to the *sefirah* associated with the matter he is requesting. For example, in the blessing of *al-ha-Ẓaddikim* (on behalf of the righteous), one should think of the *sefirah* known as *ḥesed* which is the attribute of mercy and in the blessing of *al ha-minim* (against heretics), one should think of the *sefirah* known as *gevurah* which is the attribute of justice."

This was explained to me by the aforementioned pious person regarding the Kabbalists' intentions and it is [a] very good [explanation]. But who forces us to enter into all of this? It is better to pray to God alone with concentration and He will know the way to fulfill that which is requested as the verse states, "Commit your way unto God; Trust in Him and He will bring it to pass." (Ps. 37:5). This is also what the great rabbi, R. Samson of Chinon, said as I have mentioned earlier.

I also informed you that my teacher, R. Nissim, told me privately[1] that Nahmanides involved himself much more than necessary in belief in Kabbalah. I do not involve myself in this discipline because I did not learn it from a knowledgeable Kabbalist. Although I have seen explanations of the secrets of Nahmanides they nevertheless do not reveal the roots of this discipline. They uncover one cubit and cover several cubits; it is very easy to err in such a matter. Therefore, I chose not to involve myself in hidden matters.

[With regard to] the question that you asked [viz.] whether the *sefirot* are below the level of the angels or above it, there is no doubt that the *sefirot* are above and were emanated first. From the ten [*sefirot*] emanated the angels. This was written explicitly by R. Shem Tov b. Gaon in the beginning of his commentary on the secrets of Nahmanides. R. Judah ha-Levi wrote in a finale which he composed for the Day of Atonement, which was recited in Barcelona during its tranquility, that David when he said, "Bless the Lord, you His angels . . ." (Ps. 103:20) alluded to the world of the angels and when he said, "Bless the Lord all His hosts . . .," (Ps. 103:21) he alluded to the intermediate world, and when he said, "Bless the Lord all His works . . ." (Ps. 103:22) he alluded to the lower world. . .

NOTES

1. A possible, but less likely translation of the term used, *"be-yiḥud,"* in this context is "clearly" or "explicitly"; cf. Rashi, *Beiẓah* 22b.

ALBO, *IKKARIM*

Translation by Isaac Husik

BOOK IV, CHAPTER 16

Having treated of Providence, it is proper to follow it up with a discussion of prayer. For though prayer is not a fundamental principle of the Torah, nevertheless it is a branch growing out of Providence. The acceptance of prayer necessarily indicates Providence, as we said before. And on the other hand, every one who believes in Providence must believe that prayer will help him and save him from misfortune. If one does not pray in a time of trouble, it is either because he does not believe in Providence, or because, though he does believe in Providence, he doubts God's ability to save him—both of which are forms of unbelief—or because, though he believes in Providence and doubts not God's ability to save him, for God is all powerful, he doubts whether he is worthy of the privilege of having his prayer heard.

Now it is true that a man must never be righteous in his own eyes, nevertheless this should not prevent him from praying to God to satisfy his needs. For to refrain from prayer on this account indicates a belief that the good which comes to man from God is a reward for his good deeds and not due to God's mercy and kindness. But this opinion is incorrect, as we read in the Bible: "We do not present our supplications before Thee because of our righteousness, but because of Thy great compassions."[1] The kindness of God and the mercy He bestows upon all His creatures are based upon pure loving kindness, and are not in the nature of compensation, as God said to Job: "Who hath given Me anything beforehand, that I should repay him?"[2] The Rabbis say: If a man makes a *mezuzah*[3] have I not given him the house? And if he attaches *zizit* (fringes) to his garment,[4] have I not given him the garment?[5]

The proper belief, then, is that all benefits which come from God are due purely to His loving kindness, and are not compensation for one's good deeds. This being so, benefits may come from God whether the recipient deserves to receive them or not. For prayer confers a capacity upon a person who is not by nature fit to receive a given benefit. No one else except God can do anything like this unless the recipient has a capacity, natural or artificial; because all the superlunar powers are finite and can act only upon that which is prepared to receive their influence. As fire has the power to make warm, and water to make cold, so Mars has the power, for example, to destroy, to kill and to ruin. But it can not bestow the opposite of that which the recipient is prepared to receive or vary its activity, as the fire has no power to make cool. Similarly Jupiter has the power to make prosperous and rich, but he can not change that indication and give the recipient the opposite, as water has not the power to make warm, except *per accidens.*[6] The same thing applies to the other superlunar powers.

The Rabbis explain this matter in the Talmud: "When the wicked Nebuchadnezzar cast Hananiah, Mishael and Azariah into the fiery furnace, Yurkemi, the spirit of hail, came before God and said, Lord of the world, let me go down and cool the furnace, and save the righteous men. Thereupon Gabriel rose before God, and said: This is not in consonance with the dignity of God, but let me, the spirit of fire, go and heat the furnace on the outside and cool it within so that there may be a miracle within a miracle."[7] It is clear from this that Yurkemi only had the power to cool and Gabriel had the power only to heat, except when God desired otherwise. The superlunar powers, therefore, can not act upon the recipients unless the latter have the capacity, whether the influence comes upon the recipient through a visible property or an invisible. For example, drugs act upon those who take them, either through their natural qualities or through their properties, which are invisible qualities, according as the recipients are prepared to receive the quality or property in question.

Now when the recipient prepares himself to receive the influence which comes from the visible nature of a given star, as for example, to receive moisture from the moon or heat from the sun, there is no likelihood of an erroneous opinion that the effect is due to the favor of the star. But if the recipient prepares himself to receive the influence of the star through one of those acts whose causes are unknown, like the acts of drugs which come from their properties, people are led into the erroneous opinion that the effect is due to the favor of the star. But it is not true. The fact is this, that just as the influence of the teacher affects the pupil who is prepared more than the one who is not prepared, though the teacher is not directing his instruction to the one more than the other, so the influence of the star reaches the one who is prepared more than the one who is unprepared, without any intention or will on the part of the star.

The error of the idolaters was just this, namely, that they thought that the influence which comes from the star is due to the favor of the star gained by doing those things which are of particular interest to the particular star, not knowing that the real reason is because those activities prepare the recipient. The error was due to the fact that the causes are unknown. For this reason they bowed down before the star and prayed to it, offered sacrifices, burned incense and poured out libations to it, thinking to obtain its favor through these rites.

The error here is clear, for the force of the higher powers is limited, and no one of them can do anything else than that which its nature determines. And its activity depends upon the preparation of the recipient and is not in the nature of a voluntary act. Baal Peor, for example, had the power to act as a purgative for those who performed the act of defecation before him. The Rabbis say that the priests fed the person with beets and gave him beer of *hizme* to drink.[8] The purpose was to prepare the recipient for the effect, which followed in the person who defecated before it, whether he needed it or not, thus benefiting the one who needed it, and injuring and killing the one who needed it not, for the effect was not voluntary. This is why the Bible calls that service, "sacrifices of the dead:" "They joined themselves also unto Baal of Peor, and ate the sacrifices of the dead."[9] The point of the analogy is that just as the dead have not the power to will or not to will, so the stars have not the power to will or not to will. As the fire has not the power to refrain from burning the garment of the righteous man if he comes near it, nor the power to burn the garment of the wicked when he is far away, or if the object is such that it is not subject to being burned, so the star has no power to do good or evil except as its nature dictates and as the recipient is prepared for the effect. Therefore it is not proper to pray to it since it can not act voluntarily. God alone is the one to pray to, because His activities are voluntary. He can will or not, can do a thing as well as its opposite, can do a kindness gratis, i.e. whether the recipient is deserving or not, provided he prepares himself by prayer alone.

This is stated clearly in the Bible in many places, and especially in relation to Menasseh, son of Hezekiah, king of Judah, who was a thoroughly wicked man, and never had his like before or after in disobedience and wrongdoing. And yet we read: "And when he was in distress, he besought the Lord his God . . . and he prayed unto Him; and He was entreated of him, and heard his supplication, and brought him back to Jerusalem into his kingdom."[10] We learn from this two things, one is that even though a person is thoroughly wicked like Menasseh, he may become fit to receive divine grace through prayer. The second is that prayer is heard even though it is forced by distress, as the text testifies: "And when he was in distress . . ."

This shows how wonderfully great is God's kindness to His creatures. For a human being under similar circumstances would say, "Why are ye come unto me now when ye are in distress?"[11] But God delights in loving-kindness, and His right hand is extended to receive penitents at all times. Thus the Psalmist says: "Then they cried unto the Lord in their trouble, and He delivered them . . ."[12] Jonah says: "I called out of mine affliction unto the Lord, and He answered me."[13] He means, although I did not deserve to have my prayer in distress accepted, after I ran away from Him, nevertheless He did not forbear to answer me.

NOTES

1. Dan. 9, 18.
2. Job 41, 3.
3. An inscription on the doorpost, according to Deut. 6, 9.
4. Num. 15, 38.
5. Yalkut Shim'oni ad locum.
6. I.e. by virtue of the heat of fire which has made the water hot.
7. Pesahim 118a.
8. Sanhedrin 64a. For the meaning of תרדין and שכר של הזמי see Jastrow, Dictionary s. vv. תרד and היזמא. For Baal Peor, see Num. 25, 3 and Gesenius, Lexicon. It is hard to tell whether the talmudic description of the worship has a tradition behind it or not. It surely has no basis in the biblical text, which bears a different implication. [Sanhedrin 64a cites neither biblical source nor rabbinic tradition in describing the preparatory procedure, but rather the instructions given a gentile woman by pagan priests. The description of the act of worship itself is an elucidation of the term "Peor." J.D.B.]
9. Ps. 106, 28.
10. II Chron. 33, 12–13.
11. Judg. 11, 7.
12. Ps. 107, 6.
13. Jonah 2, 3.

BOOK IV, CHAPTER 17

All kinds of loving-kindness emanate and derive from God, and there is no other being who can bestow a kindness on any one. The reason is because one can not expect an absolute kindness from any one unless the latter has the following four attributes.

1. He must be unchangeable; for if he is subject to change, the kindness coming from him can not be absolute because it will not be permanent. But God is the only unchangeable being, as I explained in Book II, chapter 2.[1]

2. He must not require the aid of any other being in bestowing the kindness or benefit in question. For if he requires the aid of another, the recipient can not be sure of the continuance of that kindness unless the aid continues. The superlunar powers are a case in point. They indicate a certain event if a certain other condition or cause is there to assist them, for example, if the rising star is in its elevation,[2] or faces a favorable star, and the like. But there is no other being who requires no assistance except God, as the Bible says: "I am the Lord that maketh all things; That stretcheth forth the heavens alone; That spread abroad the earth by Myself."[3]

3. He must be equally able to do either of two opposed things, else the recipient would not be able to obtain his desire at all times. For a person sometimes needs one thing and sometimes its opposite, for example sometimes he has to make war, and sometimes he has need of peace. Now it is well known in relation to the superlunar powers that the star which indicates war does not indicate peace, and the star which indicates destruction does not indicate building up, and the star which indicates war has no power to change its indication into one of peace. Similarly the star which indicates disease does not indicate health. Hence the recipient of a kindness can never be sure that he will always have the kindness that he needs, unless the giver has equal ability to give either of two opposite things. But there is no one else who has this power except God, as we read: "I form the light, and create darkness; I make peace and create evil; I am the Lord that doeth all these things."[4]

4. The giver must be so situated that there is no other being who can prevent him from doing his will. For if there is one who can prevent him, then the recipient of the kindness can never be sure of obtaining the favor which he desires of the giver, for the latter may be prevented from doing it. Now it is clear that every being except God can be prevented by God, but no one can prevent God from doing His will, as we read: "Behold, He snatcheth away, who can hinder Him? Who will say unto Him: 'What doest Thou?'"[5]

When these conditions are combined in the giver, the recipient is assured that he will obtain his desire and that the kindness he receives will be permanent. Now since there is no one but God who combines in him these four conditions, it is clear that one should not desire or hope for any favor from any one else. . . .

Prayer should therefore be directed to Him alone and to no one else. For how can a man pray to one who can not grant his prayer or request? Reason dictates that one should pray only to one who is able to grant one's request. For the impulse to pray comes from reason. It is true that we read in the Bible: "Lord, Thou hast heard the desire of the humble,"[12] from which it may appear that the impulse to pray is due to the faculty of desire, but it is not so. As soon as the power of desire begins to act, the rational faculty is aroused and reflects and seeks for a way to realize the desire. And when it determines that it can not be attained except through God who can do all things, and bestows kindness even upon those who are not deserving, it comes at once to the conclusion that God is the one to pray to. . .

Daniel also was told: "From the first day that thou didst set thy heart to understand, and to humble thyself before thy God, thy words were heard."[13] In explanation of this our Rabbis say,[14] "From this we learn that the intention to fast, even before the actual fasting, helps one in having his prayer received, by reason of the fact that his heart is prepared." This is the meaning of the biblical expression: "And it shall come to pass that, before they call, I will answer."[15] The meaning is, when the rational power prepares itself to pray or to submit to God and fast, even before the actual prayer and fasting take place, I will answer; and while they are talking about praying and fasting, I will hear them, even before they actually begin their prayer; provided, however, that the rational power has decided that the thing in question is a proper thing to pray for, and that it is possible of attainment, not merely so far as the giver is concerned—for God can do everything—but that the possibility is there also so far as the recipient is concerned, i.e. that he is properly prepared to receive the favor in question. For if the recipient is not capable of receiving so great a kindness, if it is something which it is not in his power to receive, it is wrong to pray for it. Thus it is wrong to pray to God that He should make one king of the whole world like Alexander the Great, though it is possible so far as the giver is concerned, since God can do everything. The reason is because the recipient is not capable of receiving so great a favor, for not every one is fit to rule over all the inhabitants of the earth, as there may be among them some one who is better prepared for it than he, and God would not deprive the other one on account of this one. The kindness of God invoked by prayer shows itself to the recipient according to the power of the latter to receive. This is what the Psalmist had in mind when he said: "Commit thy way unto the Lord . . ."[16] The meaning is that it is the wisdom of God that determines what things are beneficial to man, and who is worthy to receive His benefits.

NOTES

1. Cf. also II, 19.
2. בעל הצומח and בית כבודו are astrological terms. צומח means rising. Ibn Ezra in his ספר המולדות (Paris, Nat. Lib., Fonds Heb. 1056, fol. 46) has בהכנס מאדים אל מעלתו הצומחת. See below, IV, 43, page 433, note 2, לידע הצומח לקחת הצומח, and cf. Rosin, MGWJ, 42, p. 308; ib. p. 316 f. כבוד=elevation. See also Efros in J.Q.R., N.S., 17, 329.
3. Isa. 44, 24.
4. Ibid. 45, 7.
5. Job 9, 12.
6. Deut. 32, 39.
7. Deut. 32, 37–38.
8. Isa. 40, 25.
9. Isa. 43, 11.
10. Deut. 32, 39.
11. Ps. 130, 7.
12. Ps. 10, 17.
13. Dan. 10, 12.
14. Ta'anit 8b, ed. Malter, p. 56.
15. Isa. 65, 24.
16. Ps. 37, 5.

BOOK IV, CHAPTER 18

The reason which leads men to doubt the efficacy of prayer is the same as that which leads them to deny God's knowledge. Their argument is as follows: Either God has determined that a given person shall receive a given benefit, or He has not so determined. If He has determined, there is no need of prayer; and if He has not determined, how can prayer avail to change God's will that He should now determine to benefit the person, when He had not so determined before? For God does not change from a state of willing to a state of not willing, or vice versa. For this reason they say that right conduct is of no avail for receiving a good from God. And similarly they say that prayer does not avail to enable one to receive a benefit or to be saved from an evil which has been decreed against him.

Job argues in this manner in the name of the wicked and inclines to it. Sceptically he asks, If God takes notice of human conduct, why does He not punish tbe wicked for believing in this manner? "Wherefore do the wicked live, become old, yea, wax mighty in power? Their seed is established in their sight with them, and their offspring before their eyes . . . Yet they say unto God: 'Depart from us; for we desire not the knowledge of Thy ways. What is the Almighty, that we should serve Him? And what profit should we have, if we pray unto Him?'"[1] This shows their opinion that right conduct is of no benefit: "What is the Almighty that we should serve Him?" and that prayer is of no avail: "And what profit should we have, if we pray unto Him?" The reason for this belief is their opinion that when a certain evil has been determined for any one, it can not be annuled in any way.

That Job was inclined to sympathize with this idea appears from the remark which follows: "Lo, their prosperity is not in their hand; the counsel of the wicked is far from me."[2] The meaning is, I see that their prosperity is not in their hands, i.e. they can not increase their goods by right coduct, nor do their evil deeds injure them by taking away from them the benefits which they get. Hence I say: "The counsel of the wicked is far from me." That is, the divine plan which decides that these wicked men should spend their lives in prosperity is far from my understanding. Therefore I say that everything is pre-ordained, for if everything were not pre-ordained, and right conduct were of any benefit, the wicked should have misfortune for their deeds. But it is not so, for: "How oft is it that the lamp of the wicked is put out? That their calamity cometh upon them? That He distributeth pains in His anger?"[3] That is, how often does it happen that they are punished for their evil deeds, and that God sends misfortunes upon them in His anger on account of their wrong doing? From this it seems that Job inclined to the opinion of the wicked men who said that everything is pre-ordained, and that neither right conduct nor prayer can avail to annul the pre-determined event.

But this opinion is not true, for the influences from above come down upon the recipient when he is in a certain degree and state of preparation to receive them. And if a person does not prepare himself, he withholds the good from himself. For example, if it has been determined from on high that a given person's crops shall prosper in a given year, and he neglects to plow or sow his land that year, then God may bring the most abundant rain upon the land but his crops will not prosper, seeing that he has not plowed or sowed. He withheld the good from himself because he did not prepare himself to receive it.

Our idea therefore is that when a benefit is determined in favor of any one, it is conditional upon a certain degree of right conduct. This must be taken to be a general principle as regards the promises in the Bible. In the same way when a certain evil is determined upon some one, it is also conditional upon his being wicked in a certain degree or of being predisposed to it. And if the degree of wickedness or predisposition thereto changes, the pre-determined event or fate changes also necessarily for the better or the worse.

The matter is similar to the hypothetical case of a king who made a decree that all the uncircumcised persons in a given country should be killed, or should receive a talent of gold. Now if one of the people has himself circumcised, there is no doubt that the decree is of no effect so far as he is concerned, whether for good or for evil, by reason of the new state into which the person has been brought. The effort, therefore, to do good is essential everywhere, for it serves as a preparation for the reception of the divine influence or for the annulment of a divine decree.

This is in agreement with the statement of our Rabbis: "Rabba came to Mamla, and saw that all the people had black hair.[4] He inquired for the reason and was told that they were descendants of Eli, concerning whom it is said; 'And all the increase of thy house shall die young men.'[5] Then he said to them: Go and study the Torah, concerning which it is written: 'For she is thy life and the length of thy days.'"[6] From this it is clear that divine decrees are conditional upon the recipient being in a certain state and degree of preparation. And if that changes, the decree changes also. This is the reason why the Rabbis say that a change of name may avail to nullify a decree, as also change of conduct may have the same effect.[7]

In this way repentance benefits a wicked man, for through repentance he becomes another person, as it were, concerning whom no such decree was made. Take the case of Ahab. The Bible says concerning him: "But there was none like unto Ahab, who did give himself over to do that which was evil in the sight of the Lord,"[8] and a divine decree was made against him. And then, because he fasted, and covered himself with sackcloth, and humbled himself before God, it was said to Elijah: "Because he humbleth himself before Me, I will not bring the evil in his days; but in his son's days will I bring the evil upon his house."[9] This shows that when a decree is made upon a wicked person, it is conditional upon his maintaining his state of wickedness. But if he changes that state through repentance, he, as it were, changes into another person upon whom that decree was not made.

In this way, it is clear that prayer and right conduct help to prepare the person to receive the good influence or to nullify the evil that has been decreed concerning him, because he changes from the evil state in which he was. Zophar alludes to this argument when he blames Job for not praying to God to deliver him from his misfortune, and for not preparing himself to nullify the decree: "If thou set thy heart aright, and stretch out thy hands toward Him—If iniquity be in thy hand, put it far away . . . Surely then shalt thou lift up thy face without spot . . ."[10] That is, if you set your heart to pray and to improve your conduct, there is no doubt that through prayer and right conduct you will escape from these troubles. From this it is clear that prayer and right conduct are always helpful in nullifying a divine decree. Our Rabbis also say:[11] "The cry [of prayer] is good for a man both before the divine decision and after."

As for the objection that the divine will can not be changed by prayer, the answer is that the divine will in the first place is that the decree should be realized if the person in question continues in the same state, and that the decree should be changed if the person's state changes.

The other problem, namely that God's knowledge would change as the man's state changes through prayer, is related to the problem of the relation of God's knowledge to the category of the contingent. Now just as we do not find it necessary that God's knowledge should change because the contingent is a real category, so we do not find it necessary that it should change because of prayer, but we believe that as God's knowledge does not change because of the existence of the contingent, so it does not change because of the efficacy of prayer. We believe that the contingent is real because experience testifies to it, and similarly we believe that prayer has the effect of nullifying a divine decree because experience testifies to it, as we shall see, and though we do not know how to reconcile God's changeless knowledge with the efficacy of prayer, as we do not know how to reconcile it with the contingent, we do not on this account deny what experience proves, namely that God listens to prayer and grants the person's request, whatever it be.

This is the answer which Eliphaz gave to Job when he saw that Job was inclined to accept the view of the wicked, who say: "What is the Almighty that we should serve Him? And what profit should we have, if we pray unto Him?"[12] In answer to this Eliphaz says: "And thou sayest: 'What doth God know? Can He judge through the dark cloud? Thick clouds are a covering to Him, that He seeth not . . .'"[13] That is, since you incline to the opinion of the wicked, who say: "What profit should we have, if we pray unto Him?" thus denying the efficacy of prayer in order to save God's changeless knowledge, you must also in the same way deny God's knowledge of the contingent in order to save His changeless knowledge: "And thou sayest: 'What doth God know?'" Your opinion seems to be that the world is ruled by unchanging law, which Eliphaz calls "The way of the world," when he says to Job: "Wilt thou keep the way of the world which wicked men have trodden? . . . who said unto God: 'Depart from us;' and what could the Almighty do unto them?"[14] He calls those men wicked who say that the world is ruled by unchanging law, because they deny the efficacy of right conduct and prayer. Hence he concludes: "If thou return to the Almighty, thou shalt be built up . . . thou shalt make thy prayer unto Him, and He will hear thee . . . ,"[15] alluding, as it were, to the fact that his misfortunes came upon him because he believed that his prosperity had been due not to God, but to nature; and he entertained the same belief about the origin of his misfortune, and hence he did not pray to God concerning them. Eliphaz, therefore, says to him that if he returns to God and prays to Him and acknowledges that everything came to him from God, He will hear his prayer, will save him from his sufferings and will prosper his affairs. Hence he says: "Thou shalt make thy prayer unto Him, and He will hear thee . . . and the Almighty be thy treasure, and precious silver unto thee,"[16] i.e. through prayer your affairs will prosper. The Bible also testifies to the truth of this when it says: "And the Lord changed the fortune of Job, when he prayed for his friends."[17] When he came to believe that prayer has efficacy, he prayed to God, and immediately God changed his fortune.

NOTES

1. Job 21, 7, 15.
2. Job 21, 16.
3. Ibid. 17.
4. I.e. he saw only young men, which indicated that the inhabitants were short lived.
5. I Sam. 2, 33.
6. Deut. 30, 20; Bereshit Rabbah, 59. Albo's citation differs considerably from the midrashic text. Cf. also Yebamot 105a.
7. Rosh Hashanah 16b; Bereshit Rabbah 44, 12. For parallel passages see Theodor ad. loc.
8. I Kings 21, 25.
9. Ibid. 29.
10. Job 11, 13–15.
11. Rosh Hashanah 18a.
12. Job 21, 15.
13. Ibid. 22, 13–14.
14. Job 22, 15–17.
15. Ibid. vv. 23, 27.
16. Ibid. 25.
17. Ibid. 42, 10.

The Sixth Principle

Prophecy

INTRODUCTION

The Sixth Principle is an affirmation of the phenomenon of prophecy and of its nature. The *ani ma'amin* formulation contained in the prayerbook, which reads, "I believe with perfect faith that all the words of the Torah are true," is not an accurate paraphrase. Belief in the veracity of the words of the prophets is included in the content of the Eighth Principle, which affirms the divine nature of Scripture in its entirety. The Sixth Principle deals not with the truth of recorded prophecy but with the factual existence of the phenomenon of prophecy.

The Talmud, *Megillah* 14a, declares that during the course of Jewish history the total number of persons privileged to experience the phenomenon of prophecy will be equal to twice the number of those who participated in the Exodus from Egypt. Certainly, not all of these approximately 1,200,000 individuals are deemed to be bearers of prophetic messages worthy of incorporation in sacred writ. Scripture records the prophetic utterances of only a small fraction of this number, forty-eight prophets and seven prophetesses. The vast majority of prophets were not the bearers of prophetic messages designed to be immortalized for posterity as the word of God.

In actuality, not all prophets are bearers of divine messages. The essence of prophecy is an attachment to, or communication with, God which is experiential in nature. God may at times utilize this bond of communication as a means of transmitting a message to others through the prophet via the medium of the prophetic experience. Even prognostication and the foretelling of future events is incidental to the prophetic experience.

Saadia denies that prophets "were possessed of some peculiarity" which enabled them to know the secrets of the future as a matter of course. The prophet is selected by God to serve as a messenger to mankind. The ability to perform miracles and to obtain knowledge to which other mortals are not privy is severely limited. The prophet is permitted to perform miracles only on certain occasions, and to obtain knowledge of future occurrences only at certain times, precisely in order that there be no error with regard to the nature of prophecy, which Saadia asserts must be conferred as an act of divine grace. Were the prophet to manifest his powers constantly, prophecy might erroneously be presumed to be a natural faculty present in at least some men.

Judah Halevi views prophecy as the unique gift of the Jewish people. The propensity for the prophetic experience is transmitted in what may perhaps be described as a meta-genetic manner. The capacity to enter into the prophetic experience was part of the unique human perfection enjoyed by Adam and transmitted by him to select progeny. The prophet, for Judah Halevi, must not only be heir to a unique spiritual legacy but must nurture this faculty under ideal geographical and climatic conditions. It is for this reason that prophecy occurs only in the Land of Israel. Hasdai Crescas agrees with Halevi that the gift of prophecy is limited to Jews but denies the mystic nature of this limitation. For Crescas unique moral training is necessary in order to develop the degree of spiritual perfection which is the prerequisite of prophecy. Since this moral excellence can be achieved only through adherence to the precepts of the Torah, which is the possession of the Jewish people, prophecy is, practically speaking, limited to Jews.

Maimonides adopts the view that prophecy is natural in the sense that it is a psycho-intellectual state achieved as the culmination of moral, intellectual and spiritual perfection. As such, prophecy is the epitome of human intellectual perfection. The prophetic state is achieved through the unification of the human intellect and the Active Intellect. As man develops his rational faculty, his soul gradually frees itself from his body so that it may become united with the Active Intellect with which it shares an affinity. The ultimate communication which takes place by virtue of this unification is the prophetic experience. The Active Intellect is passive in this phenomenon. It is the human intellect which reaches out and enjoys the unparalleled intellectual bliss of contemplating the Active Intellect. This phenomenon is "natural." Any person possessing the requisite moral and intellectual perfection may achieve this state unless God intervenes in order to prevent this phenomenon from occurring.

Maimonides maintains that many of the incidents recorded in the Bible which appear to be reports of actual occurrences are, in reality, descriptions of prophetic experiences. In particular, the appearance of divine messengers to Abraham and the wrestling of Jacob with an angel are not regarded by Maimonides as having been actual historical events. Naḥmanides takes sharp issue with this position and affirms the factual nature of these incidents and of similar events recorded in the Bible.

Gersonides' view with regard to the nature of prophecy closely parallels that of Maimonides, although some details of Gersonides' theory are not present in Maimonides. Gersonides asserts that natural events are, to a large degree, determined by the heavenly bodies. These events are known to the Active Intellect, which in turn imparts a knowledge of them to man. Information may be imparted through dreams, divination or prophecy in order that man, in acquiring this information, may protect himself from evil destined to befall him by virtue of the natural order or so that he may use this information in order to benefit from natural occurrences. The Active Intellect is only indirectly responsible for imparting information by means of dreams or divination. Such phenomena are produced by the heavenly bodies which act upon the imagination. Prophecy is derived directly from the Active Intellect acting upon the material intellect. Hence, a high degree of intelligence is a requisite of prophecy.

Albo, disagreeing with both Maimonides and Gersonides, accepts the view espoused by Judah Halevi and Crescas and maintains that prophecy is a supernatural gift bestowed as an act of divine will. Normally, however, the gift of prophecy is accorded only to those who are worthy and intellectually prepared to receive it. Albo agrees with the view of Halevi that prophecy is found only among Jews and only in the Land of Israel. Prophecy is limited in this manner because it is possible only by virtue of the presence of the Divine Spirit. The ark and the tablets upon which the Divine Presence rests reflect the Divine Spirit upon those selected as recipients of the gift of prophecy.

SAADIA, *EMUNOT VE-DE'OT*

Translation by Alexander Altmann

THIRD TREATISE
COMMANDMENT AND PROHIBITION

4. *The Credentials of True Prophecy*

Having explained the necessity for the sending of prophets, it is desirable that I should now explain how their prophetic mission was verified to the rest of the people.[1] I say then that men know (the limits) of their power and ability, namely, the fact that they are unable to subdue the elements of nature or to change the essence of things. They realize that they are powerless in regard to these matters since this is the work of the Creator. He subdued the diverse elements of nature and combined them to form composite things in spite of their antagonistic character. He transformed their original natures so that, in their combinations, their essential characteristics disappeared and something new and different emerged, namely, man and plant and similar bodies. This is indisputably a sign that they are the work of a Creator. Now every prophet chosen by the Creator for a prophetic mission commences his career as soon as God furnishes him with one of the following signs; either he enables him to subdue the elements of nature, e.g. to prevent fire from burning or restraining water from flowing or cause the sphere to halt on its way, etc.; or He enables him to change the essence of the elements, e.g. to transform an organism into inorganic nature, or inorganic nature into an organism, or water into blood, or blood into water. And whenever such a sign is delivered into the hands of the prophet the people who see it are obliged to pay reverence to him and to hold his message to be true, for the Wise (God) does not deliver a sign into his hands unless he is trusted.[2] This fact, although discoverable by Reason, is also stated in the text of Scripture, as the reader will know from the story of our Teacher Moses and the wonders and miracles delivered into his hand, which, for the sake of brevity, I shall not mention here as these things are described in the text of the Book of Exodus and in other books and their Commentaries;[3] thus, he said to his people, 'The great trials which thine eyes saw' (Deut. 7.19). Those men[4] who believed[5] in him believed the truth,[6] and they were the superior ones, as is said, 'And he did the signs in the sight of the people, and the people believed' (Ex. 4.30-31). Those who did not believe in him and did not believe the truth were lost in error, as the reader will know from the story of those in regard to whom it is said, 'Because they believed not in God. . .' (Ps. 78.22).

I must here add a qualification to avoid misunderstanding, namely, that the Creator (be He exalted and glorified) does not change the essence of a thing before having announced to the people that He is going to change it. The reason for this[7] is that they may believe in the truth of His prophet. But without reason He does not make any change in the essence of things, for if we were to believe[8] that, we should have no certainty of anything, and none of us when returning to his home and people would be sure that the Creator had not changed their essences so that they would be different from what they were when we left them; similarly if a man acted as witness for a person or pronounced judgment on a person. But it is necessary for us to believe[8] that the existing things remain as they are, and that their Lord does not alter them except after having announced it beforehand.

I say furthermore that, in the judgment of wisdom, it is impossible that the messengers sent to mankind should have been angels,[9] because men do not know either the capabilities or the limitations of the angels. If they (the angels) had come and performed miracles which men are powerless to perform, people would have thought that such is the nature of all angels, and they would have had no clear proof that the miracle was a sign from the Creator. If, however, the prophets are men like ourselves and we find that they are doing things which we are actually powerless to do and which are entirely the work of the Creator, it becomes evident to us that they are sent by His Word. I maintain that for this very reason God placed the prophets and the rest of mankind on the same level in regard to death, so that men should not think that, in the same way as the prophets differ from the rest of mankind by being able to live forever, so they also differ from the rest of mankind in being able to do things which others are powerless to do. For the same reason, God did not cause them to abstain from food, drink and sexual intercourse, since this might have weakened the force of their miracles, for people might have thought that such abstinence was due to their peculiar nature and that in the same way as such a nature was granted to them, so the power of working miracles was also granted to them. For the same reason, God did not assure them of lasting bodily health, or of great fortunes, or of posterity, or of protection against oppressors seeking to beat or insult or kill them; for if He had done so, it was possible that people might attribute their miracles to their peculiar condition by virtue of which they did not belong to the same class as ordinary men; they would say that since they are shown to be exceptional in those respects, it follows that they are capable of things which all other people are powerless to do. Knowing as I do that His wisdom is above everything, I nevertheless venture to declare that the reason why He left them in every respect in the same condition as the rest of mankind, and yet at the same time made them different by enabling them to do things which all other men are powerless to do, was to verify His sign and to establish His prophecy. I declare that for this reason also, He did not cause them to perform miracles continually or to know the hidden things (of the future) continually lest the people should think that they are possessed of a peculiar quality to which this power is due, but He made them do this at certain periods and to have such knowledge at certain opportune times. In this way it became clear that this originated from the Creator and not from them.[2]

NOTES

1. Saadya explains elsewhere that the appearance of the Created Glory (*Kabod nibra*), which accompanied, as a visible element, the audible manifestation (*dibbur nibra*) of God's Word (see above, p. 90, n. 1), served as a criterion to the Prophet that he was in the presence of Divine Revelation. (Cf. *Amānat*, 99-100, 123; Hebr. 51, 63). Only in the case of Moses' prophecy did the Word speak directly, without the intermediacy of a visible manifestation. (For an explanation of Saadya's complicated theory see the Translator's article, 'Saadya's Theory of Revelation,' pp. 20 ff.). Saadya's problem, in the above chapter, is, however, the criterion of true prophecy, not for the prophet himself, but for the people to whom he is to convey the Divine message. Here the function of miracle comes in, as explained in the text. Although Saadya states (see *Amānāt*, 123; Hebr. 63) that the people saw in the 'Pillar of cloud' a testimony of God's self-manifestation to Moses and probably to the other prophets as well (cf. Ps. 99.7), he regards, not quite consistently, the performance of miracles as a necessary credential of true prophecy.

2. Saadya qualifies this statement later (see below, pp. 113-4) by saying that miracles produced in support of doctrines which are contrary to Reason cannot be accepted as evidence for their truth. For 'no miracle can prove the rationally impossible.' It is most remarkable that he unhesitatingly puts the judgment of Reason above any proof furnished by miracles. Cf. also Albo, *Ikkarim*, I, 18.

3. Arab. *tafsīr.*
4. Lit. 'servants.'
5. Arab. *'āmand.*
6. Arab, *ṣaddaḳa.*
7. I.e. the reason for changing the nature of things.
8. Arab. *'i'tiḳād.*
9. Saadya rejects the conception of angel as intermediary of Revelation. According to the *Barāhima,* who denied prophecy (cf. above, p. 103, n. 2), God communicates with men through angels. Cf. al-Sharastānī, II, 6, 42; Guttmann, p. 103, n. 2.—Saadya also repudiates the angel doctrine in the form given it by Nahawandi and the Maghāriyya sect as well as by Jewish mystics who identified the angel mentioned in Ex. 23.20 with a mediator (*meṭaṭron*), a conception closely akin to the *Logos* of Philonic tradition and bordering upon Gnostic dualism. Instead of the angel, he introduces the conception of *Kaḇod niḇra',* which is rooted in the Jewish mystical tradition. Cf. the Translator's article, 'Saadya's Theory of Revelation,' pp. 17-19; 21-5.
10. Whilst Saadya emphasizes the ordinary human quality of the prophet, Yehudah Hallevi raises the status of the prophet to a position similar to that of the angels. As to the background of Yehudah Hallevi's theory, cf. the article by I. Heinemann in *K'nesset,* 5702, pp. 267 ff., and the Translator's article in *Melilah,* pp. 14-17.

HALEVI, *KUZARI*

Translation by Hartwig Hirschfeld

PART I

95. The Rabbi: Bear with me a little while that I show the lofty station of the people. For me it is sufficient that God chose them as His people from all nations of the world, and allowed His influence to rest on all of them, and that they nearly approached being addressed by Him. It even descended on their women, among whom were prophetesses, whilst since Adam only isolated individuals had been inspired till then. Adam was perfection itself, because no flaw could be found in a work of a wise and Almighty Creator, wrought from a substance chosen by Him, and fashioned according to His own design. There was no restraining influence, no fear of atavism, no question of nutrition or education during the years of childhood and growth; neither was there the influence of climate, water, or soil to consider. For He created him in the form of an adolescent, perfect in body and mind. The soul with which he was endowed was perfect; his intellect was the loftiest which it is possible for a human being to possess, and beyond this he was gifted with the divine power of such high rank, that it brought him into connection with beings divine and spiritual, and enabled him, with slight reflection, to comprehend the great truths without instruction. We call him God's son, and we call all those who were like him also sons of God. He left many children, of whom the only one capable of taking his place was Abel, because he alone was like him. After he had been slain by Cain through jealousy of this privilege, it passed to his brother Seth, who also was like Adam, being [as it were] his essence and heart, whilst the others were like husks and rotten fruit. The essence of Seth, then, passed to Enosh, and in this way the divine influence was inherited by isolated individuals down to Noah. They are compared to the heart; they resembled Adam, and were styled sons of God. They were perfect outwardly and inwardly, their lives, knowledge and ability being likewise faultless. Their lives fix the chronology from Adam to Noah, as well as from Noah to Abraham. There were some, however, among them who did not come under divine influence, as Terah, but his son

Abraham was the disciple of his grandfather Eber, and was born in the lifetime of Noah. Thus the divine spirit descended from the grandfather to the grandchildren. Abraham represented the essence of Eber, being his disciple, and for this reason he was called *Ibri*. Eber represented the essence of Shem, the latter that of Noah, He inherited the temperate zone, the centre and principal part of which is Palestine the land of prophecy. Japheth turned towards north, and Ham towards south. The essence of Abraham passed over to Isaac, to the exclusion of the other sons who were all removed from the land, the special inheritance of Isaac. The prerogative of Isaac descended on Jacob, whilst Esau was sent from the land which belonged to Jacob. The sons of the latter were all worthy of the divine influence, as well as of the country distinguished by the divine spirit. This is the first instance of the divine influence descending on a number of people, whereas it had previously only been vouchsafed to isolated individuals. Then God tended them in Egypt, multiplied and aggrandised them, as a tree with a sound root grows until it produces perfect fruit, resembling the first fruit from which it was planted, viz. Abraham, Isaac, Jacob, Joseph and his brethren. The seed further produced Moses, Aaron and Miriam, Bezaleel, Oholiab, and the chiefs of the tribes, the seventy Elders, who were all endowed with the spirit of prophecy; then Joshua, Kaleb, Hur, and many others. Then they became worthy of having the divine light and providence made visible to them. If disobedient men existed among them, they were hated, but remained, without doubt, of the essence inasmuch as they were part of it on account of their descent and nature, and begat children who were of the same stamp. An ungodly man received consideration in proportion to the minuteness of the essence with which he was endowed, for it reappeared in his children and grandchildren according to the purity of their lineage. This is how we regard Terah and others in whom the divine afflatus was not visible, though, to a certain extent, it underlay his natural disposition, so that he begat a descendant filled with the essence, which was not the case with all the posterity of Ham and Japhet. We perceive a similar phenomenon in nature at large. Many people do not resemble their father, but take after their grandfathers. There cannot, consequently, be any doubt that this nature and resemblance was hidden in the father, although it did not become visible outwardly, as was the nature of Eber in his children, until it reappeared in Abraham. . . .

115. . . Now we do not allow any one who embraces our religion theoretically by means of a word alone to take equal rank with ourselves, but demand actual self-sacrifice, purity, knowledge, circumcision, and numerous religious ceremonies. The convert must adopt

our mode of life entirely. We must bear in mind that the rite of circumcision is a divine symbol, ordained by God to indicate that our desires should be curbed, and discretion used, so that what we engender may be fitted to receive the divine Influence. God allows him who treads this path, as well as his progeny, to approach Him very closely. Those, however, who become Jews do not take equal rank with born Israelites, who are specially privileged to attain to prophecy, whilst the former can only achieve something by learning from them, and can only become pious and learned, but never prophets. . . .

PART II

8. The Rabbi: Even so does the glory of God, which is only a ray of the divine light, benefit His people in His country.

9. Al Khazari: I understand what thou meanest by 'His people,' but less intelligible is what thou sayest about 'His country.'

10. The Rabbi: Thou wilt have no difficulty in perceiving that one country may have higher qualifications than others. There are places in which particular plants, metals, or animals are found, or where the inhabitants are distinguished by their form and character, since perfection or deficiency of the soul are produced by the mingling of the elements.

11. Al Khazari: Yet I never heard that the inhabitants of Palestine were better than other people.

12. The Rabbi: How about the hill on which you say that the vines thrive so well? If it had not been properly planted and cultivated, it would never produce grapes. Priority belongs, in the first instance, to the people which, as stated before, is the essence and kernel [of the nations]. In the second instance, it would belong to the country, on account of the religious acts connected with it, which I would compare to the cultivation of the vineyard. No other place would share the distinction of the divine influence, just as no other mountain might be able to produce good wine.

13. Al Khazari: How could this be? In the time between Adam and Moses were not prophetic visions in other places granted to Abraham in Ur of the Chaldaeans, Ezekiel and Daniel at Babylon, and Jeremiah in Egypt?

14. The Rabbi: Whosoever prophesied did so either in the [Holy] Land, or concerning it, viz. Abraham in order to reach it, Ezekiel and Daniel on account of it. The two latter had lived during the time of the first Temple, had seen the Shekhinah, through the influence of which each one who was duly prepared became of the elect, and able to prophesy. Adam lived and died in the land. Tradition tells us that in the cave [of Machpelāh] were buried the four pairs: Adam and Eve, Abraham and Sarah, Isaac and Rebeccah, Jacob and Leah. This is the land which bore the name 'before the Lord,' and of which it is stated that 'the eyes of the Lord thy God are always upon it' (Deut. xi. 12). It was also the first object of jealousy and envy between Cain and Abel, when they desired to know which of them would be Adam's successor, and heir to his essence and intrinsic perfection; to inherit the land, and to stand in connection with the divine influence, whilst the other would be a

nonentity. Then Abel was killed by Cain, and the realm was without an heir. It is stated that 'Cain' went out of the presence of Lord (Gen. iv. 16), which means that he left the land, saying: 'Behold, Thou hast driven me out this day from the face of the earth, and from Thy face shall I be hid' (*ib.* v. 14). In the same way is it said: 'But Jonah rose up to flee unto Tarshish from the presence of the Lord' (Jonah i. 3), but he only fled from the place of prophecy. God, however, brought him back there out of the belly of the fish, and appointed him prophet in the land. When Seth was born he was like Adam, as it is said: 'He begat in his own likeness, after his image' (Gen. v. 3), and took Abel's place, as it is said: For God has appointed me another seed, instead of Abel, whom Cain slew (*ib.* iv. 25). He merited the title: 'Son of God,' like Adam, and he had a claim on the land, which is the next step to paradise. The land was then the object of jealousy between Isaac and Ishmael, till the latter was rejected as worthless, although it was said concerning him: 'Behold, I have blessed him, and will multiply him exceedingly' (*ib.* xvii. 20) in worldly prosperity; but immediately after it is said: 'My covenant will I establish with Isaac' (v. 21), which refers to his connection with the divine influence and happiness in the world to come. Neither Ishmael nor Esau could boast of a covenant, although they were otherwise prosperous. Jealousy arose between Jacob and Esau for the birthright and blessing, but Esau was rejected in favour of Jacob, in spite of his strength and the latter's weakness. Jeremiah's prophecy concerning Egypt was uttered in Egypt itself. This was also the case with Moses, Aaron and Miriam. Sinai and Parān are reckoned as belonging to Palestine, because they are on this side of the Red Sea, as it is said: 'And I will set thy bounds from the Red Sea, even unto the sea of the Philistines, and from the desert unto the river' (Exod. xxiii. 31). The 'desert' is that of Paran, 'that great and terrible wilderness' (Deut. i. 19), being the southern border. 'The fourth river is Euphrates' (Gen. ii. 14), designates the northern border, where there were the altars of the Patriarchs, who were answered by fire from heaven and the divine light. The 'binding' of Isaac took place on a desolate mountain, viz. Moriah. Not till the days of David, when it was inhabited, was the secret revealed that it was the place specially prepared for the Shekhinah. Araunah, the Jebusite, tilled his land there. Thus it is said: 'And Abraham called the name of the place, *The Lord shall see*, as it is said to this day, in the mount of the Lord it shall be seen' (ib. xxii. 14). In the Book of the Chronicles it is stated more clearly that the Temple was built on mount Moriah. These are, without doubt, the places worthy of being called the gates of heaven. Dost thou not see that Jacob ascribed the vision which he saw, not to the purity of his soul, nor to his belief, nor to true integrity, but to the place, as it is said: 'How awful is this place' (ib. xxviii. 17). Prior to this it is said: 'And he lighted upon a certain place' (ver. 11), viz. the chosen one. Was not Abraham also, and after having been greatly exalted, brought into contact with the divine influence, and made the heart of this essence, removed from his country to the place in which his perfection should become complete? Thus the agriculturer finds the root of a good tree in a desert place. He transplants it into properly tilled ground, to improve it and make it grow; to change it from a wild root into a cultivated one, from one which bore fruit by chance only to one which produced a luxuriant crop. In the same way the gift of prophecy was retained among Abraham's descendants in Palestine, the property of many as long as they remained in the land, and fulfilled the required conditions, viz. purity, worship, and sacrifices, and, above all, the reverence of the Shekhinah. For the divine influence, one might say, singles out him who appears worthy of being connected with it, such as *prophets and pious men*, and is their God.

PART III

The Rabbi: According to our view a servant of God is not one who detaches himself from the world, lest he be a burden to it, and it to him; or hates life, which is one of God's bounties granted to him, as it is written: 'The number of thy days I will fulfil'; 'Thou shalt live long' (Exod. xxiii. 26). On the contrary, he loves the world and a long life, because it affords him opportunities of deserving the world to come. The more good he does the greater is his claim to the next world. He even reaches the degree of Enoch, concerning whom it is said: 'And Enoch walked with God' (Gen. v. 24); or the degree of Elijah, freed from worldly matters, and to be admitted to the realm of angels. In this case he feels no loneliness in solitude and seclusion, since they form his associates. He is rather ill at ease in a crowd, because he misses the divine presence which enables him to dispense with eating and drinking. Such persons might perhaps be happier in complete solitude; they might even welcome death, because it leads to the step beyond which there is none higher. Philosophers and scholars also love solitude to refine their thoughts, and to reap the fruits of truth from their researches, in order that all remaining doubts be dispelled by truth. They only desire the society of disciples who stimulate their research and retentiveness, just as he who is bent upon making money would only surround himself with persons with whom he could do lucrative business. Such a degree is that of Socrates and those who are like him. There is no one nowadays who feels tempted to strive for such a degree, but when the Divine Presence was still in the Holy Land among the people capable of prophecy, some few persons lived an ascetic life in deserts and associated with people of the same frame of mind. They did not seclude themselves completely, but they endeavoured to find support in the knowledge of the Law and in holy and pure actions which brought them near to that high rank. These were the disciples of prophets. He, however, who in our time, place, and people 'whilst no open vision exists' (1 Sam. iii. 1), the desire for study being small, and persons with a natural talent for it absent, would like to retire into ascetic solitude, only courts distress and sickness for soul and body. The misery of sickness is visibly upon him, but one might regard it as the consequence of humility and contrition. He considers himself in prison as it were, and despairs of life from disgust of his prison and pain, but not because he enjoys his seclusion. How could it be otherwise? He has no intercourse with the divine light, and cannot associate himself with it as the prophets. He lacks the necessary learning to be absorbed in it and to enjoy it, as the philosophers did, all the rest of his life. Suppose he is God-fearing, righteous, desires to meet his God in solitude, standing, humbly and contritely, reciting as many prayers and supplications as he possibly can remember, all this affords him satisfaction for a few days as long as it is new. Words frequently repeated by the tongue lose their influence on the soul, and he cannot give to the latter humbleness or submission. Thus he remains night and day, whilst his soul urges him to employ its innate powers in seeing, hearing, speaking, occupation, eating, cohabitation, gain, managing his house, helping the poor, upholding the law with money in case of need. Must he not regret those things to which he has tied his soul, a regret which tends to remove him from the Divine Influence, which he desired to approach?

MAIMONIDES, *MISHNEH TORAH*

Translation by Moses Hyamson

BOOK OF KNOWLEDGE, LAWS CONCERNING THE BASIC PRINCIPLES OF THE TORAH, CHAPTER 7

1. It is one of the basic principles of religion that God inspires men with the prophetic gift. But the spirit of prophecy only rests upon the wise man who is distinguished by great wisdom and strong moral character, whose passions never overcome him in anything whatsoever, but who by his rational faculty always has his passions under control, and possesses a broad and sedate mind. When one, abundantly endowed with these qualities and physically sound, enters the "Paradise" and continuously dwells upon those great and abstruse themes,—having the right mind capable of comprehending and grasping them; sanctifying himself, withdrawing from the ways of the ordinary run of men who walk in the obscurities of the times, zealously training himself not to have a single thought of the vanities of the age and its intrigues, but keeping his mind disengaged, concentrated on higher things as though bound beneath the Celestial Throne, so as to comprehend the pure and holy forms and contemplating the wisdom of God as displayed in His creatures, from the first form to the very centre of the Earth, learning thence to realize His greatness—on such a man the Holy Spirit will promptly descend. And when the spirit rests upon him, his soul will mingle with the angels called *Ishim*. He will be changed into another man and will realize that he is not the same as he had been, and has been exalted above other wise men, even as it is said of Saul "And thou shalt prophesy with them, and shalt be turned into another man." (I Sam. 10:6).

2. The prophets are of various degrees. Just as one sage is greater in wisdom than another, so, in the gift of prophecy, one prophet is greater than another. All the prophets experienced prophetic manifestations only in dreams, at night, or by day after a deep sleep had fallen upon them; as it is said, "I do make Myself known unto him in a vision. I do speak with him in a dream" (Num. 12:6). At the time when they had the prophetic experience, their limbs trembled, their physical strength failed

them, their thoughts became confused; and thus the mind was left free to comprehend the vision it saw, as is said in reference to Abraham, "And lo, an horror of great darkness fell upon him" (Gen. 15:12), and of Daniel, "And my comeliness was turned in me into corruption, and I retained no strength." (Dan. 10:8).

3. The matters communicated to the prophet in a prophetic vision are communicated to him in allegorical form. Its interpretation is immediately impressed upon his mind, simultaneously with the vision, so that he grasps what it means. Such, for example, was the case with the vision the Patriarch Jacob saw (Gen. 28:12–15) of a Ladder with angels ascending and descending it—a type of the Monarchies and their oppression of Israel; the *Chaioth* in Ezekiel's vision (Ezek. Chap. 1); the Seething Cauldron (Jerem. 1:13) and the Rod of an Almond Tree (Jerem. 1:11) seen by Jeremiah; the Scroll seen by Ezekiel (Ezekiel 2:9) and the Ephah (measure) seen by Zechariah (Zech. 5:6) and so with the rest of the prophets. Some, like these prophets, recited the allegory together with its interpretation. Others only gave forth the interpretation. Sometimes, as in the case of some prophecies of Ezekiel and Zechariah, they only recited the allegory. All the prophets prophesied in allegories and riddles.

4. The prophets did not prophesy whenever they pleased, but had to concentrate their minds, resting, joyous and cheerful, and in solitude. For the spirit of prophecy does not descend upon one who is melancholy or indolent, but comes as a result of joyousness. And therefore, the Sons of the Prophets had before them psaltery, tabret, pipe and harp, (I Sam. 10:5), and thus sought a manifestation of the prophetic gift. This is expressed in the phrase, "And they were מתנבאים (ibid. 10:5), which means, that they were on the way to prophesy, before they actually did so, as one might say, "That person is becoming great."

5. Those who sought the prophetic gift were called Sons of the Prophets. Although they concentrated their minds, the Divine Spirit might or might not rest upon them. . .

MAIMONIDES, *MOREH NEVUKHIM*

Translation by Michael Friedlander

PART II, CHAPTER 32

There are as many different opinions concerning Prophecy as concerning the Eternity or Non-Eternity of the Universe. For we have shown that those who assume the existence of God as proved may be divided into three classes, according to the view they take of the question, whether the Universe is eternal or not. Similarly there are three different opinions on Prophecy. I will not notice the view of the Atheist; he does not believe in the Existence of God, much less in Prophecy; but I will content myself with discussing the various opinions [on Prophecy] held by those who believe in God.

1. Among those who believe in Prophecy, and even among our coreligionists, there are some ignorant people who think as follows: God selects any person He pleases, inspires him with the spirit of Prophecy, and entrusts him with a mission. It makes no difference whether that person be wise or stupid, old or young; provided he be, to some extent, morally good. For these people have not yet gone so far as to maintain that God might also inspire a wicked person with His spirit. They admit that this is impossible, unless God has previously caused him to improve his ways.

2. The philosophers hold that prophecy is a certain faculty of man in a state of perfection, which can only be obtained by study. Although the faculty is common to the whole race, yet it is not fully developed in each individual, either on account of the individual's defective constitution, or on account of some other external cause. This is the case with every faculty common to a class. It is only brought to a state of perfection in some individuals, and not in all; but it is impossible that it should not be perfect in some individual of the class; and if the perfection is of such a nature that it can only be produced by an agent, such an agent must exist. Accordingly, it is impossible that an ignorant person should be a prophet; or that a person being no prophet in the evening, should, unexpectedly on the following morning, find himself a prophet, as if prophecy were a thing that could be found unintentionally. But if a person, perfect in his intellectual and moral faculties, and also perfect, as

far as possible, in his imaginative faculty, prepares himself in the manner which will be described, he must become a prophet; for prophecy is a natural faculty of man. It is impossible that a man who has the capacity for prophecy should prepare himself for it without attaining it; just as it is impossible that a person with a healthy constitution should be fed well, and yet not properly assimilate his food; and the like.

3. The third view is that which is taught in Scripture, and which forms one of the principles of our religion. It coincides with the opinion of the philosophers in all points except one. For we believe that, even if one has the capacity for prophecy, and has duly prepared himself, it may yet happen that he does not actually prophesy. It is in that case the will of God [that withholds from him the use of the faculty]. According to my opinion, this fact is as exceptional as any other miracle, and acts in the same way. For the laws of Nature demand that every one should be a prophet, who has a proper physical constitution, and has been duly prepared as regards education and training. If such a person is not a prophet, he is in the same position as a person who, like Jeroboam (1 Kings xiii. 4), is deprived of the use of his hand, or of his eyes, as was the case with the army of Syria, in the history of Elisha (2 Kings vi. 18). As for the principle which I laid down, that preparation and perfection of moral and rational faculties are the *sine qua non,* our Sages say exactly the same: "The spirit of prophecy only rests upon persons who are wise, strong, and rich." We have explained these words in our Commentary on the Mishnah, and in our large work. We stated there that the Sons of the Prophets were constantly engaged in preparation. That those who have prepared themselves may still be prevented from being prophets, may be inferred from the history of Baruch, the son of Nerijah; for he followed Jeremiah, who prepared and instructed him; and yet he hoped in vain for prophecy; comp., "I am weary with my sighing, and rest have I not found." He was then told through Jeremiah, "Thus saith the Lord, Thus shalt thou say to him, Thou seekest for thee great things, do not seek" (Jer. xlv. 5). It may perhaps be assumed that prophecy is here described as a thing "too great" for Baruch. So also the fact that "her prophets did not find visions from the Lord" (Lam. ii. 4), may be considered as the result of the exile of her prophets, as will be explained (chap. xxxvi.) There are, however, numerous passages in Scripture as well as in the writings of our Sages, which support the principle that it depends chiefly on the will of God who shall prophesy, and at what time, and that He only selects the best and the wisest. We hold that fools and ignorant people are unfit for this distinction. It is as impossible for any one of these to prophesy as it is for an ass or a frog; for prophecy is

impossible without study and training; when these have created the possibility, then it depends on the will of God whether the possibility is to be turned into reality. . . . As to the revelation on Mount Sinai, all saw the great fire, and heard the fearful thunderings, that caused such an extraordinary terror; but only those of them who were duly qualified were prophetically inspired, each one according to his capacities. Therefore it is said, "Come up unto the Lord, thou and Aaron, Nadab and Abihu." Moses rose to the highest degree of prophecy, according to the words, "And Moses alone shall come near the Lord." Aaron was below him, Nadab and Abihu below Aaron, and the seventy elders below Nadab and Abihu, and the rest below the latter, each one according to his degree of perfection. Similarly our Sages wrote: Moses had his own place and Aaron his own. Since we have touched upon the revelation on Mount Sinai, we will point out in a separate chapter what may be inferred as regards the nature of that event, both from the Scriptural text, in accordance with reasonable interpretation, and from the words of our Sages.

PART II, CHAPTER 36

Prophecy is, in truth and reality, an emanation sent forth by the Divine Being through the medium of the Active Intellect, in the first instance to man's rational faculty, and then to his imaginative faculty; it is the highest degree and greatest perfection man can attain; it consists in the most perfect development of the imaginative faculty. Prophecy is a faculty that cannot in any way be found in a person, or acquired by man, through a culture of his mental and moral faculties; for even if these latter were as good and perfect as possible, they would be of no avail, unless they were combined with the highest natural excellence of the imaginative faculty. You know that the full development of any faculty of the body, such as the imagination, depends on the condition of the organ, by means of which the faculty acts. This must be the best possible as regards its temperament and its size, and also as regards the purity of its substance. Any defect in this respect cannot in any way be supplied or remedied by training. For when any organ is defective in its temperament, proper training can in the best case restore a healthy condition to some extent, but cannot make such an organ perfect. But if the organ is defective as regards size, position, or as regards the substance and the matter of which the organ is formed, there is no remedy. You know all this, and I need not explain it to you at length.

Part of the functions of the imaginative faculty is, as you well know, to retain impressions by the senses, to combine them, and chiefly to form images. The principal and highest function is performed when the senses are at rest and pause in their action, for then it receives, to some extent, divine inspiration in the measure as it is predisposed for this influence. This is the nature of dreams which prove true, and also of prophecy, the difference being one of quantity, not of quality. Thus our Sages say, that dream is the sixtieth part of prophecy; and no such comparison could be made between two things of different kinds, for we cannot say the perfection of man is so many times the perfection of a horse. In Bereshith Rabba (sect. xvii.) the following saying of our Sages occurs, "Dream is the *nobheleth* (the unripe fruit) of prophecy." This is an excellent comparison, for the unripe fruit (*nobheleth*) is really the fruit to some extent, only it as fallen from the tree before it was fully developed and ripe. In a similar manner the action of the imaginative faculty during sleep is the same as at the time when it receives a prophecy, only in the first case it is not fully developed, and has not yet reached its highest degree. But why need I quote the words of our Sages, when I can refer to the following passage of Scripture; "If there be among you a prophet, I, the Lord, will make Myself known unto him in a vision, in a dream will I speak to him" (Num. xii. 6). Here the Lord tells us what the real essence of prophecy is, that it is a perfection acquired in a dream or in a vision (the original *mareh* is a noun derived from the verb *raah*); the imaginative faculty acquires such an efficiency in its action that it sees the thing as if it came from without, and perceives it as if through the medium of bodily senses. These two modes of prophecy, vision and dream, include all its different degrees. It is a well-known fact that the thing which engages greatly and earnestly man's attention whilst he is awake and in the full possession of his senses forms during his sleep the object of the action of his imaginative faculty. Imagination is then only influenced by the intellect in so far as it is predisposed for such influence. It would be quite useless to illustrate this by a simile, or to explain it fully, as it is clear, and every one knows it. It is like the action of the senses, the existence of which no person with common sense would ever deny. After these introductory remarks you will understand that a person must satisfy the following conditions before he can become a prophet: The substance of the brain must from the very beginning be in the most perfect condition as regards purity of matter, composition of its different parts, size and position; no part of his body must suffer from ill-health; he must in addition have studied and acquired wisdom, so that his rational faculty passes from a state of potentiality to that of actuality; his intellect must be as developed and perfect as human intellect can be; his passions pure and equally balanced; all his desires must aim at obtaining a knowledge of the hidden laws and the causes that are in force in the Universe; his thoughts must be engaged in lofty matters; his attention directed to the knowledge of God, the consideration of His works, and such other things our belief ascribes to Him. There must be an absence of the lower desires and appetites, of the seeking after pleasure in eating, drinking, and cohabitation; and, in short, every pleasure connected with the sense of touch. (Aristotle correctly says that this sense is a disgrace to us, since we possess it only in virtue of our being animals; and it does not include any specifically human element, whilst enjoyments connected with other senses, as smell, hearing, and sight, though likewise of a material nature, may sometimes include [intellectual] pleasure, appealing to man as man, according to Aristotle. This remark, although forming no part of our subject, is not superfluous, for the thoughts of the most renowned wise men are to a great extent affected by the pleasures of this sense, and filled with a desire for them. And yet people are surprised that these scholars do not prophesy, if prophesying be nothing but a certain degree in the natural development of man.) It is further necessary to suppress every thought or desire for unreal power and dominion; that is to say, for victory, increase of followers, acquisition of honour, and service from the people without any ulterior object. On the contrary, the multitude must be considered according to their true worth; some of them are undoubtedly like domesticated cattle, and others like wild beasts, and these only engage the mind of the perfect and distinguished man in so far as he desires to guard himself from injury, in case of contact with them, and to derive some benefit of them when necessary. A man who satisfies these conditions, whilst his fully developed imagination is in action, influenced by the Active Intellect according to his mental training,—such a person will undoubtedly perceive nothing but things very extraordinary and divine, and see nothing but God and His angels. His knowledge will only include that which is real knowledge, and his thought will only be directed to such general principles as would tend to improve the social relations between man and man.

We have thus described three kinds of perfection: mental perfection acquired by training, perfection of the natural constitution of the imaginative faculty, and moral perfection produced by the suppression of every thought of bodily pleasures, and of every kind of foolish or evil ambition. These qualities are, as is well known, possessed by the wise men in different degrees, and the degrees of prophetic faculty vary in accordance with this difference. Faculties of the body are, as you know, at one time weak, wearied, and corrupted, at others in a healthy state. Imagination is certainly one of the faculties of the body. You find, therefore, that prophets are deprived of the faculty of prophesying when they mourn, are angry, or are similarly affected. Our Sages say, Inspiration does not come upon a prophet when he is sad or languid. This is the reason why Jacob did not receive any revelation during the period of his mourning, when his imagination was engaged with the loss of Joseph. The same was the case with Moses, when he was in a state of depression through the multitude of his troubles, which lasted from the murmurings of the Israelites in consequence of the evil report of the spies, till the death of the warriors of that generation. He recieved no message of God, as he used to do, even though he did not receive prophetic inspiration through the medium of the imaginative faculty, but directly through the intellect. We have mentioned it several times that Moses did not, like other prophets, speak in similes. This will be further explained (chap. xlv.), but it is not the subject of the present chapter. There were also persons who prophesied for a certain time and then left off altogether, something occurring that caused them to discontinue prophesying. The same circumstance, prevalence of sadness and dullness, was undoubtedly the direct cause of the interruption of prophecy during the exile; for can there be any greater misfortune for man than this: to be a slave bought for money in the service of ignorant and voluptuous masters, and powerless against them as they unite in themselves the absence of true knowledge and the force of all animal desires? Such an evil state has been prophesied to us in the words, "They shall run to and fro to seek the word of God, but shall not find it" (Amos viii. 12); "Her king and her princes are among the nations, the law is no more, her prophets also find no vision from the Lord" (Lam. ii. 9). This is a real fact, and the cause is evident; the pre-requisites [of prophecy] have been lost. In the Messianic period—may it soon commence—prophecy will therefore again be in our midst, as has been promised by God.

PART II, CHAPTER 37

It is necessary to consider the nature of the divine influence, which enables us to think, and gives us the various degrees of intelligence. For this influence may reach a person only in a small measure, and in exactly the same proportion would then be his intellectual condition, whilst it may reach another person in such a measure that, in addition to his own perfection, he can be the means of perfection for others. The same relation may be observed throughout the whole Universe. There are some beings so perfect that they can govern other beings, but there are also beings that are only perfect in so far as they can govern themselves and cannot influence other beings. In some cases the influence of the [Active] Intellect reaches only the logical and not the imaginative faculty; either on account of the insufficiency of the influence, or on account of a defect in the constitution of the imaginative faculty, and the consequent inability of the latter to receive that influence: this is the condition of wise men or philosophers. If, however, the imaginative faculty is naturally in the most perfect condition, this influence may, as has been explained by us and by other philosophers, reach both his logical and his imaginative faculties: this is the case with prophets. But it happens sometimes that the influence only reaches the imaginative faculty on account of the insufficiency of the logical faculty, arising either from a natural defect, or from a neglect in training. This is the case with statesmen, lawgivers, diviners, charmers, and men that have true dreams, or do wonderful things by strange means and secret arts, though they are not wise men; all these belong to the third class. It is further necessary to understand that some persons belonging to the third class perceive scenes, dreams, and confused images, when awake, in the form of a prophetic vision. They then believe that they are prophets; they wonder that they perceive visions, and think that they have acquired wisdom without training. They fall into grave errors as regards important philosophical principles, and see a strange mixture of true and imaginary things. All this is the consequence of the strength of their imaginative faculty, and the weakness of their logical faculty, which has not developed, and has not passed from potentiality to actuality.

It is well known that the members of each class differ greatly from each other. Each of the first two classes is again subdivided, and contains two sections, namely, those who receive the influence only as far as is necessary for their own perfection, and those who receive it in so great a measure that it suffices for their own perfection and that of others. A member of the first class, the wise men, may have his mind influenced either only so far, that he is enabled to search, to understand, to know, and to discern, without attempting to be a teacher or an author, having neither the desire nor the capacity; but he may also be influenced to such a degree that he becomes a teacher and an author. The same is the case with the second class. A person may receive a prophecy enabling him to perfect himself but not others; but he may also receive such a prophecy as would compel him to address his fellow-men, teach them, and benefit them through his perfection. It is clear that, without this second degree of perfection, no books would have been written, nor would any prophets have persuaded others to know the truth. For a scholar does not write a book with the object to teach himself what he already knows. But the characteristic of the intellect is this: what the intellect of one receives is transmitted to another, and so on, till a person is reached that can only himself be perfected by such an influence, but is unable to communicate it to others, as has been explained in some chapters of this treatise (chap. xi.) It is further the nature of this element in man that he who possesses an additional degree of that influence is compelled to address his fellow-men, under all circumstances, whether he is listened to or not, even if he injures himself thereby. Thus we find prophets that did not leave off speaking to the people until they were slain; it is this divine influence that moves them, that does not allow them to rest in any way, though they might bring upon themselves great evils by their action. E.g., when Jeremiah was despised, like other teachers and scholars of his age, he could not, though he desired it, withhold his prophecy, or cease from reminding the people of the truths which they rejected. Comp. "For the Word of the Lord was unto me a reproach and a mocking all day, and I said, I will not mention it, nor will I again speak in His name; but it was in mine heart as a burning fire, enclosed in my bones, and I was wearied to keep it, and did not prevail" (Jer. xx. 8, 9). This is also the meaning of the words of another prophet, "The Lord God hath spoken, who shall not prophesy?" (Amos iii. 8). Note it.

PART II, CHAPTER 38

Every man possesses a certain amount of courage, otherwise he would not stir to remove anything that might injure him. This psychical force seems to me analogous to the physical force of repulsion. Energy varies like all other forces, being great in one case and small in another. There are, therefore, people who attack a lion, whilst others run away at the sight of a mouse. One attacks a whole army and fights, another is frightened and terrified by the threat of a woman. This courage requires that there be in a man's constitution a certain disposition for it. If man, in accordance with a certain view, employs it more frequently, it develops and increases, but, on the other hand, if it is employed, in accordance with the opposite view, more rarely, it will diminish. From our own youth, we remember that there are different degrees of energy among boys.

The same is the case with the intuitive faculty; all possess it, but in different degrees. Man's intuitive power is especially strong in things which he has well comprehended, and in which his mind is much engaged. Thus you may yourself guess correctly that a certain person said or did a certain thing in a certain matter. Some persons are so strong and sound in their imagination and intuitive faculty that, when they assume a thing to be in existence, the reality either entirely or partly confirms their assumption. Although the causes of this assumption are numerous, and include many preceding, succeeding, and present circumstances, by means of the intuitive faculty the intellect can pass over all these causes, and draw inferences from them very quickly, almost instantaneously. This same faculty enables some persons to foretell important coming events. The prophets must have had these two forces, courage and intuition, highly developed, and these were still more strengthened when they were under the influence of the Active Intellect. Their courage was so great that, *e.g.*, Moses, with only a staff in his hand, dared to address a great king in order to deliver a nation from his service. He was not frightened or terrified, because he had been told, "I will be with thee" (Exod. iii. 12). The prophets have not all the same degree of courage, but none of them have been entirely without it. Thus Jeremiah is told: "Be not afraid of them," &c. (Jer. i. 8), and Ezekiel is exhorted, "Do not fear them or their word" (Ezek. ii. 6). In the same manner, you find that all prophets possessed great courage. Again, through the excellence of their intuitive faculty, they could quickly foretell the future, but this excellence, as is well known, likewise admits of different degrees.

The true prophets undoubtedly conceive ideas that result from premises which human reason could not comprehend by itself; thus they tell things which men could not tell by reason and ordinary imagination alone; for [the action of the prophets' mental capacities is influenced by] the same agent that causes the perfection of the imaginative faculty, and that enables the prophet thereby to foretell a future event with such clearness as if it was a thing already perceived with the senses, and only through them conveyed to his imagination. This agent perfects the prophet's mind, and influences it in such a manner that he conceives ideas which are confirmed by reality, and are so clear to him as if he deduced them by means of syllogisms.

This should be the belief of all who choose to accept the truth. For [all things are in a certain relation to each other, and] what is noticed in one thing may be used as evidence for the existence of certain properties of another, and the knowledge of one thing leads us to the knowledge of other things. But [what we said of the extraordinary powers of our imaginative faculty] applies with special force to our intellect, which is directly influenced by the Active Intellect, and caused by it to pass from potentiality to actuality. It is through the intellect that the influence reaches the imaginative faculty. How then could the latter be so perfect as to be able to represent things not previously perceived by the senses, if the same degree of perfection were withheld from the intellect, and the latter could not comprehend things otherwise than in the usual manner, namely, by means of premise, conclusion, and inference? This is the true characteristic of prophecy, and of the disciplines to which the preparation for prophecy must exclusively be devoted. I spoke here of true prophets in order to exclude the third class, namely, those persons whose logical faculties are not fully developed, and who do not possess any wisdom, but are only endowed with imaginative and inventive powers. It may be that things perceived by these persons are nothing but ideas which they had before, and of which impressions were left in their imaginations together with those of other things; but whilst the impressions of other images are effaced and have disappeared, certain images alone remain, are seen and considered as new and objective, coming from without. The process is analogous to the following case: A person has with him in the house a thousand living individuals; all except one of them leave the house: when the person finds himself alone with that individual, he imagines that the latter has entered the house now, contrary to the fact that he has only not left the house. This is one of the many phenomena open to gross misinterpretations and dangerous errors, and many of those who believed that they were wise perished thereby.

There were, therefore, men who supported their opinion by a dream which they had, thinking that the vision during sleep was independent of what they had previously believed or heard when awake. Persons whose mental capacities are not fully developed, and who have not attained intellectual perfection, must not take any notice of these [dreams]. Those who reach that perfection may, through the influence of the divine intellect, obtain knowledge independent of that possessed by them when awake. They are true prophets, as is distinctly stated in Scripture, *ve-nabhi lebhabh chochmah* (Ps. xc. 12), "And the true prophet possesseth a heart of wisdom." This must likewise be noticed.

PART II, CHAPTER 41

I need not explain what a dream is, but I will explain the meaning of the term *mareh,* "vision," which occurs in the passage: "In a vision (*be-mareh*) do I make myself known unto him" (Num. xii. 6). The term signifies that which is also called *mareh ha-nebhuah,* "prophetic vision," *yad ha-shem,* "the hand of God," and *machazeh,* "a vision." It is something terrible and fearful which the prophet feels while awake, as is distinctly stated by Daniel: "And I saw this great vision, and there remained no strength in me, for my comeliness was turned in me into corruption, and I retained no strength" (Dan. x. 8). He afterwards continues, "Thus was I in deep sleep on my face, and my face toward the ground" (ibid., ver. 9). But it was in a prophetic vision that the angel spoke to him and "set him upon his knees." Under such circumstances the senses cease to act, and the [Active Intellect] influences the rational faculties, and through them the imaginative faculties, which become perfect and active. Sometimes the prophecy begins with a prophetic vision, the prophet greatly trembles, and is much affected in consequence of the perfect action of the imaginative faculty; and after that the prophecy follows. This was the case with Abraham. The commencement of the prophecy is, "The word of the Lord came to Abraham in a vision" (Gen. xv. 1); after this, "a deep sleep fell upon Abraham"; and at last, "he said unto Abraham," &c. When prophets speak of the fact that they received a prophecy, they say that they received it from an angel, or from God; but even in the latter case it was likewise received through an angel. Our Sages, therefore, explain the words, "And the Lord said unto her" that He spake through an angel. You must know that whenever Scripture relates that the Lord or an angel spoke to a person, this took place in a dream or in a prophetic vision.

There are four different ways in which Scripture relates the fact that a divine communication was made to the prophet. (1.) The prophet relates that he heard the words of an angel in a dream or vision; (2.) He reports the words of the angel without mentioning that they were perceived in a dream or vision, assuming that it is well known that prophecy can only originate in one of the two ways, "In a vision I will make myself known unto him, in a dream I will speak unto him" (Num. xii. 6). (3.) The prophet does not mention the angel at all; he says that God spoke to him, but he states that he received the message in a dream or a vision. (4.) He introduces his prophecy by stating that God spoke to him, or told him to do a certain thing, or speak certain words, but he does not explain that he received the message in a dream or vision, because he assumes that it is well known, and has been established as a principle that no prophecy or revelation originates otherwise than in a dream or vision, and through an angel. Instances of the first form are the following:—"And the angel of the Lord said unto me in a dream, Jacob" (Gen. xxxi. 11); "And an angel said unto Israel in a vision of night" (ibid. xlvi. 2); "And an angel came to Balaam by night," "And an angel said unto Balaam" (Num. xxii. 20–22). Instances of the second form are these: "And Elohim (an angel) said unto Jacob, Rise, go up to Bethel" (Gen. xxxv. 1); "And Elohim said unto him, Thy name is Jacob," &c. (ibid. xxxv. 10); "And an angel of the Lord called unto Abraham out of heaven the second time" (ibid. xxii. 15); "And Elohim said unto Noah" (ibid. vi. 13). The following is an instance of the third form: "The word of the Lord came unto Abraham in a vision" (ibid. xv. 1). Instances of the fourth form are: "And the Lord said unto Abraham" (ibid. xviii. 13); "And the Lord said unto Jacob, Return," &c. (ibid. xxxi. 3); "And the Lord said unto Joshua" (Josh. v. 9); "And the Lord said unto Gideon" (Judges vii. 2). Most of the prophets speak in a similar manner: "And the Lord said unto me" (Deut. ii. 2); "And the word of the Lord came unto me" (Ezek. xxx. 1); "And the word of the Lord came" (2 Sam. xxiv. 11); "And behold, the word of the Lord came unto him" (1 Kings xix. 9); "And the word of the Lord came expressly" (Ezek. i. 3); "The beginning of the word of the Lord by Hosea" (Hos. i. 2); "The hand of the Lord was upon me" (Ezek. xxxvii. 1). There are a great many instances of this class. Every passage in Scripture introduced by any of these four forms is a prophecy proclaimed by a prophet; but the phrase, "And Elohim (an angel) came to a certain person in the dream of night," does not indicate a prophecy, and the person mentioned in that phrase is not a prophet; the phrase only informs us that the attention of the person was called by God to a certain thing, and at the same time that this happened at night. For just as God may cause a person to move in order to save or kill another person, so He may cause, according to His will, certain things to rise in man's mind in a dream by night. We have no doubt that the Syrian Laban was a perfectly wicked man, and an idolator; likewise Abimelech, though a good man among his people, is told by Abraham concerning his land [Gerar] and his kingdom, "Surely there is no fear of God in this place" (Gen. xx. 11). And yet of both of them, viz., of Laban and of Abimelech, it is said [that an angel appeared to them in a dream]. Comp. "And Elohim (an angel) came to Abimelech in a dream by night" (ibid. ver. 3); and also, "And Elohim came to the Syrian Laban in the dream of the night" (ibid. xxxi. 24). Note and consider the distinction between the phrases, "And Elohim came," and "Elohim said," between "in a dream by night," and "in a vision by night." In reference to Jacob it is said, "And an angel said to Israel in the visions by night" (Gen. xlvi. 2), but in reference to Laban and Abimelech, "And Elohim came," &c. Onkelos makes the distinction clear; he translates, in the last two instances, *atha memar min kodam adonai,* "a word came from the Lord," and not *ve-ithgeli,* "and the Lord appeared." The phrase, "And the Lord said to a certain person," is employed even when this person was not really addressed by the Lord, and did not receive any prophecy, but was informed of a certain thing through a prophet. *E.g.*, "And she went to inquire of the Lord" (Gen. xxv. 22); that is, according to the explanation of our Sages, she went to the college of Ebher, and the latter gave her the answer; and this is expressed by the words, "And the Lord said unto her" (ibid. ver. 23). These words have also been explalned thus, God spoke to her through an angel; but by "angel" Ebher is meant here, for a prophet is sometimes called "angel," as will be explained; or the angel that appeared to Ebher in this vision is referred to, or the object of the Midrash explanation is merely to express that wherever God is introduced as directly speaking to a person, *i.e.*, to any of the ordinary prophets, He speaks through an angel, as has been set forth by us (chap. xxxiv.)

PART II, CHAPTER 42

We have already shown that the appearance or speech of an angel mentioned in Scripture took place in a vision or dream; it makes no difference whether this is expressly stated or not, as we have explained above. This is a point of considerable importance. In some cases the account begins by stating that the prophet saw an angel; in others, the account apparently introduces a human being, who ultimately is shown to be an angel; but it makes no difference, for if the fact that an angel has been heard is only mentioned at the end, you may rest satisfied that the whole account from the beginning describes a prophetic vision. In such visions, a prophet either sees God who speaks to him, as will be explained by us, or he sees an angel who speaks to him, or he hears some one speaking to him without seeing the speaker, or he sees a man who speaks to him, and learns afterwards that the speaker was an angel. In this latter kind of prophecies, the prophet relates that he saw a man who was doing or saying something, and that he learnt afterwards that he was an angel.

This important principle was adopted by one of our Sages, one of the most distinguished among them, R. Chiya, the Great, in the exposition of the Scriptural passage commencing, "And the Lord appeared unto him in the plain of Mamre" (Gen. xviii). The general statement that the Lord appeared to Abraham is followed by the description in what manner that appearance of the Lord took place; namely, Abraham saw first three men; he ran and spoke to them. R. Chiya, the author of the explanation, holds that the words of Abraham, "My Lord, if now I have found grace in thy sight, do not, I pray thee, pass from thy servant," were spoken by him in the prophetic visions to one of the men; for he says that Abraham addressed these words to the chief of these men. Note this well, for it is one of the great mysteries [of the Law]. The same, I hold, is the case when it is said in reference to Jacob, "And a man wrestled with him" (Gen. xxxii. 25); this took place in a prophetic vision, since it is expressly stated in the end (ver. 31) that it was an angel. The circumstances are here exactly the same as those in the vision of Abraham, where the general statement, "And the Lord appeared to him," &c., is followed by a detailed description. Similarly the account of the vision of Jacob begins, "And the angels of God met him" (Gen. xxxii. 2); then follows a detailed description how it came to pass that they met him; namely, Jacob sent messengers, and after having prepared and done certain things, "he was left alone," &c., "and a man wrestled with him" (ibid. ver. 24). By this term "*man*" [one of] the angels of God is meant, mentioned in the phrase "And angels of God met him"; the wrestling and speaking was entirely a prophetic vision. That which happened to Balaam on the way, and the speaking of the ass, took place in a prophetic vision, since further on, in the same account, an angel of God is introduced as speaking to Balaam. I also think that what Joshua perceived, when "he lifted up his eyes and saw, and behold a man stood before him" (Josh. v. 13), was a prophetic vision, since it is stated afterwards (ver. 14) that it was "the prince of the host of the Lord." But in the passages, "And an angel of the Lord came up from Gilgal" (Judges ii. 1); "And it came to pass that the angel of the Lord spake these words to all Israel" (ibid. ver. 2); the "angel" is, according to the explanation of our Sages, Phineas. They say, The angel is Phineas, for, when the Divine Glory rested upon him, he was "like an angel." We have already shown (chap. vi.) that the term "angel" is homonymous, and denotes also "prophet," as is the case in the following passages:—"And He sent an angel, and He hath brought us up out of Egypt" (Num. xx. 16); "Then spake Haggai, the angel of the Lord in the Lord's message" (Hagg. i. 13); "But they mocked the angels of God" (2 Chron. xxxvi. 16).—Comp. also the words of Daniel, "And the man Gabriel, whom I had seen in the vision at the beginning, being caused to fly swiftly, touched me about the time of the evening oblation" (Dan. ix. 11). All this passed in a prophetic vision. Do not imagine that an angel is seen or his word heard otherwise than in a prophetic vision or prophetic dream, according to the principle laid down:—"I make myself known unto him in a vision, and speak unto him in a dream" (Num. xii. 6). The instances quoted may serve as an illustration of those passages which I do not mention. From the rule laid down by us that prophecy requires preparation, and from our interpretation of the homonym "angel," you will infer that Hagar, the Egyptian woman, was not a prophetess; also Manoah and his wife were no prophets; for the speech they heard, or imagined they heard, was like the *bath-kol* (prophetic echo), which is so frequently mentioned by our Sages, and is something that may be experienced by men not prepared for prophecy. The homonymity of the name "angel" misleads in this matter. This is the principal method by which most of the difficult passages in the Bible can be explained. Consider the words, "And an angel of the Lord found her by the well of water" (Gen. xvi. 7), which are similar to the words referring to Joseph—"And a man found him, and behold, he was erring in the field" (ibid. xxxvii. 15). All the Midrashim assume that by *man* an angel is meant.

PART II, CHAPTER 44

Prophecy is given either in a vision or in a dream, as we have said so many times, and we will not constantly repeat it. We say now that when a prophet is inspired with a prophecy he may see an allegory, as we have shown frequently, or he may in a prophetic vision perceive that God speaks to him, as is said in Isaiah (vi. 8), "And I heard the voice of the Lord saying, Whom shall I send, and who will go for us?" or he hears an angel addressing him, and sees him also. This is very frequent, *e.g.*, "And the angel of God spake unto me," &c. (Gen. xxxi. 11); "And the angel that talked with me answered and said unto me, Dost thou not know what these are" (Zech. iv. 5); "And I heard one holy speaking" (Dan. viii. 13). Instances of this are innumerable. The prophet sometimes sees a man that speaks to him. Comp., "And behold there was a man, whose appearance was like the appearance of brass, and the man said to me," &c. (Ezek. xl. 3, 4), although the passage begins, "The hand of the Lord was upon me" (ibid. ver. 1). In some cases the prophet sees no figure at all, only hears in the prophetic vision the words addressed to him; *e.g.*, "And I heard the voice of a man between the banks of Ulai" (Dan. viii. 16); "There was silence, and I heard a voice" (in the speech of Eliphaz, Job iv. 16); "And I heard a voice of one that spake to me" (Ezek. i. 28). The being which Ezekiel perceived in the prophetic vision was not the same that addressed him; for at the conclusion of the strange and extraordinary scene which Ezekiel describes expressly as having been perceived by him, the object and form of the prophecy is introduced by the words, "And I heard a voice of a man that spake to me." After this remark on the different kinds of prophecy, as suggested by Scripture, I say that the prophet may perceive that which he hears with the greatest possible intensity, just as a person may hear thunder in his dream, or perceive a storm or an earthquake; such dreams are frequent. The prophet may also hear the prophecy in ordinary common speech, without anything unusual. Take, *e.g.*, the account of the prophet Samuel. When he was called in a prophetic vision, he believed that the priest Eli called him; and this happened three times consecutively. The text then explains the cause of it, saying that Samuel naturally believed that Eli had called him, because at that time he did not yet know that God addressed the prophet in this form, nor had that secret as yet been revealed to him. Comp. "And Samuel did not yet know the Lord, and the word of the Lord was not yet revealed to him," *i.e.*, he did not yet know, and it had not yet been revealed to him, that the word of God is communicated in this way. The words, "He did not yet know the Lord," may perhaps mean that Samuel had not yet received any prophecy; for in reference to a prophet's receiving divine communication it is said, "I make myself known to him in a vision, I speak to him in a dream" (Num. xii. 6). The meaning of the verse accordingly is this, Samuel had not yet received any prophecy, and therefore did not know that this was the form of prophecy. Note it.

PART II, CHAPTER 45

After having explained prophecy in accordance with reason and Scripture, I must now describe the different degrees of prophecy from these two points of view. Not all the degrees of prophecy which I will enumerate, qualify a person for the office of a prophet. The first and the second degrees are only steps leading to prophecy, and a person possessing either of these two degrees does not belong to the class of prophets whose merits we have been discussing. When such a person is occasionally called prophet, the term is used in a wider sense, and is applied to him because he is almost a prophet. You must not be misled by the fact that according to the books of the Prophets, a certain prophet, after having been inspired with one kind of prophecy, is reported to have received prophecy in another form. For it is possible for a prophet to prophesy at one time in the form of one of the degrees which I am about to enumerate, and at another time in another form. In the same manner, as the prophet does not prophesy continuously, but is inspired at one time and not at another, so he may at one time prophesy in the form of a higher degree, and at another time in that of a lower degree; it may happen that the highest degree is reached by a prophet only once in his lifetime, and afterwards remains inaccessible to him, or that a prophet remains below the highest degree until he entirely loses the faculty; for ordinary prophets must cease to prophesy a shorter or longer period before their death. Comp. "And the word of the Lord ceased from Jeremiah" (Ezra i. 1); "And these are the last words of David" (2 Sam. xxiii. 1). From these instances it can be inferred that the same is the case with all prophets. After this introduction and explanation, I will begin to enumerate the degrees of prophecy to which I have referred above.

(1.) The first degree of prophecy consists in the divine assistance which is given to a person, and induces and encourages him to do something good and grand, *e.g.*, to deliver a congregation of good men from the hands of evil-doers; to save one noble person, or to bring happiness to a large number of people; he finds in himself the cause that moves and urges him to this deed. This degree of divine influence is called "the spirit of the Lord"; and of the person who is under that influence we say that the spirit of the Lord came upon him, clothed him, or rested upon him, or the Lord was with him, and the like. All the judges of Israel possessed this degree, for the following general statement is made concerning them:—"The Lord raised up judges for them; and the Lord was with the judge, and he saved them" (Judges ii. 18). Also all the noble chiefs of Israel belonged to this class. The same is distinctly stated concerning some of the judges and the kings:—"The spirit of the Lord came upon Jephthah" (ibid. xi. 29); of Samson it is said, "The spirit of the Lord came upon him" (ibid. xiv. 19); "And the spirit of the Lord came upon Saul when he heard those words" (1 Sam. xi. 6). When Amasa was moved by the holy spirit to assist David, "A spirit clothed Amasa, who was chief of the captains, and he said, Thine are we, David," &c. (1 Chron. xii. 18). This faculty was always possessed by Moses from the time he had attained the age of manhood; it moved him to slay the Egyptian, and to prevent evil from the two men that quarrelled; it was so strong that, after he had fled from Egypt out of fear, and arrived in Midian, a trembling stranger, he could not restrain himself from interfering when he saw wrong being done; he could not bear it. Comp. "And Moses rose and saved them" (Exod. ii. 17). David likewise was filled with this spirit, when he was anointed with the oil of anointing. Comp. "And the spirit of God came upon David from that day and upward" (1 Sam. xvi. 13). He thus conquered the lion and the bear and the Philistine, and the like, by this very spirit. This faculty did not cause any of the above-named persons to speak on a certain subject, for it only aims at encouraging the person who possesses it to action; it does not encourage him to do everything, but only to help either a distinguished man or a whole congregation when oppressed, or to do something that leads to that end. Just as not all who have a true dream are prophets, so it cannot be said of every one who is assisted in a certain undertaking, as in the acquisition of property, or of some other personal advantage, that the spirit of the Lord came upon him, or that the Lord was with him, or that he performed his actions by the holy spirit. We only apply such phrases to those who have accomplished something very good and grand, or something that leads to that end; *e.g.*, the success of Joseph in the house of the Egyptian, which was the first cause leading evidently to great events that occurred subsequently.

(2.) The second degree is this: A person feels as if something came upon him, and as if he had received a new power that encourages him to speak. He treats of science, or composes hymns, exhorts his fellow-men, discusses political and theological problems; all this he does while awake, and in the full possession of his senses. Such a person is said to speak by the holy spirit. David composed the Psalms, and Solomon the Book of Proverbs, Ecclesiastes, and the Song of Solomon by this spirit; also Daniel, Job, Chronicles, and the rest of the Hagiographa were written in this holy spirit; therefore they are called *Chethubhim* (Writings, or Written), *i.e.*, written by men inspired by the holy spirit.

Our Sages mention this expressly concerning the Book of Esther. In reference to such holy spirit, David says: "The spirit of the Lord spoke in me, and His word is on my tongue" (2 Sam. xxiii. 2); *i.e.*, the spirit of the Lord caused him to utter these words. This class includes the seventy elders of whom it is said, "And it came to pass when the spirit rested upon them, that they prophesied, and did not cease" (Num. xi. 25); also Eldad and Medad (ibid. ver. 26); furthermore, every high priest that inquired [of God] by the Urim and Tumim; on whom, as our Sages say, the divine glory rested, and who spoke by the holy spirit; Yechaziel, son of Zechariah, belongs likewise to this class. Comp. "The spirit of the Lord came upon him in the midst of the assembly, and he said, Listen, all Judah and inhabitants of Jerusalem, thus saith the Lord unto you," &c. (2 Chron. xx. 14, 15); also Zechariah, son of Jehoiada the priest. Comp. "And he stood above the people and said unto them, Thus saith God" (ibid. xxiv. 20); furthermore, Azariah, son of Oded; comp. "And Azariah, son of Oded, when the spirit of the Lord came upon him, went forth before Asa," &c. (ibid. xv. 1, 2); and all who acted under similar circumstances. You must know that Balaam likewise belonged to this class, when he was good; this is indicated by the words, "And God put a word in the mouth of Balaam" (Num. xxiii. 5), *i.e.*, Balaam spoke by divine inspiration; he therefore says of himself, "Who heareth the words of God," &c. (ibid. xxiv. 4). We must especially point out that David, Solomon, and Daniel belonged to this class, and not to the class of Isaiah, Jeremiah, Nathan the prophet, Ahijah the Shilonite, and those like them. For David, Solomon, and Daniel spoke and wrote inspired by the holy spirit, and when David says, "The God of Israel spoke and said unto me, the rock of Israel" (2 Sam. xxiii. 3), he meant to say that God promised him happiness through a prophet, through Nathan or another prophet. The phrase must here be interpreted in the same manner as in the following passages, "And God said to her" (Gen. xxv. 26); "And God said unto Solomon, Because this hath been in thy heart, and thou hast not kept my convenant," &c. (1 Kings xi. 11). The latter passage undoubtedly contains a prophecy of Ahijah the Shilonite, or another prophet, who foretold Solomon that evil would befall him. The passage, "God appeared to Solomon at Gibeon in a dream by night, and God said" (ibid. iii. 5), does not contain a real prophecy, such as is introduced by the words: "The word of the Lord came to Abram in a vision, saying" (Gen. xv. 1); or "And God said to Israel in the visions of the night" (ibid. xlvi. 2), or such as the prophecies of Isaiah and Jeremiah contain; in all these cases the prophets, though receiving the prophecy in a prophetic dream, are told that it is a prophecy, and that they have received prophetic inspiration. But in the case of Solomon, the account concludes, "And Solomon awoke, and behold it was a dream" (1 Kings iii. 15); and in the account of the second divine appearance, it is said, "And God appeared to Solomon a second time, as He appeared to him at Gibeon" (ibid. ix. 2); it was evidently a dream. This kind of prophecy is a degree below that of which Scripture says, "In a dream I will speak to him" (Num. xii. 6). When prophets are inspired in a dream, they by no means call this a dream, although the prophecy reached them in a dream, but declare it decidedly to be a prophecy. Thus Jacob, our father, when awaking from a prophetic dream, did not say it was a dream, but declared, "Surely there is the Lord in this place," &c. (Gen. xxviii. 16); "God the Almighty appeared to me in Luz, in the land of Canaan" (ibid. xlviii. 3), expressing thereby that it was a prophecy. But in reference to Solomon we read:—"And Solomon awoke, and behold it was a dream" (1 Kings iii. 15). Similarly Daniel declares that he had a dream; although he sees an angel and hears his word, he speaks of the event as of a dream; even when he had received the information [concerning the dreams of Nebukadnezzar], he speaks of it in the following manner—"Then was the secret revealed to Daniel in a night vision" (Dan. ii. 19). On other occasions it is said, "He wrote down the dream"; "I saw in the visions by night," &c; "And the visions of my head confused me" (Dan. vii. 1, 2, 15); "I was surprised at the vision, and none noticed it" (ibid. viii. 27). There is no doubt that this is one degree below that form of prophecy to which the words, "In a dream I will speak to him," are applied. For this reason the nation desired to place the book of Daniel among the Hagiographa, and not among the Prophets. I have, therefore, pointed out to you, that the prophecy revealed to Daniel and Solomon, although they saw an angel in the dream, was not considered by them as a perfect prophecy, but as a dream containing correct information. They belonged to the class of men that spoke, inspired by the *ruach ha-kodesh*, "the holy spirit." Also in the order of the holy writings, no distinction is made between the books of Proverbs, Ecclesiastes, Daniel, Psalms, Ruth, and Esther; they are all written by divine inspiration. The authors of all these books are called prophets in the more general sense of the term.

(3.) The third class is the lowest [class of actual prophets, *i.e.*] of those who introduce their speech by the phrase, "And the word of the Lord came unto me," or a similar phrase. The prophet sees an allegory in a dream—under those conditions which we have mentioned when speaking of real prophecy—and in the prophetic dream itself the allegory is interpreted. Such are most of the allegories of Zechariah.

(4.) The prophet hears in a prophetic dream something clearly and distinctly, but does not see the speaker. This was the case with Samuel in the beginning of his prophetic mission, as has been explained (chap. xliv.).

(5.) A person addresses the prophet in a dream, as was the case in some of the prophecies of Ezekiel. Comp. "And the man spake unto me, Son of man," &c. (Ezek. xl. 4).

(6.) An angel speaks to him in a dream; this applies to most of the prophets; *e.g.*, "And an angel of God said to me in a dream of night" (Gen. xxxi. 11).

(7.) In a prophetic dream it appears to the prophet as if God spoke to him. Thus Isaiah says, "And I saw the Lord, and I heard the voice of the Lord saying, Whom shall I send, and who will go for us?" (Isa. vi. 1, 8). Micaiah, son of Imla, said likewise, "I saw the Lord" (1 Kings xxii. 19).

(8.) Something presents itself to the prophet in a prophetic vision; he sees allegorical figures, such as were seen by Abraham in the vision "between the pieces" (Gen. xv. 9, 10); for it was in a vision by daytime, as is distinctly stated.

(9.) The prophet hears words in a prophetic vision; as *e.g.*, is said in reference to Abraham, "And behold, the word came to him, saying, This shall not be thine heir" (ibid. xv. 4).

(10.) The prophet sees a man that speaks to him in a prophetic vision; *e.g.*, Abraham in the plain of Mamre (ibid. xviii. 1), and Joshua in Jericho (Josh. v. 13).

(11.) He sees an angel that speaks to him in the vision, as was the case when Abraham was addressed by an angel at the sacrifice of Isaac (Gen. xxii. 15). This I hold to be—if we except Moses—the highest degree a prophet can attain according to Scripture, provided he has, as reason demands, his rational faculties fully developed. But it appears to me improbable that a prophet should be able to perceive in a prophetic vision God speaking to him; the action of the imaginative faculty does not go so far, and therefore we do not notice this in the case of the ordinary prophets; Scripture says expressly, "In a *vision* I will make myself known, in a *dream* I will speak to him"; the speaking is here connected with *dream*, the influence and the action of the intellect is connected with *vision*; comp. "In a vision I will make myself known to him" (*ethvadda*, hithpael of *yada*, "to know"), but it is not said here that in a vision anything is heard from God. When I, therefore, met with statements in Scripture that a prophet heard words spoken to him, and that this took place in a vision, it occurred to me that the case in which God appears to address the prophet seems to be the only difference between a vision and a dream, according to the literal sense of the Scriptural text. But it is possible to explain the passages in which a prophet is reported to have heard in the course of a vision words spoken to him, in the following manner: at first he has had a vision, but subsequently he fell into a deep sleep, and the vision was changed into a dream. Thus we explained the words, "And a deep sleep fell upon Abram" (Gen. xv. 12); and our Sages remark thereon, "This was a deep sleep of prophecy." According to this explanation, it is only in a dream that the prophet can hear words addressed to him; it makes no difference in what manner words are spoken. Scripture supports this theory, "In a dream I will speak to him." But in a prophetic vision only allegories are perceived, or rational truths are obtained, that lead to some knowledge in science, such as can be arrived at by reasoning. This is the meaning of the words, "In a vision I will make myself *known* unto him." According to this second explanation, the degrees of prophecy are reduced to eight, the highest of them being the prophetic vision, including all kinds of vision, even the case in which a man appears to address the prophet, as has been mentioned. You will perhaps ask this question: among the different degrees of prophecy there is one in which prophets, *e.g.*, Isaiah, Micaiah, appear to hear God addressing them; how can this be reconciled with the principle that all prophets are prophetically addressed through an angel, except Moses our Teacher, in reference to whom Scripture says, "Mouth to mouth I speak to him" (Num. xii. 8)? I answer, this is really the case, the medium here being the imaginative faculty that hears in a prophetic dream God speaking; but Moses heard the voice addressing him "from above the covering of the ark from between the two cherubim" (Exod. xxv. 22), without the medium of the imaginative faculty. In Mishneh Torah we have given the characteristics of this kind of prophecy, and explained the meaning of the phrases, "Mouth to mouth I speak to him"; "As man speaketh to his neighbour" (Exod. xxxiii. 11), and the like. Study it there, and I need not repeat what has already been said.

PART II, CHAPTER 46

One individual may be taken as an illustration of the individuals of the whole species. From its properties we learn those of each individual of the species. I mean to say that the form of one account of a prophecy illustrates all accounts of the same class. After this remark you will understand that a person may sometimes dream that he has gone to a certain country, married there, stayed there for some time, and had a son, whom he gave a certain name, and who was in a certain condition [though nothing of all this really takes place]; so also in prophetic allegories certain objects are seen, acts performed—if the style of the allegory demands it—things are done by the prophet, the intervals between one act and another determined, and journeys undertaken from one place to another; but all these things are only processes of a prophetic vision, and not real things that could be perceived by the senses of the body. Some of the accounts simply relate these incidents [without premising that they are part of a vision], because it is a well-known fact that all these accounts refer to prophetic visions, and it was not necessary to repeat in each case a statement to this effect.

Thus the prophet relates: "And the Lord said unto me," and need not add the explanation that it was in a dream. The ordinary reader believes that the acts, journeys, questions, and answers of the prophets really took place, and were perceived by the senses, and did not merely form part of a prophetic vision. I will mention here an instance concerning which no person will entertain the least doubt. I will add a few more of the same kind, and these will show you how those passages must be understood which I do not cite. The following passage in Ezekiel (viii. 1, 3) is clear, and admits of no doubt: "I sat in mine house, and the elders of Judah sat before me, &c., and a spirit lifted me up between the earth and the heaven, and brought me in the visions of God to Jerusalem," &c.; also the passage, "Thus I arose and went into the plain" (iii. 2, 3),refers to a prophetic vision; just as the words, "And he brought him forth abroad, and said, Look now toward heaven and tell the stars, if thou be able to number them" (Gen. xv. 5) describe a vision. . . .

It is analogous to the description of the vision of Abraham which begins, "The word of the Lord came to Abram in a vision, saying" (Gen. xv. 1); and contains at the same time the passage, "He brought him forth abroad, and said, Look now to the heaven and count the stars" (ibid. ver. 6). It is evident that it was in a vision that Abraham saw himself brought forth from his place looking towards the heavens and being told to count the stars. This is related [without repeating the statement that it was in a vision]. . . .

The correctness of this theory cannot be doubted, and only those do not comprehend it who do not know to distinguish between that which is possible, and that which is impossible. The instances quoted may serve as an illustration of other similar Scriptural passages not quoted by me. They are all of the same kind, and in the same style. Whatever is said in the account of a vision, that the prophet heard, went forth, came out, said, was told, stood, sat, went up, went down, journeyed, asked, or was asked, is all part of the prophetic vision; even when there is a lengthened account, the details of which are well connected as regards the time, the persons referred to, and the place. After it has once been stated that the event described is to be understood figuratively, it must be assumed for certain that the whole is a prophetic vision.

NAḤMANIDES, *COMMENTARY ON THE BIBLE*

Translation by Charles B. Chavel

GENESIS 18:1

AND HE APPEARED TO HIM. Rashi comments: "To visit the sick man. Said Rabbi Chama the son of Chanina, 'It was the third day after his circumcision, and the Holy One, blessed be He, came and inquired after him.'[1] *And, lo, three men:*[2] angels who came to him in the form of men. *Three:* one to announce to Sarah that she would bear a son, one to heal Abraham, and one to overthrow Sodom. Raphael who healed Abraham went from there to rescue Lot" for these do not constitute two commissions.[3] This is because the second mission was in another place, and he was commanded thereon after [he had completed his first mission].[4] Perhaps it is because the two missions had rescue as their common goal.[5] "*And they did eat:*[6] they appeared to be eating."

In the book Moreh Nebuchim[7] it is said that this portion of Scripture consists of a general statement followed by a detailed description. Thus Scripture first says that the Eternal appeared to Abraham in the form of prophetic visions, and then explains in what manner this vision took place, namely, that he [Abraham] lifted up his eyes in the vision, *and lo, three men stood by him,*[2] *and he said, if now I have found favor in thy eyes.*[8] This is the account of what he said in the prophetic vision to one of them, namely, their chief.

Now if in the vision there appeared to Abraham only men partaking of food, how then does Scripture say, *And the Eternal appeared to him,* as God did not appear to him in vision or in thought?[9] Such is not found with respect to all the prophecies. And according to his[10] words, Sarah did not knead cakes, nor did Abraham prepare a bullock, and also, Sarah did not laugh. It was all a vision! If so, this dream came *through a multitude of business,*[11] like dreams of falsehood, for what is the purpose of showing them all this![12] Similarly did the author of the Moreh Nebuchim say[7] in the case of the verse, *And a man wrestled with him,*[13] that it was all a prophetic vision. But if this be the case, I do not know why Jacob limped on his thigh when he awoke! And why did Jacob say, *For I have seen an angel face to face, and my life is preserved?*[14] The prophets did not fear that they might die on account of having experienced prophetic visions. Jacob, moreover, had already seen a greater and more distinguished vision than this since many times, in prophetic visions, he had also seen the Revered Divinity.[15] Now according to this author's opinion, he will find it necessary for the sake of consistency to say similarly in the affair of Lot that the angels did not come to his house, nor did he bake for them *unleavened bread and they did eat.*[16] Rather, it was all a vision! But if Lot could ascend to the height of a prophetic vision, how did the wicked and sinful people of Sodom become prophets? Who told them that men had come into Lot's house? And if all these [i.e., the actions of the inhabitants of Sodom], were part of prophetic visions, then it follows that the account related in the verses, *And the angels hastened Lot, saying: Arise take thy wife. . . .And he said, Escape for thy life. . . See, I have accepted thee,*[17] as well as the entire chapter is but a vision, and if so, Lot could have remained in Sodom! But the author of the Moreh Nebuchim thinks that the events took place of themselves, but the conversations relating to all matters were in a vision! But such words contradict Scripture. It is forbidden to listen to them, all the more to believe in them!

In truth,[18] wherever Scripture mentions an angel being seen or heard speaking it is in a vision or in a dream for the human senses cannot perceive the angels. But these are not visions of prophecy since he who attains the vision of an angel or the hearing of his speech is not yet a prophet. For the matter is not as the Rabbi[19] pronounced,[20] i.e., that every prophet, Moses our teacher excepted, received his prophecy through the medium of an angel. The Sages have already said[21] concerning Daniel: "They[22] were greater than he for they were prophets and he was not a prophet." His book, likewise, was not grouped together[23] with the books of the prophets since his affair was with the angel Gabriel, even though he appeared to him and spoke with him when he was awake, as it is said in the vision concerning the second Temple: *Yea, while I was speaking in prayer, the man Gabriel,* etc.[24] The vision concerning the ultimate redemption[25] also occurred when Daniel was awake as he walked with his friends beside the Tigris River.[26] Hagar the Egyptian[27] is not included in the group of prophetesses.[28] It is also clear that hers was not a case of the *bath kol* (prophetic echo),[29] as the Rabbi[19] would have it. Scripture, furthermore, sets apart the prophecy of Moses our teacher from that of the patriarchs, as it is said, *And I appeared unto Abraham, unto Isaac, and unto Jacob, by* [the name of] *God Almighty,*[30] this name being one of the sacred names for the Creator, and not a designation for an angel. Our Rabbis also taught concerning the difference in the degree of prophecy between Moses and the other prophets, and they said:[31] "What is the difference between Moses and all the prophets? The Rabbis say that all prophets saw through unclear vision. It is to this matter that Scripture refers in saying, *And I have multiplied visions, and by the ministry of the prophets have I used similitudes.*[32] Moses saw through a clear vision. It is to this matter that Scripture refers in saying, *And the similitudes of the Eternal doth be behold,*"[33] as is explained in Vayikra Rabbah[31] and other places. But in no place did the Sages attribute the prophecy of the prophets to an angel.

Do not expose yourself to argument by quoting the verse, *I also am a prophet as thou art; and an angel spoke unto me by the word of the Eternal, saying,*[34] since its meaning is as follows: "I also am a prophet as thou art, and I know that the angel who spoke to me was by word of God, this being one of the degrees of prophecy, as the man of God said, *For so was it charged me by the word of the Eternal,*[35] and he further said, *For it was said to me by the word of the Eternal.*[36]

Our Rabbis have further stated[37] in the matter of Balaam, who said, *Now, therefore, if it displease thee, I will get me back,*[38] [that is as if Balaam commented]: "I did not go [with the messengers of Balak] until the Holy One, blessed be He, told me, *Rise up, go with them,*[39] and you [i.e., an angel], tell me that I should return. Such is His conduct! Did He not tell Abraham to sacrifice his son, after which the angel of the Eternal called to Abraham, *And he said, Lay not thy hand upon the lad.*[40] He is accustomed to saying something and to have an angel revoke it, etc." Thus the Sages were prompted to say that the prophecy comprising the first charge where God is mentioned is not like the second charge of which it is said that it was through an angel, only this was not unusual, for it is customary with the prophets that He would command by a prophecy and revoke the command through an angel since the prophet knew that the revocation was the word of God.

In the beginning of Vayikra Rabbah[41] the Sages have said: "*And He called to Moses,*[42] unlike Abraham. Concerning Abraham it is written, *And the angel of the Eternal called unto Abraham a second time out of heaven.*[43] The angel called, and God spoke the word, but here with respect to Moses, the Holy One, blessed be He, said, 'It is I Who called, and it is I Who spoke the word.'" That is to say, Abraham did not attain prophecy until he prepared his soul first to perceive an angel, and from that degree he ascended to attain the word of prophecy, but Moses was prepared for prophecy at all times.

Thus the Sages were prompted to inform us everywhere that seeing an angel is not prophecy, and those who see angels and speak with them are not included among the prophets, as I have mentioned concerning

Daniel. Rather, this is only a vision called "opening of eyes," as in the verse: *And the Eternal opened the eyes of Balaam, and he saw the angel of the Eternal;*[44] similarly: *And Elisha prayed, and said, O Eternal, I pray thee, open his eyes that he may see.*[45] But where Scripture mentions the angels as men, as is the case in this portion, and the portion concerning Lot—likewise, *And a man wrestled with him,*[13] *And a certain man found him,*[46] in the opinion of our Rabbis[47]—in all these cases there was a special glory created in the angels, called among those who know the mysteries of the Torah "a garment," perceptible to the human vision of such pure persons as the pious and the disciples of the prophets, and I cannot explain any further. And in those places in Scripture where you find the sight of God and the speech of an angel, or the sight of an angel and the speech of God, as is written concerning Moses at the outset of his prophecy,[48] and in the words of Zechariah,[49] I will yet disclose words of the living God in allusions.

NOTES

1. "After him." In our text of Rashi: "after the state of his health."
2. Verse 2 here.
3. "One angel does not carry out two commissions." (Bereshith Rabbah 50:2 and mentioned in Rashi here.) But, continues Ramban, these two missions given to the angel Raphael—healing Abraham and rescuing Lot from Sodom—do not violate the principle. See text.
4. It is as if he was sent on a new mission in another place after he had completed his mission in a different place. For it is clear that the principle of one angel not carrying out two commissions applies only to two simultaneous commissions, as explained in Mizrachi's commentary on Rashi.
5. Since healing and rescue are missions with a common purpose, one angel could be charged with both missions.
6. Verse 8 here.
7. Ibn Tibbon's translation, II, 42: in Al Charizi, Chapter 43.
8. Verse 3 here.
9. In other words, why does Scripture begin the chapter with the statement, *And the Eternal appeared to him,* when in the detailed account of the vision it is explained that he saw only angels?
10. The author of the Moreh Nebuchim.
11. See Ecclesiastes 5:2.
12. Since the vision concerning the preparation and the eating of the meal were not relevant to the prophecy of the birth of Isaac.
13. Further, 32:25. The reference deals with Jacob wrestling with the angel.

14. *Ibid.*, Verse 31.
15. *Ibid.*, 28:13.
16. *Ibid.*, 19:3.
17. *Ibid.*, Verses 17–21.
18. Ramban partially agrees with Rambam's position. He says that wherever seeing or hearing an angel is mentioned in Scripture, it refers to a vision since the human senses can not perceive an angel. However, wherever Scripture ascribes human appearances to the angels, as in the case of Abraham, then their presence is sensually perceived. Other differences of opinion between Ramban and Rambam regarding prophecy are mentioned further on in the text.
19. Rabbi Moshe ben Maimon (Maimonides). See *Seder Bereshith*, Note 139.
20. Moreh Nebuchim, II, 41.
21. Megillah 3a.
22. Haggai, Zechariah and Malachi—three prophets who lived at the beginning of the second Temple.
23. The Men of the Great Assembly redacted the books of the Bible. See Baba Bathra 15 a. They placed the book of Daniel in the section of the Writings. (*Ibid.*, 14 b).
24. Daniel 9:1.
25. From the beginning of Chapter 10 there.
26. *Ibid.*, 10:4. As for his friends, see *ibid.*, Verse 7. Tradition specifies that these were Haggai, Zechariah and Malachi (Megillah 3a.)
27. She was not a prophetess even though angels appeared to her. (Above, 16:7.) Ramban thus differs with Rambam, who had said that all prophets received the prophecy through the medium of an angel. Rambam's position is defended as follows: Rambam's intent was not that whenever an angel is seen it is an instance of prophecy. Rather his intent was that whenever prophecy comes to any of the prophets it comes through an angel. However, it is possible that an angel may appear for the purpose of conveying information to one who is not a prophet. This was the case with Daniel and Hagar.
28. In Megillah 14a, the Rabbis list seven prophetesses who arose in Israel: Sarah, Miriam, Deborah, Hannah, Abigail, Huldah and Esther. Hagar however was not listed among them. See Note 103 further.
29. Guide of the Perplexed, II, 42. See Friedlander's note on *bath kol*, p. 199, n. 2.
30. Exodus 6:3.
31. Vayikra Rabbah 1:14.
32. Hosea 12:11.
33. Numbers 12:8.
34. I Kings 13:18. From this you might argue that the prophets themselves attributed their prophecy to an angel. This is not correct, as is explained in the text.
35. *Ibid.*, Verse 9.
36. *Ibid.*, Verse 17.
37. Bamidbar Rabbah 20:13.
38. Numbers 22:34.
39. *Ibid.*, 22:20.
40. Further, 22:12.
41. 1:9.
42. Leviticus 1:1.
43. Further, 22:15.
44. Numbers 22:31.
45. II Kings 6:17.
46. Further, 37:15.
47. According to the Sages the man who wrestled with Jacob was the angel of Esau (Bereshith Rabbah 77:2), and the man who found Joseph was the angel Gabriel (Tanchuma Vayeshev 2).
48. Exodus 3:2.
49. Zechariah 1:14, etc.

GERSONIDES, *MILḤAMOT HA-SHEM*

Translation by David Wolf Silverman

SECOND TREATISE, CHAPTER 6

. . . After expounding these differences between prophecy [on the one hand] and divination and dreams [on the other] it is clear that their modes of communication do not belong to the same genus. For, if such were the case, then the differences between them would [only] be one of greater or lesser [degrees] in accordance with the preparation of the recipient power involved, since by this assumption they would all be caused essentially by the same efficient cause and possess the selfsame recipient power. Or, shall we assume that the three [modes of communication] are self-evidently not of the same genus, since the recipient power of the prophetic communication is [none other than] the hylic intellect. Once it has been perfected by the intelligibles, as we have explained above, we must infer necessarily that the level of this mode of communication is correlative with the level of perfection of the intellect to the extent that the intellect bereft of any perfection is not disposed to receive anything [whatsoever] of this emanation. Now this runs contrary to our experience in this matter, for we have already found that this mode of communication exists in some children and simple folk, and more frequently amongst them than amongst the many people who are wiser than they.

Moreover, the striking differences between prophecy, divination and dreams indicates they do not fall under a single genus, for if they were, such a striking disparity among them would not exist. Rather, they should demonstrate only a qualitative difference of greater or lesser degree, as we have said. And, since such is the case [viz., that there exist significant differences in kind and not merely differences of magnitude] there is, indeed, no problem from this aspect of the matter.

But it is still incumbent upon us to investigate, in terms of the premises available to us [concerning them] and in conformity with what is apparent from our experience of them, what is the nature of these modes of communication, what is the efficient cause involved in [the production of] each one of them, and the recipient power [involved in each]. For despite the great difficulty involved in this undertaking, due to the paucity of premises available to us, it is necessary to expound it according to the measure of our comprehension; for understanding each of the things which exist insofar as their nature can be known constitutes the essence of [human] happiness.

And we maintain also that it is now clear that if the recipient power of these modes of communication be not one and the same substance, then the efficient cause must [also] be correspondingly plural. Suppose that their recipient power is not one and the same, but that in one [mode of communication] it is the imagination, then their efficient cause cannot be the same [in both cases] since the imagination cannot receive the activity of the intellect except via the hylic intellect; [this is a requirement] inasmuch as the soul be constituted as a [realized] unity. Once this is acceptable as true, via this hypothetical syllogism, we can maintain it as evident indeed that the recipient power cannot be the same [substance] in these [different] modes of communication. As to the recipient in the case of prophecy, it is clear that it is the hylic intellect and the occurrence of prophecy is therefore congruent upon the perfection of the intellect. The recipient, however, in the case of divination and dreams cannot be the hylic intellect, for if such were the case, then their various degrees would be correlative to the [degree of] the intellect receiving them, to the extent that the more highly perfected the intellect, the greater the disposition to receive this emanation. Ergo, this mode of communication should be found with greater frequency among those who are wiser than among those children and simple folk where it now happens most frequently. And this is contrary to our experience viz., that we discover this mode of communication with greater frequency among children and simple folk than among those who are wiser than they.

Now one might object to this and claim that the reason for the frequency of such occurrences among children and simple folk is due to their lack of preoccupation with the objects of sensation and the shifting of their thoughts from the distractions usually attendant upon these, to other matters. As a result, the isolation of the hylic intellect from the other rational powers is more easily perfected in them than in other people and they would thus be disposed [all the more] to receive this emanation. We answer our objector by saying that it is impossible for those whose intellects are deficient to isolate their intellect from the other parts of their souls, for they can have no efficient cause to accomplish such an isolation. With regard to those whose intellects are perfected, however, their intellects are indeed separable as soon as they [viz., their intellects] utilize their intelligibles, for it is under this aspect that the separation of the parts of the soul actually takes place. This is obvious to any interested reader of our book.

A situation analogous to the one where thought, engaged in its proper activities separates itself from the other [rational] powers and thereby weakens the other perceptual powers [of the body] can be seen where the organs of digestion, due to their full employment during the process of digestion are isolated from the other sensory powers and draws off the natural warmth of the other sensory organs into its own operations and sleep results. This happens due to the unity of the soul, for when the soul is employed in the activity proper to one of its powers, the others are inoperative, since it cannot employ two powers simultaneously. This being so, it is clear [now] that the soul's recipient power of this emanation in dreams and in divination will be the imagination, while its recipient power in prophecy will be the hylic intellect.

That the recipient power in the case of dreams is the imagination can be determined with but slight reflection upon what is set forth in the treatise *De Sensu et Sensibili* for it is made clear there that, in general, dreams are related to the imagination. As for divination, it belongs in the same class as dreams; the difference between it and dreams is one of degree alone, and for this reason it is clear that the mode of communication involved in both belong to the same genus. This being so, it is a necessary inference that their recipient power and efficient cause be one and the same. And, since the imagination does not receive this emanation directly from the Active Intellect, another efficient cause for this mode of communication becomes necessary. However, it has already been made clear—from preceding chapters—that it is a universally necessary conclusion that the efficient cause of these modes of communication is the Active Intellect and, moreover, if we concede the possibility that another efficient cause is involved here—it becomes difficult for us to understand what this cause might be.

We shall then maintain the following: since this proposition necessarily entails the rejection of the Active Intellect as the efficient cause of the communication realized through divination and dreams, while the previous proposition entails necessarily that the Active Intellect be [considered as] the proper cause of this communication, we [must] infer that, from one point of view the Active Intellect is the efficient cause while from the other it is not. This being so, it is apparent that the Active Intellect is the efficient cause of the communication realized through divination and dreams mediately—and not directly from its own substance—and that which is directly affirmed as necessary by the proposition, i.e., that it is a universally necessary entailment that the Active Intellect is the efficient cause of this communication, does not compel it to do so directly. Nevertheless, it is a necessary entailment that it constitute the efficient cause—either mediately or immediately—and this is clear from the explanation given there. What is entailed necessarily by the proposition rejecting the Active Intellect as the efficient cause of this mode of communication excludes only direct activation of it by the Active Intellect, but does not exclude its activation of such by indirect means.

This being so, it now becomes necessary to explain what constitutes this mediator. And, we shall maintain that, since in many matters the heavenly bodies constitute the media through which the operations of the Active Intellect are accomplished, it seems that they are also the mediators for the actualization of this mode of communication. Moreover, since it has already been explained that the structural patterns to which this communication pertains are themselves derived from the heavenly bodies, and since the heavenly bodies themselves possess intellects, they must apprehend unconditionally their resultant structural pattern. This will be fully explained in the fifth treatise of this [our] book. We expound it here by way of preface to that which will be [more fully] explained there. Namely—whatever is derived as structurally patterned by one of the heavenly bodies cannot be inferred from any of the others and that the intellect of each one of the movers of the heavenly bodies apprehends only those ordered patterns resulting from its [own] operations, and not those that are structured by the other movers. Once we establish this, we can then maintain that, just as the phantasms and intelligibles are ordered directly to each and every man from the constellation ascendant or dominant at a particular time, so it will happen, that when the imagination separates itself from the other powers of the psyche, it will then be predisposed to receive the structural patterns pertinent to other men, insofar as its emanation is affected by them. And, since this mode of communication does not suffer the perfect participation of all of the heavenly bodies, as is clear to anyone acquainted with [the science of] astrology, while all of the heavenly bodies do participate in that which exists as the resultant of their structural patterns, the knowledge attained in this manner will of course be inadequate, and this accounts for the many errors which occur in these [astrological] predictions.

Since prophecy, however, is actualized by the Active Intellect which itself permeates all of the movers of the heavenly bodies, the knowledge attendant upon its actualization will be perfect [knowledge]. And, since prophecy derives from the Active Intellect, and the Active Intellect intends solely to aid man in attaining happiness—via the various perfections with which it has endowed him—for such is the final end of its [the Active Intellect's] present and past operations—prophecy [therefore] strives to lead mankind towards happiness.

Divination and dreams, however, insofar as they are to be accounted among the powers emanating in the manner explained previously from the heavenly bodies, do not, through these emanations upon man's thought and imagination, conduce towards happiness, but will, upon occasion, accomplish the opposite, so too, it will happen that this predictive mode [viz., divination and dreams] will not be conducive to happiness.

And, since the recipient power in prophecy is the hylic intellect and prophecy will then be correlative with the [degree of] perfection of the intellect, and for this reason is attainable through training—and since the recipient power in dreams and divination is the imagination, which is not correlative to the [degree of] perfection of the intellect and cannot therefore be attained via training—and since the imagination separates itself more easily from the distractions of thought and sensation in simple folk and children then in the case of other people, it can occur among some of them more often than it does among those who are wiser than they—because the instrument for receiving this emanation is solely the imagination—it becomes necessary for the imagination to sequester itself from the other perceptual powers in order that they not impair its operation. And since what has been explained in this treatise corresponds to our sensory experience of these predictive modes of communication, it is clear that these accord precisely with our conclusions regarding this matter. And with this—we have now answered all of the objections listed in this chapter.

NOTES

1. The reading *al mah sh'hunahnu* which is found in the Vatican MSS. is preferable to the elision of this phrase from the other two editions. I have translated accordingly.
2. Cf. 2 Chronicles 34:5.

CRESCAS, *OR HA-SHEM*

Translation by Warren Zev Harvey

BOOK II, PART 4

Concerning the exposition of the word "prophecy," and its subject matter, in accordance with what the Law requires and with which philosophic speculation is consistent:

Prophecy, according to what is found concerning it, is a spiritual cognitive overflow overflowing to the intellect of man from Him, may He be blessed, through a medium or not through a medium, informing him—even without the premises from which they are deducible—of some thing or things of which that man is ignorant; and it is with regard to all the modalities; and it is for the sake of his own direction or the direction of others.

As for our saying in this definition, "overflow overflowing," it is like a genus of all overflows which overflow from those effecting the overflow to those receiving the overflow.

Our saying "to the intellect of man" is to distinguish it from the overflows which overflow to the other species; e.g., to the animals and plants. And since we posited the recipient of the overflow to be his intellect, dreams and magic are excluded, since the faculty which receives them is the imagination, as was made clear in the *Parva Naturalia*.[1]

Our saying "spiritual . . . overflow" is to distinguish it from the material corporeal overflows.

Our saying "cognitive" is to distinguish it from spiritual overflows which [2] are *in potentia;* e.g., the overflow overflowing to man which renders him intellectually cognizing *in potentia.*

Our saying "from Him, may He be blessed, through a medium or not through a medium," also excludes dreams and magic, and has reference to the prophecy of Moses which was not through a medium, and that of the rest of the prophets, which was through a medium.

Our saying "informing him—even without the premises . . . —of some thing or things" is to distinguish it from the overflow which overflows to man and which renders him intellectually cognizing *in actu* in such a way that he does not intellectually cognize its truth without the premises from which are deduced the *intelligibile*. This [information] is with regard either to *intelligibilia*, to *sensibilia*, or to objects of the continuous tradition, as has been explained in its place.[2]

Now, our saying "of which that man is ignorant," is to distinguish it from the *intelligibilia prima*, of which he is not ignorant, given that the man in question is an intellectual.

And our saying "and it is with regard to all the modalities," indicates that prophecy might occur with regard to the modality of possibility, as well as with regard to the other modalities. This indeed is apparent from most of the prophecies and promises, as we have noted in Part 1[3] of this Book. On this have stumbled the feet of some of the savants of our nation, who were of the opinion that [3] God's knowledge extends over the modality of necessity alone; and while this is wholesale infidelity to the ordinance of the Law, it is itself demonstrably indefensible, as we have already shown, and as we shall argue further in Part 5,[4] God willing.

And our saying "and it is for the sake of his own direction or the direction of others," is in the slot of purpose; for purposes are well included in definitions, inasmuch as purpose is the strongest of the four causes, as has been explained in its place. Now, according to what is found in the Law and in the Writings, some prophecies may be for the sake of the direction of the prophet, like most of the prophecies which came to the Patriarchs, and some may be for the sake of the direction of others, like the prophecy of [Moses] the Master of the prophets, which was for the sake of the direction of the totality of our nation, and like the prophecies of the prophets sent to Israel and to other nations.

This is what seems fitting in exposition of the word "prophecy," according to what is found of it.

NOTES

1. Aristotle, *De Somniis*, 1, 459a.
2. Cf. Judah ha-Levi, *Kuzari*, I, 25, Ibn Tibbon's translation: הקבלה הנמשכת שהיא כמראה העין (Arabic: אלתואתר). Cf. *Ibid.*, V. 25.
3. *Or Ha-Shem*, II, 1, 1.
4. *Or Ha-Shem*, II, 5, 3–4.

ALBO, *IKKARIM*

Translation by Isaac Husik

BOOK III, CHAPTER 8

The divine inspiration which we said was necessary in order that we may know through it what things are acceptable to God and what things are not, man can not acquire by himself without divine consent. For it is not natural that the spirit of an intellect devoid of matter should rest upon a material thing. For this reason all the ancients thought it impossible that the divine spirit should rest upon man, and that the latter should prophesy by means of a supernatural power and foretell the future. And therefore the ancient peoples used to make images and burn incense and offer prayers to the stars to bring down the spiritual influence of some star upon one of their images, in order that through it the spirit of the star residing in the body of the star should rest upon man, who is a corporeal being, so that the latter might foretell the future through the spirit of the star exerting an influence upon the person. This is the meaning of divination. . .

The prophets had indeed also this power of foretelling the future as a secondary consideration, as a testimony to the truth of their prophetic teaching, in order that men may believe them. Accordingly we find that all the prophets admonish us constantly to observe the Torah and carry out the commandments. The main purpose of God in inspiring the prophets was that through them man may attain to his perfection by doing those things which are acceptable to God and not in order to give mankind a knowledge of the future, as is the case with the diviners. These foretell the future by certain practices which strengthen the power of imagination in a natural way, and not through the spirit of God, as the prophets do; unless, indeed, we say that prophecy is also a function of the imagination, as is the opinion of some of our wise men who follow the Philosopher.[1] They hold that prophecy is a natural phenomenon, pertaining solely to the power of imagination, like dreams. They go so far as to say that it is an unusual thing if a man does not prophesy being wise and prepared thereto, i.e. if his imagination is prepared for prophecy.

This is, however, contradicted both by our senses and our reason. The argument from the senses is that we never find the gift of prophecy in any one of the philosophers, though they were wise men in theoretical speculation; whereas we do find prophecy among the Jewish people. This shows that it is not a natural phenomenon associated with theoretical speculation. For if it were so, why should this gift have been kept from the other nations, so that their wise men despite their perfection of intellect and imagination are devoid of the prophetic inspiration? There is no doubt, therefore, that prophecy is a divine inspiration which comes by the will of God upon the rational power, either through the medium of the imagination or without it, as will be explained.

The argument from reason is that the diviners, the image worshippers, those who consult ghosts and familiar spirits, and those who indulge in other practices in order to strengthen the power of imagination so as to know the future, can not determine the things which are acceptable to God, because they have no means of knowing this, seeing that it is above nature and the spirit of uncleanness and the powers of the spheres, from which they obtain all their information. And for this reason they are not always correct in their prognostications. And this for two reasons, first, because the power of imagination is necessarily deceptive from its nature, for not everything that is imaginable is possible, as is known to those who are familiar with the nature of that faculty. And secondly, because God can destroy the power of the constellations and bring about the opposite of that which they determine. Therefore astrologers are necessarily liable to deception, as the Bible says: "Let now the astrologers, the star-gazers, the monthly prognosticators, stand up and save thee from the things that shall come upon thee."[2] The Rabbis[3] comment upon the expression "*from* the things," as meaning that they can save from some of the things, but not from all the things. They can not foretell truly all that has been determined for they are necessarily liable to error for the two reasons mentioned, either by reason of the nature of the imaginative faculty, or because God can nullify by His will that which is determined by the stars.

The prophet is the opposite of all this. His inspiration comes from God and is due to the will of God, and not to the powers of the spheres. Moreover it descends primarily and essentially upon the rational power. Hence there can not be any error in it. The Bible testifies to this effect concerning Samuel, "And did let none of his words fall to the ground. And all Israel from Dan even to Beer-Sheba knew that Samuel was established to be a prophet of the Lord."[4] The meaning is that the true character of his prophecy was known from the fact that none of his words fell to the ground, unlike the diviners and magicians. So Balaam says to Balak, "For there is no enchantment with Jacob, neither is there any divination with Israel; Now is it said of Jacob and of Israel: what hath God wrought!'"[5] The meaning is, Do not think that the good which is promised to Israel can be nullified in any way, as those things are nullified which are determined by the stars. No, it can not be, for they know what is determined, not by means of divination and enchantment, but through prophecy do they know "what God hath wrought," i.e. what God has decreed that He would do. Therefore it can not be nullified in any way. For God has power to destroy the constellation and the work of the diviners and the magicians as well as the results of their science, for He is "God who brought them forth out of Egypt, though they have lofty horns like those of the wild-ox."[6] The word *lo* (lit. to him) refers to the people of Egypt, though it is in the singular, as in the expression, "Egypt said, 'let me flee from the face of Israel;'"[7] "Shall Egypt be like women."[8] The meaning is that though the people of Egypt had knowledge through diviners and magic, and great strength like the horns of the wild-ox through the constellations, nevertheless God took Israel out of their power and punished their gods.

From all this it is clear that it is impossible to know all the things that are acceptable to God in any way except through the will of God, i.e. through the medium of a special inspiration coming from Him for this purpose. Accordingly the definition of prophecy from this point of view is that it is an inspiration coming from God to the rational power in man, either through the medium of the power of imagination or without it, by virtue of which information comes to him through an angel or otherwise concerning matters which a man cannot know naturally by himself. The purpose is to lead him or others to happiness, so that mankind may attain the human purpose.

In defining prophecy as coming through the medium of the imagination or without it, our purpose is to embrace all degrees of prophecy. For there are prophets to whom, in the beginning of their career, prophecy comes through the medium of the power of the imagination. For this reason they see extraordinary images in their prophetic visions by reason of their inferior status as prophets. Thus some see forms of women, as Zechariah said, "And, behold, there came forth two women, and the wind was in their wings; for they had wings like the wings of a stork. . ."[9] Others see angels with great and fearful bodies, as Daniel said, "His body also was like the beryl, and his face as the appearance of lightning, and his eyes as torches of fire. . ."[10] And there are other instances of images named by the prophets when the inspiration of the rational power came through the medium of the imagination.

Some prophets remain in that stage, while others ascend to a higher stage, some reaching so high that their prophecy comes to them without a medium. That is, the inspiration of the rational power is not associated with the activity of the imagination at all. This was the status of Moses at all times after the first revelation, when an angel of God appeared to him in a flame of fire out of the midst of the burning bush. Thereafter the Bible says, "With him do I speak mouth to mouth,"[11] i.e. without a medium. For this reason we do not find any figures of speech or allegories in his words, but his words are all plain. This was also the status of all Israel when the Torah was given, as the Bible says, "The Lord spoke with you face to face in the mount out of the midst of the fire."[12] God desired to give through Moses a law that should be free from all doubt, and hence He desired that Moses' power should be of so high a character that the power of the imagination should have no part in it, so as to avoid suspicion and doubt. And for the same reason Israel who received the law also attained to the grade of being spoken to by God face to face at the time of the Sinaitic revelation.

NOTES

1. The reference can scarcely be to Maimonides and Gersonides, for neither of them assimilates prophecy entirely to dreams, though they institute a comparison between them, and Maimonides says expressly that given all the natural requirements, a person is not a prophet unless God desires that he should be, or more precisely that one may have all the natural equipment in reason and imagination and yet not be able to prophesy if God does not impart that gift. Cf. Husik, A History of Medieval Jewish Philosophy, New York, 1916, xlix, 276 ff., 340 ff.
2. Isa. 47, 13.
3. Cf. Duran, Magen Abot, p. 74. Professor Louis Ginzberg doubts the authenticity of this alleged rabbinical interpretation.
4. I Sam. 3, 19–20.
5. Num. 23, 23.
6. Ibid. 22. Note peculiar translation.
7. Ex. 14, 25. Here both verbs, "said" (ויאמר) and "flee" (אנוסה), are singular.
8. Isa. 19, 16. The verb "shall be" (יהיה) is singular in the Hebrew.
9. Zech. 5, 9.
10. Dan. 10, 6.
11. Num. 12, 8.
12. Deut. 5, 4.

BOOK III, CHAPTER 9

A question may arise as follows: Since the prophetic inspiration comes from God, who is One, and the purpose of the prophetic message is always the same, namely to lead mankind to happiness, how is it that the prophets differ in their expressions when they treat of the same topics, and why are their visions different, one prophet seeing God under one form, another under another?

The answer is that the differences of vision and expression do not prove difference in origin, nor do they necessarily indicate a change in the nature of the author of the prophetic inspiration or in the purpose. Different effects may come from the same agent, depending upon the nature of the recipients. Thus fire, being one and the same thing, causes wax to melt and salt to harden. Similarly, though the soul, according to the consensus of philosophers, is one in essence and indivisible, nevertheless it is the cause of different activities in the body, depending upon the different parts of the body in which its activity is visible. In the brain the soul exhibits one kind of activity, in the liver another kind, in the heart still another, though all the activities are for one purpose, namely to conserve the body. In the flesh again the soul has sensation, in the bones she has no sensation, and in different members the soul shows different powers. This shows that the same agent may exhibit his power in different ways in different places, causing different activities for one and the same purpose. The difference is due either to the media through which he shows his power or to the localities in which his power appears. . .

The Rabbis explain this subject in Bereshit Rabbah[9]: "A Cuthean[10] asked Rabbi Meir, Is it possible that God, of whom it is written, 'Do not I fill heaven and earth?'[11] should have spoken to Moses from between the staves of the ark? Said Rabbi Meir, bring me large mirrors. When he brought them, R. Meir said to him, look at your reflection. He looked, and he saw they were large. Then he said, bring me small mirrors. When he brought them, R. Meir said, look at your reflection. He looked, and he saw they were small. Then R. Meir said, If you, a man of flesh and blood, can change yourself into many shapes at your pleasure, surely God who created the world can do so."

The purpose of the Cuthean was to deny that prophetic inspiration emanates from God. He thought that it was the work of the power of imagination, as the philosophers hold and those who follow after them. Their reasons are two-fold. First, God being One cannot appear to the prophet under many different forms, for this would argue multiplicity or change in the agent. The second reason is that an abstract intellect can not appear to a material being.

These arguments R. Meir refuted by means of the mirrors. The first argument is answered as follows: As in the mirrors a thing appears different in form, large or small, straight or crooked, bright or obscure, according to the nature of the mirrors through which the thing is seen, i.e. according as the mirrors are large or small, straight or crooked, clear or obscure, though the thing itself does not change, so God appears to the prophets under many and various forms according to the brightness and purity of the media, though God Himself does not multiply or change. The change and the multiplicity come from the media, as in the illustration of the mirrors. A thing seen also varies according to the difference in the person who sees. Thus, if the person who sees a thing through a mirror has sharp and clear vision, he will see the thing in one form, whereas if his vision is weak or dimmed, he will see the thing in another form, though the thing seen and the mirror are the very same which appeared to the man of clear vision.

The second argument is answered as follows: As the person or the thing seen through a mirror is different from the mirror through which he or it is seen, nor does his existence depend upon that of the mirror; and yet the likeness of the person appears in the mirror, though there is no likeness in the mirror in reality, it only appears so to the eye, so though God is separate and abstract and can not be comprehended, He nevertheless appears to the prophet in a given form, which the prophet sees speaking to him, though in reality there is no such form in existence, the voice alone which the prophet hears being the real purpose of the vision, and nothing else.

And if the question is asked, How is it possible that one should see what does not exist and yet acquire truth by means of it? The answer is, when a person sees in a true dream a man speaking to him, the things are not real, though the dreamer imagines that they are, and he hears a voice speaking to him, which does not really exist, and yet the information which the person gets through that dream is correct. In the same way, from the analogy of the dream or the mirror, in which a person sees the form or hears a sound of words, the prophet understands the meaning of the prophetic inspiration which comes to him. As in the mirror in which one sees his likeness, there really is no such likeness as he sees, so the prophet understands that there is no such form in reality as he sees, though he sees it, and that the purpose of the form which appears to him is that he should hear the voice or get the *meaning* of the vision, in which the truth resides. In the mirror, too, the likeness seen in it does not really exist, but the significance of the visible likeness is real and points to the thing seen through the likeness, which is real. So in the prophetic vision the idea signified in the vision is true, though the form itself which appears is not real. It may be that the expression, "I make myself known to him in a *vision* (מראה),"[12] is an allusion to the nature of the mirror (מראה), as we have explained.[13]

And similarly the expression, "I speak with him in a dream," has reference to our previous explanation. There is a great difference, indeed, between a dream and a prophetic vision. There is no dream without foolish elements,[14] whereas a prophetic vision is entirely correct and true. Nevertheless, since we can not imagine a voice speaking without corporeal organs except by thinking of a dream, the Bible uses the expression, "I speak with him in a dream," to indicate that as in a dream one hears a voice speaking and sees a person speaking, though in reality no such things exist, so in a prophetic vision, the truth in it is the information which the prophet obtains. This is God's purpose in sending the vision, but the voice that is heard expressing itself by means of corporeal organs is not really there. This is what the Rabbis meant when they said, "A dream is one sixtieth part of prophecy."[15]

The illustration which R. Meir employed of the mirrors has shown, therefore, that the variety and multiplicity of likenesses which appear to prophets are no indication of multiplicity and change in God, as the multiplicity and change of the mirrors or the multiplicity and change of the spectators imply no change or multiplicity in the thing seen in the mirror. It follows also from this that the variety of expression of the different prophets does not indicate change in God or in His purpose. For though the speakers use different expressions, the idea is the same necessarily since it comes from one author, and hence the purpose is the same. This is the meaning of the Rabbis when they say, "Many prophets have one idea, though no two prophets use the same expression."[16] This is what we intended to make clear in this chapter.

NOTES

1. Num. 12, 6 f.
2. Isa. 6, 1.
3. Dan. 7, 9.
4. Ex. 15, 3.
5. Rosh Hashanah, 17b. It does not say, however, in that passage that any one *saw* God in that form.
6. Dan. 10, 6.
7. Ibid. 5.
8. Zech. 1, 8.
9. Ber. Rab. 4.
10. Cuthean in the strict sense refers to the heathen population which the king of Assyria, according to II Kings, 17, 24 ff., settled in the Kingdom of Israel in 722 B.C. They were the ancestors of the Samaritans, who are in the Talmud called Cutheans. In our editions, however, the censors substituted the word incorrectly in many cases for גוי or מין, to denote an opponent of the religion of Israel, a heathen or an unbeliever.
11. Jer. 23, 24.
12. Num. 12, 6.
13. מראה in Hebrew means mirror as well as vision; cf. Ex. 38, 8, במראת הצבאת.
14. Berakot 55a.
15. Berakot 57b.
16. Sanhedrin 89a. The word סיגנון (Lat. signum, Gk. *σίγνον*) is used in two senses, meaning both the expression and the idea.

BOOK III, CHAPTER 10

We must now explain the existence of prophecy and its various grades, so that believers may find it easier to understand the existence of prophecy and the different degrees thereof. At the moment of birth the individual is devoid of all understanding. The first things that are formed in him are the five external senses, touch, taste, smell, hearing, sight. The individual does not get these all at once, but one at a time. At the moment of his appearance in the outer world he perceives only with the coarsest of the senses, that of touch. The objects of his perception at this stage are heat and cold, moisture and dryness, softness and hardness, roughness and smoothness and the like. After a further interval of time after birth, he perceives a finer and more important class of objects, namely tastes, like sweet, bitter, sour, astringent,[1] sharp, and so on. Later on he perceives another class of things still finer, namely the odors, the agreeable and the disagreeable, etc. Later still he perceives with the sense of hearing a class of objects that is still finer than those of the sense of smell, and that may be perceived at a greater distance, such as sounds and tones, and their various kinds, etc. Still later he perceives with the sense of sight another class of existents finer than all the rest, which can be perceived at a greater distance than the others, such as colors and forms according to their various kinds, and so on. One of these five senses can not perceive the objects of the others. Thus, the sense of sight can not perceive sounds, or tones or odors; nor can the senses of smell and taste perceive colors and sounds.

After he has advanced a considerable time and has become habituated to the five senses, he rises to a higher degree than that of perceiving the objects of the various senses. He now has the power of recognizing a thing when it is no longer actually perceived. He recognizes what he has once perceived when he sees it again, and though the thing has disappeared he remembers the knowledge which is impressed on his imagination and recognizes the object. This power of apprehension he acquires through the medium of the first faculty.[2]

As he grows older still, he attains to a higher degree by means of the first powers,[2] a new gate opens before him, and he acquires the power of intellectual apprehension. He strips the sensible object of its particular qualities and apprehends the general essence. For example, he takes animality and rationality in a human being and judges that these are common to the whole species and are different from those particular qualities which differ in different individuals.

As he advances further in years and acquires information, another gate opens before him which he has not entered hitherto. He now makes a distinction between substance and accident, and between the necessary, the possible and the impossible. He combines rational principles not based upon sense perception[3] with each other, and acquires all the sciences, which he could not have acquired by means of the powers mentioned before. These four stages form the limit of the human intellect, beyond which it can not go. Some individuals do not reach the highest stage, but stop with the second or the third. These then are the powers which the generality of men have.

But it is possible that in addition to these powers, still another gate may open to a person and still another degree may be attainable by him of which he has no idea. For just as, if a person who has never seen them were told about lights and colors, he would not be able to imagine them and would not understand the different colors, as a eunuch can not imagine the pleasure of sexual intercourse, so it is possible that though by the custom of nature man does not attain a greater degree than the four mentioned, nevertheless the mind may conceive of a higher degree. And experience testifies to this. For we see that beyond the four degrees above mentioned, a new gate opens before a given person which his own nature never imagined, and he speaks words of wisdom or words of song and praise to God in pure and fluent style such as he was incapable of hitherto. Everyone who hears him wonders at his knowledge and the manner of his expression, while he himself does not know whence this power came to him, as a child learns to speak without knowing whence the power came. But everybody recognizes his superiority in this respect. This degree is called the holy spirit.

Now just as the human intellect stops at the four degrees above mentioned and does not pass beyond, so there are persons who stop at the degree of the holy spirit and do not pass beyond it. There are persons whose imagination is strong by nature or who do certain things to strengthen it, like the practices of the diviners or the woman with the familiar spirit. As a result of this they have imaginative visions. There are others who have true dreams, like Pharaoh, Nebuchadnezzar, the chief butler and the chief baker. By reason of these powers some of them think they are prophets. They are the persons of whom the prophet in Scripture says that they "prophesy out of their own heart."[4] For though they sometimes speak the truth, they are bound sometimes to speak falsehood. Thus Ezekiel says, "Woe unto the vile prophets, that follow their own spirit, . . . They have seen vanity and lying divination, that say: The Lord saith; and the Lord hath not sent them, yet they hope that the word would be confirmed."[5] The intimation is that it is impossible, for though their words may be partly true, they can not but be partly false, for such is the nature of the power of imagination, the source of dreams. Our Rabbis say: As there is no wheat without straw, so there is no dream without foolishness.[6]

When, however, the rational power prevails over the imagination, then the person sees true dreams without foolishness. The explanation is given by the Rabbis: "Raba asked the question, How reconcile the statement, 'And the dreams speak falsely,'[7] with the expression, 'I do speak with him in a dream?'[8] His answer is, the two passages are not incompatible. The one passage refers to dreams that come through the medium of an angel, the other to those that come through the medium of a demon."[9] Angel stands for the rational power, demon for the power of imagination. If the rational power prevails over the power of imagination, the person sees true dreams or visions which communicate to him information he never had before. In the measure in which the rational power prevails over the imagination is the person better or less well prepared for prophetic inspiration.

There are persons whose rational power is stronger than the imagination, but the superiority is not great, and hence the power of imagination maintains its strength. And therefore though the rational power is prepared to receive the prophetic inspiration, yet on account of the strength of the imagination and its opposition to the rational power, the person receives the inspiration in trembling and pain. His limbs shake, his sinews tend to dissolve, and a great trembling comes over him, that his soul almost leaves him. And after all that pain the prophetic inspiration comes to the rational power in a dream or vision of the night, and the person dreams prophetic dreams and learns things he has never known before—ideas about the separate substances, or particular notions, or universal ideas of existence, and the like. This is the first degree of prophetic inspiration.

There are others who do not stop here. They enter still another gate that opens before them and attain to a higher degree, which sometimes comes before the first degree and sometimes after. When the two powers are equally strong, the person receives the prophetic inspiration without trembling and without toil, while sleeping on his couch, or in a deep sleep which comes upon him during the day. This degree is called vision (מחזה, מראה). In this stage he sees, by means of the power of imagination, forms which are not real, like the women and the horses seen by Zechariah,[10] or the basket of summer fruit seen by Amos,[11] and the like, which did not really exist. But by reason of the fact that the rational power is stronger than the imagination,[12] it makes the ideas indicated by the forms true, though the forms are not real. This is the second degree of prophetic inspiration.

There are others who do not stop at this degree, but enter another door that opens before them and attain a still higher degree. This happens when the rational power prevails so completely over the imagination that it subdues it and does not allow it to imagine unreal forms. The visions that such a person sees in the prophetic state are real, like the visions of Ezekiel, which were all real, representing mysteries of nature and of the divine being as represented in the mysteries of the chariot. He may also see or hear an angel speaking to him and communicating to him some particular matter for his own benefit or for the benefit of others, or he communicates to him something of a universal nature, and gives him information concerning human events that are to come in the future, particular events that are to happen to an individual, or something general that is to happen to a nation or nations or to humanity as a whole. This is the third degree of prophecy. This degree sometimes comes after the earlier ones, and sometimes it comes first, depending upon the equipment of the recipient. Samuel is a good example. At the beginning of his prophetic career he heard a voice speaking to him, and was free from trembling or toil, nor did he see any form. However, this did not take place while he was absolutely awake, but during a waking vision. A vision or appearance which one has while awake is called, "hand of the Lord," as Maimonides explains in the forty-first chapter of the second part of the *Guide of the Perplexed.* Thus we are told, "And the lamp of God was not yet gone out, and Samuel was laid down to sleep in the temple of the Lord, where the ark of God was."[13] The verse should be construed as follows: "The lamp of God was not yet gone out in the temple of the Lord, and Samuel was laid down to sleep," i.e., in his upper chamber in the court. And "the Lord called Samuel", i.e. in a vision. This is as far as all prophets attain. In every case, even if the individual has the preparation, he does not get the prophetic inspiration except by the grace of God. And it happens sometimes that after having had a prophetic experience, a prophet ceases from prophesying for a long time. And sometimes he must undertake a certain preparatory practice to receive a prophetic inspiration, as in the case of Elisha, who said, "But now bring me a minstrel. And it came to pass, when the minstrel played, that the hand of the Lord came upon him."[14]

There are others still who do not stop at these degrees, but rise to a higher degree where the power of imagination has no say at all. The person does not see or imagine any form, he does not see any angel or likeness before him, but hears a voice speaking to him and communicating to him general ideas for the benefit of a nation or nations, or a rule or rules of conduct for the human race or for a part of it, such as lead to human perfection. This inspiration comes to him without any apparition or vision, but in the daytime while he is awake. And whenever he concentrates his thoughts in reflection and considers a question, the answer comes at once while he is awake; and this happens not at great intervals, but whenever he desires. An individual who attains such a degree as this should no longer be called a human being, but an angel. There is no one among us who has reached this stage except Moses our teacher, peace be upon him, whose prophecy is distinguished from that of all the other prophets in four respects, as enumerated by Maimonides in his commentary on chapter "Helek."

These four points of difference are the four degrees of prophecy which we named, and which are referred to in the Bible, "And the Lord spoke to Moses face to face as a man speaks to his neighbour."[15] "Face to face," means that the inspiration did not come through an angel or intermediary, as is the case in the third degree. "As a man speaks," indicates that the message did not come in visions of the night or in a deep sleep that fell upon him, as in the second degree, but Moses was awake and heard the voice speaking to him, without feeling any trembling or pain, as is the case in the first degree, but "as a man speaks to his neighbour," i.e. without any pain. Whenever he desired to go into the tent of meeting, he heard the voice speaking to him, as we are told, "And when Moses went into the tent of meeting . . . then he heard the voice speaking unto him from above the ark-cover . . . from between the two cherubim."[16] We also have the testimony of Scripture in the passage, "Stay ye, that I may hear what the Lord will command concerning you."[17] And immediately the answer came to him: "If any man of you . . shall be unclean by reason of a dead body . . ."[18] Similarly in the case of the daughters of Zelophehad we read, "And Moses brought their cause before the Lord."[19] And then came the answer, "The daughters of Zelophehad speak right."[20]

No person can attain to any degree of prophetic inspiration at all unless he has the first four natural qualities which we mentioned. Our Rabbis say, "The prophetic spirit does not rest upon a person unless he is wise, strong, rich and tall."[21] Unless he has the quality of wisdom and the other natural qualities, the prophetic inspiration can not come to him at all. This is why they say that Jacob's ladder had four steps. The meaning is that Jacob's prophetic experience was not preceded by the degree of the "holy spirit," which sometimes comes before prophecy, but that the preparatory quality in Jacob was wisdom, which he learned in the school of Eber,[22] where he concealed himself for fourteen years. Without wisdom the prophetic inspiration would not have come to him even in a dream, which is the first degree of prophecy.

The prophets and the righteous and the pious differed from each other in the degree of their association with God. There are some whose souls cleaved so intimately to the celestial beings that the powers of heaven were obedient to them and exerted their influence on the matters of this world at their bidding, for their own benefit or for the benefit of others. They could cause rain to come down by their prayer, heal the sick, cause barren women to bear children, cause fire to come down from heaven, revive the dead, as in the case of Elijah and Elisha. We find that when a person thinks about a palatable article of food or sees another eating sour grapes, the salivary power is aroused and his mouth waters of its own accord;[23] and similarly when he is thinking about sexual intercourse, the seminal power is aroused and the organ stretches. In the same way the natural powers of the physical universe are obedient to the pure soul of the prophet, and dew or rain or a storm comes at his bidding. For just as the powers of the body were created to serve the powers of the soul, and therefore as soon as the psychic power determines upon anything, the corporeal powers and the limbs are impelled to carry it out, so the physical forces in the world of nature are subservient to the pure souls—the whole universe being as one individual—and obey them. Accordingly when such a pure soul conceives the coming of dew or rain or a great and mighty wind, or an earthquake or the opening of the earth, and the like, immediately the power which controls the world of genesis and decay is impelled to carry out the conception.

Sometimes the degree of the prophet or pious man goes beyond this measure, so that the celestial powers too are obedient to him and do his will, bringing down fire from heaven, reviving the dead, and the like, since all things are subject and subservient to him, whether he be a prophet or not. This power varies among righteous men, pious men and prophets according to the degree in which their souls cleave to the higher beings. In this way the prophet or the pious man rules over nature and produces signs and wonders in the world according to the measure of his communion with the higher beings.

This explains the differences among pious men. There are some who reach such a degree of communion that they can produce signs and wonders in nature, like Honi ha-Me'aggel,[24] R. Phinehas ben Yair,[25] R. Hanina ben Dosa,[26] and others, though they did not attain to the degree of prophecy. On the other hand, there are prophets who never performed any sign or miracle, like Jeremiah, Haggai, Zechariah and Malachi. Others have only one sign to their credit, like Samuel, who caused rain to come down in the season of wheat harvest by praying for it. Others again have two or three miracles recorded of them, like Isaiah, who brought about the destruction of Sennacherib, the cure of Hezekiah and the going back of the shadow a number of degrees. Some have still more miracles to their credit, like Elijah and Elisha. . .

NOTES

1. עפיץ (Ar عفص) means astringent, acerbic. Cf. Kaufman, Die Sinne, Leipzig 1884, p. 164 note 8.
2. I.e. sense faculty.
3. The axioms or fundamental laws of thought like the principles of identity, contradiction and excluded middle. Cf. Jevons, Elementary Lessons in Logic, 1920, p.117 f. For a discussion of Aristotle's ideas on the subject, cf. Zeller, Aristotle, I, 200 ff. For a more modern view, see Mill, J.S., A System of Logic, 8th ed., p. 204, §5.
4. Ezek. 13, 2.
5. Ibid. 13, 2, 6.
6. Berakot 55a.
7. Zech. 10, 2.
8. Num. 12, 6.
9. Berakot 55b.
10. Zech. 5, 9.
11. Amos 8, 1.
12. There seems to be a contradiction here, for a few lines back this stage is described as one in which the rational power and the power of imagination are equally strong. The latter expression, however, cannot be taken literally, for even in the first stage the reason is stronger than the imagination, though not a great deal.
13. I Sam. 3, 3.
14. II Kings, 3, 15.
15. Ex. 33, 11.
16. Num. 7, 89.
17. Ibid. 9, 8.
18. Ibid. 10.
19. Ibid. 27, 5.
20. Ibid. 7.
21. Shabbat 92a; Nedarim 38a.
22. See J. E., XI, 262a.
23. Lit., his jaws dissolve. הכליי in the sequel= אבר הכליי, the part of the body functioning for the particular purpose.
24. Ta'anit 23a; ed. Malter, p. 167.
25. Hullin 7a.
26. Ta'anit 25a; ed. Malter, p. 187.

The Seventh Principle

Prophecy of Moses

INTRODUCTION

The Seventh Principle, which declares the superiority of the prophecy of Moses, complements the Sixth Principle. The Seventh Principle both affirms the reality of the phenomenon which constitutes this unique form of prophecy and asserts that it was enjoyed only by Moses. Moses alone was endowed with the superior and qualitatively different form of prophecy described in this principle.

Moses differed from other prophets in that God communicated with him directly without an intermediary. This communication took place "face to face" rather than in a dream or vision. Other prophets felt a waning of strength, became enfeebled during the prophetic experience, and were overcome by fear. No such physical or emotional debilitation occurred to Moses. Finally, Moses was unique in his capacity to enter into prophetic communication with God at will.

Moses was able to enter into a direct and intense communication with God by virtue of the perfection of his intellect. Moses achieved the epitome of human intellectual perfection and hence was able to perceive God in the waking state without an intermediary because, in contradistinction to other prophets, it was not necessary for him to employ the imaginative faculty in order to achieve prophetic comprehension. He was able to enter into the prophetic state at will by virtue of his constant state of intellectual perfection. The power to transcend the corporeal state so completely was unique to Moses and places him in a class by himself.

Albo asserts that not only was the prophecy of Moses qualitatively superior to that of other prophets, but that the miracles performed by Moses were also of a different order. As distinct from those of other prophets, the miracles performed by Moses were more numerous, were public in nature and endured for lengthy periods of time.

MAIMONIDES, *MISHNEH TORAH*

Translation by Moses Hyamson

BOOK OF KNOWLEDGE, LAWS CONCERNING THE BASIC PRINCIPLES OF THE TORAH, CHAPTER 7

6. The foregoing observations refer to the manner in which prophecy was vouchsafed to all the earlier and later prophets with the exception, however, of our teacher, Moses, the chief of all the prophets. In what respects was the prophecy of Moses distinguished from that of the other prophets? All the prophets received their inspired messages in a dream or in a vision; Moses while awake and standing, as it is said, "And when Moses went into the tent of meeting, that He might speak with him, then he heard the Voice speaking unto him." (Num. 7:89). All the prophets received their messages through the medium of an angel. Hence, what they saw, they saw as an allegory or riddle—Moses received his message not through an angel, as it is said, "Mouth to mouth will I speak with him" (Num. 12:8), "The Lord spake unto Moses face to face" (Exod. 33:11); furthermore "And the similitude of the Lord doth he behold" (Num. 12:8); that is to say, that it was no allegory that was revealed to Moses but he realized the prophetic message clearly, without riddle and without parable. To this, the Torah testifies in the text, "Even manifestly, not in dark speeches" (Num. 12:8), which means that he received his prophecy not as a riddle, but had a clear and lucid vision. All the prophets (when receiving their messages) were filled with fear and consternation and became physically weak. Not so, our teacher Moses, of whom Scripture says, "As a man speaketh unto his neighbour." (Ex. 33:11). Just as a man is not startled when he hears the words of his fellow-man, so the mind of Moses was vigorous enough to comprehend the words of prophecy while retaining his normal state. None of the prophets could prophesy at their pleasure. It was otherwise with Moses. He was invested with the prophetic spirit and was clothed with the power of prophecy whenever he pleased. There was no need for him specially to concentrate his mind and prepare for the prophetic manifestations; since

he was ever intent and in readiness like the ministering angels. He therefore prophesied at all times; as it is said, "Stand ye still and I will hear what the Lord will command concerning you." (Num. 9:8). In this regard God made him a special promise, as it is said, "Go, say unto them: 'Return ye to your tents. But as for thee, stand thou here by me'." (Deut. 5:27–28). Hence it may be inferred that all the prophets, when the prophetic power left them, returned to their tents, that is, attended to the satisfaction of their physical needs. Moses, our teacher, never went back to his former tent. He accordingly permanently separated himself from his wife, and abstained from similar gratifications. His mind was closely attached to the Rock of the Universe. The Divine Glory never departed from him; the skin of his face sent forth rays of light, and he was sanctified like the angels.

7. The gift of prophecy may be vouchsafed to a prophet, intended for him alone, to develop his mind and increase his knowledge, so that he may know what hitherto he had not known concerning exalted themes. Sometimes the prophet is sent on a special mission to a particular people or to the inhabitants of a certain city or kingdom, to direct them aright, teach them what they are to do or restrain them from the evil courses they were pursuing. And when so sent, a sign or token may be given him, so that the people might know that God had in truth sent him. Not every one showing a sign or token is on that account to be accepted as a prophet. Only if a man, by reason of his wisdom and conduct wherein he stands preeminent among his contemporaries, is already recognized as worthy of the prophetic gift, and his life, in its sanctity and renunciation, is favourable to the prophetic calling,—then, when he shows a sign or token and asserts that God had sent him, it is one's duty to listen to his message, as it is said, "Unto him ye shall hearken." (Deut. 18:15). It is, however, possible that such a man may show a sign and token and yet not be a prophet. The sign may be a mystery. Nevertheless, it is a duty to listen to him, for, being a great and wise man, worthy of the prophetic gift, we give him the benefit of the presumption. For thus too are we enjoined to decide a suit on the evidence of two competent witnesses. Though it is possible that they may have given false testimony, still having accepted them as competent witnesses, we rely on their qualification. On these and such like matters, it is said, "The secret things belong unto the Lord, our God; but the things that are revealed, belong unto us and to our children" (Deut. 29:28). And further it is said, "For man looketh on the outward appearance, but the Lord looketh on the heart" (I. Sam. 16:7).

CHAPTER 8

1. Israel did not believe in Moses, our Teacher, on account of the tokens he showed. For when one's faith is founded on tokens, a lurking doubt always remains in the mind that these tokens may have been performed with the aid of occult arts and witchcraft. All the signs Moses showed in the Wilderness, he performed because they were needed, and not to support his prophetic claims. Thus, when it was necessary that the Egyptians should be drowned, he divided the Red Sea and drowned them in its depths. We needed material sustenance; he brought down the Manna for us. The people thirsted; he clave the rock for them. Korah's company denied his authority; the earth swallowed them up. And so with all the other tokens. What then were the grounds of the faith in him? The Revelation on Sinai which we saw with our own eyes, and heard with our own ears, not having to depend on the testimony of others, we ourselves witnessing the fire, the thunder, the lightning, Moses entering the thick darkness after which the Divine Voice spoke to him, while we heard the call, "Moses, Moses, go, tell them thus and thus." And so it is said, "The Lord spoke with you, face to face" (Deut. 5:4); and furthermore, "The Lord made not this covenant with our fathers only, [but with us, *even us,* who are all of us here alive this day"] (Deut. 5:3). Whence do we know that the Sinaitic Revelation is the sole proof that Moses' prophetic mission is true? From the text, "Lo, I come unto thee in a thick cloud, that the people may hear when I speak with thee, and may also believe in thee for ever." (Ex. 19:9). Hence the inference that before that event they did not believe with a faith that would endure for ever, but only with a faith followed by hesitating and doubting speculation.

2. As those to whom Moses was sent, were themselves witnesses to the truth of his prophecy, there was no need for him to show them any other sign, since they and he were witnesses to the same matter. They were like two persons who saw an event together. When giving their testimony in such a case, each of them is a witness that the other is telling the truth, and neither need bring proof of the credibility of the other. So was it with Moses, our Teacher. After the Revelation on Sinai, all Israel became witnesses for him; and there was no need for him to show them any further sign. The Almighty indicated this to Moses at the beginning of the latter's career, when He gave him signs which he was to perform in Egypt, and said to him, "They shall hearken to thy voice" (Ex. 3:18). Moses realised that belief based on signs leaves lurking doubts and is followed by musings and speculation. He therefore sought to avoid the

acceptance of his mission, and said, "But lo, they will not believe me" (Ex. 4:1), till the Almighty informed him that these signs were only to serve till our ancestors had departed from Egypt. "And when they will have gone forth and stand at the foot of this mountain," God said to Moses, "their doubts about thee will disappear. For here, I will give thee a sign by which they will know that it was I who sent thee from the first, and no vestige of doubt will linger in their mind." And this is what is meant in the text, "And this shall be a token unto thee that I have sent thee; when thou hast brought forth the people out of Egypt, ye shall serve God at this mountain" (Ex. 3:12). Hence one may conclude with regard to every prophet after Moses, that we do not believe in such a prophet because of the signs he shows, as much as to say that only if he shows a sign, we shall pay heed to him in all that he says, but we believe in him, because of the charge laid down by Moses in the Torah that if the prophet gives a sign "ye shall listen to him"; just as the Lawgiver directed that a cause is to be decided on the evidence of two witnesses even if we have no certainty as to whether they are testifying to the truth or to a falsehood. Similarly, it is our duty to listen to the prophet though we do not know if the sign he shows is genuine or has been performed with the aid of sorcery and by secret arts.

3. Hence too, if a prophet were to arise and perform signs and wonders, and seek to deny the prophetic character of Moses, our Teacher, we would not have to listen to him and would be clearly certain that those signs were wrought by secret arts and witchcraft. For Moses' authority as a prophet is not founded upon signs, in which case we might have weighed the signs of one prophet against those of another. But with our eyes we saw and with our ears we heard the divine Voice, even as he (the claimant to prophecy) also heard it. To what may this be compared? To persons testifying in the presence of a man concerning an incident which he saw with his own eyes and denying that it took place as he saw it. He will surely not accept their statement, but will be convinced that they are false witnesses. The Torah accordingly ordains that even if the sign or token takes place, you are not to listen to the words of such a prophet; since he shows a sign and token in order to deny what you saw with your own eyes. As we only accept signs (as a prophet's credentials) because we are so bidden in the commandment given us by Moses, how shall we, on the strength of such a sign, accept a man as a prophet, who seeks to repudiate Moses' prophecy for the truth of which we have the evidence of our own eyes and ears?

MAIMONIDES, *MOREH NEVUKHIM*

Translation by Michael Friedlander

PART II, CHAPTER 33

It is clear to me that what Moses experienced at the revelation on Mount Sinai was different from that which was experienced by all the other Israelites, for Moses alone was addressed by God, and for this reason the second person singular is used in the Ten Commandments; Moses then went down to the foot of the mount and told his fellow-men what he had heard. Comp., "I stood between the Lord and you at that time to tell you the word of the Lord" (Deut. v. 5). Again, "Moses spake, and God answered him with a loud voice" (Exod. xix. 19). In the Mechilta our Sages say distinctly that he brought to them every word as he had heard it. Furthermore, the words, "In order that the people hear when I speak to thee" (Exod. xix. 9), show that God spoke to Moses, and the people only heard the mighty sound, not distinct words. It is to the perception of this mighty sound that Scripture refers in the passage, "When ye hear the sound" (Deut. v. 20); again it is stated, "You heard a sound of words" (*ibid.* iv. 12), and it is not said, "You heard words"; and even where the hearing of the words is mentioned, only the perception of the sound is meant. It was only Moses that heard the words, and he reported them to the people. This is apparent from Scripture, and from the utterances of our Sages in general. There is, however, an opinion of our Sages frequently expressed in the Midrashim, and found also in the Talmud, to this effect: The Israelites heard the first and the second commandments from God, *i.e.*, they learnt the truth of the principles contained in these two commandments in the same manner as Moses, and not through Moses. For these two principles, the existence of God and His Unity, can be arrived at by means of reasoning, and whatever can be established by proof is known by the prophet in the same way as by any other person; he has no advantage in this respect. These two principles were not known through prophecy alone. Comp., "Thou hast been shown to know that," &c. (Deut. iv. 34). But the rest of the commandments are of an ethical and authoritative character, and do not contain [truths] perceived by the intellect. Notwithstanding all that has been said by our

Sages on this subject, we infer from Scripture as well as from the words of our Sages, that the Israelites heard on that occasion a certain sound which Moses understood to proclaim the first two commandments, and through Moses all other Israelites learnt them when he in intelligible sounds repeated them to the people. Our Sages mention this view, and support it by the verse, "God hath spoken once; twice have I heard this" (Ps. lxii. 11). They state distinctly, in the beginning of Midrash Chazitha, that the Israelites did not hear any other command directly from God; comp., "A loud voice, and it was not heard again" (Deut. v. 19). It was after this first sound was heard that the people were seized with the fear and terror described in Scripture, and that they said, "Behold the Lord our God has shown us, &c., and now why shall we die, &c. Come thou near," &c. Then Moses, the most distinguished of all mankind, came the second time, received successively the other commandments, and came down to the foot of the mountain to proclaim them to the people whilst the mighty phenomena continued; they saw the fire, they heard the sounds, which were those of thunder and lightning during a storm, and the loud sound of the cornet; and all that is said of the many sounds heard at that time, *e.g.*, in the verse, "and all the people perceived the sounds," &c., refers to the sound of the shofar, thunder, and similar sounds. But the voice of the Lord, that is, the voice created for that purpose, which was understood to include the diverse commandments, was only heard once, as is declared in the Law, and has been clearly stated by our Sages in the places which I have indicated to you. When the people heard this voice their soul left them; and in this voice they perceived the first two commandments. It must, however, be noticed that the people did not understand the voice in the same degree as Moses did. I will point out to you this important fact, and show you that it was a matter of tradition with the nation, and well known by our Sages. For, as a rule, Onkelos renders the word *va-yedhabber* by *u-mallel* ("and God spake"); this is also the case with this word in the beginning of the twentieth chapter of Exodus, but the words *ve-al yedabber immanu elohim*, "let not God speak to us" (Exod. xx. 19), addressed by the people to Moses, is rendered *vela yithmallel immanu min kodam adonai* ("Let not aught be spoken to us by the Lord"). Onkelos makes thus the same distinction which we made. You know that according to the Talmud Onkelos received all these excellent interpretations directly from R. Eliezer and R. Joshua, the wisest men in Israel. Note it, and remember it, for it is impossible for any person to expound the revelation on Mount Sinai more fully than our Sages have done, since it is one of the secrets of the Law. It is very difficult to have a true conception of the events, for there has never been before nor will there ever be again anything like it. Note it.

PART II, CHAPTER 35

I have already described the four points in which the prophecy of Moses our Teacher was distinguished from that of other prophets, in books accessible to every one, in the Commentary on the Mishnah and in Mishneh-torah; I have also adduced evidence for my explanation, and shown the correctness thereof. I need not repeat the subject here, nor is it included in the theme of this work. For I must tell you that whatever I say here of prophecy refers exclusively to the form of the prophecy of all prophets before and after Moses. But as to the prophecy of Moses I will not speak of it in this work with one single word, whether directly or indirectly, because, in my opinion, the term prophet is applied to Moses and other men homonymously. A similar distinction, I think, must be made between the miracles wrought by Moses and those wrought by other prophets, for his signs are not of the same class as the miracles of other prophets. That this prophecy was distinguished from that of all his predecessors is proved by the passage, "And I appeared to Abraham, &c., but by my name, the Lord, I was not known unto them" (Ex. vi. 3). We thus learn that his prophetic perception was different from that of the Patriarchs, and excelled it, *à fortiori* it must have excelled that of other prophets before Moses. As to the distinction of Moses' prophecy from that of succeeding prophets, it is stated as a fact, "And there arose not a prophet since in Israel like unto Moses, whom the Lord knew face to face" (Deut. xxxiv. 10). It is thus clear that his prophetic perception was above that of later prophets in Israel, who are "a kingdom of priests and a holy nation," and "in whose midst is the Lord"; much more is it above that of prophets among other nations.

The general distinction between the wonders of Moses and those of other prophets is this: The wonders wrought by prophets, or for them, are witnessed by a few individuals, *e.g.*, the wonders wrought by Elijah and Elisha; the king of Israel is therefore surprised, and asked Gehazi to describe to him the miracles wrought by Elisha: "Tell me, I pray thee, all the great things that Elisha hath done. And it came to pass as he was telling, &c. And Gehazi said: 'My lord, O king, this is the woman, and this is her son, whom Elisha restored to life'" (2 Kings viii. 4, 5). The same is the case with the signs of every other prophet, except Moses our Teacher. Scripture therefore, declares that no prophet will ever, like Moses, do signs publicly in the presence of friend and enemy, of his followers and his opponents; this is the meaning of the words: "And there arose not a prophet since in Israel like unto Moses, &c. In all the signs and the wonders, &c., in the sight of all Israel." Two things are here mentioned together; namely, that there will not arise a prophet that will perceive as Moses perceived, or a prophet that will do as he did; then it is pointed out that the signs were made in the presence of Pharaoh, all his servants and all his land, the opponents of Moses, and also in the presence of all the Israelites, his followers. Comp., "In the sight of all Israel." This is a distinction not possessed by any prophet before Moses; nor, as is correctly foretold, will it ever be possessed by another prophet. We must not be misled by the account that the light of the sun stood still certain hours for Joshua, when "he said in the sight of Israel," &c. (Josh. x. 12); for it is not said there "in the sight of *all* Israel," as is said in reference to Moses. So also the miracle of Elijah, at Mount Carmel, was witnessed only by a few people. When I said above that the sun stood still *certain hours,* I explain the words "*ka-jom tamim*" to mean "the longest possible day," because *tamim* means "perfect," and indicates that that day appeared to the people at Gibeon as their longest day in the summer. Your mind must comprehend the distinction of the prophecy and the wonders of Moses, and understand that his greatness in prophetic perception was the same as his power of producing miracles. If you further assume that we are unable fully to comprehend the nature of this greatness, you will understand that when I speak, in the chapters which follow this, on prophecy and the different classes of prophets, I only refer to the prophets which have not attained the high degree that Moses attained. This is what I desired to explain in this chapter.

PART II, CHAPTER 39

We have given the definition of prophecy, stated its true characteristics, and shown that the prophecy of Moses our Teacher was distinguished from that of other prophets; we will now explain that this distinction alone qualified him for the office of proclaiming the Law, a mission without a parallel in the history from Adam to Moses, or among the prophets who came after him; it is a principle in our faith that there will never be revealed another Law. Consequently we hold that there has never been, nor will there ever be, any other divine Law but that of Moses our Teacher. According to what is written in Scripture and handed down by tradition, the fact may be explained in the following way: There were prophets before Moses, as the patriarchs, Shem, Ebher, Noah, Methushelah, and Hanoch, but of these none said to any portion of mankind that God sent him to them and commanded him to convey to them a certain message or to prohibit or to command a certain thing. Such a thing is not related in Scripture, or in authentic tradition. Divine prophecy reached them as we have explained. Men like Abraham, who received a large measure of prophetic inspiration, called their fellow-men together and led them by training and instruction to the truth which they had perceived. Thus Abraham taught, and showed by philosophical arguments that there is one God, that He has created everything that exists beside Him, and that neither the constellations nor anything in the air ought to be worshipped; he trained his fellow-men in this belief, and won their attention by pleasant words as well as by acts of kindness. Abraham did not tell the people that God had sent him to them with the command concerning certain things which should or should not be done. Even when it was commanded that he, his sons, and his servants should be circumcised, he fulfilled that commandment, but he did not address his fellow-men prophetically on this subject. That Abraham induced his fellow-men to do what is right, telling them only his own will [and not that of God], may be learnt from the following passages of Scripture: "For I know him, because he *commands* his sons and his house after him, to practise righteousness and judgment" (Gen. xxiii). Also Isaac, Jacob, Levi, Kehath, and Amram influenced their fellow-men in the same way. Our Sages, when speaking of prophets before Moses, used expressions like the following: The *beth-din* (court of justice) of Ebher, the *beth-din* of Methushelah, and in the college of Methushelah; although all these were prophets, yet they taught their fellow-men in the manner of preachers, teachers, and pedagogues, but did not use such phrases as the following: "And God said to me, Speak to certain people so and so." This was the state of prophecy before Moses. But as regards Moses, you know what [God] said to him, what he said [to the people], and the words addressed to him by the whole nation: "This day we have seen that God doth talk with man, and that he liveth" (Deut. v. 21). The history of all our prophets that lived after Moses is well known to you; they performed, as it were, the function of warning the people and exhorting them to keep the Law of Moses, threatening evil to those who would neglect it, and announcing blessings to those who would submit to its guidance. This we believe will always be the case. Comp. "It is not in the heavens that one might say," &c. (ibid. xxx. 12); "For us and for our children for ever" (ibid. xxix. 28). It is but natural that it should be so. For if one individual of a class has reached the highest perfection possible in that class, every other individual must necessarily be less perfect, and deviate from the perfect measure either by surplus or deficiency. Take, *e.g.*, the normal constitution of a being, it consists in the most proper composition possible in that class; any constitution that deviates from that norm contains something too much or too little. The same is the case with the Law. It is clear that the Law is normal in this sense; for it contains "Just statutes and judgments" (Deut. iv. 8); but "just" is here identical with "equibalanced." The statutes of the Law do not impose burdens or excesses as are implied in the service of a hermit or pilgrim, and the like; but, on the other hand, they are not so deficient as to lead to gluttony or lewdness, or to prevent, as the religious laws of the heathen nations do, the development of man's moral and intellectual faculties. We intend to discuss in this treatise the reasons of the commandments, and we shall then show, as far as necessary, the justice and wisdom of the Law, on account of which it is said: "The Law of God is perfect, refreshing the heart" (Ps. xix. 8). There are persons who believe that the Law commands much exertion and great pain, but due consideration will show them their error. Later on I will show how easy it is for the perfect to obey the Law. Comp. "What does the Lord thy God ask of thee?" &c. (Deut. x. 12); "Have I been a wilderness to Israel?" (Jer. ii. 31). But this applies only to the noble ones; whilst wicked, violent, and pugnacious persons find it most injurious and hard that there should be any divine authority tending to subdue their violence. To low-minded, wanton, and passionate persons it appears most cruel that there should be an obstacle in their way to satisfy their carnal appetite, or that a punishment should be inflicted for their doings. Similarly every godless person imagines that it is too hard to abstain from the evil he has chosen in accordance with his inclination. We must not consider the Law easy or hard according as it appears to any wicked, low-minded, and immoral person, but as it appears to the judgment of the most perfect, who, according to the Law, deserve to be the example for all mankind. This Law alone is called divine; other laws, such as the political legislations among the Greeks, or the follies of the Sabeans, are the works of human leaders, but not of prophets, as I have explained several times.

ALBO, *IKKARIM*

Translation by Isaac Husik

BOOK III, CHAPTER 10

. . .All these miracles, however, performed by the prophets, have this in common that they did not last a long time, and were not performed in the presence of all or of a great concourse of people; whereas all the signs and wonders performed by Moses were not merely more numerous than all those of all the other prophets, but they were superior to them in that they were performed in public and lasted a long time, for example, the manna lasted forty years, also the pillar of cloud by day and the pillar of fire by night.

For this reason these differences between the miracles of Moses and those of the others are mentioned at the end of the Torah. First the text refers to the differences between the prophetic inspiration of Moses and that of the others in the expression, "And there hath not arisen a prophet since in Israel like unto Moses, whom the Lord knew face to face,"[1] as we explained the passage above. Then the text proceeds to explain the differences between the miracles of Moses and those of the others, "In all the signs and the wonders which the Lord sent him to do."[2] This indicates their great number. Then it says, "In the land of Egypt, to Pharaoh, and to all his servants, and to all his land,"[3] alluding to the publicity of the miracles in the presence of his opponents. Then, referring to their duration, Scripture says, "And in all the great terror, which Moses wrought in the light of all Israel." This refers, as we said, to the pillar of cloud by day and the pillar of fire by night, which lasted all the forty years that the Israelites were in the wilderness, as we read, "For the cloud of the Lord was upon the tabernacle by day, and there was fire therein by night, in the sight of all the house of Israel, throughout all their journeys."[4] This is the way to understand the conception of prophecy and its various degrees as shown logically and in the difference between the prophecy and miracles of Moses and those of the other prophets. This is what we intended to show.

NOTES

1. Deut. 34, 10.
2. Ibid. 11.
3. Ibid. 12.
4. Ex. 40, 38.

BOOK III, CHAPTER 11

What we said above concerning the manner in which the various degrees of prophetic inspiration come upon a person holds good when there is no prophet who may serve as a medium or instrument through whom inspiration may come to those who are not prepared. But when there is such a prophet, inspiration may come to those unprepared without reference to the degrees mentioned. This possibility was realized, at the time of the revelation on Sinai, when all Israel, the foolish as well as the wise, attained to the prophetic quality: "These words the Lord spoke unto all your assembly in the mount out of the midst of the fire."[1] And not merely did they attain to prophetic inspiration, but they reached the degree called "face to face," which is the highest that any one can attain and which requires the grace of God, viz. the degree attained by Moses. For we read concerning Moses, "And the Lord spoke to Moses face to face,"[2] and similarly in reference to the degree reached by all Israel at the time of the Sinaitic revelation, we read likewise, "The Lord spoke with you face to face in the mount out of the midst of the fire."[3]

Now it is clear that the six hundred thousand men who came out of Egypt on foot and had been accustomed to hard work in clay and in bricks were not worthy of so high a degree, and yet they attained it through the instrumentality of Moses. God said to him, "Go, I come unto thee in a thick cloud, that the people may hear when I speak with thee."[4] The meaning of this verse is, I wish to come to you and to reveal Myself to you in the highest degree, face to face, though you are clothed in the thickness and obscurity of matter, symbolized by "thick cloud," and are not worthy of it,—all this I do in order that the people may hear when I speak with you. This is the highest degree possible, namely that a person in the waking state should hear a voice speaking to him, without seeing any form, "Ye heard the voice of words, but ye saw no form."[5]

This degree the people attained through the grace of God and the instrumentality of Moses, in order that they might give up the doubt which they entertained concerning the possibility of a human being receiving prophetic inspiration. They expressed their wonder after the revelation, saying, "For who is there of all flesh, that hath heard the voice of the living God . . ."[6] This shows that the Israelites doubted the possibility of prophetic inspiration until that day. But Moses did not wonder at the prophetic inspiration of an individual, but at the attainment thereto by the whole people. Hence he said, "Did ever a people hear the voice of God. . ."[7] After the revelation they all acknowledged the possibility, as we read, "We have seen this day that God doth speak with man, and he liveth."[8] This proves that the experience at that time removed the doubt from their mind.

In the same way the prophetic power was communicated by Elijah to Elisha without the preparatory degrees. For there was not a single one of the sons of the prophets who did not serve Elijah and learn from him before Elisha came to serve Elijah, for only when God wanted to take Elijah away did he say to him in Horeb, "And Elisha the son of Shaphat of Abel-Meholah shalt thou anoint to be prophet in thy room."[9] Through the instrumentality of Elijah he attained to a higher degree than any of them.

Also Joshua owed the degree which he attained to the instrumentality of Moses. And hence the Rabbis in discussing this matter say, "The face of Moses was like that of the sun, the face of Joshua was like that of the moon. The elders of that generation used to say, 'Oh, the shame and disgrace!' "[10] The meaning is, Joshua himself was not worthy to attain the degree which he did. It was due to the instrumentality of Moses. Therefore Moses was like the sun, who gives of his light to the moon, while Joshua was like the moon, which receives her light from the sun, having none of her own. Hence they said, "Oh, the shame and disgrace" that Joshua himself should not have been worthy of prophecy and should get it through Moses only!

Similarly the seventy elders owed their prophetic gift to the instrumentality of Moses, not having been worthy of it in their own right: "And I will come down and speak with thee there; and I will take of the spirit which is upon thee, and will put it upon them."[11] The meaning is, though they are not worthy of it on their own account. Hence when Joshua said to Moses, "Eldad and Medad are prophesying in the camp,"[12] Moses replied, "Art thou jealous for my sake?"[13] He meant to say, You should not be jealous on my account, for the prophetic spirit comes upon them through my spirit and instrumentality, "Would that all the Lord's people were prophets"[14] on their account, worthy in their own right without my influence, "that the Lord would put His spirit upon them," not through my instrumentality, but that they should themselves be worthy of the prophetic spirit without any intermediary.

The need of a medium may be explained as follows. When a spark of sunlight strikes a bright body, like a polished mirror, it is reflected upon a dark place, which is then illuminated by the reflection, not having been illuminated before. Similarly when the divine influence descends upon a perfect prophet, it is reflected from him upon one who is not worthy, thus inspiring with the prophetic spirit one who is not perfect and not prepared, and causing him to prophesy. Still, even in case of reflection, the one who is prepared gets a greater portion than he who is not prepared.

My opinion is that this is the reason why prophecy existed among the people of Israel in the land of Palestine and not among other nations in other lands. The Shekinah rested upon the ark and the tables of stone, and from these it was reflected like a ray of sunlight, and the prophetic spirit then rested upon a person who had in him a certain preparation analogous to the contents of the ark, that is a person who really had the ideas of the Torah, which are written upon the tables of the covenant. We find this illustrated in the prophecy of Samuel. He lay in his chamber and the prophetic voice came to him from above the ark-cover which was upon the ark that was then in Shilo. Samuel himself did not know who called him, for he did not think that he was worthy of the prophetic gift, that he should hear a voice in the waking state in a prophetic vision. Therefore he rose from his bed and went to Eli, until Eli understood, as we read, "And Eli perceived that the Lord was calling the child."[15]

An inspiration of this kind, which comes in this way without the mediation of a prophet, requires preparation in the recipient, that is the recipient must be himself prepared to a certain extent. Divine inspiration of this nature comes only when the recipient has a certain degree of preparation, and upon this is dependent the degree of inspiration which comes to him. The prophetic inspiration, however, which comes through the mediation of a prophet, comes also to a person who is not worthy of prophecy, as it came to all Israel at the time of the Sinaitic revelation; or it comes to one who is not prepared for it, as it came to Aaron and Miriam through the mediation of Moses, though they were not prepared for it at that time. This is the reason why the Lord called Moses with Aaron and Miriam, so that the prophetic spirit should come upon them through the mediation of Moses. For though they were worthy of the prophetic gift, they were not prepared for it at that time. This matter requires attention, for many learned men have wondered why God called Moses with Aaron and Miriam.

It is worth noting that when the prophetic spirit comes through the mediation of a prophet upon a person who is not worthy or who is not prepared, the recipient is able to pass it to another only when the nation has in its midst the ark and the tables. Moreover after the ark disappeared, the unprepared could not get prophetic inspiration even through a prophet. This is why Baruch son of Neriyah did not receive the prophetic gift through Jeremiah, because he was not prepared for it, and the ark had been hidden. Prophetic inspiration did come to Haggai, Zechariah and Malachi, because they saw Jeremiah and Ezekiel and were more prepared for it than Baruch. But it did not reach others through them, because the ark was not there and the inspiration they received was not sufficient to pass from them to others, since there was no ark. The proof of this is that there was no prophecy during the second temple, though there were at that time pious men and men of good works more worthy of prophetic inspiration than the men of the first temple. The reason was because they did not have the ark. Ezekiel could receive his inspiration outside of Palestine because he had already received it in Palestine, as our Rabbis explain the verse in Ezekiel, "The word of the Lord came expressly unto Ezekiel the priest, the son of Buzi, in the land of the Chaldeans by the river Chebar."[16] They construe the verb (היה היה) as meaning: 'it came' because 'it had come' before.[17]

NOTES

1. Deut. 5, 19.
2. Ex. 33, 11.
3. Deut. 5, 4.
4. Ex. 19, 9.
5. Deut. 4, 12.
6. Ibid. 5, 23.
7. Deut. 4, 33.
8. Ibid. 5, 21.
9. I Kings 19, 16.
10. Baba Batra 75a.
11. Num. 11, 17.
12. Ibid. 27.
13. Ibid. 29.
14. Ibid.
15. I Sam. 3, 8.
16. Ezek. 1, 3.
17. Mo'ed Katan 25a. The emphatic form of the verb, consisting of the infinitive absolute (הָיֹה) and the perfect (הָיָה) is analyzed into two verbs, as if to signify: The word of the Lord came to Ezekiel in the land of the Chaldeans because it had already come to him before in Palestine.

BOOK III, CHAPTER 12

The principal purpose of the prophetic institution existing in the human race is not to foretell the future or to regulate particular matters that interest individuals, such as are communicated by diviners and star-gazers, but to enable a whole nation or the entire human race to attain to human perfection.

The Rabbis make this clear in the treatise Berakot[1]: Commenting upon the biblical verse, "And the Lord spoke unto Moses, Go, get thee down; for thy people . . . have dealt corruptly"[2] they say, God said to Moses, get thee down from thy greatness. I gave it thee only for the sake of Israel. Now that Israel has sinned, why do I want thee? This clearly shows that the prophetic gift of Moses was given to him solely for the sake of Israel, that they might receive the Torah and fulfil it. We find the same idea in "Torat Kohanim."[3] Commenting on the verse, "These are the commandments, which the Lord commanded Moses for the children of Israel,"[4] they say it was the merit of Israel that was responsible for Moses' receiving divine inspiration.

Hence some learned men say that the beginning of Moses' prophetic experience did not take place in the gradual manner we described in chapter ten, but that it was a miraculous phenomenon and came upon him suddenly by the will of God, though he was neither prepared nor worthy of that high degree, the purpose being that the human race or the Jewish nation as a whole should attain to the destined end of man. This is why God said to him, Now that Israel has sinned, why do I need you? That is if I can not realize My purpose, there is no need of the prophet's inspiration. This is the reason why when the Rabbis say, in the treatise Nedarim:[5] "Prophecy rests only upon a person who is wise, strong, rich and tall," they derive these requisite qualities from Moses. Since the prophetic gift is bestowed for the sake of the nation's perfection, the prophet must have the qualities of Moses, whose prophetic gift was given to him for the same purpose. Therefore one of these attributes is tall stature, so that he should be admired and respected by the people. But if a prophet has not these qualities which are for the people's benefit, there is no purpose in giving him the prophetic gift. This will also explain why we made revelation of the Torah a fundamental principle, while we considered prophecy as a derivative principle dependent upon the former, though one might suppose that the reverse is true, namely that prophecy is the fundamental thing and revelation of the Torah the derivative.

The truth is this. If the purpose of the prophetic institution among men were that people may know the particular events of the world or that by means of it signs and wonders may be produced for a particular purpose, as might seem at first sight, then the objection would be well taken. But since we have made clear that the necessity of prophecy is that men may be guided toward eternal happiness, that they may know through it what is agreeable to God and what is not, and that they may attain to the destiny intended for mankind by doing those things which are agreeable to God, the above objection does not hold. For since the purpose of prophecy is that the human race may be guided by God, which means revelation of the Torah, the latter must be a fundamental principle, because it is that which makes prophecy necessary. For this reason we consider prophecy a derivative principle dependent on revelation.

The Eighth Principle

Revelation

INTRODUCTION

The Eighth Principle embodies two distinct concepts. The first concept expressed in this principle is that the Torah in its entirety was handed down by God to Moses. The phrase "the whole of this Torah found in our hands" is crucial to the formulation of this concept. This principle affirms not simply the validity of the *mesorah*, or tradition, which postulates that the Torah was transmitted by Moses, but also the belief that the Torah which is in our possession was handed down by Moses in its entirety and that no additions or changes were made at any subsequent time. The Talmud, *Sanhedrin* 99a, declares that denial of the divine origin of a single word or letter of the Torah is tantamount to rejection of the Torah in its entirety. This principle is, in effect, an affirmation of the authenticity of the Masoretic text.

It is indeed remarkable that despite the vicissitudes of time, and the many upheavals and wanderings to which the Jewish nation has been subjected, the Scrolls of the Law in the possession of even the most far-flung and widely separated Jewish communities are identical in virtually every respect. The variant spellings of the word *daka* in Deuteronomy 23:2 are the exception which proves the rule. The word is spelled with an *alef* in many of the Torah scrolls of Western Jews but with a *heh* in Oriental scrolls[1]—a variation of textual significance only, but one which is of no significance whatsoever in terms of cognitive meaning.

Tradition relates that precautions were taken by Moses himself to prevent possible tampering with the text of the Torah. There is a midrashic comment, *Midrash Rabbah, Devarim* 9:4 and *Midrash Tehillim* 90:30, paraphrased by Maimonides in the Introduction to his *Mishneh Torah,* which reads as follows: "Moses wrote thirteen Scrolls of the Law, one for each tribe, and a thirteenth to be placed in the Ark so that the Torah would not be falsified by anyone."

In affirming the divine nature of the Torah, Maimonides stresses not only that the Written Law is of divine origin, but that the Oral Law is of divine origin as well. Maimonides, *Mishneh Torah, Hilkhot Teshuvah* 3:8, is explicit in stating that one who is *makḥish maggideha,* i.e., one

[1] See *Minḥat Shai, ad locum.*

who in any way disputes the reliability of the bearers of the tradition in which the Oral Law is expressed, is to be counted among those who deny the divinity of the Torah. The Talmud, *Sanhedrin* 99a, cites the verse "Because he has despised the words of the Lord" (Num. 15:31) and comments:

> This verse refers to one who maintains that Torah is not from heaven. And even if he maintains that the whole Torah in its entirety is from heaven but that a certain verse was not uttered by the Holy One, blessed be He, but Moses [stated it] on his own initiative, he is [included among those referred to by the verse] "Because he has despised the word of this law"; and even if he maintains that the whole Torah in its entirety is from heaven with the exception of a particular vocalized spelling (*dikduk*), a particular argument from major to minor (*kal va-ḥomer*), or a particular textual analogy (*gezerah shaveh*), he is [included among those referred to by the verse] "Because he has despised the word of the Lord."

The second concept embodied in this principle is the belief that the Torah in its entirety is of divine origin and that no part is to be attributed to the autonomous authorship of Moses. Indeed, in times gone by, those who denied the divine nature of the Torah were not given serious consideration. The argument from tradition, which, as we have seen, was formulated to prove the existence of God, is an even more potent argument with regard to the historical fact of revelation. This argument asserts that it is inconceivable that a community numbering in the millions would have accepted the claims made by Scripture itself with regard to the source and nature of revelation unless the community's own experience confirmed this claim. The scriptural account of revelation does not describe a revelational experience limited to a single individual or to a group of individuals which must be accepted on the basis of the credentials of the person or persons advancing the claim, but a public revelation in which all to whom this revelation was addressed were themselves participants. That *a* Torah was revealed was regarded as undeniable; the Eighth Principle stresses that it is the Torah which is in our possession which was the subject of this revelation, that it was revealed in its entirety, and that no additions were made by Moses. Many biblical commentaries stress that in ancient times the common heresy was not the denial of the event of revelation or of the divine origin of the Torah, but the assertion that Moses incorporated material which was not commanded by God. Thus Koraḥ, for example, argues, ". . . for all the congregation are holy, every one of them, and the Lord is among them, wherefore then lift you up yourselves above the assembly of the Lord" (Num. 16:3), but does not deny the phenomenon of revelation. Maimonides stresses, therefore, that Moses "was like a scribe writing from dictation," a mere copyist with no claim to either legal or literary originality.

Saadia stresses the role of authentic tradition or "true report," i.e., information conveyed by one person to another, as a major source of knowledge. Indeed, "true report" is no less significant than direct empirical experience as a source of knowledge. Of course, a report is liable to falsification. However, this could not have occurred with regard to the tradition concerning revelation since willful distortion cannot occur without detection when a large group of people collectively present an identical report. This notion recurs and occupies an even more central position in Judah Halevi's *Kuzari.*

Judah Halevi, in refuting the position of the Karaites, emphasizes that the Written Law would be incomprehensible in the absence of an accompanying tradition of interpretation. The text, written without vowels, could not be read, much less understood, had this tradition not been accurately preserved. The meaning of numerous words and phrases is obscure and could not be surmised, much less unequivocably accepted by an entire people, other than on the basis of an oral revelation which was preserved and transmitted from generation to generation.

Albo reiterates that the Torah which is in our possession is entirely identical with the one given to Moses on Mount Sinai. However, he is concerned with the references in rabbinic literature to the concept of *tikkun soferim,* which translated literally would mean "correction of the scribes." Albo describes *tikkun soferim* not as a willful change on the part of the scribes, but as the rabbinic phrase for a euphemism. Such usage is in the nature of what in humanly authored documents would be a euphemistic correction. In the Torah, however, all such usages were directly dictated by God Himself.[2]

[2] Cf. the strikingly similar discussion of *tikkun soferim* by R. Judah Loewe of Prague (Maharal), *Tiferet Yisrael,* chap. 66.

SAADIA, *EMUNOT VE-DE'OT*

Translation by Alexander Altmann

THIRD TREATISE
COMMANDMENT AND PROHIBITION

5. *Scripture and Tradition*

. . .I deem it proper to mention a few points in regard to the truth of Tradition. Unless men had the confidence that there exists in the world such a thing as true report, no man would build any expectations on any report he might be told about success in any branch of commerce, or of progress in any art [which we naturally believe], since it is gain which man requires and for which he exerts his strength. Nor would he fear what he should guard against, be it the dangerous state of a road, or a proclamation prohibiting a certain action. But if a man has neither hopes nor fears,[1] all his affairs will come to grief. Unless it is established that there is such a thing as true report in this world, people will not pay heed to the command of their ruler nor his prohibition, except at such time as they see him with their own eyes, and hear his words with their own ears; and when no longer in his presence, they will cease to accept his commands and prohibitions.[2] If things were like this, all management of affairs would be rendered impossible and many people would perish. And unless there was a true tradition in this world, a man would not be able to know that a certain property was owned by his father, and that this is an inheritance from his grandfather, nor would a man be able to know that he is the son of his mother, let alone that he is the son of his father. Human affairs would be in a state of perpetual doubt, so much so that people would only hold to be true what they perceive with their own senses, and this only at the actual moment of their sense perceptions, an opinion which is akin to the view of *those who affect ignorance,*[3] which I mentioned in Chapter I.

Scripture already declares that reliable tradition is as true as the things perceived by sight. Thus it says, 'For pass over to the isles of the Kittites, and see, and send unto Kedar, and consider diligently . . .' (Jer. 2.10).[4] Why does it add the words, 'And consider diligently' in connection with the matter of report? The answer is: because a report (tradition) is, unlike sense perception, liable to be falsified in two ways, either through a wrong idea or through wilful distortion. For this reason Scripture warns,'And consider diligently'. Having considered deeply how we can have faith in tradition seeing that there are these two ways (of possible falsification) I found, by way of Reason, that wrong idea and wilful distortion can only occur and remain unnoticed if they emanate from individuals, whereas, in a large collective group, the underlying ideas of the individuals who compose it will never be in agreement with one another, and if they wilfully decide and agree on inventing a story, this will not remain unnoticed amongst their people, but whenever their story is put out, there will be related, at the same time, the story of how they came to agree upon it. And when a tradition is safe against these two possibilities (of falsification), there is no third way in which it could possibly be falsified. And if the Tradition of our Fathers is viewed from the aspect of these principles, it will appear sound and safe against any attack, and true, and firmly established.[5]

NOTES

1. Saadya sees in Hope and Fear—the two cardinal themes of the Greek Tragedy—the prime movers in human affairs. Cf. above, pp. 68, 92, where he states that in the case of God it is impossible to assume that He should hope or fear.

2. Saadya seems to assume that the refusal to believe in true reports entails an inability to believe oneself in regard to the testimony of one's own memory.

3. Arab. *mutajahilun*; by this term Saadya denotes the Pyrrhonists, whose standpoint is one of absolute scepticism. He deals with this view under No. 13 of his list of cosmoligical theories. Cf. *Amānāt*, 69 ff. (36 ff.); see above, p. 62, n. 4.

4 The verse mentions two ways of verification, (1) to see for oneself; (2) to ask for reports. Both are put on the same level, which seems to Saadya an indication that sense perception and tradition have the same character of truth.

5. In a passage of the Prolegomena not included in this Selection (Amānāt, *22-3;* Hebr. 11-12), Saadya quotes Isa. 44.8 ('And ye are my witnesses') with reference to the historical experience of Israel as recorded in the Scriptures. He particularly mentions the Ten plagues, the dividing of the Red Sea, and the Sinaitic Revelation. He continues, 'I think that the most wondrous experience of all is the miracle of the Mannah; for a miracle which continues for some period is more wondrous than one which passes, for no fraudulent device can be suspected when a people of nearly a million souls is fed from nothing for a period of 40 years. . . and it cannot be assumed that the whole people should have agreed (to invent this story), for general consent is sufficient as a condition for the trustworthiness of a tradition'. The meaning of the last sentence becomes clear from the above exposition. Cf. Guttmann, p. 147-8, n. 3. Later Jewish philosophers followed the trend of this 'historical argument. It plays a most prominent part in Yehudah Hallevi's thought. Cf. *Kuzari,* I, 86, where Saadya's remark about the miracle of Mannah is literally repeated. Cf. also I, 25, 47–8.

HALEVI, *KUZARI*

Translation by Hartwig Hirschfeld

PART I

19. The Rabbi: If thou wert told that the King of India was an excellent man, commanding admiration, and deserving his high reputation, one whose actions were reflected in the justice which rules his country and the virtuous ways of his subjects, would this bind thee to revere him?

20. Al Khazari: How could this bind me, whilst I am not sure if the justice of the Indian people is natural, and not dependent on their king, or due to the king or both?

21. The Rabbi: But if his messenger came to thee bringing presents which thou knowest to be only procurable in India, and in the royal palace, accompanied by a letter in which it is distinctly stated from whom it comes, and to which are added drugs to cure thy diseases, to preserve thy health, poisons for thy enemies, and other means to fight and kill them without battle, would this make thee beholden to him?

22. Al Khazari: Certainly. For this would remove my former doubt that the Indians have a king. I should also acknowledge that a proof of his power and dominion has reached me. . .

25. The Rabbi:. . .In the same strain spoke Moses to Pharaoh, when he told him: 'The God of the Hebrews sent me to thee,' viz. the God of Abraham, Isaac and Jacob. For Abraham was well known to the nations, who also knew that the divine spirit was in contact with the patriarchs, cared for them, and performed miracles for them. He did not say: 'The God of heaven and earth,' nor 'my Creator and thine sent me.' In the same way God commenced His speech to the assembled people of Israel: 'I am the God whom you worship, who has led you out of the land of Egypt,' but He did not say: 'I am the Creator of the world and your Creator.' Now in the same style I spoke to thee, a Prince of the Khazars, when thou didst ask me about my creed. I answered thee as was fitting, and is fitting for the whole of Israel who knew these things, first from personal experience, and afterwards *through uninterrupted* tradition, which is equal to the former. . .

PART III

23. . . .What dost thou think we should adopt in order to become like our fathers, to imitate them, and not to speculate about the Law?

24. Al Khazari: We can only accomplish this through the medium of their traditional teachings, by the support of their deeds, and by endeavouring to find one who is regarded as an authority by one generation, and capable of handing down the history of another. The latter generation, however, cannot, on account of the multitude of its individuals, be suspected of having made a general agreement to carry the Law with its branches and interpretations unaltered from Moses downward either in their memories or in a volume.

25. The Rabbi: What wouldst thou think if difference were found in one or two copies?

26. Al Khazari:[One must study several copies,] the majority of which cannot be faulty. The minority can, then, be neglected. The same process applies to traditions. If the minority differs, we turn to the majority.

27. The Rabbi: Now, what is thy opinion if in the manuscripts a letter were found which is in contrast to common sense, e.g. *s̄ādū̱* (Lam. iv. 18), where we should expect *sārū*, and *nafshī* (Ps. xxiv. 4), where we should read *nafshō̱*?

28. Al Khazari: Common sense would in these and other cases alter in all volumes, first the letters, then the words, then the construction, then the vowels and accents, and consequently also the sense. There are many verses to which the reader can give an opposite meaning by altering the place of any of these appositives.

29. The Rabbi: In which form did Moses leave his book to the Israelites in thy opinion?

30. Al Khazari: Undoubtedly without either vowels or accents, just as our scrolls are written. There was as little agreement possible among the people on this point, as on the unleavened bread, or Passover, or other laws which were given as a 'remembrance of the delivery from Egypt.' These laws confirm in the minds of the Israelites the historical truth of the exodus from Egypt by means of the recurring ceremonies, which could not possibly be the result of common agreement without causing contradiction.

31. The Rabbi: There is, therefore, no doubt that the Book was preserved in memory with all its vowels, divisions of syllables and accents: by the priests, because they required them for the Temple service, and in order to teach the people; by the kings, because they were commanded: 'And it shall be with him and he shall read therein all the

days of his life' (Deut. xvii. 19). The judges had to know it to enable them to give judgment; the members of the Synhedrion, because they were warned: 'Keep therefore and do them, for this is your wisdom and understanding' (Deut. iv. 6); the pious, in order to receive reward; and, finally, the hypocrites, to acquire a good name. The seven vowels and accents were appointed as signs for forms which were regarded as Mosaic tradition. Now, how have we to judge those persons who first divided the text into verses, equipped it with vowel signs, accents, and masoretic signs, concerning full or defective orthography; and counted the letters with such accuracy that they found out that the *gimel* of *gāhōn* (Lev. xi. 42) stood right in the middle of the Tōrāh, and kept a record of all irregular vowels? Dost thou consider this work either superfluous or idle, or dutiful zeal?

32. Al Khazari: The latter no doubt. It was to serve as a fence round the law in order to leave no room for alterations. Moreover, it is a great science. The system of vowel signs and accents reveals an order which could only emanate from divinely-instilled notions, quite out of proportion to our knowledge. It can only have been received from a community of favoured ones or a single individual of the same stamp. In the latter case it must have been a prophet, or a person assisted by the Divine Influence. For a scholar who lacks this assistance can be challenged by another scholar to adopt his views in preference.

33. The Rabbi: The acknowledgment of tradition is therefore incumbent upon us as well as upon the Karaites, as upon anyone who admits that the Tōrāh, in its present shape and as it is read, *is* the Tōrāh of Moses.

34. Al Khazari: This is exactly what the Karaites say. But as they have the complete Tōrāh, they consider the tradition superfluous.

35. The Rabbi: Far from it. If the consonantic text of the Mosaic Book requires so many traditional classes of vowel signs, accents, divisions of sentences and masoretic signs for the correct pronunciation of words, how much more is this the case for the comprehension of the same? The meaning of a word is more comprehensive than its pronunciation. When God revealed the verse: 'This month shall be unto you the beginning of months' (Exod. xii. 2), there was no doubt whether He meant the calendar of the Copts—or rather the Egyptians—among whom they lived, or that of the Chaldaeans who were Abraham's people in Ur-Kasdim; or solar [or lunar months], or lunar years, which are made to agree with solar years, as is done in embolismic years. I wish the Karaites could give me a satisfactory answer to questions of this kind. I would not hesitate to adopt their view, as it pleases me to be enlightened. I further

wish to be instructed on the question as to what makes an animal lawful for food; whether 'slaughtering' means cutting its throat or any other mode of killing; why killing by gentiles makes the flesh unlawful; what is the difference between slaughtering, skinning, and the rest of it. I should desire an explanation of the forbidden fat, seeing that it lies in the stomach and entrails close to the lawful fat, as well as of the rules of cleansing the meat. Let them draw me the line between the fat which is lawful and that which is not, inasmuch as there is no difference visible. Let them explain to me where the tail of the sheep, which they declare unlawful, ends. One of them may possibly forbid the end of the tail alone, another the whole hind part. I desire an explanation of the lawful and unlawful birds, excepting the common ones, such as the pigeon and turtle dove. How do they know that the hen, goose, duck, and partridge are not unclean birds? I further desire an explanation of the words: 'Let no man go out of his place [on the seventh day]' (Exod. xvi. 29). Does this refer to the house or precincts, estate—where he can have many houses—territory, district, or country? For the word *place* can refer to all of these. I should, further, like to know where the prohibition of work on the Sabbath commences? Why pens and writing material are not admissible in the correction of a scroll of the Law (on this day), but lifting a heavy book, or a table, or eatables, entertaining guests and all cares of hospitality should be permitted, although the guests would be resting, and the host be kept employed? This applies even more to women and servants, as it is written: 'That thy manservant and thy maidservant rest as well as thou' (Deut. v. 14). Wherefore it is forbidden to ride [on the Sabbath] horses belonging to gentiles, or to trade. Then, again, I wish to see a Karaite give judgment between two parties according to the chapters Exodus xxi. and Deuteronomy xxi. 10 sqq. For that which appears plain in the Tōrāh, is yet obscure, and much more so are the obscure passages, because the oral supplement was relied upon. I should wish to hear the deductions he draws from the case of the daughters of Zelophehād to questions of inheritance in general. I want to know the details of circumcision, fringes and tabernacle; why it is incumbent on him to say prayers; whence he derives his belief in reward and punishment in the world after death; how to deal with laws which interfere with each other, as circumcision or Paschal lamb with Sabbath, which must yield to which, and many other matters which cannot be enumerated in general, much less in detail. Hast thou ever heard, O King of the Khazars, that the Karaites possess a book which contains a fixed tradition on one of the subjects just mentioned, and which allows no differences on readings, vowel signs, accents, or lawful or unlawful matters, or decisions? . . .

38. Al Khazari: All thou sayest is convincing, because the Law enjoins that there shall be 'one Tōrāh and one statute.' Should Karaite methods prevail there would be as many different codes as opinions. Not one individual would remain constant to one code. For every day he forms new opinions, increases his knowledge, or meets with someone who refutes him with some argument and converts him to his views. But whenever we find them agreeing, we know that they follow the tradition of one or many of their ancestors. In such a case we should not believe their views, and say: 'How is it that you agree concerning this regulation, whilst reason allows the word of God to be interpreted in various ways?' If the answer be that this was the opinion of Anan, or Benjamin, Saul, or others, then they admit the authority of tradition received from people who lived before them, and of the best tradition, viz. that of the Sages. For they were many, whilst those Karaite teachers were but single individuals. The view of the Rabbis is based on the tradition of the Prophets; the other, however, on speculation alone. The Sages are in concord, the Karaites in discord. The sayings of the Sages originate with 'the place which God shall choose,' and we must therefore accept even their individual opinions. The Karaites have nothing of the kind. I wish I knew their answer regarding the calculation of the new moon. I see that their authorities follow Rabbanite practice in the intercalation of Adar. Nevertheless they taunt the Rabbanites, when the Tishri new moon appears, with the question: 'How could it happen that you [once] kept the fast of the day of Atonement on the *ninth* of Tishri?' Are they not ashamed not to know, when intercalating, whether the month is Ellul or Tishri; or Tishri or Marḥeshwān, if they do not intercalate? They ought rather to say: 'I am drowning, but fear not the wet!' We do not know whether the month is Tishri, Marḥeshwān, or Ellul. How can we criticise those in whose steps we follow, and whose teachings we adopt, and ask: Do you fast on the ninth or tenth of Tishri?

39. The Rabbi: Our law is linked to the 'ordination given to Moses on Sinai,' or sprung 'from the place which the Lord shall choose' (Is. ii. 3), 'for from Zion goes forth the Law, and the word of God from Jerusalem.' Its mediators were the Judges, Overseers, Priests, and the members of the Synhedrion. It is incumbent upon us to obey the Judge appointed for the time being, as it is written: 'Or to the judge who will be in those days . . . and thou shalt inquire, and they shall tell thee the sentence of judgment, and thou shalt do according to the word which they tell thee . . . from the place which the Lord shall choose . . . and thou shall take heed to do according to all they teach thee' (Deut. xvii. 9 sqq.). Further: 'The man who doeth presumptuously not to listen to the priest . . . this man shall die, and thou shalt remove the evil from thy midst.' Disobedience to the

Priest or Judge is placed on a par with the gravest transgressions, in the words: 'Thou shalt remove the evil from thy midst.' This concludes with the words: 'And all the people shall hear and fear, and do no more presumptuously.' This refers to the time when the order of the Temple service and the Synhedrion, and the sections [of the Levites], who completed the organization, were still intact, and the Divine Influence was undeniably among them either in the form of prophecy or inspiration, as was the case during the time of the second Temple. Among these persons no agreement or convention was possible. In a similar manner arose the duty of reading the Book of Esther on Purim, and the ordination of Ḥanuccah, and we can say: 'He who has commanded us to read the Megillāh' and 'to kindle the light of Ḥanuccah,' or 'to complete' or 'to read' the Hallēl, 'to wash the hands,' 'the ordination of the Erūb,' and the like. Had our traditional customs arisen after the exile, they could not have been called by this name, nor would they require a blessing, but there would be a regulation or rather a custom. The bulk of our laws, however, derives its origin from Moses, as an 'ordination given to Moses from Sinai.' This also explains how a people obtained during forty years sufficient food and clothing, in spite of their large number. Moses was with them, and the Shekhinah did not forsake them, giving them general as well as special laws. Is it not absurd to assume that they refrained from inquiring occasionally into the details, and handing down their explanations and subdivisions? Take the verse: 'And I will make known the laws of God and His statutes' (Exod. xviii.16), which is supplemented by the other: 'For this is your wisdom and understanding in the eyes of the nations, which shall hear all these laws, and they will say, surely this great nation is a wise and understanding people' (Deut. iv. 6). He who wishes to gainsay this verse may look at the Karaites; but he who desires to confirm it, let him behold the branches of knowledge embodied in the Talmud, which form only a small portion of the natural, metaphysical, mathematical, and astronomical studies [in which the Sages indulged]. He will, then, see that they deserve praise above all nations for their learning.

MAIMONIDES, *COMMENTARY ON THE MISHNAH*

Translation by Fred Rosner

INTRODUCTION TO SEDER ZERAIM

Know[1] that every commandment which the Holy One Blessed Be He gave to Moses our Teacher, may he rest in peace,[2] was given with its clarification. First He told him the commandment and then He expounded on its explanation and content, including all that which is included in the Torah. The manner of its transmittal to Israel occurred as stated in the Gemara:[3] Moses entered into the Tent, and first Aaron entered unto him. Moses then stated to him a single time the commandment he had received, and taught him its explanation, (following which) Aaron retreated to the right of Moses, our teacher. Thereupon, Elazar and Ithamar, Aaron's sons, entered and Moses told them what he had told Aaron, and then they stepped back. One sat to the left of Moses, our Teacher, and the other on the right of Aaron. Then the seventy Elders arrived, and Moses taught them, just as he had taught Aaron and his sons. Following this came the masses of people and every one seeking God, and he (Moses) placed before them that commandment, until all had heard it from his mouth. The result is that Aaron heard that precept from the mouth of Moses four times, his sons three times, the Elders twice, and the remainder of the populace once. Moses then left and Aaron repeated the explanation of that commandment which he had learned, having heard it from the mouth of Moses four times as we have mentioned, to all those present. Aaron then left, after his sons had heard the precept four times; three times from Moses, and once from Aaron. After Aaron had departed, Elazar and Ithamar repeated and taught that commandment to the entire populace that was present, and then ceased their teaching. Thus we find that the seventy Elders heard the precept four times; twice from Moses, once from Aaron, and once from Elazar and Ithamar. The Elders themselves then repeated and expounded the commandment to the populace once and, (as a result), we find that the entire congregation heard the precept in question four times; once from Moses, once from Aaron, a third time from his sons, and the fourth time from the Elders. After this, all the people went to teach one another what they had heard from Moses and to write that commandment on scrolls. The leaders roamed over all of Israel to (insure that the people) learn and apply themselves until they would know the traditional version of that commandment and were fluent in reading it. They would then teach the explanations of that God-given precept. That explanation would include all aspects, and they would write the precept and learn by heart the oral tradition.

Thus, our Sages, of Blessed Memory, said in the *Beraitha:*[4] *And the Lord spoke unto Moses at Mount Sinai.*[5] Why does the teaching state specifically *at Mount Sinai?* Was not the entire Torah given[6] at Sinai? But (the lesson is) to tell us that just as the law of *Shemita*[7] was stated with its generalities, specifics and fine details at Sinai, so too all the commandments were stated with their generalities, specifics and fine details at Sinai. You have an example of this when the Holy One Blessed Be He told Moses: *Ye shall dwell in booths for seven days,*[8] following which He informed him that his *Succah*[9] is an obligation upon males and not females, and that sick people are not so obligated, nor travelers; also the covering of the *Succah* should only be of that which grows from the earth, and that one should not use wool or silk or utensils for a covering even when these utensils are made of products which grow from the earth, such as mattresses, pillows and clothing. He (God) also clearly indicated that eating, drinking and sleeping therein are all obligatory for the entire seven (days of *Succoth*). Furthermore, its (interior) space should not be less than seven handbreadths in length by seven handbreadths in width, nor shall the height of the *Succah* be less than ten handbreadths. And when the prophet (Moses), may he rest in peace, came, he was given this commandment with its explanation, and so too the 613 precepts with their explanations; the commandments in writing, and the explanations by oral transmission.

And it came to pass in the fortieth year, in the eleventh month[10] on the day of the New Moon of the month of Shebat, that he (Moses) gathered the people and told them: *The time of my death has arrived. If there is any one among you who heared a law and forgot it, let him come and ask me and I will explain it. Also, let anyone to whom a question remains in doubt come and I will clarify it* as it is written: *Moses began to explain this Torah saying . . .*[11] Thus too did the Sages state in *Sifre:*[12] "Let he who has forgotten (even) one single law come and relearn it and whoever is in need of explanation, let him come and it will be explained".[13] From his (Moses) mouth they received clarification of the law and learned the explanations during the entire period, from the New Moon of Shebat till the seventh of Adar.[14] When he was close to death he began to write the Torah on scrolls[15], and wrote thirteen Torah scrolls, all of rolled parchment, from the (letter) *Beth of Bereishith*[16] to the (last) *Lamed of L'ainai Kol Yisrael.*[17] He gave one scroll to each tribe to conduct itself accordingly, and to follow its laws. He gave the thirteenth scroll to the Levites and told them: *Take this book of the law*[18], after which he ascended the Mount at noon[19] of the seventh day[20] of the month of Adar,[21] as tradition has deduced. We would consider that particular process[22] which occurred to him death, because we lost him and missed him. However, he lives in the glory of the (greater) height to which he ascended. So too is it stated "Moses our Teacher, did not die; rather he ascended and is serving in heaven".[23] Discussions in these matters (of death) can be extremely lengthy, and this is not the place (to expound upon the details). He died, may he rest in peace, after having bequeathed to Joshua that which was endowed to him (Joshua) in the way of interpretation and wisdom, and he became wise. And Joshua and the people of his generation studied it.

Of all that he (Joshua) or one of the Elders received from Moses, there was no need for further discussion, since no disagreement occurred thereon. He who did not hear the decision directly from the prophet (Moses), of blessed memory, concerning questions arising therefrom[24], derived the laws by means of reasoning or by means of the thirteen principles given at Mount Sinai through which the Torah may be expounded.[25] These interpreted laws were sometimes free of argumentation, everyone agreeing (to a single view). On some of them, however, differences of opinion occurred between two views, the one stating thusly and the other thusly, the former deducing his view and, by means of reason, strengthening it in his own mind, and the latter also presenting reason to strengthen his opinion. It is because of the pitfall of analogy[26] by means of reasoning that this happening (i.e. the difference) in their opinions occurs. When such a difference of opinion does occur, then one follows the (ruling of the) majority as it is written: *Thou shalt follow the majority.*[27]

Know, too, that prophecy is not helpful in the interpretation of the Torah, nor in the derivation of the details of commandments through the thirteen principles (mentioned above). Rather, that which Joshua and Pinchas wrought was (not through prophecy but) through deliberation and logical derivation, much the same as did Rabina and Rav Ashi.[28] The advantage of a prophet and his accomplishment in the matter of any commandment, if you inquire into this, is, by my life,[29] among the great principles upon which the faith is supported and founded.

NOTES

1. This introduction to Tractate Berachoth serves as the general introduction to the entire Commentary on the Mishnah. It is sometimes spoken of as the introduction to Seder Zeraim since Maimonides wrote separate introductions for the other sections or orders of the Mishnah.
2. Lit: peace be upon him.
3. Tractate Erubin 54b.
4. *Torath Kohanim,* a *halachik* Commentary on Leviticus.
5. Levit. 25, 1.
6. Lit: said.
7. Resting of the soil and cancellation of debts in the Sabbatical year.
8. Levit. 23, 42.
9. Booth or hut or tabernacle.
10. Deut. 1, 3.
11. Deut. 1, 5.
12. Maimonides explains *Beraitha, Sifra & Sifre* later in his Introduction to the Commentary.
13. *Sifre,* Deut. 1, 5.
14. One month and seven days.
15. lit: books.
16. The first word in the Torah.
17. The last three words in the Torah. They begin and end with the letter *lamed.* See Tractate Baba Bathra 15a.
18. Deut. 31, 26.
19. lit: half.
20. *Sifre* Deut. 32, 1.
21. Tractate Megillah 13b.
22. The death of Moses.
23. Tractate Sotah 13b.
24. Questions whose answers can be derived from the explicit law.
25. *Sifra* 1, also known as the *Beraitha* of Rabbi Ishmael which enunciates the thirteen principles of Rabbinic exegesis. See Hertz, *Authorized Daily Prayer Book,* New York. Bloch Publishers, 1959, p. 43.
26. Between two Biblical laws.
27. Exodus 23, 2.
28. Compilers of the *Gemara* of the Babylonian Talmud.
29. Lit: let my soul live; an expression of oath common among the prophets.

MAIMONIDES, *MISHNEH TORAH*

Translation by Moses Hyamson

INTRODUCTION

All the precepts which Moses received on Sinai, were given together with their interpretation, as it is said "And I will give unto thee the tables of stone, and the law, and the commandment." (Exodus 24:12). "The law" refers to the Written Law; "and the commandment," to its interpretation. God bade us fulfil the Law in accordance with "the commandment." This commandment refers to that which is called the Oral Law. The whole of the Law was written by Moses, our teacher, before his death, in his own hand. He presented a scroll to each tribe and deposited one in the Ark for a testimony, as it is said "Take this book of the law and put it by the side of the Ark of the Covenant of the Lord your God, that it may be there for a witness against thee" (Deut. 31:26). "The commandment," which is the Interpretation of the Law, he did not write down but gave a charge concerning it to the Elders, to Joshua and to the rest of Israel, as it is said "All this which I command you, that shall ye observe to do; thou shalt not add thereto, nor diminish from it." (Deut. 4:2). Hence, it is styled the Oral Law.

Although the Oral Law was not committed to writing, Moses taught the whole of it, in his court, to the seventy elders as well as to Eleazar, Phineas and Joshua — all three of whom received it from Moses. To Joshua, his disciple, our teacher, Moses, delivered the Oral Law and charged him concerning it. So too, Joshua, throughout his life, taught orally. Many elders received the Oral Law from Joshua. Eli received it from the elders and from Phineas. Samuel, from Eli and his court. David, from Samuel and his court. Ahijah, the Shilonite, was among those who had come forth from Egypt. He was a Levite and had heard the Law from Moses, in his childhood. He received the Oral Law from David and his court. Elijah received it from Ahijah, the Shilonite, and his court. Elisha from Elijah and his court. Jehoiada the Priest, from Elisha and his court. Zechariah, from Jehoiada and his court. Hosea, from Zechariah and his court. Amos, from Hosea and his court. Isaiah, from Amos and his court. Micah, from Isaiah and his court. Joel, from Micah and his court. Nahum, from Joel and his court. Habakkuk, from Nahum and his court. Zephaniah, from Habakkuk and his court. Jeremiah, from Zephaniah and his court. Baruch, the son of Neriah, from Jeremiah and his court. Ezra and his court received it from Baruch and his court. The members of Ezra's court are called "The Men of the Great Synagogue." They were Haggai, Zechariah, Malachi, Daniel, Hananiah, Mishael and Azariah, Nehemiah, the son of Hachaliah, Mordecai, Zerubabel and many other sages, numbering altogether one hundred and twenty elders. The last of them was Simon the Just, who is included among the hundred and twenty. He received the Oral Law from all of them and was a high priest after Ezra. Antigonos of Socho and his court received the Oral Law from Simon the Just and his court. José, the son of Joezer of Zeredah, and Joseph, the son of Johanan of Jerusalem, and their court, from Antigonos and his court. Joshua, the son of Perahiah, and Nitai the Arbelite and their court, from Jose the son of Joezer and Joseph the son of Johanan and their court. Judah, the son of Tabbai, and Simeon, the son of Shetah and their court received from Joshua, the son of Perahiah and Nitai the Arbelite and their court. Shemaiah and Abtalion, proselytes of righteousness,[1] and their court received from Judah and Simon and their court. Hillel and Shammai and their court received from Shemaiah and Abtalion and their court. Rabban Johanan, the son of Zaccai, and Rabban Simeon, the son of Hillel received from Hillel and his court. Rabban Johanan ben Zaccai had five disciples who were the most distinguished among the scholars who received the Oral Law from him. They were Rabbi Eliezer the Great,[2] Rabbi Joshua, Rabbi José the Priest, Rabbi Simeon, the son of Nathaniel and Rabbi Eleazar, the son of Arach. Rabbi Akiba, the son of Joseph, received the Oral Law from Rabbi Eliezer the Great. Joseph, his father, was a proselyte of righteousness. Rabbi Ishmael and Rabbi Meir, the son of a proselyte of righteousness, received the Oral Law from Rabbi Akiba. Rabbi Meir and his colleagues also received it from Rabbi Ishmael. The colleagues of Rabbi Meir were Rabbi Judah, Rabbi José, Rabbi Simeon, Rabbi Nehemiah, Rabbi Eleazar, the son of Shammua, Rabbi Johanan, the sandal-maker, Simeon the son of Azzai and Rabbi Hananiah the son of Teradion. Rabbi Akiba's colleagues received the Oral Law also from Rabbi Eliezer the Great. The colleagues of Rabbi Akiba were Rabbi Tarfon, the teacher of Rabbi José the Galilean, Rabbi Simeon, the son of Eleazar, and Rabbi Johanan, the son of Nuri. Rabban Gamaliel the Elder received the Oral Law from Rabban Simeon, his father, a son of Hillel the Elder. Rabban Simeon, his son, received it from him. Rabban Gamaliel, his son, received it from him. Rabban Simeon, his son, received it from him. Rabbi Judah, the son of Rabban Simeon, is the Rabbi, called Our Teacher, the Saint. He received the Law from his father and from Rabbi Eleazar, the son of Shammua and from Rabbi Simeon, his father's colleagues. Our Teacher, the Saint, compiled the Mishnah. From the time of Moses to that of Our Teacher, the Saint, no work had been composed from which the Oral Law was publicly taught. But in each generation, the head of the then existing court or the prophet of that time wrote down for his private use a memorandum of the traditions which he had heard from his teachers, and which he taught orally in public. So too, every student wrote down, according to his ability, the exposition of the Torah and of its laws, as he heard them, as well as the new matter evolved in each generation, which had not been received by tradition but had been deduced by application of the thirteen hermeneutical rules and had been adopted by the Supreme Court. This was the method in vogue till the time of Our Teacher, the Saint.

He gathered together all the traditions, enactments, interpretations and expositions of every portion of the Torah, that had either come down from Moses, our Master, or had been deduced by the courts in successive generations. All this material he redacted in the Mishnah, which was diligently taught in public, and thus became universally known among the Jewish people. Copies of it were made and widely disseminated, so that the Oral Law might not be forgotten in Israel.

Why did our Teacher, the Saint, act so and not leave things as they were? Because he observed that the number of disciples was diminishing, fresh calamities were continually happening, the wicked Government was extending its domain and increasing in power, and Israelites were wandering and emigrating to distant countries. He therefore composed a work to serve as a handbook for all, and the contents of which could be rapidly studied and would not be forgotten. Throughout his life, he and his colleagues were engaged in giving public instruction in the Mishnah. Among the sages who were members of our sainted master's court and received instruction in the Oral Law from him, the following were the most distinguished: his sons, Simeon and Gamaliel; Rabbi Efes; Rabbi Yohanan and Rabbi Hoshaia. These were the most illustrious of the sages who received instruction from him; besides thousands and tens of thousands other scholars. Although these eleven are named as having received instruction from our sainted teacher and attended his college, Rabbi Yohanan was a child at the time, and, at a subsequent period, a pupil of Rabbi Yannai from whom he received instruction. Rav also received instruction from Rabbi Yannai; as Samuel did from Rabbi

Hanina, son of Hama. Rav compiled the *Sifra* and the *Sifrē*, the purpose of which is to expound and teach the principles of the Mishnah. R. Hiya compiled the *Tosefta*, to explain the subject matter of the Mishnah. So too, Rabbi Hoshaia and Bar Kappara compiled *Boraithas*, to elucidate the text of the Mishnah. Rabbi Yohanan composed the Jerusalem Talmud in Palestine, approximately three centuries after the destruction of the Second Temple. Among the distinguished sages who received the Law from Rav and Samuel were Rav Huna, Rav Judah, Rav Nahman and Rav Kahana. Among the distinguished sages who received such instruction from Rabbi Johanan were Rabbah, grandson of Hanah, Rav Ami, Rav Asi, Rav Dimi and Rav Abin. Among the sages who were thus instructed by Rav Huna and Rav Judah, were Rabbah and Rav Joseph. Among the disciples of Rabbah and Rav Joseph were Abaié and Rava. The last two were also instructed by Rav Nahman. Among Rava's disciples were Rav Ashi and Ravina. Mar, son of Rav Ashi was instructed by his father, Rav Ashi and by Ravina.

Accordingly, counting back from Rav Ashi to Moses, our teacher, (upon whom be peace), there were forty generations of scholars (who received the Oral Law each from his predecessors in unbroken succession) as follows:

(1) Rav Ashi received from Rava; (2) Rava from Rabbah; (3) Rabbah from Rav Huna; (4) Rav Huna from Rabbi Johanan, Rav and Samuel; (5) Rabbi Johanan, Rav and Samuel from Our Teacher, the Saint; (6) Our Teacher, the Saint, from his father, Rabbi Simeon; (7) Rabbi Simeon from his father, Rabban Gamaliel; (8) Rabban Gamaliel from his father, Rabban Simeon; (9) Rabban Simeon from his father Rabban Gamaliel (the Elder); (10) Rabban Gamaliel (the Elder) from his father, Rabban Simeon; (11) Rabban Simeon from his father, Hillel and from Shammai; (12) Hillel and Shammai from Shemaiah and Abtalion; (13) Shemaiah and Abtalion from Judah and Simeon; (14) Judah and Simeon from Joshua, (the son of Perahiah) and Nitai (the Arbelite); (15) Joshua and Nitai (the Arbelite) from Joseph (the son of Joezer) and Joseph, (the son of Johanan); (16) Joseph, (son of Joezer) and Joseph (son of Johanan) from Antigonos; (17) Antigonos from Simon the Just; (18) Simon the Just from Ezra; (19) Ezra from Baruch; (20) Baruch from Jeremiah; (21) Jeremiah from Zephaniah; (22) Zephaniah from Habakkuk; (23) Habakkuk from Nahum; (24) Nahum from Joel; (25) Joel from Micah; (26) Micah from Isaiah; (27) Isaiah from Amos; (28) Amos from Hosea; (29) Hosea from Zechariah; (30) Zechariah from Jehoiadah; (31) Jehoiadah from Elisha; (32) Elisha from Elijah; (33) Elijah from Ahijah; (34) Ahijah from David; (35) David from Samuel; (36) Samuel from Eli;

(37) Eli from Phineas; (38) Phineas from Joshua; (39) Joshua from Moses, our teacher; (40) Moses, our teacher, the teacher of all prophets, from the Eternal, God of Israel.

All the sages here mentioned were the great men of the successive generations; some of them were presidents of colleges, some exilarchs, and some were members of the great Synhedria; besides them were thousands and myriads of disciples and fellow-students. Ravina and Rav Ashi closed the list of the sages of the Talmud. Rav Ashi it was who compiled the Babylonian Talmud in the land of Shinar (Babylon), about a century after Rabbi Johanan had compiled the Jerusalem Talmud. These two Talmuds contain an exposition of the text of the Mishnah and an elucidation of its abstruse points and of the new subject-matter that had been added by the various courts from the days of Our Teacher, the Saint, till the compilation of the Talmud. The two Talmuds, the *Tosefta,* the *Sifra* and the *Sifrẹ,* and the *Toseftoth* are the sources, from all of which is elucidated what is forbidden and what is permitted, what is unclean and what is clean, what is a penal violation and what involves no penalty, what is fit to be used and what is unfit for use, all in accordance with the traditions received by the sages from their predecessors in unbroken succession up to the teachings of Moses as he received them on Sinai. From these sources too, are ascertained the decrees, instituted by the sages and prophets, in each generation, to serve as a protecting fence about the Law, in accordance with Moses' express injunction, "Ye shall keep my charge" (Lev. 18:30), that is, "Ordain a charge to preserve My charge." From these sources a clear conception is also obtained of the customs and ordinances, either formally introduced in various generations by their respective authorities or that came into use with their sanction; from these it is forbidden to depart, as it is said, "Thou shalt not turn aside from the sentence which they shall declare unto thee, to the right hand; nor to the left." (Deut. 17:11). So too these works contain the clearly established judgments and rules not received from Moses, but which the Supreme Court of each generation deduced by applying the hermeneutical principles for the interpretation of the Law, and which were decided by those venerable authorities to be the Law,—all of which, accumulated from the days of Moses to his own time, Rav Ashi put together in the Gemara. The sages of the Mishnah composed other works to expound the words of the Torah. Rabbi Hoshiah, a disciple of Our Teacher, the Saint, wrote an exposition of the book of Genesis; and Rabbi Ishmael, a commentary on the Pentateuch, from the beginning of the book of Exodus to the end of the Pentateuch. This work is called Mechilta. Rabbi Akiba also wrote a Mechilta. Other sages, who lived subsequently, compiled Midrashim. All these works were composed before the Babylonian Talmud. Ravina and Rav Ashi and their colleagues were the last of the great sages who firmly established the Oral Law, made decrees, and ordinances and introduced customs. Their decrees, ordinances and customs obtained universal acceptance among Israelites wherever they settled.

After the Court of Rav Ashi, who compiled the Gemara which was finally completed in the days of his son, an extraordinarily great dispersion of Israel throughout the world took place. The people emigrated to remote parts and distant isles. The prevalence of wars and the march of armies made travel insecure. The study of the Torah declined. The Jewish people did not flock to the colleges in their thousands and tens of thousands as heretofore; but in each city and country, individuals who felt the divine call gathered together and occupied themselves with the Torah; studied all the works of the sages; and from these, learnt the method of legal interpretation.

If a court established in any country, after the time of the Talmud, made decrees and ordinances or introduced customs for those residing in its particular country or for residents of other countries, its enactments did not obtain the acceptance of all Israel because of the remoteness of the Jewish settlements and the difficulties of travel. And as the court of any particular country consisted of individuals (whose authority was not universally recognised), while the Supreme Court of seventy-one members had, several years before the compilation of the Talmud, ceased to exist, no compulsion is exercised on those living in one country to observe the customs of another country; nor is any court directed to issue a decree that had been issued by another court in the same country. So too, if one of the *Geonim* taught that a certain way of judgmment was correct, and it became clear to a court at a later date that this was not in accordance with the view of the Gemara, the earlier authority is not necessarily followed but that view is adopted which seems more reasonable, whether it be that of an earlier or later authority.

The foregoing observations refer to rules, decrees, ordinances and customs that originated after the Talmud had been compiled. But whatever is already mentioned in the Babylonian Talmud is binding on all Israel. And every city and country is bound to observe all the customs observed by the sages of the Gemara, promulgate their decrees, and uphold their institutions, on the ground that all these customs, decrees, and institutions mentioned in the Talmud received the assent of all Israel, and those sages who instituted the ordinances, issued the decrees, introduced the customs, gave the decisions and taught that a certain ruling was correct, constituted the total body or the majority of Israel's wise men. They were the leaders who received from each other the traditions concerning the fundamentals of Judaism, in unbroken succession back to Moses, our teacher, upon whom be peace.

The sages, however, who arose after the compilation of the Talmud, studied it deeply, and became famous for their wisdom, are those called Geonim. All these Geonim who flourished in the land of Israel Shinar,[3] Spain and France, taught the method of the Talmud, elucidated its obscurities, and expounded the various topics with which it deals. For its method is exceedingly profound. Furthermore, the work is composed in Aramaic mixed with other languages—this having been the vernacular of the Babylonian Jews at the time when it was compiled. In other countries, however, as also in Babylon in the days of the Geonim, no one, unless specially taught, understood that dialect. Many applications were made to the Gaon of the day by residents of different cities, asking for explanations of difficulties in the Talmud. These, the Geonim answered, according to their ability. Those who had put the questions collected the responses which they made into books for study. The Geonim also, at different periods, composed commentaries on the Talmud. Some of them explained specific laws; other, particular chapters that presented difficulties to their contemporaries; others again expounded complete treatises and entire orders of the Talmud. They also made compilations of settled rules as to things permitted or forbidden, as to infractions which were penal or were not liable to a penalty. All these dealt with matters in regard to which compendia were needed, that could be studied by one not capable of penetrating to the depths of the Talmud. This is the godly work in which all the Geonim of Israel engaged, from the completion of the Talmud to the present date which is the eighth year of the eleventh century after the destruction of the Second Temple.[4]

In our days, severe vicissitudes prevail, and all feel the pressure of hard times. The wisdom of our wise men has disappeared; the understanding of our prudent men is hidden. Hence, the commentaries of the Geonim and their compilations of laws and responses, which they took care to make clear, have in our times become hard to understand so that only a few individuals properly comprehend them. Needless to add that such is the case in regard to the Talmud itself—the Babylonian as well as the Palestinian—the *Sifra*, the *Sifri* and the *Tosefta*, all of which works require, for their comprehension, a broad mind, a wise soul and considerable study, and then one can learn from them the correct practice as to what is forbidden or permitted, and the other rules of the Torah.

On these grounds, I, Moses the son of Maimon *the Sefardi,* bestirred myself, and, relying on the help of God, blessed be He, intently studied all these works, with the view of putting together the results obtained from them in regard to what is forbidden or permitted, clean or unclean, and the other rules of the Torah—all in plain language and terse style, so that thus the entire Oral Law might become systematically known to all, without citing difficulties and solutions or differences of view, one person saying so, and another something else,—but consisting of statements, clear and convincing and in accordance with the conclusions drawn from all these compilations and commentaries that have appeared from the time of Moses to the present, so that all the rules shall be accessible to young and old, whether these appertain to the (Pentateuchal) precepts or to the institutions extablished by the sages and prophets, so that no other work should be needed for ascertaining any of the laws of Israel, but that this work might serve as a compendium of the entire Oral Law, including the ordinances, customs and decress instituted from the days of our teacher Moses till the compilation of the Talmud, as expounded for us by the Geonim in all the works composed by them since the completion of the Talmud. Hence, I have entitled this work *Mishneh Torah* (Repetition of the Law), for the reason that a person, who first reads the Written Law and then this compilation, will know from it the whole of the Oral Law, without having occasion to consult any other book between them.

NOTES

1. I.e., full proselytes in contradistinction to proselytes of the gate who only accepted the obligation of the seven Noachide precepts.
2. Rabbi Eliezer, son of Hyrcanus.
3. Babylon.
4. Corresponding to 4937 A.M. (1177 C.E.).

ALBO, *IKKARIM*

Translation by Isaac Husik

BOOK III, CHAPTER 22

The Torah which we have to-day and which has been handed down to us by unbroken tradition from father to son is the same that was given to Moses on Sinai, without any change. It could not have received change in the time of the first temple when the priests and teachers were in the temple and the Torah was well known to everybody. And though there were among them kings who worshipped idols, they also had prophets during the entire period until the time of the destruction, who admonished the people to observe the Torah. And as for the great alarm which Josiah felt when the priest Hilkiah found a book of the Torah in the house of the Lord,[1] this does not signify that they had no copy of the Torah, for Jeremiah was alive then. But the reason was this. Amon and Menasseh were worshippers of idols and offended God, so much so that our Rabbis say,[2] Menasseh cut the names of God out of the Torah and substituted names of idols in their place. Accordingly one of the priests who feared that the king might do the same with the original copy of the Torah which Moses wrote, if it got into his hands, hid it in the walls of the building. Later, in the days of Josiah, who returned to the Lord with all his heart, with all his soul and with all his might in accordance with the law of Moses, they looked for this book and could not find it. And when they repaired the temple, Hilkiah found it in the wall and was very much elated over it, as if he had found a great treasure. He then sent a message to the king, saying, I have found *the* book of the Law, the well known book which Moses wrote; he did not say I found *a* book of the Law. Now the reason that king Josiah was so alarmed at the find and rent his garments when he heard the words of the book, is as our Rabbis explain in the Jerusalem Talmud.[3] The Torah which Moses wrote was rolled up so that it opened on the beginning of Genesis, whereas the manuscript which they found opened on the verse in Deuteronomy:[4] "The Lord will bring thee, and thy king whom thou shalt set over thee, unto a nation that thou has not known. . ." This is the reason why the king was alarmed, and not because the people had forgotten the Torah, God forbid!

Nor could the Torah have undergone change when the Israelites were exiled to Babylon. For in the beginning of the exile under Jehoiachin, before the destruction of the temple, the craftsmen and the smiths and the leaders of the wise men of Israel were exiled, Daniel was among them and also the prophet Ezekiel, as we read, "One that had escaped out of Jerusalem came unto me, saying: 'The city is smitten'."[5] And all the Jewish exiles who were scattered through all the land of Assyria had in their possession a copy of the Law, for even the Cutheans,[6] whom the king of Assyria settled in the cities of Samaria, had a copy of the Torah. When the temple was destroyed, the Torah had already spread through all Babylonia and could not have undergone any change by reason of the destruction of the temple.

When Ezra returned from Babylon, only a few went with him, while the leaders of Israel and the wise men and those of noble lineage, all remained in Babylon. Thus our Rabbis say, Ezra did not leave Babylon until he made it like fine flour;[7] that is to say, he left those of pure descent and took with him those who were not pure, because he knew that in Palestine he would be able to prevent the Israelites from mixing with them. Thus none of the tribe of Levi returned with him, as we read: "And I viewed the people and the priests, and found there none of the sons of Levi."[8] He, therefore, sent to Babylon, and they sent him eighteen persons of the sons of Mahli. Since, therefore, all the great men who were conversant with the Torah remained in Babylon, Ezra would not have dared to make any changes in the Torah, for then his Torah would not have agreed with that of all those who remained in Babylon, and who lived in the cities of Samaria and in the land of Assyria and in other places, who refused to return with him. . .

The differences in word and expression which are found in the Torah among the other nations are due to errors of translation into the other languages by unskilled persons. The Jews were very careful about the letters of the Torah, the *plene* and *defective* writings. They prided themselves on knowing the number of letters and verses, which they recorded in the margins of their copies, calling it Masorah—a practice which the other nations did not follow. "Why were they (sc. the Scribes) called 'Soferim' (lit. counters)? Because they counted all the letters of the Torah."[9] This shows that they kept it in the form in which it was given to Moses without any change. A proof of this is that the Torah is exactly the same to-day without any change among all Israel who are scattered all over the world from the extreme east to the farthest west.

The Rabbis speak of certain words in the Torah as being corrections of the Scribes, for example in reference to the verse, "But Abraham stood yet before the Lord,"[10] they say that the reading ought to be, "The Lord stood yet before Abraham," but the expression was changed by the Scribes. Also, "Let me not look upon my wretchedness,"[11] they say, is a correction of the Scribes for "Let me not look upon *Thy* wretchedness,"[12] and they say the same thing about other expressions. But this does not mean that anybody changed any words in the Torah, God forbid! No one who falsifies a book would admit that he falsified it or made changes in it. How then could the Rabbis say that the Soferim (Scribes) made changes? The meaning is that from the context it would seem that Moses should have said, "Let me not look upon *Thy* wretchedness." The reason for the changed reading, "*my* wretchedness," is like a correction which a scribe makes out of respect to God. Moses was not speaking in reference to himself, but in reference to God, but he changed the expression by divine order, as a scribe changes an expression by way of euphemism. The other instances must be explained in the same way. Similarly we must explain the dots which we find in the Torah over the ואהרן (and Aaron) in the verse, "Whom Moses and Aaron numbered";[13] over the words לנו ולבנינו (unto us and to our children),[14] and in other passages. The word in question remains in the text, and the dot indicates something intermediate between retaining the word and deleting it. The meaning is that though the text reads, "Whom Moses and Aaron numbered," the one who did the numbering was Moses, while Aaron was merely with him, and his name is mentioned out of respect, for Moses was the important person in the act and not Aaron. Similarly the dots on לנו ולבנינו are intended to show that though children may be obligated by the parents, the obligation is not of the same degree as when the parents obligate themselves. The other cases must be explained in a similar manner.

NOTES

1. II Kings 22.
2. Sanhedrin 103b.
3. Not in our texts, but the statement is frequently quoted. See Ginzberg, "Legends of the Jews," VI, p. 377, note 116.
4. 28, 36.
5. Ezek. 33, 21.
6. See II Kings 17, 24 f.
7. Kiddushin 69b.
8. Ezra 8, 15.
9. Kiddushin 30a.
10. Gen. 18, 21.
11. Num. 11, 15.
12. Yalkut Shim'oni, §736. The reading in Yalkut is ברעתם, in *their* wickedness, which makes better sense. Rashi ad locum also has ברעתם.
13. Num. 3, 39.
14. Deut. 29, 29.

The Ninth Principle

Immutability of Torah

INTRODUCTION

The immutable and unchanging nature of the Law of Moses is without question the most distinctive belief of Judaism. Acceptance of this principle is in itself sufficient grounds for total rejection of the claims of both Christianity and Islam. A law which is immutable cannot be abrogated, annulled, rescinded or supplanted. Nor, for that matter, can it be supplemented.

A person claiming to be a prophet and claiming that he bears a prophetic message commanding the permanent abrogation of any precept stands convicted by his own mouth of false prophecy. Such prophecy is in direct contradiction to the prophecy of Moses. Maimonides declares that a prophet may not even claim prophetic power to resolve an ambiguity or doubt with regard to a fine point of law. Even though it in no way contradicts the revelation at Mount Sinai, resolution of such an ambiguity would constitute an addition to the Torah, and any addition, even if only clarificatory in nature, constitutes a "change" in the corpus of law revealed to Moses.[1]

[1] In disagreement with Maimonides, *Tosafot, Yevamot* 14a and *Ḥullin* 44a, recognize the possibility of resolution of a doubtful matter of *halakhah* by means of a "heavenly voice." Rabbi Abraham I. Kook, *Mishpat Kohen* (Jerusalem, 1937), no. 92, narrows the area of disagreement. He asserts that *Tosafot* accept the authority of a *bat kol* or of prophetic revelation in matters of law in only one of two situations. One possibility is that law may be established on the basis of prophecy only when this form of revelation is a spontaneous communication as distinct from a solicited response. Moses alone was priviliged to elicit *halakhah* as a response to his query. Another possibility is that law may be established on the basis of prophecy only in cases in which both sides of a question or two conflicting opinions are fully formulated, with cogent and equally valid arguments advanced in support of each contingent position. In such situations revelation serves only to determine which of the two theoretical positions is to be accepted as normative. The latter interpretation is espoused by Rabbi Chaim Joseph David Azulai, *Shem ha-Gedolim, Ma'arekhet Gedolim, yud,* no. 224 and apparently also by Rabbi Israel Salanter, *Or Yisra'el,* note appended to chapter 30.

For narrower interpretations of Maimonides' position see Rabbi Meir Simchah ha-Kohen of Dvinsk, *Or Sameaḥ, Hilkhot Yesodei ha-Torah* 9:4; Rabbi Menachem Krakovsky, *Avodat ha-Melekh, Hilkhot Yesodei ha-Torah* 9:4; Rabbi Chaim Joseph David Azulai, *loc. cit.;* and *idem, Birkei Yosef, Oraḥ Ḥayyim* 32:4. Cf., Maharam ibn Ḥabib, *Tosefot Yom ha-Kippurim,* p. 3a f.

Maimonides argues that the Torah itself proclaims its inherent immutability. In his *Mishneh Torah, Hilkhot Yosodei ha-Torah* 9:1, Maimonides cites four different proof-texts which establish this teaching in three different ways. Any subsequent change must perforce involve either an expansion or a diminution of the Law of Moses. This is excluded by virtue of the admonition "Thou shalt not add to it, nor diminish from it" (Deut. 13:1). Moreover, the Torah proclaims itself to be eternally binding, as evidenced by two separate citations: ". . . but the things that are revealed belong unto us and to our children forever, that we may do all the words of this Law" (Deut. 29:28); and the recurring phrase, "an eternal statute unto your generations," which indicates the nature of the Law as being of eternal validity. Finally, the Torah declares that the Law "is not in heaven, that thou shouldst say: 'Who shall go up to heaven and bring it unto us, and make us to hear it, that we may do it?'" (Deut. 30:12). It is this last verse which is invoked by the Talmud, *Baba Meẓi'a* 59b, in rejecting the authority of a heavenly voice in resolving a dispute among the sages concerning a matter of ritual purity. The Law, having been revealed to man, is no longer in heaven; there can be no supplemental revelation.

In the *Guide*, III, 34, Maimonides adds another consideration auguring against the possibility that the Torah might be changed. The Torah is harmonious and perfect. That which is harmonious and perfect can only be marred if anything is added or taken away. Although Maimonides does not himself cite a scriptural source, Albo cites the verse "The Law of the Lord is perfect, restoring the soul" (Ps. 19:8) in his paraphrase of Maimonides' argument.

Saadia similarly declares that the Torah will never be abrogated. He emphasizes that acceptance of the prophecy of Moses is not predicated upon wonders and miracles. Hence, alleged performance of miracles by a prophet in support of a new revelation is not a compelling factor which would warrant abrogation of the Torah.

Albo points out that divine law did indeed change, at least in a limited manner. The flesh of animals was denied to Adam as food but was permitted to Noah. Abraham was the first to be given the commandment concerning circumcision. Most significantly, the Sinaitic revelation superseded the earlier Noachide Code. Divine law was thus modified in accordance with the changed nature and character of the recipients of the law.

Under what circumstances may divine law be changed? Albo answers that such change must be revealed directly by God. The veracity of any such revelation may be established in two ways: (1) the prophet introducing any change must be greater than the prophet through whom the law was originally revealed; or (2) the evidence establishing the credentials of the second prophet must be at least as convincing as the evidence which established the genuine nature of the mission of the prophet who established the law originally. Moses was greater than all of the prophets who preceded him, and the Bible itself declares there will be no prophet greater than Moses. The prophecy of Moses was verified in a most wondrous manner. All of Israel heard God speaking to Moses. Thus no prophet could change the law of Moses unless God were to reveal Himself to Israel directly and publicly as He did in revealing Himself to Moses in the presence of 600,000 people.

Although the notion is modified somewhat by Albo, both Crescas and Albo do accept the basic truth of the immutability of the Torah but deny that it is a fundamental principle. These philosophers maintain that immutability is not a fundamental principle of divine law in general or of the law of Moses in particular. Nevertheless, both Albo and Crescas agree that the principle should be accepted by every believing Jew.

The dispute between Maimonides and his opponents is, then, not so much one of fact but one of classification. Indeed, Maimonides does not advance philosophical proofs demonstrating the principle of immutability but bases himself upon the statements contained in the Torah itself. Immutability of the Torah is thus, for Maimonides, a matter of dogma rather than of reason. Whether such matters should or should not be included among the fundamental principles of belief is directly contingent upon how the notion of a principle is defined. As has been explained, it is precisely the definition of the notion of a principle which lies at the crux of the differences in classification between Maimonides, Crescas and Albo.

SAADIA, *EMUNOT VE-DE'OT*

Translation by Alexander Altmann

THIRD TREATISE
COMMANDMENT AND PROHIBITION

6. *The Eternal Validity of the Law*

Having dealt with these matters (i.e. the character of Scripture and Tradition), I deem it right to add to my remarks a word on the Abrogation of the Law,[1] since this seems to be the proper place for it. I declare that the Children of Israel, according to an accepted tradition,[2] were told by the prophets that the laws of the Torah shall never be abrogated.[3] They assert that they heard this in clear terms which allowed no room for misunderstanding or allegorical interpretation. I thereupon searched in the Scriptures and found support for this tradition. First, in regard to most of the laws it is written that they are 'a covenant for ever'[4] and 'for your generations.' There is, furthermore, the phrase which occurs in the Torah, 'Moses commanded us a law, an inheritance of the congregation of Jacob' (Deut. 33.4). Moreover, our people, the Children of Israel, are a people only by virtue of our laws, and since the Creator has declared that our people should exist as long as heaven and earth exist, it necessarily follows that our laws should continue to exist as long as heaven and earth are in being, and this is what he says, 'Thus saith the Lord, who giveth the sun for a light by day, and the ordinances of the moon and of the stars for a light by night, who stirreth up the sea, that the waves thereof roar, the Lord of Hosts is His name: If these ordinances depart from before Me, saith the Lord, then the seed of Israel also shall cease from being a nation before Me for ever' (Jer. 31.35-36).[5]

I found that in the last period of prophecy God exhorted (his people) that they should keep the Law of Moses until the Day of Judgment, which will be preceded by the advent of Elijah; He says, 'Remember ye the law of Moses, My servant, which I commanded unto him in Horeb for all Israel, even statutes and ordinances. Behold I will send you Elijah the prophet before the coming of the great and terrible day of the Lord' (Mal. 3.22-23).

Some people say that in the same way as the reason for our believing in Moses was his performance of wonders and miracles, so it follows that the reason for believing in some other prophet would be the performance of wonders and miracles by the latter. I was greatly astonished when I heard this remark. For the reason of our belief in Moses lies not in the wonders and miracles only, but the reason for our belief in him and all other prophets lies in the fact that they admonished us in the first place to do what was right,[6] and only after we had heard the prophet's message and found that it was right did we ask him to produce miracles in support of it. If he performed them, we believed in him. But if we hear his call and find it, at the outset, to be wrong, we do not ask him for miracles, for no miracle can prove the (rationally) impossible. The case is similar to that of two people Reuben and Simon appearing before the judge. If Reuben claims from Simon something within the realm of the possible, saying for instance, 'He owes me a thousand dinar,' then the judge will ask him to produce evidence, and if he can establish the claim, the money will be awarded to him. But if he claims something in the nature of the impossible, as by saying, 'He owes me the river Tigris,' his claim will be void from the outset since nobody owns the Tigris, and it would not be correct for the judge to ask him for evidence for his claim.

So it is with everyone who claims to be a prophet. If he tells us, 'My Lord commands you to fast to-day,' we ask him for a sign of his prophecy, and if we see it, we believe it and shall fast. But if he says, 'My Lord commands you to commit adultery and to steal' or, 'He announces to you that He will flood the world again' or, 'He informs you that He created heaven and earth in one year (without allegory),[7] we shall not ask him for a sign because he brings us a message which neither Reason nor Tradition can sanction. Some people carried the discussion a stage further and said, "What, if he does not pay regard to us, but shows us wonders and miracles, and willy-nilly we see them, what shall we say to him then?' I replied: 'We shall tell him then the same as we would say in case someone showed us wonders and miracles in support of a doctrine which runs counter to the innate dictates of our Reason, with regard to the approval of truth and the disapproval of falsehood, etc.'[8] He would be driven to assert that the disapproval of falsehood and the approval of truth are not dictated by Reason, but are matters of (legal) commandment and prohibition,[9] and so likewise the condemnation of murder, adultery, theft, etc. But when he comes down to that, he is no longer worthy of my notice, and I see no purpose in further discussion with him.[10]

NOTES

1. The question whether the Biblical Law was given for all time or whether it was to be abrogated at a certain period, formed the subject of many disputes amongst Jews, Christians, and Muhammedans. The famous historian al-Mas'ūdī (died 957) reports that he had numerous discussions on this point with Abū Kathir, the teacher of Saadya. Cf. Ventura, [*La Philosophie de Saadia Gaon*, Paris, 1934], pp. 201–2.

2. Arab. *nakl*; Tibbon translates it by *ḳabbalah*.

3. Cf. *p. Megillah*,I, 5: R. Yohanan said, 'The Prophets and the Writings will be abolished in the Future World, but the Five Books of the Torah will never be abolished . . . R. Shimeon b. Levi said, 'Not even the Scroll of Esther nor the laws (*halakōt*) will ever be abolished.' In some Midrashic utterances, however, the possibility of an abrogation of certain laws in the Future World is considered. Cf. *Lev. R.* 13.3; *Midr. Shoḥer Tob* on Ps. 146.7 ('The Lord looseth the prisoners'—*mattīr 'assurīm*—in the sense of *mattīr 'issurīm*, 'permitteth that which is forbidden'); *Yalk. Shimeoni Prov.* §944. See also *Tossafot Niddah* 61 b. In Halachic literature the view is predominant that even in the Future World not a single law nor letter of the Torah will be changed. The Midrashic passages quoted above are explained either with reference to the state of man after death when his soul is free from the Law (cf. *b. Niddah* 61 b; *Yad Mal.*437), or as a temporary suspension of certain laws (cf. *Sedeh Ḥemed*, Vol. II; ch. 3.7), or in a merely homiletical fashion (cf. *Responsa R. Shelomo b. 'Adret* 93). Maimonides (*Comm. Mishnah Sanh.* X, 9; *Yes. Hat.* 9) declares with reference to Deut. 13.1 that the Law will never be modified nor changed for another Law (cf. the line in the *Yigdal Hymn*, 'God will not alter nor change His Law to everlasting for any other'). In *Moreh* III, 34, he makes the same statement. He explains that the Law, being perfect (Ps. 19.8), is not subject to change. Albo (*'Iḳḳarim* III, 14-20) argues against Maimonides that, on principle, the Law could be altered (with the exception of the Decalogue) if the prophet who announced a new law were superior to Moses; but this possibility, he emphasizes, is precluded by Deut. 34.10. In Jewish mysticism, the Midrashic utterances quoted above are given depth and significance by the theory of World Periods (*Shemitōt*) as explained in the book *Temunah* (about 1250). It teaches that the Torah is to be read in different ways during the various successive periods without, however, being changed in its outward form. In the current period which is that of Stern Judgment, commandments and prohibitions are necessary, in accordance with the present reading of the Torah. But in the coming Aeon the Torah will no longer contain prohibitions since the power of evil will be broken. Cf. Scholem [*Major Trends in Jewish Mysticism*, Jerusalem, 1941], pp. 175-6; see also pp. 228, 275. The followers of the Jewish Pseudo-Messiah Sabbatai Z'bi, especially the Frankist movement, made ample use of this bold theory, by which they sought to sanction their antinomian doctrine. Cf. Scholem's article in *K'nesset*, 5697, pp. 370 ff.

4. *le-'olam*—Albo (*'Iḳḳarim*, III, 16) denies that the Hebrew word *'olam* necessarily means eternity; it may also be applied, he says, to limited periods, in the same way as the word *neṣaḥ*. In a passage not included in this Selection (*Amānāt*, 138-9; Hebr. 71), Saadya admits that *'olam* can denote a limited period, but asserts that such a meaning is exceptional and cannot be applied without cogent reasons. On the etymology and meaning of *'olam* cf. the Translator's article 'Olam und Aion' in *Festschrift für Jakob Freimann* (1937), pp. 1-14.

5. Some of the Church Fathers, notably Justin and Eusebius, sought to prove the abrogation of the Biblical Law by reference to Jer. 31.31-4, where mention is made of the 'new covenant' which God will make with the House of Judah. Saadya quotes here verses 35-6 of that very chapter in order to prove that the Law of the Torah is destined to be valid eternally. A direct answer to the Christian exegesis of Jer. 31.31–4 is given in a subsequent passage, not included in this Selection (*Amānāt*, 135; Hebr. 69) where Saadya points out

that the 'new covenant' is nothing but the old Law fulfilled and no longer broken by Israel. He refers to verses 32-3 in support of his interpretation.

6. Arab. *jā'iz*; lawful, right, i.e., conforming to the innate cognition of Reason.
7. Arab. *bilā tāwīl*; i.e. in a literal sense.
8. i.e. We shall reply that no miracle can prove the rationally impossible.
9. The Ash'arite view. Cf. above, p. 96, n. 4.
10. The authority of Reason is above discussion and cannot be disproved by miracles.

MAIMONIDES, *MISHNEH TORAH*

Translation by Moses Hyamson

BOOK OF KNOWLEDGE, LAWS CONCERNING THE BASIC PRINCIPLES OF THE TORAH, CHAPTER 9

1. It is clearly and explicitly set forth in the Torah that its ordinances will endure for ever without variation, diminution or addition; as it is said, "All this word which I command you, that shall ye observe to do; thou shalt not add to it, nor take away from it" (Deut. 13:1); and further it is said "but the things that are revealed belong unto us and to our children for ever, that we may do all the words of this Law" (Deut. 29:28). Hence the inference that to fulfil all the behests of the Torah is an obligation incumbent upon us for ever, as it is said, "It is an everlasting statute throughout your generations." (Lev. 23:14, Num. 18:23). It is also said, "It is not in heaven" (Deut. 30:12). Hence the inference that a prophet is forbidden to make innovations in the Torah. Accordingly, if any one should arise, whether among the Gentiles or among the Israelites, and, showing a sign and token, declare that God had sent him to add a precept to the Torah or take away a precept from the Torah, or give an interpretation to any of the commandments, such as we had not heard from Moses; or should assert that the commandments ordained to Israel are not of perpetual obligation for all generations but only temporary, such a man is a false prophet, because he sets out to deny the prophecy of Moses. He is to be put to death by strangling because he spoke perversely in the name of God that which God had not bidden him, for the Lord enjoined Moses that this Commandment shall be unto us and to our children after us for ever. And God is not a man that he should lie.

2. Since this is so, why is it said in the Torah, "I will raise them up a prophet from among their brethren, like unto thee" (Deut. 18:18)? The answer is that the prophet here referred to, will come, not to found a religion, but to charge the people concerning the words of the Torah and exhort them not to transgress it; as the last of the prophets expressed it, "Remember ye the law of Moses, My servant" (Malachi 3:22). And so, if the prophet gives an order in regard to things permissible, as for instance, if he says "Go to that place" or "Do not go to it," "Wage war

today" or "Do not wage war," "Build this wall" or "Do not build it," it is a duty to obey him. Whoever transgresses his instructions incurs the penalty of death by the hand of God, as it is said, "And it shall come to pass, that whosoever will not hearken unto the words of the prophet which he shall speak in My Name, I will require it of him." (Deut. 18:19).

3. So too, a prophet who acts contrary to his own exhortations or suppresses the prophetic message he is charged to deliver, incurs the penalty of death by the hand of God. To all the above three offences applies the text "I will require it of him" (Deut. 18:19). So also, if one, who is known to us as a prophet, bids us transgress on a certain occasion any precept of the Torah or several such precepts—whether minor or major—it is our duty to obey him. For thus were we taught by the ancient sages, on the authority of tradition, that if the prophet tells you to transgress the precepts of the Torah, as Elijah did on Mount Carmel, obey him in all matters, unless the commandment be to worship idols; this is the rule however only when the prophet's instruction is for a single occasion. Such was the case of Elijah at Mount Carmel. He offered up burnt offerings outside the Temple, while the Sanctuary in Jerusalem was the place appointed for such sacrifices, and any one who offered them up outside the appointed place incurred the penalty of excision. But because Elijah was a prophet, it was obligatory to heed him, and even in the above case the rule applied "Unto him shall ye hearken" (Deut. 18:15). If Elijah's contemporaries had asked him, "How dare we abrogate the precept, "Take heed to thyself that thou offer not thy offering in any place" (Deut. 12:13), the prophet would have replied, "This verse only refers to one who constantly offers up sacrifices outside the Sanctuary; such a person incurs the penalty of excision prescribed by Moses. But *I* propose to offer up sacrifices outside the Temple, this day only, by the express commandment of God, for the purpose of discrediting the prophets of Baal." And thus, if prophets order the violation of a precept for a set time, it is a duty to obey the direction. But if they declare that the precept is abrogated for ever, they incur the penalty of death by strangling, for the Torah said "Unto us and to our children for ever." (Deut. 29:28).

4. So too, if a prophet attempts to rescind any of the institutions that have come down to us by tradition, or if, in reference to a moot point, he asserts that the Almighty had instructed him as to what was the decision and that the rule was according to the view of a certain teacher, he is a false prophet, and should be strangled, even if he showed a token, since he proposes to deny the Torah which has laid down the principle "It is not in Heaven" (Deut. 30:12). But if his direction be only for a single occasion, we obey him in all things.

5. These rules apply to all precepts but not to the prohibition of idolatry. If a prophet bids us worship idols even on a single occasion, we are not to listen to him. And though he performs great signs and wonders, if he says that the Almighty commanded him that an idol should be worshipped this day only or this hour only, he speaks perversely against the Eternal. Scripture charges us in such a case, "And even if the sign or wonder come to pass . . . thou shalt not hearken unto the words of that prophet. . . ., because he hath spoken perversely against the Lord, your God." (Deut. 13:3-4-6). Since he seeks to discredit the teaching of Moses, we know for certain that he is a false prophet; and whatever he did, was done by secret arts and with the aid of witchcraft, and he is to be strangled.

ALBO, *IKKARIM*

Translation by Isaac Husik

BOOK III, CHAPTER 13

We now desire to investigate whether it is possible that a given divine law of a given people should change in time, or whether it can not change but must be eternal.

It would seem that a divine law can not change, for reasons based upon a consideration of the giver, of the recipient, and of the law itself. Considering the giver, it would seem inconceivable that God who is the giver should desire one thing at one time and then change His will and desire its opposite at another time. It can not be that God should desire right at one time and wrong at another. Why then should God change His law for another?

Considering the recipient, we can not see why, since the nation is the same, the law should change in the course of time. We can not use the analogy of the individual and say that just as the rules of health for a child are different from those of a young man and those of a young man are different from those of an old man, as the time changes from childhood to youth and from youth to old age, so the rules of divine law must change with the times. For while it may be true in the case of an individual that his behavior is bound to change as the period of his life changes, the rule does not apply to a political group in which there is no such change from childhood to youth and to old age, for the convention of law is that all the times are the same. Hence we can not see that divine law should change by reason of the recipient.

Now if we consider the law itself, it would seem that since the purpose of the divine Torah is to teach men intellectual conceptions and true opinions, there can be no reason for its changing at any time. For true opinions can never change. Monotheism can not be true at one time and dualism or trinitarianism at another, any more than it is possible that a thing that has already been should change and not have been. It seems clear therefore that there can be no change in a divine law, whether we consider the law itself, the giver, or the recipient.

Nevertheless, if we consider the matter carefully, we shall find that it does not necessarily follow that a divine law can not be changed for one and the same people. For though the ideas themselves do not change, nor the giver, a change may occur on the part of the recipient. A perfect agent does his work in a manner corresponding to the preparation of the recipient. As that changes, the work of the agent changes, no doubt. Nor does this imply any change in the agent. A physician prescribes a certain regimen to his patient for a term known to himself, which he does not reveal to the patient. When that time passes and the patient gets better, the physician changes his regimen, allows what he prohibited before and forbids what he formerly permitted. The patient has no reason to wonder at this, for it does not imply any change in the physician's original intention or imperfection in the physican because he did not in the first place prescribe a regimen good for all time. When the physician prescribed the first regimen, he knew the length of time that the patient would have to conform to it. And though he did not say anything to the patient, he knew when that regimen would have to change, estimating as he did, from the condition of the patient, the time required to pass from disease to health. When he prescribed the first regimen, his purpose was to improve the condition of the patient so that he might be ready and prepared to follow the second regimen, which was to come after its work had been done by the first. And when the time came he changed the first regimen for another which he had in mind in the first place.

In the same way it argues no defect in God if He did not give at the beginning a law and a regimen that would suffice for all times. For when He gave the Torah He knew that that law would suffice for the time which in His wisdom He estimated would be required to prepare the recipients and improve their condition so as to fit them to receive the second regimen, though He did not reveal this purpose of His to any one. When the time comes, He gives the second regimen, which may contain rules different from and opposed to the first, but it was in His mind from the beginning. On the contrary, as it would show a defect in the physician if he prescribed solid and substantial food, like bread and meat and wine, for convalescents and children and infants before they grow up or are strong enough to stand such food, so it would argue a defect in the giver of the Torah if He gave the same law for all time to novices and to habituates. The proper thing is to change it according to the change in the capacity of the recipients. As soon as they are accustomed to an easy regimen, He can advance them to a more difficult one, suitable to their nature, like bread and meat and wine and other substantial foods which, though unsuitable for children, are fit and proper for adults. And children, as they grow up and become accustomed to solid foods, change their mode of sustenance. A teacher treats his pupil in a similar manner. First he trains him in matters easy to understand until he gets accumstomed to study little by little. Then he advances him to a more difficult and more profound plane for which he was not fit at the beginning before he became accustomed to study.

And if one object that it is not fitting to suppose that God's power is so limited that He can not prescribe a rule of conduct that will embrace all men, young and old, for all time, his objection would be analogous to the question that is asked, why did not God create all men righteous and eager to worship Him so that there be not one that is crooked? assuming that this would show perfection. The fact is not so, as Maimonides has shown, touching this and similar matters, in the thirty-second chapter of the third part of the *Guide of the Perplexed.* We do not say that perfection would require that God should have created all animals with reason to praise Him, because it is contrary to nature. Similarly we do not say that it would be a credit to God if all things happened by way of miracle and not in accordance with natural law. For all theologians are agreed that nature is precious to God and He does not change it except when it is absolutely necessary. We are here discussing this subject as reason demands and as a study of the Torah suggests. Any one who chooses may disagree and insist that God constantly creates miracles in opposition to nature. When the Rabbis say that the Torah is a panacea and a drug that gives life to all,[1] they mean for all the organs of the body. Similarly they say that[2] "the words of the Torah are a salve for the eye, an emollient for the heart, and a medicine for the bowels. . . as is said, and health to all their flesh,'"[3]but they do not say that it is the same for all men, women and children, and for all time. The truth of our statement will be made clear in the following chapter.

NOTES

1. Kiddushin 30b.
2. Vayyikra Rabbah, XII, 3.
3. Prov. 4, 22.

BOOK III, CHAPTER 14

If we investigate the divine laws of the world, we find that they changed from time to time, forbidding what was originally permitted, and then again permitting what had been forbidden. Thus in the beginning Adam was given a few commandments which, according to the tradition of our Rabbis, mankind followed till the time of Noah. Noah was permitted to eat animal food, which was forbidden to Adam. Originally animal food was forbidden to Adam, plants alone being permitted, "Behold, I have given you every herb yielding seed, which is upon the face of all the earth, and every tree, in which is the fruit of a tree yielding seed—to you it shall be for food." [1] Later, Noah was given permission to eat animal food, "Every moving thing that liveth shall be for food for you; as the green herb have I given you all."[2] An additional commandment was given to him, forbidding him to eat a limb cut from the living animal. Abraham was given the additional commandment of circumcision. Moses received many other commandments. Also God prohibited certain marriages of relations which were permitted to the Noahites and permitted certain matters which were forbidden to the Noahites. Thus an Israelite may eat an animal after it is slaughtered even though it is still struggling, whereas a Noahite would deserve the penalty of death if he ate the animal before it died, for it would come under the prohibition of eating the limb of a living animal. Similarly a Noahite is punishable with death if he is guilty of robbery, even to the extent of less than a *perutah*,[3] not so an Israelite. Also a Noahite seeing another committing a robbery without preventing him is guilty of a capital crime. This is why all the inhabitants of Shechem deserved the punishment of death, because they saw Shechem committing a robbery and did not prosecute him, as Maimonides says in "Sefer Shofetim."[4] Also a Noahite who marries a half sister on the father's side goes unpunished, whereas an Israelite guilty of such an act is punishable with death . . . .

The opinion of Maimonides is that the Torah will never change in whole or in part. Hence one of his principal dogmas is the immutability of the Torah. Now inasmuch as we have found that the divine laws which existed before Moses did undergo changes in the matter of permission and prohibition, immutability would be a principle peculiar to the Mosaic law. Maimonides[5] bases this dogma upon the scriptural passage, "Thou shalt not add thereto, nor diminish from it."[6] The reason he gives, in the *Guide of the Perplexed*,[7] is because a thing which is harmonious and perfect can not have anything added to it or taken away from it, as the harmony and perfection would be destroyed. But the

Torah is perfect, as Scripture testifies, "The law of the Lord is perfect, restoring the soul,"[7a] therefore it can never be changed. This is the gist of Maimonides' opinion in this matter, as expressed in a number of places.

But his ideas on this point require careful consideration in respect to their source. The dogma is surely of great importance, nevertheless we must know whether Maimonides derives it from tradition or from his own ratiocination. If the former, we must gracefully accept it, but if it is the latter, we have something to say about it. . . .

The Bible merely warns us not to add to or take away from the commandments on our own account. But what can there be to prevent God Himself from adding or diminishing as His wisdom decrees? As for the argument that the equal and the mean can never be added to or taken away from, that applies to the true and absolute mean, whereas the relative mean may very well change with the nature of the recipients.[8] Thus food that is fitting for a child is milk, while for an adult, the proper food is bread and meat and wine. . . .

NOTES

1. Gen. 1, 29.
2. Ibid. 9, 3.
3. A small coin, one eighth of an *as* (אִיסָר).
4. The fourteenth book of Maimonides' Code, Yad ha-Hazakah, is called "Sefer Shofetim," Book of Judges. The discussion of the Noachian laws is found in the last division of the Sefer Shofetim, entitled "Hilkot Melakim," Rules concerning Kings, chapters 9 and 10, and the statement in the text about Shechem is found in ch. 9, paragraph 14. See also J. E., s. v. Laws, Noachian, VII, 648.
5. Commentary on Chapter Helek, art. 9; Madda', ch. 9.
6. Deut. 13, 1.
7. III, 34.

7a. Ps. 19, 8.

8. For the relative and absolute mean, see Arist. *Nic. Eth.* II, 6, p. 1105b 28f.: *ἐν παντὶ δὴ συνεχεῖ καί διαιρετῷ ἔστι λαβεῖν τὸ μὲν πλεῖον τὸ δ' ἔλαττον τὸ δ' ἴσον, καὶ ταῦτα ἢ κατ' αὐτὸ τὸ πρᾶγμα ἢ πρὸς ἡμᾶς. τὸ δ' ἴσον μέσον τι . . . λέγω δὲ τοῦ μὲν πράγματος μέσον τὸ ἴσον ἀπέχον . . . ὅπερ ἐστὶν ἕν καὶ ταὐτὸν πᾶσιν, πρὸς ἡμᾶς δὲ . . . τοῦτο δ' οὐχ ἕν, οὐδὲ ταὐτὸν πᾶσιν.*

BOOK III, CHAPTER 19

From what we have said it is clear that a divine law can not change in respect to the three general principles which we mentioned. For when they heard the first two commandments from God, they were convinced of the reality of revelation and the existence of God who gave the commandments, also that He takes notice of, and punishes those who transgress His will, while He rewards those who fear Him, freeing them from bondage, as they saw how He punished the Egyptians and delivered the Israelites. The expression, "Who brought thee out of the land of Egypt, out of the house of bondage,"[1] shows the extent of divine providence, from which we conclude that we must not worship any one else even as a mediator. All this is contained in the expression, "Thou shalt have no other gods before Me," as we have seen. It is clear, therefore, as we have written in the twenty-fifth chapter of the First Book, that the difference between divine laws does not lie in their general principles. What still remains to be explained is whether the other commandments in the law of Moses may be changed by a prophet or not.

Now as there is a difference between the first two commandments and the others in that the former were spoken by God without the mediation of Moses, while the latter, though heard from God, were explained by Moses, so we can say that there is a difference between the ten commandments and the other precepts in that the ten commandments were heard from God, whereas the others were commanded by Moses. And as we have found that the last eight commandments of the decalogue may be changed by a prophet temporarily, so we may say that the other precepts of the Mosaic law can be changed by a prophet even permanently. And it is for this reason that they could abolish counting the months from Nisan in the time of the second temple by the command of Jeremiah, as we have seen.

But if it were true that any prophet or any one who professes to be a prophet is authorized to change any commandment of the divine law except those of the decalogue, or to say that the time has come to change it, the entire law would fall and it would have no permanence at all. On the other hand, if we say that no prophet has the right to change the commandments of the divine law given by another prophet, it would cause grave difficulty, for if this were the case, then why did Israel believe Moses when he changed the Noachian law which they had received by a continuous tradition from their ancestors, who were prophets?. . .

Our opinion therefore is, as the matter appears from an investigation of the Torah, that one is not permitted to budge from his traditional belief which came down to him by a continuous chain of communication, going back to the teaching of a prophet, provided he is convinced that the principles, fundamental and derivative, of the belief in question are true, as we explained in the First Book of this treatise,[2] unless he is absolutely certain that God desires to abolish the words of the first prophet from whom the traditional belief came down to him.

The manner in which one can have this latter certainty is by having an absolute verification of the genuine character of the second divine messenger. This proof can not consist in the performance of miracles, since we see many other persons who are not prophets performing miracles either by creating an illusion or by magic, like the Egyptian magicians, or through some other art. Moreover, we find that those prophets who are not sent to announce a law also perform miracles, hence we can not tell whether the miracle performed by the person in question shows that he has been sent to promulgate a law, or whether it merely indicates that he is a prophet. It is clear therfore that a miracle is no proof that the messenger is genuine, as was explained in the eighteenth chapter of the First Book, but the proof must be derived from the law of Moses for the reason given in the eleventh chapter of the First Book. Accordingly, if his misssion is proved in the same manner as was that of Moses, it is proper to listen to the second prophet even if he desires to abolish the precepts of the first.

This is the reason why the Israelites believed the words of Moses, even though some of his precepts were opposed to the Noachian law, as we said before, which they knew by tradition as divine. But they were absolutely convinced that God desired to promulgate a law through Moses; else they would not have had the right to budge from their tradition, from the law which came down to them by an unbroken tradition from their ancestors, going back ultimately to Adam and Noah. This conviction was reached in two ways. They felt certain that the last prophet, who was introducing changes, was greater than the first; and they verified the genuineness of the last prophet's mission as firmly as that of the first. Both of these kinds of proof applied absolutely in Moses' case.

He was a greater prophet than those who lived before him, for he performed wonderful miracles, such as had never been performed before. The Bible makes this clear when it says, "And I appeared unto Abraham, unto Isaac, and unto Jacob, as God Almighty, but by My name *Jhvh* I made Me not known to them."[3] The meaning is that God revealed Himself to Moses with His great name, by means of which he was able to perform miracles openly and publicly, changing the laws of nature, such as had never been done for the earlier prophets, who could only perform invisible miracles, to deliver them from death in time of famine, and from the sword in time of war. The mission of Moses was verified, because all Israel heard the voice speaking to Moses, as the Bible says, "That the people may hear when I speak with thee";[4] for I desire to promulgate a law through thee, and this will make them believe what thou sayest. For this reason Israel was obliged to believe his words, even though he were to abolish all that was said by the prophets before him, since his mission was verified, as we explained in the eighteenth chapter of the First Book, and his prophetic grade was superior to all the rest, as we explained in chapter ten of this Book.

Whether in the future there may come another prophet who will abolish the words of Moses and whom we shall be obliged to believe—this can happen only, as we have said, in one of two ways. Either the new prophet will be proved to be greater than Moses, or his mission will be verified as was that of Moses. Now the Bible says that there can not be a prophet greater than Moses, "If there be a prophet among you, I the Lord do make Myself known unto him in a vision,. . . My servant Moses is not so; he is trusted in all My house; with him do I speak mouth to mouth."[5] It seems then that Moses' prophecy is superior to any other. And at the end of the Torah we read that there will never arise another prophet like Moses whom God knew face to face. This is the degree which Moses asked for and it was granted to him, as we read at the end of the Torah, "And there hath not arisen a prophet since in Israel like unto Moses, whom the Lord knew face to face."[6]

Therefore if any prophet or any one professing to be a prophet should come and say that he has attained a higher grade than Moses, which is impossible, and should say that we should listen to him and abolish any of the commands of Moses, not as a temporary measure merely, we will refuse to listen to him, but will tell him that he must prove his superiority to Moses and all the prophets who came after him and who were his disciples, by performing miracles greater and more wonderful than those performed by Moses and all the other prophets; by humiliating all those who dispute with him, as Moses did to Korah and his assembly; by triumphing over and overcoming all the wise men of his age and all his opponents, as Moses did to Pharaoh and to all the magicians and wise men of Egypt; by performing miracles in public and in the presence of all the people, as Moses did in the presence of Pharaoh and of all Israel; and by maintaining the miracles a long time, as Moses caused to go before the people a pillar of cloud by day and a pillar of fire by night, and caused the manna to come down for forty years without ceasing, except on the Sabbath day, when it did not come down, in order to show the sanctity of the Sabbath and the truth of his words; and by fulfilling many other conditions of this kind, without which he can not make good his claim.

The reason the Israelites obeyed Jeremiah and abolished counting the months from Nisan, as we have seen, is perhaps because they based their action upon the interpretation of a biblical verse, as we find in the Tosafot[7] on the first chapter of the treatise Megillah,[8] that the reason Ezra changed the written characters when he returned from the exile was because of his interpretation of a biblical verse. "He shall write him a copy of this law (משנה התורה),"[9] he interpreted to mean, a writing that is destined to change (*mishne*, משנה, from the rabbinic *shanah*, שנה, to change). Or it may be that they obeyed Jeremiah because his precept did not concern any of the ten commandments, or because there was no intention to abolish any of the Mosaic commandments, but to commemorate the second redemption as they commemorated the first. For they had a tradition that it should be commemorated, provided that the exodus from Egypt should not be ignored, as the Rabbis say, "Not that the exodus from Egypt should be entirely removed."[10]

But if a prophet or one professing to be a prophet should come and say that he has been sent by God to promulgate a law, abolishing permanently the words of Moses, he must not be believed so far as concerns the ten commandments, since they were heard from God. But neither must he be believed in respect to the other commandments outside of the decalogue, unless he can verify his mission as Moses verified his, when all Israel heard the voice saying to Moses, "Go say to them: Return ye to your tents. But as for thee, stand thou here by Me, and I will speak unto thee all the commandment, and the statutes, and the ordinances, which thou shalt teach them."[11]

This is the reason why God revealed Himself to all Israel and spoke to them face to face, in order that Moses' mission should be absolutely verified. Therefore God said to Moses, "Lo, I come unto thee in a thick cloud, that the people may hear when I speak with thee, and may also believe thee forever."[12] The meaning is: God said to Moses that He desired to reveal Himself to him face to face despite the fact that he (Moses) was in a thick cloud, i.e. wrapped in the coarseness and obscurity of matter and unworthy of such a dignity, for the sake of two advantages to follow: one was with reference to the immediate present, namely, "that the people may hear when I speak with thee," and obey all his commandments even if they are opposed to the Noachian law. The other concerned the future: that they should believe in Moses forever as the messenger of God.

Hence they will not listen to any prophet who may come to abolish the words of Moses, unless they hear from God that he was sent for that purpose. For to obey a prophet and permanently violate a Mosaic command, is like obeying a prophet and violating that which one has heard from God Himself. In such a case one must not obey a prophet. It is for a thing of this kind that the prophet Iddo[13] was punished by being devoured by a lion, because he obeyed another prophet and violated that which he himself heard from God. It is clear therefore that we must believe no one, whether he be a prophet or one professing to be a prophet, if he says that he was sent by God to abolish the words of Moses, or if he says that they are temporary and that the time has come for their abolition, unless his mission can be proved as publicly as the mission of Moses was proved in the presence of six hundred thousand people.

As to the question whether there will ever be in the future such a great publicity as the first, when all Israel will hear the voice of the Lord God speaking to them out of the midst of the fire, the opinion of our Rabbis is that there will be such an event. Thus we read in Midrash Hazit,[14] on the biblical verse, "Let him kiss me with the kisses of his mouth,"[15] "Said Rabbi Judah, when the Israelites heard the first two commandments, the Torah was impressed upon their minds and they learned without forgetting. Then they came to Moses and said, Moses our teacher, You be the messenger between us, as is said, 'Speak thou with us and we will hear.'[16] Thereupon they learned and later forgot. They said then, as Moses who is made of flesh and blood is temporary, so is his teaching temporary, i.e. it is forgotten. Hence they went back to Moses and said: we should wish that God would reveal Himself to us again, 'Let Him kiss me with the kisses of His mouth.' Said Moses in reply, not now, but in the future He will, as is written, 'I will put My law in their inward parts.'"[17] It is clear from this that the Rabbis are of the opinion that in the future all Israel will experience a second revelation like the first, which will come directly from God without any mediation.

My own opinion is that since this does not necessarily follow from an interpretation of the biblical verses, it is more proper to say that this matter depends upon the will of God. According to the Torah it belongs neither to the category of the necessary nor to that of the impossible. Our position at present is that of a prophet who heard something from God. He must not listen to any other prophet who advises him to act contrary to the command he himself received from God, unless he himself hears to the same effect from God. And even if we can verify the mission of a new prophet as the mission of Moses was verified, we will refuse to listen to him if he bids us abolish any one of the ten commandments which we ourselves heard from God.

In this way we can reply to our opponents, who argue from the verse in the Torah: "I will raise them up a prophet from among their brethren, like unto thee; and I will put My words in his mouth, and he shall speak unto them all that I shall command him."[18] This verse signifies, they say, that a law will be given through the new prophet as it was given through Moses; also that "from among their brethren" means from the brethren of Israel and not from Israel itself. Our reply to these men is that granting that, according to the verse quoted, a prophet will come to give a law, as Moses did before, the expression, "I will raise them up a prophet. . . like unto thee," signifies that his "raising up" and the verification of his prophetic mission, which is a fundamental dogma of divine law, as we have seen, must be of the same kind as the verification of Moses' prophetic mission, which took place in the presence of six hundred thousand people, so that there was no doubt and no suspicion of any kind.

NOTES

1. Ex. 20, 2.
2. Ch. 15.
3. Ex. 6, 3.
4. Ex. 19, 9.
5. Num. 12, 6.
6. Deut. 34, 10.
7. "Critical and explanatory glosses on the Talmud, printed in almost all editions on the outer margin and opposite Rashi's notes." See J.E., s.v.
8. This quotation goes back to R. Solomon Ibn Adret who, in his commentary on Megillah 2b, quotes the statement from Tosafot, but it is not found in our Tosafot. There were a good many collections of Tosafot of which those which happened to come into the hands of the early printers in the fifteenth and the sixteenth centuries appear in our editions. Many of the old authorities had other collections of this kind.
9. Deut. 17, 18.
10. Berakot 12b.
11. Deut. 5, 27-28.
12. Ex. 19, 9.
13. See above, p. 155, note 3.
14. See above, p. 12, note 1. The citation is found in the first section, ed. Lublin, p. 123.
15. Cant. 1, 2.
16. Ex. 20, 19.
17. Jer. 31, 33.
18. Deut. 18, 18.

The Tenth Principle

Omniscience

INTRODUCTION

The threat to the notion of the unity of God posed by the doctrine of divine omniscience often comes as somewhat of an intellectual shock to persons not acquainted with the writings of medieval philosophers. The problem is a formidable one. If God is an absolute unity admitting of no attributes or predicates whatsoever, then it is difficult to understand how God may possess knowledge. Knowledge is something with which a person or being is endowed, something distinct and separate which is superimposed or added. It follows, that, logically, one cannot speak of God as a simple substance and then proceed to deny this simplicity by positing knowledge as an attribute. Moreover, God is unchanging. Were knowledge to be ascribed to the Deity, it would seem that the knowledge ascribed to God could not be described as unchanging. For God to know any transient thing implies that His knowledge changes in a manner commensurate with changes which occur in that which is known. God cannot know that something now exists if it has not come into existence or if it has been destroyed. Yet, modification in the state of divine knowledge is tantamount to change in the nature of God.

On the other hand, the concept of divine perfection demands that God be viewed as omniscient. Ignorance is certainly an imperfection. Furthermore, in the absence of knowledge of the deeds of man, reward and punishment are impossible. The religionist is thus caught on the horns of a philosophical dilemma. Either he must affirm the unity of a God who is less than perfect or else he must affirm the perfection of a God who is not a unity.

In order to bridge the gap, some Neoplatonist philosophers posited the existence of a Logos, a transcendental intellect which stands between God and man. Wisdom and providental guardianship are ascribed to this intermediary rather than to God Himself. Thus, no violence is done to the notion of God as an absolute unity, while knowledge which is necessary for the governance of the universe is ascribed to a lesser being. It is but a short step from this view to the notion that the Logos is itself divine. This was the view of the early Church Fathers, who interpreted the opening passage of the book of John as affirming the position that the Logos is a member of the Trinity, a position antithetical to the doctrine of divine unity.

Aristotelian philosophers opted for a different solution in defending the unity of God. Some maintained that God cannot know anything which is transient and changeable. His knowledge, they maintained, is limited to knowledge of that which is constant and unchanging; i.e., the only created objects of which God has knowledge are the heavenly spheres. The notion of divine perfection is preserved and defended by arguing that all transient beings are imperfect; hence knowledge of them is itself an imperfection which is not to be ascribed to God. This, however, leaves unresolved the question of knowledge as an attribute, a problem which threatens the concept of divine unity. As a result of this problem, other Aristotelians were led to concede that all forms of knowledge are incompatible with the oneness of God. Accordingly, they asserted that God can know only His own essence and maintained that it is only God's knowledge of Himself which constitutes perfection.

Maimonides resolves this problem by drawing upon his already formulated doctrine that the essence of God's nature is unfathomable by the human mind. Both assertions made in positing the dilemma are correct. God cannot be ignorant, for that would be an imperfection in His nature; God cannot possess knowledge, for that would compromise His oneness. No attribute may be ascribed to God, neither that of knowledge nor that of ignorance. Only negative attributes may be ascribed to God. Thus one may not, strictly speaking, describe God as being possessed of knowledge. But, by the same token, He is not ignorant. His "knowledge" is identical with His essence; He possesses "knowledge" by virtue of His essence and not in a manner comparable to the way mortals possess knowledge. The nature of this "knowledge" cannot be comprehended by the human mind precisely because it is identical with His essence, which assuredly cannot be fathomed by the human mind. This position was adopted by Albo as well.

Ibn Daud perceives a contradiction between absolute freedom of the will and God's foreknowledge. It is inconceivable that a just God would punish man if he were not master of his own actions. Therefore, man must be free. Ibn Daud maintains, however, that this entails a significant modification of the notion of divine omniscience. If man is free, and if freedom and foreknowledge are incompatible, it must follow that God does not have prior knowledge of man's choices. Nevertheless, argues Ibn Daud, this in no way constitutes an imperfection in the nature of God. If a contingent action is truly contingent, he contends, it cannot be known in advance. To know an action as contingent is to know it as it is.

Hence, not to be able to foretell that which is contingent is not ignorance. Therefore, this does not constitute an imperfection in the nature of God. Indeed, it is God who created the contingent and endowed it with its nature.

Gersonides resolves the matter in a similar, but somewhat different, manner. He agrees with Ibn Daud that man is free and that God's knowledge is limited in a certain sense. God has absolute knowledge of universals, which are eternal and not subject to change. God's knowledge of particulars is somewhat different. He knows them in one sense, but does not know them in another. Human events are ordered by the heavenly bodies. However, man is endowed with reason and will, and he may choose to perform actions which counteract that which is otherwise ordained for him by the heavenly bodies. Thus human events are in part determined and in part the result of free choice. God's knowledge of particulars is similarly bifurcated. God knows particulars insofar as they are ordered, but He does not know them insofar as they are contingent upon human choice. God knows particulars by virtue of His knowledge of the universal order. Hence, He knows them only to the extent that they are ordered by nature. This is not an imperfection in the nature of God because He knows the contingent in its true nature.

Crescas adopts precisely the opposite position. Confronted, as were Ibn Daud and Gersonides, with what he perceived to be a contradiction between divine omniscience and human freedom, Crescas was prepared to sacrifice the notion of human freedom in order to affirm God's omniscience. Crescas is not a fatalist. His position is very similar to what, in contemporary philosophy, is known as "soft determinism." All actions are caused. Human effort and divine commands are themselves causes. God has full knowledge of all causes and hence knows in advance how man will act. This leaves Crescas with the problem of divine justice. How can God punish man for actions resulting from causes over which man has no control? Crescas answers that punishment is a natural consequence of wrongdoing. Fire burns the person who comes into contact with it. The burn is not a punishment. Such a phenomenon is a necessary result of a physical act. Similarly, reward and punishment flow naturally from human actions which are governed by human will. Nevertheless, an act performed as the result of coercion is not punished because it is not the product of man's will. Acts of will lead naturally to reward and punishment even though, in a fundamental sense, the will is itself determined.[1]

[1] See also the introduction to the Eleventh Principle.

IBN DAUD, *EMUNAH RAMAH*

Translation by Norbert M. Samuelson

PART II, BASIC PRINCIPLE 6, CHAPTER 2

[Which Deals] With The Sources Of Goods And Evils[1], The Ordering And Enumeration Of Causes[2], And An Explanation Of Providence And The Secret Of Ability.[3] We Presented[4] This Book For The Sake And Because Of [The Subject Matter Of This] Chapter, Which Is The First Principle Of Thought And The Final [End] Of Action.[5]

I say that God, may He be exalted, knows His essence. This was already explained before. His knowledge of everything that is more abstract than matter or what is like matter, i.e. [than what has] the possibility of existence, is more perfect. [The reason for this is] that we have already explained that lack of knowledge [occurs] with respect to matter. However every lack and every evil is born by what is in a thing potentially, and everything that is more remote from that which a certain thing possesses potentially is more perfect and more remote from the ways of deficiency and what is short of perfection.

Since God[6], may He be exalted, conceives of His essence and His essence, may He be exalted, is the most esteemed of the attributes of perfection and since God, may He be exalted, conceives of it with respect to the most perfect [instance] of true knowledge, behold He also knows that His perfection is not only directed at His essence. Rather there is a respect in which it overflows from Him to something else and from [that] something else to something else so that existents are remote from Him in order. It is known that[7] He conceives of everything whose existence is remote from his in order[8] with deficiency[9] [that is] proportional to the remoteness [of the thing known], and its ordering also is [proportionally] short of perfection.

The conception of their deficiency [has] very many levels. What is above all of these ordered things in level moves them. Also what is below them in level moves them, so that existents have two extremes. One [can] not imagine the like of [one][10] extreme in its[11] perfection and its remoteness. With respect to its holiness it is clear of every manner of deficiency. It moves all things without [itself] being moved. [Conversely][12] one [can] not imagine the like of [the other] extreme in its deficiency and its remoteness with respect to the perfection of all of them.[13] It is moved by all [other] things through ordering and through mediators without [itself] moving [any]thing. This is what we call "hyle". All of this already has been explained. . .[14]

The order of existence necessitated that [some things] at one extreme in it have more virtue, [others] at [the other] extreme [have] more vice, and [others] are in between [the two extremes]. At times [either] in the mixture [that resulted from] the issuing of semen or from the womb or [from] both of them [someone] has little warmth and [his] heart is colder than is appropriate in consequence of which [that] man is stupid and simple, without knowing or fearing anything. [Such a man] neither sees that the good is good nor that the base is base. He is fervent about his passions, acting (in a way that) is good for those who are blind.[15] In order to oppose all of these base characteristics God, may He be exalted, established men who are free from all of these [base] characteristics [who] brought to those infected by them the commandments and warnings of God, may He be exalted. Afterwards [for] those who are infected by these base characteristics to oppose them is not completely impossible, for if it were so, God may He be exalted, would not command something impossible. Also if it were necessary in all respects for man to do them,[16] as (man) breathes by drawing the cold air to his heart and sending forth the warm air in it, it would not have been necessary to introduce the commandments of God, may He be exalted, about this, just as His commandments do not come to us with [the stipulation] to breathe in order to preserve our lives [even] though it is possible.

We already made known to you in the first treatise that just as God, may He be exalted, created things and gave to them certain necessary attributes like rationality to man — because when one is a man he is rational in all respects, i.e. [he is] internally rational and he can conceive — and just as He created things and gave to them impossible attributes like rationality to a stone, so God created things and gave to them certain possible attributes. This is no deficiency in His knowledge, may He be exalted, because there are two kinds of possibility. [One kind of] possibility is possibility with respect to ignorance, an example of which is whether the king of Babylon died today or is alive. [The reason that it is a possibility is] because we the men of Spain do not know this [state of affairs). Rather both alternatives are equal to us. This is because of our ignorance of what is remote from us. But since [this] matter in itself is not possible, of necessity one of the alternatives is correct and God, may He be exalted, knows in [cases] like this that one of the alternatives is necessary as it is in itself. For example [He knows] whether there will be an eclipse this month or not. [The reason for this is] that this [event] is possible to those who are ignorant of Astronomy and the equinox of the stars, but in itself one of the alternatives is necessary, and God, may He be exalted, knows the necessary alternative. God already made this known to the masters of Astronomy and equinoxes. To them it is not a possibility as it is a possibility to the masses. All the more so would it [not][17] be to God a possibility, because this kind of possibility which is [a possibility] with respect to ignorance does not occur to God, may He be praised and exalted.[18]

The second [kind of] possibility is [that] which is possible because God, may He be exalted, gave it possibility. He created it [as] a thing that [can] bear one or the other of two contrary attributes. How a possibility like this occurs or [does] not [occur] is not remote from God's knowledge, may He be exalted. [In both cases] He, may He be exalted, created that possibility. If a sophist would be sophistical and say 'Is God, may He be exalted, ignorant of the end of the matter?', we [would] say [in response that] this is not ignorance. The desire of he who says this[19] is to reverse all of the attributes. For example [he wants to say] that He gives to eclipses either necessity or impossibility in all respects and [he claims that] God did not create anything that has a possible attribute or its contrary. By this [kind of reasoning would follow] the destruction of the world and the corruption of civilization in this world as well as life in the world to come. [The reason for this is] that it [would be] vanity for a man to plough and to build buildings and to plant plants and to subjugate beasts and to increase acts of mercy and to choose weapons with which to fight, since what will happen already is decreed. Similarly it [would be] vanity to worship God, may He be exalted, since prosperity or its opposite already is decreed. The matter is clear that the truth is the opposite of this. [The reason for this is] that God created contingents [that are] possible and He knows the contingents such as eclipses. [The reason for] this is that all of their causes are not from Him by a primary intention. Rather some of them are from Him, may He be exalted, by a primary intention, and this is by His knowledge of all of their attributes which [renders] necessary for them what is necessary and [renders] impossible for them what is impossible. And some of them are entrusted to nature by the will of God, may He be exalted,so that they benefit he who properly uses them and they harm he who uses them in [a way that is] less or more than what is proper. God, may He be exalted,[20] already decreed that there be causes in this way. Our rabbis, may they be remembered for a blessing, said concerning this [that] "everything is in the hands of heaven except thorns [and] snares".[21,22] As it is said, "Thorns [and] snares are in the way of someone wicked; he who watches his soul keeps far from them".[23] In this way one must guard against those foods and drugs that cause death.

The causes of some of them are accidents. Also it is proper to guard against these [states of affairs]. Also their content is transmitted to man. Therefore there are religious warnings to guard against them in which they are described as being contingencies, as when He, may He be exalted, said, "Who is the man who is fearful and faint of heart etc.[24]"[25] and the rest of what is mentioned in that portion. Similarly (the same point is made) when He, may He be exalted, said "When you build a new house, then you should make a parapet for your roof[26]"[27]. I have already mentioned in the preceeding treatise what is testified concerning some of these states of affairs being contingencies to God, may He be exalted. [An example would be] the statement of David, peace be unto him, "Your servant has indeed heard that saul seeks to come to Keilah to destroy the city on my account. Will [the men of Keilah] deliver me up? etc."[28] He repeats the question and says, "Will the citizens of Keilah deliver up me and my men into the hand of Saul? And The Lord said, They will deliver up."[29] [It is the case] that the meaning of "they will deliver up" here in the response of God, may He be exalted, is that it is possible that they will do this. Therefore [David] benefits from being diligent. As Scripture testifies, "And David and his men who were about six hundred arose and went forth from Keilah and went where they would go. And it was told to Saul that David[30] fled[31] from Keilah, and he forebore to leave."[32] If [their capture at Keilah] were not contingent to God, may He be exalted, [David] would not have escaped from it.

In a certain respect the causes are of four kinds or in a certain [other] respect they are of one kind. [The explanation of] this is that some of them are divine, i.e. by a primary intention of God, may He be exalted, some of them are natural, some of them are accidental and some of them are voluntary. David, peace be unto him, already enumerated three in one passage by saying [the following]: "And David said, As the Lord lives, either the Lord will smite him"[33] — This is the divine kind which happens when the servant embarks on rebellion and the decree of God smites him [when] nature either does or does not decree this. — "or his day will come and he will die"[33] — This is the natural kind against which a servant has no power to guard himself — "Or he will descend in war and be swept away."[33] — This is the accidental kind against which the servant has the power to guard himself, and it is also in his hand to transmit himself into this [fate] and fall [victim to it). Concerning what is like it [Solomon] said, "Thorns and snares are in the way of a wicked person".[34] Also here are choices as [when] David came to Keilah and departed from it. There are many [texts] like these. Furthermore[35] also concerning the doing of the commandment and [its] violation there is choice. If it were not so, the prophets would not have come and they would have testified neither about reward nor about punishment, and the Torah would destroy the ways of goods and blessings. When it happens that certain evil accidents [which are either] accidental or natural are created from which follow shameful characteristics[36] and deeds, it is possible to oppose them.[37] Also there are different gradations of people who are subject to [these misfortunes]. [It is the case] that some [people] have no evil in them, so that they have no need to oppose [a bad character] while [others] of them accept it, [namely] he who is at an extreme distance from the good, so that opposition would not [even] benefit him a little. Even if he tries he will not succeed at [opposing it]. Between these two [extremes] there are enumerable intermediate gradations. For some [people] reproof is sufficient [to change them] and for [others] of them reprimand [is sufficient], and for [still others] of them chastisements and punishments [are sufficient].

Concerning the possibility of [either] the fear of God or rebellion [against God] in man, God may He be exalted, said [the following] to the nation when He testified to them in the Torah: "I call to testimony against you today the heavens and the earth etc.[38]"[39] Life [lies] in [obeying] the Torah and in the conquering of the [evil] inclination. Death [lies] in accidents which are in matter. The punishment is proper for not conquering one's [evil] inclination and the reward is proper for conquering [it].

He who opposes a shameful characteristic is near to God, may He be exalted. Concerning this our rabbis, may they be remembered for a blessing, said "Everything is in the hands of heaven except the fear of heaven".[40] When someone who seeks virtue conquers his beastly characteristics and he rules them even a little, a longing for this attaches [to him and] that longing leads him to additional conquest, and additional conquest adds to the longing. Then he will acquire for himself virtues and he will have no defect when he is strengthened in this by God and by the angels who are appointed to guard man, about some of whom it is said, "the angel who redeemed me from all evil etc."[41] [with] supervision and prosperity. This is what was said to Abimelech. "Also I know that you did this in the purity of your heart".[46] Concerning this our rabbis, may they be remembered for a blessing, said "If one comes to cleanse himself he is helped",[43] because the divine aspect governs over he who entrusts his spirit to Him.

When the opposite of this happens, he is far from [God]. He is forsaken to the evil of his [own] counsel. [The rabbis] say [the following] about this [matter]: "If one comes to defile himself he is given an opening".[44] Since choice is that to which the intellect and also the tradition testify, it is that by which a commandment befalls a nation, and [that] by which an oath departs from God, may He be exalted, when He said, "As I live, says the Lord,[45] I have no delight in the death of the wicked; rather [I desire] the wicked to turn away from his path that he may live".[46] It is proper to believe these verses according to their literal meaning, and not to rush to make an interpretation for them. And it is proper to interpret the verses that contradict them, for the truth is not in two extremities.

We already have made known to you that he who entrusts his spirit into the hand of God is supervised, since he tries to enter into the section of the notable substances, and the notable substances have supervision over existents in this world in general and over the human species in particular. Behold in all respects [the human species] is singled out by providence in great measure because of its diligence to entrust its spirit with Him. As we have said, "If one comes to cleanse himself he is helped".[47]

Concerning this providence that follows for those who entrust their spirit with Him, Scripture says [the following]: "I will make you walk in my statutes",[48] "And I will take away the heart of stone from your flesh[49] etc.",[50] and the like of these, particularly after the going forth of the principle of contact from the heart of man.

Concerning what exists without being guarded and what is delivered into the evil of one's [own] choice, [the following] is said: "And I will harden the heart of Pharaoh",[51] "for the Lord your God hardened his spirit",[52] which [means] being forsaken and abandoned after the going forth of the principle of evil from the heart of man. Concerning the providence that follows for those who entrust their spirit with Him, the prophet cries out saying, "Why O Lord do you make us err from your ways, hardening our heart from the fear of You?",[53] i.e. being forsaken and abandoned to bad advice.

When you investigate all of the verses [seemingly] about predestination, [you will see that] all of them depart in this way. Know concerning belief in choice that our ancestors said "everything is in the hands of heaven except the fear of heaven",[54] and some of the sages of the gaonim [who] followed them came [to understand] their words according to their literal meaning. They did not interpret them. Rather they believed their truth. When you examine the words of our master Saadia, may he be remembered for a blessing,[55] in his book *Beliefs and Opinions* and the words of other wise men of our nation, you will find that it is so.

NOTES

This chapter is from a joint project by Norbert Samuelson and Gershom Weiss to prepare a critical edition and English translation of the whole of *The Exalted Faith.* Their study is based on the following nine manuscripts of the Selomo Ben Labi Hebrew translation: Vatican mss. 259 and 341, British Museum ms. 1069, Montefiore ms. 274 at Jews College in London, Munich Hebrew ms. 201, Bodleian Mich. 57, and the Jewish Theological Seminary of America mss. 2238, 2239 and 2243. The *editio princeps* is Bodleian Mich. 57. In addition the Mantua ms. 81 of the Selomo Motot Hebrew translation was consulted. Wherever relevant, variations in meaning between any of these manuscripts and the *editio princeps* are noted.

1. I.e. states of affairs that are judged morally good or bad.
2. I.e. of the causes of these good and evil states of affairs.
3. Y^{e}KÔLÊT. I.e. Ibn Daud claims that he will present the solution to the problem of how creatures [notably humans] can have potentialities that need not be or not be realized given God's perfect power and knowledge. Although the term Y^{e}KÔLÊT can mean "free will", no such doctrine is discussed by Ibn Daud.
4. The British Museum ms. 1069 [henceforth referred to as ms. 1069] and the Jewish Theological Seminary of America ms. 2239 [henceforth referred to as ms. 2239] of the Shlomo Ben Labi translation read "we composed". The term "we" should be treated as an editorial we whose sole referent is Ibn Daud.
5. Ibn Daud elaborates upon the first half of this sentence in his introduction to the book as a whole where he also explains what he means by the second half of this sentence. The subject matter of the chapter is how God as final cause gives the best possible [i.e. perfect] moral ordering to the universe. Ibn Daud's deity is the first principle of his Aristotelian universe; hence God as orderer is the first principle of thought. Similarly Ibn Daud's deity is the ultimate end towards which all events are directed; hence God as moral agent, which is what the end of natural processes are in the ethics of an Aristotelian universe, is the final end of moral or practical action.
6. All mss. of the Ben Labi translation except the editio princeps [Oxford, Bodleian ms. mich. 57] read HARI'ŠÔN instead of HAŠHEM.
7. "It is known that" is missing from the Jews College Montefiore ms. 274 [henceforth referred to as ms. 274], the Jewish Theological Seminary of America ms. 2238 [henceforth referred to as ms. 2238], ms 1069 and the editio princeps.
8. Instead of "everything — in order" mss. 1069, 274 and the editio princeps read "them".
9. The deficiency resides in the objects known and not in how God kows them. Instances of God's knowledge are inferior or superior relative to the inferiority or superiority of what He knows. But in these instances the inferiority of His knowledge is the most perfect knowledge possible of the objects known.
10. I.e. God's essence.
11. "Its" is omitted from ms. 274 and from the *editio princeps.*
12. At this point the Mantua ms. 81 manuscript of the Shmuel Motot translation entitled 'EMUNAH HANISSA'AH [henceforth referred to as "Motot"] begins to include the material covered in this chapter.
13. I.e. this second extreme is so deficient as compared to everything else that the extent of its deficiency is inconceivable.
14. In Part I, chapter 2.
15. All mss. except the *editio princeps* and ms. 2239 read "ostriches". The Motot ms. reads "beasts". What Ibn Daud means is that the kind of person whom he is describing here acts like an irrational animal.
16. I.e. to perform acts which follow from one's character, be it noble or base.
17. Only the Motot manuscript includes "not".
18. Ms. 274 and ms. 51 read "God, may He be exalted, to give it".

19. Viz., what the sophist says.
20. "May He be exalted" is omitted from Vatican ms. 259 [henceforth referred to as ms. 259], ms. 341, ms. 274, Munich Hebrew ms. 201, ms. 2239 and the *editio princeps.*
21. Ms. 274 and the *editio princeps* read "except the fear of heaven, thorns and snares".
22. Babylonian Talmud, Baba Metzia 107b, Baba Batra 144b, Avodah Zarah 3b.
23. Proverbs 22:5.
24. "etc." is omitted from ms. 274 and the *editio princeps.*
25. Deuteronomy 20:8.
26. Ms. 259, ms. 1069 and ms. 2239 add "etc.".
27. Deuteronomy 22:8.
28. I Samuel 23:10-11.
29. I Samuel 23:12.
30. Ms. 274 and the *editio princeps* read "one".
31. The Biblical text reads "escaped".
32. I Samuel 23:13.
33. I Samuel 26:10.
34. Proverbs 22:5.
35. The *editio princeps* omits "Furthermore".
36. Ms. 341, ms. 274, ms. 2239 and the *editio princeps* read L^{e}MIDÔT instead of MIDÔT.
37. Viz. the consequent development of a bad character and bad actions from certain kinds of misfortunes.
38. "etc." is omitted from ms. 274, ms. 2238 and the *editio princeps.*
39. Deuteronomy 4:26.
40. Babylonian Talmud, Berachot 33b, Megillah 25a, Niddah 16b.
41. Genesis 48:16.
42. Genesis 20:6.
43. Babylonian Talmud, Shabbat 104a.
44. Babylonian Talmud, Shabbat 104a.
45. The Biblical text reads "my lord God".
46. Ezekiel 33:11.
47. Babylonian Talmud, Shabbat 104a.
48. Ezekiel 36:27.
49. "from your flesh" is omitted from ms. 341, ms. 2239 and the *editio princeps.*
50. Ezekiel 36:26.
51. Exodus 7:3.
52. Deuteronomy 2:3.
53. Isaiah 63:17.
54. Babylonian Talmud, Berachot 33b; Megillah 25a; Niddah 16b.
55. "may he be remembered for a blessing" is omitted from ms. 274 and the *editio princeps.*

MAIMONIDES, *MISHNEH TORAH*

Translation by Moses Hyamson

BOOK OF KNOWLEDGE, LAWS CONCERNING THE BASIC PRINCIPLES OF THE TORAH, CHAPTER 2

9. All beings, except the Creator, from the highest angelic form to the tiniest insect that is in the interior of the earth, exist by the power of God's essential existence. And as He has self-knowledge, and realizes His greatness, glory and truth, He knows all, and nought is hidden from Him.

10. The Holy One, blessed be He, realizes His true being, and knows it as it is, not with a knowledge external to Himself, as is our knowledge. For our knowledge and ourselves are separate. But as for the Creator, blessed be He, His knowledge and His life are One, in all aspects, from every point of view, and however we conceive Unity. If the Creator lived as other living creatures live, and His knowledge were external to Himself, there would be a plurality of deities, namely; He himself, His life, and His knowledge. This however, is not so. He is One in every aspect, from every angle, and in all ways in which Unity is conceived. Hence the conclusion that God is the One who knows, is known, and is the knowledge (of Himself)—all these being One. This is beyond the power of speech to express, beyond the capacity of the ear to hear, and of the human mind to apprehend clearly. Scripture, accordingly says "By the life of Pharaoh" and "By the life of thy soul" but not "By the life of the Eternal." The phrase employed is "As God liveth"; because the Creator and His life are not dual, as is the case with the life of living bodies or of angels. Hence too, God does not apprehend creatures and know them because of them, as we kenow them, but He knows them because of Himself. Knowing Himself, He knows everything, for everything is attached to Him, in His Being.

11. What has been said on this topic in these two chapters is but a drop in the ocean, compared with what has to be elucidated on this subject. The exposition of all the principles alluded to in these two chapters forms the so-called *Maaseh Mercabah*—"Account of the Divine Chariot" (Ezekiel Chap. 1).

12. The ancient sages enjoined us only to discuss these subjects privately, with one individual, and then only if he be wise and capable of independent reasoning. In this case, the heads of the topics are communicated to him, and he is instructed in a minute portion of the subject. It is left to him to develop the conclusions for himself and to penetrate to the depths of the subject. These topics are exceedingly profound; and not every intellect is able to grasp them. Solomon, in his wisdom, said, in regard to them, by way of parable: "The lambs[1] will be for thy clothing" (Prov. 27:26). Thus have the sages said, in the exposition of this parable, "matters that deal with the mystery of the universe shall be for thy garment, that is, for thee alone; do not expound them in public." So too, Solomon said concerning these topics "Let them be for thee alone and not for strangers with thee" (Prov. 5:17).

And he further said concerning these subjects "Honey and milk are under thy tongue" (Solomon's song 4:11). This text the ancient sages have thus explained, "The things that are like milk and honey shall be under thy tongue."

NOTES

1. A play upon כבשים which means "lambs" and כבשים "secrets."

MAIMONIDES, *MOREH NEVUKHIM*

Translation by Michael Friedlander

PART III, CHAPTER 16

The philosophers have uttered very perverse ideas as regards God's Omniscience of everything beside Himself; they have stumbled in such a manner that they cannot rise again, nor can those who adopt their views. I will further on tell you the doubts that led them to these perverse utterances on this question; and I will also tell you the opinion which is taught by our religion, and which differs from the evil and wrong principles of the philosophers as regards God's Omniscience.

The principal reason that first induced the philosophers to adopt their theory is this: at first thought we notice an absence of system in human affairs. Some pious men live a miserable and painful life, whilst some wicked people enjoy a happy and pleasant life. On this account the philosophers assumed as possible the cases which you will now hear. They said that only one of two things is possible, either God is ignorant of the individual or particular things on earth, and does not perceive them, or He perceives and knows them. These are all the cases possible. They then continued thus: If He perceives and knows all individual things, one of the following three cases must take place: (1.) God arranges and manages human affairs well, perfectly and faultlessly; (2.) He is overcome by obstacles, and is too weak and powerless to manage human affairs; (3.) He knows [all things] and can arrange and manage them, but leaves and abandons them, as too base, low, and vile, or from jealousy; as we may also notice among ourselves some who are able to make another person happy, well knowing what he wants for his happiness, and still in consequence of their evil disposition, their wickedness and jealousy against him, they do not help him to his happiness.— This is likewise a complete enumeration of all possible cases. For those who have a knowledge of a certain thing necessarily either (1.) take care of the thing which they know, and manage it, or (2.) neglect it (as we, *e.g.*, neglect and forget the cats in our house, or things of less importance); or (3.) while taking care of it, have not sufficient power and strength for its management, although they have the will to do so.

Having enumerated these different cases, the philosophers emphatically decided that of the three cases possible [as regards the management of a thing] by one who knows [that thing], two are inadmissible in reference to God—viz., want of power, or absence of will; because they imply either evil disposition or weakness, neither of which can by any means be attributed to Him. Consequently there remains only the alternative that God is altogether ignorant of human affairs, or that He knows them and manages them well. Since we, however, notice that events do not follow a certain order, that they cannot be determined by analogy, and are not in accordance with what is wanted, we conclude that God has no knowledge of them in any way or for any reason. This is the argument which led the philosophers to speak such blasphemous words. In the treatise "On Providence," by Alexander Aphrodisiensis, you will find the same as I have said about the different views of the philosophers, and as I have stated as to the source of their error.

You must notice with surprise that the evil into which these philosophers have fallen is greater than that from which they sought to escape, and that they ignore the very thing which they constantly pointed out and explained to us. They have fallen into a greater evil than that from which they sought to escape, because they refuse to say that God neglects or forgets a thing, and yet they maintain that His knowledge is imperfect, that He is ignorant of what is going on here on earth, that He does not perceive it. They also ignore, what they constantly point out to us, in as much as they judge the whole universe by that which befalls individual men, although, according to their own view, frequently stated and explained, the evils of man originate in himself, or form part of his material nature. We have already discussed this sufficiently. After having laid this foundation, which is the ruin of all good principles, and destroys the majesty of all true knowledge, they sought to remove the opprobrium by declaring that for many reasons it is impossible that God should have a knowledge of earthly things, for the individual members of a species can only be perceived by the senses, and not by reason; but God does not perceive by means of any of the senses. Again, the individuals are infinite, but knowledge comprehends and circumscribes the object of its action, and the infinite cannot be comprehended or circumscribed; furthermore, knowledge of individual beings, that are subject to change, necessitates some change in him who possesses it, because this knowledge itself changes constantly. They have also raised the following two objections against those who hold, in accordance with the teaching of Scripture, that God knows things before they come into existence. First, their theory implies that there can be knowledge of a thing that does not exist at all; secondly, it leads to the conclusion that the knowledge of an object *in potentiâ* is identical with the knowledge of that same object in reality. They have indeed come to very evil conclusions, and some of them assumed that God only knows the species, not the individual beings, whilst others went as far as to contend that God knows nothing beside Himself, because they believe that God cannot have more than one knowledge.

Some of the great philosophers who lived before Aristotle agree with us, that God knows everything, and that nothing is hidden from Him. Alexander also refers to them in the above-mentioned treatise; he differs from them, and says that the principal objection against this theory is based on the fact that we clearly see evils befalling good men, and wicked men enjoying happiness.

In short, you see that if these philosophers would find human affairs managed according to rules laid down by the common people, they would not venture or presume to speak on this subject. They are only led to this speculation because they examine the affairs of the good and the wicked, and consider them as being contrary to all rule, and say in the words of the foolish in our nation, "The way of the Lord in not right" (Ezek. xxxiii. 17).

After having shown that knowledge and Providence are connected with each other, I will now proceed to expound the opinions of thinkers on Providence, and then I shall attempt to remove their doubts as to God's knowledge of individual beings.

PART III, CHAPTER 19

It is undoubtedly an innate idea that God must be perfect in every respect and cannot be deficient in anything. It is almost an innate idea that ignorance in anything is a deficiency, and that God can therefore not be ignorant of anything. But some thinkers assume, as I said before, haughtily and exultingly, that God knows certain things and is ignorant of certain other things. They did so because they imagined that they discovered a certain absence of order in man's affairs, most of which are not only the result of physical properties, but also of those faculties which he possesses as a being endowed with free will and reason. The Prophets have already stated the proof which ignorant persons offer for their belief that God does not know our actions; viz., the fact that wicked people are seen in happiness, ease, and peace. This fact leads also righteous and pious persons to think that it is of no use for them to aim at that which is good and to suffer for it through the opposition of other people. But the Prophets at the same time relate how their own thoughts were engaged on this question, and how they were at last convinced that in the instances to which these arguments refer, only the end and not the beginning ought to be taken into account. The following is a description of these reflections (Ps. lxxiii. 11, *seq.*): "And they say, How does God know? and is there knowledge in the Most High? Behold, these are the ungodly who prosper in the world; they increase in riches. Verily I have cleansed my heart in vain, and washed my hands in innocence." He then continues, "When I thought to know this, it was too painful for me, until I went into the sanctuary of God; then understood I their end. Surely thou didst set them in slippery places; thou castedst them down into destruction. How are they brought into desolation, as in a moment! They are utterly consumed with terrors." The very same ideas have also been expressed by the prophet Malachi, for he says thus (Mal. iii. 13-18): "Your words have been stout against Me, saith the Lord. As you have said, It is vain to serve God; and what profit is it that we have kept His ordinance, and that we have walked mournfully before the Lord of hosts? And now we call the proud happy; yea, they that work wickedness are set up; yea, they that tempt God are even delivered. Then they that feared the Lord spake often one to another, &c. Then shall ye return and discern between the righteous and the wicked, between him that serveth God and him that serveth Him not." David likewise shows how general this view was in his time, and how it led and caused people to sin and to oppress one another. At first he argues against this theory and then he declares that God is omniscient. He says as follows:— "They slay the widow and the stranger, and murder the fatherless. Yet they say, The Lord shall not see, neither shall the God of Jacob regard it. Understand, ye brutish among the people, and ye fools, when will you be wise? He that planted the ear, shall He not hear? He that formed the eye, shall He not see? He that chastiseth nations, shall not He correct? or He that teacheth man knowledge?" I will now show you the meaning of these arguments, but first I will point out how the opponents to the words of the Prophets misunderstood this passage. Many years ago some intelligent co-religionists—they were physicians —told me that they were surprised at the words of David; for it would follow from his arguments that the Creator of the mouth must eat and the Creator of the lungs must cry; the same applies to all other organs of our body. You who study this treatise of mine, consider how grossly they misunderstood David's arguments. Hear now what its true meaning is: He who produces a vessel must have had in his mind an idea of the use of that instrument, otherwise he could not have produced it. If, *e.g.*, the smith had not formed an idea of sewing and possessed a knowledge of it, the needle would not have had the form so indispensable for sewing. The same is the case with all instruments. When some philosopher thought that God, whose perception is purely intellectual, has no knowledge of individual things, which are perceivable only by the senses, David takes his argument from the existence of the senses, and argues thus:—If the sense of sight had been utterly unknown to God, how could He have produced that organ of the sense of light? Do you think that it was by chance that a transparent humour was formed, and then another humour with certain similar properties, and besides a membrane which by accident had a hole covered with a hardened transparent substance? in short, considering the humour of the eye, its membranes and nerves, with their well-known functions, and their adaptation to the purpose of sight, can any intelligent person imagine that all this is due to chance? Certainly not; we see here necessarily design in nature, as has been shown by all physicians and philosophers; but as nature is not an intellectual being, and is not capable of governing [the universe], as has been accepted by all philosophers, the government [of the universe], which shows signs of design, originates, according to the philosophers, in an intellectual cause, but is according to our view the result of the action of an intellectual being, that endows everything with its natural properties. If this intellect were incapable of perceiving or knowing any of the actions of earthly beings, how could He have created, or, according to the other theory, caused to emanate from Himself, properties that bring about those actions of which He is supposed to have no knowledge? David correctly calls those who believe in this theory brutes and fools. He then proceeds to explain that the error is due to our defective understanding; that God endowed us with the intellect which is the means of our comprehension, and which on account of its insufficiency to form a true idea of God has become the source of great doubts; that He therefore knows what our defects are, and how worthless the doubts are which originate in our faulty reasoning. The Psalmist therefore says: "He who teaches man knowledge, the Lord, knoweth the thoughts of man that they are vanity" (ibid. xciv. 10-11).

My object in this chapter was to show how the belief of the ignorant that God does not notice the affairs of man because they are uncertain and unsystematic, is very ancient. Comp. "And the Israelites uttered things that were not right against the Lord" (2 Kings xvii. 9). In reference to this passage the Midrash says: "What have they uttered? This Pillar [*i.e.*, God] does not see, nor hear, nor speak"; *i.e.*, they imagine that God takes no notice of earthly affairs, that the Prophets received of God neither affirmative nor negative precepts; they imagine so, simply because human affairs are not arranged as every person would think it desirable. Seeing that these are not in accordance with their wish, they say, "The Lord does not see us" (Ezek. viii. 12). Zephaniah (i. 12) also describes those ignorant persons "who say in their heart the Lord will not do good, neither will He do evil." I will tell you my own opinion as regards the theory that God knows all things on earth, but I will before state some propositions which are generally adopted, and the correctness of which no intelligent person can dispute.

PART III, CHAPTER 20

It is generally agreed upon that God cannot at a certain time acquire knowledge which He did not possess previously; it is further impossible that His knowledge should include any plurality, even according to those who admit the Divine attributes. As these things have been fully proved, we, who assert the teaching of the Law, believe that God's knowledge of many things does not imply any plurality; His knowledge does not change like ours when the objects of His knowledge change. Similarly we say that the various events are known to Him before they take place; He constantly knows them, and therefore no fresh knowledge is acquired by Him. *E.g.* He knows that a certain person is non-existent at present, will come to existence at a certain time, will continue to exist for some time, and will then cease to exist. When this person, in accordance with God's foreknowledge concerning him, comes to existence, God's knowledge is not increased; it contains nothing that it did not contain before, but something has taken place that was known previously exactly as it has taken place. This theory implies that God's knowledge extends to things not in existence, and includes also the infinite. We nevertheless accept it, and contend that we may attribute to God the knowledge of a thing which does not yet exist, but the existence of which God foresees and is able to effect. But that which never exists cannot be an object of His knowledge; just as our knowledge does not comprise things which we consider as non-existing. A doubt has been raised, however, whether His knowledge includes the infinite. Some thinkers assume that knowledge has species for its object, and therefore extends at the same time to all individual members of the species. This view is taken by every man who adheres to a revealed religion and follows the dictates of reason. Philosophers, however, have decided that the object of knowledge cannot be a non-existing thing, and that it cannot comprise that which is infinite. Since, therefore, God's knowledge does not admit of any increase, it is impossible that He should know any transient thing. He only knows that which is constant and unchangeable. Other philosophers raised the following objection: God does not know even things that remain constant; for His knowledge would then include a plurality according to the number of objects known; the knowledge of every thing being distinguished by a certain peculiarity of the thing. God therefore only knows His own essence.

My opinion is this: the cause of the error of all these schools is their belief that God's knowledge is like ours; each school points to something withheld from our knowledge, and either assumes that the same must be the case in God's knowledge, or at least finds some difficulty how to explain it. We must blame the philosophers in this respect more than any other persons, because they demonstrated that there is no plurality in God, and that He has no attribute that is not identical with His essence; His knowledge and His essence are one and the same thing; they likewise demonstrated, as we have shown, that our intellect and our knowledge are insufficient to comprehend the true idea of His essence. How then can they imagine that they comprehend His knowledge, which is identical with His essence; seeing that our incapacity to comprehend His essence prevents us from understanding the way how He knows objects; for His knowledge is not of the same kind as ours, but totally different from it and admitting of no analogy. And as there is an Essence of independent existence, which is, as the philosophers call it, the Cause of the existence of all things, or, as we say, the Creator of everything that exists beside Him, so we also assume that this Essence knows everything, that nothing whatever of all that exists is hidden from it, and that the knowledge attributed to this essence has nothing in common with our knowledge, just as that essence is in no way like our essence. The homonymity of the term "knowledge" misled people; [they forgot that] only the words are the same, but the things designated by them are different; and therefore they came to the absurd conclusion that that which is required for our knowledge is also required for God's knowledge.

Besides, I find it expressed in various passages of Scripture that the fact that God knows things while in a state of possibility, when their existence belongs to the future, does not change the nature of the possible in any way; that nature remains unchanged; and the knowledge of the realisation of one of several possibilities does not yet effect that realisation. This is likewise one of the fundamental principles of the Law of Moses, concerning which there is no doubt nor any dispute. Otherwise it would not have been said, "And thou shalt make a battlement for thy roof," &c. (Deut. xxii. 8), or "Lest he die in the battle, and another man take her" (ibid. xx. 7). The fact that laws were given to man, both affirmative and negative, supports the principle, that God's knowledge of future [and possible] events does not change their character. The great doubt that presents itself to our mind is the result of the insufficiency of our intellect. Consider in how many ways His knowledge is distinguished from ours according to all the teaching of every revealed religion. First, His knowledge is one, and yet embraces many different kinds of objects. Secondly, it is applied to things not in existence. Thirdly, it comprehends the infinite. Fourthly, it remains unchanged, though it comprises the knowledge of changeable things; whilst it seems [in reference to ourselves] that the knowledge of a thing that is to come into existence is different from the knowledge of the thing when it has come into existence; because there is the additional knowledge of its transition from a state of potentiality into that of reality. Fifthly, according to the teaching of our Law, God's knowledge of one of two eventualities does not determine it, however certain that knowledge may be concerning the future occurrence of the one eventuality.—Now I wonder what our knowledge has in common with God's knowledge, according to those who treat God's knowledge as an attribute. Is there anything else common to both besides the mere name? According to our theory that God's knowledge is not different from His essence, there is an essential distinction between His knowledge and ours, like the distinction between the substance of the heavens and that of the earth. The Prophets have clearly expressed this. Comp. "For My thoughts are not your thoughts, neither are your ways My ways, saith the Lord. For as the heavens are higher than the earth, so are My ways higher than your ways" (Is. lv. 8-9). In short, as we cannot accurately comprehend His essence, and yet we know that His existence is most perfect, free from all admixture of deficiency, change, or passiveness, so we have no correct notion of His knowledge, because it is nothing but His essence, and yet we are convinced that He does not at one time obtain knowledge which He had not before; *i.e.* He obtains no new knowledge, He does not increase it, and it is not finite; nothing of all existing things escapes His knowledge, but their nature is not changed thereby; that which is possible remains possible. Every argument that seems to contradict any of these statements, is founded on the nature of our knowledge, that has only the name common with God's knowledge. The same applies to the term intention; it is homonymously employed to designate our intention towards a certain thing, and the intention of God. The term "management" (Providence) is likewise homonymously used of our management of a certain thing and of God's management. In fact management, knowledge, and intention are not the same when ascribed to us and when ascribed to God. When these three terms are taken in both cases in the same sense, great difficulties must arise; but when it is noticed that there is a great difference whether a thing is predicated of God or of us, the truth will become clear. The difference between that which is ascribed to God and that which is ascribed to man is expressed in the words above mentioned, "And your ways are not My ways."

PART III, CHAPTER 21

There is a great difference between the knowledge which the producer of a thing possesses concerning it, and the knowledge which other persons possess concerning the same thing. Suppose a thing is produced in accordance with the knowledge of the producer, the producer was then guided by his knowledge in the act of producing the thing. Other people, however, who examine this work and acquire a knowledge of the whole of it, depend for that knowledge on the work itself. *E.g.* An artisan makes a box in which weights move with the running of the water, and thus indicate how many hours have passed of the day and of the night. The whole quantity of the water that is to run out, the different ways in which it runs, every thread that is drawn, and every little ball that descends—all this is fully perceived by him who makes the clock; and his knowledge is not the result of observing the movements as they are actually going on; but, on the contrary, the movements are produced in accordance with his knowledge. But another person who looks at that instrument, will receive fresh knowledge at every movement he perceives; the longer he looks on, the more knowledge does he acquire; he will gradually increase his knowledge, till he fully understands the machinery. If an infinite number of movements were assumed for this instrument, he would never be able to complete his knowledge. Besides, he cannot know any of the movements before they take place, since he only knows them from their actual occurrence. The same is the case with every object, and its relation to our knowledge and God's knowledge of it. Whatever we know of the things is derived from observation; on that account it is impossible for us to know that which will take place in future, or that which is infinite.

Our knowledge is acquired and increased in proportion to the things known by us. This is not the case with God. His knowledge of things is not derived from the things themselves; if this were the case, there would be change and plurality in His knowledge; on the contrary, the things are in accordance with His eternal knowledge, which has established their actual properties, and made part of them purely spiritual, another part material and constant as regards its individual members, a third part material and changeable as regards the individual beings according to eternal and constant laws. Plurality, acquisition, and change in His knowledge is therefore impossible. He fully knows His unchangeable essence, and has thus a knowledge of all that results from any of His acts. If we were to try to understand in what manner this is done, it would be the same as if we tried to be the same as God, and to make our knowledge identical with His knowledge. Those who seek the truth, and admit what is true, must believe that nothing is hidden from God; that everything is revealed to His knowledge, which is identical with His essence; that this kind of knowledge cannot be comprehended by us; for if we knew its method, we would possess that intellect by which such knowledge could be acquired. Such intellect does not exist except in God, and is at the same time His essence. Note this well, for I think that this is an excellent idea, and leads to correct views; no error will be found in it; no dialectical argument; it does not lead to any absurd conclusion, nor to ascribing any defect to God. These sublime and profound themes admit of no proof whatever, neither according to our opinion who believe in the teaching of Scripture, nor according to the philosophers who disagree and are much divided on this question. In all questions that cannot be demonstrated, we must adopt the method which we have adopted in this question about God's Omniscience. Note it.

GERSONIDES, *MILHAMOT HA-SHEM*[1]

Translation by Norbert M. Samuelson

THIRD TREATISE

On God's Knowledge of Things, May He Be Blessed

CHAPTER 1

In which we shall mention the arguments used by our predecessors on this question.

It is proper that we should investigate whether or not God, may He be blessed, knows contingent particulars which exist in this world, and if He knows them, in what way He knows them. Since the philosophers and the sages who are the masters of the Torah are divided in this subject, it is proper that we examine first their views. What we find to be correct we shall take from them, and we shall make clear with what we do not find to be correct the way in which what follows from it concerning these two views is true.

We say that on this subject there are two views of our predecessors whose words we find to be worthy of investigation. The first is the view of the Philosopher[2] and his followers, and the second is the view of the great sages of our Torah. The Philosopher had believed that God, may He be blessed, did not know particulars. His followers are divided into two views on this issue. The one group thinks that the view of Aristotle was that God, may He be blessed, does not know either the universals or the particulars which exist in this world. The reason is that if He knows either the universals or the particulars there would be plurality in His knowledge, and there would be here plurality in His essence. In general His essence would be divided into what is more perfect and what is less perfect, as is the case with things that have a definition. This is because part of what is in a definition possesses a greater degree of perfection than its other part.

The second group thinks that the view of the Philosopher was that God, may He be blessed, knows those things which exist in this world insofar as they possess a universal nature, (*121*) i.e. essences, [but He does] not [know] them insofar as they are particular, i.e. contingents. In this way there is no plurality in His essence, because He only knows Himself and in His knowledge of Himself He knows everything which exists insofar as it possesses a universal nature. The reason for this is that He is the *nomos*, the order and the arrangement of existing beings. Yet He does not know particulars. Therefore they possess a lack of order from this aspect, although they do possess order and arrangement from the aspect by which He knows them. It will be clear from what we say in the fifth treatise of this book, God willing, that this latter view was the view of the Philosopher.

The great sages of our Torah, such as the exalted philosopher the Master, the Guide, may his memory be blessed, and other great sages of our Torah who agree with his view, believed that God, may He be blessed, knows all of these contingent particulars as particulars. They say that God, may He be blessed, knows by a single act of knowing all these things which are infinite. . . .

THIRD TREATISE, CHAPTER 3

In which we shall investigate whether or not the arguments of the Guide, may his memory be blessed, logically suffice. . .

We say that it would appear that this view of the Master, the Guide, may his memory be blessed, concerning the knowledge of God, may He be blessed, did not result from speculative foundations. This is because Philosophical Thought rejects this (position), as I shall explain. Rather it would appear that the Torah put great pressure on him in this matter. However, whether (or not) this view is necessitated by the Torah is what we will investigate after we have completed this investigation into what Philosophic Thought decrees concerning it.

That Philosophic Thought rejects what the Master, the Guide, may his memory be blessed, posited concerning the knowledge of God, may He be blessed, will be clear from what I will say. It would seem that His knowledge, may He be blessed, is equivocal with our knowledge by priority and posteriority. I mean to say that the term, "knowledge," is said of God, may He be blessed, priorly and of any other being posteriorly. This is because He has His knowledge from His own essence, whereas the knowledge of other beings is caused by His knowledge, and in the case of anything of this kind the term is said of it priorly and of the other things of which it is said it is (said) posteriorly. . .

This being the case, it would seem that there is no difference between the knowledge of God, may He be blessed, and our knowledge except that the knowledge of God, may He be blessed, is more perfect than our knowledge. This is because this is the case with terms applied priorly and posteriorly. If the case is as we have posited, it being clear that the knowledge (*133*) which is most perfect is more true in precision and clarity, then it would seem to follow necessarily from this that the knowledge of God, may He be blessed, is more true (than our knowledge) in precision and clarity. Therefore it is impossible that His knowledge should be designated as what with reference to us is opinion or error or confusion.

It is clear in another way by Philosophic Thought that the knowledge of God, may He be blessed, is not different from our knowledge in the way that the Master, may his memory be blessed, maintained. This is because it is clear that we derive matters that we affirm of God, may He be blessed, from matters that are (affirmed) of us. I mean to say that we affirm of God, may He be blessed, that He has knowledge because of the knowledge found in us. For example, because what we conceptually know existing in our intellect is a perfection of the intellect, otherwise impossible, as an actual intellect, we affirm that God, may He be blessed, has knowledge, from the point of view that it is clear to us beyond any doubt concerning Him that He is an actual intellect.

Now it is self-evident concerning any predicate when it is affirmed of a certain thing on the basis of its existence in some other thing, that it is not said of both things in absolute nominal equivocation. This is because between things which are absolutely equivocal there is no analogy. For example, just as it is not possible to say that man is rational because body is continuous, so this (above case) is not possible even if we posit one term for (both) "rational" and "continuous" said of both in absolute equivocation. This is self-evident.

This being so, it is clear that the (term) "knowledge" is not said of (both) God, may He be blessed, and us in absolute equivocation. And since it is also impossible that it should be said of (both) God and us univocally, then it is clear that the only remaining alternative is that it is said of Him, may He be blessed, and us priorly and posteriorly. Similarly this is clear with the other things which are said of (both) God and us. Therefore, it is clear that there is no difference between the knowledge of God, may He be blessed, and our knowledge except that the knowledge of God, may He be blessed, is immeasurably more perfect, and this kind of knowledge is truer in level and clarity.

In general, the equivocation between His knowledge, may He be blessed, and our knowledge is like the equivocation between His essence and the essence of our acquired intellect. This is because the knowledge and the knower are numerically one, as was explained above. Just as His essence is more perfect than the essence of our acquired intellect, so is it essentially the case with His knowledge (as compared) with our knowledge.

This (conclusion) — i.e., that the knowledge of God, may He be blessed, is not different from our knowledge in the way mentioned by the Master, the Guide, may his memory be blessed — is clear by Philosophic Thought in another way. Concerning the things that we investigate whether they are affirmed of or negated from God, may He be blessed, it is clear that we judge those predicates to have a single meaning (both) in the affirmation and in the negation. For example, when we investigate whether God, may He be blessed, is a body or is not a body, it is clear that the term "body" has for us in some way a single reference in both of these alternatives. The reason for this is that if the term "body" in the negative one of these alternatives were said by us (*134*) in absolute equivocation with what would be said of Him in the affirmative, these alternatives would not be conceived by us to be contradictory. This is self-evident. For example, just as no one would say, "I will investigate whether the wall is body or is not colored" so this cannot be said even if the same term is posited for body and color. This is because such alternatives as these would not be contradictory.

This being so, and it (further) being clear that when we negate from God, may He be blessed, the things affirmed of us, no given predicate refers to Him, may He be blessed, and to us in absolute equivocation, so (also) is it the case when we affirm of Him things affirmed of us. For example, we say that God, may He be blessed, is motionless since if He had motion He would be body, because this is a necessary entailment of motion as motion. Now it is clear that the term "motion" in this proposition is not applied in absolute equivocation with the term "motion" applied to what is (known) to us. The reason is that if this were so, there would be no proof here that God, may He be blessed, is motionless. This is because the motion that would entail necessarily that He would be body is the (same) motion which is applied to what is (known) by us. But the motion which is said of Him in absolute equivocation would not entail necessarily that He would be body.

This being so and it (further) being clear that the predicates which we negate from God, may He be blessed, are not said of Him, may He be blessed, and of us in absolute equivocation, it is clear that the predicates which we affirm of Him, may He be blessed, are not said of Him, may He be blessed, and of us in absolute equivocation. This is because it would be uncertain at first, according to the capability of our thought, whether these predicates should be affirmed of or negated from Him, may He be blessed, prior to a full investigation. (Only) afterwards could we affirm them of or negate them from Him.

In general, if the things that we affirm of Him, may He be blessed, are said of Him, may He be blessed, and of us in absolute equivocation, (then) not one of the terms for things which are (known) to us would be more appropriate in negation from God, may He be blessed, than in affirmation, or (more appropriate) in affirmation than in negation. This is because someone could say, for example, that God, may He be blessed, is body, without meaning by this term "body" something which has quantity but (rather) something which is absolutely equivocal with what we call (ordinarily) "body." Similarly it could be said that God is unknowing, since in this proposition the term "knowledge" would not designate with regard to Him what it designates when we call something "knowledge."

One may not reply that we negate corporeality from Him because it is a deficiency with reference to us, and that we affirm knowledge of Him because with reference to us it is a perfection. (One may not say this) because the term "corporeality" is not a deficiency, which is what we negate from Him. Rather its meaning is a deficiency. Similarly it is not the term "knowledge" which is a perfection, but its meaning. The proof (for this) is the fact that if we designate by the term "corporeality" what is designated (ordinarily) by the term "knowledge," and (if we designate) by the term "knowledge" what is designated (ordinarily) by the term "corporeality," (then) corporeality would be a perfection for us and knowledge a deficiency.

Futhermore, we neither affirm nor negate anything of God, may He be blessed, unless we first investigate whether or not the existence of that thing is or is not appropriate to Him, may He be blessed, without considering in this our investigation whether or not that something is a perfection with reference to us. This being the case, it is clear that Philosophic Thought rejects (the view that) the term "knowledge" is said of both Him, may He be blessed, and of us in absolute equivocation.

(*135*) It is clear in another way that Philosophic Thought rejects what the Master, the Guide, may his memory be blessed, posited on the question of the knowledge of God, may He be blessed. This is because even if we assume that the knowledge of God, may He be blessed, is absolutely equivocal with our knowledge it is impossible that contradictions should be included in this knowledge, namely that it should be without generation and without change while it is generating and changing. However, the Master, the Guide, may his memory be blessed, accepted these contradictions with regard to this knowledge, as we explained, from what he posited as a fundamental principle of this knowledge.

Furthermore, he (himself) fled from relating the term "ignorance" to God, may He be blessed.[3] Because of this he said that He knows everything. But its meaning remained for him in accordance with what was explained that he posited as a fundamental principle concerning the knowledge of God, may He be blessed, namely that such knowledge as this is called "ignorance" by us, (and) not knowledge.

However, the Torah forced the Master, may his memory be blessed, to hold this kind of belief concerning the knowledge of God, may He be blessed, as we already have mentioned. Having been of the view that Philosophic Thought greatly disputes this belief, he said what he said concerning the knowledge of God, may He be blessed, in order to rid himself of all of these arguments and to establish what the Torah, according to him, affirms of Him. But we will investigate this after we have concluded our investigation here.

There is, in a certain way, an aspect of plausibility to what the Master, the Guide, may his memory be blessed, said, (namely) that the term "knowledge" is said of (both) God, may He be blessed, and us in absolute equivocation. This is that clearly there is no relation between God, may He be blessed, and existing things; therefore, it is not possible that anything should be said of Him which is said of His created things, except in absolute equivocation. Furthermore it is not proper that any attribute should be predicated of God, may He be blessed, it being the case that any predicate entails necessarily complexity, be it a qualitative or a substantive attribute. Thus, it also is clear that when any attribute is predicated of God it is predicated of Him, may He be blessed, and us in absolute equivocation. This is because it designates in Him, may He be blessed, a quality which is in itself the essence of what is described. The Master, the Guide, may his memory be blessed, already explained this (matter) at length in his honorable book *The Guide of the Perplexed.*[4]

After this argument it would seem to follow necessarily that attributes which are predicated of (both) Him, may He be blessed, and us are predicated in absolute equivocation. But the above arguments which we have presented on this (question) necessarily entail that these attributes may not be said (of God and us) in absolute eqivocation. Thus, would that I knew how the matter could be like this!

We say that with a good deal of reflection it will be apparent that there are predicates which are said of God, may He be blessed, and other beings priorly and posteriorly which do not necessarily entail that there is complexity in Him. The reason for this is that not every statement that is said of some thing in a certain manner necessarily entails complexity in that thing. Rather, it indeed necessarily will entail complexity in it if the one part is related to the other part as the subject of existence. However, if it is not related to it as a subject in existence, even though it is a subject in the statement, it does not entail necessarily that there is complexity in it. For example, when we say about a certain redness that it is a red color, it does not follow necessarily because of this that the redness in question would be composed of color and redness. This is because color is not something existent as a subject for redness. Rather (*136*) it is a subject only in the statement. This also will be the case if individuations bring about what they bring about. (For example) if you would say that "it is a color intermediate between black and white, leaning more towards black than white," then all of them designate only one simple thing. The plurality of conditions and individuation (only) serve to explain which of the simple colors is this color.

This also is essentially the case with things which have no (real or existent) subject, i.e., that the statement which is said concerning them does not designate complexity in them. To illustrate, if we say of that intelligence which moves the sphere of the sun, for example, that "it is the intelligence which conceives of a certain *nomos* by which that sphere's movements are ordered," (then) this sentence would not designate complexity (in the subject). This is because the term "the intelligence" is a subject only in the sentence, not in existence. Even though the (term) "intelligence" may be said of what is other than separate intelligences, in this case they do not agree in subject and differ in (their) differences. Rather (it is the case that) we state in the sentence which one it is of the simple entities that the term "intelligence" comprehends (to which we are referring). The reason for this is that concerning these intelligences, some of them differ essentially from others of them without any agreement between them in any thing. The reason for this is that if it were so, (then) they would be complex entities (and) not simple entities. Indeed, the way in which (these) intelligences differ is the same way in which the objects of their conception differ. This being the case, it is clear that when some (one) attribute or multiplicity of attributes is predicated of God, may He be blessed, these attributes do not entail necessarily complexity in Him, because He has no subject. Therefore, all of these attributes in Him do not designate anything but a simple entity.

It still can be demonstrated that the predicates which are said of God, may He be blessed, are said of Him priorly and of other existent entities posteriorly even if we grant that there is no relation between God, may He be blessed, and His creatures. This is because one will find such cases among the terms which are said priorly and posteriorly. For example, the term, "existent," is said of the entity priorly and the accidents posteriorly, as has been explained in the *Metaphysics.*[5] But it is clear that there is no relation between entity and accidents.

It is proper that you should know that in this world there are attributes which necessarily must be predicated of God, may He be blessed. For example, if you say that He is an entity, the term "entity" cannot be said of Him and other things univocally. Rather it is said priorly and posteriorly. This is because (where) a (certain) thing determines the way in which a given attribute is predicated of everything (else) of which that attribute is predicated, because of what they have acquired from it essentially and primarily it is more fitting that it should be called by that term. Now God, may He be blessed, determines all other things to be characterized as entities. This is because He caused them to acquire their being. Thus it is more proper that He should be called "entity." Furthermore, (this is so) because His essence exists from His essence while all other existent things (exist because of) something other than themselves, and what exists and persists from its own essence is more properly called "entity" than what exists and persists from what is other than itself.

In this way it should be clear that it is more proper to call God, may He be blessed, "existent" and "one" than anything else. We already have explained in our commentary on the *Metaphysics* with respect to this the error of Ibn Sina's argument to deny that these attributes can be predicated of God, may He be blessed.[6] (*137*) And the Torah agrees (with the view that) both of these attributes more (properly) designate His being than anything else. Therefore it singles Him out by means of the Tetragrammaton which designates being and existence. Concerning the (term) "one," (it also is the case, namely that the Torah singles out God by this term for unique reference) as is clear in the statement, "Hear O Israel YHWH our God, YHWH is one." This is also clear from the case where our master Moses, peace be unto him, asks, "And (if) they say to me, 'What is His name?' what shall I say to them?" and the reply came to him, "EHEYEH ASHER EHEYEH" for it is a term which designates being and existence.

In this (way) it should be clear that God necessarily must be described as being "intellect," "living," "comprehending," "benevolent," "powerful," "willing," and "doing," and that He is more deserving of these names than anything else. This is clear with little reflection by him who studies this book on what preceded this topic. Furthermore it will be clear completely, God willing, in Treatise Five of this book. However, these many terms only signify one perfectly simple thing, as we have explained.

Now the distance in meaning between these predicates and those like them, when they are said of Him, may He be blessed, and (these predicates) when they are said of anything other than Him, is like the distance between His level of existence, may He be blessed, and their level of existence in terms of the perfection and excellence of being. I mean to say that they are said in a more perfect way of God, may He be blessed, than the way in which they are said of what is other than Him.

After all of this is established, it is clear with respect to Philosophic Thought that the (term) "knowledge" can be said of God, may He be blessed, and of other things priorly and posteriorly, (and) not in absolute equivocation, and that Philosophic Thought rejects what the Master, the Guide, may his memory be blessed, established as a fundamental principle concerning the knowledge of God, may He be blessed, in order to refute the arguments of the philosophers.

THIRD TREATISE, CHAPTER 4

In which we shall complete the discussion of how God, may He be blessed, knows things as considered from the speculative point of view, and we shall make clear that nothing in the arguments of our predecessors disproves what is evident to us concerning this knowledge.

After explaining that Philosophic Thought refutes what the Master, the Guide, may his memory be blessed, posited in order to refute the arguments of the philosophers, and it being clear that properly there should be disagreement about the rejection of their arguments in terms of Philosophic Thought and not only in terms of the Torah, it is proper that we should investigate the arguments of the philosophers which affirm that God, may He be blessed, does not know any of the contingent particulars. (We should investigate) whether or not (these arguments) are correct, and if they are correct, whether or not what they claim to follow necessarily from them does (in fact) follow from them. However, before we examine their arguments, we have seen fit to complete the investigation of the knowledge of God, may He be blessed, according to our limitations. This is because in this way what I shall say about the arguments of the philosophers will be more complete and better understood to him who investigates our words.

We say that it seems that God, may He be blessed, knows these particulars from (the following) aspects.

—(The first) of these (aspects) is that since it is clear that God, may He be blessed, is the cause of everything, substances and accidents, that is subject to generation and corruption in this lower world, and (it also is clear) that the Active Intellect and the heavenly bodies are His instruments, — this is because all of these things emanate from the overflow which overflows upon them from God, may He be blessed, *(138)* — it being clear in the case of an instrument *qua* instrument that it cannot move to do that for which it is an instrument except by means of the knowledge of the craftsman, it therefore clearly is apparent from this that God, may He be blessed, knows all of these particulars.

— (The second) of these (aspects) is that since it is the case necessarily that God, may He be blessed, knows His essence at a level (which is equal to the level) of His existence, and (since) His essence is such that all existents emanate from Him by degrees, it (therefore) necessarily follows that God, may He be blessed, knows of all existents which emanate from Him. The reason for this is that if He did not know them, His knowledge of His own essence would be deficient. This is because He would not know what could possibly emanate from Him in accordance with that existence which He possesses. This being so, and it (further) being clear that every substance and accident which is subject to generation emanates from Him, (therefore) it is clear that He knows every substance and accident which is subject to generation which emanates (from Him). Therefore, it clearly follows necessarily from this that God, may He be blessed, knows all of these particulars.

— (The third) of these (aspects) is that it is clear from what was stated above that the Active Intellect in some way knows these things subject to generation in this lower world. This being so, and it (further) being (the case) that God, may He be blessed, is the cause, the form, and the end of all other separate intelligences, as is explained in the *Metaphysics*,[7] it necessarily follows that congnitions of all other intelligences are found in God. This is because those cognitions proceed materially from the cognition of God, may He be blessed. Similarly it is necessarily the case that an architect of a house should know the form of the bricks and the beams which these workmen know who are engaged in those arts which aid the art of architecture. But he who is engaged in the primary art will have more perfect knowledge of them with respect to their being part of (the total plan of) the house, as was mentioned above. This being so, it is clear beyond any doubt that these cognitions which the Active Intellect has of these things (are possessed) by God, may He be blessed, in a more perfect manner. This also shows that God, may He be blessed, knows particulars.

It now is established that these arguments affirm (the view) that God, may He be blessed, knows these particulars, while the above-mentioned arguments of the philosophers refute (the affirmation of) His knowledge of them. Therefore there remains no alternative but (to posit) that in one way He knows them and in another way He does not know them. Would that Ie knew what these two ways are!

We say that it already was made clear above[8] that these contingents are defined and ordered in one respect and are contingents in another respect. This being so, it is clear that the respect in which He knows them is the respect in which they are ordered and defined. Similarly, (this) is the case with the Active Intellect, according to what was explained, because (only) in this respect is it possible that they should be known. The respect in which He does not know them is the respect in which they are not ordered, which is the respect in which they are contingents. This is because in this respect it is impossible that they should be known. However, from this (latter) respect He knows that they are contingents which possibly will not be actualized with regard to the choice which God, may He be blessed, gave to man (*139*) in order to perfect what was lacking in the governance of the heavenly bodies, as was explained in the preceding treatise.[9] But He does not know which of the two possible alternatives will be actualized from the point of view that they are contingents. The reason for this is that if this were so, there could be no contingency in this world at all.

His lack of knowledge, may He be blessed, of which of two possible alternatives *qua* possible will be actualized is not a deficiency in Him. This is because perfect knowledge of a thing consists in knowing the nature of the thing. Were (the thing) to be conceived to be other than it is, this would be error and not knowledge. This being so, (it is clear that) He knows all these things in the most perfect way possible. This is because He knows them with respect to their being ordered in a clear and definitive way. In addition He knows those respects in which they are contingent with regard to choice, according to their contingency. Therefore, by means of His prophets God, may He be blessed, could command individuals upon whom evil was about to come that they should improve their ways so that they might be saved, as (when) He commanded Zedekiah to make peace with the king of Babylonia.[10] This is one (of the Biblical texts) which shows that (concerning) the future events which God, may He be blessed, knows, He knows that they need not come about. However, He knows it with respect to its being ordered in connection with His knowing that possibly it will not be actualized with respect to its being contingent.

We shall (now) explain that the above-mentioned arguments to affirm that God, may He be blessed, knows these things, do not demonstrate that He knows them in a greater degree than this. And (we also shall explain) that the above-mentioned arguments of the philosophers to deny the knowledge of God, may He be blessed, of (these) things does not truly deny the kind of knowledge which we have affirmed of God, may He be blessed.

It is clear that it does not follow necessarily from the above-mentioned arguments that God, may He be blessed, knows (particulars) in a greater degree than this. This is because the first argument demonstrated that God, may He be blessed, knows these things since the Active Intellect and the heavenly bodies are His instruments in performing these acts. It is clear that this argument only necessitates the consequence that He knows the orderings from which these acts emanate. This is because a separate (intelligence), insofar as it is separate, moves all that which is prepared to receive its moving without being aware of each particular instance (which is moved) of this class. (It is) in this way (that) the Active Intellect moves all of these things, as is clear from what was said above.

However, with regard to the action of a corporeal being *qua* corporeal being, it is correct that it does not act upon something in a craftsmanlike way if it has no awareness of this particular upon which it acts. Thus craftsmanlike actions are (brought about) by the mediation of the intellect and the imagination, as is explained in the *De Anima.*[11] This is so since (a given thing) must necessarily be proximate to what made it. This is because what is moved cannot receive (the mover's) intention unless it meets (its mover), and (only) then can (the mover) place upon (the moved) the desired form. However, matter receives the intention of the incorporeal cause with great ease, and therefore it is not necessary that the incorporeal cause be aware of the particular which it makes as this particular.

We can understand the ease with which matter receives the intention of the form by understanding (*140*) the motions which a man determines by his conception. For example, when a man desires to sing some song which he has conceived in his mind, (his) voice organ is moved immediately on the basis of that conception with such wonderful movements that no activity with any musical instrument could bring about such movements as these. Similarly, the fingers of the musician, as a result of his mind's conception, move back and forth on the musical instrument with great ease without his contemplating the motion itself as to how it should be executed properly. Similarly when a man speaks, he does so by using the intended letters with ease without contemplating in his speech each letter (as to) how the voice box should be used so that each letter would be spoken properly. This being so, it clearly is established that God, may He be blessed, can move these (particular) things without comprehending them with respect to their particularity, although He does comprehend them in a more perfect way.

The second argument establishes that God, may He be blessed, has knowledge of these things with respect to His own essence. It also is clear (in this case) that this argument only necessitates that God knows the intelligible ordering of these things from which their existence emanates.

The third argument establishes that God, may He be blessed, knows these things since the Active Intellect has knowledge of them. It also is clear that this argument only necessitates that God knows the intelligible ordering which these things possess. This is because this is the way in which the Active Intellect has knowledge of them, as was explained above. However, God's knowledge, may He be blessed, of this ordering is different from the Active Intellect's knowledge of it in that God's knowledge, may He be blessed, of this ordering is more perfect, as was explained above. This explanation will be made clear completely, God willing, in the fifth treatise of this book.

Similarly we say that it does not follow necessarily that God, may He be blessed, knows these things to a greater degree than this from what we mentioned that the Master, the Guide, may his memory be blessed, argued in order to establish that God, may He be blessed, knows all of these things. The reason for this is that the first argument (of Maimonides) establishes that God, may He be blessed, knows all of these things by denying of Him the imperfection of ignorance, but it is clear that when He knows things in the way that we have explained, there remains no ignorance in His knowledge of them. Rather, He knows them perfectly as what they are.

(Furthermore) we already have mentioned when we stated the second argument (of Maimonides) that it (only) seems to necessitate (the conclusion) that God, may He be blessed, knows the intelligible ordering of these things from which the existence of these things emanates, and no greater degree (of knowledge) than this. But this is what we posit here concerning the knowledge of God, may He be blessed.

This being clear, we shall explain that none of the arguments of the philosophers which we mentioned necessitates (the conclusion) that God, may He be blessed, does not know these things in the way that we have posited (that He knows them).

The reasons for this are (the following): The first of these arguments which we ascribed to the philosophers — which states that God, may He be blessed, cannot perceive particulars since He has no hylic faculty — does not necessitate (the view) that God, may He be blessed, does not know the intelligible ordering (*141*) which these things possess with respect to their being ordered and defined. Rather, all that (this argument) necessitates is (the conclusion) that God, may He be blessed, cannot know them with respect to their particularity and concreteness. This is self-evident.

The second argument states that God, may He be blessed, cannot possibly perceive these particulars since they are temporal. It also is clear that (this argument) does not necessitate the denial of what we postulated concerning God's knowledge, may He be blessed, of these things. This is because we did not postulate that He knows them with respect to their being temporal. Rather we postulated that He knows their intelligible ordering with respect to their being ordered by it, and in this respect they are not temporal.

The third argument states that God, may He be blessed, cannot possibly perceive these things, neither in their universality nor in their particularity, since it this were possible, the excellent would be perfected by the deficient, and this clearly is absurd. When we examine it we find that what is inferred from the premise of this conditional syllogism does not follow necessarily. This is because from our postulating that God, may He be blessed, knows the intelligible ordering of substances and accidents which inhere in things that exist in this world, it does not follow necessarily that God, may He be blessed, is perfected by these things. This is because God, may He be blessed, does not acquire this knowledge from these things which exist in this world. Rather His knowledge of them is dependent upon their intelligible ordering within Him. Therefore, it is clear that God, may He be blessed, is not perfected in this knowledge by anything other than Himself. Rather, this intelligible ordering which is within God, may He be blessed, Himself is that which caused these things to acquire their existence. This being so, it is clear that this argument is not correct.

The fourth argument states that if God, may He be blessed, perceives these things His essence would be complex, and therefore it necessarily follows that God, may He be blessed, does not know these things which are in this world, neither what is common to these things, which are their essences, nor that through which they are particulars, which are contingencies. Indeed, with investigation it becomes clear that what is inferred does not follow necessarily from the premise. The reason for this is that from our positing that God, may He be blessed, knows these things which are in this world it does not follow necessarily that His essence is complex. The reason for this is that the orderings which all these things possess are unified. In other words, there is a respect in which they are one, as we have mentioned many times before, and it is from this respect that God, may He be blessed, perceives them, not from the respect in which they are not unified, which is the respect in which they possess particularity and concreteness. This is because from this (latter) respect they could be perceived only by a hylic faculty. But perception in this way also would be a deficient perception. This is because it is not (perception of a thing) as it (truly) is. Rather it is (perception of a thing) in terms of its being an accident. Therefore, (such perception) cannot possibly be attributed to God, may He be blessed.

What is said in it, (namely) that if God, may He be blessed, perceives these things, His essence would be divisible into what is most deficient and into what is most perfect, is not correct. This is because the Active Intellect is one (and) simple, as is the Acquired Intellect, (even) with this kind of plurality in their perception. (*142*) This matter is explained fully, God willing, in the fifth treatise of this book.

The fifth argument states that particulars are infinite, and (that) therefore knowledge cannot encompass them. It is clear that the negation of what we posited concerning God's knowledge, may He be blessed, of these things does not necessarily follow from it. The reason for this is that the intelligible orderings which these things possess are not infinite but necessarily are finite, and it is from this respect that knowledge of them is possible. What does necessarily follow from this argument is that there can be no knowledge of them from the respect in which they are particulars, which is the respect in which they are infinite.

The sixth argument states that God, may He be blessed, cannot possibly know these things subject to generation. The reason for this is that if this were possible, either He would know them before they come to be or He would know them only with their coming to be. If He knew them before they came to be His knowledge would be related to what does not exist. Furthermore, it would follow necessarily, if this were so, either that He knows them according to their nature as contingent beings, so that the contradictory of what He knows will be actualized remains a possibility, or that He knows perfectly which one of these contradictory alternatives would be actualized, and its contradictory does not remain possible. If we assume that He knows them according to their nature as contingent beings, it necessarily follows that His knowledge of these entities before they come to be changes with their coming to be. This is because they were possibilities which either could be actualized or could not be actualized before their generation, but after their generation the possibility is eliminated. Since the intellect is actualized by what it knows, it necessarily follows that the essence of God, may He be blessed, is in continuous flux. But this is absolutely absurd.

If we assume that God, may He be blessed, knows perfectly which one of the pair of possibilities will be actualized, then the nature of the contingent would be eliminated. If it is assumed that God, may He be blessed, knows these things only with their coming to be, then His knowledge is in continuous flux, and (thus) His essence is in continuous flux. Since all of this is absurd, (the philosophers) necessarily concluded from it that God, may He be blessed, does not know these things at all.

We say that clearly the denial of what we posited concerning God's knowledge, may He be blessed, of these things does not follow necessarily from this argument. The reason for this is that when we posited that God, may He be blessed, knows these things in this world with respect to their being ordered, and (that) He also knows their contingent nature with respect to human choice, none of the absurdities stated in this argument necessarily follow. The reason for this is that it does not follow necessarily from this that His knowledge is related to what does not exist. This is because we posit (that) His knowledge of these things is related to the intelligible ordering in His intellect, (and is) not (related to) these things subject to generation (themselves). Furthermore, it does not follow necessarily from this (argument) that God's knowledge, may He be blessed, changes with the generation of these things. This is because we did not posit that His knowledge is related to these particulars. Rather (we posited that it is related to) their intelligible ordering which is in His intellect, and this ordering is eternally in His intellect as a single unchanging thing. Furthermore, one need not deny the nature of the contingent by our positing that He knows which one of the set of possible alternatives (*143*) will be actualized. This is because we postulated (that) He (only) knows (concerning) this alternative that it is proper that it should be actualized with respect to these things being ordered, (but) not absolutely. This is because He reckons that it is possible that it will not be actualized with respect to choice which is the respect in which these things are contingents.

The seventh argument states that if God, may He be blessed, knows these particulars, it is proper that He should give them a good and perfect ordering, but this is the opposite of what our senses find (to be the case) concerning these particulars. I mean to say that we find much evil and disorder in them. However, since it is clear that this ordering which these contingents possess and the contingency which was posited concerning them is just ultimately and a good ordering, (then the validity of) this argument is negated. We have explained this fully in our commentary on the Book of Job, and it also is explained, God willing, in Treatise Four of this book.

The eighth argument states that if God, may He be blessed, knows all of these things in this world, it necessarily follows from this that the impossible is possible. This is because it is clear concerning the nature of continuous quantity that everything divisible remains capable of (further) division *qua* quantity. If it is assumed that God, may He be blessed, knows all these things, it would follow necessarily that He knows all the parts into which this continuous magnitude could be divided. If this were so, continuous magnitude must possess parts which cannot possibly receive division, which are the parts to which the knowledge of God, may He be blessed, is limited. The reason for this is that if the case were not so posited, God's knowledge, may He be blessed, of this part would be deficient.

We say that (this argument) is not correct. This is because if we grant that God, may He be blessed, knows, for example, the nature of each part of every material body, it does not follow necessarily from this that the division (itself) is limited. Rather, He knows this division according to its nature. I mean to say that He knows that everything which is divisible can be divided (further) in that it is continuous magnitude, (but) He does not know the limit of the divisibility which by nature is limitless. (He does not know this) because such knowledge would be called error rather than knowledge.

Furthermore, we say, according to what we have explained concerning the nature of the knowledge of God, may He be blessed, that He knows the universal nature of quantity *qua* quantity, (namely that it) is divisible infinitely into what is divisible (itself), (but) He does not know this concerning each instance of quantity. The reason for this is that if this were the case, His knowledge in this matter would be deficient. This is because (that knowledge) would not be about the nature of the thing. I mean to say that this division into each particular is only insofar as it is quantity, and not, for example, insofar as it is made of wood or copper.

Some contemporaries have explained concerning this argument that magnitude is composed of indivisible parts, since they grant that God, may He be blessed, knows perfectly this possible division of magnitude. The reason for this is that if those possible parts were divided (actually), God's knowledge, may He be blessed, would not encompass all of the parts into which it is possible that the magnitude is divisible. (*144*)

(This argument) also is clearly absurd. The reason for this is that it does not follow necessarily from our granting that God, may He be blessed, knows all of these things that He knows every part into which this (given) magnitude could possibly be divided. This is because this statement is clearly absurd. In other words, we (may) say (that God knows) "all parts," (only) because by this statement we render (in thought) universal what is not (in actuality) universal, because what is infinite is not universal. It necessarily follows from this that He knows that every part into which a magnitude is divided remains (itself) capable of division into what is magnitude. This possibility is known in this way according to its nature as what is infinite, (but this is) not (to say) that He knows the limit of what is limitless by nature. This is because anything like this would be error and not knowledge.

This problem is similar to the problem mentioned by the Philosopher in (his) book, *De Generatione Et Corruptione,*[12] which states (the following) in order to explain (the doctrine) that body is not infinitely divisible: Assume that body is divisible completely into all that into which it possibly can be divided. This (division) might not (in actuality) be able to occur, but its occurrence is not a logical impossibility. However, when this is assumed, the body (must) be divided into indivisible parts, since, if they were divisible, the body would not be divided into every possible part according to what was assumed. This being so, it would seem that it necessarily follows from this (argument) that body is divisible into what is indivisible. . .

We say in solution to this problem that no absurdity occurs in our positing that a possibility exists when the existence of what is possible is posited. But when the existence of what is not possible is posited an absurdity occurs. But it is clear that this statement posits the existence of what is not possible. This is clear because from our positing that when a continuum is divided it is divided into what is (itself) divisible, as was explained (above) in various places, it necessarily follows that it is impossible that it can be divided into what is not capable of division. When we posit that body in actuality is divisible into all that into which it is capable of division, we posit the existence of what is not possible, because it can only be divided into divisible parts. The reason that error occurs at this point is with respect to their positing the existence in unity and completeness of the possible which essentially is neither unified nor complete.

This is also the more (adequate) solution for the aforementioned problem of the contemporaries concerning the divisibility of the continuum with respect to God's knowledge, may He be blessed. This is because it does not follow necessarily from our positing that God, may He be blessed, knows perfectly this division of a continuum that God's knowledge, may He be blessed, completes this division into what is indivisible. Rather, what does follow necessarily is that He knows this division according to its nature, (namely) that everything into which a continuum is divisible is (itself) something which is capable of division. It is not (the case) that He knows the limit of the division of what by nature has no limit. . .

It is now clear that there is nothing in the aforementioned arguments of the philosophers that necessitates the view that God, may He be blessed, does not know these things in this world in the way in which we posited God's knowledge, may He be blessed, of these things.

THIRD TREATISE, CHAPTER 5

In which it will be made clear completely that what is evident to us concerning this knowledge is very adequate in every respect.

What will add complete clarity to what we have mentioned concerning God's knowledge, may He be blessed, of these things is that none of the negations which necessarily follow from what the Master, the Guide, may his memory be blessed, posited concerning God's knowledge, may He be blessed, — these being the five aforementioned cases which, according to that postulate, are characteristic of the knowledge of God, may He be blessed, each of which is inconceivable (as characteristic) of our knowledge — necessarily follows for this postulate.

The first of them is that a single (act of) knowledge is equal to and agrees with many different species of things. It also necessarily follows in the case of our knowledge. (This also is the case for us) when we know a plurality of things with respect to their being one, which is when we intelligibly comprehend their intelligible orderings and we conceive concerning them that some of them are the form and perfection of others of them. Since we posited that God, may He be blessed, knows this plurality of things in this way — i.e., He knows their intelligible orderings with respect to their being ordered, and He knows them with respect to their being one — clearly it does not follow necessarily from this respect that we should posit the distinction between the knowledge of God, may He be blessed, and our knowledge that the Master, the Guide, may his memory be blessed, posited. The distinction between these two (instances of) knowledge consists for us in the fact that these intelligible things are one in Him. This is because the difference between the unity of what is actualized from this in our intellects and the unity which is in the intellect of God, may He be blessed, is very great, so that there is utterly no relation between them, which is clear from what was said above in the first treatise of this book.

The second of them is that His knowledge is connected with nonexistence. It is something that does not follow necessarily from what we posited concerning God's knowledge, may He be blessed, of these things which exist in this world. The reason for this is that we say that God's knowledge, (*148*) may He be blessed, of these things with respect to their being ordered in Him is dependent upon the intelligible ordering which they have in God, which exists eternally. (It is) not (dependent) upon these things (themselves) subject to generation. This is because He does not acquire knowledge of them. Rather, they acquire (their) existence from His knowledge of them, i.e., because their existence is caused by the intelligible ordering which they have in God, may He be blessed. This being so, it does not follow necessarily from this that His knowledge is connected with non-existence. Rather it is connected with something that exists eternally in unchanging unity.

The third of them is that God's knowledge, may He be blessed, encompasses what is infinite with respect to its being infinite. It also is something which does not follow necessarily from what we posited concerning the knowledge of God, may He be blessed. The reason for this is that we say that He knows them with respect to their being one. (But He does) not (know them) with respect to their being infinite and non-unified, which is the respect in which they are particulars.

The fourth of them is that His knowledge, may He be blessed, of things which will come to be in the future does not necessitate that the known will be actuated; rather its contradictory remains possible. This is also the case with our knowledge when we gain knowledge of such things by a dream or by a vision or by prophecy. This is because we know them with respect to their being ordered, but they remain contingent with respect to choice. It is from this respect that we have this information in order that we may reckon with the evil that is ready to come upon us and that we may beware (in order) that (the evil) would not be realized, as all of this was explained in the preceding treatise.

We can confirm this (view) by investigating what the prophets, peace be unto them, said when they predicted a certain evil, (namely) that it is found (written) that they gave advice in order to beware of that (particular) evil (in order) that it would not be realized. Similarly, in the case of what Joseph interpreted for Pharoah you find that he gave him advice in order that the famine would not be realized in the way that it was ready to be realized on the basis of what was revealed in his dream.[13] Similarly, in the case of what Daniel, peace be unto him, interpreted for Nebuchadnezzar from what he dreamed concerning the troubling of his mind and his being like the beasts for seven years, you find that (Daniel) gave him advice in order to beware of that evil so that it would not be realized.[14]

Since we posited that God, may He be blessed, knows these things with respect to their being ordered, it is not strange that they should remain contingent with respect to choice. In this way the problem is solved, (a problem) which men have never been able to solve, namely, how it is possible for God, may He be blessed, to know things which are subject to generation while they remain contingent. (A solution is possible) because this is from two respects, (and) not from one respect.

The fifth of them is that God's knowledge, may He be blessed, of things subject to generation does not change with the generation of these things of which He has knowledge prior to their coming to be even though the object with which that knowledge is connected changes. (The reason for this is) that at first it was a possibility and afterwards it actually existed.

This also must be the case with our knowledge when we attain knowledge of things with respect to their ordering. The reason for this is that even though the contrary of what (we) have knowledge is actualized, that knowledge remains as it is (*149*) with respect to the ordering of these things. I mean to say that from this respect what was known that it would be actualized would have been actualized were it not for the human choice which caused what is fitting to be actualized not to be actualized.

Since God, may He be blessed, has this knowledge with respect to the intelligible ordering which is in Him and this ordering is always in Him in unity, it is clear that His knowledge does not change with the generation of these things. This is because His knowledge, may He be blessed, is not connected with them. Rather it is connected with the intelligible ordering which they have in Him, may He be blessed.

One may not reply that by God, may He be blessed, knowing that these things are contingent with respect to choice (His knowledge) changes with the generation of what is subject to generation. (One may not say this) because we do not maintain that God, may He be blessed, acquires knowledge from things subject to generation. Similarly, He does not know them with respect to the specification which these things possess. Rather, (He knows them) by way of (their) genus and universality, and from this respect the contingency in His knowledge, may He be blessed, of them is not removed. This is very clear to him who investigates this book.

THIRD TREATISE, CHAPTER 6

In which it will be explained that our conclusion from Philosophic Thought concerning His knowledge is the view of our Torah.

It is proper that we should explain that this view which was concluded from Philosophic Thought is also the view of our Torah. We say that the basic tenet of the Torah and the axis upon which it revolves is that in this world there exist contingents. Therefore the Torah can command (us) to do certain actions and to refrain from doing certain (other) actions. (At the same time) the basic tenet of the words of the prophets in general, peace be unto them, is that God, may He be blessed, made known to the prophets, peace be unto them, these contingents prior to their coming to be. As (Scripture) says, "Surely the Lord God does nothing without revealing His secret to His servants the prophets."[15] But it does not follow necessarily from their testifying to a certain evil that it will be actualized. As (Joel) said, peace be unto him, "For the Lord is gracious . . . and repents of evil."[16] Thus a combination of these two tenets is possible only if it is posited that these contingents are ordered in one respect, namely the respect in which knowledge of them occurs, and that they are not ordered in another respect, namely the respect in which they are contingent. (Furthermore) since God, may He be blessed, knows all of these things with respect to their being ordered, and He knows that they are contingent, it is clear that the view of our Torah is (in agreement with) what was concluded from Philosophic Thought concerning the knowledge of God, may He be blessed.

Furthermore, it clearly is the view of the Torah that God, may He be blessed, knows these things universally (and) not particularly. (This view) is clear from what (Scripture) says, (viz.) "He who fashions the hearts of them as one, and comprehends all of their deeds,"[17] i.e., He fashions the heart and thoughts of mankind as one by making these orderings which the heavenly bodies possess from which generally they are ordered. In this way, (God) comprehends all of their deeds, i.e., in unity. (But it is) not (the case) that His knowledge is connected with the particularity of a particular. Thus it is clear that He understands all of their deeds generally.

Furthermore, it is the view of our Torah that the will of God, may He be blessed, does not change. As (Scripture) says, "I the Lord do not change."[18] (*150*) (Similarly,) Balaam said at the time that he was a prophet, "God is not man that He should lie, or a son of man that He should repent."[19] However, it is found in the words of the prophets, peace be unto them, that God, may He be blessed, does repent of some things. As (Scripture) says, "And the Lord repented of the evil which He thought to do to His people,"[20] (and) "For the Lord is gracious . . . and repents of evil."[21]

If it is impossible that this problem be solved by our positing that God, may He be blessed, knows particulars with respect to their being particulars while it can easily be solved by our positing that He, may He be blessed, knows them in the way that we posited (that He knows them), then clearly it is proper with respect to the Torah that one should posit that God, May He be blessed, knows these things which exist in this world in the way that we posited (that He knows them). It is evident that this problem is solved easily according to what we posited concerning the knowledge of God, may He be blessed. The reason for this is that He, may He be blessed, as knower does not judge that a particular event will be actualized for this (particular) man. Rather He judges everything which is ordered by this ordering from the respect in which these events are ordered. In addition, He, may He be blessed, knows that this thing is a contingent which need not be realized with respect to human choice. However, when we posit that He has such knowledge about this particular man *qua* particular, then it must follow that His will, may He be blessed, is subject to change.

In general there is nothing in the words of the prophets, peace be unto them, which would necessitate (the view) that the knowledge of God, may He be blessed, differs from what we posit according to the conclusion of Philosophic Thought. This being so, clearly it is proper that we should follow Philosophic Thought in this matter. The reason for this is that whenever the Torah, according to what appears from the external meaning of its words, disagrees with some things which are clear from the point of view of Philosophic Thought, it is proper that we should interpret them in a manner which is in agreement with Philosophic Thought. In this (way) none of the tenets of (our) revealed religion will be destroyed. (In following such a procedure we act) as did the Master, the Guide, may his memory be blessed, with many things in his honorable book *The Guide of the Perplexed.*[22] How much more proper is it that we should not disagree with Philosophic Thought when we do not find the Torah disagreeing with it.

In Part III, chapter twenty of his honorable book *The Guide of the Perplexed,* the Master, the Guide, may his memory be blessed, says that some philosophers were inclined to say that knowledge is connected with species and at the same time extends to all individual members of that species.[23] (Maimonides) says that this is the view of every master of the Torah, according to what they of necessity concluded from Philosophic

Thought. So it is clear that (Maimonides) was of the opinion that this view also agrees with the view of our Torah.

(Furthermore) it seems that the sage Rabbi Abraham Ibn Ezra, may his memory be blessed, is in the same class. This is because he stated in his commentary on the words of the Torah that the truth is that He knows every individual generally but not individually.

The demonstration that the view of our Torah concerning the knowledge of God, may He be blessed, agrees with the conclusion of Philosophic Thought will be presented more completely in the following treatise on Providence, according to the view of our Torah.

Treatise Three of this book is hereby concluded. Praised be to God, may He be blessed, who has helped us in the writing of it. By His loving kindness He will aid us to have knowledge of Him, to love Him, to observe His Torah, and to arrive at the truth in which no doubt can occur. Amen.

NOTES

1. The library of the Hebrew Union College—Jewish Institute of Religion in Cincinnati, Ohio possesses two first editions of *The Wars of the Lord* published in 1560 in Riva di Trento. One of these copies contains manuscript notes written in an Italian hand in the seventeenth or eighteenth century. These notes for the most part are variant readings from an evidently better manuscript than the one that the *editio princeps* is based upon. All variations are apparently recorded in these notes, and on the basis of them it is possible to conclude that the author must have had before him one of the best manuscripts in existence. The readings are better than any manuscript readings given by Kellermann in his German translation of *The Wars of the Lord* with the exception of those taken from the Oxford manuscript, to which latter our manuscript notes are closest. Furthermore, of the one hundred and fifty-three text corrections listed by Charles Touati, ninety-six of them are included among these readings and of Touati's remaining fifty-seven text corrections only twelve of them in any significant sense affect the meaning of the passages in question.

These manuscript notes extend over the whole of the book. These glosses, together with the textual corrections suggested by Touati on the basis of his examination of eight other manuscripts (see Charles Touati, *Les Guerres Du Seigneur, Livres III et IV*, Paris Mouton & Co., 1968, pp. 31–36) have been incorporated into the Hebrew text that served as the basis for the English translation presented here. The pagination of the Leipzig edition is included in parentheses in the body of the text itself.

The translation is taken from *The Problem of God's Knowledge in Gersonides* by Norbert Samuelson, Toronto, Pontifical Institute of Mediaeval Studies, 1977. In that translation Samuelson stipulated that he has tried to be as literal as possible without losing the text's meaning, leaving commentary on the text for footnotes.

2. I.e. Aristotle
3. *The Guide of the Perplexed* III, 19.
4. I, 50–55.
5. See *Metaphysica* B, 3, 998b22; H, 6, 104a35–1045b7; Δ , 28, 1024b10–15; T, 2, 1003a33–1003b8; Z, 1, 1028a10–30; Z, 4, 1030a31–1030b4, Δ , 7, 101a6–1017b10.
6. Cf. Ibn Sina, *Najat* III, Metaphysics.
7. *Metaphysica* 2, chapter 7–9.
8. Pp. 120–127 of the Leipzig edition.
9. Cf. chapter 5, pp. 165-6 of the Leipzig edition.
10. Jeremiah chapter 22.
11. III, 8, 432a3–8.
12. I, 2, 316a, 24 ff.
13. Genesis 41:1–48.
14. Daniel, chapter 4.
15. Amos 3:7.
16. Joel 2:13.
17. Psalms 33:15.
18. Malachi 3:6.
19. Numbers 23:19.
20. Exodus 2:13.
21. Joel 2:13.
22. Cf. *The Guide of the Perplexed*, I, Introduction and 46.
23. *The Guide of the Perplexed*, III, 20.

CRESCAS, *OR HA-SHEM*

Translation by Warren Zev Harvey

BOOK II, PART 1

Concerning God's knowledge of existing things.

CHAPTER 1

Concerning the demonstration of this Fundament, in accordance with what the Law decrees: . . .

Now, as regards the mode of His knowledge, the commentators have differed greatly. However, that which is necessary according to the roots of the Law, as we understand it, are three things:

[I] The first, that His knowledge, may He be exalted, encompasses the infinite.

[II] The second: His knowledge, may He be exalted, extends over that which does not [now] exist.

[III] The third; His knowledge, may He be exalted, extends over the [disjunctive] parts of the possible, without changing the nature of the possible. . .

BOOK II, PART 1, CHAPTER 2

Concerning the objections which may be brought against this Fundament, as it has been posited:

Now, whereas some of [the objections] are general and some are particular, we shall mention first the general ones, i.e., those which are objections pertaining to [all] three of the things which were posited of God's knowledge, may He be blessed, of existing things; and they are five: . . .

The second [general objection] is that if God were to know an existing thing other than Himself, then, since [according to the philosophers] the intellect becomes constituted as a substance out of what it knows, a plurality would be necessarily implied in His essence, namely, His [previous] essence *and* that which He knows, while it would be necessarily implied that the Noble would become constituted as a substance [1] out the inferior. Now, if the objects known are many, the plurality will be in accordance with the number of the objects known; and if they are infinite [in number], the plurality will be infinite [in number]. This is perfectly absurd and ridiculous . . .

As for the particular [objections]: . . .

Concerning [II] the second thing, that His knowledge, may He be blessed, extends over that which does not [now] exist, there are. . .two objections: . . .

As for the second [objection concerning II]: inasmuch as knowledge of that which does not [now] exist, if it is true [knowledge], is of that which does not yet exist, that it will exist in the future, and when it does come to exist knowledge of it is that it exists, then it is inescapable that there occur a change in His knowledge. And since the intellect [according to the philosophers] becomes constituted as a substance out of what it knows, it is necessarily implied that His essence will change, and that is perfectly absurd.

Concerning [III] the third thing, namely, our statement that His knowlege, may He be blessed, extends over the [disjunctive] parts of the possible, without changing the nature of the possible, there are also two objections:

The first is that if His knowledge were of the attainment of one of the parts of the possible, and its contradictory remained possible, as would appear to be the case here, then when that one part has been attained, the possible will have vanished, and His knowledge will be of it [alone], and His knowledge will have undergone change. And since the intellect [according to the philosophers] becomes constituted as a substance out of what it knows, it would be necessarily implied that His essence undergoes change, and that is perfectly absurd.

The second is that if it is posited that His knowledge of the attainment of the one part of the possible [3] is such that its contradictory [part] remains possible, and it is evident with regard to the possible that no falsity will follow from its being posited as existing, then when we posit the part contradictory to His knowledge as existing, no falsity should follow from its being so posited. Yet when we do posit it as existing, two falsities necessarily follow: the first, a change in His knowledge and His essence, since [according to the philosophers] the intellect becomes constituted as a substance out of what it knows; the second, that the "knowledge" was not knowledge, but an erroneous guess. All this is perfectly absurd and ridiculous.

These are the objections which moved some of the former thinkers to dispute this Fundament in the manner it has been posited, to the extent that some of them did away entirely with [God's] knowledge of anything other than Himself, and some of them did away with [God's] knowledge of the generated and corrupted particulars, but accepted it with regard to the universals and the eternal individuals. . .

BOOK II, PART 1, CHAPTER 4

Concerning the resolution of the objections which they set down against this Fundament, in accordance with the opinion of the Law:. . .

It now remains for us to say in resolution of the objections, in a special way, what will suffice for it, as we have promised. We preface this by saying that the special difference between His knowledge, may He be blessed, and our knowledge—according to what has been demonstrated from the points of view of philosophic speculation and of the true tradition, and will be further demonstrated in our remarks in Book III, God willing—is that from His knowledge and the concept of His will the objects known acquire existence, while our knowledge is emanated and acquired from the objects known by means of the senses and the imagination as [4] has been demonstrated in Aristotle's *De Anima.*[1] This is the special true foundation by which most of the objections may be done away with. . .

As for the second [general objection], which is derived from a certain proposition which says that the intellect becomes constituted as a substance out of what it knows, and, therefore, if the knower is other than [what is known], it might be thought that it is necessary that he become constituted as a substance out of something other than himself, and that a plurality, in accordance with the number of the objects known, be necessitated in his essence: now, if that proposition is accepted, inasmuch as it is established concerning His knowledge that it imparts existence and essence to the things other than Himself, He most evidently does not become constituted as a substance out of something other than Himself, and His knowledge of [things other than Himself] does not necessitate a plurality in His essence, although it indeed would necessitate a plurality in His essence if He did become constituted as a substance out of them. However, after it has been established that He is that which imparts essence to things other than Himself, then indeed He is the one simple Source and Fountain, Who in His essential preexistent Will imparts existence to what is other than Him, whether one or many. Now *a fortiori,* if that proposition which was taken as accepted is in fact false, as will be shown in Book III, God willing, there is no room for this objection. . .

As for the second [particular] objection [concerning II], which is based on a change in [God's] knowledge, which would result in a change in His essence, since [according to the philosophers] the intellect becomes constituted as a substance out of what it knows: now, its resolution is of no difficulty, in view of what has already been said, that that proposition is false. But [even] if we were to accept it, inasmuch as [5] it is in His preexistent Will that that thing will come to be at the time which His wisdom has decreed, when that time does come and that thing does come to be, no change will thereby occur in the essence of His knowledge.

As for the first [particular] objection concerning [III] the third thing, which is based also on a change in [God's] knowledge, in that when one part of the possible is attained the nature of the possible will have been done away with: its resolution is in analogy to that of the previous objection. For once we do not accept that the intellect becomes constituted as a substance out of what it knows, there is no room for this objection. But even if we do accept it, inasmuch as it is His preexistent knowledge that at that time the nature of the possible will change, when that time does come and that thing does come to be, in accordance with His knowledge, there is in this no change in His knowledge.

As for the second [particular] objection [concerning III], whose basis is that if we posit as possible the contradictory of the [disjunctive] part that He knows, and if we then posit it as existing, two falsities will follow — the first, a change in His knowledge [since, according to the philosophers, the intellect becomes constituted as a substance out of what it knows], and the second, that his prior "knowledge" was not knowledge but an erroneous guess: now, it is evident that when we reason analogously from our knowledge to His knowledge, we have no escape but to suppose that the [disjunctive] part which He knows is possible in some respect and necessary in some respect, and that from the standpoint of its being necessary no change will occur in His knowledge and His essence, while from the standpoint of its being possible the nature of the possible will not be denied of possible things. This will be clarified by what I shall say. There is no doubt that a thing's being necessitated in some respect does not necessarily entail the thing's necessity in its essence. This is demonstrable of things which are possible in their essence [6] and which now exist perceived by the senses. For a man's knowledge of them, that a certain possible thing exists, necessarily entails its existence such that its contradictory [disjunctive part] cannot exist in any respect. Yet this necessity does not change the nature of the thing's possibility, and does not entail the thing's necessity in its essence. Thus, the knowledge of God, may He be blessed, in the respect that [His] choice occurs in it, does not entail necessity in His essence, and does not change the nature of the possible at all. This will be demonstrated more extensively in Part 4,[2] God willing, for there the veracity of this shall be proved beyond doubt. The feet of most of the philosophizers have stumbled on this, for they could not conceive how the divine justice of the Law could permit necessity.[3]

This suffices with regard to what was our intent in this Chapter.

NOTES

1. Aristotle, *De Anima*, II, 5 - III, 8.
2. II, 4, 3. However, the main discussion of this subject is in II, 5, 4; cf. note 3 below.
3. Cf. *Light*, II, 5, 4: ובכאן הותר הספק הגדול אשר יעדנו בכלל הראשון מזה המאמר להתירו בכאן, אשר מעדו בו רגלי הרבה מן הראשונים כי לא שערו בחיוב אשר יסכים עם היושר האלהי התוריי ואם היה שלא יסבלהו היושר המדיני ההמוני וכ״ש לפי דעת התורה, והוא הנכון שיסכים בו היושר המדיני ההמוני, ודעהו!.

CRESCAS, *OR HA-SHEM*

Translation by Seymour Feldman

BOOK II, PART 5, INTRODUCTION

It has already been stated that choice is one of the foundations of religion and that freedom has been granted to man, since a commandment [cannot be given if] the person to whom the command is addressed is compelled and forced to do a fixed thing. On the contraty, it is necessary that his simple will[1] be able to do any of the alternatives; then a commandment to him will be appropriate and relevant. Now the principle of choice is tantamount to the claim that the nature of the possible exists. [Nevertheless], our predecessors have had doubts about this point and we have found among their writings that have reached us a variety of opinions on this matter. Hence, it is incumbent upon us to examine their views according to [their compatibility with] the Torah and with philosophical analysis. Since the opinions we have found on this subject correspond exactly to its two contradictory alternatives, [i.e. there is or there is no such thing as choice], we have divided [our discussion of] this principle into three parts. The first two parts deal with the two [opposing] opinions and the arguments in their behalf, as are implicit in the presentations of these views. In the third part we shall indicate according to our view what the Torah and philosophical analysis imply. It is important that we be zealous in this investigation; for this principle is a fundamental pillar [for the belief] in God's knowledge of existent things, as we have alluded to [in our discussion of that belief] in Principle 1. Indeed, an error in this principle [i.e. choice] is bound lead to serious and weighty errors in connection with the beliefs in God's knowledge of existent things and His providence. Accordingly, we have added three chapters, as will be evident from our discussion of this principle.

This belief can be verified by means of philosophical analysis and the Torah. There are several philosophical methods whereby this opinion has been defended. Firstly, it is evident that things are either natural or artifacts and that they exist only by virtue of the four causes: the agent, matter, form and the goal, as has been demonstrated in the *Physics*

[Aristotle, *Physics* II:1]. Now in some things we see that some of their causes are present, whereas some are not and that it is possible for all of these causes or only some of them to be present. But it is [precisely] from this possibility [of the pressence or non-prescence] of the causes of things that the possibility of the things themselves follows.

Secondly, we observe that many things do depend upon the will. And since it is evident that man has the capacity to will [to do some thing] or not to will [to do it],—for if he were compelled [to do or not to do it], there would be no will but [just] compulsion and necessity—, it is obvious that if this is so the possible exists.

Thirdly, it has been demonstrated in the *Physics* that some things come about by chance or spontaneously [Aristotle, *Physics* II:4-6]. But if all things were necessitated, which would follow if there were no such thing as the possible, then everything [from the class of chance or class of spontaneous events] would necessarily exist. But of what necessarily exists cannot be predicated the term 'chance'; [e.g.] the rising of the sun tomorrow is not a case of a chance event. Therefore, not all things are necessitated and thte possible exists.

Fourthly, if the possible did not exist and man were compelled in his deeds, effort and endeavor would be otiose. Similarly, teaching, learning, perparations and preliminary [studies and procedures], would be futile; also, zeal in the acquisition of possessions and useful things as well as the avoidance of harmful things [would also be otiose]. But all this is contrary to what is well-known and perceptible.

Fifthly, since the will is consequent upon the rational [part of] the soul which is separate from matter, it is not appropriate for it to be affected by material things, e.g. the heavenly bodies that influence bodies in the terrestrial world; for it is evident that the incorporeal is particularly fit to act, whereas the corporeal is particularly fit to be effected, as has been explained in *Methaphics* [Aristotle, *Metaphysics* IX:8]. Thus, it is not proper to conceive of the heavenly bodies, which are, [after all], bodies, acting upon and compelling the human soul. Rather, man's soul is independent of and free from all necessity. Accordingly, from all these arguments it can be seen from the point of view of philosophical reasoning that the possible exists.

But it is also evident from the Torah too that the possible exists. Firstly, if all things were necessitated and man were compelled in his actions, all the commandments and admonitions [in the Torah] would be pointless; for they would be useless in so far as man's deeds are [on this hypothesis] compelled and he has no power or volition over them.

Secondly, if man were compelled in his deeds, reward and punishment for these deeds would be an injustice attributable to God; for it is obvious that reward and punishment in deeds have a place only in voluntary human actions. Deeds that are compelled and forced do not admit of reward and punishment. And since reward and punishment are among the roots of the Torah [Maimonides, *Mishneh Torah,* Hilchot Tshuvah, chapter 5], it is necessary that man have an independent will in his deeds, free from any force or compulsion. From that it is evident that the possible exists. Q.E.D.

BOOK II, PART 5, CHAPTER 2

The view that the possible does not exist.

This thesis has also been defended by means of philosophical reasoning as well as from the Torah. There have been several philosophical arguments in favor of this claim. Firstly, since it has been demonstrated in the sciences that in the domain of generable and corruptible things four causes precede their occurrence and that by virtue of the existence of the causes the existence of the effects is necessary, the existence of the effects is accordingly necessary, not possible.[2] Now when we examine the existence of the causes as well, other causes must exist prior to them whose existence necessarily leads to their existence, such that their existence is necessary, not possible. But if we look for the causes of the [second] set of causes, the same reasoning holds, so that we ultimately reach one *necessarily* existent being (may His name be blessed). Thus, the possible does not exist.

Secondly, it is obvious and agreed upon that a state of affairs that can or cannot exist[3] is such that it requires a cause that preponderates existence over non-existence; otherwise it would be non-existent. Thus, if we assume that some possible state of affairs obtains, there must have been some antecedent cause that necessitated and brought about its existence rather than its non-existence. [Hence], the existent which was alleged to be possible turns out to be necessary. And when we examine similarly the prior cause, if it is assumed to be possible and to obtain, that which was necessary with respect to the first assumed possible [state of affairss] is [again] implied, until we reach a first cause, a first being that *necessarily* exists (may He be blessed).

Thirdly, it is self-evident and known to all that whatever proceeds from potentiality to actuality requires an external cause that brings it out of [the state of potentiality] [Aristotle *Physics* III:2-4]. Thus, when there is generated in man a volition to do some thing, the volition which was [originally] in potentiality [but now] in actuality required a cause that was other than itself. This was the thing that moved the appetitive faculty to get together and to agree with the power of imagination, as was explained in *On the Soul* [Aristotle, *On the Soul* III:9-10]; for this is the cause of the will, [or of volition]. Now if this is the case, when there exists such a union [of the appetitive and imaginative faculties], which is the cause of volition, the volition is necessary and the union is also necessary if the mover, [or agent], is present. Now if we say that the mover of the [original] volition is the will itself, which is [by nature] contrary to necessity, either of two absurdities follows. Firstly, either something can move itself and bring itself from potentiality to actuality, which is contary to the well-known principle [previously adduced]; or there is for the will a prior will that moves it and brings it out of potentiality to actuality and to the prior will another will prior [to it] and consequently and *infinite* number of wills for this latter will—which is completely absurd. In addition, each such will would follow from the preceding one and hence would not be possible, [or contingent].

Fourthly, it is self-evident, as we have said, that everything that comes into being requires a cause that brings it into being; for a thing cannot make itself exist. Thus, if one could conceive of two men having exactly identical situations, internal constitutions, dispositions, and exactly the same relation to some thing, it would not be possible for one of them to choose the existence of that thing, whereas the other [prefer] its non-existence. Rather, the one must choose what the other chose and desired. For if they were to differ in their choices and desires by virtue of some supervenient change, there must be a cause of this change. Would that I knew the identity of this cause, especially since they agree in internal constitution, birth, and disposition in every respect. Even if the truth [of the matter] is that such [identical] individuals cannot exist, still the necessity [of their choices being identical] does not derive from the impossiblity [of those individuals existing] but from the possibility [of their existing].[4] And when it has been demonstrated that it is necessary for these men to have the same will, it is also the case that the will is necessitated and hence not contingent.

Fifthly, it has already been demonstrated in Principle I of Book II that God's knowledge encompasses all particulars in so far as they are particulars, even if they are non-existent, not [yet] having come into existence. Therefore, it follows that if God knows which one of the two possible alternatives will occur, it follows necessarily that it will occur. If not, there would be no knowledge, but just opinion or error. Accordingly, what was [initially] assumed to be a possible [state of affairs] turns out to be necessary [and] inevitable.

Sixthly, if the possible did not exist, we would have to admit that the existence of a will for one of two opposite alternatives without a necessitating cause is possible. Accordingly, it would follow that God's knowledge of this alternative does not derive from His essence, in so far as His knowledge of existent things [results from] His being their cause; rather, His knowledge would be acquired and derived from their existence. But it is absolutely false to claim that His knowledge has a cause other than Himself.

Seventhly, it is evident that knowledge of particulars, in so far as it is not in terms of the general order [in God's mind], is impossible without a corporeal power, which is not attributable to God. Now the existence of one alternative [of a pair of opposing possiblilities] without a cause necessitating it is not known by means of the general order. [Hence, God would, on the hypothesis of the existence of genuine contingencies, not know these events, which is contrary to Principle 1.] It is therefore clear from all these philosophical arguments that there is no real contingency.

[Let us now consider this thesis from the point of view of the Torah.] It has already been indubitably shown from what is mentioned in the Torah concerning God's knowledge, i.e. it encompasses *all* particulars, even if they are non-existent, and from what the Prophets [record] of their conveying information [to Israel] about many particular events before they happen, even if these events are not necessary in themselves (i.e. they depend upon choice), e.g. the case of Pharaoh,[5] that there is no such thing as genuine contingency. Q.E.D.

BOOK II, PART 5, CHAPTER 3

The True View According to What the Torah and Philosophy Require.

Since there are arguments that imply both the existence and the non-existence of the possible, the only alternative is to admit that the possible exists in one sense but does not exist in another sense. Would that I knew what these senses are!

Now when we examine the affirmative arguments, we see that these arguments entail only the existence of the possible in itself, [or as such].[6] The first affirmative argument—since some things are such that all their causes *may or may not* exist, [and hence are possible in this sense]—begs the question. For the very possibility [alleged to be inherent] in those causes is itself also in question! Hence, this argument is completely invalid in this context.

Secondly, the argument based upon the will—man has the obvious capacity to will or not to will [to do something]—also begs the question. For the person who denies the existence of the possible could argue that the will has a mover that moves it necessarily to will that thing or its contrary and that this mover is the cause of the will. Hence, the mover is that which necessitates the volition, although the will remains a will [and] there is no necessity or compulsion. For the will in itself would have been able to choose indifferently one of the two alternatives had not the mover necessitated it to opt for the other. Nor does the will feel [in this case] any compulsion or force. And since in itself it can indifferently choose either of the alternatives it is called a will, not compulsion.

Thirdly, the argument drawn from the phenomena of chance and spontaneity that are found in nature does not entail the existence of the possible except in the sense of the possible in itself. In that sense there are accidental, [or chance], phenomena. But this does not preclude the existence of causes that necessitate their existence.

Fourthly, the argument based upon effort and endeavor clearly implies only the possible in the sense of the possible in itself. For example, if a particular man were compelled to be rich as such, [i.e. his being rich is an essential feature of his condition], then any effort [on his part] to acquire possessions would be otiose. But if this [wealth] is considered as a possibility as such but as necessary by virtue of its causes, which are in fact effort and endeavor, then the latter are *not* otiose but are the essential causes of the acquisition of possessions and this acquisition is the effect of these causes. One cannot say that the cause is superfluous relative to the effect except when the effect is necessary in itself, either with our without the cause. But then it would not be an effect.

Fifthly, the argument based upon the incorporeality of the rational soul is also invalid. For the rational soul is not a separate [substance] but is corporeal and affected by the internal constitution of the organism. Thus, it is possible for the heavenly bodies, all the more so their movers, to affect the internal constitution of the organism and move the appetitive faculty, which through its coordination with the imagination, constitutes the will, as has been explained in *On the Soul* [Aristotle, *On the Soul* III: 9-11]. But whether this influence [from the heavenly bodies] is necessary or manifests some contingency has not yet been determined by this argument. It is therefore clear that none of the affirmative philosophical arguments entails the existence of the possible except in the sense of the possible in itself, but not in the sense of their causes.

Nor do the arguments drawn from the Torah establish [the thesis that the possible exists] except in the sense of the possible in itself. For the argument based upon the commandments and admonitions of the Torah — i.e. if all things were necessary, the commandments and admonitions would be pointless — clearly entails only the possibility of things in themselves. For, indeed, if things were necessary in themselves, the commandments and admonitions would be pointless. But if things are possible in themselves and necessary by virtue of their causes, the commandments and admonitions do have a purpose, indeed an important one. For [they] are moving causes of things that are in themselves possible [i.e. actions] in the same way as causes [in general] are causes of the effects, as for example, effort and zeal [are causes] of the acquisition of possessions and useful things and [things] that lead [us] away from harm. Therefore, this argument does not entail that the possible exists by virtue of its causes.

Secondly, the argument based upon reward and punishment [in the Torah]—if man were compelled and forced in his deeds, reward and punishment would be an injustice of God — appears to be a strong argument against any kind of necessity. However, a close examination shows that it can be easily dissipated. For, if reward and punishment follow from the [obedient] deeds and sins in the way that effects follow from causes, there would be no injustice attributable to God; no more than there is an injustice if someone is burned when he approaches fire, even if his approach is involuntary. It will be demonstrated (with God's help) in Book III that this is the meaning of reward and punishment, as we shall treat in detail there the reason thereof. Therefore, it is evident that none of these arguments, either from philosophy or from the Torah, entails the existence of the possible in terms of its cause. [That is, causal determinism is true. Although logically speaking certain events are abstractly possible, they are necessary given some causal sequence of prior events.]

Similarly, when we examine the arguments that entail the non-existence of the possible, we see that they imply [its non-existence] only in the sense of the possible in terms of its cause. [Causal determinism is, Crescas repeats, compatible with the *logical* possiblity, or contingency, of events.] For, the first, second, and third arguments—which are based upon the causes and movers of things that bring them out of a state of potentiality to actuality—, and the fourth argument, which is hypothetical, as well clearly imply only that [phenomena are necessary] in terms of their causes. But with respect to [the nature of the events] themselves they remain possible. For example, primary matter can by its very nature receive forms one after the other. However, with respect to [its] efficient causes verdigris [copper sulfate] must be generated from copper from the aspect of its causes. [Matter qua copper necessarily becomes copper sulfate given a specific causal context.] Yet, in itself the copper can, [abstractly speaking] remain copper. Accordingly, in the generation of verdigris there is a temporary case of necessity in terms of its causes, which is transitory; [whereas] there is an [abstract, logical] possibility considered in terms of itself that is eternal and will not disappear.

Analogously, the arguments based upon God's foreknowledge and prophetic predictions, even if choice is made a condition [of such knowledge], clearly does not imply the annulment of possibility in itself. Rather, the phenomena are possible in themselves yet necessary in terms of their causes; and in so far as they are necessary there is knowledge prior to their necessary [occurrence]. And thus, it has been shown that none of these arguments [in behalf of determinism], either philosophical or from the Torah, entails that phenomena are in themselves necessary. Hence, the complete truth [of the matter], as both philosophy and the Torah have shown, is that possibility as such does exist in things but not in terms of their causes. [Phenomena are logically, or abstractly considered, contingent; but as elements in a causal nexus they are necessary.] Yet, to make this idea well-known amongst the masses would cause harm, for they would think that [this doctrine] furnishes an excuse for evil-doers and they would not perceive that punishment follows from transgressions, as the effect follows the cause. Accordingly, God's wisdom made these commandments and admonitions effective means and strong inducements to guide man to human happiness.[7] This [guidance] is indeed attributable to God's absolute mercy and goodness, which is alluded to in the passage, "as a man chaseneth his son, so the

Lord thy God chaseneth thee" [Deuteronomy 8:5]. For just as it is evident that a father does not reprove his son out of vengence nor out of the principle of [absolute] justice but only for the benefit of the son, so too when God chastens man, the aim is not vengeance nor the principle of political justice — which is appropriate only if man is completely voluntary under no compulsion or force whatever, — but the intended good is [the good] of the whole community. Thus, it would be appropriate even when [man's deeds] are necessitated by virtue of their causes; for this would be beneficial to him.

However, it is important to realize that this necessity is fitting when the man does not feel any force or compulsion; [indeed], this is the very foundation of choice and the will. [Causal determinism is compatible, i.e. "fitting," only if the doer does not feel compelled.] But when a man performs deeds in which he feels compelled and forced, not doing them willingly, since he does not do them in a condition wherein his appetitive faculty is in agreement with his imagination, this deed is not [really] his own. [In this case], punishment is not appropriate. For admonitions and commands have no bearing upon deeds that are forced such that they could stimulate a man to do these deeds or to avoid them. Where a man's [own efforts] have no bearing upon [what he does] there cannot be any command or admonition; and punishment for transgressions would not be [consistent with] divine justice, since no good would result from the punishment.

However, if it is necessary to say that the nature of the will is such that implies [the capacity] to will or not to will [to do something] without any external cause — and[8] this is the true doctrine of the Torah, — it is possible to apply the distinction we used in Principle 1 of Book II, [i.e. the principle of divine cognition of existent things]. For something can be possible itself and in terms of its causes, yet be necessary in terms of God's foreknowledge, just as the possible when it is assumed to be actual and known [i.e. some present contingent state of affairs] is possible in itself but necessary in so far as it is existent then and known, even if God knows things before they occur. Accordingly, those who believe that what is necessary before it occurs is not possible [fail to realize that] the event is not possible *by virtue of God's knowledge*, but it is possible in itself. [Moreover], since God's knowledge does not fall under time, His knowledge of the future is like His knowledge of existent things, in which there is no necessity nor compulsion in the things themselves. But if someone objects and says, "does God's knowledge derive from existent things" (an objection raised earlier in the last two difficulties [Crescas appears to be referring back to Principle 1.]), we reply as follows. We do not really know how God knows, since His knowledge is [identical with] His essence. This is the method adopted by Maimonides, according to our opinion. Yet something more can be said by way of an answer to this objection. It is evident that things are known not as they are in themselves but according to the nature of the knower [Thomas Aquinas, *Summa Theologiae* I, q. 85, article 1, ad 1]. This is quite obvious in the case of sense-preception: for the sense of touch apprehends its object when it approaches it and touches it, and it perceives only in the place of the touched object cold or hot, hardness or softness. On the other hand, the sense of vision apprehends from afar a place and its features. The same is true in the other [senses].[9] Hence, if the knower is eternal and is not conditioned by time [in any way], it is appropriate that such a knower apprehend the object according to its mode [of cognition], which is not conditioned by time; indeed, [it knows] by virtue of its essence. Thus, it apprehends what is non-existent by an eternal cognition as if it were existent eternally.

The principle that emerges out of these discussions [is] that [concerning] this possible matter[10] in something where there is no choice [whatever], it must be necessary by virtue of its causes and possible in terms of itself.[11] But in things where there is choice, if we say that it is the nature of the will to desire or not desire [to do something] without an external cause, and this is the true view of the Torah, things would be possible by virtue of their causes and in terms of themselves, yet necessary with respect to God's knowledge of them. And since they are possible in themselves effort would be appropriate in their case. [Moreover], the commands, admonitions, rewards and punishments are relevant, since if [a man] were to choose the opposite [of what he in fact does choose], God would have known his choice of the opposite[12].

The only question that now remains is, how does God know possible states of affairs? But we have already replied to this question, either by means of Maimonides' theory or by means of our own view. In short, since God has endowed existence to all other existent things, knowledge of them is fitting and necessary. No matter how this whole principle is [to be construed], there is no way of avoiding the conclusion that there is possibility in some sense and there is necessity in some sense. The perfect one [Rabbi Akiba], who entered and left [Paradise] in peace, already pointed out all the profundities [in this doctrine] by means of a short saying: "Everything is foreseen, yet freedom is given; and the world is judged according to goodness, and everything [is reckoned] according to the majority of the deed(s)." [*Mishnah,* Avot III:15]. Now the phrase "everything is foreseen" means that all things are ordered and known [by

God]. This is an important principle whose truth cannot be doubted, about which, [however], some of our scholars have been in error. For this reason I have been led to reveal the secret [implicit in this principle], since many of our nation have fallen into error on this point.[13] The phrase "freedom is given" hints at the secret of choice and will; for freedom is given to all men as such [i.e. abstractly], since there cannot be any commanding [when the recipient of the command] is compelled and forced. The phrase "the world is judged according to goodness" refers to God's fairness in judgment, i.e. in reward and punishment, which is not concerned with vengeance nor with the ordinary, political principle of equity. For [reward and punishment] are not implied just by virtue of [their] causes but because of the good [resulting therefrom], as we have already explained. [Finally], the phrase "all is [reckoned] according to the majority of the deeds" can refer to the necessity of causes, both proximate and remote, [operative] in this context, as is referred to in the saying, "one higher than the high watcheth [and there are higher than they]" [Ecclesiastes 5:7]. Or perhaps this phrase alludes to the traditional and well-known principle that the world is judged according to the principle of the majority. Or, perhaps it is alluding to another important principle that will be discussed (with God's help) in the Sixth Principle.

[We shall now provide] an additional explanation of this view by means of the solution of a very difficult problem about which our predecessors have never ceased to be perplexed: how can divine justice with respect to reward and punishment be reconciled with necessity? [Moreover], if a reconciliation is feasible, what is the difference between the necessity by virtue of causality in which there is no feeling of force and compulsion and the necessity in which there is such a feeling? It might be thought that if the doing of the command or the transgression is the cause, whereas the reward or the punishment is their necessary effect, it would be inappropriate to distinguish the necessity without the feeling of compulsion from the necessity with such compulsion if the reward and punishment are the effects of one but not the effects of the other; for in either case there is an ineluctible necessity. [That is, where there is felt compulsion the reward and punishment are not, one might argue, genuine effects of the deeds.] [Furthermore], even if we were to admit that there is such a difference [such that] where force or compulsion is felt there is no reward or punishment, since in that case the person is not a voluntary [agent], whereas where the person does not feel force or compulsion he is called a voluntary agent, even if he is necessitated, how can [we speak of] reward and punishment in the domain of beliefs concerning the foundations of the Torah? It is evident from tradition that the punishment in these matters is severe, as of it the [Rabbis] have said, "But heretics and apostates who deny [the divinity of] the Torah and [the belief] in resurrection of the dead [*Rosh Hashanah* 7a]; or "The following are those who have no portion in the World To Come. . ." [*Mishnah* Sanhedrin X].

Now it would seem from the following arguments that concerning beliefs there is no volition or choice at all. Firstly, if will were necessarily involved in beliefs, belief would have nothing to do with [the confirmation of] truth; for the will has the capacity to will or not to will [something] and it would be always possible to believe two contradictory opinions one after the other, and this [is so] if one wants to. But this is absurd. Secondly, if the will were necessarily involved in beliefs, the moving cause that generates that belief would [itself] be in doubt about the truth of that belief. For, if the moving cause were not in doubt about the truth at all, there would be no need for the will at all; but if the generating [cause of the belief] were in doubt about the truth, then the belief itself would be doubtful. Thirdly, it would seem that in the following respect there is no element of will involved in the beliefs. For belief is nothing but the affirmation that a thing outside the soul corresponds to [the conception of it] in the soul; but what is outside the soul is not conditional upon the will [for] the belief that this is the way it is.[14] Hence, belief does not depend upon the will.

Having demonstrated this point I now claim that someone who believes [in some proposition], especially if it is a belief that has been demonstrated, cannot but feel a complete compulsion to believe in that propositon. For since the moving cause [of that belief] is a strong [kind of] necessity [i.e. the logical necessity], it is unavoidable; [indeed], it is an absolute demonstration, since we have assumed that belief is a demonstrated belief.[15] The necessity and compulsion [in this case] are evident, obvious and felt by the believer, who *cannot* believe in the contradictory of that belief. Accordingly, if this type of compulsion, i.e. the kind that is felt, is inappropriate for reward and punishment to be ascribed to it (as has been assumed), I do not know how there can be reward and punishment in beliefs! I shall now try to say something appropriate to the solution of these difficulties.

Firstly, [with respect to the first question raised at the beginning of chapter 5], since divine justice is always directed towards the good and perfection, and since the good and perfection bring forth causes motivating good actions, it was necessary (according to divine justice) to bring forth commandments, and the reward and punishment associated with them, because they [i.e., the commandments] are causes motivating good actions; they are motivating causes since reward and punishment follow from them, just as the effect follows the cause. Thus, they [i.e. the commandments] move the will and choice towards whatever is proper and away from [what is not proper]. Hence, it has been established that it is fitting that divine justice in reward and punishment agree with the necessity.[16] Despite its awkwardness I have translated the passage using the literal rendering. Crescas' meaning seems to be this. The good is the highest goal, or final cause. As a final cause it serves to stimulate man to do good. But a goal, or end, needs means for the attainment of that end; hence, the goal, the good, gives rise to commandments, which are the means for the realization of the end. The commandments are the appropriate means, or stimulants, for good actions because rewards or punishments are necessarily implicated in them. In sum, we have a goal, the good, which necessarily gives rise to means, the commandments, whereby people are stimulated to pursue to goal, and these means have associated with them consequences, i.e. rewards and punishments, which also serve as means whereby people are stimulated to follow the good.

[With respect to the second difficulty], the difference between the necessity in which no compulsion and force are felt and the necessity wherein compulsion and force are felt requires some explanation. It will be explained (with God's help) in the sixth Principle, both by means of philosophical argument as well as from Scripture which agree with various Rabbinic sayings, that the desired goal in good actions is the joy and pleasure implicit in them, which [joy] is nothing but the pleasure of the will in doing the good; for God [Himself] is at the highest level of love and pleasure in bestowing and doing good. Connection and closeness [with God] is therefore to walk in His ways as far as possible. Hence, when the desire and this pleasure are present in the soul, there is [a genuine case of] a mental act, by virtue of which there can be closeness with or separation [from God]. Accordingly, reward and punishment appropriately follow from it [i.e. the pleasure or lack of it], just as the effect follows from the cause. But when this desire is lacking in the soul, as when a man feels force and compulsion in his deeds, the soul is not the [real] agent of that deed, and closeness or separation is not consequent upon it; for the deed is [in this case] divorced from the volition of the soul. Thus, reward and punishment are altogether inappropriate in this case. The difference then between [the necessity involving felt compulsion and the necessity without such compulsion] has been explicated.

Yet, although this difference has been explicated, how can reward and punishment in belief be explained?[17] For the promises of reward or punishment in beliefs cannot move the will or choice to [the adoption of] beliefs, nor are they efficient causes of beliefs, since it has been assumed that a person has no choice over his beliefs and that the will has no bearing upon them. Some of our scholars have gone astray on this score, as it would seem from their writings, [and have claimed] that reward in beliefs is not inconsistent with divine justice. For reward is natural and follows necessarily upon the acquisition of knowledge; e.g., when a person's soul has been convinced of the truth of certain beliefs and they are apprehended by him as they are in reality, his soul is constituted by these beliefs and becomes immortal. This is [in their view] the highest reward for man[18]. Now it is evident that this theory has nothing to do with the Torah, as will be shown in the sequel (with God's help)! If this view were correct, it would have been sufficient for our purposes for the Torah to give us some guidance by means of a few ideas stated therein; we would have no need for the extraordinarily many commandments and their various ramifications, unless they were the consequences of philosophy. The number of such beliefs found in the Torah is, [however], quite small. [Moreover], if the soul were constituted by the [acquisition] of theoretical truths, there are many such truths in [Euclid's] *Elements* and [Appolonius'] *Book of Cones,* and soul of the geometer would embrace more of these truths than the follower of the Torah, [and hence on this view be more worthy of immortality]. But this opinion is obviously false according to the Torah; in addition it is highly improbable, as will be shown later, that reward consists merely in the permanence of the object of knowledge. Would that I knew in the case of a soul that has apprehended some principle, which has been proved in the *Elements* (e.g. the interior angles of a triangle equal 180°), but has not apprehended anything else, if this soul is constituted by this one object of knowledge and becomes immortal thereby? And if it does become immortal, is it like the soul that has been constituted by the principle, also proved in the *Elements,* that the square of the diagonal of a rectangle is equal to the sum of the squares of the two sides of the rectangle, or some other such principle? Or, if the souls differ, *how* do they differ? The whole idea is preposterous and self-defeating! Since Aristotle was not enlightened by the Torah and was led to teach immortality of the soul by other considerations of some weight, he concocted various fictions and arguments to bolster these teachings, even if they are quite remote from reason, all the more so from the Torah. Let us therefore put aside his way!

Since it has been demonstrated that the will has no bearing upon beliefs but that the believer feels the compulsion of what be believes, it is clear that we must locate the element of volition and choice [in belief] in something closely connected and associated with belief, i.e., the joy and pleasure which God has graciously granted us in [giving us] the belief in Him and the endeavor to understand the truth of this belief. This [joy] is indubitably voluntary and free; for one can conceive of a case where the believer in certain truths does not feel any arousal of joy in being a believer in those truths. Accordingly, the arousal of joy and the effort to examine the truth of these beliefs are matters that follow upon the will and choice, which [fact] resolves the question of reward and punishment [in beliefs], as will be explained later (with God's help).

Moreover, there are actions such that when you examine them closely you will see that their reward does not consist primarily in the doing of the act itself but in the choice of the act when the act is done. For when a man does some act, he brings into actuality one of two contrary things that were indifferent in the power of his choice. And since it is evident that whatever is in actuality is not in potentiality and possible for him by virtue of the fact that it is actual, but is instead necessary for him, it follows that reward and punishment deriving from volition and choice concern not the act itself when it is done, but the choice of the act when it is performed. This saying of our Rabbis is quite apt: "The thought of sin is worse than the sin itself" (*Yoma* 29a). For, since the sin is a composite of two elements—the act itself and the volition and choice [to do it]—and since the punishment resulting therefrom derives from the volition and choice, which in this Rabbinic saying are designated by the term הרהור, it is evident that the volition [to do evil], or the thought, is the more serious of the two. This point can be verified when we conceive [either] the act separated from the thought and volition, as in the case of a forced action, or the volition without the deed. Punishment accrues to the thought and the will [i.e. the second alternative], as has been pointed out by authentic tradition: "A burnt-offering atones for evil thoughts" (*Leviticus Rabbah* 7). But punishment does not accrue to a case of [forced] action, as [one of our traditional] principles indicates: "God forgives the person who is forced." (*Nedarim* 27a). However, much more severe is the punishment in the case where volition is joined with the action than where there is just volition but no act. This indicates that punishment does pertain to the act, but it is more severe when it pertains to the will, particularly when the will is joined with the act. This is indubitably true. This very difficult problem has, therefore, been solved: reward and punishment in beliefs pertain to the pleasure and joy experienced by us [when we have such] beliefs and to the endeavor to apprehend them. Q.E.D.

BOOK II, PART 5, CHAPTER 6

In explanation of what has become clear with regard to this on the basis of philosophy.

In this chapter I shall show how the position we have demonstrated by means of philosophy is compatible with the view of our Rabbis. This position amounts to two theses: 1) beliefs are not acquired by means of the will; 2) reward and punishment pertain to the will, i.e. the reward consists in the desire in the endeavor for and the joy in being an adherent of that belief and the punishment consists in the opposite. Now both of these points are alluded to in a saying that occurs in *Shabbat* 88a: " 'They stood at the bottom of the mountain' . . . (Exodus 19:17). This teaches that the Holy One (blessed be He) overturned the mountain upon them like an [inverted] cask, and said to them, 'If ye accept the Torah, 'tis well; if not, there shall be your burial.' R. Aha b. Jacob observed: This furnishes a strong protest against the Torah. Said Raba, yet even so, they re-accepted it in the days of Ahasuerus, for it is written, '[the Jews] confirmed and took upon them . . .' [Esther 9:27] i.e. they confirmed what they had accepted long before."

The explanation given by this saying is as follows: Since it has been shown that belief is acquired by means of theoretical premises, all the more so by means of prophecy, which was manifested at the great revelation [at Sinai], the will has no bearing upon belief. Hence, the Israelites *had* to believe in God, willy-nilly; thus they were compelled in their belief. [The Rabbis] likened this to God overturning the mountain upon them like a cask in order that they accept [the Torah] against their will; if not they would die there. This is obviously a case of compulsion. The same is true in many of the great miracles. And at the end of that great revelation they believed in the Torah through compulsion; and if they departed from it, they would be turning away from the correct [path] and the way of life, which is designated 'death' and 'burial'. Thus, the first sage said: "This furnishes a strong protest against the Torah." For, although the Torah is indubitably true, since however their belief was compulsory, the will had no bearing upon it; and perhaps they would not have accepted it out of their free will, which is what [normally] compels us to follow it. For it is clear that although this belief is indubitably true, if we did not accept it [willingly], there would be no possibility of severe punishment as there would be if we agreed to follow after it willingly. Accordingly, the [second sage] replied: "They accepted it again in the days of Ahasuerus . . .", i.e. by virtue of the joy experienced as a result of the miracles and salvation that were done for them at that time, they reaffirmed what they had already accepted, and the protest became invalid. For the pleasure and joy, on which reward in beliefs depends, was perfect in the days of Ahasuerus. This saying is a complete analogue to our analysis, both with respect to the claims that theoretical beliefs are acquired without volition and that reward pertains to the willingness and the joy [experienced by the person] in being a believer [in that idea]; such that this joy is pleasure and benefit to the believer.

NOTES

This translation was originally made from the editio princeps (the Ferrara) and the Vienna edition, neither of which is wholly satisfactory. I later obtained copies of two manuscripts (Ms. #2428: Adler Collection, and Ms. #2514: Bamberger Collection) which I used in part to control the translation.

1. The term רצון can mean both *will* and *volition*, depending upon the context. I shall translate this term accordingly.

2. Here and throughout the term אפשר, 'possible', should be understood as *contingent*, the contrary of *necessary* (Aristotle, *Prior Analytics*, I:3).

3. Here Crescas defines the possible for the first time.

4. Crescas claims here that the principle adduced earlier in the paragraph does not hinge upon the existence or non-existence of two individuals who are exactly alike. No matter whether such individuals do not or cannot exist; all that matters is that we can *conceive or imagine* them existing and draw out in our minds what the logical consequences are of such a "thought-experiment". One such consequence is that their choices would be identical. And this is the point that Crescas wants to drive home. This point is in fact an instance of the logical principle known as the Law of Identity: if two names refer to the same individual then every property true of the individual denoted by one name is true of the individual denoted by the other name.

5. Crescas is apparently, referring to the passages in Exodus about God hardening Pharaoh's heart so that he will not hearken to Moses.

6. See H. Wolfson, *The Philosophy of Spinoza* (New York, 1969) vol. I. 309 ff.

7. The commandments are *causes* that lead to happiness in the sense that they are *means* whereby man reaches his perfection. The means-end relationship is, Crescas suggests, a causal relation.

8. This passage is difficult and has occasioned a controversy amongst several modern interpreters of Crescas. If the passage is read as it stands, Crescas seems to be retracting his defense of determinism, which he now appears to admit is incompatible with the Torah. Accordingly, as Urbach suggests, Crescas would seem to be committed to some kind of "double truth theory" (Urbach, S., *The Philosophic Teachings of R. Hasdai Crescas* (Hebrew) (Jerusalem 1961) 296, n. 214). This was the interpretation suggested by P. Bloch

100 years ago (Bloch, P. *Die Willensfreiheit*, 6–7). Nevertheless, this interpretation of Crescas was challenged by Guttmann, who argued that the term [אם] הוא הצעת הנכון that appears in the beginning of this sentence serves to introduce a disjunctive question and has to be understood as re-appearing before the second disjunct.

In other words אם corresponds here to the Latin 'utrum . . . and . . . ' (J. Guttmann, *Dat U'Mada* (Jerusalem 1955). 163 n. 22). However, this interpretation would require in addition altering והוא into הוא. Moreover, it is unusual for the second אם in disjunctive questions to be omitted, which fact is confirmed by even a random reading of Wolfson's critical edition of Book I of Crescas' *Or Adonai* (Wolfson, *Crescas' Critique of Aristotle*).

It is possible to construe this passage as a hypothesis which Crescas is entertaining for the purpose of showing its irrelevance to his own theory. That is, even though one *were* to say that the Torah implies indeterminism, i.e. no external cause determines the will, nevertheless the theory of divine cognition developed earlier by Crescas shows that, although events may be possible in themselves, they are necessary in terms of God's knowledge of them. Accordingly, whether or not we are committed to causal determinism and regardless of how the Torah is to be construed on this score, it still remains true that events are not contingent in so far as God has antecedent knowledge of them, although such events may be contingent in themselves.

9. Each sense organ perceives its objects differently. Some require actual contact between the organ and its object, e.g. touch and taste; others do not, e.g. vision and hearing (Aristotle, *On the Soul*, Book II, 6–11. Urbach, op. cit. 297).

10. Or alternatively rendered, 'matter in which there is possibility', i.e. in the domain of corporeal entities.

11. If it were not possible in itself, the whole question of choice would be besides the point. E.g. if the sum of the interior angles of a Eucledian plane triangle *must* equal 180°, even when we consider these angles *in themselves*, then choice is irrelevant. The question of choice arises whenever there is at least logical contingency, i.e. the logical possibility that p or not-p.

12. This paragraph is especially difficult because of the significant divergence in manuscript readings. My translation is that of the fuller text. In addition, it should be observed that this passage repeats the difficult phrase that occasioned the controversy amongst Bloch, Guttmann and Urbach noted earlier: והוא הדרך הנכון לפי התורה. In the face of these textual and interpretative obstacles it is a bit rash to venture a solution; but I shall try to suggest a plausible reading of this passage.

The one point that Crescas wants to stress throughout Principles 1 and 5 of Book II is that human behavior exhibits two aspects: from one point of view human acts are contingent in so far as their contradictories are logically possible; from another point of view they are necessary either because they are members of a causal series of events or because they are known by God, or both. Now, if someone were to claim that the Torah implies indeterminism of the will with respect to external causes, the previous point is still valid. For all the Torah requires, Crescas insists, is that human actions be contingent, logically possible in themselves. This last condition is, he claims, enough to justify reward and punishment. This condition is secured whether or not we believe in causal determinism and even though we accept divine foreknowledge.

The resolution of this issue is clearly dependent upon the establishment of a critical text. But it also hinges, at least to some extent, on the interpretation of other issues in Crescas' philosophy. Of special importance in this particular context is Crescas' doctrine of creation. For there he argues in support of the idea that the universe is *eternally created* by God, although he admits that the Torah teaches the *temporal origin* of the universe, and hence we are obliged to believe in latter doctrine. This ambiguity has probably led to Urbach's suggestion that Crescas was inclined towards the "double-truth theory" both here and on the question of free-will. The matter still is open. (Cf. D. Neumark, "Crescas and Spinoza", in his *Essays in Jewish Philosophy* (Central Conference of American Rabbis, 1929), 314–315.

13. The secret is the doctrine of the compatibility of causal determinism with abstract, or logical, possibility, and hence qualified freedom (Urbach, op. cit. 297–298. Guttmann, op. cit. passim). Urbach suggests that Crescas is referring to Gersonides in particular.

14. Reality does not depend upon our beliefs, whereas our beliefs do depend, or at least they should depend, upon reality (Maimonides, *Guide* I: 50).

15. In a case of a demonstrative proof, or scientific syllogism, the logical compulsion is of the strongest type. We cannot but believe the conclusion, since it is necessarily true following from premises that are themselves necessarily true (Aristotle, *Posterior Analytics*, I:205).

16. The word המצאת, occurring three times in this paragraph, is especially difficult to render into English. Literally, it means 'bringing forth of', 'bringing into existence of' (Pines' translation of Maimonides' *Guide* I, chapter 7). Despite its awkwardness I have translated the passage using the literal rendering. Crescas' meaning seems to be this. The good is the highest goal, or final cause. As a final cause it serves to stimulate man to do good. But a goal, or end, needs means for the attainment of that end; hence, the goal, the good, gives rise to commandments, which are the means for the realization of the end. The commandments are the appropriate means, or stimulants, for good actions because rewards or punishments are necessarily implicated in them. In sum, we have a goal, the good, which necessarily gives rise to means, the commandments, whereby people are stimulated to pursue the goal, and these means have associated with them consequences, i.e. rewards and punishments, which also serve as means whereby people are stimulated to follow the good.

17. This was the third difficulty originally raised by Crescas.

18. This was a common view amongst Muslim and some Jewish philosophers, such as Gersonides. (Gersonides, *The Wars of the Lord*, Book I. Jehudah Halevi, *The Kuzari*, Book I:1).

ALBO, *IKKARIM*

Translation by Isaac Husik

BOOK IV, CHAPTER 3

Having shown that the exponents of the different sciences differ from one another in their assumptions, we must find for everything a basis in sense perception, and pay no regard to anybody's ideas, except where they are in agreement with sense data.

Now the senses testify, in agreement with the theologian, that the contingent exists; also that God communicates through the prophets knowledge concerning particular and individual things; also we know that God provides specially for particular individuals, witness the pătriarchs in all their relations, according to the continuous tradition which has come down to us, the exodus from Egypt, and other special individuals mentioned in the books of the Prophets. Hence we pay no regard to those who deny these things. For we do not deny what we see with our senses despite the speculations of philosopher, as we do not deny that a sphere revolves about two stationary poles, though the physicist according to his theory denies it. We must use the senses as a basis in everything, even though the reason is not able to know the cause thereof. . . .

But if you ask, how is it possible to maintain both of these opinions, viz. to maintain the reality of the contingent and at the same time to hold that God's knowledge embraces it? Our answer is the same as that of Maimonides: who says:[1] that since God's knowledge is essential in Him and not something added to His essence, the investigation of the character of His knowledge is tantamount to an investigation of His essence. But His essence is absolutely unknown, hence the character of His knowledge is also absolutely unknown. As there is no comparison or similarity between His existence and the existence of other things, so there is no comparison between His knowledge and the knowledge of others. Hence though if we picture His knowledge on the analogy of our own, a great many objections follow, such as that we must either deny the reality of the contingent or assume that His knowledge embraces that which we can not conceive as knowable, for He would have to know the infinite, or His knowledge would change with the change of the objects, and other difficulties of this sort—this would follow only if we conceive of His knowledge on the analogy of our own, but since His knowledge is not of the same kind as ours, these difficulties do not follow. God's knowledge is infinite, and infinite knowledge is not liable to these difficulties. . . .

We challenge therefore the one who believes in the eternity of the world and denies God's knowledge to tell us how a corporeal thing can come from a separate and unchangeable Intelligence. He will have to admit that for a material thing to come from a Separate Intelligence is such a change as the coming of something out of nothing, of which the human intellect can give no explanation. We also challenge him to explain how a finite world can come from a being whose power is infinite. We must therefore admit that this matter rests in God's knowledge in so far as it is infinite, and that He knows the explanation of all this, though we with our knowledge are unable to conceive it. Similarly we must say that the error of those who deny God's knowledge and say, "My way is hid from the Lord,"[2] is due to the fact that they compare God's knowledge with human knowledge. Human knowledge being finite, all the difficulties that we mentioned present themselves, namely that the knowledge changes with the change of the objects, and that it can not embrace the unembraceable, namely the infinite, so far as we can conceive with our knowledge. But as God's knowledge is infinite, it can embrace the infinite and the non-existent, without necessitating a change in God. Hence he concludes the verse, "His discernment is past searching out." Likewise when you say, "and my judgment is passed over from my God,"[3] which means that your choice of and determination upon one of the two possible alternatives can not be known by God, or else the contingent would cease to exist—your statement is not true. For such an inference may apply to finite knowledge, but the discernment of God is past searching out, and since His knowledge is infinite, the category of the contingent is not destroyed thereby, though we do not know the nature of His knowledge any more than we know the character of His essence.

This is Maimonides' conception of God's knowledge. He says, as we can not compare His essence with our essence, so we can not compare His knowledge with our knowledge, for the term knowledge is applied to God and to us as a pure homonym.[4] Maimonides does not mean that the term as applied to us means knowledge and as applied to God means ignorance, or vice versa, as absolute homonymity would signify.[5] By no means. What he means is this. The term existence is applied to God and to ourselves in an absolutely homonymous manner. Yet there is no doubt that though God's existence is absolutely different from the existence of anything else, nevertheless the term does not denote existence in the one case and non-existence in the other. So far as the negative signification is concerned, i.e. the denial of non-existence, the term has the same meaning in both cases, as is explained in Book Two, chapter 30. The term existence denotes the negation of non-existence, whether applied to us or to God. The absolute homonymity of the term applies to its positive signification, because there is no comparison at all between God's existence and the existence of anything else. Similarly the term knowledge, both as applied to God and as applied to us, means negation of ignorance. In this respect, i.e. in respect of its negative signification, the relation of the two applications, i.e. to God and to us, is one of priority and posteriority,[6] and not of absolute homonymity. In respect of the positive signification, on the other hand, the term knowledge is applied to God and to us as a pure homonym, and God's knowledge is absolutely unknown as His essence is absolutely unknown.

If we understand the words of Maimonides concerning God's knowledge in this manner, all the objections adduced by later writers will disappear. The result of all this is that God's knowledge, being infinite, embraces everything that happens in the world without necessitating change in God, and without destroying the category of the contingent. It also embraces the infinite. I have selected this view as the best in this matter. Our Rabbis also adopt it,[7] expressing the idea anonymously and without naming any opponent thereof: "All is foreseen, yet permission is given." "All is foreseen," signifies that God's knowledge embraces everything that happens in the world, and that nothing happens by accident without being known in advance. "Yet permission is given," signifies that the category of the contingent is real and God's knowledge does not destroy it. This is the truth in reference to this matter, though our knowledge is not sufficient to understand the possibility of this thing. This much will suffice as a brief discussion of God's knowledge.

NOTES

1. Guide of the Perplexed, III, 20.
2. Isa. 40, 27.
3. Ibid. The word משפט = judgment is understood by Albo in the sense of a determination in the field of the contingent, like a voluntary choice.
4. See vol. II, p. 45, note 3.
5. If there is nothing in common in two applications of a homonymous term, it follows that if one of them denotes knowledge, the other denotes not-knowledge, or ignorance.
6. See vol. II, p. 174, note 1.
7. Abot, ch. 3.

The Eleventh Principle

Reward and Punishment

INTRODUCTION

Affirmation of the belief that God rewards and punishes man gives rise to one of the most difficult of theological problems. Reward is meaningless and punishment unjust unless man is author of his own actions. Yet affirmation of human freedom poses two difficulties. The Ashariya philosophers believed freedom of the will to be precluded by the principle of divine omnipotence. God is not only all-powerful in the sense of potentially controlling all events, but is, in actuality, the author of all human events, even those ostensibly controlled by human volition. Human freedom may indeed be reconciled with the notion of divine omnipotence, but only by means of an explanation which states that God permits man to exercise independent volition. The Mishnah, *Avot* 3:19, states, "Everything is foreseen, but freedom of choice is given," i.e., God made freedom of human activity contingently possible. God, then, is omnipotent in the sense that He is a *kol yakhol*, i.e., He could control human will, but does not do so in order to make reward and punishment possible. Since the concept of divine justice mandates freedom of the will as a necessary condition of reward and punishment, God has indeed endowed man with freedom of the will.

More difficult is reconciliation of the concept of freedom of the will with belief in divine omniscience as asserted in the Tenth Principle. Here we seem to become involved in a logical contradiction. Knowledge, by definition, is of that which is certain. If God knows in advance the deeds of man, then those actions will surely come to be. When performed, those actions may hardly be deemed to be free since they can occur only in a manner compatible with God's already existent knowledge. Man certainly cannot act contrary to divine knowledge, thereby rendering God ignorant. If man cannot act contrary to divine knowledge, are his actions really free?

Maimonides finds the solution to this paradox in his thesis concerning the nature of the divine essence. Some questions have answers; others turn out not to be questions at all. For Maimonides this problem does not admit of a solution; rather, when subjected to careful scrutiny, the problem simply disappears. In speaking of the nature of God, in discussing the problem of attributes, and in formulating his concept of the nature of divine knowledge, Maimonides has stressed that the term "knowledge" as ascribed to God does not have the same connotation as the identical term applied to the human phenomenon of knowledge. The term "knowledge" is a homonym and, when applied to God, it is simply a denial of ignorance. As already noted, divine knowledge is identical with divine essence, not a quality added or superimposed. The paradox arises only because prescient "knowledge" is incompatible with subsequent freedom. No such paradox arises with regard to the compatibility of divine knowledge and human freedom simply because divine knowledge" is not knowledge in the conventional sense at all. Since God's knowledge is identical with His essence, divine knowledge can no more be comprehended by human reason than the essence of God can be fathomed by the human mind. All that can be said is that ignorance is antithetical to the divine nature, but since God does not possess "knowledge" in the usual sense of the term, His cognition does not prejudice human freedom. Maimonides' solution is not presented in the form of a resolution contrived to provide an escape from between the horns of a dilemma but emerges as an integral part of his philosophical system.

Saadia presents a more conventional resolution to this problem. Saadia accepts both the principle of divine omniscience and the reality of human freedom, and denies any incompatability between these doctrines. For Saadia divine knowledge is not causative in nature. This can best be understood in light of the proposition that God transcends time. To God, past, present and future are one and the same. God knows the future not in the present which would entail the conclusion that future volition cannot contradict present knowledge, but in a manner contemporaneous with the future. God sees all events in an eternal now. Human knowledge of contemporary events is certainly not causative. Since God is outside time, present and future are one and the same. The Catholic philosopher Thomas Aquinas, in formulating a similar explanation, offers the illustration of men passing single file through a deep gorge or ravine. A person standing at the side of the gorge can see only individual men passing through, but a person standing on a cliff overlooking the file of people sees them all at once. Man perceives only a single quantum of time as the "now," but God perceives all of eternity as the transcendental present.

Halevi accepts Saadia's position and explains that God transcends time and hence is able to know an act before it occurs, just as a man can know the act of another person after it has occurred. The act itself is entirely free; God simply knows how man will choose to act.

Less well known are the views of Abraham Ibn Daud and Ḥasdai Crescas. Selections from the writings of these philosophers have been included in the unit on the Tenth Principle since those readings relate more directly to the question of divine omniscience. Ibn Daud upholds human freedom at the expense of divine omniscience. Man is free and God does not know in advance how man will exercise the volition with which he has been endowed. Yet this in no way mitigates divine omniscience. Even God can know only that which is the subject of knowledge. According to Ibn Daud, it is illogical and a contradiction in terms to speak of knowledge of the contingent. With regard to the contingent one can only know that it is contingent. To claim any other knowledge of the contingent is to betray ignorance. God is certainly not ignorant, and hence He can know only the contingent nature of acts governed by human volition.

Crescas affirms divine omniscience at the expense of human freedom. God knows all things in advance and this knowledge does, indeed, render human freedom a nullity. Retribution is not punishment, which would be unjust, but the natural effect of human acts. A child who disobeys a parent's command not to place his hand in the fire will burn his hand. This phenomenon is not a punishment but rather the natural result of the child's folly. Human actions when good produce beneficial results or rewards; when evil they result in misfortune or punishment. Such actions and their results are connected in an entirely natural, causal manner.

Yet, as has been stated earlier, Crescas is not a fatalist. He is a "soft" determinist in that his position allows for commandments and prohibitions as factors which influence the determination of human conduct. This form of behaviorism recognizes that man's actions, although determined by physical and psychological forces, are the result of many different, and often contradictory, vector forces. Commandments and prohibitions thus become significant factors in determining human conduct by virtue of their psychological impact. God's knowledge is absolute because He is able to assess the relative strength of the various motivating forces which may be present in any given situation involving human choice and to predict with unerring accuracy how the human personality will respond.

The doctrine that God rewards and punishes man for his conduct entails acceptance of the notion that God regulates occurrences which befall man and exercises providence over His creatures. Aristotle accepted the notion of a providence limited in its governance to those things in the universe whose existence is permanent. As understood by Maimonides, this providence extends only to the intelligences and the heavenly spheres, including the sphere of the moon. Providence, according to Aristotle, extends only to entities whose existence is eternal. Indeed, it is this providence which, in accordance with Aristotle's theory of the eternity of the universe, guarantees the permanence and constancy of these entities. This selfsame providence influences terrestrial affairs to the extent of assuring immortality and constancy with regard to the various species without establishing permanence for the individual members of the species. Individual beings are, however, endowed with such properties as are necessary for the preservation of the species to which these individuals belong. Thus indirectly, through the activities of the spheres, providence influences earthly beings by providing for the permanent existence of the various species and the transient existence of individual members of those species. According to this analysis, providence manifests itself in the laws of nature and is expressed through the constancy and invariability of these laws and their operation. That which is not constant and does not follow a definite and certain rule is the result of change or accident and cannot be ascribed to divine providence.

Maimonides enumerates five theories regarding providence and discusses each at length, culminating in an analysis of his own view. The final view cited by Maimonides is identified by him as that of the Torah and is formulated in two different ways. The first of these formulations is in accordance with the literal meaning of statements found in Scripture and is the view accepted by "the multitude of our scholars." This opinion asserts that *all* calamities and beneficial occurrences which befall mankind are determined according to the deserts of the individuals involved. According to this view, afflictions bestowed solely in order to increase reward would not be in accordance with divine justice. The talmudic dictum "There is no death without sin, nor suffering without transgression" is cited as evidence. These scholars also deny that irrational beings are subject to reward. Some of the later *Ge'onim*, influenced by the Mu'tazila, accepted the notion of "sufferings of love," according to which misfortunes at times occur, not because of prior sin, but in order to enhance future reward.

The second formulation represents Maimonides' own view. He maintains that in the sublunar world man alone enjoys individual providence. Individual members of other species are subject to the haphazard occurrences of chance, as was the opinion of Aristotle according to Alexander's interpretation. There are, however, varying degrees of providence corresponding to the extent to which the individual is subject to the influence of the Active Intellect. Accordingly, not all individuals of the human species enjoy the same degree of providence; the protection and guidance of providence varies in accordance with a person's character and achievement. The highest form of providence is extended to the prophets; a lesser one is associated with the pious and with wise men. Maimonides diverges from the opinion of "the multitude of our scholars" in maintaining that an ignorant and sinful person is neglected and left to the governance of chance. Furthermore, even individuals possessing the requisite intellectual perfection enjoy the protection of providence only so long as they meditate on God. When thought is directed to mundane matters, the bond linking the human and the divine is broken, and providence departs from them while their thoughts are centered upon other matters. It is only those whose perception of God is so perfect that their minds contemplate Him constantly—this constant intercourse between the human intellect and the Active Intellect being the highest perfection man can attain—who are the recipients of providential guardianship at all times. Accordingly, Maimonides further differs from "the multitude of scholars" in another manner as well. Maimonides' theory necessarily entails that calamities and misfortunes may occur as a result of chance to individuals not accorded the protection of providence. The absence of providential guardianship may result from imperfect development of the intellect or from the temporary interruption of the contemplation of God. Such calamities and misfortunes are clearly not positive acts of divine judgment.

Gersonides rejects the contention of the "adherents of the Torah" that providence extends to all individuals on the threefold basis of philosophical argument, experience and the authority of Scripture itself. The contention that God rewards and punishes individuals by means of providence is deemed untenable by Gersonides since it is predicated upon divine knowledge of particulars, a thesis which, as we have seen, is rejected by Gersonides. According to Gersonides, God knows things only as ordered by the heavenly bodies by virtue of His knowledge of the genera. He also knows that, exercising freedom of will, man may prevent events ordained by the constellations from actually taking place. That God rewards and punishes on the basis of deeds destined by heavenly bodies is unthinkable. This would constitute a base injustice. Such retribution would result in punishment for misdeeds not actually committed since, according to this hypothesis, through exercise of free will man can contravene the dictates of the heavenly bodies. Nor can God reward and punish on the basis of deeds actually performed, since this would require that He have knowledge of them as particulars, and Gersonides denies that God has such knowledge.

Since Gersonides refutes both the view that providence does not extend to any individual and the opposite view that providences extends to all individuals, the intermediate position, namely, that providence extends to some individuals and not to others, emerges as the only tenable theory. This is perfectly reasonable because, as Aristotle notes in the

De Animalium, providence accorded to lesser species also varies in degree according to closeness to the Active Intellect. Preservation of the various species is assured by providing members of the genus with various organs and natural instincts to safeguard their existence; the more noble the genus, the more numerous its means of preservation. Human perfection is achieved by attaining closeness to the Active Intellect. Divine solicitude increases in direct correlation with the closeness of this bond. Those individuals who do not develop this capacity are provided for only as members of the species.

The relationship between man and the Active Intellect can be demonstated in another manner as well. All ideas are actually known by God, while man has the capacity of coming to know them in some fashion. Accordingly, it may be said that these ideas exist in man potentially, and in coming to know them, that which previously existed in potentiality is brought into actuality. However, this transition from potentiality to actuality requires the causal action of something existing in actuality. Therefore, it is God, in whom these ideas are actual, who leads man from potentiality to actuality. Since the agent, or efficient cause, becomes united in some way with that which is acted upon, man, in realizing his intellectual potentialities, becomes in some way united with, or attached to, the Active Intellect. At such times man may be said to be the recipient of divine providence.

Some individuals are privileged to receive knowledge of causal events leading to future benefits and misfortunes. This enables them to arrange their affairs so that they may receive benefits and be preserved from misfortunes. Such knowledge is conveyed through intuition, dreams, divination or, in its highest level, by means of prophecy. The extent of this form of providence varies directly with the individual's closeness or attachment to the Active Intellect. The greater the affinity of the individual with the Active Intellect, the greater and clearer is the knowledge of the ideas present in the Active Intellect. Accordingly, providence does not extend to the individual as a considered act on the part of God, but is a direct result of the intellectual and spiritual perfection of the recipient.

Albo agrees that providence is commensurate with the degree of intellectual perfection attained by the individual, but he does not present an explication of the nature and essence of providence. For Albo the crucial question is whether the world is governed by providence or by the celestial bodies. Albo accepts the validity of astrological influences, as did Gersonides, but denies that they are necessary causes in a deterministic sense. Albo asserts that astrological influences can be nullified or circumvented through exercise of free will, by reason of merit and, most importantly, by the will of God.

SAADIA, *EMUNOT VE-DE'OT*

Translation by Alexander Altmann

FOURTH TREATISE
ON OBEDIENCE AND DISOBEDIENCE: CUMPULSION AND JUSTICE

2. *The freedom of the will*

Having explained the way in which we should approach these questions relating to the Justice of God,[1] I say this: It accords with the justice of the Creator and His mercy towards man that He should have granted him the power[2] and ability[3] to do what He commanded him to do, and to refrain from what He forbade him to do. This is established by Reason and by Scripture. By Reason, because the Wise will not insist that a person should do a thing which lies beyond his ability and strength; by Scripture, as it says, 'O My people, what Have I done unto thee? and wherein have I wearied thee? Testify against Me' (Micah 6.3). Furthermore, it is said in Scripture, They that wait for the Lord shall renew their strength' (Isa. 40.31); moreover, 'Keep silence before Me, O Islands, and let the peoples renew their strength' (Isa. 41.1), and '. . .When the morning is light, they execute it, because it is in the power of their hand' (Micah 2.1).

I also found that the ability to act must necessarily exist before the act, so as to give man the free choice of either acting or abstaining from the act. For if the ability to act came into existence only at the moment of the act and were co-existent with it, the two would be either mutually interdependent or neither of them would be the cause of the other. If, on the other hand, the ability to act were to arise only after the act, man would have the power to take back an act which he had already performed. This is absurd, and the other alternative which we mentioned before is likewise absurd. It, therefore, follows that man's power to act must exist before his action so that, by his power, he may be able perfectly to fulfil the commandment of his Lord and God.[4]

I deem it important to make clear that in the same way as a man's action is a positive act, his abstention from a certain action is likewise a positive act, for by abstaining from that action he does, in fact, the opposite of it. This is not the case with the Creator (be He exalted and glorified), whose abstention from creating things is not an act. For if He abstains from creating the substances and their qualities, [5] it is something to which there exists no opposite, whereas man, whenever he abstains from doing one thing, actually chooses the opposite since his action concerns accidents only: if he does not love, he hates; if he is not favourably disposed, he is angry; there is no intermediate position between these.[6] Thus Scripture says, 'Therefore shall ye keep My charge, that ye do not any of these abominable customs, which were done before you' (Lev. 18.30), and furthermore, 'Yea, they do not unrighteousness; they walk in His ways'[7] (Ps. 119.3).

I must further explain that man does not perform any action unless he chooses to do it, since it is impossible for one to act if he has no free will or fails to exercise his free will.[8] The fact that the Law does not prescribe punishment for one who commits an illicit act unintentionally is not because he has no free will, but because of his ignorance of the cause and effect of his particular action. Thus, we say of one who killed a person unintentionally that, for instance, the hewing of the wood was done intentionally and with his free will, whereas his failure to prevent the accident was unintentional.[9] Or to quote the case of one who has desecrated the Sabbath,[10] the gathering of the sticks may have been intentional, but the person forgot that that particular day was the Sabbath.

Having dealt with all these points, I maintain further that the Creator (be He exalted) does not allow His power to interfere in the least with the actions of men, nor does He compel them to be either obedient or disobedient. I have proofs for this doctrine founded on sense perception, Reason, Scripture and Tradition.

In regard to sense perception, I have found that a man observes from his own experience that he has the power to speak and to be silent, the power to seize a thing and to abandon it; he does not notice any other force that would hinder him in any way from exercising his will-power. The simple truth is that he directs the impulses of his nature by his Reason, and if he follows the bidding of Reason, he is prudent, if he does not, he is a fool.

As to the proof based on Reason, our previous arguments have already shown how untenable is the idea that one action can be attributed to two agents.[11] Now one who thinks that the Creator (be He exalted and glorified) interferes with the actions of men, does in fact ascribe one single action to God and Man together. Furthermore, if God used compulsion against man, there would be no sense in His giving him commandments and prohibitions. Moreover, if He compelled him to do a certain action, it would be inadmissible to punish him for it. In addition, if men acted under compulsion, it would be necessary to mete out reward to believers and infidels alike, since each of them did only what he was ordered to do. If a wise man employs two workmen, the one that he may build, and the other that he may destroy, it is his duty to pay wages to both. Moreover, it is impossible to assume that man acts under compulsion, for if this were the case, he would have to be excused since one knows that man is unable to prevail against the power of God, and if the infidel offered the excuse that it was not within his power to believe in God, it would be necessary to consider him as justified and to accept his excuse.

As to the proofs based on Scripture, we have already mentioned the verse, 'Therefore choose life' (Deut. 30.19). The sinners are told, 'This has been of your doing; will He accept any of your persons?' (Mal. 1.9). Moreover, the Creator explains clearly that He is innocent with regard to their sins, as He says, 'Woe to the rebellious children, saith the Lord, that take counsel, but not of Me' (Isa. 30.1). He makes it clear that He is innocent with regard to the doings of the false prophets, saying 'I have not sent these prophets, yet they ran; I have not spoken to them, yet they prophesied' (Jer. 23.21), and other similar pronouncements.

As to the proofs based on Tradition, our ancient Teachers have told us, 'Everything lies in the hands of God except the fear of God, as it says, "And now, Israel, what doth the Lord Thy God require of thee, but to fear the Lord Thy God"' (Deut. 10.12).[12]

NOTES

1. Next to the problem of the Unity of God, that of God's Justice forms the main subject of Mu'tazilite theology.

2. Arab. *ḳadar,* which denotes, in the first place, God's 'measure,' 'decree,' but, in the view of the Mu'tazilites, also man's 'power' over his actions. For this reason, the Mu'tazilites were called *Ḳadarīyya.*

3. Arab. *'isti'dāt.*

4. This line of argument is only intelligible against the background of the Islamic controversy about the freedom of the will. The extreme orthodox view denied the freedom of the will altogether. Some Mu'tazilite schools suggested the compromise view that the

ability to act, i.e. the freedom of the will, arises not before the act but simultaneously with it: Man's freedom consists in the mere act of consent and thus accompanies the act without causing it. Saadya rejects this view, as seen above. He postulates the absolute freedom of the will.

5. Lit. 'The bodies and what is in them.'

6. Saadya distinguishes between God's and man's actions: God acts by creating the substances, and when He does not create He does not act at all. Man, who is incapable of creative activity, only acts by producing accidental conditions. He, therefore, is acting even if he abstains from an explicit act: if he fails to love, he hates, etc. Saadya introduced this distinction first in connection with the problem of Creation in Chapter I (ed. Landauer 71; ed. Slucki 38). There he points out that before God created the world He did not act at all. In this chapter Saadya wishes to make clear *(a)* that man's freedom of the will ('his ability to act') is present both in his action and abstention from action, since even his passivity has the positive character of an act; *(b)* that, on the other hand, God's non-interference with man's freedom must not be understood as an act in analogy with man's abstention from acting, but as absolute passivity. Thus, man's freedom is completely assured.

7. In both Scriptural passages man's abstention from acting against God's will is described in terms of *doing* something, i.e. keeping God's charge and walking in His ways.

8. Saadya means to say that the term *action* in its full sense implies free choice and responsibility.

9. Cf. Deut. 19.1-3.

10. Cf. Num. 15.32-36.

11. Cf. *Amānāt*, pp. 50-1 (26-7).

12. *b. Ber.* 33 b.

3. *Providence and Free Will*

All this explanation brings me to the following question, which will no doubt be asked: 'If what you have said is true, viz. that the will of God has no share in the disobedience of those who disobey Him, how is it possible that there should exist in His world anything which does not find His approval, or to which He does not give His consent?'[1] The answer to this is not far to seek. It is this: *we* regard it as strange that a wise man should tolerate within the realm of his power anything which is undesirable from his point of view, and to which he cannot give his consent. This is intelligible in the case of a human being since he dreads those things which cause him harm, but our Lord does not dread disobedience on account of Himself, since it is impossible to assume that any sort of accident should affect Him. He abhors disobedience for our own sakes because it has a harmful effect on us. For if we sin against Him and fail to acknowledge His Truth, we act foolishly, and if we sin against each other, we endanger our lives and positions. Since this is quite clear and manifest,[2] it is not strange that there should exist in His world things which we consider to be strange. When He explains to us that He abhors certain things, He does so for our own sakes in His way of mercy, as He made it clear in Scripture by saying, 'Do they provoke Me? saith the Lord; do they not provoke themselves, to the confusion of their own faces?' (Jer. 7.19).

Perhaps, someone will ask further: 'If God knows that which is going to be before it comes into being, He knows in advance if a certain person will disobey Him; now that person must by necessity disobey God, for otherwise God's foreknowledge would not prove to be correct.'[3] The fallacy underlying this question is even more evident than that underlying the previous one. It is this: He who makes this assertion has no proof that the knowledge of the Creator concerning things is the cause of their existence. He merely imagines this to be so, or chooses to believe it. The fallacy of this assumption becomes quite clear when we consider that, if God's knowledge of things were the cause of their existence, they would have existed from eternity, since God's knowledge of them is eternal.[4] We do, however, believe that God knows things as they exist in reality, i.e. of those things which He creates, He knows in advance that He is going to create them, and of those things which are subject to man's free will He knows in advance that man is going to choose them. Should one object, 'If God knows that a certain person will speak, is it possible for that person to be silent?' we answer quite simply that if that person was to keep silent instead of speaking we should have said in our original statement that God knew that this man would be silent, and we were not entitled to state that God knew that this person would speak. For God knows man's ultimate action such as it will be whether sooner or later after all his planning; for God knows man's nature,[5] as is said, 'The Lord knoweth the thoughts of man' (Ps. 94.11), and furthermore, 'For I know their inclination how they do even now' (Deut. 31.21).

I found people who asked on this point: 'How can it be reconciled with God's wisdom that He gives commandments and prohibitions to the righteous knowing as He does that they will always obey Him?'[6] I found there are four ways of answering this question. (1) The commandments were given in order to inform man what God desired of him; (2) in order that man's reward should be complete, for if he acted in conformity to God's will without being commanded to do so, he would have no claim to reward;[7] (3) if it were proper for God to bestow reward upon man for something concerning which He did not command him, it would be equally proper to punish him for something concerning which he issued no prohibition. This, however, would be unjust; (4) the commandments were given in order to enjoin, for a second time, through the prophet, the commandments which are already established by Reason so that man, being warned and well prepared, should be particularly careful to perform them, as it says, 'If Thou warn the righteous man, that the righteous sin not, he shall surely live, because he took warning' (Ezek. 3.21).

People ask further: 'How can it be reconciled with God's wisdom that he sends prophets to those who deny Him, knowing as He does in advance that they will refuse to believe? Does this not seem to be useless?' I found there are six ways of answering this argument. (1) If God did not send a prophetic message to those who deny Him calling on them to believe, they would be able to offer the excuse: if only the prophet had come to us, we would have believed in God.[8] (2) If that which exists in God's foreknowledge has not yet become reality in the form of a human act, God cannot mete out retribution, since otherwise reward and punishment would follow God's foreknowledge, not man's actions.[9] (3) In the same way as He established in the world[10] rational and sensible proofs of His existence for believers and unbelievers alike, so it is necessary that the proofs of prophecy should likewise be universal and embrace believers and unbelievers alike. (4) It is evident to us that if a man bids another person commit a crime which that person refuses to do, he has tried to harm that person and must be called a fool; in the same way, one who bids another person do something good which that other person refuses to do has, nevertheless, tried to benefit that person and must be called a wise man. (5) If the command of one who bids a person do something good is to be regarded as foolish when that person refuses to accept the command, simply because of that person's refusal, then the command of one who bids a person commit a crime would have to be regarded as wisdom in the case of that person accepting it. The essential natures of good and evil would thus be liable to be reversed according as they are accepted or not, which is absurd. (6) In the same way as God put the two classes on the same footing so far as Reason and Free Will are concerned, so it was necessary to put them on the same footing so far as the commandments and the prophetic message are concerned.

In addition to all these arguments I maintain that only that which arises from an action which does not benefit anybody can be called useless, whereas the prophetic message of God to the unbelievers, although they have chosen not to benefit nor to derive improvement from it, is yet one from which the believers and the rest of mankind did benefit in that they paid good heed to it, as one can see from the fact that to this day people have recounted, and will do so in the future, the stories of the Flood, of the people of Sodom, of Pharaoh, and so forth.[11]

NOTES

1. Mu'tazilite theology formulates the above problem as follows: 'whether God has power over the evil deeds and injustices.' Cf. al-Sharastānī, I, 53, 60; Guttmann, p. 169, n. 2.

2. An alternative translation: 'since the Commandment (of God) has been revealed for this purpose.'

3. Saadya formulates here for the first time in Jewish philosophical thought a problem which has since occupied the minds of both Jewish and non-Jewish scholastic thinkers, i.e. the problem of the reconciliation of man's freedom of will with the foreknowledge of God.

4. Cf. Yehudah Hallevi, *Kuzari*, V, 20 (ed. Cassel, pp. 415, 418, n. 4), where the above argument is stated in the name of the Mutakallimūn. Yehudah Hallevi adopts Saadya's solution of the problem, whereas Albo (*'Iḳḳarim*, IV, 1 ff.), after quoting both Saadya and Hallevi, expresses the view that it is no solution at all: if reality, he says, does not depend on God's knowledge, but, on the contrary, God's knowledge depends on reality, God's omniscience is no longer upheld.

5. God knows the nature of man and is therefore able to foresee the mental processes of his deliberations. The Scriptural verses quoted above confirm this interpretation of this

obscure passage. 'Nature' (*'ayn;* lit. 'essence') can hardly refer to *God's* essence in the sense of Maimonides' solution of the problem (cf *Hil. Teshubah,* V; *Moreh,* III, 16 ff.), since Saadya gives no hint of such an interpretation.

6. 'Obedience' must be taken here in the sense of conformity, on the basis of Reason, to the Divine will. Cf. above, pp. 95-7.

7. Although good and evil can be determined on rational grounds, Saadya holds that reward and punishment pre-suppose a Divine revelation. Cf. above, pp. 93-4. This constitutes an interesting compromise between the Ash'ariya, who held that without Revelation there was neither obligation (*taklif*) nor reward, and the Mu'tazilites, who believed that both were independent of Revelation.

8. Cf. al-Sharastānī, I, 67.

9. The above interpretation of the text (which is corrupt) follows Guttmann (p. 171, n. 3).

10. Wolff's emendation *fi-l-'ilmi* ('in the knowledge') for *fi-l-'almi* ('in the world') is unnecessary.

11. Saadya means to say that although God's commandments were rejected by the unbelievers, a fact which God could foresee, they helped the righteous to appreciate the binding character of the Law: in remembering the stories of the Flood, etc., they were strengthened in their belief in the God of Justice.

HALEVI, *KUZARI*

Translation by Hartwig Hirschfeld

PART V

19. Al Khazari: This is sufficient to refresh my memory. There is no doubt that thy discourse on the soul and reason, as well as these axioms, was quoted from other authorities. Now I desire to hear thy own opinion and principles of faith. Thou didst declare thy willingness to examine this and similar points. It seems to me that it will not be possible to omit the questions of predestination and human free will, since they are of actual importance. Now tell me thy mind.

20. The Rabbi: Only a perverse, heretical person would deny the nature of what is possible, making assertions of opinions in which he does not believe. Yet from the preparations he makes for events he hopes for or fears, one can see that he believes in their possibility, and that his preparations may be useful. If he believed in absolute necessity, he would simply submit, and not equip himself with weapons against his enemy, or with food against his hunger. If he, on the other hand, thinks that either preparation or the omission of the same is necessary in accordance with the nature of the case, he admits intermediary causes, as well as their consequences. He will encounter his desire in every intermediary cause, and if he is just and not perverse, he will find himself placed between himself and his desire to obtain achievable objects, which he can pursue or abandon as he likes. Such a belief is not incompatible with a belief in Divine Providence, but everything is led back to him in various ways, as I am going to explain. My opinion is that everything of which we are conscious is referred to the Prime Cause in two ways, either as an immediate expression of the divine will, or through intermediaries. An instance of the first kind is found in the synthetic arrangement visible in animals, plants and spheres, objects which no intelligent observer would trace back to accident, but to a creative and wise will, which gives everything its place and portion. An instance of the second kind is to be found in the burning of a beam. Fire is a fine, hot, and active substance, whilst wood is a porous and passive one. It is the nature of the fine and active substance to affect its object, whilst heat and dryness warm and

volatilize the moisture of the object till it is completely dissolved. If thou seekest the causes of these processes, active as well as passive, thou wilt not fail to discover them. Thou mayest even discover the causes of their causes till thou arrivest at the spheres, then at their causes, and finally at the Prime Cause. One might justly say that everything is ordained by God, and another is equally right in making man's free will or accident responsible for it, without, however, bringing it outside the divine providence. If thou likest thou mayest render the matter more intelligible by means of the following classification. Effects are either of divine or of natural origin, either accidental or arbitrary. The *divine* ones issue forth actively, having no other causes except God's will. The *natural* ones are derived from intermediate, preparatory causes which bring them to the desired end, as long as no obstacle arises from one of the other three classes. The *accidental* ones are likewise the result of intermediary causes, but accidentally, not by nature or arrangement, or by will power. They are not prepared to be brought to completion and standstill, and they stand apart from the other three classes. As regards the arbitrary actions, they have their roots in the free will of man, when he is in a position to exercise it. Free will belongs to the class of intermediary causes, and possesses causes which reduce it, chainlike, to the Prime Cause. This course is not compulsory, because the whole thing is potential, and the mind wavers between an opinion and its opposite, being permitted to turn where it chooses. The result is praise or blame for the choice, which is not the case in the other classes. An accidental or natural cause cannot be blamed, although some of them admit a possibility. But one cannot blame a child or a sleeping person for harm done. The opposite was possible just the same, and they cannot be blamed, because they lack judgment. Dost thou think that those who deny the potential are not wroth with those who injure them purposely? Or do they acquiesce in being robbed of their garments, and consequently also in suffering from cold, just as they would expose themselves to the north wind on a cold day? Or do they believe that the anger about it is but a fallacious exertion, instituted for no purpose, that man may feel anger about one particular thing, or give praise and blame, show hatred etc.? In these cases free will, as such, has no forcing cause, because it is itself reduced to compulsion. Man's language, then, would be as little free as the beating of his pulse. This would be against evident appearances. Thou perceivest that speaking or being silent is in thy power as long as thou art in possession of thy reason, and not controlled by other casualties. If all incidents would be the result of the original will of the Prime Cause, they would, each in its turn, be created anew in every moment. We might then say that the Creator created anew the whole world this very moment. The servant of God would be no better than the wicked, as both would be obedient, and only do that for which they are fated. A conviction of this kind has many objections, whilst the refutation of appearances is most difficult, as we said before. The objection made against those who assert that some matters are removed from the bounds of Providence by human free will is to be refuted by what was said before, viz. that they are completely outside the control of Providence, but are indirectly linked to it. There is still another objection, viz. that these matters are outside the divine omniscience, because the absolutely potential is naturally an unknown quantity. The Mutakallims considered this matter in detail, with the result that the divine knowledge of the potential is but casual, and that the knowledge of a thing is neither the cause of its coming into existence, nor of its disappearance therefrom. There is, withal, a possibility of existence and non-existence. For the knowledge of events to come is not the cause of their existence, just as is the case with the knowledge of things which have been. This is but a proof that the knowledge belongs to God, or to the angels, or the prophets, or the priests. If this knowledge were the cause of the existence of a thing, many people would be placed in paradise solely for the sake of the divine knowledge that they are pious, even if they have done no pious act. Others would be in Gehenna, because God knows them to be wicked, without their having committed a sin. Man should also be satisfied without having eaten, because he knows that he is accustomed to be satisfied at certain times. Another consequence would be that intermediary causes would cease to exist, and their disappearance would be shared by that of the intermediary factors. . .

But I have diverged a little from my subject. Returning to the same, I say that David laid down three causes of death, viz. 'God may slay him,' i.e. divine cause; 'Or his day shall come to die,' i.e. natural cause; 'Or he shall descend into battle and perish,' i.e. accidental cause (I Sam. xxvi. 10). He omits the fourth possibility, viz. suicide, because no rational being seeks death voluntarily. If Saul killed himself, it was not to seek death, but to escape torture and derision. A similar classification can be made with regard to speech. The speech of a prophet at the time when he is enwrapped by the Holy Spirit is in every part directed by the Divine Influence, the prophet himself being powerless to alter one word. Natural speech consists in communications and hints which conform to the subject to be discussed, and the mind follows without previous convention. Conventional languages are composed of natural and arbitrary elements. Accidental speech is that of a madman, and is neither in harmony with a subject, nor to the purpose. Free speech is that of a prophet when not inspired, or the words of an intelligent, thinking person who connects his words, and chooses his expressions in accordance with the subject under consideration. If he wished he could replace each word by another, could even drop the whole subject and take up another. All these cases, however, can be reduced indirectly to God, but not as immediate issues of the Prime Will, otherwise the words of a child, and mad people, the speech of an orator, and the song of a poet were the words of God. Far be this from Him. The excuse of a slothful person who tells the energetic one that that which is to be, exists previously in the knowledge of God, is inconclusive. For should he even assert that that which shall be must be, he is told: 'Quite so; but this argument should not prevent thee to take the best counsel, to prepare weapons against thy enemy, and food for hunger, as soon as thou art aware that that both thy safety and destruction depend upon intermediary causes.' One of them, which is the most frequent, is the application of energy and industry, or of lassitude and indolence. Do not try to refute me with those rare and accidental cases, viz. that a circumspect person perishes, whilst the careless and unprotected one is saved. For the word safety means something quite different from the word risk. A sensible person will not flee from a place of safety to one of risk, just as one flees from a dangerous place to a safe one. If safety accrues in the place of danger this is considered rare, but if a person perishes in a safe place, it is called an extraordinary occurrence. One should, therefore, employ circumspection. One of the causes of carelessness is the view opposite to this advice. Everything, however, is indirectly related to God. Whatever happens through direct ordination belongs to the class of strange and miraculous events, and can dispense with intermediary causes. In some cases they are, however, necessary, as in the preservation of Moses during his fast of forty days, when he was without food, or in the destruction of Sanherib's army without a visible cause—unless through a divine one—which we cannot consider as such, as we do not know what it is. Of such we say that preparation avails them not, viz. preparation in the concrete sense. Moral preparation, however, based on the secret of the law, benefits him who knows and understands it, because it brings what is good, and repels what is bad. If man aids intermediary causes with energy, having left to God the objects of his fear with a pure mind, he fares well and suffers no loss. He, however, who courts danger [transgresses the warning: 'You shall not tempt the Lord' (Deut. vi. 16), in spite of his confidence in God. But if one considers it absurd] to give commands to a person who, as he knows beforehand, may either disobey or obey him, this is not absurd. We have shown previously that disobedience and obedience depend upon intermediary causes. The cause of obedience is the command for it. [The obeying person knew beforehand that he would do so and that the cause of it was that he had heard reproof.] He also keeps in mind that disobedience depends on intermediary causes, which are to be found either in the companionship of wicked people, or in the preponderance of evil temperament, or inclination for comfort and rest. Finally, he knew that his disobedience was lessened through reproof. Reproof, as is known, impresses the mind in any case, and even the soul of an insubordinate person is in some small way influenced by reproof. In a higher degree this takes place in a multitude, because there is at any rate one person to be found who accepts it. Far from being useless, reproof is, therefore, useful.

MAIMONIDES, *MISHNEH TORAH*

Translation by Moses Hyamson

BOOK OF KNOWLEDGE, LAWS OF REPENTANCE, CHAPTER 3

1. Every human being has merits and iniquities. One whose merits exceed his iniquities is righteous. He whose iniquities exceed his merits is wicked. If the two balance in an individual, he belongs to the intermediate class. II. So it is with a country. If the merits of all its inhabitants exceed their iniquities, the country is righteous. If their iniquities preponderate, it is a wicked country. So too is it with regard to the whole of the world.

2. III. A person whose iniquities exceed his merits perishes forthwith in his wickedness, as it is said, "For the multitude of thy iniquity" (Hosea. 9:7). So too, a country, the iniquities of whose inhabitants preponderate, perishes forthwith, as it is said, "the cry of Sodom and Gomorrah, because it is great" (Gen. 18:20). So, with the entire world, if the iniquities of its human population exceed their merits, they are destroyed forthwith, as it is said, "And the Lord saw that the wickedness of man was great in the earth" (Gen. 6:5). IV. This valuation takes into account not the number but the magnitude of merits and iniquities. There may be a single merit that outweighs many iniquities, as it is said, "Because in him there is found some good thing" (I. Kings 14:13). And there may be one iniquity that counterbalances many merits, as it is said "But one sinner[1] destroyeth much good" (Eccles. 9:19). The valuation is according to the knowledge of the Omniscient God. He alone knows how to set off merit against iniquities.

3. V. Whoever regrets the precepts that he had fulfilled and wonders at his meritorious deeds, saying to himself, 'What profit have I of them? Would that I had not done them,' forfeits the credit for all of them, and none of his meritorious deeds is ever remembered in his favour, as it is said, "The righteousness of the righteous shall not deliver him on the day of his transgression" (Ezek. 33:12); that is, if he regrets his former good deeds. VI. And even as a man's meritorious deeds and iniquities are balanced at the hour of death, so are the iniquities of every single

inhabitant of the Earth weighed against his merits annually on the New Year Feast. He who is found righteous is sealed unto life; he who is found wicked is sealed unto death. If one belongs to the intermediate class, sentence on him is suspended till the Day of Atonement. If he repents, he is sealed unto life; if he does not do so, he is sealed unto death.

4. VII. Although the Sounding of the Shofar on the New Year is a decree of Holy Writ,[2] still it has a deep meaning, as if saying, "Awake, awake, O sleepers, from your sleep; O slumberers, arouse ye from your slumbers; and examine your deeds, return in repentance, and remember your Creator. Those of you who forget the truth in the follies of the times and go astray, the whole year, in vanity and emptiness, which neither profit nor save, look to your souls; improve your ways and works. Abandon, everyone of you, his evil course and the thought that is not good." VIII. It is necessary therefore that every one, throughout the year, should regard himself as if he were half innocent and half guilty; and should regard the whole of mankind as half innocent and half guilty. If then he commits one more sin, he presses down the scale of guilt against himself and the whole world and causes his destruction. If he fulfills one commandment, he turns the scale of merit in his favour and in that of the whole world, and brings salvation and deliverance to all his fellow-creatures and to himself, as it is said, "the righteous man is the foundation of the world" (Prov. 10:25); that is to say, that he who acts justly presses down the scale of merit in favour of all the world and saves it. IX. And because of these considerations, the whole house of Israel have the custom to increase their charities and other good deeds from the New Year to the Day of Atonement and engage in religious duties at this period to a larger extent than during the rest of the year. So too, during these ten days, all rise up while it is still night, and pray in the synagogues till dawn, with fervent entreaties and supplications.

5. X. When a person's iniquities and merits are weighed, the first offence that he committed is not counted, nor yet the second. The reckoning starts from the third offence. And if his iniquities, from the third onwards, are found to exceed his merits, the first two sins are also included in the demerits and he is judged for all of them. XI. But if his merits and iniquities—counting from the third offence—are found to balance, then all his iniquities are cancelled, one after another. The third is regarded as if it had been the first, the first two having already been forgiven. Then the fourth is regarded as if it had been the first, the third having been forgiven; and so on to the last. XII. This applies to an individual, as it is said, "Lo, all these things does God do; twice, yea, thrice with a man" (Job. 33:29). As to a community, (punishment for)

their first offence as well as for their second and third, is suspended, as it is said "For three transgressions of Israel,—yea, for four, I will not reverse it" (Amos. 2:6). When account is taken of the merits and demerits of a community, their sins are reckoned from the fourth onwards, after the manner already described. XIII. As to those who belong to the intermediate class, if among half of an individual's deeds which constitute offences there is included the sin of never having put on phylacteries,[3] he is judged according to his sins but will have a portion in the world to come. So too, all wicked persons whose iniquities exceed their merits are judged according to their sins and have a portion in the world to come; for all Israelites, notwithstanding that they have sinned, have a portion in the life hereafter, as it is said, "Thy people shall all be righteous, they shall inherit the land for ever" (Isaiah. 60:21). The expression *land* is a metaphor for the land of life, that is, the world to come. And so too, the saints among the gentile peoples have a portion in the world to come.

BOOK OF KNOWLEDGE, LAWS OF REPENTANCE, CHAPTER 5

1. Free Will is bestowed on every human being. If one desires to turn towards the good way and be righteous, he has the power to do so. If one wishes to turn towards the evil way and be wicked, he is at liberty to do so. And thus is it written in the Torah, "Behold, the man is become as one of us, to know good and evil" (Gen. 3:22)—which means that the human species had become unique in the world—there being no other species like it in the following respect, namely, that man, of himself and by the exercise of his own intelligence and reason, knows what is good and what is evil, and there is none who can prevent him from doing that which is good or that which is evil. And since this is so (there is reason to fear) "lest he put forth his hand etc." (ibid.).

2. II. Let not the notion, expressed by foolish gentiles and most of the senseless folk among Israelites, pass through your mind that at the beginning of a person's existence, the Almighty decrees that he is to be either righteous or wicked. This is not so. Every human being may become righteous like Moses, our teacher, or wicked like Jeroboam; wise or foolish, merciful or cruel; niggardly or generous; and so with all other qualities. III. There is no one that coerces him or decrees what he is to do, or draws him to either of the two ways; but every person turns to the way which he desires, spontaneously and of his own volition. Thus Jeremiah said, "out of the mouth of the Most High, proceedeth not evil and good" (Lam. 3:38); that is to say, the Creator does not decree either that a man shall be good or that he shall be wicked. IV. Accordingly it follows that it is the sinner who has inflicted injury on himself; and he should therefore weep for, and bewail what he has done to his soul—how he has mistreated it. This is expressed in the next verse, "Wherefore doth a living man complain, a strong man, because of his sins" (Lam. 3:39). The prophet continues: since liberty of action is in our hands and we have, of our free will, committed all these evils, it behoves us to return in a spirit of repentance, and forsake our wickedness, for we have the power to do so. This thought is expressed in the next verse, "Let us search and try our ways, and return to the Lord" (Lam. 3.40).

3. V. This doctrine is an important principle, the pillar of the Law and the Commandment, as it is said, "see, I set before thee this day life and good, and death and evil" (Deut. 30:15); and again it is written, 'Behold, I set before you this day, a blessing and a curse" (Deut. 11: 26). This means that the power is in your hands, and whatever a man desires to do among the things that human beings do, he can do, whether they are good or evil; and, because of this faculty, it is said, "O that they had such

a heart as this always" (Deut. 5:26), which implies that the Creator neither puts compulsion on the children of men nor decrees that they should do either good, or evil, but it is all left to their discretion.

4. VI. If God had decreed that a person should be either righteous or wicked, or if there were some force inherent in his nature which irresistibly drew him to a particular course, or to a special branch of knowledge, to special views or activities, as the foolish astrologers, out of their own fancy, pretend, how would the Almighty have charged us, through the prophets: 'Do this and do not do that, improve your ways, do not follow your wicked impulses,' when, from the beginning of his existence, his destiny had already been decreed, or his innate constitution irresistibly drew him to that from which he could not set himself free? What room would there be for the whole of the Torah? By what right or justice could God punish the wicked or reward the righteous? "Shall not the Judge of all the earth act justly?" (Gen. 18:25). VII. Do not, however, wonder: how can a man do whatever he desires, and act according to his discretion? Can aught in the world be done without the Master's Will and pleasure? The Scripture itself says, "Whatsoever the Lord pleased, that hath He done in heaven and on earth" (Ps. 135:6). Know then that everything takes place according to His pleasure, notwithstanding that our acts are in our power. VIII. How so? Just as it was the pleasure of the Creator that fire and air shall ascend, earth and water descend, and that the sphere shall revolve in a circle, and all other things in the Universe shall exist in their special ways which He desired, so it was His pleasure that Man should have liberty of will, and all his acts should be left to his discretion; that nothing should coerce him or draw him to aught, but that, of himself and by the exercise of his own mind which God had given him, he should do whatever it is in a man's power to do. IX. Hence, he is judged according to his deeds. If he does well, good is done to him; and if he does ill, evil is done to him. So the prophet says, "This hath been of your doing" (Mal. 1:9); "Yea, they have chosen their own ways" (Is. 66:3). On this theme Solomon said, "Rejoice, O young man, in thy youth. . .but know thou, that for all these things God will bring thee into judgment" (Eccles. 11:9); that is to say, realize that what you do is in your power, and that you will have to render an account.

5. X. Perchance you will say, "Does not the Almighty know everything that will be before it happens?" He either knows that this person will be righteous or wicked, or He does not know. If He knows that he will be righteous, it is impossible that he should not be righteous; and if you say that He knows that he will be righteous and yet it is possible for him to be wicked, then He does not know the matter clearly.

XI. As to the solution of this problem, understand that "the measure thereof is longer than the earth and wider than the sea" (Job. 11:9), and many important principles of the highest sublimity are connected with it. You, however, need only to know and comprehend what I am about to say. XII. In the Second Chapter of the laws relating to the fundamental principles of the Torah, we have already explained that God does not know with a knowledge external to Himself, like human beings whose knowledge and self are separate entities, but He, blessed be His Name, and His knowledge are One. This, the human intellect cannot clearly apprehend. And just as it is not in human power to apprehend or discover the Creator's Real Essence, as it is said, "For there shall no man see Me and live" (Ex. 33:20), so it is not in human power to apprehend or discover the Creator's knowledge. So the prophet said, "For My thoughts are not your thoughts, neither are your ways My ways" (Is. 55:8). This being the case, we lack the capacity to know how God knows all creatures and their activities. XIII. Yet we do know beyond doubt that a human being's activities are in his own hands and the Almighty neither draws him on, nor decrees that he should act thus or not act thus. It is not religious tradition alone by which this is known. It is also supported by clear proofs furnished by science. Hence, it is said in the Prophetic writings that a man will be judged for all his deeds, according to his deeds, whether they be good or evil. And this is the principle on which all the words of Prophecy depend.

BOOK OF KNOWLEDGE, LAWS OF REPENTANCE, CHAPTER 9

1. It is known that the reward for the fulfilment of the commandments and the good to which we will attain if we have kept the way of the Lord, as prescribed in the Law, is life in the World to Come, as it is said, "That it may be well with thee, and that thou mayest prolong thy days" (Deut. 22:7), while the retribution exacted from the wicked who have abandoned the ways of righteousness prescribed in the Torah is excision, as it is said, "that soul shall be utterly cut off; his iniquity shall be upon him" (Num. 15:31). What then is the meaning of the statement found everywhere in the Torah that 'if ye obey, it will happen to you thus; if ye do not obey, it will be otherwise; and all these happenings will take place in this world, such as war and peace; sovereignty and subjection; residence in the Promised Land, and exile; prosperity in one's activities and failure, and all the other things predicted in the words of the Covenant (Lev. ch. 26. Deut. ch. 28)? II. All those promises were (once) truly (fulfilled) and will again be so. When we fulfil all the commandments of the Torah, all the good things of this world will come to us. When however we transgress the precepts, the evils that are written in the Torah will befall us. But nevertheless, those good things are not the final reward for the fulfilment of the commandments, nor are those evils the last penalty exacted from one who transgresses all the commandments. These matters are to be understood as follows: III. The Holy One, blessed be He, gave us this Law—a tree of life. Whoever fulfills what is written therein and knows it with a complete and correct knowledge will attain thereby life in the World to Come. According to the greatness of his deeds and abundance of his knowledge will be the measure in which he will attain that life. He has further promised us in the Torah, that, if we observe its behests joyously and cheerfully, and continually meditate on its wisdom, He will remove from us the obstacles that hinder us in its observance, such as sickness, war, famine, and other calamities; and will bestow upon us all the material benefits which will strengthen our ability to fulfil the Law, such as plenty, peace, abundance of silver and gold. IV. Thus we will not be engaged, all our days, in providing for our bodily needs, but will have leisure to study wisdom and fulfil the commandment, and thus attain life in the World to Come. Hence, after the assurance of material benefits, it is said in the Torah, "And it shall be righteousness unto us, if we observe to do all this commandment before the Lord, our God, as He hath commanded us" (Deut. 6:25). V. So too, He taught us in the Torah that if we deliberately forsake it and occupy ourselves with temporal follies, as the text says,

"But Jeshurun waxed fat and kicked" (Deut. 32:15),—the true Judge will deprive the forsakers of all those material benefits which only served to encourage them to be recalcitrant, and will send upon them all the calamities that will prevent their attaining the life hereafter, so that they will perish in their wickedness. This is expressed by the Torah in the text: "Because thou didst not serve the Lord, thy God, with joyfulness and with gladness of heart, by reason of the abundance of all things, therefore shalt thou serve thine enemy whom the Lord shall send against thee"[1] (Deut. 28:47–48). VI. Hence, all those benedictions and maledictions are to be explained as follows: If you have served God with joy and observed His way, He will bestow upon you those blessings and avert from you those curses, so that you will have leisure to become wise in the Torah and occupy yourselves therewith, and thus attain life hereafter, and then it will be well with you in the world which is entirely blissful and you will enjoy length of days in an existence which is everlasting. So you will enjoy both worlds,—a happy life on earth leading to the life in the World to Come. For if wisdom is not acquired and good deeds are not performed here, there will be nought meriting a recompense hereafter, as it is said, "for there is no work, nor device, nor knowledge nor wisdom in the grave" (Eccles. 9:10). VII. But if you have forsaken the Lord and have erred in eating, drinking, fornication, and similar things, He will bring upon you all those curses and withhold from you all those blessings till your days will end in confusion and terror, and you will have neither the free mind nor the healthy body requisite for the fulfilment of the commandments so that you will suffer perdition in the life hereafter and will thus have lost both worlds,—for when one is troubled here on earth with diseases, war or famine, he does not occupy himself with the acquisition of wisdom or the performance of religious precepts by which life hereafter is gained.

2. VIII. Hence, all Israelites, their prophets and sages, longed for the advent of Messianic times, that they might have relief from the wicked tyranny that does not permit them properly to occupy themselves with the study of the Torah and the observance of the commandments; that they might have ease, devote themselves to getting wisdom, and thus attain to life in the World to Come. IX. For in those days, knowledge, wisdom and truth will increase, as it is said "For the earth will be full of the knowledge of the Lord" (Is. 11:9), and it is said, "They will no more teach everyone his brother and everyone his neighbour" (Jer. 31:34), and further, "I will remove the heart of stone from your flesh" (Ezek. 36:26). X. Because the King who will arise from the seed of David will possess more wisdom than Solomon and will be a great prophet, approaching

Moses, our teacher,[2] he will teach the whole of the Jewish people and instruct them in the way of God; and all nations will come to hear him, as it is said, "And at the end of days it shall come to pass that the Mount of the Lord's house shall be established as the top of the mountains" (Micah 4:1, Is. 2:2). XI. The ultimate and perfect reward, the final bliss which will suffer neither interruption nor diminution is the life in the world to come. The Messianic era, on the other hand, will be realized in this world; which will continue in its normal course except that independent sovereignty will be restored to Israel. The ancient sages already said, "The only difference between the present and the Messianic era is that political oppression will then cease."

NOTES

1. The order of the sentences in this text, correctly given as it is in the Torah, is reversed in the Hebrew manuscript, possibly not to end with calamitous maledictions.

2. In the MS. "nearer than our teacher Moses," ונביא גדול הוא קרוב ממשה. This may be a scribal error, and should be corrected to קרוב למשה.

MAIMONIDES, *MOREH NEVUKHIM*

Translation by Michael Friedlander

PART III, CHAPTER 10

The Mutakallemim, as I have already told you, apply the term non-existence only to absolute non-existence, and not to the absence of properties. A property and the absence of that property are considered by them as two opposites, they treat, *e.g.*, blindness and sight, death and life, in the same way as heat and cold. Therefore they say, without any qualification, non-existence does not require any agent, an agent is required when *something* is produced. From a certain point of view this is correct. Although they hold that non-existence does not require an agent, they say in accordance with their principle that God causes blindness and deafness, and gives rest to anything that moves, for they consider these negative conditions as positive properties. We must now state our opinion in accordance with the results of philosophical research. You know that he who removes the obstacle of motion is to some extent the cause of the motion, *e.g.*, if one removes the pillar which supports the beam he causes the beam to move, as has been stated by Aristotle in Physics (VIII., chap. iv.); in this sense we say of him who removed a certain property that he produced the absence of that property, although absence of a property is nothing positive. Just as we say of him who puts out the light at night that he has produced darkness, so we say of him who destroyed the sight of any being that he produced blindness, although darkness and blindness are negative properties, and require no agent. In accordance with this view we explain the following passage of Isaiah: "I form the light and create (*bore*) darkness; I make peace, and create (*bore*) evil" (Isa. xlv. 7), for darkness and evil are non-existing things. Consider that the prophet does not say, I make (*oseh*) darkness, I make (*oseh*) evil, because darkness and evil are not things in positive existence to which the verb "to make" would apply; the verb *bara* "to create" is used, because in Hebrew this verb is applied to non-existing things, *e.g.*, "In the beginning God created" (*bara*), &c.; here the creation took place from nothing. Only in this sense can non-existence be said to be produced by a certain action of the agent. In the same way we must explain the following passage: "Who hath made man's mouth? or who maketh the dumb, or deaf, or the seeing," &c. (Exod. iv. 11). The passage can also be explained as follows: Who has made man able to speak? or can create him without the capacity of speaking, *i.e.*, create a substance that is incapable of acquiring this property? for he who produces a substance that cannot acquire a certain property may be called the producer of that privation. Thus we say, if any one abstains from delivering a fellow-man from death, although he is able to do so, that he killed him. It is now clear that according to all these different views the action of an agent cannot be directly connected with a thing that does not exist; only indirectly is non-existence described as the result of the action of an agent, whilst in a direct manner an action can only influence a thing really in existence; accordingly, whoever the agent may be, he can only act upon an existing thing.

After this explanation you must recall to memory that, as has been proved, the [so-called] evils are evils only in relation to a certain thing, and that which is evil in reference to a certain existing thing, either includes the non-existence of that thing or the non-existence of some of its good conditions. The proposition has therefore been laid down in the most general terms, "All evils are negations." Thus for man death is evil; death is his non-existence. Illness, poverty, and ignorance are evils for man; all these are privations of properties. If you examine all single cases to which this general proposition applies, you will find that there is not one case in which the proposition is wrong, except in the opinion of those who do not make any distinction between negative and positive properties, or between two opposites, or do not know the nature of things,—who, *e.g.*, do not know that health in general denotes a certain equilibrium, and is a relative term. The absence of that relation is illness in general, and death is the absence of life in the case of any animal. The destruction of other things is likewise nothing but the absence of their form.

After these propositions, it must be admitted as a fact that it cannot be said of God that He directly creates evil, or He has the direct intention to produce evil; this is impossible. His works are all perfectly good. He only produces existence, and all existence is good; whilst evils are of a negative character, and cannot be acted upon. Evil can only be attributed to Him in the way we have mentioned. He creates evil only in so far as He produces the corporeal element such as it actually is; it is always connected with negatives, and on that account the source of all destruction and evil. Those beings that do not possess this corporeal element are not subject to destruction or evil; consequently the true work of God is all good, since it is existence. The book which enlightened the darkness of the world says therefore, "And God saw everything that He had made, and, behold, it was very good" (Gen. i. 31). Even the existence of this corporeal element, low as it in reality is, because it is the source of death and all evils, is likewise good for the permanence of the Universe and the continuation of the order of things, so that one thing departs and the other succeeds. Rabbi Meir therefore explains the words "and behold it was very good" (*tobh m'od*); that even death was good in accordance with what we have observed in this chapter. Remember what I said in this chapter, consider it, and you will understand all that the prophets and our Sages remarked about the perfect goodness of all the direct works of God. In Bereshith Rabba (chap. i.) the same idea is expressed thus: "No evil comes down from above."

PART III, CHAPTER 11

All the great evils which men cause to each other because of certain intentions, desires, opinions, or religious principles, are likewise due to non-existence, because they originate in ignorance, which is absence of wisdom. A blind man, for example, who has no guide, stumbles constantly, because he cannot see, and causes injury and harm to himself and others. In the same manner various classes of men, each man in proportion to his ignorance, bring great evils upon themselves and upon other individual members of the species. If men possessed wisdom, which stands in the same relation to the form of man as the sight to the eye, they would not cause any injury to thmselves or to others; for the knowledge of truth removes hatred and quarrels, and prevents mutual injuries. This state of society is promised to us by the prophet in the words: "And the wolf shall dwell with the lamb," &c.; "and the cow and the bear shall feed together," &c.; and "the sucking child shall play on the hole of the asp," &c. (Isa. xi. 6 *seq.*) The prophet also points out what will be the cause of this change; for he says that hatred, quarrel, and fighting will come to an end, because men will then have a true knowledge of God. "They shall not hurt nor destroy in all my holy mountain: for the earth shall be full of the knowledge of the Lord, as waters that cover the sea" (ibid. ver. 9). Note it.

PART III, CHAPTER 12

Men frequently think that the evils in the world are more numerous than the good things; many sayings and songs of the nations dwell on this idea. They say that a good thing is found only exceptionally, whilst evil things are numerous and lasting. Not only common people make this mistake, but even many who believe that they are wise. Al-Razi wrote a well-known book "On Metaphysics" [or Theology]. Among other mad and foolish things, it contains also the idea, discovered by him, that there exists more evil than good. For if the happiness of man and his pleasure in the times of prosperity be compared with the mishaps that befall him,—such as grief, acute pain, defects, paralysis of the limbs, fears, anxieties, and troubles,—it would seem as if the existence of man is a punishment and a great evil for him. This author commenced to verify his opinion by counting all the evils one by one; by this means he opposed those who hold the correct view of the benefits bestowed by God and His evident kindness, viz., that God is perfect goodness, and that all that comes from Him is absolutely good. The origin of the error is to be found in the circumstance that this ignorant man, and his party among the common people, judge the whole universe by examining one single person. For an ignorant man believes that the whole universe only exists for him; as if nothing else required any consideration. If, therefore, anything happens to him contrary to his expectation, he at once concludes that the whole universe is evil. If, however, he would take into consideration the whole universe, form an idea of it, and comprehend what a small portion he is of the Universe, he will find the truth. For it is clear that persons who have fallen into this wide-spread error as regards the multitude of evils in the world, do not find the evils among the angels, the spheres and stars, the elements, and that which is formed of them, viz., minerals and plants, or in the various species of living beings, but only in some individual instances of mankind. They wonder that a person, who became leprous in consequence of bad food, should be afflicted with so great an illness and suffer such a misfortune; or that he who indulges so much in sensuality as to weaken his sight, should be struck with blindness! and the like. What we have, in truth, to consider is this:—The whole mankind at present in existence, and *a fortiori*, every other species of animals, form an infinitesimal portion of the permanent universe. Comp. "Man is like to vanity" (Ps. cxliv. 4); "How much less man, that is a worm; and the son of man, which is a worm" (Job xxv. 6); "How much less in them who dwell in houses of clay" (ibid. iv. 19); "Behold, the nations are as a drop of the bucket" (Isa. xl. 15). There are many other passages in the books of the prophets expressing the same idea. It is of great advantage that man should know his station, and not erroneously imagine that the whole universe exists only for him. We hold that the universe exists because the Creator wills it so; that mankind is low in rank as compared with the uppermost portion of the universe, viz., with the spheres and the stars; but, as regards the angels, there cannot be any real comparison between man and angels, although man is the highest of all beings on earth; *i.e.*, of all beings formed of the four elements. Man's existence is nevertheless a great boon to him, and his distinction and perfection is a divine gift. The numerous evils to which individual persons are exposed are due to the defects existing in the persons themselves. We complain and seek relief from our own faults; we suffer from the evils which we, by our own free will, inflict on ourselves and ascribe them to God, who is far from being connected with them! Comp. "Is destruction His [work]? No. Ye [who call yourselves] wrongly His sons, you are a perverse and crooked generation" (Deut. xxxii. 5). This is explained by Solomon, who says, "The foolishness of man preverteth his way, and his heart fretteth against the Lord" (Prov. xix. 3).

I explain this theory in the following manner. The evils that befall man are of three kinds:—

(1.) The first kind of evil is that which is caused to man by the circumstance that he is subject to genesis and destruction, or that he possesses a body. It is on account of the body that some persons happen to have great deformities or paralysis of some of the organs. This evil may be part of the natural constitution of these persons, or may have developed subsequently in consequence of changes in the elements, *e.g.*, through bad air, or thunderstorms, or landslips. We have already shown that, in accordance with the divine wisdom, genesis can only take place through destruction, and without the destruction of the individual members of the species the species themselves would not exist permanently. Thus the true kindness, and beneficence, and goodness of God is clear. He who thinks that he can have flesh and bones without being subject to any external influence, or any of the accidents of matter, unconsciously wishes to reconcile two opposites, viz., to be at the same time subject and not subject to change. If man were never subject to change there could be no generation; there would be one single being, but no individuals forming a species. Galen, in the third section of his book, "The Use of the Limbs," says correctly that it would be in vain to expect to see living beings formed of the blood of menstruous women and the semen virile, who will not die, will never feel pain, or will move perpetually, or shine like the sun. This dictum of Galen is part of the following more general proposition:—Whatever is formed of any matter receives the most perfect form possible in that species of matter; in each individual case the defects are in accordance with the defects of that individual matter. The best and most perfect being that can be formed of the blood and the semen is the species of man, for as far as man's nature is known, he is living, reasonable, and mortal. It is therefore impossible that man should be free from this species of evil. You will, nevertheless, find that the evils of the above kind which befall man are very few and rare; for you find countries that have not been flooded or burned for thousands of years; there are thousands of men in perfect health, deformed individuals are a strange and exceptional occurrence, or say few in number if you object to the term exceptional,—they are not one-hundredth, not even one-thousandth part of those that are perfectly normal.

(2.) The second class of evils comprises such evils as people cause to each other, when, *e.g.*, some of them use their strength against others. These evils are more numerous than those of the first kind; their causes are numerous and known; they likewise originate in ourselves, though the sufferer himself cannot avert them. This kind of evil is nevertheless not widespread in any country of the whole world. It is of rare occurrence that a man plans to kill his neighbour or to rob him of his property by night. Many persons are, however, afflicted with this kind of evil in great wars; but these are not frequent, if the whole inhabited part of the earth is taken into consideration.

(3.) The third class of evils comprises those which every one causes to himself by his own action. This is the largest class, and is far more numerous than the second class. It is especially of these evils that all men complain,—only few men are found that do not sin against themselves by this kind of evil. Those that are afflicted with it are therefore justly blamed in the words of the prophet, "This hath been by your means" (Mal. i. 9); the same is expressed in the following passage, "He that doeth it destroyeth his own soul" (Prov. vi. 32). In reference to this kind of evil, Solomon says, "The foolishness of man perverteth his way" (ibid. xix. 3). In the following passage he explains also that this kind of evil is man's own work, "Lo, this only have I found, that God hath made man upright, but they have thought out many inventions" (Eccles. vii. 29), and these inventions bring the evils upon him. The same subject is referred to in Job (v. 6), "For affliction cometh not forth of the dust, neither doth trouble spring out of the ground." These words are immediately followed by the explanation that man himself is the author of this class of evils. "But man is born unto trouble." This class of evils originates in man's vices, such as excessive desire for eating, drinking, and love; indulgence in these things in undue measure, or in improper manner, or partaking of bad food. This course brings diseases and afflictions upon body and soul alike. The sufferings of the body in consequence of these evils are well known; those of the soul are twofold:— First, such evils of the soul as are the necessary consequence of changes in the body, in so far as the soul is a force residing in the body; it has therefore been said that the properties of the soul depend on the condition of the body. Secondly, the soul, when accustomed to superfluous things, acquires a strong habit of desiring things which are neither necessary for the preservation of the individual nor for that of the species. This desire is without a limit, whilst things which are necessary are few in number and restricted within certain limits; but what is superfluous is without end—*e.g.*, you desire to have your vessels of silver, but golden vessels are still better: others have even vessels of sapphire, or perhaps they can be made of emerald or rubies, or any other substance that could be suggested. Those who are ignorant and perverse in their thought are constantly in trouble and pain, because they cannot get as much of superfluous things as a certain other person possesses. They as a rule expose themselves to great dangers, *e.g.*, by sea-voyage, or service of kings, and all this for the purpose of obtaining that which is superfluous and not necessary. When they thus meet with the consequences of the course which they adopt, they complain of the decrees and judgments of God; they begin to blame the time, and wonder at the want of justice in its changes; that it has not enabled them to acquire great riches, with which they could buy large quantities of wine for the purpose of making themselves drunk, and numerous concubines adorned with various kind of ornaments of gold, embroidery, and jewels, for the purpose of driving themselves to voluptuousness beyond their capacities, as if the whole Universe existed exclusively for the purpose of giving pleasure to these low people. The error of the ignorant goes so far as to say that God's power is insufficient, because He has given to this Universe the properties which they imagine cause these great evils, and which do not help all evil-disposed persons to obtain the evil which they seek, and to bring their evil souls to the aim of their desires, though these, as we have shown, are really without limit. The virtuous and wise, however, see and comprehend the wisdom of God displayed in the Universe. Thus David says, "All the paths of the Lord are mercy and truth unto such as keep His covenant and His testimonies" (Ps. xxv. 10). For those who observe the nature of the Universe and the commandments of the Law, and know their purpose, see clearly God's mercy and truth in everything; they seek, therefore, that which the Creator intended to be the aim of man, viz., comprehension. Forced by the claims of the body, they seek also that which is necessary for the preservation of the body, "bread to eat and garment to clothe," and this is very little; but they seek nothing superfluous; with very slight exertion man can obtain it, so long as he is contented with that which is indispensable. All the difficulties and troubles we meet in this respect are due to the desire for superfluous things; when we seek unnecessary things, we have difficulty even in finding that which is indispensable. For the more we desire for that which is superfluous, the more we meet with difficulties; our strength and possessions are spent in unnecessary things, and are wanting when required for that which is necessary. Observe how Nature proves the correctness of this assertion. The more necessary a thing is for living beings, the more easily it is found and the cheaper it is; the less necessary it is, the rarer and dearer it is. *E.g.*, air, water, and food are indispensable to man: air is most necessary, for if man is without air a short time he dies; whilst he can be without water a day or two. Air is also undoubtedly found more easily and cheaper [than water]. Water is more necessary than food; for some people can be four or five days without food, provided they have water; water also exists in every country in larger quantities than food, and is also cheaper. The same proportion can be noticed in the different kinds of food; that which is more necessary in a certain place exists there in larger quantities and is cheaper than that which is less necessary. No intelligent person, I think, considers musk, amber, rubies, and emerald as very necessary for man except as medicines; and they, as well as other like substances, can be replaced for this purpose by herbs and minerals. This shows the kindness of God to His creatures, even to us weak beings. His righteousness and justice as regards all animals are well known; for in the transient world there is among the various kinds of animals no individual being distinguished from the rest of the same species by a peculiar property or an additional limb. On the contrary, all physical, psychical, and vital forces and organs that are possessed by one individual are found also in the other individuals. If any one is somehow different it is by accident, in consequence of some exception, and not by a natural property; it is also a rare occurrence. There is no difference between individuals of a species in the due course of Nature; the difference originates in the various dispositions of their substances. This is the necessary consequence of the nature of the substance of that species; the nature of the species is not more favourable to one individual than to the other. It is no wrong or injustice that one has many bags of finest myrrh and garments embroidered with gold, while another has not those things, which are not necessary for our maintenance; he who has them has not thereby obtained control over anything that could be an essential addition to his nature, but has only obtained something illusory or deceptive. The other, who does not possess that which is not wanted for his maintenance, does not miss anything indispensable: "He that gathered much had nothing over, and he that gathered little had no lack: they gathered every man according to his eating" (Exod. xvi. 18). This is the rule at all times and in all places; no notice should be taken of exceptional cases, as we have explained.

In these two ways you will see the mercy of God toward His creatures, how He has provided that which is required, in proper proportions, and treated all individual beings of the same species with perfect equality. In accordance with this correct reflection the chief of the wise men says, "All His ways are judgment" (Deut. xxxii. 4); David likewise says: "All the paths of the Lord are mercy and truth" (Ps. xxv. 10); he also says expressly, "The Lord is good to all; and His tender mercies are over all His works" (ibid. cxlv. 9); for it is an act of great and perfect goodness that He gave us existence; and the creation of the controlling faculty in animals is a proof of His mercy towards them, as has been shown by us.

PART III, CHAPTER 17

There are four different theories concerning Divine Providence; they are all ancient, known since the time of the Prophets, when the true Law was revealed to enlighten these dark regions.

First Theory.—There is no Providence at all for anything in the Universe; all parts of the Universe, the heavens and what they contain, owe their origin to accident and chance; there exists no being that rules and governs them or provides for them. This is the theory of Epicurus, who assumes also that the Universe consists of atoms, that these have combined by chance, and have received their various forms by mere accident. There have been atheists among the Israelites who have expressed the same view; it is reported of them: "They have denied the Lord, and said He is not" (Jer. v. 12). Aristotle has proved the absurdity of the theory, that the whole Universe could have originated by chance; he has shown that, on the contrary, there is a being that rules and governs the Universe. We have already touched upon this subject in the present treatise.

Second Theory.—Whilst one part of the Universe owes its existence to Providence and is under the control of a ruler and governor, another part is abandoned and left to chance. This is the view of Aristotle about Providence, and I will now explain to you his theory. He holds that God controls the spheres and what they contain: therefore the individual beings in the spheres remain permanently in the same form. Alexander has also expressed it in his writings that Divine Providence extends down to, and ends with, the sphere of the moon. This view results from his theory of the Eternity of the Universe; he believes that Providence is in accordance with the nature of the Universe: consequently in the case of the spheres with their contents, where each individual being has a permanent existence, Providence gives permanency and constancy. From the existence of the spheres other beings derive existence, which are constant in their species but not in their individuals: in the same manner it is said that Providence sends forth [from the spheres to the earth] sufficient influence to secure the immortality and constancy of the species, without securing at the same time permanence for the individual beings of the species. But the individual beings in each species have not been entirely abandoned, that portion of the *materia prima* which has been purified and refined, and has received the faculty of growth, is endowed with properties that enable it to exist a certain time, to attract what is useful and to repel what is useless. That portion of the *materia prima* which has been subject to a further development, and has received the faculty of sensation, is endowed with other properties for its protection and preservation; it has a new faculty of moving freely toward that which is conducive to, and away from that which is contrary to its well-being. Each individual being received besides such properties as are required for the preservation of the species to which it belongs. The portion of the *materia prima* which is still more refined, and is endowed with the intellectual faculty, possesses a special property by which each individual, according to the degree of his perfection, is enabled to manage, to calculate, and to discover what is conducive both to the temporary existence of the individual and to the preservation of the species. All other movements, however, which are made by the individual members of each species are due to accident; they are not, according to Aristotle, the result of rule and management; *e.g.*, when a storm or gale blows, it causes undoubtedly some leaves of a tree to drop, breaks off some branches of another tree, tears away a stone from a heap of stones, raises dust over herbs and spoils them, and stirs up the sea so that a ship goes down with the whole or part of her contents. Aristotle sees no difference between the falling of a leaf or a stone and the death of the good and noble people in the ship; nor does he distinguish between the destruction of a multitude of ants caused by an ox depositing on them his excrement and the death of worshippers killed by the fall of the house when its foundations give way; nor does he discriminate between the case of a cat killing a mouse that happens to come in her way, that of a spider catching a fly, and that of a hungry lion meeting a prophet and tearing him. In short, the opinion of Aristotle is this: Everything is the result of management which is constant, which does not come to an end and does not change any of its properties, as *e.g.*, the heavenly beings, and everything which continues according to a certain rule, and deviates from it only rarely and exceptionally, as is the case in objects of Nature. All these are the result of management, *i.e.*, in a close relation to Divine Providence. But that which is not constant, and does not follow a certain rule, as *e.g.*, incidents in the existence of the individual beings in each species of plants or animals, whether rational or irrational, is due to chance and not to management; it is in no relation to Divine Providence. Aristotle holds that it is even impossible to ascribe to Providence the management of these things. This view is closely connected with his theory of the Eternity of the Universe, and with his opinion that everything different from the existing order of things in Nature is impossible. It is the belief of those who turned away from our Law, and said: "God hath forsaken the earth" (Ezek. ix. 9).

Third Theory.—This theory is the reverse of the second. According to this theory, there is nothing in the whole Universe, neither a class nor an individual being, that is due to chance; everything is the result of will, intention, and rule. It is a matter of course that he who rules must know [that which is under his control]. The Mahometan Ashariyah adhere to this theory, notwithstanding evident absurdities implied in it; for they admit that Aristotle is correct in assuming one and the same cause [the wind] for the fall of leaves [from the tree] and for the death of a man [drowned in the sea]. But they hold at the same time that the wind did not blow by chance; it is God that caused it to move; it is not therefore the wind that caused the leaves to fall; each leaf falls according to the Divine decree; it is God who caused it to fall at a certain time and in a certain place; it could not have fallen before or after that time or in another place, as this has previously been decreed. The Ashariyah were therefore compelled to assume that motion and rest of living beings are predestined, and that it is not in the power of man to do a certain thing or to leave it undone. The theory further implies a denial of possibility in these things; they can only be either necessary or impossible. The followers of this theory accepted also the last-mentioned proposition, and say, that we call certain things possible, as *e.g.*, the facts that Zeid stands, and that Amr is coming; but they are only possible for us, whilst in their relation to God they cannot be called possible; they are either necessary or impossible. It follows also from this theory, that precepts are perfectly useless, since the people to whom any law is given are unable to do anything: they can neither do what they are commanded nor abstain from what they are forbidden. The supporters of this theory hold that it was the will of God to send prophets, to command, to forbid, to promise, and to threaten, although we have no power [over our actions]. A duty would thus be imposed upon us which is impossible for us to carry out, and it is even possible that we may suffer punishment when obeying the command and receive reward when disobeying it. According to this theory, it must also be assumed that the actions of God have no final cause. All these absurdities are admitted by the Ashariyah for the purpose of saving this theory. When we see a person born blind or leprous, who could not have merited a punishment for previous sins, they say, It is the will of God; when a pious worshipper is tortured and slain, it is likewise the will of God; and no injustice can be asserted to Him for that, for according to their opinion it is proper that God should afflict the innocent and do good to the sinner. Their views on these matters are well known.

Fourth Theory.—Man has free will; it is therefore intelligible that the Law contains commands and prohibitions, with announcements of reward and punishment. All acts of God are due to wisdom; no injustice is found in Him, and He does not afflict the good. The Mu'tazila profess this theory, although they do not believe in man's absolute free will. They hold also that God takes notice of the falling of the leaf and the destruction of the ant, and that His Providence extends over all beings. This theory likewise implies contradictions and absurdities. The absurdities are these: The fact that some persons are born with defects, although they have not sinned previously, is ascribed to the wisdom of God, it being better for those persons to be in such a condition than to be in a normal state, though we do not see why it is better; and they do not suffer thereby any punishment at all, but, on the contrary, enjoy God's goodness. In a similar manner the slaughter of the pious is explained as being for them the source of an increase of reward in future life. They go even further in their absurdities. We ask them why is God only just to man and not to other beings, and how has the irrational animal sinned, that it is condemned to be slaughtered? and they reply it is good for the animal, for it will receive reward for it in the world to come; also the flea and the louse will there receive compensation for their untimely death: the same reasoning they apply to the mouse torn by a cat or vulture; the wisdom of God decreed this for the mouse, in order to reward it after death for the mishap. I do not consider it proper to blame the followers of any of the [last named] three theories on Providence, for they have been driven to accept them by weighty considerations. Aristotle was guided by that which appears to be the nature of things. The Ashariyah refused to ascribe to God ignorance about anything, and to say that God whilst knowing one individual being or one portion of the Universe is ignorant of another portion; they preferred to admit the above-mentioned absurdities. The Mu'tazilites refused to assume that God does what is wrong and unjust; on the other hand, they would not contradict common sense and say that it was not wrong to inflict pain on the guiltless, or that the mission of the Prophets and the giving of the Law had no intelligible reason. They likewise preferred to admit the above-named absurdities. But they even contradicted themselves, because they believe on the one hand that God knows everything, and on the other that man has free will. By a little consideration we discover the contradiction.

Fifth Theory.—This is our theory, or that of our Law. I will show you [first] the view expressed on this subject in our prophetical books, and generally accepted by our Sages. I will then give the opinion of some later authors among us, and lastly, I will explain my own belief. The theory of man's perfectly free will is one of the fundamental principles of the Law of our Teacher Moses, and of those who follow the Law. According to this principle man does what is in his power to do, by his nature, his choice, and his will; and his action is not due to any faculty created for the purpose. All species of irrational animals likewise move by their own free will. This is the Will of God; that is to say, it is due to the eternal divine will that all living beings should move freely, and that man should have power to act according to his will or choice within the limits of his capacity. Against this principle we hear, thank God, no opposition on the part of our nation. Another fundamental principle taught by the Law of Moses is this: Wrong cannot be ascribed to God in any way whatever; all evils and afflictions as well as all kinds of happiness of man, whether they concern one individual person or a community, are distributed according to justice; they are the result of strict judgment that admits no wrong whatever. Even when a person suffers pain in consequence of a thorn having entered into his hand, although it is at once drawn out, it is a punishment that has been inflicted on him [for sin], and the least pleasure he enjoys is a reward [for some good action]; all this is meted out by strict justice; as is said in Scripture, "all His ways are judgment" (Deut. xxxii. 4); we are only ignorant of the working of that judgment.

The different theories are now fully explained to you; everything in the varying human affairs is due to chance, according to Aristotle, to the Divine Will alone according to the Ashariyah, to Divine Wisdom according to the Mu'tazilites, to the merits of man according to our opinion. It is therefore possible, according to the Ashariyah, that God inflicts pain on a good and pious man in this world, and keeps him for ever in fire, which is assumed to rage in the world to come; they simply say it is the Will of God. The Mu'tazilites would consider this as injustice, and therefore assume that every being, even an ant, that is stricken with pain [in this world], has compensation for it, as has been mentioned above; and it is due to God's Wisdom, that a being is struck and afflicted in order to receive compensation. We, however, believe that all these human affairs are managed with justice; far be it from God to do wrong, to punish any one unless the punishment is necessary and merited. It is distinctly stated in the Law, that all is done in accordance with justice; and the words of our Sages generally express the same idea. They clearly say: "There is no death without sin, no sufferings without transgression." Again, "The deserts of man are meted out to him in the same measure which he himself employs." These are the words of the

Mishnah. Our Sages declare it wherever opportunity is given, that the idea of God necessarily implies justice; that He will reward the most pious for all their pure and upright actions, although no direct commandment was given them through a prophet; and that He will punish all the evil deeds of men, although they have not been prohibited by a prophet, if common sense warns against them, as *e.g.*, injustice and violence. Thus our Sages say: "God does not deprive any being of the full reward [of its good deed];" again, "He who says that God remits part of a punishment, will be punished severely; He is long-suffering, but is sure to enact payment." Another saying is this: "He who has received a commandment and acts accordingly is not like him who acts in the same manner without being commanded to do so"; and it is distinctly added that he who does a good thing without being commanded, receives nevertheless his reward. The same principle is expressed in all sayings of our Sages. But they contain an additional doctrine which is not found in the Law; viz., the doctrine of "afflictions of love," as taught by some of our Sages. According to this doctrine it is possible that a person be afflicted without having previously committed any sin, in order that his future reward may be increased; a view which is held by the Mu'tazilites, but is not supported by any Scriptural text. Be not misled by the accounts of trials, such as "God tried Abraham" (Gen. xxii. 1); "He afflicted thee and made thee hungry" (Deut. vii. 3); for you will hear more on this subject later on (chap. xxiv.). Our Law is only concerned with the relations of men; but the idea that irrational living beings should receive a reward, has never before been heard of in our nation; the wise men mentioned in the Talmud do not notice it; only some of the later Geonim were pleased with it when they heard it from the sect of the Mu'tazilites, and accepted it.

My opinion on this principle of Divine Providence I will now explain to you. In the principle which I now proceed to expound I do not rely on demonstrative proof, but on my conception of the spirit of the Divine Law, and the writings of the Prophets. The Principle which I accept is far less open to objections, and is more reasonable than the opinions mentioned before. It is this: In the lower or sublunary portion of the Universe Divine Providence does not extend to the individual members of species except in the case of mankind. It is only in this species that the incidents in the existence of the individual beings, their good and evil fortunes, are the result of justice, in accordance with the words, "For all His ways are judgment." But I agree with Aristotle as regards all other living beings, and *a fortiori* as regards plants and all the rest of earthly creatures. For I do not believe that it is through the interference of Divine

Providence that a certain leaf drops [from a tree], nor do I hold that when a certain spider catches a certain fly, that this is the direct result of a special decree and will of God in that moment; it is not by a particular Divine decree that the spittle of a certain person moved, fell on a certain gnat in a certain place, and killed it; nor is it by the direct will of God that a certain fish catches and swallows a certain worm on the surface of the water. In all these cases the action is, according to my opinion, entirely due to chance, as taught by Aristotle. Divine Providence is connected with Divine intellectual influence, and the same beings which are benefited by the latter so as to become intellectual, and to comprehend things comprehensible to rational beings, are also under the control of Divine Providence, which examines all their deeds with a view of rewarding or punishing them. It may be by mere chance that a ship goes down with her contents, as in the above-mentioned instance, or the roof of a house falls upon those within; but it is not due to chance, according to our view, that in the one instance the men went into the ship, or remained in the house in the other instance; it is due to the will of God, and is in accordance with the justice of His judgments, the method of which our mind is incapable of understanding. I have been induced to accept this theory by the circumstance that I have not met in any of the prophetical books with a description of God's Providence otherwise than in relation to human beings. The prophets even express their surprise that God should take notice of man, who is too little and too unimportant to be worthy of the attention of the Creator; how, then, should other living creatures be considered as proper subjects for Divine Providence! Comp. "What is man, that Thou takest knowledge of him?" (Ps. cxliv. 3); "What is man, that Thou art mindful of him?" (ibid. viii. 8). It is clearly expressed in many Scriptural passages that God provides for all men, and controls all their deeds—*e.g.*, "He fashioneth their hearts alike, He considereth all their works" (ibid. xxxiii. 15); "For Thine eyes are open upon all the ways of the sons of men, to give every one according to his ways" (Jer. xxxii. 19). Again: "For His eyes are upon the ways of man, and He seeth all his goings" (Job xxxii. 21). In the Law there occur instances of the fact that men are governed by God, and that their actions are examined by Him. Comp. "In the day when I visit I will visit their sin upon them" (Exod. xxxii. 34); "I will even appoint over you terror" (Lev. xxvi. 16); "Whosoever hath sinned against me, him will I blot out of my book" (Exod. xxxii. 33); "The same soul will I destroy" (Lev. xxiii. 30); "I will even set my face against that soul" (ibid. xx. 6). There are many instances of this kind. All that is mentioned of the history of Abraham, Isaac, and Jacob is a perfect proof that Divine

Providence extends to every man individually. But the condition of the individual beings of other living creatures is undoubtedly the same as has been stated by Aristotle. On that account it is allowed, even commanded, to kill animals; we are permitted to use them according to our pleasure. The view that other living beings are only governed by Divine Providence in the way described by Aristotle, is supported by the words of the Prophet Habakkuk. When he perceived the victories of Nebuchadnezzar, and saw the multitude of those slain by him, he said, "O God, it is as if men were abandoned, neglected, and unprotected like fish and like worms of the earth." He thus shows that these classes are abandoned. This is expressed in the following passage: "And makest men as the fishes of the sea, as the creeping things, that have no ruler over them. They take up all of them with the angle," &c. (Hab. i. 14, 15). The prophet then declares that such is not the case; for the events referred to are not the result of abandonment, forsaking, and absence of Providence, but are intended as a punishment for the people, who well deserved all that befell them. He therefore says: "O Lord, Thou hast ordained them for judgment, and O mighty God, Thou hast established them for correction" (ibid. ver. 12). Our opinion is not contradicted by Scriptural passages like the following: "He giveth to the beast his food" (Ps. cxlvii. 9); "The young lions roar after their prey, and seek their meat from God" (ibid. civ. 21); "Thou openest Thine hand, and satisfiest the desire of every living thing" (ibid. cxlv. 16); or by the saying of our Sages: "He sitteth and feedeth all, from the horns of the unicorns even unto the eggs of insects." There are many similar sayings extant in the writings of our Sages, but they imply nothing that is contrary to my view. All these passages refer to Providence in relation to species, and not to Providence in relation to individual animals. The acts of God are as it were enumerated; how He provides for every species the necessary food and the means of subsistence. This is clear and plain. Aristotle likewise holds that this kind of Providence is necessary, and in actual existence. Alexander also notices this fact in the name of Aristotle, viz., that every species has its nourishment prepared for its individual members; otherwise the species would undoubtedly have perished. It does not require much consideration to understand this. There is a rule laid down by our Sages that it is directly prohibited in the Law to cause pain to an animal, and is based on the words: "Wherefore hast thou smitten thine ass?" &c. (Num. xxii. 32). But the object of this rule is to make us perfect; that we should not assume cruel habits; and that we should not uselessly cause pain to others; that, on the contrary, we should be prepared to show pity and mercy to all living creatures, except when necessity demands the contrary: "When thy soul longeth to eat flesh" (Deut. xii. 20). We should not kill animals for the purpose of practising cruelty, or for the purpose of play. It cannot be objected to this theory, Why should God select mankind as the object of His special Providence, and not other living beings? For he who asks this question must also inquire, Why has man alone, of all species of animals, been endowed with intellect? The answer to this second question must be, according to the three aforementioned theories: It was the Will of God, it is the decree of His Wisdom, or it is in accordance with the laws of Nature. The same answers apply to the first question. Understand thoroughly my theory, that I do not ascribe to God ignorance of anything or any kind of weakness; I hold that Divine Providence is related and closely connected with the intellect, because Providence can only proceed from an intelligent being, from a being that is itself the most perfect Intellect. Those creatures, therefore, which receive part of that intellectual influence, will become subject to the action of Providence in the same proportion as they are acted upon by the Intellect. This theory is in accordance with reason and with the teaching of Scripture, whilst the other theories previously mentioned either exaggerate Divine Providence or detract from it. In the former case they lead to confusion and entire nonsense, and cause us to deny reason and to contradict that which is perceived with the senses. The latter case, viz., the theory that Divine Providence does not extend to man, and that there is no difference between man and other animals, implies very bad notions about God; it disturbs all social order, removes and destroys all the moral and intellectual virtues of man.

PART III, CHAPTER 18

Having shown in the preceding chapter that of all living beings mankind alone is directly under the control of Divine Providence, I will now add the following remarks: It is an established fact that species have no existence except in our own minds. Species and other classes are merely ideas formed in our minds, whilst everything in real existence is an individual object, or an aggregate of individual objects. This being granted, it must further be admitted that the result of the existing Divine influence, that reaches mankind through the human intellect, is identical with individual intellects really in existence, with which, *e.g.*, Zeid, Amr, Kaled and Bekr, are endowed. Hence it follows, in accordance with what I have mentioned in the preceding chapter, that the greater the proportion which a person has obtained of this Divine influence, on account of both his physical predisposition and his training, the greater must also be the effect of Divine Providence upon him, for the action of Divine Providence is proportional to the endowment of intellect, as has been mentioned above. The relation of Divine Providence is therefore not the same to all men; the greater the human perfection a person has attained, the greater the benefit he derives from Divine Providence. This benefit is very great in the case of prophets, and varies according to the degree of their prophetic faculty; as it varies in the case of pious and good men according to their piety and uprightness. For it is the intensity of the Divine intellectual influence that has inspired the prophets, guided the good in their actions, and perfected the wisdom of the pious. In the same proportion as ignorant and disobedient persons are deficient in that Divine influence, their condition is inferior, and their rank equal to that of irrational beings; and they are "like unto the beasts" (Ps. xlix. 21). For this reason it was not only considered a light thing to slay them, but it was even directly commanded for the benefit of mankind. This belief that God provides for every individual human being in accordance with his merits is one of the fundamental principles on which the Law is founded.

Consider how the action of Divine Providence is described in reference to every incident in the lives of the patriarchs, to their occupations, and even to their passions, and how God promised to direct His attention to them. Thus God said to Abraham, "I am thy shield" (Gen. xv. 1); to Isaac, "I will be with thee, and I will bless thee" (ibid. xxvi. 3); to Jacob, "I am with thee, and will keep thee" (ibid. xxviii. 15); to [Moses] the chief of the Prophets, "Certainly I will be with thee, and this shall be a token unto thee" (Exod. iii. 12); to Joshua, "As I was with Moses, so I shall be with thee" (Josh. i. 5). It is clear that in all these cases the action of Providence has been proportional to man's perfection. The following verse describes how Providence protects good and pious men, and abandons fools; "He will keep the feet of His saints, and the wicked shall be silent in darkness; for by strength shall no man prevail" (1 Sam. ii. 9). When we see that some men escape plagues and mishaps, whilst others perish by them, we must not attribute this to a difference in the properties of their bodies, or in their physical constitution, "for by strength shall no man prevail"; but it must be attributed to their different degrees of perfection, some approaching God, whilst others moving away from Him. Those who approach Him are best protected, and "He will keep the feet of His saints"; but those who keep far away from Him are left exposed to what may befall them; there is nothing that could protect them from what might happen; they are like those who walk in darkness, and are certain to stumble. The protection of the pious by Providence is also expressed in the following passages:—"He keepeth all his bones," &c. (Ps. xxiv. 21); "The eyes of the Lord are upon the righteous," &c. (ibid. xci. 15). There are in Scripture many more passages expressing the principle that men enjoy Divine protection in proportion to their perfection and piety. The philosophers have likewise discussed this subject. Abu-nasr, in the Introduction to his "Commentary on Aristotle's Nikomachean Ethics," says as follows:—Those who possess the faculty of raising their souls from virtue to virtue obtain, according to Plato, Divine protection to a higher degree.

Now consider how by this method of reasoning we have arrived at the truth taught by the Prophets, that every person has his individual share of Divine Providence in proportion to his perfection. For philosophical research leads to this conclusion, when we assume, as has been mentioned above, that Divine Providence is in each case proportional to the person's intellectual development. It is wrong to say that Divine Providence extends only to the species, and not to individual beings, as some of the philosophers teach. For only individual beings have real existence, and individual beings are endowed with Divine Intellect; Divine Providence acts, therefore, upon these individual beings.

Study this chapter as it ought to be studied; you will find in it all the fundamental principles of the Law; you will see that these are in conformity with philosophical speculation, and all difficulties will be removed; you will have a clear idea of Divine Providence.

GERSONIDES, *MILḤAMOT HA-SHEM*

Translation by J. David Bleich

FOURTH TREATISE, CHAPTER 4

Clarifying In Part The Nature Of This Providence

Now that it has been demonstrated that it is false that Divine Providence does not extend to any individual human being by virtue of [his] individual nature and it has also been demonstrated that it is false that Providence extends to each one by virtue of [his] individual nature it is clear that this necessitates that Providence must extend to some and not to others. This will be seen also in another manner. I mean that Divine Providence, does extend to individual human beings by virtue of the individual nature and that it extends to some and not to others; that is, it is evident that God exercises a greater degree of Providence over [the creature] which is more noble and closer in stature to the Active Intellect and has placed in [that creature] additional organs to safeguard its existence. This is clear from what is demonstrated in the *De Animalium,*[1] for you will find that the more noble the creature, the more organs have been allotted to it in order to safeguard its existence. Since with regard to mankind there [exist] varying degrees of closeness and distance with regard to the Active Intellect by virtue of the individual nature, it follows that those most strongly attached to [the Active Intellect] enjoy a greater degree of Providence by virtue of the individual nature. Since some people remain with [only] the predisposition they possess by virtue of the nature of the species and do not attempt to pursue the perfection which would bring them closer to the Active Intellect, [and] since some instead add defects to the defects which are theirs stemming from nature by virtue of the nature of the species, it is clear that to this group of people Divine Providence can extend only in relation to the nature of the species; for there is no other way in which Providence can be extended to them by virtue of the individual nature. Since this is the case, it is clear that Divine Providence extends to some people in varying degrees by virtue of the individual nature and in others is not to be found at all. This can also be seen in another way; namely, it is self-evident that God knows all intelligibles and man is well prepared to receive intelligibles to the extent that he has the ability to receive all of them in some way. Since this is the case, I mean that God is Master of the intelligibles in actuality and man is master of the predisposition to receive them and it is clear that something existing in actuality will actualize that which exists in potentiality and bring it into actuality, it is [therefore] clear that God actualizes that which is potentially in man and brings it into actuality. Since in bringing the potential into actuality with regard to intelligibles the agent and that which is acted upon are united in some way it is clear that man in this way receives some[2] manner of unification and conjunction with God. Since this is its nature,[3] it is clear that Providence will properly be something wondrous with regard to [man] by virtue of this unification and conjunction. It is not the case that God forsakes [man] in disdain because he is lowly and despised in comparison to Him; [the case is not] as [some people] say that there is no Divine Providence with regard to individuals by virtue of their specific nature since man is lowly and too disdainful in comparison to God. Since this unification is a result of the actualization of intelligibles in man, not of the potentiality which is the nature of the species, it is clear that it is proper that Divine Providence extend to men possessing intelligence, by virtue of the individual nature.

NOTES

1. For relevant passages *vide De Partibus Animalium,* trans. A.L. Peck, The Loeb Classical Library (Cambridge, 1937), II, 10, p. 173, and also *De Generatione Animalium,* trans. A. L. Peck, The Loeb Classical Library (Cambridge, 1953), I, 23, p. 123. The Islamic philosophers viewed the *Historia Animalium,* the *De Partibus Animalium* and the *De Generatione Animalium* as comprising a single three-part work entitled כתאב אלחיואן and translated by the Hebrew writers as ספר בעל חיים by which title the work is here cited. *Vide* Steinschnedier, *Hebraeische Ubersetzungen,* p. 143.

2. Following the manuscript reading האתאחדות מה ודבקות rather than התאחדות מהדבקות of the text. *Vide* Benzion Kellerman, *Die Kampfe Gottes von Lewi ben Gerson,* Berlin, 1914, II, 236, note 2.

3. I.e., the nature of this form of Providence. The phrase ומה שזה דרכו may perhaps refer to "that the nature of which" is to receive unification and conjunction with God.

FOURTH TREATISE, CHAPTER 5

Clarifying The Manner In Which That Which Has Been Explained Regarding This Providence May Be Posited In Order That It May Be Compatible With That Which Has Been Explained Concerning Divine Knowledge of Things

Now that it has been made clear that Divine Providence extends to some individuals by virtue of the individual nature it is proper that we investigate the manner in which it is possible to posit, simultaneously with this, the preservation of the principle which has been explained in the preceding [treatise] concerning Divine Knowledge; I mean [the principle] that [God's] knowledge does not extend to a particular in so far as it is particular. For it would seem that this involves such difficulty that one may deem a person who wishes to accept both these opinions together to be in the position of one who wishes to accept two contradictories simultaneously.

We maintain that it has become clear through investigation that the Active Intellect exercises Providence over existent beings by placing in them physical organs possessing animate powers so that the possessors of those organs may protect their existence through them and drive away that which might harm them or remove themselves from [that which might harm them], e.g., the Active Intellect gave horns, round hoofs and teeth to some animals in order to protect them from anyone who might seek to harm them and [gave these organs] to carnivorous animals in order to capture prey.[1] With regard to some [existent beings] it exercises Providence by giving them animate instincts[2] alone or activities which are comparable to animate instincts: e.g., the [Active Intellect] has instilled in the lamb a natural instinct to run from the wolf when it sees him even though it does not perceive that [the wolf] is harmful and has not seen him previously. In this manner many [animals] flee from birds of prey even though they have not seen them previously. Many birds go south in the winter and north in the summer with intent without [consciously] recognizing the landmarks to be found in the places to which they migrate. [Another example is the fact that] the swallow places a certain herb on the eyes of its young when they are pecked without knowing that this is a remedy for their eyes. As an example of activities [which are manifestations of Providence] one might say that [the Active Intellect] instilled in bees a skill with regard to making honeycombs[3] in which they procreate and to make honey from which they are nourished when food is lacking without [the bees] possessing productive intellect[4] from which these activities might arise. This form of Providence is found in regard to man in much more perfect a manner. To him has been allotted productive intellect from which are ordered many works which aid him in self-protection; to him has been allotted intellect from which arise the instincts to flee from many things which are harmful and to seek many things which are beneficial. With regard to some people this Providence may be still more perfect; I mean that God makes known to them, by means of prophecy, misfortunes and benefits which are about to come upon them so that they may guard against [those] misfortunes and seek [those] benefits, as has been explained in the Second Treatise of this book.[5] This is as is fitting, that is, that God does not refrain from conferring good and perfection according to that which is possible to each creature. Since this is the manner of Providence with which He watches over many animals, i.e., by instilling in them animate instincts to flee from evil and to seek good without weighing that good or that evil, it is possible that [this Providence] extends to some people in a more perfect way, i.e., that He make known to them the evil and good about to come upon them that they may flee from the evil and seek the good. It is proper that Providence extend to them in this manner. In some instances He exercises Providence over individual existent beings by causing them some form of pain so that through it they may safeguard themselves. For example, God put black bile in the stomach that it may tickle the orifice of the stomach at such times as there is need of food. [The individual] in experiencing this feels pain and seeks food, for in this way the person is safeguarded. Another example—[God] placed a vessel in a certain species of living creatures to guard its seed so that if in becoming afraid of other animals it happens that fear causes [the animal] to cast its seed, it is hidden in [the vessel.][6]

Now that the various forms of Providence which are found to be exercised by God with regard to [these] things here in the sublunar world have been established, and it has been explained that God exercises Providence with regard to some individual human beings in varying degrees by virtue of the individual nature, it is proper that we investigate which of the forms of Providence that we have mentioned it is possible for this Providence to assume. It is clear that it is impossible that this Providence [take the form of] God giving those people [who are] under the greater influence of Providence additional limbs to safeguard their existence, since men are all of one species and the individuals of a single species are alike by virtue of the laws of nature with regard to the number of limbs [they possess], their form and in the animate powers they possess. I swear! The multiplicity of limbs in individuals is determined by matter; and that which is of this nature is not due to Providence and benevolence. Since this is the case, it seems that this Providence must assume one of the remaining forms or some [form] which is in accordance with them. Since it is clear from what has preceded that God, exercising Providence in protecting them, makes known to some people the benefits and misfortunes which will befall them in the future, it would appear from this that God's Providence in regard to individual human beings consists of making known to them the benefits and misfortunes about to come upon them so that they may guard against the misfortunes and direct themselves to the benefits.

This fore-knowledge comes from Him in different ways according to the varying degrees of closeness and distance of individuals from the Active Intellect, that is, people who are closely united with the Active Intellect receive this fore-knowledge in a perfect manner by way of prophecy. This also occurs in varying degrees according to the variations in the degree of conjunction. Toward those whose degree [of closeness] does not enable them to receive the communication in this manner God exercises Providence by instilling in them animate instincts causing them to seek those things through which benefits will come to them without their weighing these benefits and to flee from other things from which, because of the order proceeding from the heavenly bodies, comes misfortune without their weighing that misfortune. However, this fore-knowledge is weak. In this way fear occurs to some people at about the time that misfortune is about to befall them without their weighing what is the cause of their fear. This is in some way similar to the experience of those having poor vision who do not see things themselves which give off light but perceive their glow and rays. Of similar [situations] our Rabbis, of blessed memory, said, "Even though he does not perceive, his *Mazal* perceives."[7] The meaning of this adage becomes clear with [but] a little reflection on the basis of what we have explained in the Second Treatise of this book. For this reason you will also find that some people remove themselves from some things not understanding why they remove themselves and later it becomes clear to them that if they had not removed themselves from [those things] they would have experienced misfortune; and some people draw near to some things not understanding why they were stimulated to draw near and later it becomes clear to them that their drawing near to those things was a cause of receiving benefits. With regard to those whose degree [of perfection] does not reach [the point] where this desire can be instilled in them it is possible that Providence is effected with regard to them by bringing upon them by way of Providence things which cause pain in order to protect them from other things—worse than these—which had been about to come upon them—or else with the intention that benefits be received by them. An example of something [designed] to protect them from misfortune is the case of a righteous man who sets out on a journey with merchants to travel the seas and a splinter enters his foot so that he cannot go with them and this is the cause of his escape from drowning in the sea. Regarding such things it is said:[8]

> I will give thanks unto thee, O Lord;
> For though Thou wast angry with me,
> Thine anger is turned away and Thou comfortest me.[9]

An example of something the intention of which is to cause the receiving of benefits is the case of a certain person who desires to travel with a caravan and a splinter enters his foot. This is the cause of his refraining from accompanying the caravan and remaining in the city and [as a result] he achieves great successes [which] he would not have achieved if he had not remained there. All these, and things similar to them, our Sages called "afflictions of love."[10]

NOTES

1. Averroes regards the tactile sense as the primary vehicle of providential guardianship of the animal kingdom with the faculty of reason serving the same function in the human species. The organs noted by Gersonides are of course rendered efficacious through the sense of touch. Cf., Averroes, *Metaphysik*, p. 204:

> Betrachte jedoch die göttliche Vorsehung, die sich auf das Tier erstreckt, wie sie ihm die Fähigkeit des Tastsinnes verlieh. Sonst könnte sie dasselbe nicht in seiner Natur erhalten und es von Gegenständen der sinnlichen Wahrnehmung entfernen, die schädlich sind. Diese Wahrnehmung vollzieht sich nach Massgabe der Natur dieses Tieres, so dass es sich anderen Dingen (die nützlich sind) nähert.

2. Literally: "desire." The term תשוקה is clearly used in this context in the sense of an instinctive desire.

3. Reading בעשיית ששיותיהם. *Vide* Kellermann, p. 238, n. 2.

4. I have rendered שכל מעשי as "productive intellect" rather than "practical intellect" because the Aristotelian term *praktikos* or "practical knowledge" is restricted to the category of knowledge concerned with human action.

5. Chap. 5.

6. I have been unsuccessful in locating a source for this example.

7. *Talmud Babli, Megilla* 3a. The term is understood by Gersonides as having reference to the configuration of the heavenly bodies responsible for the astral influences governing events which effect human lives. *Vide Milhamot,* III, 2, p. 98. The Talmudic quotation is accordingly understood by Gersonides as stating that although the individual may not have clear knowledge of such events or of their effect upon his welfare such events are nevertheless determined by astral influences. This knowledge which is "perceived" by the *Mazal* may communicate itself to him in an unclear manner. For a somewhat different interpretation of the Talmudic passage in question, cf., Rashi's commentary on *Megilla* 3a.

8. Here also the words אמר דוד are in error. *Vide* Kellermann, p. 245, n. 1. Cf., above p. 124, note 27.

9. Isaiah 12:1.

10. *Talmud Babli, Berakhot* 5a. For different interpretations of "afflictions of love" cf., Maimonides, *Guide,* III, 17 and Nachmanides, *Sha'ar ha-G'mul,* included in *Kitbe Ramban,* ed. Charles B. Chavel (Jerusalem, 1964), II, 264–311.

FOURTH TREATISE, CHAPTER 6

Explaining Therein That What Has Been Clarified Regarding Providence Is Of The Things Which Cannot In Any Way Be Doubted, Either On The Basis Of Philosophical Speculation, or On The Basis Of Sense Perception, or On The Basis Of [The Teachings Of] The Torah

It is proper that we clarify that this manner of Divine Providence which we have posited [as extending] to some individual human beings gives rise to no doubt, whether on the basis of philosophical speculation or on the basis of sense perception or on the basis of the [teachings of the] Torah, which is difficult to resolve. On the contrary, they [all] agree with this premise in every respect, for when this is clarified our treatise with regard to Providence will be more complete; that is, we will recognize that we have arrived at the ultimate verification in each detail when there remains no doubt regarding it. For this reason, it is proper that we first explain that the arguments employed in substantiating their opinions [both] of those who say that Divine Providence does not extend to individual human beings in regard to their individual nature and of those who say that it extends to every individual of the human species do not necessitate the refutation of this premise.

We maintain that upon a little reflection in conjunction with the discussion which has preceded it is self-evident that these arguments contain nothing which necessitates the refutation of that which we have postulated with regard to Divine Providence. It is clear that the arguments advanced by the Aristotelians to substantiate [the opinion] that Divine Providence does not extend to any individual human being by virtue of the individual nature, because it is impossible that His knowledge extend to individual things in so far as they are individual, do not contradict this premise. This is so because the Providence which we have posited is compatible with our admission that God's knowledge does not extend to particular things *qua* particulars. That is, the Providence which accrues to the righteous by virtue of fore-knowledge regarding benefits and misfortunes which are imminent can be perfected even though the One from Whom this fore-knowledge emanates does not perceive the individual who receives the emanation [and] even though the particular details which are the [subject of] fore-knowledge are not known to the One from Whom [it] emanates *qua* particulars. We have already explained this in the Second Treatise of this work. There[1] we have explained that fore-knowledge with regard to particulars is received from the Active Intellect by the recipient of the emanation by virtue of [his] sentient existence. The Providence which brings fear [to people] in order to preserve [them] from misfortunes and in order to instill in them other animate instincts [to prompt them] to strive for things which bring benefit and to draw away from things which bring misfortune is also a weak form of fore-knowledge, as we have explained in what has preceded, but its [nature] is the same as that of perfect fore-knowledge with regard to this matter. This is self-evident; I mean that just as God does not prevent the receiving of perfect fore-knowledge with regard to particulars so also does He not prevent that fore-knowledge be received from Him which is not perfect with regard to particular things since the lack of perfection which is found in this fore-knowledge is due to the recipient. [The recipient] perceives that this particular thing is about to come to him in this manner [rather than] it being the emanation which is concerned with particulars.

Now concerning our premise that it is possible that Providence may bring misfortune upon the righteous in order to preserve them from greater misfortune or in order to bestow upon them some benefit, if it is the case that this is true, it is possible that this be so without God having knowledge of a particular thing *qua* particular. Rather, this [Providence] is received from Him because it is its nature that it be received by all who are prepared to receive this manner of Providence, just as the Active Intellect activates all who are prepared to receive its action despite the fact that it has no knowledge of the particular *qua* particular. Since this is the case, it is clear that from our admission that God's knowledge does not extend to the particular *qua* particular it does not follow that this Providence does not extend to some individual human beings by virtue of their individual natures in the manner which we have posited.

Now it is clear that that which has been argued with regard to this on the basis of the poor order which is found with regard to the benefits and misfortunes which occur to individual human beings does not contradict what we have posited concerning Providence; that is, our assumption does not necessitate that it be impossible for the wicked to receive the benefits destined by the constellations to come upon them; we have said rather that the wicked are forsaken and left to those happenings which are ordered by the heavenly bodies and [that] God does not preserve them from the misfortunes destined to come upon them through the constellations since they are not on a level at which it is possible for this Divine Providence to attach [itself] to them. According to our assumption it is also not impossible for misfortunes to befall the righteous at such times as they pursue sensory pleasures [thereby] severing the bond and the conjunction between themselves and God by virtue of which they are the recipients of Providence. For at such times this Providence turns aside from them and they become the goal of the oppression of chance occurrences. Since this is the case, it is clear that no doubt arises from this direction regarding what we have posited concerning Divine Providence.

However, one may question [one aspect] of what we have posited concerning those things which admit of lack of order. We have already admitted that it is not impossible that very great benefits may befall the wicked by virtue of the arrangements of the heavenly bodies and misfortunes [may befall] the righteous at such time as they sever the bond and conjunction which [exists] between themselves and God. Since this is the case, one might say that the order which God ordained for individual human beings through the heavenly bodies from which occurs the lack of order found in the benefits and misfortunes which befall them, according to what we have posited, must inescapably be attributed to Him as an injustice or inability and shortcoming since He has knowledge of this order as has been explained in what has preceded; that is, since [these things are] ordained for the wicked and the righteous at such time as they sever the bond and the conjunction which [exists] between them and God, He knows that it is possible that [this order] may cause misfortune to the just and benefits to the wicked. Since this is the case, the dichotomy is inescapable: either God can so order [these occurrences] so that each man be compensated according to his deeds but does not attempt [to do] this [in which case] there is, without doubt, unrighteousness in regard to Him—Heaven forbid! or He is unable [to do] this—which is also an imperfection in regard to Him.

We maintain that if[2] those benefits and misfortunes in which a lack of order and justice is found [constitute] reward and punishment there would be some basis for this doubt; but it can be seen with but little reflection that true reward and punishment are not to be found in these perceptible misfortunes; that is, it is fitting that reward and punishment befalling man as a human being be through human goods and human misfortunes,[3] not through benefits and misfortunes which are not human. Since this is the case, and [since] human goods consist of acquiring well-being of the soul[4]—for this belongs to man by virtue of his humanity—not in acquiring sweet foods and [pleasant] sensory objects, for nutrition and sensation do not belong to man by virtue of his humanity, and also since human misfortune consists of the absence of well-being of the soul—I mean that its development be inadequate—it is clear that reward and punishment which befalls man by virtue of his humanity lies in the well-being of the soul and in the lack of such well-being, not in those perceptible benefits and misfortunes[5] which are governed by the heavenly bodies. Since acquisition of well-being of the soul itself depends upon good and just actions and its absence is the result of base actions it is clear that true reward and punishment, i.e., the good and evil which befall man by virtue of his humanity, proceed without exception in accordance with order and justice. Also, when the patterns arranged by the heavenly bodies through which the perceptible benefits and misfortunes which befall man are arranged are investigated, nothing can be found in them which could possibly be attributed to God as an injustice or shortcoming. [On the contrary] they are found [to be] the most perfect possible as a result of the goodness and beneficence of Providence and with regard to these things existing here [in the sublunar world] for through them this sublunar existence which contains in itself good and perfection which the human intellect cannot grasp perfectly is preserved. This is so because they preserve in the most perfect way possible the contrary elements through which all compounds exist and they preserve the elementary heat in each existing thing as long as possible in the most perfect manner of preservation possible—to the point that if one should imagine that the activity of the heavenly bodies be removed for a short time from the things existing here [in the sublunar world] the good and perfection found in them would be absent and life would not remain in any creature. They are found to guide man more than they guide other [creatures] to the extent that all [man's] actions are governed by them. It is necessary that this Providence attach itself to [man] more than it attaches itself to other things existing here [in the sublunar world] because of the subtlety of his matter as a result of which he is easily affected by external things. If not for the great protection received by [man] through the heavenly bodies he would easily be destroyed. Also because of the great diversity in the composition [of the humors] great differences[6] would be necessitated according to the [various] compositions of people. Since the predispositions of the soul vary according to variations of the composition [of the humors] it follows that great diversity occurs between individual human beings with regard to the predispositions of their souls and because of this [human beings] would necessarily be constantly engaged in strife and quarrels so that they would kill one another if not for this protection. The extent of this protection which is received from [the heavenly bodies] has already been made clear in reflecting upon the misfortunes which befall people at the hands of the wicked. Although [the wicked] are numerous and try with all their strength to do evil to others and constantly apply their ingenuity to this in so far as is possible for them—despite all this—the misfortunes which befall men through them are found to be few. Since this is the case, it is clear that the patterns which God arranged by means of the heavenly bodies contain in themselves righteousness, justice and compassion in an immeasurable [degree]; even though, of necessity, some misfortune proceeds from these patterns by chance since they safeguard the contrary [elements], through which all compounds exist, by [allowing] at times one [of these elements] to dominate and at times the other and as a result it may occur with regard to some people that misfortune becomes dominant. That God did not arrange the heavenly bodies in a way such that no misfortune proceed from them does not involve any shortcoming or weakness on His part. This is so because He placed in man an instrument by means of which he may escape these misfortunes, i.e., the intellect. Man may escape these misfortunes either through proper exercise of free will or by virtue of Providence in accordance with one of the preceding ways. One who does not engage in the perfection of the intellect to the degree which is proper [and] in a manner such that this Providence becomes attached to him should not complain other than of himself when those misfortunes come upon him because [these misfortunes] occur to him by his own doing.

Also, those misfortunes which in a minority of cases occur due to the constellations [have a purpose] which is clearly beneficial, i.e., that [readily] perceived evil occurs thereby to the wicked and other people are chastised by [these misfortunes] and escape from their wickedness. [It is] as if these misfortunes which are received from the constellations by chance were intended for this purpose as it is said:

> The Lord hath made everything
> for His own purpose,
> Yea, even the wicked for the day of evil.[7]

In general, one who does not wish that the few misfortunes which occur by chance here [in the sublunar world] be arranged by the heavenly bodies wishes that none of the wondrous benefits which God made to exist by means of them should exist here [in the sublunar world]. It is clear that it is not proper for God to refrain from producing[8] these wondrous benefits which occur through the heavenly bodies because of the little misfortune which occurs by chance. This is so because it is the nature of God to benefit a creature in so far as [the creature] is able to receive benefit and perfection. Just as it is not proper that God refrain from giving forms to those things which exist here [in the sublunar world] because they will eventually be destroyed, which is a misfortune, so is it not proper that He refrain from producing these wondrous benefits through the mediation of the heavenly bodies because of the little misfortune which occurs through them by chance. Since this is the case, it is clear that not arranging these constellations in such a way that no misfortune occur through them involves no shortcoming in God. We further maintain that there is nothing in the benefits and misfortunes occurring to individuals which are found to proceed without justice because of these constellations which can possibly be attributed to God as an injustice. This is so because the absence of order found with regard to these matters is of two kinds: either with regard to the benefits which are found to befall the wicked or with regard to the misfortunes which are found to befall the righteous; and it has already been explained that with regard to neither of these two is there anything which it is possible to attribute to injustice.

Indeed that the receiving of benefits by the wicked through the constellations [arranged by] the heavenly bodies is not an injustice is clear on the basis of what I shall say: that is, benefits come to [the wicked] by virtue of general Providence: I mean, by virtue of those constellations which [influence] man *qua* human being. Therefore, these goods accrue to [the wicked] because of the particular position of the stars when they were born, not because they are wicked. It is clear that it is not fitting that God refrain from exercising this form of Providence over the human species—[a Providence] which is necessary for its protection—because of the wicked who may be among [its recipients]. It would, however, be an injustice if they were to receive benefits by virtue of their being wicked or because of [their] individual nature. Just as it is not correct to say that the Providence which God exercised in creating man by placing in him many organs to safeguard his existence in the most perfect manner possible is an injustice because this beneficence extends also to the wicked despite their extraordinary wickedness, so it is not correct to say that this beneficence which accrues to the wicked by virtue of these constellations [ordered by] the heavenly bodies is an injustice. This is so because it is not fitting that God refrain from benefitting the human species by way of general Providence because of the wicked who may possibly be among [its recipients] and also because it is God's way to benefit creatures in the highest degree possible. This is clear from the abundance of good and compassion found in the nature of each individual existent being, so much so that it is possible [for a creature] to grasp but a little [of this good and compassion]. If it would be possible that each individual creature receive the greatest possible perfection He would not [bestow] less than [that amount of perfection]. There should, therefore, be no doubt concerning the benefits which accrue to the wicked. In general, just as it is not an injustice if food and pleasure are made available to one of the irrational animals or beasts of prey, so it is not an injustice if these false benefits are found in wicked human beings whose [spiritual] level is that of beasts of prey. It would, however, be an injustice if they were found to possess human benefits. We have explained herewith that the receiving of benefits by the wicked in this manner is not an injustice.

However, that the receiving of misfortune by the righteous is not an injustice is clear on the basis of what I shall say: that is, it is possible that misfortunes may occur to the righteous as a result of one of four causes and not one of them [constitutes] an injustice. The misfortunes which befall the righteous can be attributed to one of these four causes. The first of these is the pursuit of sensory [pleasures] by these righteous [individuals] and their severance of the bond and conjunction between themselves and God by virtue of which they are the recipients of Providence. For when the situation is in accordance with this description they are cast aside and left to the misfortunes which are received by chance through the arrangements of the heavenly bodies. If these non-human misfortunes occur to them at such times it is not an injustice since God has endeavored [to protect them] by instilling in them an instrument to guard against [these misfortunes] according to their ability, i.e., the intellect. Therefore, it is clear that they themselves are the cause of their receiving these misfortunes—not God.

The second is that it may occur that these righteous [individuals] live in [a state of] misfortune from the time of their birth because severe misfortunes occurred to their parents [and] it is difficult for their descendants to emerge from them unless they are in the ultimate [state] of worthiness, righteousness and conjunction with God. Therefore, it happens that their descendants are righteous but are [nevertheless] encumbered by these misfortunes since they have not reached such a degree of strong attachment to God that He cause them to escape from these misfortunes by way of extraordinary Providence or that they might escape the misfortunes [which occur] through the constellations. In a similar vein the prophet, may he rest in peace, said, "Our fathers have sinned and are no more; but we bear their sins,"[9] meaning by this, according to my interpretation, that, when our forefathers sinned in a manner which necessitated their being exiled among the nations it became necessary that their descendants following them bear this punishment; that they not be privileged to possess their land again[10] other than by means of many actions effected by God through extraordinary Providence. Since they have not attained this degree of attachment they remain with that punishment. If their forebears had not received this punishment the children would be in [their land] in the same manner as [the fathers were] previously and would not depart from it except by doing evil things which would make them culpable for this punishment either by virtue of Providence, as will be explained, or through the withholding of Providence. It is possible that this verse may have another interpretation and we shall note it, God willing, at the end of the treatise.[11] In a similar vein [Scripture] also says, "The fathers ate unripe grapes and the children's teeth are weakened."[12]

It is clear that the occurrence of misfortune of the righteous in this manner is not an injustice on the part of God since He instilled in them the instrument [with which] to escape these misfortunes with which they were created. It would seem that our teachers, of blessed memory, were referring to this type of misfortune in their statement, "A righteous man in misfortune—this is a righteous man who is the son of a wicked person."[13] It is clear that in a similar way it is possible that wicked people may receive benefits by virtue of their having been created with them and such benefits continue to occur to them as long as misfortune which would remove these benefits does not occur to them through the constellations. It would seem that our teachers, of blessed memory, were referring to this in their statement, "A wicked man in good fortune—this is a wicked man who is the son of a righteous person."[14] According to this principle it is possible that the wondrous good which befalls a man of perfect righteousness should continue for many generations after him since the misfortune which might possibly come through the constellations to remove these benefits is minute and might also be nullified if that generation is subject to Providence. The misfortune which extends from the wicked to their descendants cannot possibly be extended for many generations because the benefits ordained by the constellations are great. Therefore it is impossible that [the benefits] be nullified in a shorter period of time. In this way it is possible for it to be said that God "visits the iniquity of the fathers upon the children unto the third or fourth generation of them that hate Me and shows mercy unto the thousandth generation"[15] without there being injustice with regard to this.

The third of these causes is that it may happen that God causes misfortune to befall the righteous in order to save them from greater misfortunes about to come upon them through the constellations; and one of the aspects of Providence is to preserve the just from misfortunes about to come upon them. Since the occurrence of this misfortune is by way of beneficence and mercy to the good person it is clear that it is not an injustice.

The fourth of these causes is that it may happen that God brings misfortune upon the righteous by virtue of Providence in order to preserve them from the minor disobedience in which they have begun to become enmeshed. In a similar vein Elihu said, "He openeth their eyes to rebuke and commandeth that they return from iniquity."[16] That is, if God endeavors in this way to preserve [individuals] from perceptible misfortunes which are not human [in nature] certainly it is fitting that these misfortunes be received by them in order to save them from misfortunes of the soul, for [misfortunes] of the soul are human [in nature]. . .

Now [with regard to] the argument of the Aristotelians substantiating [the opinion] that it is impossible for Divine Providence to extend to individuals because man is inferior and contemptible in relation to God, it has already become clear from our words that the opposite is the case. For through reason man has some sort of unification and conjunction[17] with God and because of this it is not proper that God forget him.[18] Rather, it is proper that Providence be wondrous in regard to him because of this unification and conjunction. Furthermore, the Philosopher admits that Divine Providence extends to species because they are eternal and to individuals which are eternal such as the heavenly bodies.[19] If, according to him, Providence extends to individuals by virtue of the nature of the species and in this way they are eternal [in the species], it is also possible that Divine Providence extend to each individual of the human species who achieves intellectual perfection through the eternal nature which unifies [those individuals]—that is the Acquired Intellect.[20] It becomes clear herewith that none of the arguments which we have mentioned in order to substantiate the opinion of the Philosopher necessitates the refutation of that which we have postulated with regard to Providence. . .

Now that the problem has been resolved with regard to the doubts which might be raised regarding our premise on the basis of the arguments substantiating the remaining opinions with regard to Providence and with regard to the doubt which might be raised because of the lack of order which is found by the senses and with regard to the benefits and misfortunes of individual human beings and since there are other doubts regarding our assumption concerning Providence based upon philosophic speculation and sense perception it is proper that we attempt to resolve [the latter]. First let us state that doubts may be raised with regard to what we have posited concerning the fore-knowledge received by the righteous by way of Providence. The first of these is that it is possible, according to this premise, that this Providence attach itself to the wicked when they are intellectually accomplished. I mean that it may happen to them that this fore-knowledge reach them because of their conjunction with God by virtue of the actualization of their intellect even though their actions are not just. That this should be so is something improper in regard to Divine Justice. I mean, [it is improper] that this individual Providence should extend to the righteous and the wicked in the same degree. The second is that it is clear on the basis of sense perception that this fore-knowledge is also received by those lacking in intelligence and by minors even though they do not perform just actions. That is, this fore-knowledge may be received by those lacking in intelligence and by children through dreams or magic. We have already discussed fully the cause of this in the Second Treatise of this book.[21] It is clear that with regard to the nature of Divine justice it is not proper that this individual Providence reach people such as these. The third is that it is clear on the basis of sense perception that this fore-knowledge may reach wicked people through the intermediacy of righteous people who receive this fore-knowledge; I mean, that these people know that some [instances of] benefit and misfortune may possibly occur to them and they may receive the selfsame protection which they would have received if they had received the information themselves. Since this is the case, those who are unfit for it are [also] guided by this individual Providence and this is something improper with regard to the nature of Divine justice. These are the questions which, it seems to us, may be raised with regard to what we have posited regarding Providence.

It is proper that we attempt to resolve [these questions]. We maintain that, if according to our premise, this fore-knowledge were by way of a true reward to the righteous [person] in so far as he is righteous there would be a basis for these doubts. But it is clear from what has preceded in our discussion that this fore-knowledge is not in the nature of a true reward to the righteous [person] in so far as he is righteous since for [the righteous] the true reward is the well-being of the soul. Therefore it is clear in a general manner that no doubt can arise in these ways regarding our assumption regarding Providence. It is possible that we resolve each one of the questions in a particular manner. That is, the question which arose with regard to this [premise] on the basis of the possibility of this fore-knowledge reaching those of perfect intellect even though they be wicked being the same as the possibility of [this fore-knowledge] reaching them if they were righteous [is based on an assumption which] is not true; that is, if one who is accomplished in the understanding of intelligibles turns to shameful activities, the unification and conjunction with God which he possessed will necessarily be diminished. This is so because shameful actions are necessarily a cause of a lack of use of the intellect for [understanding] intelligibles and of a deficiency in achieving actualization of the intellect. [This occurs] because of the intellect's turning to material pleasures and because the bodily powers rule [the individual] so that, besides preventing him from endeavoring to perfect his intellect, they prevent him from contemplating the intelligibles which he has already grasped. Since this is the case and [since] a deficiency in achieving intellectual perfection is [the] cause of an inferior degree of fore-knowledge and [since] refraining from making use of intelligibles is [the] cause of interrupting [the receiving of this fore-knowledge] in some manner, it is clear that the degree of fore-knowledge [manifested] to one who has reached some degree of intellectual perfection but has turned to shameful activities is not of the same quality as it would have been if he had not turned to shameful activities. This is the opposite of what was assumed in [raising] this question. Therefore, it is clear that no doubt can occur on this account with regard to what we have posited regarding Providence.

However, the question which has been raised on account of this fore-knowledge reaching those lacking in intelligence and to minors even though they do not possess[22] just actions is not difficult to resolve since this fore-knowledge is not [manifested] to them other than by way of Providence which extends to the species. Therefore, there is no problem with regard to this [even] if benefit accrues to them because of this fore-knowledge, just as no doubt arises with regard to that which occurs to the wicked by way of the Providence which extends to the species. Also, there is a wondrous difference to be found between this fore-knowledge and the fore-knowledge which is [manifested] to the righteous by virtue of individual Providence. It has already been explained in the Second Treatise of this work that this fore-knowledge is an extremely imperfect [form of] fore-knowledge. Therefore, it is clear that the [same] benefit which would be received through a perfect [form of] fore-knowledge will not be received through [this imperfect form of fore-knowledge]. On the contrary, it is possible that some harm may occur through it because of the imperfection of this fore-knowledge. This is so because one whom this fore-knowledge reaches in an imperfect way will not know to be wary of that of which he would be wary if he were to know perfectly which benefits and misfortunes were about to come upon him, since he does not know definitely [on the basis of this fore-knowledge] what is about to occur to him. He will, for example, exchange one misfortune for another or in removing himself from the misfortune against which he had judged himself to have been warned by the fore-knowledge received by him it may sometimes happen that he will draw closer to the misfortune which was in truth about to come upon him. In this way it will become clear that it is possible that he may experience harm[23] as a result of the imperfect fore-knowledge he has received concerning benefits about to come upon him. Therefore, it is clear that the difference between this fore-knowledge and the fore-knowledge which the righteous receive by way of individual Providence is great. Since this is the case no problem arises herein on this account because the difference between these [forms of] fore-knowledge is great. In general, it has been explained that if it were possible that existence be ordered in a way such that no misfortune befall any existing being God would not fail [to do][24] this. Therefore, it is clear that [even] if some benefit is received as a result of this fore-knowledge which occurs to people of imperfect intellect and to minors no doubt arises on this account.

Now, doubts which may be raised because this fore-knowledge is received by wicked people through the intermediacy of prophets, dreamers and sorcerers are not difficult to resolve. That is, it will be evident upon [but] a little reflection that the benefits reaching them from this fore-knowledge are not of the same degree of benefit as that received by [the person] who himself received this fore-knowledge. This is so because it may happen that these individuals do not believe the people who make known to them what may possibly happen to them and because of this the benefits which would properly be received as a result of the fore-knowledge are lacking to them. This is something which occurs to them fittingly because they do not accept as being undoubtedly true that which these people tell them. This is clearly demonstrated by what is found in the words of the Prophets, may they rest in peace, in that they used to tell Israel the misfortunes about to come upon them but they did not believe [the prophets] and fell into those misfortunes. This matter is also clear from experience on the basis of that which we find that sorcerers tell people. That is, it occurs that they do not believe [the sorcerers'] words and because of this it happens at times that they fall into the [selfsame] misfortune which was about to come upon them as is recounted [concerning] what happened to one man who was told by a sorceress that if he were to go in a certain direction he would be killed; he did not believe her and was killed in that land. Since this is the case, it is clear that the difference between these [forms of] fore-knowledge is great. Therefore, it is clear that no doubt arises herein on this account.

It is clear from what we have mentioned that it is not proper that doubts be raised [concerning our opinion because] it happens that some benefit occurs to wicked people as a result of this fore-knowledge since God would not fail[25] to cause as much good as possible to emanate to His creatures. For this reason you will find that the Prophets, may they rest in peace, in making known to people what is due to come upon them guide them at the same time so that they might follow righteous and just actions and [so that] they forsake evil and violence. In this they follow the intention of the Torah which endeavored [to cause] all men [to become] righteous in the most perfect manner possible. With this we have resolved these questions in their entirety. . .

You will also find the opinion of our Sages, of blessed memory, [to be] that true reward and punishment is in the world to come and that it is not necessary that there be reward and punishment here [in the sublunar world] according to righteousness and wickedness [in the form of] bodily benefits and misfortunes. [Our Sages] said, "There is no reward in this world for [the performance of] a precept."[26] It is proper that we infer from this that the case is the same with regard to punishment, meaning that it is not to be found in bodily things because since reward and punishment are opposites their underlying subject is necessarily the same. I mean that the medium in which reward is to be found is itself the selfsame medium in which punishment is to be found. Our teachers, of blessed memory, said:[27]

> Take the case of a [person] whose father says to him, 'Ascend to the loft and bring me the nestlings.' He ascends, chases away the mother and takes the young and in returning falls and dies. Where is the 'prolonging of days' of this person? And where is the 'good' accorded to this person?[28] Rather 'that good be done unto thee'[29] refers to a world which is wholly good and 'that thou [mayest] prolong thy days'[30] to a world which is wholly long.[31] It is [also] stated there:[32] Rabbi Joseph said, 'If Aher[33] had interpreted this verse in the manner of Rabbi Jacob, his daughter's son, he would not have sinned.'[34] What is it [that caused Aher to sin]? Some say he witnessed an event such as the one described. Others say he saw the tongue of a great person[35] being dragged along by a swine [and] said 'Is it fitting that a mouth which spouted pearls [of wisdom] should lick dust?' [Aher] did not know that 'that good be done unto thee'[36] refers to a world which is wholly good and 'that thy days may be prolonged'[37] refers to a world which is wholly long.

They have [herein] explained to you that reward and punishment are not to be found in bodily benefits and misfortunes and therefore it is not impossible that they proceed without order and justice. [Our Sages] said, "Life, children, and sustenance do not depend upon merit; they depend rather upon the constellations."[38] There is no doubt that they did not intend in this dictum to dispute the Torah which in many places foretells that such bodily benefits will occur to those who walk in her ways; they meant rather that in general this matter depends upon the constellations. Therefore, it is not proper that doubts be raised if benefits similar to these occur to the wicked for they occur to them through the constellations, not through their evil actions.

Now that this has been resolved it is proper that we mention those doubts which may be raised concerning our premise with regard to Providence on the basis of what appears in the words of the prophets, may they rest in peace; and it is proper that we should attempt to resolve them. One of them [is based on] that which is mentioned in the Torah concerning the awesome punishments which come upon Israel when they are very wicked in punishment for their great disobedience. [The Torah] explains that [these punishments] do not occur by accident but by direct intention. It is stated, "If you walk with me *b'keri*,"[39]—the Torah means by this that if they ascribe the occurrence of these misfortunes to chance and do not accept them as an admonition, God will continue to smite them in harsh anger until it becomes clear to them that this does not occur by accident. [The case is] similar with regard to that which appears in the Torah and in the words of the prophets, may they rest in peace, concerning the receiving from God of what are in their essence misfortunes by other nations e.g., that which the Torah recounts concerning the bringing of wondrous plagues upon Pharaoh and upon his people on account of Israel[40] and that which is mentioned concerning the smiting of the camp of Ashur by the angel of the Lord[41] and things similar to these. For all of this seemingly disagrees with our assumption, since according to our assumption it is impossible that these misfortunes befall wicked people other than by chance. The second [concerns] that which appears in the Torah and in the words of the prophets, may they rest in peace, mentioning that man is judged in regard to all of his actions, be they good or bad. It is stated, "The Rock, His work is perfect for all His ways are just."[42] It is stated, ". . .Whose eyes are open upon all the ways of the sons of men to give every one according to his ways, and according to the fruit of his doings."[43] "Say ye of the righteous, that it shall be well with him; for they shall eat the fruit of their doings. Woe unto the wicked! It shall be ill with him; for the work of his hands shall be done to him."[44] "For the work of a man will He requite unto him, and cause every man to find according to his ways."[45] This matter may also be thought to disagree with our premise.

These are the doubts which may be raised with regard to our premise on the basis of what appears in the Torah and in the words of the prophets, may they rest in peace; and it is fitting that we attempt to resolve them. With regard to the first doubts which may be raised regarding our assumption on the basis of that which the Torah foretells concerning the receiving by Israel, from God, of what are in their essence wondrous punishments in accordance with their great disobedience, we maintain that [the] resolution [of this question] is not difficult. That is, we maintain that these matters[46] and punishments are by way of Providence so that [the people affected] turn away from their evil way for in this manner it is possible that what is in essence evil may come from God as has [been explained in what has] preceded. However, it is possible that Providence attach itself in this way to those who have been exceedingly disobedient because of the nation as a whole which is righteous and it is proper that Providence attach itself [to those people][47] in this manner. Therefore, when some individual [members] of the nation become enmeshed in shameful activities God endeavors to admonish them by means of the Providence [exercised] with regard to the nation as a whole so that that this disobedience shall not spread among them all. That is, just as the Providence which has its basis in the constellations extends to people in two ways—either in an individual manner, i.e., that which is arranged by the constellations for each individual person, or in a general way, i.e., that which is arranged by the constellations for the nation as a whole or for the state as a whole—so also is the case with regard to this Providence; I mean that it attaches itself to an [individual] person when he is righteous and attaches itself to the people as a whole when they are righteous. For this reason Divine Providence attaches itself to the nation as a whole and because of this [Providence] may reprove some of its members, if they are wicked, on account of the evil in which they have begun to become enmeshed so that they may return to the righteous path and receive well-being of the soul. It is said, ". . .as a man chasteneth his son, so the Lord thy God chastenth thee";[48] "In vain have I smitten your children—They received no correction."[49] The curses which are mentioned in the Torah for those who turn aside from the ways of God are mentioned for this reason and it is stated that they do not occur by chance; rather, they are with intent on the part of God. Of that which points to the fact that these punishments are sent by way of Providence rather than by way of punishment is the verse ". . .and I will chastise you seven times for your sins."[50] If this were by way of punishment there would be therein an injustice which could not be ignored, but since this is by way of Providence it is appropriate. I mean that when God sends afflictions upon [individuals] by way of reproof, but they are not chastised, continuing rather in disobedience, it is proper that He chastise them on account of their sins. This is so because the reproof of one who has become only a little enmeshed in disobedience is not the same as the reproof of one who has been persistent in it and in whom that evil trait has become a firm habit. This is so because one who is steeped in shameful actions will not emerge from them other than through strong reproofs. In this way the statement ". . .and also in the iniquities of their fathers shall they pine away with them"[51] is possible without there being an injustice in this;[52] that is, if the forebears become accustomed to disobedience and their children hold to their ways this base tendency becomes a firm habit in them so that they will not abandon it except through strong reproofs. Therefore, it is proper that greater misfortune come upon them by way of reproof that they may be chastised by it, than would have occurred to them if their forebears had not been wicked. Perhaps [the verse] "He visits the iniquity of the fathers on the children"[53] [and] "The fathers have eaten sour grapes, and the children's teeth are weakened"[54] is said in the same vein. It would seem that just as the misfortune which occurs to the righteous person through Providence in order to reprove him regarding the disobedience in which he has begun to become enmeshed is not permanent—rather, as he becomes confirmed in [his] disobedience this Providence turns aside from him since it is then not fitting that this Providence be attached to him—so also is the situation with regard to the Providence which is attached to the nation as a whole; I mean, that when this multitude conducts itself in a manner which is not righteous, this Providence turns aside from it and God does not then reprove them regarding their sins. It is stated, ". . .this people will rise up and go astray after the foreign gods of the land, whither they go to be among them and will forsake Me and break My covenant which I have made with them. Then My anger shall be kindled against them in that day and I will forsake them and I will hide My face from them and they shall be devoured. . ."[55] in explaining[56] to you that when the nation will become idolatrous God's Providence will turn aside from them. In a [vein] similar to this it is stated [by way] of foretelling evil, "I will not punish your daughters when they commit adultery."[57] It has already been explained to you that because of their extreme disobedience this Divine Providence ceases from [the members of the nation]; I mean, that He does not reprove them for their disobedience but leaves them to the chance occurrences of time.

It seems that there is a difference between the misfortune which occurs to the righteous person by way of Providence in order to reprove him regarding the evil in which he has become a little enmeshed[58] and the misfortune which occurs to the multitude as a whole by way of Providence in order to reprove them regarding the evil in which that group[59] has become enmeshed, that is, that when misfortune occurs to a righteous person by way of reproof it is not possible that it be in a manner such that he die as a result of it, for if it were to occur in such a manner it would be impossible to say that it [occurs] by way of Providence. However, with regard to that misfortune which befalls the nation as a whole by way of reproof it is not impossible that many die through [those misfortunes] in order that those who remain and the generations which follow take heed[60] so that all of them shall not persist in their disobedience, for this is better for the nation as a whole since it is impossible that they be admonished other than by means of this form of reproof. Therefore, you will find that regarding these reproofs the Torah foretells [that] which may result in death.

Herewith are resolved the doubts raised by the first question based upon what appears to be [contained] in the Torah foretelling that evil in essence will be received by Israel from God when they do not walk in God's ways. Now the questions concerning [our premise] which may be raised on the basis of what appears in the Torah and in the words of the prophets, may they rest in peace, concerning the receiving of evil in essence by other nations from God, such as that which the Torah relates concerning the afflictions with which God smote Pharaoh[61] and Sihon[62] and how He hardened their hearts so that He might bring punishment upon them and that which is mentioned concerning the smiting of the angel of God in the camp of Ashur[63] and that which is found concerning the wars of Israel with other nations regarding which it is said that God aided them as a result of which they vanquished [the enemy], is not difficult to resolve. This is so because the receiving of misfortune by the wicked from God in this manner is, in some instances, in the nature of a miracle, e.g. the drowning of the Egyptians in the Red Sea,[64] the slaying of the first-born[65] and the other plagues which befell the Egyptians,[66] the smiting of the camp of Ashur by the angel of God[67] and those [misfortunes] which are similar to these. Those occurrences which fit this description do not contradict our premise because we speak here solely concerning that which proceeds from Providence in a manner compatible with the order of existence, not concerning that through which a change is effected in the natural order. Furthermore, those misfortunes which befall the wicked in the form of miracles are in the nature of Providence with regard to the righteous whom those wicked people attempt to harm; that is, if righteous people may experience Providence in a manner such that misfortune befalls them in order that they may be preserved from a greater misfortune it is certainly proper that they be safeguarded by Providence through the occurrence of misfortune to the wicked who do harm to them so that their [attempted] harm be deflected from [the righteous].

Now, [regarding] that which has been mentioned concerning the hardening of Pharaoh's heart in a manner which involved increased misfortune for Israel, this too was by way of Providence in order to instill in them proper faith; when Pharaoh became culpable for punishment and it was possible for Israel to receive benefit by means of [Pharaoh] receiving [punishment] in this manner, [that is] in a way which might impress upon their hearts that God exists and in order that His strength and power might be proven to them to be verified by means of the multiplication of miracles, God caused Pharaoh to harden his heart in such a manner that His miracles might be multiplied and the true faith become manifest to Israel. This is the meaning of the statement: "Go unto Pharaoh; for I have hardened his heart and the heart of his servants, that I might show these My signs in the midst of them; and that thou mayest tell in the ears of thy son, and of thy son's son what I have wrought upon Egypt . . . that ye may know that I am the Lord."[68]

I have already explained to you[69] that the hardening of Pharaoh's heart was for the purpose of increasing miracles and the multiplication of miracles was for the purpose of making manifest to Israel and to succeeding generations that there exists a God Who does whatsoever He desires. Regarding that which has been mentioned concerning the misfortune befalling the wicked[70] when they wage wars against Israel which is not by way of miracle, [this misfortune] is either by way of Providence with regard to Israel, for this is not impossible according to our premise as has [been explained] in what preceded, or else this misfortune is brought upon those wicked people through the constellations, for this also is attributable to God since all things are caused by Him. Now, regarding that which has been mentioned in the Torah concerning the hardening of the spirit of Sihon:[71] [this] was either through Providence with regard to Israel causing misfortune to befall Sihon so that Israel might inherit his land, in which case the matter proceeded from God in the nature of a miracle; or else [this] was a misfortune destined to come upon [Sihon] and the hardening of his spirit arranged by the heavenly bodies [was] one of the means of bringing the misfortune upon him. This matter is attributable to God even though it occurred in accordance with this description because of His being the cause of what occurs regardless of the manner in which it occurs. This problem is herewith resolved.

NOTES

1. Chap. 6, p. 106.
2. According to the manuscript reading שאם היה ראוי שיהוה, the phrase "it was fitting that" should be inserted in the translation. *Vide* Kellermann, p. 250, n. 3.
3. According to the manuscripts which add the phrase וברעות האנושיות. *Vide* Kellermann, p. 205, n. 4. The term "human excellences" or "virtues" occurs in Aristotle's *Nicomachean Ethics*, 1098a. Aristotle describes human "happiness" as being identical with the highest development and operation of man's intellectual faculty. Cf., Maimonides, *Guide*, III, 27, where Maimonides asserts that the welfare of the soul consists of the perfection of the intellect.
4. I.e., intellect. *Vide* Aristotle, *De Anima*, III, 4–6 and Maimonides, *Eight Chapters*, Chap. 1, for a description of the "rational soul" as being unique to man.
5. *Vide Commentary on the Bible*, Job. Chap. 14, p. 19, ". . . according to some of the ancients as mentioned in the *Ethics* (Aristotle, *Nicomachaen Ethics*, IX, 9) death is preferable to life which is not human [in nature]. However, human benefits [even when they occur] together with misfortunes which are not human [in nature] are praiseworthy in themselves."
6. The addition of the word רב, "great" in the manuscript reading היה מחויב שיהיה התחלפות בין מזגי האנשים רב should be understood as modifying "differences." Cf., Kellermann, p. 257, n. 1.
7. Proverbs 16:4.
8. Literally: "causing to emanate."
9. Lamentations 5:7.
10. Some manuscripts add the words באופן הקודם, "in the previous manner." *Vide* Kellermann, p. 265, n. 2.
11. Above, p. 94. The verse there cited is Exodus 34:7, "He visits the iniquity of the fathers upon the children," rather than Lamentations 5:7. The two verses are, of course, similar in import. "The fathers have eaten sour grapes. . ." is also cited there in a similar vein.
12. Jeremiah 31:29; Ezekiel 18:2.
13. Berakhot 7a.
14. *Loc. cit.*
15. Exodus 20:5–6.
16. Job 36:10.
17. It seems to me that the text should read ודבקות. The word לדבקות which appears in both the Riva and Leipzig editions is obviously an error.
18. The manuscript reading is שימאסהו according to which the translation would be "disdain him." *Vide* Kellermann, p. 268, n. 2.

19. *Vide* Averroes, *Hauptlehren*, p. 62.

20. The argument seems to run as follows: Providence safeguards the continuity of the species. This is accomplished through preserving an endless series of individuals, each of which is transient in itself but participates in the eternity of the species. Thus, while the eternity of the species is contingent upon the preservation of successive individual members, Providence, which safeguards these individuals, is possible only by virtue of the eternal nature of the species. With regard to the human species it is the Acquired Intellect which constitutes the nature of the species assuring its continuity by means of its influence upon individual members. Since the nature of the human species is intellectual it is, therefore, not surprising that individual human beings who have achieved intellectual perfection be capable of availing themselves as individuals of Providential guardianship in the form of intellectual communication since the Providence extended to them as members of the species is conveyed through the medium of the intellect.

21. Chap. 6, p. 105 and p. 111 ff.

22. Literally: "are not the possessors of."

23. Reading חזק rather than החשק which is an obvious corruption of the text. *Vide* Kellermann, p. 278, n. 2.

24. Literally: "fall short of [doing]."

25. Literally: "fall short of causing."

26. *Talmud Babli, Kiddushin* 39b.

27. *Loc. cit.*

28. The standard texts of the Talmud read היכן טובת ימיו של זה והיכן אריכת ימיו של זה—where, is the goodness of days of this person? And where is the prolonging of days of this person? The reading cited by Gersonides is: היכן אריכת ימיו של זה והיכן טובתו של זה.

30. *Loc. cit.* The verse here quoted, ". . .that good be done unto thee and that thou mayest prolong thy days" indicates the compensation for fulfilling the precept contained in Deuteronomy 22:6–7; this precept is termed "the dismissal of the nest." A similar verse, ". . .that thy days may be prolonged and that good be done unto thee" (Deuteronomy 5:16) contains the promise of a similar reward in connection with honoring one's parents. The standard texts of the Talmud cite the latter למען יאריכון ימיך of verse 5:16 rather than והארכת ימים of 22:7. The Talmud, on the basis of our texts, apparently chose to quote a section of each verse since the illustration is of an individual who experiences misfortune in the very act of fulfilling both the commandment to honor one's father and the precept of dismissal of the nest.

31. I.e., both references are to the world to come. This Talmudic statement is cited as evidence that bodily benefits and misfortunes do not constitute reward and punishment.

32. *Kiddushin* 39b.

33. Elisha b. Abuyah, a renowned scholar of the Tannaitic period and teacher of R. Meir who later became a heretic, whereupon he was dubbed *aher*, a different person, a stranger.

34. Having interpreted these verses literally as having reference to this world he became an unbeliever when he saw that these promises were not fulfilled.

35. The Talmudic texts read: ". . .the tongue of Huzpith the Interpreter. . ." Huzpith was one of the martyrs slain in the Hadrianic persecution after the fall of Bethar. The interpreter was a religious functionary who translated the public readings of the Torah to the people.

36. Probably Deuteronomy 22:7 as apparently is the citation in *Kiddushin* 39b, although it is possible that Deuteronomy 5:16 is intended as well.

37. Deuteronomy 5:16. In this paraphrase Gersonides' citation conforms with that of our text of *Kiddushin* 39b.

38. *Talmud Babli, Mo'ed Katan* 28a.

39. Leviticus 26:21. The word אמר is absent in the texts. *Vide* Kellermann, p. 285, n. 1.

40. Exodus 7:14–11:10; Exodus 12:20–30.

41. II Kings 19:35; Isaiah 37:36.
42. Deuteronomy 32:40.
43. Jeremiah 32:19.
44. Isaiah 3:10.
45. Job 34:11.
46. The word העניניים is omitted in the manuscripts. *Vide* Kellermann, p. 286, n. 1.
47. Reading בהם rather than בו. *Vide* Kellermann, p. 286, n. 2.
48. Deuteronomy 8:5.
49. Jeremiah 2:30.
50. Leviticus 26:28.
51. Leviticus 26:39.
52. Cf., Maimonides, *Guide*, III, 46.
53. Exodus 34:7.
54. Jeremiah 31:29; Ezekiel 18:2.
55. Deuteronomy 31:16–17.
56. Literally: "when [Scripture] explains to you."
57. Hosea 4:14.
58. Some manuscripts have a variant reading: אשר החל להסתבך בו, "regarding the evil in which he has begun to become enmeshed." *Vide* Kellermann, p. 289, n. 2.
59. The above cited manuscripts have the reading: אשר הסתבך בו קצת הכלל, "in which some of that group have become enmeshed." *Vide* Kellermann, p. 299, n. 3.
60. Literally: "take admonition."
61. Exodus 7:17–11:80; Exodus 12:39-40.
62. Numbers 21:21–30.
63. II Kings 19:35; Isaiah 37:36.
64. Exodus 14:23–28.
65. Exodus 12:29–30.
66. Exodus 7:17–11:8.
67. II Kings 19:35; Isaiah 37:36.
68. Exodus 10:1–2.
69. According to the manuscript reading כבר באר לך, "explaining to you," this is a continuation of the previous sentence and intended to clarify the meaning of the verse cited. The translation, "I have already explained to you," follows the text of both Leipzig and Riva.
70. I.e., being sent upon them by God.
71. Deuteronomy 3:30.

ALBO, *IKKARIM*

Translation by Isaac Husik

BOOK IV, CHAPTER 29

We will now treat of reward and punishment, which is the third of the general principles of a divine law. It takes the place of the purpose intended by all laws. It is true that he who serves God from love does not concern himself at all about reward and punishment, having no other purpose except to fulfil the will of the object of his love, as the Rabbis say: "Be not like servants who serve their master in order to receive compensation . . ."[1] But this does not mean that there is no reward and punishment, Heaven forbid! The above statement simply means that one who serves God from love must not be prompted in his service by love of reward and fear of punishment, though he believes that there is reward in store for those who believe and fear God and think on His name. All this reward is as nothing in his sight as compared with the purpose of fulfilling the will of the object of his love. Service of this sort leads to the ultimate reward and punishment that is intended in all laws.

Now inasmuch as the purpose of a divine law is different from those of conventional laws, as we said before,[2] we laid it down as a general principle of divine law. We analyze the possibilities as follows: Either there is reward and punishment or there is not. If there is, it is either all corporeal and in this world, or all spiritual and in the other world, or there is both corporeal reward in this world and spiritual reward in the next world.

Opinion, we find, is divided in the matter of reward and punishment into four classes according to the four possibilities of which the situation admits. Some believe there is no reward and punishment, either corporeal or spiritual. Some believe there is both corporeal and spiritual reward. Some believe there is corporeal reward but no spiritual, and some believe there is spiritual reward but no corporeal.

This difference of opinion is based upon the division of opinion among men concerning the nature of the soul. Some say that the human soul is not superior to the animal soul except that man has more shrewdness than the other animals in devising means and inventing arts necessary for arranging his life in a complete manner, as in the animal world some are superior to others in this respect. For this reason those who hold this opinion think that there is no reward or punishment at all, either corporeal or spiritual. They hold that man is governed by accident like the other animals, concerning which the divine purpose is directed merely to the preservation of the species. This opinion has been given its deathblow by the philosophers,[3] who say that the human soul can not be compared to the animal souls. The latter have only knowledge of particulars, while man has knowledge of universals. Moreover, man can perceive a thing when it is no longer present to the sense, while an animal can not. Man, moreover, distinguishes between substance and accident, and so on, all of which shows the great difference between the human soul and the animal soul. Hence there must be a special purpose that is peculiar to the human soul, as we explained before.[4] Hence, though there is no spiritual perfection in animals, there must be such in man. The Jewish sages were also opposed to this opinion and maintained that there ought to be reward and punishment for man, either spiritual in the world to come, or corporeal in this world through divine providence, as we explained when we treated of Providence.[5]

The second opinion is that there is reward and punishment, but that it is corporeal and in this world. Some believe that the human soul is superior to that of the animals because it has a rational power through which the divine spirit cleaves to man and provides for him according to the superiority of his intellect. But since this superiority is merely a capacity or preparation,[6] it always requires, they say, a subject; and when the union between soul and body is sundered, the soul disappears. A certain school of philosophers erroneously adopt this view, saying that we can not conceive of any perfection of soul without the body. The Zadokites and the Boethusians[7] adopted this view. They believed in the Torah of Moses and in Providence, but maintained at the same time that reward and punishment are only corporeal and in this world, as is mentioned in Abot de Rabbi Natan,[8] and denied spiritual reward after death altogether. They adduced as proof of their opinion the fact that in the Law of Moses there is no mention at all of spiritual reward, but only of physical prosperity. They adopted this erroneous opinion because they thought that the human soul is composed of various faculties, such as nutrition, growth, sensation, reason. And since we see that the other powers disappear when the union between soul and body is sundered, they said that the power of understanding which it has will also disappear along with the conceptions which it already has, and therefore the human soul will cease to exist like the souls of animals, and the one will die like the other.

The great philosophers, however, have refuted this opinion, saying that the variety of activities emanating from an agent does not necessarily prove multiplicity in the essence of the agent, as we explained above.[9] Nor does the cessation of the life of the body necessarily prove the cessation of the rational soul, any more than the cessation of the power of growth after forty makes necessary the cessation of the soul. The body is an instrument through which some of the activities of the soul become visible. Hence when the instrument is destroyed, these functions alone disappear, like nutrition, growth, sensation. But it does not follow from this that the essence of the soul should disappear. For the existence of the reason is not dependent upon the body like the other corporeal powers. On the contrary, the reason grows stronger after the age of forty, when the corporeal powers grow weaker. Moreover, the reason is not like the corporeal powers, for it can perceive itself as well as its instruments, which is not the case in the corporeal powers. They adduce also other strong and irrefutable arguments to show that the human soul can not be compared with the soul of animals, but there is no need to expatiate upon this matter.

As an indication of the erroneous character of this opinion, Maimonides says in the Introduction to his commentary on Abot[10] that the term soul in its application to the soul of man and that of animal is a homonym.[11] And though we see that the functions emanating from the one are similar to those emanating from the other, it does not follow from this that the respective agents are similar in essence. The light of the sun and the light of a lamp are similar in that they illumine dark places, but this does not show that the agencies are alike. The light of the sun is permanent and does not go out, it illumines also where the sun does not shine; while a lamp goes out, is not permanent and illumines only where the ray strikes. It does not follow, therefore, that because the soul of the animal is destroyed, the human soul too is destroyed and ceases to be when it is separated from the body, since they admit that it is superior to the soul of the animal. As for the argument which the Zadokites and the Boethusians adduce in favor of their view from the fact that no mention is made in the Law of Moses of spiritual reward, but only of corporeal, the facts are not as they say. Corporeal reward is mentioned only in those cases where there is no room for spiritual reward, and spiritual reward is mentioned by allusion, for a reason which we will explain later with the help of God.

The third opinion is the converse of the second, and is adopted by some of our Rabbis, who say: There is no reward for good deeds in this world.[12] They adduce an argument from experience. A father says to his son, Go up upon the tower and bring me some pigeons. The son goes up upon the tower, sends away the mother pigeon and takes the young,[13] and on his return he falls down and is killed. Where is his good and where is his length of days? The answer is that the scriptural promise, "That it may be well with thee,"[14] has reference to that world which is wholly good; and the promise, "That thou mayest prolong thy days," refers to that world which is altogether long (eternal). The world that is wholly good and altogether long is none other than the world to come after death, and the promise has reference to spiritual reward.

This opinion is also adopted by a great school of philosophers, and some learned men of the Torah follow them. Their opinion is that man has no perfection *qua* man except after death, when the intellect is separated from matter and corporeal things. This follows from the fact that rational things are graded according to their degree of understanding, the one that understands more is superior to the one that understands less. Since, therefore, man's superiority to animals consists in his reason, his perfection must be a degree of excellence based upon intelligence alone. For if it consisted in a corporeal thing which is common to him and the animals, the perfection and rational superiority which were given to him above the animals would be a tantalizing punishment rather than a degree of perfection. For the animals, being devoid of reason and intelligence, are not troubled by the thought of misfortune which is fated to come upon them and are not grieved by the knowledge that they must die, as man does, nor do they anticipate in imagination the pain which is to come to them, and they worry about nothing; whereas man feels all this; he is worried and grieved on account of the evil that is destined to come upon him and lives in sorrow. Nay, the greater his power of understanding the more does he grieve for the evil that is destined to come upon him. For this reason they say that it is not likely that the perfection to be attained by reason is something corporeal that is common to the lower animals, but that it must be something which distinguishes man from the animal, viz. intellect, and not a corporeal thing. This is the opinion of the Philosopher in this matter.[15] Although he denies Providence, nevertheless he believes that the soul of man has a perfection after death, when it is separated from the body. And many of the sages of the Torah follow his opinion.[16]

But there is a difficulty in this explanation. For though these arguments are a sound reply to the second opinion, still they do not prove that man's perfection is after death. For since perfection and permanence can pertain only to a rational thing, as they maintain, and the rational power in man is merely a preparation or capacity,[17] how can we conceive of its surviving the body, since a capacity can not exist by itself? The statement in reply to this, namely that the acquired intellect becomes a substance through the concepts, so that the intellect and the concepts become identical,[18] is unintelligible. For if the rational faculty in man is a hylic (material) power whose nature it is to cease to exist except through the activity of understanding, how can that activity exist by itself? And how can we conceive of its identifying itself with the Active Intellect? All this is very unlikely, as we explained before.[19] Hence, some scholars[20] say that the soul is a spiritual substance, having independent existence and the capacity of understanding. It can not therefore cease to exist, since it is an independent substance, and it feels pleasure according to its activity in cognition. But this is not correct, either. For, even though the soul be an independent substance, nevertheless, since it has the capacity of cognition, the perfection of this capacity would be in vain if the soul should not attain this cognition, and not one in a thousand would attain the perfection of the soul, and possibly no one at all, as we explained above;[21] unless we say that the perfection of cognition consists in an understanding of the axioms. But if so, the righteous and the wicked would stand on the same plane, an idea which never occurred to any one before.

It seems to us therefore that the proper and correct opinion of the Torah is that the soul is a spiritual substance, having the capacity to understand the service of God, and not mere understanding. Hence when a person attains any degree of understanding of God's service, by reason of attaining some idea or notion of God, be it great or small, he immediately attains a certain degree of life in the world to come. The Rabbis also say,[22] commenting on the verse: "A seed shall serve Him,"[23] When do small children deserve the future life? Said they in the name of Rabbi Meir: As soon as they are able to say Amen, as is written: "Open ye the gates, That the righteous nation that keepeth faithfulness (*emunim*) may enter in."[24] Read not: "That keepeth (*shomer*) faithfulness (*emunim*)," but: "That sayeth (*she-omer*) Amens (*amenim*)." The meaning of this is made clear from our explanation above, namely that the soul's perfection consists in understanding the service of God, whatever it be; so that when a child attains understanding of the least important service, viz. to say Amen to any benediction, he merits some degree of future life. This is in agreement with what we have written before,[25] namely, that a man may attain a certain degree of future life by the fulfilment of one precept. . .

The fourth opinion is that some reward is corporeal in this world and some is spiritual in the next world, after death. This is the opinion of our sacred Torah, which makes specific material promises to the righteous, like the patriarchs and others, and also spiritual promises for the soul alone, punishment or reward, as we shall explain with the help of God. This is also the opinion of our Rabbis in many places, and particularly in Sifre,[26] where, commenting on the verse in Deuteronomy,[27] they say: "That your days may be multiplied"—in this world; "And the days of your children"—in the times of the Messiah; "As the days of the heavens above the earth"—in the world to come. It is clear from this that the Bible promises, for the fulfilment of the commandments, reward in this world and in the next. This is a general statement of human opinion concerning reward and punishment and the opinion of our Torah on the subject.

NOTES

1. Abot 1, 3.
2. I, 9, p. 93 f.
3. Aristotle's De Anima is the authority for Albo's statements. Cf. Zeller, Aristotle and the Earlier Peripatetics, London, 1897, II, 22 sq., 92 sq.
4. III, 2, p.14.
5. IV, 7-15, pp. 49-144.
6. This is the view of Alexander of Aphrodisias concerning the so-called passive intellect. Cf. Husik, A History of Mediaeval Jewish Philosophy, p. 332 f.
7. The Sadducees are thus designated in the Talmud, according to which they were led astray by two individuals, Zadok and Boethus. See J. E., s. v. Sadducees, X, 631.
8. Ch. 5.
9. II, 8, p. 43.
10. Chapter 1 of the so-called "Eight Chapters" or "Shemonah Perakim."
11. See II, p.45, note 3, end.
12. Kiddushin 39b.
13. According to the commandment, Deut. 22, 6–7.
14. Ibid.
15. Aristotle of course holds that reason is the distinctive faculty of man of which the lower animals are devoid, and that the active intellect does not die with the individual, but I am not aware that he states any such reason for his opinion as Albo gives.
16. Maimonides and Gersonides and the other Jewish Aristotelians would no doubt come under this category, though they would scarcely deny all reward in this world, maintaining merely that the main reward is spiritual and in the future world. Cf. Husik, A History of Mediaeval Jewish Philosophy, 339 ff.

17. See above, note 6.

18. Cf. Maimonides, Guide, I, 68; ed. Munk, I, p. 307 note. The precise expression Albo seems to have borrowed from Crescas, Or Adonai, Book II, sect. 6, ch. 1: שהוא מוסכם מהם שהשכל יתעצם במה שישיגהו מהמושכלות ויתחדש מהם שכל נקנה בלתי מעורב עם השכל ההיולני.

19. III, 3; cf. III, p. 24, note 1.

20. Crescas, Or Adonai, Book II, section 6, ch. 1: נפש האדם אשר היא צורתו עצם רוחני מוכן אל ההשכלה ובלתי משכיל בפעל בעצמו. Later on in the same chapter Crescas says: למה שנתאמת . . . היות נפש האדם עצם רוחני היה אפשר בו ההשארות אחר ההפרד למה שאין לו סבות ההפסד להיותו אז בלתי חמר והיה ההפרד אפשרי בו להיותו עצם שכלי . . . ואחר שקיומו בעצמו אפשרי בו בהפרדו מהדבר אשר הוא לו צורה הנה הנצחיות מחוייב בו כפי טבעו להיותו משולל מהחמריות אשר הוא סבת ההפסד. Albo, however, seems to be mistaken in ascribing to Crescas the opinion that the soul's pleasure is dependent upon the degree of its understanding. Crescas deliberately opposes this view when he says that the perfection of the soul consists in love and that love has nothing to do with intellect: השלם לעצמותו אוהב הטוב והשלמות וחפץ בו וכפי השלמות תהיה האהבה והערבות בחפץ . . . האהבה והערבות בחפץ זולת ההשכלה. Later on he says: ולפי שהתבאר . . . שכפי השלמות תהיה האהבה אל הטוב והערבות ההוא מבואר שלפי מדרגת האהוב הטוב תהיה מדרגת השלמות. ולפי שהתבאר . . . שהאהבה והערבות בה זולת ההשכלה הנה העצמיי לשלמות הנפש הוא דבר זולת ההשכלה והוא האהבה. See Joel, Don Chasdai Creskas' religionsphilosophische Lehren, Breslau, 1866, p. 77 f.

21. III, 3, p. 24 f.

22. Sanhedrin 110b.

23. Ps. 22, 31.

24. Isa. 26, 2.

25. III, 29, p. 2, 3 ff.

26. Ed. Friedmann, p. 83, §47.

27. 11, 21.

BOOK IV, CHAPTER 30

Concerning the spiritual reward which comes to a man after death, the later Jewish scholars are divided into two schools. The one holds that while it is true that the perfectly righteous receive in this world reward for their deeds, as did the patriarchs, nevertheless, the main reward is spiritual, bestowed upon the soul alone in the world to come, i.e. the world which comes to a person after death as soon as the soul is separated from the body—a world in which there is no eating or drinking or any of the physical pleasures. As our Rabbis say:[1] Rab was accustomed to say: In the next world there is neither eating nor drinking, nor hatred, nor envy, nor strife, but the righteous sit with their crowns on their heads and enjoy the splendor of the Shekinah. The meaning is: the crown of a good name resulting from their good deeds stands above their heads and confers upon them the privilege of enjoying the splendor of the Shekinah.

The men of this opinion also hold that while the main reward is purely spiritual, there is also another corporeal reward in this world at the time of the Messiah. This is the same as the time of the resurrection, when the perfectly righteous will come to life, either in order to publish God's miracles and truth, or in order that they may receive some corporeal pleasure corresponding to the pain they suffered during life, or more, according as the divine Wisdom shall decree, or in order that they may acquire a higher perfection than before; in case they were not able in their lifetime to attain the degree to which they were entitled, considering their upright character, on account of external hindrances and the yoke of the exile. Then they will die again and return to dust, and then the souls will, by reason of their attainments during the second life, be privileged to enjoy the future world in a higher degree than the one they enjoyed before resurrection. This is the view of Maimonides[2] and the distinguished men who came after him and adopted his opinion. If we examine this view, we find that it is correct and inevitable logically, and in agreement with the Torah. . . .

We find that the prophet or the perfectly pious man can influence the matter of the sublunar world, as the Separate Intelligences do, because the principle of his soul comes from a Separate Intelligence. The Torah testifies to this, for we find in the account of creation that the Bible ascribes the animal soul to a material principle solely. Thus in the creation of the animals, the text says: "Let the earth bring forth the living creature after its kind."[3] But in the creation of man the Bible ascribes the soul to a rational principle: "Then the Lord God formed man of the dust of the ground, and breathed into his nostrils the breath of life," concluding: "And man became a living soul,"[4] thus indicating that the vital power in man comes from the rational power which God breathed into his nostrils, and not from another principle, as in the lower animals.

Now since the vital soul in animals and the human soul which has intelligence come from two different principles, it does not follow because the vital powers in animals disappear as soon as the union between them and the body is sundered (because they come from the power of the sphere, which is a material thing, and from its soul, which is a material power), that the human soul ceases to exist, since it comes from another principle, a rational principle separate from matter, not having in it the possibility of dissolution at all, as a material thing has. Therefore if we find that the powers of growth and nutrition and sensation in man and the other powers disappear in death, this is merely because the union has ceased between the soul and the body, which was the instrument through which the soul performed those functions. On the other hand, since we see the power of reason existing in angels without the other powers, and we also see the powers of growth and of life disappear by themselves in plants and animals, we infer that since man has in him both material powers and a rational power, even though the material powers cease to exist as soon as the instrument is removed, the rational power is not destroyed with the destruction of the vital power, any more than the vital power is destroyed with the destruction of the power of growth in animals, for the vital power is a preparation and background for the rational soul, as the power of growth is a preparation and background for the vital power.

And since we find that the intellect in angels exists by itself without matter, and the intellectual power in man similarly has a function peculiar to itself, viz. the apprehension of the separate substances and things abstracted from matter, we infer that since this intellect depends upon something permanent, it is not destroyed with the destruction of the body and the disappearance of the material powers. But when it is separated from the body it will, by reason of its obedience to God's will, unite with the permanent thing which it apprehended. It will thus attain the degree of the angels, whose perfection essentially consists in their obedience to God's will, as was explained above.[5] This is the purpose of man, and the essence of the reward and punishment which the Torah[6] promises to man after death when the soul parts from the body. This is the correct conception of this subject, as Maimonides and his followers understand it.

The second opinion is that though the perfectly righteous get material reward in this world, yet since their number is small, and the great majority of righteous men do not get corporeal reward in this world, there should be in the next world corporeal as well as spiritual reward. This comes, they say, after the resurrection when the soul and the body will exist in conjunction, but without food and drink, as Moses lived forty days and forty nights with body and soul without eating and drinking. This is what, according to them, the Rabbis call the world to come, when they say concerning the righteous that they are prepared for the life of the world to come. They believe at the same time that the human soul does not die when the body dies, but that there is a stage of existence called *Gan Eden* (Paradise) where, immediately after death, the souls of the righteous are kept until they rise in resurrection and obtain the life in the world to come after the resurrection. This is what the Rabbis mean when they relate concerning Rabban Simon ben Gamaliel that he said to Rabbi Ishmael, who was weeping when he was condemned to die: Master, why weepest thou? In a brief moment thou wilt be placed in *Gan Eden* in the community of the righteous.[7] We are also told[8] that Rabbah bar Rab Huna said concerning Rabbah bar Shela, who died a short time before him: He preceded me in *Gan Eden* by a brief hour. This is the opinion of Nahmanides,[9] of R. Meir Halevi,[10] and a number of modern writers who follow them, may they all be blessed.

The argument in favor of this opinion is explained by one of the great disciples of Nahmanides in the following way. There are three degrees of rational creatures: 1. Pure intellect existing without body. This is the most perfect existence. 2. Intellect joined with a body existing forever. These are the spheres. 3. Intellect joined with a body that is subject to destruction. This is man, the lowest in rank of the intellectual creatures. Those that come after, namely the lower animals, which consist of body and soul, both subject to dissolution; and plants, consisting of body that is subject to dissolution and having no animal soul, all these are for the sake of man. Man was created last because of his perfection. The lower creatures were made for his sake, they reached their perfection in his creation, and are all embraced in him—the four elements, the power of growth, the animal power, and in addition to all he has reason. Therefore he rules over all of them, and he came last to complete their activity and to rule over them, because he possesses reason, which has immortality. But it needs the body for its perfection, hence the expression that the souls of the righteous are "hidden" under the throne of glory or in *Gan Eden*. For the word, "hidden," denotes something incomplete, i.e. they need the body and are not complete without the body. But at the end he will be an honorable and permanent body. This is their idea of the human intellect, as R. Aaron Halevi[11] says.

NOTES

1. Berakot 17a.
2. See his אגרת תחיית המתים.
3. Gen. 1, 24.
4. Gen. 2, 7.
5. III, 5, p. 41.
6. The text has the plural בתורות; the meaning of which is not clear to me. Does Albo have reference to other religions besides Judaism?
7. Semahot, ch. 8. Albo's text differs considerably from the talmudic.
8. These words are said to have been uttered by the leader of the Pharisees at the time of the Maccabean revolt. Cf. Bereshit Rabbah LXVI, end, where our texts have בשעה, but Midrash Tehillim XI, end, has לשעה. [Ginzberg].
9. See his שער הגמול.
10. Meir ben Todros Halevi Abulafia, Spanish Talmudist (1180–1244), and opponent of Maimonides. See J. E., s.v. Abulafia, I, 142; כתאב אל רסאייל, ed. Brill, Paris, 1871, pp. 52–53.
11. Spanish Talmudist of the end of the thirteenth century (d. before 1303). Wrote "commentaries on the Halakot of Alfasi of which the portions on Berakot and Ta'anit have been published by S. and N. Bamberger (Mainz, 1874) under the title 'Pekudat ha-Lewiyim.'" He was also the author of talmudic commentaries and of a criticism of a code of Ibn Adret. See J. E., s. v. Aaron b. Joseph Ha-Levi, I, 13b. The statement in the text is taken from his commentary on Alfasi's Hilkot Berakot, chapter dealing with Birkat ha-Lebanah, or blessing of the moon, pp. 81–82 of edition above mentioned.

BOOK IV, CHAPTER 31

The foundation upon which the advocates of this second opinion base their great idea[1] that the world to come is a degree of reward to which a man can not attain until after the resurrection, is a passage in the Mishnah:[2] "These have no share in the world to come—He who says that the resurrection of the dead is not referred to in the Torah . . ." The Gemara, commenting upon this statement, says: He denies the resurrection of the dead, therefore he will have no share therein. From this passage they inferred that the world to come, which is the main reward referred to in the statement of the Rabbis that all Israel have a share in the world to come, comes after the resurrection of the dead and only to those who deserve resurrection.

But the inference is invalid, for we may say that the expression, "resurrection," in this place denotes the reward of the soul and its life in the world of souls, which comes right after death. They call it resurrection of the dead in opposition to the Sadducees and the Samaritans,[3] who denied the immortality of the soul and said that the soul dies with the body. This follows also from the language of the Gemara in that place.[4] R. Eliezer son of R. Jose said: I showed the Cutheans[5] that their books are corrupt. They say that the resurrection is not mentioned in the Torah. So I said to them: You corrupted your Torah but accomplished nothing. You say that the resurrection is not mentioned in the Torah, but it says: "That soul shall utterly be cut off, his iniquity shall be upon him"[6]—"Shall utterly be cut off" (*hikkaret tikkaret*), refers to this world; "His iniquity shall be upon him," refers to the next world. Said Rab Papa to Abaye, why could he not have inferred both worlds from the expression, "Shall utterly be cut off" (*hikkaret tikkaret*)? Answer: They would have replied that the Torah uses a current expression. From this it would seem that his intention was to prove to them from the Torah that the soul has an existence after death, and nothing else. But this can not be, for this would be in conflict with the accepted belief among our people concerning the resurrection of the dead, and any one who denies it is ascribing a defect to God's power. It is one of those beliefs which every adherent of the Mosaic Law must hold, as we explained above.[7]

I say, therefore, that the expression in the Mishnah: "All Israel have a share in the world to come," refers to the reward of the soul after death, both that degree which man has after the resurrection and that which he has immediately after death. This is proved by the statement of the Rabbis that the pious men of other nations have a share in the world to come.[8] Now if the world to come denoted only a stage which comes after the resurrection, how could they say that the pious men of other nations enjoy it, since that stage is reserved exclusively for the perfectly righteous, as they say:[9] "The benefit of rain is for the righteous as well as for the wicked, the resurrection of the dead is for the perfectly righteous only?" The expression, "world to come," in this place must therefore mean that degree which a man attains after death, at the expiration of the twelve months during which the soul is purged of its material habits.

The stage which a man attains immediately after death, within the twelve months, is called in the language of the Rabbis, *Gan Eden* (Paradise). And it is in reference to this that it is said that the whole nation enjoys it, entering this stage immediately at death. Thus we find:[10] "Rab Judah said in the name of Samuel: When Moses died and entered *Gan Eden,* he said to Joshua: 'Ask me all the things about which you are in doubt. . .'" It seems therefore that the reward or the degree of existence which Moses enjoyed as soon as he died was *Gan Eden.* The Rabbis also say:[11] Jose ben Joezer dozed off and saw the bed of Yorkis of Zereda flying in the air. He said then: "He has preceded me in *Gan Eden* by a brief hour." This stage is incomplete before the end of twelve months. After twelve months one rises to one of the stages of the 'world to come,' which is a degree of perfection and glory. Thus we are told:[12] The souls of the righteous are hidden beneath the Throne of Glory, as is said: "The soul of my Lord shall be bound in the bundle of life with the Lord thy God."[13] Also we find:[14] "The inside thereof being inlaid with love from the daughters of Jerusalem"[15]—these are the souls of the righteous which are with Him in heaven. In the Midrash on Psalms[16] they say that this degree is attained right after death and before the resurrection. Commenting on the verse in the Psalms:[17] "Let the saints exult in glory," they say: In what glory? Answer: In the glory which God confers upon the righteous when they depart this world. And they praise God, who bound them in the bundle of life, as is said: "The soul of my lord shall be bound in the bundle of life." Also in the treatise Hagigah:[18] "Arabot is the place in which are righteousness and judgment, treasures of life and treasures of peace and treasures of blessing, and the souls of the righteous. There are the Ofannim and the Seraphim and the Holy Hayyot and the attending angels and the Throne of Glory, while the Living and Eternal King, high and exalted, dwells above them." Here it is stated clearly that the degree occupied by the souls of the righteous after they leave the body and before resurrection is the same as that of the attending angels. The literal meaning of the verse in Zechariah[19] points to the same thing: "I will give thee free access among these that stand by." This degree is called in the Mishnah,[20] "world to come," because it comes to a man after death. The statement: "All Israel have a share in the world to come," refers to it.

But there is another degree which is also called "world to come" without qualification. This is that which comes after resurrection. This is referred to in the Mishnah above mentioned, where the Gemara says that the one who denies resurrection will have no share in resurrection. For it appears from that passage that "the world to come" is a state of reward which comes after resurrection, a reward which is accepted traditionally among our people as conferred upon those whom God brings back to life at the resurrection. The same thing appears also from the statement of the Rabbis.[21] "There are three classes on the day of judgment . . . the perfectly righteous are immediately written down, and their destiny is sealed for life in the world to come." This shows that the world to come is a state which comes to a person after the great day of judgment, i.e. after the resurrection, as is traditionally accepted among our people. . . .

It appears therefore that there are four different periods of reward: 1. This world. 2. The world to come after death, either before resurrection or after resurrection. 3. The days of the Messiah. 4. Resurrection. These rewards are all different from each other. Some are fortunate enough to receive reward in all these periods, namely the perfectly righteous. Some are rewarded in this world only, viz. the wicked, who are paid for the few good deeds they have to their credit in this world, so that they may be punished in the next. Then there are good men who have not the privilege of receiving reward in this world. They enjoy life in the world to come right after death, but not resurrection. Then there are some who have the privilege of resurrection also, and some there are who merit the days of the Messiah also.

The four different expressions for reward which occur in the Yozer[22] prayers for the Sabbath probably refer to the four different kinds of reward which we have mentioned. The expressions are: "There is none to compare with Thee," "There is none beside Thee," "No other, save Thee," "Who is like unto Thee?" And the explanation of these various expressions as referring to the four different periods and kinds of reward follows in the immediate sequel: "There is none to compare with Thee, O Lord our Lord, in this world, and there is none beside Thee, our King, in the life of the world to come." These are the two general periods of reward. Then he speaks of the best reward in this world, which was mentioned first: "There is no other save Thee, our Redeemer, in the days of the Messiah," and then comes the best reward in the world to come after death, at the time of resurrection: ["And there will be none like

Thee, our Saviour, at the resurrection of the dead]."[23] The "world to come" is mentioned right after this world because it comes right after death for every one, before the days of the Messiah and before resurrection. This is more in agreement with the words of Maimonides. For according to Nahmanides, *Gan Eden* should have been mentioned after this world, because that is the state which comes after this world and not life in the world to come, which is the last stage, according to him. Since *Gan Eden* is not mentioned at all, it seems that the term, "world to come," includes all the stages which come after death. But he speaks of "life in the world to come," because it is the best of all.

NOTES

1. Lit., "turrets of silver," after Cant. 8, 9.
2. Sanhedrin 90a.
3. Lit. Cutheans. See III, p. 79, note 9.
4. Sanhedrin 90b.
5. See III, p. 79, note 9.
6. Num. 15, 31.
7. I, 23, p. 184.
8. See I, p. 184, note 1.
9. Ta'anit 7a; ed. Malter, p. 39, 1. 5.
10. Temurah 16a.
11. Bereshit Rabbah 65.
12. Shabbat 152b.
13. I Sam. 25, 29.
14. Midrash Shir ha-Shirim 9, 3.
15. Cant. 3, 10.
16. Our texts of the Midrash have not this passage on the verse in question. The editions of Prague and Amsterdam read: בא וראה היאך הצדיקים מתעננים בשעה שעוברים בג"ע.
17. 149, 5.
18. 12b.
19. 3, 7.
20. Sanhedrin 90a.
21. Rosh Hashanah 16b.
22. See Singer Prayer Book, p. 187.
23. Hasdai Crescas, Or Adonai, Book III, section 4, ch. 4, cites the same passage.

BOOK IV, CHAPTER 32

Every change from the customary, even though natural and for the person's good, causes him pain so long as he does not understand the good. Thus when a child leaves his mother's womb, he passes from potentiality to actuality and to a form of existence superior to and more worthy than the first, being prepared to see the light, to perceive objects with his senses, and to apprehend concepts with his intellect. And yet he cries because he can not understand the good. Similarly when he is weaned and his milk food is discontinued, he cries, although the change is for better and more substantial food and such as is more fitting and wholesome. Yet he feels pain because it is a change from that to which he has been accustomed. Similarly if one is accustomed to sit in darkness a long time and he suddenly comes out into the light, the light is difficult for him and causes discomfort until he gets gradually accustomed to it. So in the day of death, although a person changes for a superior and worthier existence and for a perpetual birghtness which the intellect can not know while it is sunk in matter, yet he is extremely grieved by death—not because he is removed from existence to non-existence, as those think who hold that the human intellect can not exist without the body, but because the change from that to which a person has been accustomed is hard and painful until he becomes gradually accustomed to the new. Hence the Rabbis say,[1] concerning the souls of the righteous, that during the entire twelve months [following the person's death] the soul comes up and then comes down again, i.e. because it is hard for her to be taken away from the corporeal things to which she was accustomed.

And although after she is separated from the body, she does not need to pay any attention to it, nor does she require sensations in order to receive the spiritual influence which she was prepared to receive during life when the body and its powers hindered and prevented her from complete communion with the spiritual, whereas as soon as the hindrance of the body and the corporeal powers is removed in death the veil is removed, the obstacle is taken away and the communion is constant,—nevertheless the soul is grieved at the time of death, and after death it is hard for her to be separated from the body and the corporeal things of which she made use, because she was accustomed to them at first when she needed the sensations and the corporeal powers in order by means of them to acquire the sensible images, from which the soul removed the element of particularity, which is perishable, and retained the element of universality, which is permanent. Thus of Reuben and

Simeon the soul retains only animality and rationality in general, but not the particular. Similarly in all things the soul removes the elements of particularity and retains the elements of universality. This universality, however, the soul can not comprehend except by means of the particular sensations which the corporeal powers receive.

A human being is like a house of five gates, through which there come into the house all the moneys and possessions and provisions which are needed by the master of the house. They are all gathered at first in one house, and later all the possessions and provisions are distributed from that house into the various rooms, each thing being placed in the appropriate room. After all the rooms have been filled with the moneys and possessions, each room according to its capacity, the open gates are no longer needed to bring anything into the house or to keep the valuable possessions. It is better for the house that the gates should be shut in order that the valuable contents should be safe in their rooms.

So the human being has five senses by means of which all sensations are perceived. After being all taken into the common sense,[2] the perceptions are distributed among the various compartments in a proper manner. The power of imagination takes from them that which is appropriate to it, while the rational power takes their universal element and essence, removing the elements of particularity, and separating the accidents from the substances. And after the universal elements of things enter the soul, she does not need any longer the senses and the sense perceptions, as the house no longer needs the open gates after the rooms are filled with all the valuable things. And as it is best to shut the gates in order to keep the valuable property, so it is better for the soul to abandon the corporeal powers. The sense perceptions, in relation to the soul, are like a net or like a ship or animal which bring a man to his destination. When he has arrived there, he has no longer any need of the ship or the animal and they become a great trouble and a heavy burden, though at first he could not have reached his destination without them. Similarly the sense perceptions and the corporeal powers, after the ideas have been apprehended, are no longer needed to keep the ideas in the soul; on the contrary, they hinder and prevent the soul from comprehending the idea completely and from being in constant communion with it, because the Active Intellect is abstract, pure and free from matter.[3] Hence the soul can not properly unite with it as long as she is entangled in matter.

But despite all this it is hard for the soul to get away from the things to which she has been accustomed, and she feels pain in death, for every man feels pain in parting from that to which he has been accustomed.

Our Rabbis say:[4] " 'All the days of the poor are evil'[5]—even their Sabbaths and holy days, as Samuel said: Change of habit is the beginning of intestinal disease." The meaning is, it is hard for a poor man to change his habits even if the change be to a state of greater pleasure. In the same way it is hard for the soul to give up corporeal things until she gets accustomed to it in the course of twelve months. Hence our Rabbis say: The entire twelve months the soul goes up and comes down, after twelve months the soul goes up but does not come down.[6]

Therefore the man of intelligence who understands the good which comes to a person after death will not grieve on account of death, but will be eager for it, because he knows that the body and its powers hinder the soul from obtaining that good and from the enjoyment of continual delight. He will understand that a man's grief at the time of death is like the child's pain when it leaves its mother's womb, which it feels because it does not know the good which it obtains in birth. The reason we find righteous men, like Moses and others, being grieved on account of death, is because they knew that the degree which the soul attains in the world to come depends upon its service in this world. Hence they wanted to acquire more perfection during life in this world in order that they might merit a greater degree of existence in the world to come, because they knew how great the reward and the pleasure in the other world are. Their grief was not because they thought that they were passing from existence to non-existence because the soul can not exist without the body, as the fools think, far be it!

NOTES

1. Shabbat 152b.
2. The Aristotelian *αἴσθησις κοινή*, which perceives motion, rest, figure, magnitude, number, unity. Cf. De Anima, III, 1, p. 425a 27: *τῶν δὲ κοινῶν ἤδη ἔχομεν αἴσθησιν κοινήν*; Zeller, Aristotle and the Earlier Peripatetics, II, 68 f.; Husik, *A History of Mediaeval Jewish Philosophy*, 179, 211.
3. Cf. The Aristotelian characterization of the active intellect as *χωριστὸς καὶ ἀπαθὴς καὶ ἀμιγής* . . ., De Anima, III, 5, p. 430a 17.
4. Baba Batra 146b.
5. Prov. 15, 15.
6. Shabbat 192b.

BOOK IV, CHAPTER 33

. . .As for the nature of the soul's pain and punishment, that is to be explained as follows: If a person in his lifetime pursued his desires and physical pleasures, and his soul departed from doing the will of God and accommodated her acts to the nature of the body, which is opposed to her own nature, then when this soul is separated from the body, she longs for those things to which she was accustomed and feels a desire for them, but has no instruments with which to obtain them. On the other hand, by reason of her own nature she will desire to unite with the higher forms and the immaterial substances, and will experience a longing for them. But she has not learned the elements, nor been accustomed to the service of God, the delight in which can not be enjoyed except by one who has accustomed and prepared himself for it, as the Rabbis say:[1] The Lord gives wisdom to him only who has wisdom, for it says: "He giveth wisdom unto the wise."[2] Accordingly the soul will be drawn in two directions at once, upwards and downwards, the one by reason of her nature, the other by reason of her habit and custom. But she will have no instruments for obtaining the lower desires and no preparation to obtain the higher. This will cause her great pain and suffering, greater than any pain in the world or any kind of fracture—more pain than the burning of fire or cold and terrible frost, more than the wounds of knives and swords or the stings of snakes and scorpions.

When a person is burned by fire, he feels pain, but it is not the body that feels the pain, but the soul. And the soul feels pain not because the fire has any effect upon the soul — fire can not affect a spiritual thing—but because the vital power is a corporeal power residing in the body when its parts are united to each other. Now when the soul becomes aware of the separation of the parts of the body one from another through fire or cold or a sword or any other agency having a similar effect, and perceives the pain which the vital power feels when the parts of the body which are its seat are divided, and the grief which it suffers on account of the dissolution of the body upon whose integrity it depends—then the soul feels pain on account of the pain of the vital power which is the seat of the soul, and is grieved on account of the separation of their union. In a similar way when the soul herself is separated from the body and is drawn in two opposite directions, as said before, by her own nature upward and by habit downward, she experiences great pain as if her parts were torn asunder. To be sure, the soul has no parts, but we use this expression to give an imaginary idea, the point being that she has two contrary desires and can not follow either one of them alone. This is the meaning of the rabbinic statement:[3] R. Eliezer said: "The souls of the righteous are hidden under the Throne of Glory, as is said: 'The soul of my lord shall be bound in the bundle of life with the Lord thy God.'[4] As to the souls of the wicked, one angel stands at one end of the world and another at the other end and they throw it to each other, as is said: 'And the souls of thine enemies, them shall he sling out, as from the hollow of a sling.'[5]" This is an allusion to the two contrary desires which she has. But the soul of the righteous has no downward desire, hence she is united at once with that which is akin to her nature, namely the Throne of Glory under which she dwells. As the pleasure is greater than any that can be imagined, as we said before, so is the pain greater than any imaginable pain.

We have already explained above[6] that though the soul is not in place, not being a corporeal thing, nevertheless she is confined by direction, so that she can feel pain, as she is confined by the body, though she is not in place. This is the meaning of the rabbinic statement:[7] "Antoninus said to Rabbi: The body and the soul can both evade the day of judgment. The body can say: It is the soul that has sinned, for since she has parted from me I am lying in the grave like a stone. The soul will say: It is the body that sinned, for since I parted from it, I am like a bird flying in the air. Said Rabbi to Antoninus, I will give you a parable. This is similar to the case of a human king . . .[8] So God takes the soul, throws her into the body and judges them together, as is said: 'He calleth to the heavens above, and to the earth, that He may judge His people.'[9] 'The heavens above,' signifies the soul, 'And to the earth, that He may judge His people,' refers to the body."

It seems to me that they mean to say that though the soul is a spiritual thing which can not be held in place, God does confine her in a place, which they call body, in order that she may receive punishment and be afflicted with pain for her conduct. This place is called gehenna. They call it body to indicate that just as the body confines the soul in a place—for though the soul does not occupy space, nevertheless since she is not outside of the body she is necessarily confined by the body—so the place of gehenna, which is called body, also confines the soul in order that she may receive her punishment there.

Note carefully that they make this statement only concerning pain and punishment, for we can not conceive of the soul receiving punishment unless she is confined in a place. But the statement does not apply to spiritual reward and delight. For we can conceive the soul receiving this without being confined to a place. Perhaps this is the error of those who say that the bodies must be purified to receive their reward and that the soul is not rewarded without the body. They think that just as a definite place is mentioned for judgment, i.e. punishment, so is a definite place necessary for reward. But it is not so, for both punishment and reward are given to the soul alone, but a definite place is necessary for punishment, not for reward, as we have explained.

NOTES

1. Berakot 55a.
2. Dan. 2, 21.
3. Shabbat 152b.
4. I Sam. 25, 29.
5. *Ibid.*
6. II, 17, p. 103 f.
7. Sanhedrin 91a.
8. The omitted portion is as follows: The king had an orchard in which figs were ripening. He put a lame man and a blind man to watch the orchard. Said the lame man to the blind: I see beautiful ripe figs, let me get on your back and we will get the figs and eat them. The lame man got on the back of the blind man, and they picked off the figs and ate them. After a while the owner of the orchard came along and said, where are the beautiful ripe figs? Said the lame man, I cannot walk [hence I did not take them]. Said the blind man, I cannot see. What did the king do? He put the lame man on the back of the blind and punished them together.
9. Ps. 50, 4.

BOOK IV, CHAPTER 34

The punishment of which we have been speaking, which is inflicted upon the body and the soul together or upon the soul alone, differs according to the different degrees of the individuals. If a person has a few good deeds to his credit and is also guilty of a few transgressions, he can not be continually punished in the extraordinary manner that we mentioned, for a limited period will make him forget his habit [of committing sins]. According to the Rabbis,[1] this period lasts twelve months. After twelve months of punishment, the individual attains to some degree [of reward] according to the number of good deeds which he has to his credit. Then there are individuals who, after they have forgotten their habits through twelve months' punishment, have no good deeds to entitle them to any degree of reward, and so they become non-existent, since they have no preparation at all for receiving spiritual reward. This is what the Bible means when it speaks of the soul being cut off. In reference to these the Rabbis say that after twelve months their body is destroyed, their soul is burned, and they are scattered by the wind under the soles of the feet of the righteous.[2]

Then there are other wicked men who are punished eternally for their misdeeds, those, for example, who deny the principles of the Torah, as we shall see later with the help of God. The souls of these men must be confined in a place that they may receive continuous punishment, as we explained before. There are others who after twelve months attain a great degree, as the Rabbis say concerning Samuel, who was a perfectly righteous man, that the entire twelve months his soul went up and down,[3] and that this was the reason the witch was able to bring him up, because it was within the twelve months, as she said: "I see a god-like being coming up out of the earth."[4] But after twelve months the soul goes up but does not come down. This shows that even perfectly righteous men find it hard to give up the material things to which they have been accustomed, until they have been purified for a certain length of time. This purification lasts twelve months, a period embracing the four seasons, which include all temporal changes. This is the meaning of the passage[5] in which we are told concerning Rabbah bar Nahamani that shortly before his death, when he was fleeing from a horseman, an officer of the king who wanted to capture him, he saw or heard in a dream or in a vision that after death the souls study the laws of the plagues as they used to do in life, and he heard them discussing: "If the bright spot comes before white hair . . .[6] If it is doubtful, the celestial college said, the man was unclean and God said, he was clean. Then he heard them say: Who shall decide the matter? Answer: Rabbah bar Nahamani, who is an expert in the subject of clean and unclean . . ." From the entire context there it is clear that the souls after death are eager to occupy themselves with the things to which they were accustomed in life, for even the souls of the righteous are engaged in studying the laws of the plagues and of the clean and unclean with which they occupied themselves in life. This desire, they say, disappears after twelve months.

The Rabbis speak of this frequently in different places. Concerning Rabbi Judah ha-Nasi they say[7] that he came to his house every Friday evening and pronounced the Sabbath benediction, thus indicating that even after death the souls of the righteous are eager to perform the commandments which they were accustomed to perform during life, so much so that R. Judah ha-Nasi came home every Sabbath eve to pronounce the Kiddush. We find the same thing in a few other pious men, but it never lasts more than twelve months, as the Rabbis say: After twelve months the soul goes up but she does not come down. The case of Elijah, who goes up and down all the time, is unique even now among the righteous men, as we find in the Zohar on the section "Vayakhel":[8] "We find a mystery in the book of Adam,[9] which says that among the generations of the world there will be one spirit that will go down to the earth and clothe itself in a body. His name is Elijah. In this body he will go up, put it off and leave it in the storm. Then he will put on another body of light, in which he will remain among the angels. Later he will go down again and put on the body which remained in the storm, and appear in it down below. With the other body he appears above. This is the mystery contained in the words: 'Who hath ascended up into heaven, and descended?' There is no human being whose spirit ascended to heaven and then came down, except Elijah. He it is who ascended above and then descended." This is also the mystery of the "garment," which is mentioned in the works of the Cabalists, but I can not say more.

NOTES

1. Rosh Hashanah 17a.
2. Ibid.
3. Shabbat 152b.
4. I Sam. 28, 13.
5. Baba Mezi'a 86a.
6. Cf. Lev. 13.
7. Ketubot 103a.
8. One of the weekly sections of the Pentateuch according to the annual pericope. It extends from Exodus 35, 1 to 38, 20.
9. On the Book of Adam, see J. E., s. v. "Adam, Book of," I, 179.

The Twelfth Principle

The Messiah

INTRODUCTION

Saadia's discussion of the Messiah is based upon the rabbinic tradition which regards the time of the coming of the Messiah as fixed in one of two alternate ways. The Messiah must appear no later than upon culmination of the ordained period of exile and suffering. His appearance will not be delayed beyond that time—a time which is preordained but which is unknown to us. However, the Messiah may appear earlier, at such time as the people of Israel repent of their iniquities. It is thus within the power of man to hasten the redemption.

For Maimonides, as is clear from his formulation of the Twelfth Principle and his statements in the *Mishneh Torah,* the belief in the coming of the Messiah is essentially the belief in the restoration of the monarchy of the House of David. Included in this principle is the belief that the Messiah will be the direct lineal descendant of David and Solomon. According to Maimonides, this principle negates the legitimacy of a monarchy other than that of the Davidic dynasty even prior to the advent of the Messiah.

Maimonides' discussion in the *Mishneh Torah, Hilkhot Melakhim,* chapter 11, underscores the monarchical nature of the Messiah. The qualifications of the Messiah are those of a king. Noteworthy is the fact that nowhere in the formulation of this principle in his introduction to *Ḥelek* or in his codification in *Hilkhot Melakhim* does Maimonides indicate that the Messiah will be possessed of prophetic powers, although this fact is recorded in *Hilkhot Teshuvah* 9:2, where it is stated that the Messiah will be a great prophet "approaching [the greatness of] our teacher Moses." The implication is inescapable. The Messiah will indeed be a prophet, but his prophetic powers are essentially extrinsic to his role as Messiah.

In the *Mishneh Torah,* Maimonides carefully indicates how the Messiah may establish his claim. Most illuminating is his distinction between criteria which establish acceptance *be-ḥezkat mashiaḥ* and others which establish that the person is indeed *mashiaḥ be-vadai.* The first is simply a *prima facie* claim which is accepted with full realization that the claim may subsequently prove to be spurious. It is only when the claimant succeeds in "rebuilding the Temple on its proper site and in the ingathering of the dispersed of Israel" that his claim must be regarded as having been established irrefutably. Maimonides is here declaring that the claims of a false messiah may have halakhic legitimacy in the sense that they must be accepted provisionally by the community. This was indeed the case when Rabbi Akiva accepted Bar Kochba as the Messiah. Even though subsequent events disproved Bar Kochba's claim, Rabbi Akiva acted in accordance with halakhic criteria in granting tentative credence to the claim presented. This explanation accounts in part for the credence given to a number of pseudo-messiahs who have appeared at various points in Jewish history.

The discussion in *Hilkhot Melakhim* is a striking parallel to Maimonides' discussion of prophecy in chapter 8 of *Hilkhot Yesodei ha-Torah*. There, too, there is expressed a candid recognition that not every prophetic claim is authentic. Yet, under certain conditions, the claim of the prophet must be accorded a form of *prima facie* validity despite the clear recognition that it may indeed be false. In that discussion, Maimonides draws an analogy to the credence given to the testimony of witnesses in a court of law. Certainly the judges are fully aware of the fact that witnesses have been known to commit perjury. Nevertheless, the testimony of witnesses who have undergone the proper examination must be accepted and the fear of possible perjury must be set aside. The court must act in this manner because such is the divine command as embodied in the laws of testimony. Were this not the case, no testimony could ever be accepted by a court of law, with the result that the judicial system would collapse and anarchy would reign. In accepting the testimony of apparently reliable witnesses, the judges are fully cognizant of the possibility of false testimony and do not pretend that the veracity of the witnesses has been infallibly demonstrated. There is a clear distinction between legal credibility in terms of judicial procedure and absolute belief as an epistemological phenomenon. A similar suspension of human critical judgment is required in the examination of the credentials of a self-announced prophet. Halakhic criteria of credibility are established. When these criteria are satisfied, the prophet's claim must be accorded credence and his fellows must comport themselves accordingly, but they may, and indeed must, remain mindful that acceptance of the prophetic claim is merely tentative in nature. The same is the case with regard to the messianic claim advanced by any individual. In the case of the Messiah, absolute confirmation of this claim must await the rebuilding of the Temple and the ingathering of the exiles. Only when these feats are performed can it be known with certainty that this person is indeed the Messiah.

Maimonides' statement that the messianic claim can be authenticated only upon the rebuilding of the Temple would indicate that, in his opinion, the Temple will not be rebuilt prior to the advent of the Messiah. Maimonides' remarks in Book III, chapter 32, of the *Guide* to the effect that biblical commandments concerning sacrifice were a concession to the idolatrous habits of the generation of the Exodus are well known and often quoted. These comments notwithstanding, in the *Mishneh Torah* Maimonides clearly affirms that the sacrificial rites will be reinstituted in the time of the Messiah and that the Messiah's success in this matter is a *sina qua non* for authenticating his claim. Moreover, in *Hilkhot Me'ilah* 8:8, Maimonides describes the sacrificial rites as included in the category of *ḥukkim,* i.e., commandments whose rationale is beyond human understanding.

Albo stresses that belief in the advent of the Messiah is not merely confirmed by tradition but is rooted in specific prophetic passages which refer to the messianic period. He emphatically rejects the view that those prophecies may be understood as referring to events which have already transpired.

SAADIA, *EMUNOT VE-DE'OT*

Translation by Alexander Altmann

EIGHTH TREATISE
ON THE REDEMPTION OF ISRAEL

1. *'They that sow in tears . . .'*

. . .The fact of Redemption is undeniable for various reasons: (1) Because it is confirmed by the miracles performed by Moses, the first prophet, in announcing the message of Redemption, and because it is confirmed by the miracles which happened to the prophet Isaiah and to the other prophets who announced the Redemption of Israel. If God sent these prophets as His messengers, then undoubtedly He will fulfil his message, as is said, 'That confirmeth the word of His servant, and performeth the counsel of His messengers' (Isa. 44.26). (2) Because He is just and will not do wrong. Having inflicted on our people heavy and prolonged sufferings — some, no doubt, as punishment, and some as a test[1] — He must certainly have set a time limit to them. It cannot be thought that they should be unlimited. When the end comes,[2] He will assuredly punish those who oppressed us and reward those who suffered, as it says, 'Bid Jerusalem take heart and proclaim unto her that her time of service is accomplished, that her guilt is paid off; that she hath received of the Lord's hand double for all her sins' (Isa. 40.2). (3) He is a faithful keeper of His promises, His word endureth and His commandment stands for ever, as it says, 'The grass withereth, the flower fadeth; but the word of our God shall stand for ever' (Isa. 40.8). (4) We judge the promise of final Redemption from the first promise at the time when we were living as exiles in Egypt and God promised us in more precise terms that He would mete out judgment to our oppressors and reward us with great wealth, as it says, 'And also that nation, whom they shall serve, will I judge; and afterwards they shall come out with great substance' (Gen. 15.14). Our eyes have seen the things which He performed for us in dividing the Sea, in feeding us with the manna and the quails, in giving us the Law on Sinai, in causing the sun to stand still and similar things. For the future, He promised us wonderful and immeasurable bliss and happiness, and that honour, glory and distinction which He will bestow upon us as a double reward for all the humiliation and misery which He brought upon us, as it says, 'For your shame which was double . . . therefore in their land they shall possess double' (Isa. 61.7). Of that which we endured in the past God speaks of as a brief moment, transient like the twinkling of the eye, but of the reward He will give us in the future He speaks in terms of a boundless compassion, as it says, 'For a small moment have I forsaken thee, but with great compassion will I gather thee' (Isa. 54.7). For the trials and ordeals of the past He will give us the double of our double share,[3] which is over and above that which He promised, an amount of bliss not quickly or easily to be measured. Thus it is said, 'And He will do thee good, and multiply thee above thy fathers' (Deut. 30.5). For this reason He mentions to us the Exodus from Egypt so frequently and in so many places. He wants us to remember the things we experienced.[4] If anything which He did for us in the course of the redemption from Egypt is not explicitly included in the promise of the final Redemption, it is implied in the statement 'As in the days of thy coming forth out of the land of Egypt, will I show unto him marvellous things' (Micah 7.15).

For this reason one finds that we patiently endure our sufferings, and wait for Him without casting any doubt on His promise. We do not expire nor does our courage falter, but we grow in strength and in firmness, as it says, 'Be strong and let your heart take courage, all ye that wait for the Lord' (Ps. 31.21). One who sees us in our misfortune is either astounded at us or considers us fools because he has never experienced what we experienced, nor has he the strong faith which we have. He is like one who has never known what it is to sow seed; when he sees, for the first time, the farmer throwing grain into the fissures of the earth to sprout there, he is likely to consider him a fool. But he will realize his own ignorance at the time of harvesting when he will see that each measure has yielded 20 to 30 measures. We find an image similar to this in Scripture: 'They that sow in tears shall reap in joy' (Ps. 126.5). He is also like one who has never seen the bringing up of a child, and when he sees, for the first time, a parent willingly bearing all the sacrifices entailed in the rearing of a child, he will mock at him and ask, 'What is this man hoping for?' But after the son has grown up and has become a scholar or a philosopher or a governor or a general, then that person will realize that he has made himself ridiculous. In comparing our hope to the expectation of a child, the prophet says, 'Before she travailed, she brought forth; before her pain came, she was delivered of a man-child' (Isa. 66.7). . .

It would be wrong on our part to imagine that God does not know the position in which we find ourselves, or that He is unjust or without compassion. Such a view, if held by us, has already been rebuked by the prophet when he says, 'Why sayest thou, O Jacob . . . my way is hid from the Lord?' (Isa. 40.27). Nor must we say that He is unable to help us and to answer our prayers, since it says, 'Behold, the Lord's hand is not shortened, that it cannot save, neither His ear heavy, that it cannot hear' (Isa. 59.1). Nor must we say that He has rejected us and cast us away, 'For the Lord thy God is a merciful God; He will not fail thee, neither destroy thee, nor forget the covenant of thy fathers which He swore unto them' (Deut. 4.31).

NOTES

1. Cf. pp. 137–9.
2. With the beginning of the messianic era, the period of retribution will be initiated, although the principal reward and punishment will be left over to the 'Future World' (*'ōlam habā'*).
3. Our double share of suffering entails a double measure of the originally promised reward.
4. The Exodus from Egypt serves as both the model and the assurance of the final Redemption in the messianic era. The Midrash makes ample use of the analogy between the Exodus from Egypt and the future Redemption of Israel.

2. *The Two Roads to Redemption*

We believe that God has appointed two alternative periods for the duration of our servitude in exile, one extending until such time as we do penitence (*Teshubah*), the other being terminated at a fixed time (*ḳeṣ*). Whichever of these times arrives first, it carries Redemption with it: if our repentance (*teshubah*) is complete, the *fixed time (ḳeṣ)* will be disregarded and the words of the Torah will come true, 'It shall come to pass when all these things are come upon thee . . . and thou shalt return unto the Lord thy God . . . that then the Lord thy God will turn thy captivity . . .' (Deut. 30.1–10). If, however, our repentance is slow, we shall have to wait until the *fixed time* is reached.[1] In this case some of us will have to bear suffering as a punishment, others as a test,[2] as we know happens in every general disaster at any time, be it famine, war or pestilence: some people will suffer because they deserve to be punished, others because they are put to a test. Thus, in the Flood there must have perished many young children and infants who were tried so as to be later rewarded; nor can we doubt that amongst our forefathers in Egypt there were many pious people who had to endure their trials until the time arrived which was fixed for their redemption. Let nobody tell us, 'If there were pious men amongst you to-day, your redemption would come to pass.' for Moses, Aaron and Miriam (and with them many more pious peole like them) had to remain in servitude for over eighty years until the moment of the *fixed time* arrived.

We have learned that in case our repentance is not complete, we must wait until the *fixed time* has arrived. When it is come, and we have not yet repented of our sins, it would not be fitting that salvation should come to us whilst we are still entangled in our sins. God exiled us because of our sins, and should He restore us merely because our stay in exile has been prolonged even though we have not returned to him, and we have not bettered our ways? That would make no sense. Our ancient prophets have, however, handed down to us a tradition, according to which hardships and sufferings will, at the *fixed time,* come upon us in such overwhelming measure that under their impact we shall be forced to choose the way of repentance, and thus become worthy of Redemption. This is what our ancestors said: 'If Israel will do penitence, they will be redeemed; if not, The Holy One (blessed be He) will appoint a king whose harsh decrees will be more terrible than those of Haman, whereupon they will do penitence, and then they will be redeemed.'[3] They say further that this chain of events will be started by the appearance of a man from the descendants of Joseph[4] on the mount of

Galilee. Many of the chief leaders of the nation will gather round him, and he will make his way to the place of the Temple, which will previously have been in the possession of Rome. There he will stay for some while. Later on a man called Armilius[5] will wage war against them. He will fight them, conquer the city, and slay and capture and humiliate the people. That man of the descendants of Joseph will be amongst the multitude of the slain. Terrible hardships will overtake the nation at that time, and the hardest of all will be their degradation amongst the nations, which will lead to their expulsion into the desert and waste places, where they will be left to starvation and misery. Under the pressure of their sufferings, many of them will abandon their faith, but a purified remnant will remain steadfast, and unto them the prophet Elijah will appear to bring them Redemption.

I say furthermore that in either of the two cases, that is to say, in case we fail to do penitence and thus have to go through the experiences which will accompany the advent of the Messiah of the House of Joseph, or, alternatively, we do penitence and shall be spared those sufferings, there will appear unto us the Messiah of the House of David. If he is preceded by the Messiah of the House of Joseph, the latter will act as his messenger, prepare the nation, and pave the way of Redemption, as is said, 'Behold, I send My messenger and he shall clear the way before Me' (Mal. 3.1).

Then the resurrection of the dead will take place as explained in the preceding chapter. First and foremost amongst them will be the Messiah of the House of Joseph, for he is a pious man who suffered trials and merits great reward. Then our Lord (be He exalted and glorified) will renew His Holy Place in the way He described to us, 'When the Lord hath built up Zion, when He hath appeared in His glory' (Ps. 102.17), and its chambers and innermost sanctuary as Ezekiel explained them (Ezek. ch. 40); and in them will be the precious stones and rubies which Isaiah mentioned, 'And I will make thy pinnacles of rubies, and thy gates of carbuncles, and all thy border of precious stones' (Isa. 54.12). The whole country will be inhabited so that there will not remain in it a waste or empty place, as it says, 'And the parched land shall become a pool, and the thirsty ground springs of water' (Isa. 35.7). Then the light of the Divine Presence (*Shek̲īnāh*) will shine over the Temple so brilliantly that all the lights around it will seem dim and faint, for, as I have already explained in Chapter II, it surpasses in radiance all light,[6] as it says, 'Arise, shine, for thy light is come, and the glory of the Lord is risen upon thee. For, behold, darkness shall cover the earth . . . but upon thee the Lord will arise' (Isa. 60.1–2). Such will be its brilliance that one who does not know the way to the Temple will only have to follow the direction of that light, which will extend from heaven to earth, as is said, 'And nations shall walk at thy light, and kings at the brightness of thy rising' (Isa. 60.3). Then the gift of prophecy will abound amongst our nation so that even our children and servants will prophesy, as it says, 'And it shall come to pass afterward that I will pour out my spirit upon all flesh; and your sons and your daughters shall prophesy . . . and also upon the servants and upon the handmaids' (Joel 3.1–2). So much so that if one of them goes to any other country and says there, 'I am an Israelite,'[7] people will ask him, 'Tell us what happened yesterday, and what will happen tomorrow,' if they are desirous to know the things that are hid from them. If he is able to tell them about these things, they will be convinced that he is an Israelite, as it says, 'And their seed shall be known amongst the nations, and their offspring among the peoples' (Isa. 61.9).

The Israelites will remain in this position for the whole duration of this world thenceforward, and their condition will not change, as it says, 'O Israel, that are saved by the Lord with an everlasting salvation; he shall not be ashamed nor confounded for evermore' (Isa. 45.17). I have an idea that the expression, 'for evermore' (*'ad 'olmē 'ad*)[8] in this and other passages is only used in order to emphasize the assurance of salvation by means of the strongest expression possible and to repudiate the opinion of those who claim that our salvation will be limited in time and vanish. God furthermore informed us that the people will, in that time, choose obedience towards God, not disobedience, as is explained in Chapter 30 of Deuteronomy, where it is said, 'And the Lord thy God will circumcise thy heart' (6), and in Chapter 36 of Ezekiel, where it is said, 'A new heart also will I give you, and a new spirit will I put within you' (26). They will choose this path for a number of reasons: because of their witnessing the light of the Divine Presence; because of the descent of Divine Inspiration upon them; because of their existence as an independent kingdom in prosperity and freedom from oppression; because of the absence of poverty and distress; because of their complete happiness in every respect. For God has informed us that pestilence, diseases, and calamities will completely vanish, and likewise all grief and sorrow. For them the world will be one of complete joy and gladness so that it will appear to them as if a new heaven and a new earth had been created for them, as is explained in Chapter 65 of Isaiah: 'For, behold, I create new heavens and a new earth; and the former things shall not be remembered nor come into mind. But be ye glad and rejoice for ever in that which I create; for, behold, I create Jerusalem a rejoicing, and her people a joy. And I will rejoice in Jerusalem, and joy in my people; and the voice of weeping shall be no more heard in her, nor the voice of crying' (17–19). How wonderful will such a world be that is full of joy and gladness, full of obedience and service, full of the treasures of reward! . . .

(1) In the messianic age it is expected that all creatures will believe in God and proclaim His unity, as is said, 'And the Lord shall be King over all the earth; in that day shall the Lord be one and His name One' (Zech. 14.9), but do we not see them still clinging to their errors and denial of God? (2) In the messianic age the faithful are supposed to be free and not forced to pay tribute in money and food to other nations, as it says, 'The Lord hath sworn by His right hand . . . Surely I will no more give thy corn to be food for thine enemies; and strangers shall not drink thy wine for which thou hast laboured' (Isa. 62.8). But do we not see that every nation is compelled to pay tribute and obedience to the nation to which it is subject? (3) In the messianic age we expect the abolition of all wars between men and complete disarmament, as it says, 'And they shall beat their swords into ploughshares, and their spears into pruning-hooks; nation shall not lift up sword against nation, neither shall they learn war any more' (Isa. 2.4). But do we not see the nations fighting and contending with each other more violently than ever before? Should one try to explain that Scripture only means to say that there will be no more wars under the banner of religion, is it not the fact that religious wars and quarrels are to-day more intense than ever? (4) In the messianic age the animals are expected to live peacefully one beside the other, the wolf feeding with the lamb, the lion eating straw, and the young child playing with a snake and the basilisk, as is said, 'And the wolf shall dwell with the lamb . . . and the cow and the bear shall feed . . . They shall not hurt nor destroy. . . .' (Isa. 11.6–9), whereas we see that the evil nature of the wild animals is still the same and they have not changed in any way. Should, again, someone explain that Scripture only means to say that the wicked people will live peacefully alongside with the virtuous,[9] the facts are precisely to the contrary. For nowadays the tyranny and violence of the strong against the weak are more ruthless than ever before.

All these facts prove conclusively that the prophetic messages of comfort have not yet been fulfilled. Our refutation of the opinion held by the people we have referred to applies also to the Christians.

NOTES

1. According to the apocalyptic tradition (notably Daniel 12.7), Redemption has to wait until the time fixed for it has arrived. According to the Jewish prophetic tradition, Redemption depends solely on Israel's return to God. The problem formed the subject of a famous dispute between R. Eliezer b. Hyrkanos and R. Joshua b. Ḥananyah. The former held that repentance was the decisive factor, whereas the latter believed that redemption was sure to come at the appointed time (*ḳeṣ*) even without repentance. Their views were harmonized later by R. Joshua b. Levi in the dictum, 'If Israel fail to prove worthy, Redemption has to wait until the appointed time; if they prove worthy, Redemption will be hastened.' A similar compromise can already be found in IV Ezra (4.35). Saadya's theory as set out above follows the Talmudic tradition in combining the two elements of Repentance and *fixed time*. Cf. Marmorstein, "The Doctrine of Redemption in Saadya's Theological System," *Saadya Studies* (ed. E.I.J. Rosenthal), 1943, pp. 103–18.

2. Cf. pp. 137–9.

3. The well-known view of R. Eliezer, based on Jer. 30.7, 'A time of tribulation will come over Jacob, and thence will come salvation.' See *p. Ta'anit*, I, 1; *b. Sanh.* 97b.

4. According to a Midrashic tradition, which can be traced back to a Tannaitic source (*b. Sukkah* 52b), the real Messiah of the House of David will be preceded by another Messiah of the descendants of Joseph, who will fall in battle. Later Midrashim have elaborated this theme of the suffering Messiah under Gnostic and, to some extent, Christian influences. Cf. G. Dalman, *Der Leidende und Sterbende Messias in der Synagoge;* Israel Lēvi in *REJ,* Vol. 74, 77. [Such influences in the development of Messianic concepts would be emphatically denied by rabbinic scholars. In light of the obvious Tannaitic source for the Messiah ben Joseph who will fall in battle there is no reason to postulate such influences in the development of the idea here presented by Saadya.—J.D.B.]

5. Probably identical with Romulus, who stands for Rome. According to the Jewish apocalyptic tradition, Rome is the arch-enemy of the Kingdom of God. Although in Saadya's time, Palestine was in the hands of the Caliphs, Saadya still retains the ancient tradition, which sees in the fall of the Roman Empire a preliminary to the establishment of God's Kingdom on earth. Cf. Marmorstein, *loc. cit.*, pp. 113–4.

6. Cf. above, pp. 90–1.

7. Lit. 'One of the Believers.'

8. Which cannot be taken literally since the present world including the messianic era will come to an end when the Future World (*'ōlam hābā'*) is created.

9. This is in fact the symbolic interpretation which Maimonides was later to apply to this messianic prophecy. Cf. *Hil. Melaḵīm* 12.1.

MAIMONIDES, *MISHNEH TORAH*

Translation by Abraham M. Hershman

BOOK OF JUDGES, LAWS OF KINGS, CHAPTER 11

1. King Messiah will arise and restore the kingdom of David to its former state and original sovereignty. He will rebuild the sanctuary and gather the dispersed of Israel. All the ancient laws will be reinstituted in his days; sacrifices will again be offered; the Sabbatical and Jubilee years will again be observed in accordance with the commandments set forth in the Law.

He who does not believe in a restoration or does not look forward to the coming of the Messiah denies not only the teachings of the Prophets but also those of the Law and Moses, our teacher, for Scripture affirms the rehabilitation of Israel, as it is said: *Then the Lord thy God will turn thy captivity, and have compassion upon thee, and will return and gather thee . . . if any of thine that are dispersed be in the uttermost parts of heaven . . . and the Lord thy God will bring thee into the land which thy fathers possessed* (Deut. 30:3, 4, 5). These words stated in Scripture include all that the Prophets said (on the subject). They recur in the section treating of Balaam. The prophecy in that section bears upon the two Messiahs: the first, namely, David, who saved Israel from the hand of their enemies; and the later Messiah, a descendant of David, who will achieve the final salvation of Israel. There it is said: *I see him, but not now* (Num. 24:17), this refers to David; *I behold him, but not nigh (ibid.),* this refers to King Messiah. *There shall step forth a star out of Jacob (ibid.),* this refers to David; *And a sceptre shall rise out of Israel (ibid.),* this refers to King Messiah. *And shall smite through the corners of Moab (ibid.),* this refers to David, for we are told: *And he smote Moab, and measured them with the line* (II Sam. 8:2); *and break down all the sons of Seth* (Num. 24:17), this refers to King Messiah, as it is written concerning him: *And his dominion shall be from sea to sea* (Zech. 9:10). *And Edom shall be a possession* (Num. 24:18), this refers to David, as it is written: *And all the Edomites became servants to David* (II Sam. 8:14); *And Seir shall be a possession* (Num. 24:18), this refers to (the days of) King Messiah, as it is written: *And saviours shall come up on Mount Zion to judge the mount of Esau* (Obad. 1:21).

2. So too, with reference to the cities of refuge, the Bible says: *And if the Lord thy God enlarge thy borders . . . then thou shalt add three cities more for thee* (Deut. 19:8, 9)—a precept which has never been carried out. Yet, not in vain did the Holy One, blessed be He, give us this commandment. As for the prophetic utterances on the subject (of the Messiah), no citations are necessary, as all their books are full of this theme.

3. Do not think that King Messiah will have to perform signs and wonders, bring anything new into being, revive the dead, or do similar things. It is not so. Rabbi Akiba was a great sage, a teacher of the Mishnah, yet he was also the armor-bearer of Ben Kozba. He affirmed that the latter was King Messiah; he and all the wise men of his generation shared this belief until Ben Kozba was slain in (his) iniquity, when it became known that he was not (the Messiah). Yet the Rabbis had not asked him for a sign or token. The general principle is: this Law of ours with its statutes and ordinances [is not subject to change]. It is for ever and all eternity; it is not to be added to or to be taken away from. [Whoever adds aught to it, or takes away aught from it, or misinterprets it, and strips the commandments of their literal sense is an impostor, a wicked man, and a heretic.]

4. If there arise a king from the House of David who meditates on the Torah, occupies himself with the commandments, as did his ancestor David, observes the precepts prescribed in the Written and the Oral Law, prevails upon Israel to walk in the way of the Torah and to repair its breaches, and fights the battles of the Lord, it may be assumed that he is the Messiah. If he does these things and succeeds, rebuilds the sanctuary on its site, and gathers the dispersed of Israel, he is beyond all doubt the Messiah. He will prepare the whole world to serve the Lord with one accord, as it is written: *For then will I turn to the peoples a pure language, that they may all call upon the name of the Lord to serve Him with one consent* (Zeph. 3:9). [But if he does not meet with full success, or is slain, it is obvious that he is not the Messiah promised in the Torah. He is to be regarded like all the other wholehearted and worthy kings of the House of David who died and whom the Holy One, blessed be He, raised up to test the multitude, as it is written *And some of them that are wise shall stumble, to refine among them, and to purify, and to make white, even to the time of the end; for it is yet for the time appointed* (Dan. 11:35).

Even of Jesus of Nazareth, who imagined that he was the Messiah, but was put to death by the court, Daniel had prophesied, as it is written *And the children of the violent among thy people shall lift themselves up to establish the vision; but they shall stumble* (Dan. 11:14). For has there ever been a greater stumbling than this? All the Prophets affirmed that the Messiah would redeem Israel, save them, gather their dispersed, and confirm the commandments. But he caused Israel to be destroyed by the sword, their remnant to be dispersed and humiliated. He was instrumental in changing the Torah and causing the world to err and serve another beside God.

But it is beyond the human mind to fathom the designs of the Creator; for our ways are not His ways, neither are our thoughts His thoughts. All these matters relating to Jesus of Nazareth and the Ishmaelite (Mohammed) who came after him, only served to clear the way for King Messiah, to prepare the whole world to worship God with one accord, as it is written *For then will I turn to the peoples a pure language, that they may all call upon the name of the Lord to serve Him with one consent* (Zeph. 3:9). Thus the messianic hope, the Torah, and the commandments have become familiar topics — topics of conversation (among inhabitants) of the far isles and many peoples, uncircumcized of heart and flesh. They are discussing these matters and the commandments of the Torah. Some say, "Those commandments were true, but have lost their validity and are no longer binding"; others declare that they had an esoteric meaning and were not intended to be taken literally; that the Messiah has already come and revealed their occult significance. But when the true King Messiah will appear and succeed, be exalted and lifted up, they will forthwith recant and realize that they have inherited naught but lies from their fathers, that their prophets and forbears led them astray.][1]

NOTES

1. This section appears in the manuscript versions, as well as in the early printed editions of the *Mishneh Torah.* It was deleted in the Venice edition (1574–76), apparently by reason of censorship, and does not appear in any subsequent edition, with the exception of the Amsterdam edition (1702) and the recent vocalized *Rambam la-Am,* published by Mossad ha-Rav Kook (Jerusalem, 1962).—J.D.B.

BOOK OF JUDGES, LAWS OF KINGS, CHAPTER 12

1. Let no one think that in the days of the Messiah any of the laws of nature will be set aside, or any innovation be introduced into creation. The world will follow its normal course. The words of Isaiah: *And the wolf shall dwell with the lamb, and the leopard shall lie down with the kid* (Isa. 11:6) are to be understood figuratively, meaning that Israel will live securely among the wicked of the heathens who are likened to wolves and leopards, as it is written: *A wolf of the deserts doth spoil them, a leopard watcheth over their cities* (Jer. 5:6). They will all accept the true religion, and will neither plunder nor destroy, and together with Israel earn a comfortable living in a legitimate way, as it is written: *And the lion shall eat straw like the ox* (Isa. 11:7). All similar expressions used in connection with the Messianic age are metaphorical. In the days of King Messiah the full meaning of those metaphors and their allusions will become clear to all.

2. Said the Rabbis: *The sole difference between the present and the Messianic days is delivery from servitude to foreign powers* (B. San 91b). Taking the words of the Prophets in their literal sense, it appears that the inauguration of the Messianic era will be marked by the war of Gog and Magog; that prior to that war, a prophet will arise to guide Israel and set their hearts aright, as it is written: *Behold, I will send you Elijah the prophet* (Mal. 3:23). He (Elijah) will come neither to declare the clean unclean, nor the unclean clean; neither to disqualify those who are presumed to be of legitimate descent, nor to pronounce qualified those who are presumed to be of illegitimate descent, but to bring peace in the world, as it is said: *And he shall turn the hearts of the fathers to the children* (Mal. 3:24).

Some of our Sages say that the coming of Elijah will precede the advent of the Messiah. But no one is in a position to know the details of this and similar things until they have come to pass. They are not explicitly stated by the Prophets. Nor have the Rabbis any tradition with regard to these matters. They are guided solely by what the scriptural texts seem to imply. Hence there is a divergence of opinion on the subject. But be that as it may, neither the exact sequence of those events nor the details thereof constitute religious dogmas. No one should ever occupy himself with the legendary themes or spend much time on midrashic statements bearing on this and like subjects. He should not deem them of prime importance, since they lead neither to the fear of God nor to the love of Him. Nor should one calculate the end. Said the Rabbis: *Blasted be those who reckon out the end* (B. San 97b). One should wait (for his coming) and accept in principle this article of faith, as we have stated before.

3. In the days of King Messiah, when his kingdom will be established and all Israel will gather around him, their pedigrees will be determined by him through the Holy Spirit which will rest upon him, as it is written: *And he shall sit as a refiner and purifier . . .* (Mal. 3:3). First he will purify the descendants of Levi, declaring: "This one, of good birth, is a priest; this one, of good birth, is a Levite." Those who are not of good birth will be demoted to the rank of (lay) Israelites, for it is written: *And the Tirshatha said unto them that they should not eat of the most holy things, till there stood up a priest with Urim and Tummim* (Ezra 2:63). It is inferred therefrom that the geneaology of those considered to be of good lineage will be traced by means of the Holy Spirit, and those found to be of good birth will be made known. The descent of the Israelites will be recorded according to their tribes. He will announce: "This one is of such-and-such a tribe, and this one of such-and-such a tribe." But he will not say concerning those who are presumed to be of pure descent: "This is a bastard; this is a slave." For the rule is: once a family has been intermingled with others, it retains its status.

4. The Sages and Prophets did not long for the days of the Messiah that Israel might exercise dominion over the world, or rule over the heathens, or be exalted by the nations, or that it might eat and drink and rejoice. Their aspiration was that Israel be free to devote itself to the Law and its wisdom, with no one to oppress or disturb it, and thus be worthy of life in the world to come.

5. In that era there will be neither famine nor war, neither jealousy nor strife. Blessings will be abundant, comforts within the reach of all. The one preoccupation of the whole world will be to know the Lord. Hence Israelites will be very wise, they will know the things that are now concealed and will attain an understanding of their Creator to the utmost capacity of the human mind, as it is written: *For the earth shall be full of the knowledge of the Lord, as the waters cover the sea* (Isa. 11:9).

ALBO, *IKKARIM*

Translation by Isaac Husik

BOOK IV, CHAPTER 42[1]

Every adherent of the Law of Moses is obliged to believe in the coming of the Messiah, as we explained above.[2] The Torah expressly commands us to believe the words of the prophet: "Unto him ye shall hearken."[3] But the prophets announced the coming of the Messiah, hence it is clear that any one who does not believe in the coming of the Messiah denies the words of the prophets and transgresses a mandatory precept. But the belief in the coming of the Messiah is not a fundamental principle, denial of which would nullify the entire Torah. . .

We say, therefore, that belief in the coming of the Messiah is not such a fundamental principle that he who denies it should be called an infidel. But it is a true belief which every adherent of the Mosaic law must believe. We do not intend in this part of our treatise to mention the specific prophecies which refer to his coming, as that would take too long, for the commentators differ as to which are the Messianic prophecies, though they all agree that the Messiah will come. Some of the sages of the Gemara hold that all the prophecies which refer to the Messiah have already been fulfilled—according to some they were all fulfilled in the days of Hezekiah, king of Judah: "Israel has no Messiah, for they consumed him in the days of Hezekiah king of Judah."[4] Rab Ashi contradicts this opinion, and cites Zechariah in his favor: "Behold thy king cometh unto thee . . .,"[5] but this was not at the time of the second temple. Since he does not cite Isaiah, it seems that according to Rab Ashi too there is no conclusive refutation of the former statement in the prophecies of Isaiah. Our Rabbis agree that the prophecies were said concerning Hezekiah, but were not fulfilled in him: "God wanted to make Hezekiah the Messiah, etc."[6] The passage in Ezekiel,[7] "And I will make them one nation in the land, upon the mountains of Israel, and one king shall be king to them all," is also interpreted as referring to the second temple. A proof of this is the statement[8] by Rabbi Akiba that the ten tribes are not destined to return, etc. Now if the prophecy of Ezekiel referred to the distant future, how could R. Akiba say that the ten tribes will not return, when Ezekiel says the opposite? It seems, therefore, that R. Akiba referred the words of Ezekiel to the time of the second temple. The words: "And one king shall be king to them all," may refer to Zerubbabel, the satrap of Judah, or to Nehemiah, if he was a different person from Zerubbabel,[9] or to the Nasi,[10] or to the reigning king of the Hasmoneans.

Some of the commentators also say that all the prophecies of Isaiah were fulfilled at the time of the second temple, which Cyrus ordered to be built: "And let the expenses be given out of the king's house."[11] The passage in Isaiah, beginning: "And kings shall be thy foster fathers . . .,"[12] and the whole section there refers to Cyrus and the kings of Media and Persia. In the beginning of the second commonwealth they were poor, while later in the days of the Hasmoneans they became very rich, thereby fulfilling the prophecy: "For brass I will bring gold . . ."[13] In the beginning they were so poor that they made the candelabrum of tin and covered it with brass, while the other vessels were made of brass. When they became rich, they made them of gold, as the Rabbis say[14] about king Yannai[15] that he ate with the Pharisees at tables of gold. In Herod's temple, which was more beautiful than that of Solomon, was fulfilled the prophecy: "And I Will make thy pinnacles of rubies . . ."[16] . . .

R. Hayim Galipapa[17] also writes in an epistle, called *Epistle of Redemption*, that all the prophecies of Daniel refer to the second temple only. The words in Daniel:[18] "And [he] shall wear out the saints of the Most High; and he shall think to change the seasons and the law; and they shall be given into his hand until a time and times and half a time," all refer to Antiochus. Also the words: "But the saints of the Most High shall receive the kingdom,"[19] refer, he says, to the Hasmoneans. As for the words: "And possess the kingdom for ever, even for ever and ever (*'ad 'alma vee'ad 'alam 'almaya*),"[20] he says that *'olam* means one jubilee, a short and definite time during which the Hasmoneans ruled. The words: "And one that was ancient of days did sit,"[21] he refers to Mattathias the high priest, who was the head of the Hasmoneans, a very old man, all of whose sons reigned after him. He supports this interpretation by citing a statement of the Rabbis[22] in reference to the words: "For the day of vengeance that was in My heart and My year of redemption are come"[23]—"If the heart has not revealed it to the mouth, to whom can the mouth reveal it?" From this it appears that even the angels do not know when the redemption will come, because God did not reveal it to them; whereas in the words which the angel says to Daniel it seems that the angel knew the time, but Daniel did not understand him. . .

These commentators, therefore, say that the belief in the Messiah is mainly traditional in character, and there is no prophecy in the Torah or in the Prophets which must necessarily refer to the Messiah, for they can all be interpreted in accordance with their context as referring to an event that is past. Thus the words: "The sceptre shall not depart from Judah,"[24] may be interpreted: "The greatness and the dignity of the tribe will not depart from Judah," for Judah will always be the first to fight the battles until Shiloh is destroyed. [The verb *yabo* in *ki yabo shiloh,* has the same meaning as in *uba hashemesh vetaher,*[25] i.e. until the setting of Shiloh, namely its destruction.] The reason is because after the destruction of Shiloh, when Saul was anointed king, that rule departed from Judah, who no longer went first to battle. Hence the words: "Until the setting of Shiloh." Or the words may be translated, "Until his son (*shiloh*) comes," alluding to David [*shiloh* having the same meaning as *ubeshilyatah*[26] (=after-birth)]. The meaning would then be, "The scepter will not come to Judah" [*yasur* having the same meaning as *surah adonai surah elai*[27]—*turn in,* my Lord, *turn in* to me], i.e. the rule and the law-giver will not come from Judah until David comes, to whom all the tribes will gather [the word *'ammim* in the expression *velo yikhat 'ammim* having the same meaning as in the phrase *'ammim har yikrau,*[28] which Onkelos[29] translates, "the tribes of Israel"]. And the words may be interpreted in still another way in agreement with the other interpretations, as Ibn Ezra explains it. . .

In the same way they explain all the prophecies in this manner and refer them to the past, maintaining that the belief in the coming of the Messiah is mainly traditional. Onkelos,[30] the proselyte, a disciple of Shemayah and Abtalyon, who lived in the time of the second temple, refers the words: "The sceptre shall not depart from Judah . . ."[31] to the Messiah. This is the traditional interpretation to this day and we can not deny tradition, because if we were to deny tradition, then we would deny even the fundamental principles of the faith and interpret the texts differently. But the basis of all is tradition.

Our opinion is, however, that if there is no conclusive evidence in the text, tradition alone is not decisive, because one may say that even though he had not yet come in the time of Onkelos, may be he came later, as the Rabbis say:[32] "If they deserve it, he will come 'with the clouds of heaven';[33] if they do not deserve it, then, 'Lowly and riding upon an ass.'"[34] One might therefore say that he came after the time of Onkelos, but because of our sins the good things which were promised to come through him were not fulfilled and the people did not regard him as the Messiah.

The truth of the matter is that there are in the Torah and in the Prophets passages definitely indicating the growth of Israel's dignity, which have never yet been fulfilled in whole or in part, for example: "There shall step forth a star out of Jacob, and a sceptre shall rise out of Israel, and shall smite through the corners of Moab, and break down all the sons of Seth."[35] The Rabbis say:[36] "Shall smite through the corners of Moab," refers to David; "and break down all the sons of Seth," refers to the Messianic king. And their interpretation must be true, for David did not rule over all the sons of Seth and there has never been in all Israel a king who ruled over the whole world, who are the sons of Seth. Again, in Isaiah we read: "For this is as the waters of Noah unto Me; For as I have sworn that the waters of Noah should no more go over the earth, so have I sworn that I would not be wroth with thee . . .,"[37] and yet we are still in exile to-day, which shows that the prophecy has not yet been fulfilled. We also read in Isaiah: "For as the new heavens and the new earth, which I will make, shall remain before Me, saith the Lord, so shall your seed and your name remain,"[38] a promise which without doubt points to the permanent existence of the whole nation and to its ultimate grandeur.

There are nations, like the Philistines, the Ammonites, the Amalekites and others whose name has disappeared from the world, although their descendants are still existing, for there is no Philistine or Amalekite or Ammonite or Moabite nation. On the other hand, there are other nations whose name remains but not their descendants, like Egypt, which was destroyed several times, as Ezekiel prophesied. And when it was settled again, all those who came to live there were called Egyptians, although they were not of Egyptian descent—the name remained but not the race. There is no nation which continues to exist both in name and in race except that of Israel, of whom this thing was foretold: "Shall your seed and your name remain." The prophet connects it with the continuance of the new heavens and the new earth, for otherwise one might say that everything that comes into existence also passes out of existence. The other nations came into being and then disappeared and Israel too will necessarily disappear, since it came into being. To anticipate this notion, he says that it is not necessarily true that whatever is subject to genesis is also subject to destruction, for the heavens and the earth are new, that is, have come into being, according to the opinion of those who adhere to the Torah and believe in the creation of the world in time, and yet they exist before the Lord continually, i.e. they are eternal, as David says: "He hath also established them for ever and ever; He hath made a decree which shall not be transgressed."[39] Hence the seed of Israel as well as their name will also remain forever and will not disappear.

Jeremiah also says: "Thus saith the Lord, who giveth the sun for a light by day, and the ordinances of the moon and of the stars for a light by night . . . If these ordinances depart from before Me, saith the Lord, Then the seed of Israel also shall cease from being a nation before Me for ever."[40] This is also a promise of Israel's continuance and grandeur, for if the promise were that Israel will remain forever in exile, it would be a curse and not a blessing. The same thing applies to the prophecy of Ezekiel containing a description of the temple. Some portion of it was indeed fulfilled in the second temple, as appears from the words of the Rabbis in tractate Menahot.[41] Commenting on the verse: "Thus saith the Lord God: In the first month, in the first day of the month, thou shalt take a young bullock without blemish; and thou shalt purify (*vehitteta*) the sanctuary,"[42] they say, "Why a sin offering? It should be a burnt-offering."[43] Said R. Johanan, "Elijah will explain this passage," thus indicating that it refers to the Messianic period. R. Ashi said: "They offered installation sacrifices in the days of Ezra as they offered them in the days of Moses,"[44] indicating that this prophecy was fulfilled in the days of Ezra. In tractate "Middot,"[45] it also appears that in building the second temple they followed Ezekiel as far as they were able. Nevertheless it is clear that there are many things in Ezekiel that were not fulfilled in the days of Ezra or in the second commonwealth, for example the division of the land into tribes was not carried out in the second commonwealth. They were all mixed up and there was no special possession for each tribe or prince as Ezekiel describes.[46]

The prophecy concerning Gog[47] was not fulfilled at any time. To judge from the account given by Joseph ben Gorion, the priest[48] of the war of Antiochus king of Greece against Jerusalem and his defeat by the Hasmoneans, it does not agree with the prophecy concerning Gog at all. We also find in Spanish history an account of the coming of the Goths, who are descendants of Gog, to Spain, having conquered Rome and all Italy from the Greeks. But the rule of the Goths did not extend at that time over Palestine, nor did they subdue it, nor did Israel dwell at that time in their own land, as is stated in the prophecy concerning Gog. The words of Jeremiah in Lamentations: "The punishment of thine iniquity is accomplished, O daughter of Zion, He will no more carry thee away into captivity,"[49] must refer to the last exile, that is, the exile after the second temple, for after the Babylonian exile at the time of the first temple, we were exiled again by Titus. To this reference is made in the words: "He will punish thine iniquity, O daughter of Edom,"[50] which surely refers to the Roman exile, which is the last one. . .

Nor is it possible to refer all the statements mentioned in Daniel in connection with the rule of the fourth beast to any events in Israel's past or to the sinners of Israel so as to account for all the details. And there are many other prophecies of the same kind that can not be referred to the past, especially that of Malachi, the last of the prophets, who says: "Behold, I will send you Elijah the prophet before the coming of the great and terrible day of the Lord. And he shall turn the heart of the fathers to the children, and the heart of the children to their fathers,"[51] an event which has not been fulfilled.

NOTES

1. Cf. S. Schechter, Some Aspects of Rabbinic Theology, p. 346, 1. 3.
2. I, 23, p. 186.
3. Deut. 18, 15.
4. Sanhedrin 98b.
5. Zech. 9, 9.
6. Sanhedrin 94a.
7. 37, 22.
8. Sanhedrin 110b.
9. There is an haggadic opinion that Nehemiah and Zerubbabel were the same person. See Sanhedrin 38a.
10. The patriarch who, by Jews and Christians alike, was considered as the legitimate head of the Jews and hence might be referred to in Scripture as מלך; cf. Sanhedrin 5a; Horayot 11b; Hullin 92a and the passages from the patristic literature referred to by Schürer, Geschichte, vol. III, 120, last edition.
11. Ezra 6, 4.
12. Isa. 49, 23.
13. Ibid. 60, 17.
14. Kiddushin 66a.
15. John Hyrcanus.
16. Isa. 54, 12.
17. Spanish Rabbi; born at Monzon about 1310, died about 1380. See J. E., s. v. Galipapa, Hayim.
18. 7, 25.
19. Ibid. 18.
20. Ibid.
21. Ibid. 9.
22. Midrash Shohar Tob, 9, 2; cf. Sanhedrin 99a.
23. Isa. 63, 4.
24. Gen. 49, 10.
25. Lev. 22, 7.

26. Deut. 28, 57.
27. Judg. 4, 18.
28. Deut. 33, 19.
29. See I, p. 52, note 1.
30. See J. E., s. v. Onkelos; also above I, 52, note 1.
31. Gen. 49, 10.
32. Sanhedrin 98a.
33. Dan. 7, 13.
34. Zech. 9, 9.
35. Num. 24, 17.
36. Midrash Agada, Balak, ed. Buber.
37. Isa. 54, 9.
38. Ibid. 66, 22.
39. Ps. 148, 6.
40. Jer. 31, 35–36.
41. 45a.
42. Ezek. 45, 18.
43. The verb וחטאת, thou shalt purify, suggests a sin-offering (חטאת), but in Num. 28, 11 a burnt-offering is prescribed for the first day of the month.
44. Lev. 8.
45. 4, 2.
46. Ch. 48.
47. Chs. 38 and 39.
48. He is apparently referring to Josephus, though he no doubt read Pseudo-Josephus or Josippon or Yosippon, a mediaeval work of uncertain data based upon the material in Josephus and other authors. See J. E., s. v. Joseph ben Gorion; S. Zeitlin, J.Q.R., N.S., XVIII, 246–247, XIX, 77–78.
49. Lam. 4, 22.
50. *Ibid.*
51. Mal. 3, 23.

The Thirteenth Principle

Resurrection

INTRODUCTION

The belief in resurrection of the dead is stated tersely, without elaboration, in Maimonides' formulation of his Thirteen Principles: "The Thirteenth Principle: Resurrection of the dead, and we have already explained it." The explanation to which Maimonides refers is contained in the introductory exposition which prefaces his formulation of the Thirteenth Principle. There Maimonides asserts the belief that resurrection of the dead is "one of the principles of Moses, our teacher, and there is no religion or attachment to the Jewish religion for one who does not believe this." Again, in his *Mishneh Torah, Hilkhot Teshuvah* 3:5, Maimonides declares explicitly that one who denies the resurrection of the dead is denied a share in the world-to-come. These succinct but unequivocal statements notwithstanding, during his own lifetime Maimonides was accused of denying resurrection. In order to dispel any such impression, and in order to correct certain heretical views which had come to be more widely accepted since they were associated with as illustrious a figure as himself, Maimonides composed the *Treatise on the Resurrection of the Dead,* in which this principle is not only reaffirmed but is explained in greater detail.

In his *Treatise on the Resurrection of the Dead,* Maimonides explains his previous brevity by stating that resurrection of the body is a matter of belief, to be accepted on faith, rather than a conclusion which may be reached by a process of philosophical investigation. In the *Treatise,* Maimonides does add one very significant point with regard to the nature of resurrection. He asserts that at some point following the physical resurrection, all those revived will die again: "And so it appears to me from these verses that the individuals whose souls will return to their bodies will eat, drink, marry and procreate and then die after enjoying that very long span of life characteristic of the messianic era." Maimonides' belief that those resurrected will ultimately die after the lapse of an undetermined period of time is based upon the talmudic statement that in the world-to-come there is no eating, drinking or physical pleasure. There is, thus, no need for bodily organs in the world-to-come. Maimonides argues that since divine wisdom decrees that nothing be created without purpose, it follows that the resurrected subsequently die and their souls enter into a blissful existence unencumbered by corporeal bodies. This position is adopted by Albo as well.

Naḥmanides, in his *Sha'ar ha-Gemul,* takes sharp issue with Maimonides' view concerning the ultimate destruction of the body. Naḥmanides maintains that following resurrection, both the bodies and the souls of those restored to life will live on for all of eternity. Naḥmanides asserts that upon resurrection the body will not be quite the same as the body which we possess in our present existence, but will be a specially refined body which will not experience physical need, but which will be suitable for a wholly spiritual existence.

A third view is advanced by Saadia. Saadia asserts that there will be not one resurrection, but two resurrections. The first will take place at the time of the Messiah and will be limited to the righteous of Israel. Other persons will be restored to life on the occasion of the second resurrection, which will take place at a subsequent time and will usher in the age referred to as "the world-to-come." The righteous of Israel, who will be resurrected in the messianic era, will not die subsequently, but will be transferred to the world-to-come. According to Saadia, the resurrected bodies will remain to share the spiritual bliss of the world-to-come.

This view is also advanced by Abraham Ibn Ezra in his commentary on Daniel 12:2, but with one important modification. According to Ibn Ezra, the righteous of Israel who are restored to life during the messianic era will subsequently die and be restored to life a second time at the time of the resurrection ushering in the world-to-come. The verse upon which Ibn Ezra bases his view reads, "And many of them that sleep in the dust of the earth shall awake, some to everlasting life, and some to reproaches and everlasting abhorrence." In a short and succinct comment, Ibn Ezra states, "In my opinion, the righteous who died in exile will be resurrected when the Redeemer comes. . . . They will then delight in the Leviathan, the Ẓiẓ, and the Behemoth and die a second time, to live at the resurrection of the dead when they will be in the world-to-come [in which] they will not eat or drink, but enjoy the radiance of the *Shekhinah.*"

A quite different view is advanced by Crescas. Crescas asserts that the resurrection will occur after the rebuilding of the Temple, which, in turn, will occur at some unspecified time after the coming of the Messiah. According to Crescas, not every person will be resurrected. Resurrection will be limited to the completely righteous and the completely wicked of the people of Israel. The righteous will experience reward, and the wicked will be punished. The souls of persons of an intermediary status, as well as of the righteous of the nations of the world, will be rewarded, but they will not merit the wondrous miracle of resurrection.

Crescas also differs from Saadia with regard to another point. According to Saadia, the actual decomposed parts of the human body are reconstituted as the new body at the time of the resurrection. For Crescas it is not necessary that the body be regenerated from its original components. A body will be fashioned which will be identical with the original, and it is into this body that the soul will enter. Those resurrected will be endowed with memory. Hence, even though the corporeal substances may be new, the identity of individuals will be preserved.

SAADIA, *EMUNOT VE-DE'OT*

Translation by Alexander Altmann

SEVENTH TREATISE
THE RESURRECTION OF THE DEAD IN THE PRESENT WORLD[1]

1. *Refutation of the Allegorist Interpretation*

As to the Resurrection of the Dead, regarding which our Lord has informed us that it will take place in the Future World of Reward,[2] this is something on which our whole people is agreed. Their agreement is based on the view already mentioned in the preceding chapters,[3] that Man is the final object of Creation; that the reason of his distinction lies in his obedience (to God); and that the fruit of his obedience is the eternal life in the World of Reward.[4] Prior to this period God deemed it right to separate soul and body only until such time as the (number of) souls was completed and all of them were gathered together as I explained.[5] We know of no Jew who opposes this doctrine,[6] or finds it difficult from the point of view of his Reason that God should revive the dead, since it has already become clear to him that God created the world *ex nihilo*. He can find no difficulty therefore in believing that God should, by a second act, create something from something disintegrated and dissolved.[7]

God stated, furthermore, in Scripture that there will take place for us a Resurrection of the Dead at the time of the Redemption of Israel.[8] His prophets have established this doctrine for us by miracles. I found, nevertheless, that in regard to this doctrine of the Resurrection of the Dead in the Present World opinions are divided. The large majority of our people declare that there will be a resurrection at the time of the messianic Redemption, and they interpret all that is found in the Scriptural passages on the Resurrection of the Dead according to its plain meaning,[9] and fixed its time without question for the time of the Redemption. I saw only a small minority of the whole nation interpret figuratively the passages which speak of the Resurrection of the Dead at the time of the Redemption as references to the revival of our Kingdom and the restoration of the people.[10] That which is not fixed for the time of the Redemption they transfer to the Future World.[11] I have reserved this chapter for a treatment of this point.

I declare in regard to this matter that after careful examination I have ascertained beyond doubt for myself what forms the opinion of the majority of the nation, namely, that a resurrection of the dead will take place at the time of the Redemption. I deemed it right to confirm this so that it may serve as a guide and give a lead[12] (to our people) like the matters dealt with before. I declare in the first place that one of the things of which we can be certain[13] is that every statement found in the Scriptures must be taken in its plain sense. Only for one of four reasons it is not permitted to take a statement in its plain sense. These four reasons are the following: (1) If sense perception rejects the plain sense of the passage, as in the statement, 'And the man called his wife's name Eve; because she was the mother of all living' (Gen. 3.20), seeing that we witness the fact that ox and lion are not the children of woman so that it is necessary for us to believe that the statement refers only to man;[14] (2) in case Reason repudiates it, as in the statement, 'For the Lord thy God is a devouring fire, a jealous God' (Deut. 4.24), seeing that the fire is something created, required for use and extinguishable; it is, therefore, not permitted, from the point of view of Reason, to assume that God should be like it; it, therefore, follows that we must understand the statement in an elliptical sense, namely, that God's *punishment* is like a devouring fire, in the same way it says, 'For all the earth shall be devoured with the fire of My jealousy' (Zeph. 3.8); (3) in case there exists some clear text which renders the plain meaning of a passage impossible; it then follows that this clear text should be used to interpret the text which is not clear, as in the statement, 'Ye shall not try the Lord your God, as ye tried Him in Massah' (Deut. 6.16), and it is further said, 'And try Me now herewith—if I will not open you the windows of heaven' (Mal. 3.10). Both statements agree in this respect, that one should not try our Lord as to whether or not He is able to do a certain thing, after the manner of those of whom it was said, 'And they tried God in their hearts by asking food for their craving; yea, they spoke against God, they said: "Can God prepare a table in the wilderness?"' (Ps. 78.18–19). Of these it is said, 'As ye tried Him in Massah.' But man[15] may try the power of his Lord as to whether or not He is able to produce a sign and miracle for him, in the same way as Gideon asked, 'Let me make trial, I pray thee, but this once with the fleece' (Judges 6.39), or as Hezekiah asked (II Kings 20.8), and others besides them, which is permissible; (4) if to the statement of Scripture is attached some tradition[16] which modifies it, we must interpret the passage in conformity with the reliable tradition, as in the case of the tradition that flogging consists of 39 stripes, although it is written, 'Forty stripes he may give him' (Deut. 25.3). We take this to be a figure of speech;[17] the flogging consists of 39 stripes, and the text of Scripture mentions a round figure,[18] in the same way as it says, 'After the number of the days in which ye spied out the land, even 40 days, for every day a year . . .' (Num. 14.34), although in fact it was only 39 (years) because in the first year they had not yet entered into this punishment.[19]

There are only these four reasons which necessitate the interpretation of the plain meaning of the Scriptural passages in an allegorical sense;[20] there exists no fifth reason which would justify an allegorical interpretation. Now we find that the Resurrection of the Dead is not rejected by sense experience because we do not assert that the dead will be revived by themselves, but we say that their Creator will revive them. Nor is it rejected by Reason because the second creation of a thing which was already in existence and became dissolved, is more acceptable to Reason than the *creatio ex nihilo*. Nor is it precluded by any other text of Scripture; on the contrary, other texts corroborate it by stating in clear terms that the son of the woman of Zarephat (I Kings 17.17–24) and the son of the Shunammite woman (II Kings 4.32–7) were revived in this world. Nor does any tradition make it necessary to interpret it in an allegorical sense; on the contrary, the whole of tradition supports it. Thus it follows that this doctrine must be left in its original meaning in accordance with the clear sense of the text, namely, that God will revive the dead of His people at the time of the Redemption.[21]

2. *Evidence from Scripture*[22]

I consider that the Song of Moses (*Shīrat Ha'azīnū*) outlines the whole history of Israel. It commences with the beginnings of our election[23] by God, and says, 'Remember the days of old, consider the years of many generations . . . when the Most High gave to the nations their inheritance . . . for the portion of the Lord is His people' (Deut. 32.7–9). Then, at the second stage, the Song mentions God's favours towards us, and says, 'He found him in a desert land . . . He compassed him about, He cared for him, He kept him as the apple of His eye' (10). Then, at the third stage, it mentions our prosperity[24] and sinfulness, and says, 'But Jeshurun waxed fat, and kicked . . .' (15). Then, at the fourth stage, it mentions our punishment, and says, 'And the Lord saw, and spurned . . . and He said: "I will hide My face from them" . . .' and what follows

(19–25). Then, at the fifth stage, it mentions the punishment of our enemies, and says, 'For their vine is of the vine of Sodom . . .' (32–5). Then, at the sixth stage, it speaks of our relief and succour, namely from the verse, 'See now that I, even I, am He, and there is no god with Me' (39) until the end of the Song. And within this historical account[25] occurs the statement, 'I kill and I make alive; I have wounded, an I heal' (39), namely, in the days of Redemption. And lest we imagine that the meaning of the verse is, 'He killeth some people and maketh other people live,'[26] as is the way[27] of the world, He says, 'I have wounded, and I heal,' so as to let us know that in the same way as it is the sick body which is healed, so it is the dead body which will be revived.[28] And all this will take place at the time of the Redemption as is evident from the following verses:[29] 'For I lift up my hand to heaven and say, "As I live for ever, if I whet My glittering sword, and My hand take hold on judgment" . . .' (40–42); 'Sing aloud, O ye nations, of His people,' the meaning of which is the same as in the verse, 'Sing with gladness for Jacob . . .' (Jer. 31.7).[30]

I declare furthermore: 'The Creator knew that whispers might reach us of the difficulty of believing in the Resurrection of the Dead of our people.[33] He, therefore, met this point in advance by the prophecy of Ezekiel. He said unto him, 'Son of man, those bones are the whole house of Israel; behold, they say: "Our bones are dried up, and our hope is lost; we are clean cut off"' (Ezek. 37.11). Then He commanded him to announce to us that we shall rise from our graves, and that all of our dead will be revived, in the following words, 'Therefore, prophesy, and say unto them: . . . "Behold, I will open your graves, and cause you to come up out of your graves, O my people"' (12). And lest we should think that this promise only relates to the Future World, He added at the end of this verse, 'And I will bring you into the Land of Israel' (12), so that we may be sure that it will happen in the present world. And He further added that every one of us, when revived by God, will remember that he is the one who lived and died and was revived. Thus He says, 'And ye shall know that I am the Lord, when I have opened your graves . . . and ye shall know that I the Lord have spoken, and performed it . . .' (13–14). And He repeats the mention of Palestine in order to corroborate our belief that it will happen in this world, as He says, 'And I will put My spirit in you, and ye shall live, and I will place you in your own land' (14).[32]

I declare furthermore: The prophet (Isaiah) has announced something similar to this promise when he says, 'Thy dead shall live' (Is. 26.19), which in effect corresponds to Ezekiel's statement,[33] 'They say: "Our bones are dried up, and our hope is lost.'"[34] This state (of Resurrection) resembles the condition of one who awakens from his slumber, as it says, 'Awake and sing' (*ibid.*), which corresponds to Ezekiel's statement, 'And ye shall know that I am the Lord, when I have opened your graves.'[35] The Resurrection is also likened to the 'Dew of light' (*ibid.*), because man's nature[36] is built up from the four elements: The earth is there already, and the moisture God brings to it from the essence[37] of dew; then He brings to it the spirit[38] from the essence of light, because the soul is luminous like the light (as we explained).[39] 'And the earth shall cause the shades to fall' (*ibid.*)[40] means to say that the unbelievers[41] will be cast down to earth and humbled, as we explained, and they are those who ignored the commandment and prohibition of God. Thus it is said, 'The man that strayeth out of the way of understanding shall rest in the congregation of the shades' (Prov. 21.16).

I declare furthermore: I found that our Lord informed Daniel as to what will happen in the end of time, in 47 verses.[42] One verse, namely the first one, describes what will happen in the final period of the Persian Kingdom (Dan. 11.2); 13 verses inform us about the Greek Kingdom, namely, from 11.3 to 16; 20 verses inform us about the Roman Empire, namely from 11.16 to 36; 10 verses inform us about the Arab Kingdom, namely from 11.36 to 12.1; and the last 3 verses deal with the Redemption (of Israel), and one of them reads as follows, And many of them that sleep in the dust of the earth shall awake, some to everlasting life, and some to reproaches and everlasting abhorrence' (12.2). He only says, 'And *many* of them that sleep'; he does not say, '*All* of them that sleep,' because that would include all children of Adam, whereas this promise[43] includes only the children of Israel. Therefore, he says, 'Many.' And he says, 'Some to everlasting life, and some to reproaches.' which does not mean that some of those revived will be rewarded and some punished, since at the time of the Redemption God will not revive those who deserve punishment.[44] But the meaning of the distinction made in this verse is that those who will awake will awake to life everlasting, and those who will not awake will be marked for eternal shame, because all the righteous and penitent will be revived, and only the unbelievers and those who died without repentance will be left over. All this applies to the time of the Redemption.[45]

3. *A Knotty Point*[46]

Having explained these statements,[47] I declare: If one by the exercise of his Reason tries to penetrate more deeply into the subject of (the Resurrection of the Dead—an event which will take place at the time of the Redemption[48] and, for all mankind, in the Future World)—he will, perhaps, be led in the course of his reflections to the following objection: When any human body, as it exists at its first stage,[49] dissolves into its elements after death, all its parts return to their elemental sources,[50] that is to say the bodily warmth joins the fire, the moisture and the humours the air, the coldness the water, and the dryness remains with the earth. Then the Creator forms the bodies of the second stage from the same materials of which the parts of the first stage were composed. Then the human body of the second stage dies, and, again, its parts return to their elemental sources. Then the Creator forms from them a third stage which, again, is composed in the same way as the two preceding stages. And so with the fourth and the fifth. Now how is it possible to assume that the first stage should be perfect, and the second stage also perfect, and the third stage also perfect, seeing that the parts of every stage have already entered into existence at other stages?[51] To remove all misgivings on this matter I say: God would have need to use the dissolved parts of the bodies of the first stage for His composition of the second bodies only if there remained amongst the existing things nothing else but those parts. In this case He would have had to use them over and over again in perpetuity.[52] I will make this clear by an illustration.[53] Suppose a man possesses a vessel of silver of a thousand drachms weight, and possesses nothing else of worth. Whenever this vessel breaks, he has to renew it by casting it into the mould and handing it to the silversmith. But a man who has houses full of treasures is in a different position: If any of his vessels breaks he puts its fragments aside until he wants to renew this very same vessel. But everything which he casts into the mould until such time is fresh, taken from (the gold of) his treasure house, and there are not mixed with it the fragments of broken pieces; these he lays aside until such time as he renews the broken vessels, as he may have promised to do.[54] I searched and found that, in a similar way, the original elements of air and fire which form the atmosphere between the air and the first layer[55] of the heaven are equal to the volume of the entire body of the earth including its mountains and oceans, multiplied by 1089.[56] And since the elements[57] are of such a magnitude,[58] there is no necessity that the Creator should compose the bodies of the second stage from the dissolved bodies of the first stage. Thus he stores them away until the time comes for him to fulfil what he has promosed them.

Perhaps on further reflection one will say: 'If a man has been eaten by a lion, and the lion was drowned and a fish ate it, and then the fish was caught and a man ate it, then the man was burned to ashes, whence can the Creator retrieve the first man? From the lion, or from the fish, or from the second man, or from the fire, or from the ashes?'[59] I have an idea that this is a question which greatly perplexes the faithful. Before I answer it, I think it is right to state this: We have to remember that no body which exists in this world can destroy another body. Thus, the fire which is quick to burn only separates the parts of a thing so that each part rejoins its element, and the earthly part becomes dust; but it does not destroy anything. It is out of the question to assume that anything should be able to destroy anything so as to reduce it to nothing, except the Creator who created the things from nothing. Since this is clear beyond question, any animal which eats any body does not destroy it, but merely dissolves its parts . . . And since things can be explained in this way, the parts of those men who were consumed are not destroyed, but all of them are stored away, no matter whether they belong to a pious one or to a criminal, until such time as all of them are made anew.[60] This is nothing to wonder at in the case of Him who created them originally.

NOTES

1. The text of this chapter differs widely in the two extant MSS. (i.e. the Oxford and Leningrad Recensions). The above translation is based on Landauer's text, which follows the Oxford Recension. For our reason see Introduction, pp. 21–2. Tibbon's translation is based on the text which is given in the Leningrad Recension. The anonymous Paraphrase follows partly one and partly the other recension. An abridged version of Chapter VII as it appears in the Paraphrase was published as a separate treatise in Mantua (1556) under the title *Sefer ha-teḥiyyah* ('Book on Resurrection'). Cf. Malter, pp. 362–4. On the subject of Resurrection cf. A. Löwinger, 'Die Auferstehung in der jüd. Tradition' in *Jahrbuch für Jüdische Volkskunde,* ed. Max Grunwald (1923), Vol. 25, pp. 23–122. An exposition of Saadya's view is given there on pp. 99–104. See also Israel Lévi, 'Les Morts et l'avènement de l'ère messianique' *in REJ* (1919), Vol. 69.

2. Arab. *dār al-'āchir* (Hebr. *'ōlam habā');* in contradistinction to *dār al-dunyā* (Hebr. *'ōlam hazeh*), which occurs in the title of the chapter. Saadya teaches that the messianic period will be initiated by the resurrection of the pious of Israel, who will thus receive a special reward for the suffering they had to endure during the long period of Israel's exile. This resurrection will take place in the present world as part of the scheme of Israel's Redemption, and constitutes an act of justice on God's part. Cf. *Amānāt,* p. 225–6. This

resurrection of the pious of Israel will later be followed by the resurrection of the dead of all peoples at the time when the Future World, the World of Reward, will be inaugurated. In this Future World God will mete out justice to every man, pious and impious. In this chapter Saadya deals with the resurrection in the messianic period.

3. Cf. above, pp. 115–7.

4. Saadya deals with the World of Reward in Chapter IX.

5. Cf. above, p. 154.

6. Arab. *'amānāt;* i.e. of the Resurrection in the Future World.

7. The same argument occurs also in the Leningrad Recension. Cf. ed. Bacher, p. 100; ed. Slucki 107.

8. The term used by Saadya throughout this chapter for the Redemption of Israel is the Hebrew word *yeshu'ah,* salvation, which he invariably cites in Hebrew characters. In Chapter VIII he uses the Arabic *furḳān.* Cf. below, p. 167, n. 1.

9. Arab. *ẓāhir*: manifest, literal (meaning).

10. Abū Yūsuf Ya'ḳūb al-Ḳirḳisānī, a contemporary of Saadya's mentions that some Ḳaraites asserted that the messianic salvation had already taken place during the time of the Second Temple (cf. below, pp. 175 ff), and that others interpreted the Scriptural passages dealing with the Resurrection of the Dead in the sense of allegorical descriptions of Israel's rise from exile. Cf. Bacher, *loc. cit.,* p. 224.

11. I.e. the references to Resurrection which are unconnected with the Redemption of Israel they understood to apply to the Resurrection in the Future World. With this Saadya agrees.

12. According to the Leningrad Recension, Saadya's meaning is that the belief in the Resurrection of the pious of Israel in the messianic era is bound to guide and strengthen the people amidst the trials of exile. Cf. ed. Bacher 99; ed. Slucki 106.

13. Lit. 'according to our knowledge of the true realities of things.' Cf. above, p. 107.

14. I.e. 'All living' means 'All men.'

15. Lit. 'Servant' (of God).

16. Arab. *athar.*

17. Arab. *majāz.* Cf. above, p. 88, n. 3.

18. Arab. *jabara;* lit. 're-unite broken parts'; the word *Algebra* is derived from this Arabic root.

19. The Leningrad Recension contains the same exegetical canon, but in a slightly less elaborate form than presented here. Cf. ed. Bacher 102–3; ed. Slucki 109. A similar exegetical canon was evolved by Ibn Ḥazm, but with the omission of a possible conflict between Scripture and Reason. Cf. I. Goldziher, *Die Zahiriten,* pp. 122–3; 142–5.

20. Arab. *tā'wīl.* Cf. above, p. 88, n. 3.

21. In a passage not included in this Selection (ed. Landauer 216–8; ed. Bacher 106–7; ed. Slucki 112–3), Saadya seriously considers whether the Resurrection of the Dead may not, after all, merely express, in symbolic language, the promised rise of the Jewish kingdom 'From its dust.' He quotes Ps. 113.7, II Kings 16.2, Ps. 88.5–6, 31.13, 71.20 as evidence that Scripture is wont to use such and similar expressions for the rise of man from humbleness to glory. His counter-argument is that unless we are prepared to accept the doctrine of Resurrection in its plain literal sense, there is nothing to prevent us from dissolving the whole Torah, its laws and miracles, into a nebulous allegorism. Saadya's anti-allegorism is in striking contrast to Philo's allegorical interpretation of the Torah, including its laws.

22. According to the Mishnah (*Sanh.* 10.1), 'One who declares that the Resurrection of the Dead is not proclaimed by the Torah, has no share in the Future World.' Saadya endeavours to trace this doctrine both in the Torah and the later Scriptures. In so doing he elaborates some of the arguments produced by the Talmud in order to prove that this doctrine is already found in the Torah.

23. Arab. *'iṣṭafā;* cf. below, p. 167, n. 2.

24. Lit. 'High rank' (Arab. *chaṭar*); the Leningrad Recension reads *ṭarhum*, 'their sprouting.' Cf. ed. Bacher, 108.

25. Lit. 'Arrangement' (Arab. *naẕām*); the same expression is used in the opening sentence of this paragraph.

26. I.e. not that God revives those who are killed, but He kills people and causes others to live.

27. Lit. 'nature'; Arab. *binya*.

28. Saadya borrows this argument from the Talmud (*b. Sanh.* 91 b).

29. Since the verses following upon the announcement of the Resurrection speak of the messianic Redemption, the Resurrection must necessarily form part of this period.

30. The same paragraph occurs, in a slightly different form, also in the Leningrad Recension. Cf. ed. Bacher 108; ed. Slucki 113–4.

31. Lit. 'The resurrection of the dead amongst us.' The reference is to the special resurrection of the pious of Israel in the messianic period prior to the general resurrection in the Future World.

32. The above paragraph on Ezekiel's prophecy appears in a different version also in the Leningrad Recension. Cf. ed. Bacher 104–5; ed. Slucki 111. In the Talmud (*b. Sanh.* 92 b), opinions are divided as to whether Ezekiel's vision was in the nature of a simile (*mashal*) or portrayed a real event.

33. Lit. 'to what is said there.' i.e. in Ezekiel, chap. 37.

34. In the Leningrad Recension this paragraph occurs in a modified form. Cf. ed. Bacher 105; ed. Slucki 111. There Isaiah's words, 'Thy dead shall live,' are said to correspond to Ezekiel's words, 'Behold, I open your graves;' and the second part of Isaiah's verse, 'My dead bodies shall arise' is stated to correspond to Ezekiel's words, 'I will cause you to come up out of your graves'. The answer to the despairing words, 'Our bones are dried up,' is said to be given by Isaiah's words, 'For Thy dew is a dew of light.'

35. The Leningrad Recension elaborates this point by adding, 'For one who awakens relates in his waking state what he saw in his dream, and knows that it is he who slept and awoke.'

36. Arab. *binya*.

37. Arab. *ma'nā*.

38. Arab. *ruḥ*; Saadya takes the spirit (breath) to consist of air and fire.

39. Cf. above, pp. 145–6.—In the Leningrad Recension the plural 'lights' (*'orōt*) which occurs in Isa. 26.19 is explained with reference to the sixteen faculties of the soul, a conception which strangely contrasts with Saadya's notion of three faculties of the soul as explained in Chapter VI.

40. This is how Saadya understands the verse. The Authorized Version renders it, 'And the earth shall bring to life the shades.'

41. Arab. *al-kuffār*; Saadya holds that the souls of the unbelievers roam about in the universe until the time of their punishment in the Future World arrives. Cf. above, p. 153.

42. Cf. Dan. 11.2–45; 12.1–3.

43. I.e. of Resurrection in the messianic period as distinct from the life in the Future World.

44. Only the pious of Israel will be revived in the messianic period.

45. The above paragraph on Daniel occurs with some variation in the Leningrad Recension as well. Cf. ed. Bacher 105–6; ed. Slucki 111–2.

46. The exposition which follows occurs, with some modifications, also in the Leningrad Recension. Cf. ed. Bacher 100–101; ed. Slucki 107–8. There it is introduced as an answer to a possible objection which natural science might raise against the doctrine of Resurrection.

47. Saadya refers to the Scriptural passages quoted before and a number of Talmudic utterances on the subject, quoted on pp. 219–20 (ed. Landauer). See also ed. Bacher 108–9; ed. Slucki 114.

48. I.e. for the pious of Israel.

49. Arab. *ṭabaḳa*; layer, stage, grade. The assumption is that the elements into which man dissolves after death are used again in the process of generation on earth so that the very same materials which formed the body of a man at stage 1 may appear again in the body of another man (stage 2), and so forth.

50. Arab. *ma'din*. Cf. above, p. 69, n. 7.

51. The trend of the argument is this: If we assume that there exists only a limited amount of elementary matter in the universe, then the same matter which has been used already will have to form the substance of all subsequent generation. But if this is the case, its quality must necessarily degenerate. If so, how can we imagine that at the time of Resurrection the human body will still be 'perfect'? The idea that, in a biological sense, mankind is in a process of degeneration has been advanced, from a different point of view, by such modern thinkers as L. Klages and Th. Lessing. The notion that the world grows old is already found in IV Ezra 5.53–5; 14.10, 16; syr. Baruch 85.10.

52. But in fact, as Saadya explains later, the amount of elementary matter in the universe is so ample that the decomposed parts of the human body can be left unused for the process of continued generation, and only appear again in the resurrected bodies.

53. The Leningrad Recension does not contain this simile.

54. The rich man has no need to cast the fragments of his broken vessels into the mould since he has plenty of silver and gold in his treasury to have new and fresh vessels made. He, therefore, reserves the broken pieces until such time as he is interested in renewing the very same old vessles. In the same way, God has no need to use the decomposed parts of the bodies for keeping the process of the world going, but will use them again only at the promised time of Resurrection.

55. Lit. 'Part'; cf. p. 54, n. 3.

56. In the Leningrad Recension (ed. Bacher 100 ed; ed. Slucki 107), Saadya explains in greater detail that according to the knowledge of the learned (*'ulamā'*) the atmosphere between the earth and the first layer of heaven is 33 times 33 (=1089) times larger than the volume of the earth. In his *Comm. Yes.*, p. 84 (107), Saadya mentions that the measures of the earth and the heavenly bodies have been determined by the ancient scholars with the help of astronomical instruments and geometrical principles. As S. Gandz has shown Saadya's main source is al-Farghānī's *Elementa Astronomica.* Al-Farghānī flourished under the famous caliph al-Mamum (813-833), who organized an expedition of mathematicians and astronomers to measure one degree of the meridian of the earth. *Saadya Anniversary Volume*, New York, pp. 189-93.

57. Lit. 'Things.'

58. Lit. 'Width.'

59. The Leningrad Recension quotes the same questions, but does not give the detailed example as above. Augustine, *De Civitate Dei* XXII, 12, poses the same problem. Cf. Ventura, p. 249.

60. i.e., in the Future World when the pious and the wicked of all nations will be judged.

NINTH TREATISE
ON REWARD AND PUNISHMENT IN THE FUTURE WORLD[1]

1. *A postulate of Reason*

Our Lord (be He blessed and exalted) has informed us that He has fixed a time for the reward of the righteous, and that, at such time, He will distinguish between them and the unbelievers, as it says, 'And they shall be Mine, saith the Lord of Hosts, in the day that I do make . . . Then shall ye again discern between the righteous and the wicked . . .' (Mal. 3.17–18). The prophets established this doctrine for us by wonders and miracles, and we accepted it.

It is desirable that I should adduce positive proofs concerning this time called the Future World, from the evidence of Reason, Scripture and Tradition, according to the method, which I laid down in the opening of the book, of finding the prophetic teachings demonstrated by the arguments of Reason. I affirm, in the first place, that it has already become clear from what I stated in Chapters III, IV and VI that heaven and earth and all that is between them have been created solely for the sake of man, for this reason, he was placed in the centre with all things surrounding him; and for this reason God endowed the soul with distinction and excellence, that is to say, with Reason and Wisdom; for this reason He imposed on it the duty of obeying commandment and prohibition, and through them He made it fit for life everlasting[2]; and this life (of the Future World) will supervene when there will be completed (the number of) the human beings which His wisdom has decided to create,[3] whereupon He will place them in a Second World in which to bestow upon them their reward. We have established this by proofs from Reason, Scripture and Tradition in the chapters mentioned, which can serve us as a sufficient preparation for this chapter. I deemed it proper to add some more points which strengthen and corroborate this belief, and to elucidate it further from the three sources[4] which we mentioned.

I affirm: It is, in addition, a postulate of Reason[5] that, from what we can discern of the wisdom and power of the Creator as well as of His goodness towards His creatures, it is not permissible to assume that the measure of happiness which He intended for the human soul should be limited to what it finds in this world in the shape of earthly pleasure and delight. For every pleasure in this world is associated with evil, every happiness with misery, every delight with pain, and every joy with sadness. I find that either these aspects are equal or that the sorrows outweigh the joys. This being so beyond doubt, it would be absurd to think that the Wise (be He glorified in His glory) should have limited the highest good of the soul to what it can attain under these conditions. No, it is necessary that He should have prepared for it a place where it can find everlasting life and true happiness, to which He may lead it. Moreover, I find that the human beings whom I have known are neither content nor at rest in this world, even if they have attained the summit of power in the kingdom or the highest rank. And this lies in the nature of the soul only because it knows that it has a place more excellent than all the excellencies of this place, and it turns towards it in longing, and its eyes look out for it; but for this, the soul would be satisfied and at rest (in this world). Moreover, God has made loathsome to man's Reason things for which his natural disposition[6] lusts, such as adultery, theft, boasting and revenge by killing and similar things.[7] And when he obeys these commandments, he does so with a sense of grievance and repining, which causes him pain and distress at heart. Surely God would not have treated man thus, unless he intended to give him his recompense. Likewise, God has made attractive to man's Reason the idea of Truth and Justice as well as the commandment of loving-kindness and the prohibition of reprehensible deeds.[8] But if a man seeks to act in this way, he will be pursued by the enmity and hatred of those whom he brought to justice, and of those whom he directed by command and prohibition because he interfered between them and their passions; they may even vilify, beat and kill him. Surely God would not have brought him into such a sorry position by making these ideas attractive to his Reason unless He intended for him, in return, abounding reward.

Moreover, we find that some people treat their fellow men wrongfully, and the wrong-doer as well as the wronged may live either in happiness or in misery. Then both die, and since He (be He glorified in His glory) is the God of Justice, it follows that He must have prepared for both a second place where He will judge between them in equity, and mete out reward to the one according to the pain he suffered at the hands of the wrong-doer, and bring punishment upon the other according to the pleasure which, from his natural disposition,[9] he derived from his wrongdoings and evil acts.

Moreover, we see that unbelievers live in happiness in this world and believers suffer misery in this world. The conclusion can therefore not be avoided that to both classes a second place is allotted where truth and justice decide their fate. Moreover, we find that one who murders one person is killed, and one who murdered ten persons is also killed; similarly, one who committed adultery once and one who committed adultery twenty times. It follows that the justice which remains to be executed for each one of a person's offences will reach him in the Second World. And similarly with everything which belongs to this category.

Someone may ask: Why is it that the Wise (be He glorified in His glory) did not create man from the beginning of things in the Future World so as to save him both the pain and its reward? My answer to this question is the same as we have already explained before in Chapter III.[10]

4. Paradise and Hell

I consider that reward and punishment are two subtle essences[11] which our Lord (be He exalted and glorified) will create at the time of Judgment,[12] and which He will assign to every man[13] according to his merit or guilt. They both consist of the same essence,[14] an essence which resembles the particular quality of fire in its capacity both to burn and illumine. It[15] will illumine the righteous, but not the wrong-doers; and it will burn the wrong-doers, but not the righteous. In regard to this, the text of Scripture states, 'For, behold, the day cometh, it burneth as a furnace; and all the proud, and all that work wickedness, shall be stubble; and the day that cometh shall set them ablaze . . . But unto you that fear My name shall the sun of righteousness arise with healing in its wings . . .' (Mal. 3.19–21). How apt is this comparison with the double activity of the sun in producing both the heat of the day and the bright daylight. The expressions 'The day . . . burneth' and 'The sun of righteousness shall arise' both speak of the same thing; for we do find the sun alluded to in the term 'day.' (Cf. Judges 19.11 and 19.9.) The root of this essence which the Creator (be He exalted and glorified) will call into being will resemble the sun, but there is a difference between it and the sun. For in the case of the sun, heat and light are mixed together, and neither of the two can subdue the other, whereas this essence will be at the disposal of the Creator (be He glorified in His glory) to confine its light to the righteous, and gather its heat for the wrong-doers, either by virtue of a particular quality which He will impart to it, or by specially providing[16] that the one group should be guarded from its heat while its light is hidden from the others. The second theory seems the more probable one. For we have seen that God did something similar in Egypt when He gathered the light for the believers and the darkness for the unbelievers by a special provision emanating from His command.[17]

On the basis of these remarks I now affirm that for this reason Scripture calls the reward of the righteous, Light, and every punishment for the wrong-doers, Fire. As to reward, it is said, 'For with Thee is the fountain of life; in Thy light do we see light' (Ps. 36.10). (See further Ps. 97.11; Prov. 13.9; Job 33.30; and other passages of a similar character.) In regard to punishment, it is said, 'And the strong shall be as tow, and his work as a spark; and they shall both burn together, and none shall quench them' (Isa. 1.31). (See further Isa. 33.11, 26.11, 30.33; Job 15.34, 22.20, 20.26; Ps. 11.6, 140.11, and other passages of a similar character.)

If someone asks us to give him an example as to how body and soul can live everlastingly without food,[18] we quote the example of our Teacher Moses, whom God (be His name blessed) kept alive for 40 days and 40 nights three times without food, as it says, 'And He was there with the Lord 40 days and 40 nights; he did neither eat bread, nor drink water' (Ex. 34.28). What kept him alive was the light which God created for him and which He caused to radiate from his face, as it says, 'And Moses knew not that the skin of his face sent forth beams' (Ex. 34.29). This can furnish our Reason with an illustration and an analogy of the way in which the life of the righteous can be sustained by Light, without food. In this sense God said to him, 'Before all thy people I will do marvels, such as have not been wrought in all the earth, nor in any nation' (Ex. 34.10). And this is similar to the words of the prophet regarding the righteous, 'And whereof from of old men have not heard, nor perceived by the ear, neither hath the eye seen a god beside Thee, Who worketh for him that waiteth for Him' (Isa. 64.3). But how will God keep alive those who will be undergoing the eternal and everlasting punishment of fire? We do not find amongst the people of the past anyone to whom anything similar occurred so that we could point to him as an example. And since we do not find anything similar to it, Scripture mentions it especially, and says of the unbelievers, 'For their worm shall not die, neither shall their fire be quenched' (Isa. 66.24).

Now, the Reward is called Paradise (*gan 'eden*), because in this world there is found nothing more exalted than this garden in which God placed Adam. And the punishment is called Hell (*Gehinnom*), which is the name of a place in the neighbourhood of the Temple, which Scripture also calls *Tophet*, as it says, 'It shall no more be called Tophet nor the valley (*gey*) of the son of Hinnom' (Jer. 7.32). The *Gehinnom* is also mentioned in the book of Joshua (15.8).

NOTES

1. An analysis of the origin and background of the Rabbinic conception of the Future World (*'ōlam habā'*) is attempted in the Translator's article 'Olam und Aion' in *Festschrift für Dr. Jakob Freimann* (1937), pp. 1–14.

2. Arab. *al-ḥayāt ad-dā'ima*; Tibbon: *ha-ḥayyīm ha-matmīdīm.*

3. Cf. above, p. 141.

4. Arab. *mawād*; Tibbon: *meshakīm.* Cf. above, p. 36. n. 1.

5. Lit. 'Of that which Reason further demands.'—Cf. I. Kant, *Kritik der prakischen Vernunft* I, 2, 2 (4), where the belief in a Future Life is developed as a "Postulate of Reason.'

6. Arab. *ṭab'*.—Saadya contrasts man's natural disposition (*ṭab'*) with his Reason (*'akl*). The conflict between Nature and Reason is particularly stressed in his *Comm. Prov.* Cf. E. I. J. Rosenthal, 'Saadya Gaon: An Appreciation of his Biblical Exegesis,' in *Bulletin of the John Rylands Library*, Vol. 27, 1. See also the Translator's article, 'Saadya's Conception of the Law' in *Bulletin of the John Rylands Library*, Vol. 28, 2.

7. Cf. above, p. 97.

8. Arab. *munkar.* Cf. above, p. 99. n. 2.

9. Cf. above, p. 182, n. 3.

10. I.e.That this world gives man an opportunity of earning reward and thus makes his happiness in the Future World the greater. Cf. above, pp. 93–4.

11. Arab. *ma'nā.*

12. Lit. 'Reward.'

13. Lit. 'Servant' (of God).

14. Arab. *'ayn.* Cf. above, p. 185, n. 2. Tibbon renders it here by *eṣem.*

15. I.e. the 'subtle essence' which God will create as a medium of reward and punishment.

16. Arab. *'araḍ* (accident); i.e. by creative acts which cause the effect desired in each particular case.

17. Saadya's theory that the Light of the Future World will have opposite effects on the righteous and wicked is obviously based on the Talmudic passage, *b. Ned.* 8 b. On the origin of the Rabbinic conception of the 'Light which is stored up for the righteous' see the Translator's article, 'Gnostic Themes in Rabbinic Cosmology' in *Essays in Honour of the Very Rev. Dr. J.H. Hertz*, pp. 28 ff.

18. The above question arises out of Saadya's statement that reward and punishment in the Future World will be in the nature of Light. Since the men who will be revived in the Future World will be 'men with body and soul' (see *Amānāt*, p. 269; ed. Slucki, p. 136), the question naturally arises how they will be able to live. Saadya explains that their life will be of a purely spiritual nature. Cf. *b. Berakot* 17 a.

MAIMONIDES, *MA'AMAR TEḤIYAT HA-METIM*

Translation by Sabato Morais

It is not at all improbable, that an argument elucidated in a manner which ought to place it beyond the possibility of misconstruction, may nevertheless be understood by the ignorant to convey the opposite idea to that which the writer sought to communicate. A proof of this is the important sentence by which the Almighty wishes to erase from our minds any belief in the division of his Essence, but which has been interpreted by those who entertain that erroneous opinion, as a demonstration in favour of their creed. They have stated that term אחד "One" qualifies the nature of the three divine beings mentioned before it, that is; "Adonai," "Elohenu," "Adonai," the three forming a unity. (May the Lord preserve us from such hallucination!) Now, if the words of the Most High have been subject to misapprehension, surely those of mortals cannot but be subject still more to it. Thus it happened that while endeavoring to illustrate a cardinal point of our religion, that had been lost sight of, we involuntarily occasioned a doubt touching our faith in another universally known and avowed by our people. However, when we felt impelled to undertake the exposition of the law and its behests, we designed obtaining the favor of our Maker, and not human approbation.

We applied ourselves to rendering the knowledge imparted by our predecessors accessible to the unenlightened and we think we succeeded in simplifying what was abstruse, and in condensing in proper order what was scattered in voluminous works. If we are correct in our impression, and our labor has really proved useful to our fellow creatures, we are amply repaid; if we are mistaken, then suffice it to experience the satisfaction that our intention was good, and he who looks at the heart will grant us a full reward. But as with that object in view, we had set forth, in comprehensive and clear style the injunctions of our religion, we deemed it also and ever more important to dwell on the fundamental principles thereof; especially so, because we met with a man regarded as learned in the law, and who truly from his early age was accustomed to discuss its merits, who still doubted whether God was a bodily form,—

for the reason that Holy Writ represents Him so—,or only a pure spirit. In fact, we have heard some proclaimed Him altogether corporeal and denounced as infidels those opposed to that opinion, citing in their support sundry passages which they understood literally. We then saw how far the human mind had gone astray; and concluded to introduce in our theological writings certain cardinal points, which, without being advanced and substantiated in a scientific manner—too high for intellects untutored in science—might be the means of communicating religious truths to the generality of our readers. Wherefore, in our preface to the commentary on the Mishna, we explained what is essential to be believed respecting prophecy and tradition, and what touching the oral law. So likewise in the chapter חלק of treatise Sanhedrin, we elucidated, in addition to other principal tenets of our religion, those which relate to the Unity of God and a future existence.

And in the extensive work called "Mishna Torah,"—which can be rightly appreciated only by those who possess a well-cultivated and upright mind,—we followed the same course, for, in it are comprised both Scriptural and Talmudical subjects of the highest import, and so methodically arranged, that scholars may, by degrees, become acquainted with the learning of the Sages; and at the same time, imbibe correct notions with regard to the Deity, which will lead them to seek His favor alone by approaching Him through their moral perfection.

One of the essential points, to which we awakened the attention of our readers is the existence of an endless futurity. We treated of that grand truth, and descanted thereon adducing proof from the Bible and the Rabbins, sufficient to satisfy the intelligent. And in the chapter חלק we, alleged the reason which has induced us to speak at large of the future existence, in preference to the resurrection of the dead, mentioning that as the latter had been made exclusively the subject of discussion, and the former had been altogether neglected, we esteemed it necessary to dispel any misgivings as to whether a reward and punishment hereafter was pointed out in the divine law. Besides, we stated also there, that the resurrection of the dead, though an essential creed of the Mosaic religion, is not our final destination, but that, life after death can solely be termed so, as frequently indicated in the heavenly volumes by the term "Karet" "excision" according to oral interpretation. And upon the same topics we expatiated in the "Rules of penitence," with the exception that in the chapter חלק, after we had argued on the dogmas of immortality, we added that, "notwithstanding the resurrection of the dead is not our final destination, yet whoever denies it cannot be called an Israelite." Moreover, in our extensive work, we enumerated among those that have no share in the world to come, he who disbelieves in the resurrection of the dead. And in connection with our spiritual existence hereafter, we said that *that* is our final destination, expressing ourselves as follows "it is a reward which is above every other and a happiness which is the loftiest ever to be attained," for we demonstrated that when our spirit is divested of all perishable matter, by which it acted during its abode on earth, it will most assuredly enjoy eternity.

So have our Sages written. "In the world to come, neither eating nor drinking, nor any of the functions indispensable to the maintenance of the body will be needed," and verily it cannot be supposed that in such a state, we could still bear a material form, for, of what use would it be to us, when its agency is at an end? The Almighty who assigns to every created thing its particular aim, would not give us limbs, organs, sinews, etc., to no purpose. Now, to dispute such a truism by some Talmudical legends taken in their outward garb, would be the height of folly. And they who have attempted to gainsay our position by instancing Moses and Elijah, that for a period lived spiritually, although they were possessed of bodies, drew a very absurd inference, for, Moses and Elijah, before and after the miracle of which they were the recipients, required the aid of their corporeal substance, like all other men; hence they cannot serve as a criterion to judge thereby of a state which is to endure for ever, and as our Rabbis style it "the world of unalloyed felicity, and of eternity."

But they who strove to controvert our opinion, are unable to understand how derogatory of the wisdom of God it would be to attribute to Him a creation without any design; and, on the other hand, the masses cannot disjoin the idea of permanency from that of matter. As for the properties inherent in the body, which in the abstract they must admit to be incorporeal, they attribute to them, for the reason, a shorter duration. But to ascribe existence to that which is neither a body, nor a quality thereof, is repugnant to their belief. Therefore it ensues, as a natural consequence, that the majority of these superficial thinkers represent to themselves the Deity in a corporeal form. However, they who are really wise acknowledge, on the contrary, that what is free of materiality has more permanence, or I should say rather, has a more true existence than that which is material, for it is not liable to changes. And such ones have also learned that, beyond a shadow of doubt, the Omnipotent is incorporeal,—and therefore is his existence infinite and unalterable,—and that moreover, whatever is not termed as angelic beings and the intellect, is, without comparison, more durable than its opposite. We then firmly believe that angels are not bodies, and that the participants of the world to come are disembodied souls or intelligences.

Already in our work called "The Teacher of the Perplexed" we have offered evidences from the Pentateuch that corroborate our assertion; and if some unenlightened person refuse to abide thereby, it being more congenial with his thoughts to believe that angels possess a body and partake of food, because in the book of Genesis is written "and they did eat," also that after death we still retain our corporeal form, we will not take offence at it, nor call such an infidel and avoid him. And should any one observe, that an opinion so proposterous evinces the folly of him that entertains it, we would answer: nay, let us rest satisfied if that folly does not go so far as to induce a belief in the corporeity of God.

If the untutored will not even stop to consider which of the two opinions is right, tenaciously persisting that he holds the correct one, and we are in error, we will not impute it to sin, but readily pardon him.

We have on other occasions, exhibited his mental deficiencies, and all the Talmudical legends that he renders literally, will be insufficient to refute us; no more than the Scriptural passages, from which it might appear that God has eyes, ears, etc., but which reason and reflection show us in the proper light, agreeably to the maxim of the Rabbins, namely, "Holy Writ has employed human language, because it was intended for human understanding." But so wise a conclusion would not be consonant with the ideas imbued by the individuals above referred to, so that while we regard simply as a metaphor, whatever has been said materially of angels and of the life after death, they, on the contrary, accept to the very letter; maintaining withal that the knowledge of the existence of both, could have been derived from no other source than the Bible, and as in it they are represented in a material garb, they must needs consist of materiality.

From this false position have they started, who conceive they have dived into sublime truths, in one moment, without serious meditation and deep researches, and with no other escort than the outward construction of the sacred pages, as if our instructor had not explicitly said, that the law has an open and a hidden meaning, or as if they had not alluded in the least to this "hidden meaning," which the unenlightened totally reject. As to ourselves, we have offered to the world, upon these subjects, in the "Teacher of the Perplexed," what will convince the intelligent; strengthening our arguments with the opinions of our Sages and by the quotation of their own words.

However, when our productions found circulation in various countries, we were apprised of the fact that a certain scholar from Damascus asserted, that there will not be a resurrection of the dead, for the soul cannot return into the body after it was severed from it. Having been called to task by his colleagues, he attempted to prove that we taught so, in stating that our final destination is a spiritual existence after our decease. The others then remarked that the instruction of the Rabbis as well as the universal belief in Israel belied him, and he rejoined, that it is all allegorical. This incident was reported to us, but we remained silent, deeming it a rare case of a misconstruction of that which we have clearly written.

But in the year 1500 of the Grecian era, we received a letter from the southern countries, the purport of which was to inform us that several individuals had arrived at the conclusion that the body will dissolve and never more be reunited with the soul, fastening that opinion on our expressions touching the world-to-come. And as the well known sayings of the Rabbins and some sentences of the Prophets were brought forward in refutation of their avowal, they retorted, that they are mere allegories capable of a different exposition. We were therefore earnestly requested to give a reply, inasmuch as that opinion was spreading fast in those climes, and nothing to the contrary would be heeded.

The reply we gave was, that the resurrection of the dead is a cardinal point of our religion, to wit, the reunion of the body with the soul, which cannot admit of any other interpretation, and that the world to come will succeed it, as we had stated in the chapter חלק, and added no more, thinking we had said enough. But again two years later, sundry of our friends wrote to us from Babylon, that a Hebrew from the southern countries had questioned upon the same theme, the chief of the College, R. Samuel Hallevi, lately invested with ecclesiastical authority in Bagdad, and he had composed a treatise upon the resurrection of the dead, wherein he represented our opinions partly as erroneous, and partly as justifiable, endeavoring himself to use his pen in our defence. Subsequently to the receipt of that intelligence the treatise itself was forwarded to us; and there we read a collection of legends and figurative expressions of the Rabbins, which every one knows ought to be explained in a manner consistent with human reason, and not to the letter. And that which to us seems surprising among the startling sentiments he advances concerning the soul, is that he prefers them as the opinion of philosophers, thus proving at once that he honors with that appellation every idle talker. And yet there is something even more wonderful in that all-wonderful production, namely: his declaring that philosophers do not judge it incompatible with reason, that the soul should be reunited to the body; by which he again displays his ignorance of the distinction that philosophers draw between the real, the improbable and the probable. He likewise introduces a portion of a discourse on future reward by Aben

Sina, which he refutes philosophically. The same learned author moreover gives as his decision, that philosophers do not admit the immortality of the soul, because they dispute about it, but we wonder whom he styles such.

Something also has excited our astonishment, in that treatise, and that is, that the mind is never mentioned in it, so that we are at a loss to discover, whether he means that the mind and the soul are precisely the same, or whether the former is to perish and the latter to last, or vice versa, for he certainly affirms that philosophers do not acknowledge a separate existence of the soul, but one of their notions is that it is perfectly identical with the blood. Perchance he conceives that the mind is a mere property of the body and if thus has been decided by those whom he calls philosophers, then our spirit must surely perish. Verily, it would have been more in accordance with the mind of the sapient writer to have confined himself to the collection of Rabbinical legends and tales, and to the exposition of passages which he interprets as a demonstration that the dogma of the resurrection of the dead has been plainly spoken of in the books of Moses. In fine, whatever was stated by R. Samuel Hallevi has been, either in full, or in part, already said before him, and it is not our purpose to confute or even quote him, only necessity constrained us to mention as much as we have, prior to our entering into our explanation: the aim of which is to benefit the reflecting student and not self-aggrandizement; for, we leave controversies and disputations to whomsoever likes them. And may the help of God be with us in this undertaking and in all others.

Let the intelligent reader know that our object in the present discourse is to explain what we believe touching an essential tenet of our religion, which has given rise to controversy among scholars; viz., the resurrection of the dead. We shall not advance in it new ideas, for that cannot be expected, but will repeat at some length what we have propounded in our commentary to the Mishna, in a manner adapted to the untutored.

To commence: we would premise that the dogma of the resurrection of the dead,—universally acknowledged by our people; incorporated in our usual prayers, (composed by wise and inspired men,) and to which the Talmud frequently reverts,—is capable of no other signification than the literal. It would therefore be un-Jewish to disbelieve that the soul will be reunited with the body, for there has been no dissenting voice raised against it among our nation. We will now proceed to show why we do not interpret some biblical passage relative to it in an allegorical sense, as we are wont in other cases.

The resurrection of the dead or the reunion of the soul with the body is mentioned in Daniel, couched in such words that it is impossible to render them otherwise than according to the very letter. "And many of those that sleep in the dust of the earth shall awake," and the Angel who spoke concluded, "As for thyself, go to thy final destination, there thou shalt rest and stand up again for thy allotted portion at the end of days." Whosoever, then, accuses us of having said that the scriptural passage is figurative, has uttered a flagrant falsehood. Our productions have already been published; let the reader point out where we have stated so, unless we have been misunderstood, when we wrote that the resuscitated bodies referred to in the book of Ezekiel, might be a parable, for the reason that a question to that effect has been mooted among the Talmudists; adding that on a point concerning which the Rabbins differ,—if it does not imply the performance of a divine precept,—it is immaterial which of their opinions we accept. This we repeated in our commentary on the Mishna. But to return to the main topic.

The expressions of our Sages allow free scope to our assumption that the bodies restored to life will eat, drink, generate and die after a prolonged existence, as at the time of the Messiah, but that the life which is not destined to end, is that in which the spirit will not be confined in bodily tenements. This truth is obvious to the mind of every intelligent person, I mean that in the world to come, we must be incorporeal as angelic beings, for he comprehends how the body ministers to the soul, and is directed in all its operations,—wherefore has nature supplied it with the means of its own preservation by endowing it with diverse organs; with those of nutrition, as the mouth, the stomach, the liver and intestines; with those of procreation, and with the others which complete the corporeal construction, such as the senses, the arteries, the bones, the ligaments &c., whereby the living being is enabled to go in quest of his food and of whatever is calculated to benefit him, and flee from its opposite. But as the furnishing of his aliment demands the knowledge of several arts and of arrangements that can only be the effect of thought and memory, man has been gifted with those faculties. He is besides possessed of hands and feet, which, in a great measure, become subservient to the same purpose. However, all further details on this topic concern the physiologists; we merely sought to illustrate how the whole system of the human frame tends to the satisfaction of its necessities and the propagation of the race.

It thence follows that when that object is no longer to be attained, the existence of the body is rendered useless. And so it would be indeed after our decease in the world to come, when, as our Rabbins teach, "neither eating nor drinking nor any of the functions by which the animal economy is carried on will be needed." For to suppose the existence of a body in such a state, would be tantamount to saying that the actions of the Most Wise are like those of the heathen, who fashion their idols with eyes that cannot see, with ears that cannot hear, and nose that cannot smell. Aye, we would harbour an irreverent thought, if we deemed it possible that he should give us limbs unnecessarily.

It might be presumed that our opponents do not exactly mean that the participants of the future life are framed with limbs, but that they are nevertheless bodies, either in a spherical, in a conical, or an equilateral form, but really the idea is so ludicrous that the following verse of Job may well be applied to its supporters, "Oh that ye would altogether hold your peace, for that would be your wisdom!!" We have demonstrated above that the source whence this stupendous error proceeds is the incapacity of the ignorant to conceive the notion of existence distinct from matter, for whatever is not a body or a property thereof, is with them a nonentity; and on the contrary whenever they wish to exhibit a subject with more force, they materialize it to a very high degree. We have without demur dwelt on this fact in our "Teacher of the Perplexed," and are perfectly satisfied to bear the reproach of those who lay it as a charge against us, for as we wrote in the same work, if only one endowed with a bright intellect accepts our definition of sublime truths, we heed not the thousands that refuse us a hearing.

Still, what we deny and declare ourselves innocent of before God is our disbelief in the resurrection, or the reunion of the soul with the body, and our having said that a want of faith in that dogma would not be conducive to the rejection of other miracles chronicled in the law, for we do consider it in that light, and regard the resurrection of the dead as a cardinal point of our religion, concerning which we never expressed a doubt in all our writings. Let him now who chooses to slander us by perverting our meaning be judged by the Almighty with the severity due to the wicked who accuse the guiltless. No one can possibly be misled by our words and infer therefrom that all the biblical verses allusive to a resurrection are figurative, because we have unequivocally stated that while several are evidently so, and others are of an uncertain interpretation, yet the one from the book of Daniel is positively literal, as the whole context shows, and as learned men and expositors among the Andalusians have instructed us. And even should that passage stand alone in support of the dogma, it would by no means invalidate it, for religious truths gain nothing by frequent repetitions, and lose nothing by a rare or solitary mention. Every Jew is aware that the Unity of God was taught us by two words which occur but once in the law "Adonai Echad, The Eternal is One." Suffice it then to know that the sentence of the inspired writer admits but one signification, and that is, the return of the soul into the body. Now, were the word "reviving" wherever it happens in Holy Writ, capable of being construed as an allusion to the resurrection, or were we to think that all other sentences, save the one in Daniel, are allegories, it would be entirely immaterial.

In short, the prophetical imparting of the resurrection is met with once or more; it has been referred to innumerable times by the wise men of Israel both ancient and modern; it has spread among our people, and has been universally acknowledged by them. It matters not therefore, if scholars or authors ignore it altogether. Some individuals, however, have been deceived by the following words which we penned towards the close of our extensive work: "Do not imagine that the King Messiah must perform extraordinary signs and wonders, alter the course of nature, *revive the dead*, etc., for it is not so," illustrating at the same time our assertion. The weakminded thought that a denial of the resurrection, and a flat contradiction of what we had stated elsewhere. But, verily, there is no contradiction; we simply explained that the Messiah will not be asked to prove his mission by dividing the sea, or reviving the dead, since the prophets whose predictions have, in other respects, been verified, have foretold his advent. But that does not imply that the Almighty will not cause the resurrection whenever He wills, and on behalf of whomsoever He wills, either at the time of the Messiah, or after his demise. In fine, there is nought in our productions that can be misunderstood except by mere tyros.

We have also been censured for having written that when Isaiah speaks of the wolf dwelling with the lamb, he employs a rhetorical figure; but that has not been said only by us, for our predecessors who labored in the field of literature, such as R. Moses Gaetela, Aben Bilaam and others have formed the same judgment; as it is corroborated by the conclusion of the subject, "They shall not hurt nor destroy in all my holy mountain, for the earth shall be full of the knowledge of the Lord." Here the reason is given why they shall no longer injure or devastate; namely, because they shall know the Lord. Is there an Israelite with a sane mind that pictures to himself the lion, which now tears and devours, impressed at a future period with the knowledge of the Supreme, which will impel him to feed on straw, and not upon the lacerated flesh of his victims? If so, it would be actually the realization of another prophecy, "The whole vision was to them like the words of a sealed book."

But we have already reverted to this topic in the "Teacher of the

Perplexed," and in our extensive work we substantiated our position by the dictum of the Rabbins, that the Messianic era will not differ in the divine economy of the world from our own. Still we dare not offer our opinion touching the language used by the prophets in this and other cases, as an incontrovertible decision; for we have not received a celestial communication to that effect, nor has it been so handed down by our wise ancestors; only we would remark in connection with this matter, that our aim and that of a few others is greatly at variance with that of the commonalty. They place the law of God and human reason far apart from each other, and transfigure every thing incomprehensible to them from its natural aspect into a supernatural one, attaching an extraordinary importance to whatever is recorded of the past, to that which is discernible at the present time, and to what will happen in future. We, on the contrary, strive to reconcile the law of God with the human reason, and regard every thing in its natural light, unless it bears within itself the evidence of its miraculous production. On other occasions, we have dwelt alike on Biblical and Rabbinical expressions, not less than on the parables used by the Prophets, and so minutely expounded by them, that no one but an ignoramus can refuse recognising therein a figurative character, as represented by us and sundry eminent commentators.

With regard to the passage under discussion, we might, if we wish to divest it of its allegorical garb, argue like Aristotle, when he reasons why in Egypt animals do not destroy each other to the same extent as in other countries, that proportionately as the world will be more thickly populated, ferocious beasts will become more easily tamed and subserve man's purposes. Or it might be a sheer hyperbole in which inspired writers occasionally indulge. Or even if it is strictly literal, it will be a wonder exhibited solely in Jerusalem, as we read in "all my holy mountain," agreeably to what our Sages recount touching the absence of noisome reptiles in that sacred city in the days of yore. In short, this is not a cardinal point of our religion, and every one may adopt the opinions most consonant with his reason; provided he believes in the restoration itself—which God may soon bring to pass—for it is then that we shall learn the definite sense of the prediction.

As for ourselves, we are averse to admit an inversion of the order of nature, and allow those to believe it, who ever they may be, who are unable to discriminate between marvelous events, which happened because indispensable in the dealings of the Lord with his redeemed people, or because necessary to accredit a prophet, and the sublunary occurrences, fixed by the law of the Creator, which continue unaltered.

Thus have written our Sages "The world proceeds in a regular manner," and on other occasions "Miracles serve not as a criterion." Influenced by the same idea, Solomon declared that "whatsoever God doeth shall be for ever; nothing can be put to it, nor anything taken from it." It is, then, proved that natural incidents follow an even course precisely as we explained in our "Teacher of the Perplexed," when speaking of the creation.

But what may, in all likelihood, have led men to misjudge us, is the fact that while we dilate on the dogma of immortality, offering appropriate illustrations alike from Scriptural and Rabbinical authorities, we are, on the contrary, very brief when alluding to the resurrection, and content ourselves with the mere assertion that it is an essential creed of our religion. But our motive for pursuing that course is twofold. Firstly: that we have in all our productions determined to be as comprehensive as the subject can permit, in order to avoid crowding our pages with foreign matter; wherefore we generally epitomize and explain only what absolutely requires elucidation in a concise diction. Secondly: that one's design in descanting on any point must be either to exhibit to view all its various features, or to prove it incontestably true. This, however, can be the aim of an author, when he treats of sciences, such as theology, natural philosophy and metaphysics, for oftentimes they are presented to the mind in a form so obscure that only by the aid of a lengthy dissertation can some light be shed thereupon. But that which partakes of the supernatural, cannot be placed in the same category, for what has happened miraculously, or what will come to pass according to divine promise, cannot be proved true by human ratiocination. It must fall under our own senses, or it must be credited because related by reliable witnesses. Therefore, we expatiate on our future existence in order that the intellect may obviously discover how immortality is a direct consequence of the essence of the soul, but are brief touching the resurrection of the dead, because it demands no explanation at our hands. It is faith and not reason that can persuade us that it will occur, just as we have learned with certainty that other miracles have been performed in our behalf. But as it does not appertain to the natural, no proof can be advanced in support thereof. How then could it be expected that we should have discussed at large? Are we to devote our time in commenting on the legends and tales, which were written about that looked-for event? It may suit others so to do, but not ourselves who have invariably avoided launching into polemics. Verily, could we condense the whole Talmud in a single chapter, we would not give it room in two. Hence it is vain to ask of us to introduce in our works all which has been said in parables by our predecessors. A repetition of them would be of no utility: let those who are anxious to be instructed thereby, seek them in their respective places. But we apprehend that our discourse has been hitherto uninteresting, for it contains the identical statements which we have made in our exposition of the Mishna, in our extensive work. Therefore, in order that it may not prove altogether void of instruction, we purpose elucidating two points connected with it. The first is, the difficulty we encounter in sundry passages of Holy Writ, which are in open antagonism to the dogma of resurrection; for instance "Shall a man die and live again?" (Job 14.14) "As the cloud is consumed and vanishes away, so he that goeth down to the grave shall come up no more" (Idem. 7.9.) "Before I go whence I shall not return" (Idem. 10.21.) besides other numerous sentences in the same book. So also did king Hezekiah exclaim "They that go down into the pit cannot hope for Thy truth; but the living, the living, they shall praise Thee" (Isaiah 38.18.19.), thus demonstrating that "they who go down into the pit" are for ever dead. In the same spirit can only be understood the following speech of the wise woman of Tekoah: "For we must needs die, and become as water spilt on the ground which cannot be gathered up again." (2d Samuel 14. 14.). So we find likewise "Shall the dead arise and praise Thee?" (Psalms 88. 11.) "For He remembered that they were but flesh, a wind that passeth and cometh not again." (Idem 78. 79.). And in general when we accurately peruse the Bible, we discover that it abounds with passages that gainsay the resurrection of the dead. We must, however, except a few in Isaiah, which are capable also of a figurative interpretation, and the two registered in the book of Daniel, to wit: "And many of those that sleep in the dust of the earth shall awake." "As for thyself, go to thy final destination, there thou shalt rest, but stand up again for thy allotted portion at the end of days."

So it has happened that those contradictions with which Holy Writ is fraught touching the resurrection, gave rise to a great deal of controversy. Some have altogether doubted the veracity of the dogma, and others who faithfully believed in it were compelled to strain the sense of the verses aforecited.

The second point which we intend to explain is why the Pentateuch does not in plain terms refer to the resurrection,—for we cannot accept as an evidence thereof the faint allusions which some presume to have discovered in those holy volumes, since the Rabbins differ as to their correct signification. When it concerns a subject of such magnitude, the language should be sufficiently comprehensible and not enigmatic, like that of one who wishes to conceal his own ideas. In solving the first query, we would remark that the inspired writings are simply the exponent of the laws which nature has ordained, namely; that the connection of the sexes must produce young of their various species, which will also gradually attain a full size and strength, and then decay and nevermore be reconstructed, but dissolve into the different elements of which they are formed. That this decomposition of material substances will be slow, but nevertheless so certain that in the lapse of time not one part will be distinguished from the other; but that man in whom God Himself breathed a heavenly spirit must needs survive the consumption of his body. Such is the gist of the passages above quoted, which coincides in toto with the decision of those who have deeply searched into this momentous topic. Moreover, the sacred pages afford a palpable demonstration of our argument by placing the soul, or the spirit in juxtaposition of the body, as we read in Ecclesiastes "The dust shall return to the earth, as it was, but the spirit shall return unto God who gave it." So that humanly speaking, the question of Job "whether a man that dieth can live again" is not any more startling than that of Moses, when he wrathfully exclaimed "Shall we draw water for you out of this rock?" both the occurrences being *naturally* beyond the range of possibility. Still through a miracle the water did issue out of the rock, so will also the dead revive by the same marvelous agency. In like manner, there exists no difference between Jeremiah's inquiry, "whether an Ethiopian can ever change his swarthy skin," and the ejaculation of the Psalmist "Will the dead arise and praise Thee?" Yet in a miraculous manner did once a purely healthy hand assume a snowy white colour. Furthermore, if one should assert that an inanimate object is not endowed with the power of motion, he would utter what is true in accordance with the order of nature, but it would not invalidate the fact, that a wand in the hand of the ancient Seer was converted into a living serpent; because that was a wonder; hence we maintain that whenever Biblical expressions are in opposition to the dogma of resurrection, they simply describe natural causes and effects; and do not by any means subvert a creed universally accepted, because the Almighty can, at his will, infuse new life into the dead bodies. This appears to us the most logical conclusion to be arrived at in scanning the Scriptural passages under discussion; so that we need not adopt the far-fetched rendering of some who imagined to uphold thereby the dogma of resurrection, but have on the contrary, supplied its opponents with arms to combat it. But let us now see for what reasons will the latter reject it. Is it because the laws of nature would in that case be inverted? Why, are not the miracles recorded in the holy volumes so many instances of the same kind? Or is it because they have failed in meeting with a sentence which in a plain, unequivocal manner states that the dead bodies will resuscitate, as it is with the passages which contain the narrative of marvelous occurrences? Well, they must then give a satisfactory explanation to the two verses in Daniel, which are doubtless the groundwork of the creed. And should they succeed in persuading themselves that they admit of a meaning consonant with the order of nature, it would only show their disbelief in the Bible, for as we have observed in the "Teacher of the Perplexed," the truth that the Almighty Being brought forth the universe out of uncreated matter, is a sufficient evidence of His ability to alter nature at his will, and consequently of the authenticity of miracles. Wherefore we are not at all justified in supposing that the words of the prophet which are so very explicit, bear a hidden sense, notwithstanding that we are forced to do so, when the Deity is represented in a corporeal form.

However, there may be some who agree that a resurrection will take place, but deny the reunion of *body* and soul, inasmuch as the occurrence is inconceivable to the human mind; but then they must needs for the same reason, reject all the miracles chronicled in Holy Writ, by which they would place themselves beyond the pale of Judaism. For whosoever believes that God has created the world out of nothing, must concede the possibility of miracles, and surely no one can style himself a follower of Abraham and Moses who doubts that verity. Resting upon the solidity of this argument, we have numbered the resurrection of the dead among the essential creeds of our religion, and chosen the two verses in the last chapter of Daniel, as the basis of that dogma, because they cannot be understood but in that sense.

We will now proceed with the solution of the second query we have started, namely; why the dogma of resurrection is not mentioned in the Pentateuch. It is universally known that the law to which we adhere is a direct inspiration from the Almighty, and not the offspring of the mind of Moses; we are, therefore, impelled reverently to seek for the motive which actuated its wise Author in alluding to the immortality of the soul, and remaining perfectly silent respecting the resurrection. We have already explained that the resuscitation of dead bodies can only be the effect of a miracle, and not of natural causes; ergo, the knowledge of that extraordinary event can be derived but from a prophet. Now, at the period in which the law was promulgated, mankind were mostly Sabeans—a sect who believed that the world never had a beginning, and who identified the Supreme with the motion of the heavenly bodies.—The false notions which they entertained led directly to a denial of prophecy and of all miracles, which they attributed to the possession of a neoromantic power. Thus we perceive the Egyptians offering an attempt to belie the mission of Moses, by resorting to enchantments, with a view of imitating his stupendous deeds. Thus we likewise hear the Hebrews themselves exclaim, "This day have we seen that God doth speak to man while he liveth," acknowledging thereby that prophecy was before that time incredible to them. Such being the case, how could the law impart a dogma, which demands as a pre-requisite for its acceptance an implicit reliance on the words of a prophet, to men whose mind was unprepared to admit prophecy itself? They who believe that the world has ever existed, must reject altogether the possibility of miracles, and a non-admission of the latter implies also a denial of the resurrection. Consequently, when it pleased the Most High to reveal His law to man, and by the medium of prophets to disseminate the knowledge of His existence and His tenets, throughout the habitable globe, He had recourse to the marvelous acts recorded in the Pentateuch, in order to accredit by them His righteous messengers, and instill the belief that the creation has emanated from Him "who spoke and it was"; for as we have illustrated in the "Teacher of the Perplexed" a true miracle is the strongest testimony to corroborate the universally known verity, that the world was created out-of nothing.

But the divine Legislator did not carry his instructions beyond what concerns this terrestrial existence (to which he assigned a reward and punishment) and what is a logical deduction, viz., the immortality of the soul, or its perdition, as expressed by the term "Karet."

And so it was His gracious will to continue, until, after the lapse of ages, those fundamental principles of religion had struck deep root in the minds of men, and removed every misgiving touching prophecy and its concomitant truth—the performance of miracles. When *that* was accomplished, the Lord inspired his servants to foretell the resurrection of the dead, for the acceptation of which mortal beings had become qualified by the knowledge previously imbibed. This we regard to be in perfect consonance with the ways of Providence, for it is obviously illustrated by the fact, that the Redeemer of Israel, thought it advisable to guide His liberated people through an indirect path at their exit from Egypt, to avoid the encounter of a Philistine army, which might awe them back to the land of servitude. If on that occasion, the precaution used was urged by the apprehension of failing in the work of deliverance, on the other, it was demanded by the inaptitude of the mind to receive an incomprehensible notion; that is, the resurrection of the dead. Centuries had, therefore, to elapse ere Israel could become the repository of all truths. It is well known that the individuals to whom the Almighty delivered His law were impressed with very erroneous ideas, so much so that towards the expiration of forty years, their leader said, "The Lord hath not given you a heart to perceive, nor eyes to see, nor ears to hear unto this day." He that "searcheth the reins" understood how repugnant would have been yet to them the belief in the resurrection, and forebore communicating it. Moreover, if they had been then told that a requital of their doings upon earth, would be meted out to them at a period exceedingly distant, their proneness to sin might have remained uncurbed; but as, on the contrary, they were admonished and promised a speedy recompense according to their deserts, they were deterred from vice and incited to virtue. And here we may opportunely remark that this wise ordination of a reward and punishment following closely one's conduct in this terrestrial career, is best calculated to maintain it in the right balance. Certain it is, that the execution of this divine fiat, has always been discernible in the Jewish nation: they flourished when they observed the law, and they were brought low when they swerved from it; precisely in accordance with the denunciatory words of Moses, "these curses shall be as a token and as a wonderful sign in thee and in thy seed for ever, because thou hast not served the Lord thy God." To carry out the same view, our Sages have declared "Israel are not under the influence of the constellations," meaning that their happiness and their tribulations must not be ascribed to natural causes, but to a peculiar watching of Providence in connection with their obedience or disobedience with His Torah. This is really the greatest of all wonders, for, as we have elucidated elsewhere, it is exemplified alike nationally and individually. Most appropriately was therefore written "they shall be as a token and a wonderful sign in thee and in thy seed." Our Rabbins have evinced their full comprehension of this sentence, when they recommended "If trials come upon man, let him scrutinize his action. But in addition to the above, Holy Writ contains another passage, which obviously conveys the same idea, to wit "Lest thou lift up thine eyes unto heaven, and when thou seest the sun, and the moon and the stars, even all the host of heaven—*which the Lord thy God hath set apart for all the nations under the whole heaven,* thou shouldst be driven to worship and serve them. For, as to yourselves, the Lord hath taken you and brought you forth out of the iron furnace, even out of Egypt, to be unto Him a people of inheritance, as ye are this day," purporting to signify that while in His government of the world, Providence allows certain natural laws to work out His design either in favor or against nations; in His guidance of Israel, He demonstrates how He awards a condign retribution to their conduct, in an extraordinary manner.

As we have finished offering our views upon the two objections that might be advanced respecting the dogma of the resurrection, we purpose now speaking of a subject, which commends itself, more than all which has been said above, to the serious reflection of our readers. We would then say, that miracles vary in their character. Some are an entire inversion of the laws of nature, as for instance, the transformation of the rod of Moses into a living serpent; the sudden disruption of the earth which swallowed Korah and his followers, and the division of the Red Sea. Others again display themselves in a manner consistent with those fixed laws, for example: the devastation caused in the land of Egypt by the locust, by the hail, and the pestilence; for, the same occurrences may happen at different times, in diverse places. In this category we would also enumerate the rending of the altar constructed by Jeroboam, at the bidding of the prophet. As we read (I. Kings, 13. 3.) "This is the sign of which the Lord spoke; behold! the altar shall be rent, and the ashes that are upon it shall be poured out," because, it is not extraordinary that a building may break down, particularly so, when newly erected. Likewise, the inundating rain that fell at the harvest season through the prayer of Samuel, and the blessings and curses pronounced in the Torah as a reward or punishment, might be brought under the same head; for, each of those events may be experienced in any country, at any period of the year, ergo, they are within the range of probability. However, these very incidents which assume the aspect of natural issues, attest their wonderful emanation, by exhibiting either one or all of the three following peculiar features. Firstly: By being produced just at the time appointed by the prophet, as it is chronicled, that Samuel declared he would bring down rain and occasion thunders at his invocation, and no sooner had he besought the Eternal, than the rain descended, and the thunders were heard. Equally wondrous was the deed performed by the man of God, who came from Judah. Jeroboam deemed his prediction a vain threat, but scarcely had he ordered the arrest of the Seer, than it was literally verified; "The altar was rent, and the ashes poured out from it." Secondly: By appearing in a guise unparalleled in history: as the locust, concerning which we are informed, that never before or after did any of that species prove so terribly destructive. And as for the hail, we read that since Egypt had become a nation, so severe an infliction had not been suffered. Touching the pestilence, the distinguishing feature consisted in leaving the cattle of Israel totally uninjured. Thirdly: By the protraction and renewal thereof; as the blessings and curses recorded in the Pentateuch, for, had they befallen our nation only once, they might be attributed to mere chance, but when they can be discerned at all times and under all circumstances, they must convince every mind of their preternatural origin. Wherefore does Holy Writ express itself as follows: "If ye will walk with me by *casualty*, then I will also walk with you in anger through that *casualty*"; (Leviticus xxvi. 27. 28.) purporting to signify that if we regarded those tribulations as fortuitous occurrences, and not as a condign requital of our evil doings, the Almighty would then suffer the same calamities to continue upon us, as a chastisement for refusing to acknowledge in them a divine judgment.

But while the miracles accomplished by means of nature's established ordinances, will endure an indefinite time and be also reiterated, those which appertain altogether to the supernatural, can neither last nor be frequently repeated; for in that case they might awaken a doubt as to their true emanation; thus, by way of example: if the rod of Moses had remained a serpent, we might have suspected its having been so always, and by pure delusion having appeared once otherwise; consequently the miracle was proved genuine only when the serpent became again in the hand of the man of God a simple rod. Thus likewise, if the earth which opened itself to engulf the seditious Korah and his adherents had left its chasm continually visible, the miracle would have been incomplete and doubtful, but when it was closed so as to leave no perceptible trace of its disruption, the reality of the wonder was rendered obvious to all. The same argument will hold good touching the division of the Red Sea. That portentous event was perfected when, "toward the morn the sea resumed its course." The reasons hitherto adduced show us as a fact that a miracle inverting the order of nature, cannot be protracted, and that, on the contrary, the one which is performed through a natural medium, will be more strongly substantiated the longer it continues. We therefore firmly believe the blessings and the curses pronounced in the law are a mighty wonder, by which the Eternal rewards Israel's obedience, and punishes their dereliction. Let no one now ask why we have been promised so explicitly that compensation, and not the resurrection of our bodies, or the immortality of our souls. We have already demonstrated herein the wisdom of God in acting thus, besides which there may exist motives which our finite understanding is unable to comprehend. Such queries, after all, can never be entirely solved, no more than if one should inquire of us, why among the marvelous deeds achieved by Moses, a stone was not converted into a lion; for, we cannot fathom the designs of the Omnipotent in the smallest degree.

In conclusion, we would request our learned readers not to criticize our present discourse, either because of its unnecessary length, or on account of the repetition of the same idea; for, we have composed it solely to disabuse the mind of the untutored, who misconstrued our words, and satisfy those who had noticed the brevity wherewith we treated the dogma of resurrection.

We are perfectly aware that mere hints suffice the intelligent, and that without frequently reverting to the same ideas, or expatiating thereon, a few cursory strictures supply the wise with a light through which they will search and discover grand truths. Such is, in fact, the plan we followed in writing our "Teacher of the Perplexed" conformably with the axiom of our Sages "a wise man requires neither elucidations nor repetitions." To that, we would add the adage of King Solomon, "Give (little) to the wise, and he will grow wiser." However, the commonalty require both lengthy argumentations and repetitions, "a rule upon a rule," "a line upon a line," and by that means they acquire the ability of understanding "here a little and there a little." Consequently we have deemed it needful to suit our language to the mind of our various readers.

May the Almighty, for the sake of His mercy, direct our sayings and our actions, that we may eschew sin and error now and evermore.

NAḤMANIDES, *SHA'AR HA-GEMUL*

Translation by Eugene B. Korn

How precious are the words of the great Master, Rabbi Moses, of blessed memory, who wrote in [his commentaries to] chapter *Helek* concerning this world in words which are both brief and comprehensive. He said,[1] "In the World-to-Come our souls will comprehend the mysteries of the Creator in the same way that the angels and the spheres comprehend those mysteries or in an even greater measure. Thus our Rabbis said, 'In the World-to-Come there is neither eating nor drinking. Rather, the righteous sit with crowns upon their heads and derive enjoyment from the splendor of the Divine Presence.' 'Crowns upon their heads,' denotes the existence of the intelligent soul through the existence of the object of knowledge. The two are a single entity as philosophers who understand the matter have stated. When they say, 'derive enjoyment from the splendor of the Divine Presence,' they mean that these souls receive enjoyment from what they comprehend and know of the mystery of God. Therefore, the greatest recompense and the ultimate end is for men to reach this highest reward and to be included in this category. The existence of the soul, as we have stated, will be eternal by virtue of the existence of the Creator, may He be blessed, for He is the cause of the soul's existence by virtue of the soul's comprehension of Him." These are the words of the master, and they are words of purity.

All these statements have already appeared in the words of the Sages, of blessed memory. [The Master] has mentioned the pleasure of the soul during its continued existence and has categorized it as comparable to that of the angels and holy beings, just as the Sages have said that [the soul] is placed beneath the Throne of Glory . . . . They have also mentioned that the soul exists by virtue of the existence of the object of its knowledge and that the soul and [the objects of its knowledge] are a single entity. This is the explanation of what is said in the Torah: "You shall cleave unto Him."[2] [Scripture] also says, "The soul of my master will be bound up in the bond of life with the Lord, Your God." . . .[3] Our Rabbis understood and explained this matter of unification. [This does not mean] that man can achieve knowledge of the essence of God, for knowledge itself constitutes unification. Regarding this they stated, "All of the prophets prophesied only with regard to the days of the Messiah.

However, [with regard to] the World-to-Come no eye has seen it, O God, besides You."[4] The Master quotes this dictum and explains, "The Sages have made known to us that man does not have the ability to comprehend properly the goodness of the World-to-Come and cannot know its greatness and beauty. [This can be comprehended] only by the Holy One, blessed be He."[5] These statements of the Master concerning the World-to-Come and its enjoyment are correct statements. We can agree with them and praise their virtues to their author, of blessed memory.

In response to a question he wrote further, "Greek and Arabic scholars have concluded that the soul is form without matter and without body. Rather it is pure and radiant and the source of knowledge, without need of a body. Therefore, when the body is destroyed, the soul is not destroyed, but exists by itself and endures, as do angels. It derives enjoyment from, and perceives by means of, the light of the world, which is the World-to-Come." These are all his words.

Nevertheless, he has changed the order of tradition for he has made out this world to be the world of the souls in which the body has no part, as he has explained in many places in his books. Similarly, it appears from his statements that he has changed the epoch of the World-to-Come. According to his opinion, it comes to man immediately after death. [The existence after death] is the enjoyment and pleasure that we have referred to as the Garden of Eden. Thus he writes in the Book of Knowledge:[6] "That which the Sages refer to as the World to Come, is not referred to in this way because it does not exist at present or that this world will be destroyed and afterwards that World will come into being. This is not the case. Rather, [the World-to-Come] exists [at present], as it is written, 'How abundant is Your goodness which You have laid up for those that fear You.'[7] They called it the World-to-Come only because it is that life which comes to man after life in this world, in which we exist with body and soul. It [i.e. the World-to-Come] is the first existence which comes to all men [subsequent to death]." It deems from these statements that the World-to-Come is the world of the souls which comes immediately after the death of the body.

He writes further:[8] "There is no body or material substance in the World-to-Come, but only the souls of the righteous without bodies, like the ministering angels. Since there are no bodies there, there is neither eating nor drinking nor any physical thing which the bodies of men require in this world. Nor does there occur in [the World-to-Come] any of the things which occur to the body in this world, e.g., sitting, standing, sleeping, seeing, pain, laughter, and the like. Thus the early Sages stated, 'In the World-to-Come, there is neither eating, nor drinking, nor sexual intercourse. Rather the righteous are seated with crowns upon their heads and they derive enjoyment from the splendor of the Divine Presence.'" It has thus been made clear to you that there is no body since there is no eating or drinking. When they say, "the righteous are seated," it is a metaphor meaning that the souls of the righteous are present there without any physical exertion or toil. Similarly, when they say, "with crowns upon their heads" they mean that the knowledge which the righteous acquire by virtue of which they merit the World-to-Come remains with them and it is their crown. What do they mean when they say, "they derive enjoyment from the splendor of the Divine Presence?" [They mean] that they know and grasp the true nature of the Holy One, blessed be He, which they did not know while they had dark and lowly bodies. . .

One may wonder why he found it necessary to adduce so many proofs and demonstrations showing that in the World-to-Come there are no bodies but only souls, since he believed that the World-to-Come is the place of man's existence immediately after death. The youngest Jewish student knows that when a righteous person dies "his soul abides in prosperity,"[9] in the goodness of the higher world without any matter or body whatsoever. Its good does not consist of eating, drinking, annointing, or sexual activity, for these pleasures do not pertain to the soul, but rather the soul is preserved only by virtue of the splendor of the Divine Presence as it is said, "Your righteousness shall go before you and the splendor of the Lord shall be gathered unto you."[10]

Even though the hidden meaning of these matters is known only to an elite few and only the Lord, may He be blessed, is able to understand their full truth, their plain meaning is known to all. Why, then, did the Master feel the need to write the following in his *Essay on the Resurrection of the Dead?*: "The life following which there is no death is life in the World-to-Come, because there is therein no body. For we believe, and it is correct according to all men of knowledge, that the inhabitants of the World-to-Come are souls without bodies, like angels. The proof of this is that the body is composed of organs which function for the activity of the soul. In general, the necessity for the existence of the body is for one end, namely the eating of food in order to sustain the body and to procreate a similar body so that the species be preserved. The Sages intend to say that when this end is removed and there is no need for [the body] in the World-to-Come—as the multitude of Sages have stated in explaining that there is neither eating nor drinking nor sexual activity in [the World-to-Come]—there is [then] no body in [the

World-to-Come]. For God, may He be blessed, does not create a useless object. He makes entities only for the sake of some purpose. Heaven forbid that His true works be as the working of [the] idol-worshippers: "They have eyes but do not see; ears but do not hear."[11] So the Creator, in the eyes of those who think in this manner, creates limbs for no function. Perhaps, according to these people, the inhabitants of the World-to-Come possess no limbs but only bodies. Perhaps they are circular [bodies] or pillars or rectangular in stature. The opinion of these fools is but the object of derision among all nations. Would that they hold their silence and it would be wisdom for them."[12] All these are the statements of the Master, of blessed memory, and many more statements are added to them.

Now, since he believes that the explanation of the World-to-Come is that it is the World-to-Come for souls immediately after the death of the body, one may wonder why he needs these arguments. It is known by all that after the soul is stripped from the body of a dead person, the body is left to decay. Scripture testifies to this: "The dust returns to the earth as it was, and the spirit returns to God who gave it."[13] However, it appears that the intention of the Master, of blessed memory, is that according to him, the [term] "World-to-Come" is used to denote all the worlds of the souls and all that occurs to [the souls] throughout all of eternity. Indeed [the Master] truly believes that the meaning of resurrection of the dead, which is a fundamental axiom of the Torah, is that the soul will return to its body according to the Will of the Creator. The souls will exit from the World-to-Come and will return to their bodies in the days of the resurrection. These privileged men will derive pleasure from the goodness of this world during the Messianic Era, and they will merit therein a status higher than their original status. However, after this the Master, of blessed memory, decrees the death of the Messiah and of his generation. Their souls will exist in the goodness of the World-to-Come without bodies, as they had originally, but in yet a greater status since they merit [that status] by virtue of the commandments which they performed during the Messianic Era. They will exist for all eternity.

The Master, of blessed memory, goes to great lengths in making numerous statements in order to demonstrate that the inhabitants of the World-to-Come have no bodies for two reasons: [First] he knows that the men of our tradition believe that there is no death following the resurrection of the dead on the basis of their explanation [of the verse] "He will swallow up death forever."[14] They declared, "The dead which the Holy One, blessed be He, will revive do not return to dust."[15] According to this opinion, the inhabitants of the World-to-Come will exist in that world with their bodies after the resurrection. The Master negates this opinion with all his ability. Therefore, many of the wise men of these generations have disagreed with him concerning this, as is found in their statements. That the World-to-Come after death is [only] for the souls, no man disputes—whether he be wise or not. There is no need for the statements which the Master wrote in many places, for it is well known that the body has no share or privilege [in the World-to-Come after death].

Furthermore, the Master, of blessed memory, intended as a second purpose to strengthen [the concept of] the soul itself; viz. that it is neither a body nor a force within a body, but is a transcendental intellect as are angels. Thus he said in the *Treatise on the Resurrection of the Dead,*[16] ". . . The cause of all this is what occurs to the minds of the masses who believe that there is no existence other than the existence of the body. That which is not a body or an accident of a body does not exist in the thought of these persons who are bereft of thought. Therefore, most of them believe that the Creator is corporeal, for were He not corporeal, He would not exist according to their thinking. However, those who may truly be called wise . . . know demonstrably that anything which transcends the corporeal has a stronger and more enduring existence than that which has a body. It is not even correct to say 'more enduring,' rather transcendental existence is the true existence because it is not subject to change. They are wise to whom it has become clear by means of demonstration that the Creator is not corporeal and therefore His existence is the ultimate of duration. Similarly, the existence of every transcendental being, i.e., angels and the Intelligences, is stronger and more enduring than any corporeal being. Therefore, we believe that angels are not corporeal and that the inhabitants of the World-to-Come are transcendent souls."

The Master, of blessed memory[17] states further: "How could one imagine that these foolish people would understand that angels transcend the corporeal since their very existence, that is, the existence of angels and inhabitants of the World-to-Come is thought by them to be known only by virtue of tradition on the basis of the Torah and that there is no mode of investigation which can prove the existence of angels or the continued existence of souls, etc." This passage teaches you, on the basis of the statements of the Master, of blessed memory, the meaning of the World-to-Come, namely, that it is the continued existence of the souls alone after death, and that it is a matter which became clear to [the wise] by means of proof and investigation and not by tradition, for the matter of the World-to-Come after resurrection, in truth, requires the statements of the Torah and the explanation of tradition. Thus the belief of the Master, of blessed memory, in explaining the World-to-Come, as well as ours, has been explained.

In truth, one can find that some of the wise men of Spain, in their scholarly writings and in their prayers, agree with the opinion that the World-to-Come is the world of the souls. Rabbi Solomon ibn Gabirol, of blessed memory, says in his prayer: "Under Your throne of glory is a stand for the souls of Your followers and there they experience enjoyment without limit or end." This is the World-to-Come. Thus he would pray, "At the proper time take me out of this world; bring me in peace to the World-to-Come." But we are hearkened to, since we have stated the matter correctly, and we have brought proof from the statements of our Rabbis. I later found that R. Saadia Gaon, in his commentary on the book of Daniel, explains the World-to-Come as we have explained it. It is the tradition of the early [generations]; you should not forget their teaching. In any event, there are only semantic differences between us. Everyone agrees with regard to the [nature of] resurrection of the dead and the existence of that era both in general and in its details as I have explained, except [for] the opinion of the Master, Rabbi Moses, of blessed memory, who imposes a limit on the period of the resurrection and [claims that] everyone returns to the world of the souls, as we have mentioned above. However, we maintain that those resurrected exist forever from the era of resurrection to the World-to-Come, which is an eternally long world. May the Master of mercy cause us to merit the goodness which He has hidden for those who fear Him and has made for His servants according to His compassion and His mercies. Amen and amen.

NOTES

1. *Commentary on the Mishnah,* introduction to *Helek.*
2. Deuteronomy 11:22.
3. I Samuel 25:29.
4. *Berakhot* 34 b.
5. *Commentary on the Mishnah,* introduction to *Helek.*
6. *Mishneh Torah,* Laws of Repentance 8:8.
7. Psalms 31:20.
8. *Mishneh Torah,* Laws of Repentance 8:2.
9. Psalms 25:13.
10. Isaiah 58:8.
11. Psalms 115:5.
12. Job 13:5.
13. Psalms 12:7.
14. Isaiah 25:8.
15. *Sanhedrin* 92a.
16. Chapter 4.
17. *Ibid.*, Chapter 2.

CRESCAS, *OR HA-SHEM*

Translation by Warren Zev Harvey

BOOK III, FIRST SECTION, PART 2

Concerning the survival of the soul, wherein the discourse is of two subjects: [1] the quiddity of the soul, and [2] its survival. As for the quiddity, we have discoursed on it in Part 6 of Book II, sufficiently for the intent of this book. Thus, there remains for us the exposition of its survival; and our discourse on it shall be in accordance with our custom: that is, on the one hand, the exposition of how it should be understood according to what the Law and philosophic speculation decree, and, on the other hand, the way of our coming to know it. Thus we have put the chapters of this Part at two.

CHAPTER 1

Concerning the exposition of how it should be understood according to what the Law and philosophic speculation decree.

I say that the soul which survives after death survives eternally by nature, enduring *per se*, and not changing qua species or qua individual — according to what the Law has decreed, and with which philosophic speculation is consistent.

We said, "which survives after death," for the souls of men do not all survive, but some of them perish in their hour, like the souls of some of the wicked, as will be discussed in Part 3,[1] God willing.

And we said, "survives eternally by nature," for it does not contain in itself causes of corruption.[2] Therefore, unless by reason of punishment — in accordance with what appears in the tradition, and which we shall discuss subsequently — it will survive eternally by nature.

And we said, "enduring *per se*," for it has been established in its definition that it is a substance — not a disposition alone, as imagined Averroes.

And our saying, "not changing qua species," indicates the worthlessness of the opinion of him who imagined that what survives of the souls unites with the Active Intellect in such a manner that it is it. For inasmuch as the soul of man is different from the Active Intellect, if it were to unite with it in such a manner that our saying "it is it"[3] is correct, then it will have changed in species!

And our saying, "and not qua individual," indicates the worthlessness of the opinion of him who maintains that souls, after separation [from the body], cannot be many but are one in number. This is a very worthless opinion according to the tradition, and according to philosophic speculation itself.

BOOK III, FIRST SECTION, PART 2, CHAPTER 2

Concerning the way of our coming to know it:

I say that we come to know the survival of the soul, in the sense that it has been set down, from [IA] the Law and [IB] the tradition, and that [II] philosophic speculation is consistent with this.

[IA] As for the Law, although it is not stated explicitly in it as a promise of requital, many texts[4] testify to it as an elementary thing accepted among the nation and well known among them. First of all, it is found concerning Enoch: "and he was not, for God took him,"[5] which is to say, He *took* him to his portion in the ranks of his angels.[6] The same language[7] [i.e., the term "to take"] is found with regard to Elijah: "Today the Lord will take away thy master from thy head."[8] This [doctrine of the survival of the soul] was so well-known, that Balaam yearned to be like Israel in the end, saying: "Let my soul die the death of the righteous, and let my end be like his."[9] And because it was well-known among [the Israelites], Abigail said: "Yet the soul of my Lord shall be bound in the bundle of life; and the souls of thine enemies, them shall He sling out, as from the hollow of a sling."[10] Moreover, He, may He be blessed, said: "See, I have set before thee this day life and good."[11] Ezekiel promised this life as a reward, saying: "Turn ye, and live!"[12] Now, there is no doubt that [what is here spoken of] is not material life, for [material] life and death are common to the righteous and the wicked.[13] And the poet, in his Psalms, called the wicked "dead," saying: "The dead praise not the Lord."[14] He continued: "But we shall bless the Lord, from this time forth and forever." [15] And he said, testifying to this [belief in the survival of the soul]: "But God will redeem my soul from the power of Sheol, for He shall take me. Selah."[16] And he said elsewhere: "Until I entered into the sanctuary of God, and considered their end."[17] And Solomon his son said explicitly: "And the spirit shall return unto God who gave it."[18] And so on [one could continue to cite biblical texts testifying to belief in the survival of the soul], in the manner of another scholar[19] who has already elaborated on this subject.

Nevertheless, it was only the material requital which was set down explicitly as a promise, owing to a reason which we shall mention in Part 6,[20] God willing.

[IB] As for the tradition, this [doctrine of the survival of the soul] was well-known to our Sages. They mentioned the subject of the world-to-come in many places, and there is no need to reiterate them.

[I] Thus, the matter of the survival [of the soul] is very evident according to [A] the Law, and [B] the tradition.

[IA] Now, that the soul which survives changes neither qua species nor qua individual, as premised, will be seen from the standpoint of the Law. For inasmuch as the true reward and punishment of man is in the survival of souls after the separation [from the bodies], if it were the case that the soul unites with the Active Intellect, or that a plurality of souls unite and all become one — as one of the servants of our nation imagined, and tripped up here owing to his following the way of the Greeks —, then the reward would not be appropriate, since there would be no preeminence of the servant [of God] over someone who does not attain to one thousandth of his level!

[IB] Now, in the statements of our Rabbis of blessed memory, this [i.e., that the surviving soul does not lose its individuality] is very evident. There is their statement: "The righteous sit with their crowns on their heads, enjoying the radiance of the Indwelling."[21] And they said: "The face of Moses is like the face of the sun; the face of Joshua, like the face of the moon."[22] They said: "It teaches that each is given a dwelling in accordance with his honor."[23] There are many other statements besides these. However, a lengthly exposition of this would be superfluous.

[II] As for philosophic speculation being consistent with this:

With regard to survival [of the soul] itself, the commentators on the books of Aristotle have been perplexed. Some of them deny its existence. Some of them affirm it. They multiplied words and arguments concerning it. Consequently, it would be appropriate for us to present that which reinforced their opinions from among those things which deserve attention, and this in exceeding brevity; in this way, the true reality of what we intended shall become clear.

I say[24] that that upon which they all agreed, and upon which they constructed edifices, comprises three propositions:

The *first:* that the human intellect becomes constituted as a substance out of its *intelligibilia.*[25] And they called it the "acquired intellect."

The *second:* that all that is generated will be corrupted, and all that is corrupted was generated.[26]

And the *third:* that if the cognition by the human intellect of the Active Intellect is presumed to be possible, it will necessarily become eternal.

However, there is a division of opinion among them concerning two propositions:

The *first:* whether the *intelligibilia* of our world are generated or not generated.

And the *second:* is it possible for the human intellect to cognize the Active Intellect?[27]

The faction which denies the survival [of the soul] is of the opinion that the *intelligibilia* of this world are generated, and that it is impossible for the human intellect to cognize the Active Intellect.[28] Now, it follows from this that it is impossible for the human intellect to become eternal. For when it is accepted by them as true that the intellect becomes constituted as a substance out of its *intelligibilia,* as established in the *first* commonly agreed-upon proposition, and if the *intelligibilia* of this world are generated, then [the intellect] will by necessity be corrupted, in accord with the *second* commonly agreed-upon proposition. This, to be sure, is as long as it does not intellectually cognize the Active Intellect. But when it is accepted by them as true that it is impossible for it to cognize the Active Intellect, it follows necessarily that it is impossible for the human intellect to become eternal.

As for the faction which affirms the survival [of the soul], there is one among them who is of the opinion that the *intelligibilia* of this world are not generated.[29] Now, when it is accepted by him as true that the intellect becomes constituted as a substance out of its *intelligibilia,* as established in the *first* commonly agreed-upon proposition, then [the intellect] will necessarily become eternal because the *intelligibilia* are eternal, since they are not generated, in accord with the *second* commonly agreed-upon proposition. He deduces from this the affirmation of survival. Also, there is one among them [in the faction affirming survival] who is of the opinion that it is possible for the human intellect to cognize the Active Intellect.[30] He deduces, with appeal to the *third* commonly agreed-upon proposition, the affirmation of survival of the human intellect, upon its intellectually cognizing the Active Intellect.

These are the poles of their theory.

We, however, shall say, with regard to the *first* commonly agreed-upon proposition, which is the foundation of the whole edifice, that, indeed, its falsity has been proved beyond any doubt in Part 6 of Book II.[31] Likewise the second [commonly agreed-upon] proposition, whereas Rabbi Levi [Gersonides] has already smote it on the head,[32] yet even if it is presumed to be true, it will not be applicable to voluntaristic generation;[33] and it has been demonstrated earlier[34] that the universal generation is voluntary *ex nihilo,* and *a fortiori* eternality is possible in it. As for the *third* [commonly agreed-upon] proposition, its falsity is facilely demonstrated by the falsity of the first [commonly agreed-upon proposition]; for the intellectual cognition by the human intellect of the Active Intellect will not impart eternality to the human intellect, unless we say that the intellect becomes constituted as a substance out of its *intelligibilia;* this is self-evident.

Now, therefore, what ought to be said in affirmation of the survival of the soul is that, once it has been established in the definition of the soul that it is an intellectual substance, not containing within it causes of corruption;[35] then, when the soul becomes perfected in conjunction and love, by means of what it apprehends of the Law and of the wonders of the Lord, may He be blessed, it should remain in its perfection and in a strong conjunction and in the shining forth of unremitting light, owing to the removal of the obstacle which darkens its intrinsic reality, which [obstacle] is matter.[36] This being so, it is clear that philosophic speculation does not deny anything concerning survival. Rather, it will be seen to affirm it.

For inasmuch as it has been demonstrated of a compound undergoing corruption, and which decomposes into its simple parts, that each [simple part] returns to its simple essence; and since man is compounded of a material part and of an essential spiritual part, which is an overflow from an overflowing intellectual substance, be that overflowing agent an angel or something else, it is fitting and necessary that that spiritual part not undergo corruption, just as it is clear with regard to the material part, that it returns to its simple components and to the four elements.

Thus, the survival [of the soul] is demonstrated and necessary *per se,* according to the true philosophic speculation.

It was to it that Solomon referred in his dictum: "The dust shall return to the earth as it was, and the spirit shall return unto God who gave it."[37] However, the distinction between the material part and the spiritual part is that the simple components of the material part return to their elements and unite with them, owing to their being homogeneous parts and to their not having acquired in matter a stable perfection, since matter is mobile and in flux; while the spiritual part, since it acquired in man, by means of his attaining perfection and adhesion unto the Supreme Light, which is stable and unchanging, it is fitting and necessary that it remain stable in its substance and in its perfection.[38]

With regard to the affirmation of the survival [of the soul] this will suffice, according to the intent of the book.

Now, that [the soul] will be unchanging both qua species and qua individual — is very obvious from what preceded. For it is self-evident that that which changes qua species or qua individual is transformed from essence to essence, be it a species or an individual. And the essence from which it is transformed necessarily undergoes corruption. For were it not to undergo corruption, then one and the same thing would have two essences, and this is something whose absurdity has been demonstrated. And since it has been established of the intellectual soul that it does not have causes of corruption, it follows necessarily, therefore, that it is unchanging qua species and qua individual.

Yet, what brought some of the commentators on Aristotle's books to this error is their acceptance of the premise which says that the human intellect becomes constituted as a substance out of its *intelligibilia*. And when it was accepted by them as true that the intellectually cognizing subject, the *intelligibile*, and intellectual cognition are one thing,[39] and that intellectual cognition admits of no plurality qua individual, it followed necessarily for them that the souls after the separation [from the bodies] are one thing. But we have already made clear in what preceded the humbuggery and falsity of that proposition.[40]

For the soul has an essence other than intellectual cognition, even though its quiddity is inscrutable to us. Our Rabbis of blessed memory called [the soul] in several places, "light." And Scripture says: "The soul of man is the lamp of the Lord."[41] And it well deserves this name, for it is a lamp enlightening the eyes of the blind and of them who are in darkness. For this reason, [the Rabbis] associated this light with the Indwelling, saying: "enjoying the radiance of the Indwelling."[42] And [Daniel] said: "the light dwelleth with Him."[43] Thus, one is dumbfounded at [the philosophers], for if intellectual cognition itself is one and does not admit of plurality, and intellectual cognition and the *intelligibile* are one thing, then the *intelligibilia*, with their multitudinous plurality, are one individual![44] This is perfect nonsense and ridiculous. Rather, all that they said concerning this is a fantastic contrivance, besides being total infidelity according to the Law and the tradition, as preceded.[45]

Here has been demonstrated what we saw fit to demonstrate in this Part. Praise to God alone, high above all blessing and praise. Amen. Amen.

NOTES

1. *Or ha-Shem*, IIIA, 3, 3.
2. *Or ha-Shem*, II, 6, 1.
3. On this formula [Hebrew: הוא הוא; Arabic: هو هو], which appears in Judah ha-Levi, *Kuzari*, IV, 13, and which goes back to Avicenna, see Vajda, *Recherches*, p. 28, n. 3 (note begins on p. 27).
4. Crescas' scriptural argumentation, including nine of his source-texts, may be traced to

the following text in Abraham ibn Daud, *Emunah Ramah*, I, 17, pp. 39–40. The numbers in parentheses following biblical references or quotations indicate the order in which those references or quotations appear in the *Or ha-Shem*.

ויתהלך חנוך את האלהים ואיננו כי לקח אתו אלהים (1), אין זה מיתה כמיתת מי שקדמו, אבל הוא
הפרד מזה על צד האלהי, באופן זר עלינו. ואם היה מיתה, יאמר עליו: וימת כמו שאמר על זולתו. ולא
היה בלא ספק, אלא כדרך מה שקרה ג״כ לאליהו זכור לטוב (2), והוא, שיותך הגשם כלו, ותשאר
הנפש במחיצת המלאכים ...עד שאחד החכמים מזולת אומתנו, למה ששיער מי שיעד טוב מהם יעודם
אחר המות אמר תמות נפשי מות ישרים ותהי אחריתי כמוהו (3), עד שהנשים בעלות תבונה היו
יודעות בזה, כמאמר אביגיל לדוד ע״ה: והיתה נפש אדני צרורה בצרור החיים את ה׳ אלהיך ואת נפש
איוביך יקלענה בתוך כף הקלע (4). ובהעיר האומה לקבל התורה אמר ית׳ וית׳: נתתי לפניך היום את
החיים ואת הטוב (5) ...ויאמר ית׳ ית׳ על יד יחזקאל ע״ה ...השיבו וחיו (6). ואלה החיים אשר ייעדו
אותנו בהם משה ויחזקאל ע״ה אינם הגשם, כי גשמי הצדיקים והרשעים תכליתם המות, ואינם אלא
חיי נפש. ונמצא החכם שלמה ע״ה יאמר בפירוש: ...והרוח תשוב אל האלהים אשר נתנה. (10)
...ויאמר אביו ע״ה: ...לא המתים יהללויה ולא כל יורדי דומה, והוא אמנם יקרא מתים ...הרשעים
...ולזה תמצא דוד ע״ה יסמוך לאמרו לא המתים יהללויה, אמרו: ואנחנו נברך יה מעתה ועד עולם (7)
...אך אלהים נפשי מיד שאול כי יקחני סלה (8) ...ודע כי מילת לקיחה באמרו כי יקחני סלה ...כי לקח
אתו אלהים (1), ה׳ לקח אדנך מעל ראשך (2), הנרצה בכלם, הגיע הנפש במחיצת המלאכים ...

5. Gen. 5:24.

6. Cf. Targum Yonatan, *ad loc.*; Gen. *Rabba* 25:1. Cf. Rashi, *ad loc.*; Judah ha-Levi, *Kuzari*, III, 1; Abraham ibn Daud, *Emunah Ramah*, cf. note 1 above.

7. On this comparison of Enoch and Elijah based on the term "to take," see *Gen. Rabbah* 25:1. Cf. Abraham ibn Ezra, *ad loc.*; Bahya ben Asher, *ad loc.*; Abraham ibn Daud, *Emunah Ramah*, cf. note 1 above. Cf. *Or ha-Shem*, IIIA, 4, 3.

8. II Kings 2:3,5. Cf. Abraham ibn Daud, *Emunah Ramah*, cf. note 1 above. Cf. *Or ha-Shem*, IIIA, 3, 3.

9. Num. 23:10. Cf. Abraham ibn Daud, *Emunah Ramah*, cf. note 1 above.

10. I Sam. 25:29. Cf. Abraham ibn Daud, *Emunah Ramah*. Cf. Maimonides, *Guide*, I, 41, p.91.

11. Deut. 30:15. Cf. Abraham ibn Daud, *Emunah Ramah*. Cf. Maimonides, *Guide*, I, 42, p. 93.

12. Ezek. 18:32.

13. Cf. Abraham ibn Daud, *Emunah Ramah*.

14. Ps. 115:17. Cf. Abraham ibn Daud, *Emunah Ramah*.

15. *Ps. 115:18. Cf. Abraham ibn Daud*, Emunah Ramah.

16. Ps. 49:16. Cf. Abraham ibn Daud, *Emunah Ramah*. Cf. with the following text from Bernat Metge, *Lo somni*, I, p. 35: "*David, sobira propheta, sabent clarament la dita inmortalitat, dix: 'Senyor, no jaquesques la mia (anima) en infern'* [verse ?]. *E en altre loch: 'Nostre Senyor Deu, reembra la mia anima de la ma d infern, com haura reebut mi'* [Ps. 49:16]. *E pus auant: 'Senyor, tu has desliurada d infern la.mia anima, e has saluat mi dels deuallants al lach'* [Ps. 30:4]. *E en altre loch: 'Tu, Senyor, has conegut la mia resurrectio'* [verse ?]. *Salamo, fill seu, ja t he dit dessus qu en dix a la fi dels (sic) Ecclesiastes, quel espirit tornara a Deu, qui ha donat aquell'* [Eccles. 12:7]."

17. Ps. 73:17. This verse is not cited in Abraham ibn Daud, *Emunah Ramah*. Cf. Maimonides, *Guide*, III, 19; Joseph Kaspi, *Commentary on Psalms*, *ad loc.*; Samuel ibn Tibbon, *Ma'amar Yiqqavu ha-Mayim*, XIV, pp. 88–91.

18. Eccles. 12:7. Cf. Maimonides, *Guide*, I, 40. For Bernat Metge's use of this verse, see note 16 above.

19. Abraham ibn Daud.

20. *Or ha-Shem*, IIIA, 3, 3.

21. BT *Berakhot* 17a. Cf. *Or ha-Shem*, IIIA, 4, 4.
22. BT *Baba Batra* 75a.
23. Cf. *ibid.* and BT *Shabbat* 152a.
24. Much of Crescas' following summary may be traced to Gersonides, *Wars*, I, 8–9; cf. notes below.
25. Cf. *Or ha-Shem*, I, 3, 3; II, 1, 2; II, 5, 5; II, 6, 1; IV, 11.
26. Gersonides, *Wars*, I, 8, p. 52. cf. Maimonides, *Guide*, I, 72, p. 186; II, 14, pp. 286–287. Cf. Aristotle, *De Caelo*, I, 10–12.
27. Cf. Gersonides, *Wars*, I, 9, p. 52; cf. I, 11.
28. Gersonides attributes this position to Alfarabi; *Wars*, I, 8, p. 52.
29. Gersonides, citing Averroes, Epitome of the *De Anima*, attributes this position to Avicenna; *Wars*, I, 8, p. 52.
30. Gersonides, citing Averroes, Epitome of the *De Anima*, attributes this position to Alexander of Aphrodisias, Themistius, and Averroes; *Wars*, I, 8, p. 52.
31. *Or ha-Shem*, II, 6, 1.
32. Gersonides, *Wars*, VIA, 27; cf. I, 10, pp. 74, 81.
33. Cf. *Or ha-Shem*, I, 2, 10; IIIA, 1, 3–5.
34. *Or ha-Shem*, IIIA, 1, 5.
35. *Or ha-Shem* II, 6, 1; IIIA, 2, 1.
36. Cf. Ran, *12 Derushim*, I, p. 9:

הנה נגלה אם כן שהגוף וכחותיה אינן נותנים קיום והעמדה לנפש, אבל מחשיכים כחותיה, עד שראוי שכאשר יופסד המונע תהיה אז הנפש יותר שלמה, וכל יעודי התורה שבאו בענינים גופנים על זה הצד שאם יראה לחוש שיש לאדם דבקות בענין האלהי והוא עומד בענין מונע אותו מהשיג שהוא גוף, אין ספק שיהיה מובטח להיות הדבקות שלם כפי מה שאפשר, כאשר יוסר המציק המונע ...

Cf. Pseudo-Maimonides, *De Beatitudine*, pp. 37–39.

37. Eccles. 12:7. Cf. *Or ha-Shem*, II, 6, 1.
38. Cf. Ran, *12 Derushim*, I.
39. Cf. *Or ha-Shem*, I, 3, 3; II, 2, 2; II, 6, 1; IV, 11; IV, 13.
40. *Or ha-Shem*, II, 6, 1.
41. Prov. 20:27. Cf. *Or ha-Shem*, Introduction.
42. BT *Berakhot* 17a. Cf. *Or ha-Shem*, IIIA, 4, 4.
43. Dan. 2:22. Cf. Gersonides, *Wars*, I, 12, p. 88.
44. Cf. *Or ha-Shem*, II, 6, 1; IV, 11.
45. *Or ha-Shem*, II, 6, 1.

BOOK III, FIRST SECTION, PART 4, CHAPTER 2

Concerning the purpose intended in this wonderful miracle, and its benefits:

I say, moreover, that in this miracle there is another purpose which is also intended in it, for which it is appropriate that it be performed by Elijah the prophet — may he be remembered for good! — and not by someone else. For inasmuch as the true reward and punishment should attain to the very same one who serves [God] or transgresses, and not to another, according to political justice and, *a fortiori*, in the ordinance of divine justice,[1] the reward or punishment which attains to the soul upon its separation from the body is not sufficient — even notwithstanding that the service [of God] or the transgression should be accounted more to the most noble part of man [sc., the soul], which, while in the body, did not attain to its reward or punishment, as was explained previously. Thus, were it not for this miracle [of the resurrection], there would be a lack — Heaven forbid! — in the ordinance of divine justice. Therefore, the divine Wisdom decreed this great miracle, in which are realized in perfection the divine justice and all manners of rectitude. Now, inasmuch as what intended in this miracle is reward and punishment in body-and-soul, it is appropriate that this miracle be performed through the medium of the first prophet who merited this degree in body and soul, and he is Elijah, may he be remembered for good! For although it is recorded in a midrash[2] that Enoch also merited this, he was before the [giving of] the Law. In addition, there is [Elijah's] vigorous striving concerning this purpose in the days of Ahab, in his saying: "How long halt ye between two opinions,"[3] etc. In any event, that midrash [concerning Enoch] is not incontestable, for Onkelos the Proselyte disputes it in his translation of "and he was not, for God took him."[4] And although our Rabbis of blessed memory have related to us that pious ones other than him have merited this rank, the first prophet who merited it and who strove concerning this purpose, was Elijah, may he be remembered for good! Therefore, it is appropriate and necessary in the ordinance of divine justice that this miracle be performed through the medium of him.

I say, moreover, that in this act the purpose of the creation of the human species will be realized in perfection, and that is one and the same with the purpose intended in the Law, as we established at the end of Book II. And this is the case whether from the standpoint of the Creator, may He be blessed, it is the greatest possible bestowal of good. All this has been demonstrated there [in Book II, Part 6, Chapter 1]. This being so, it is appropriate that [the purpose] be perfected through the medium of him who merited this union in perpetuity. He is Elijah, may he be remembered for good!

NOTES

1. Cf. *Or ha-Shem*, II, 6, 1 and IIIA, 3, 3.
2. *Genesis Rabba* 25:1. Cf. *Or ha-Shem*, IIIA, 2, 2.
3. I Kings 18:21.
4. Gen. 5:24. *Or ha-Shem*, IIIA, 2, 2. Onkelos translates the Hebrew לקח ("took") with the Aramaic אמית, ("killed"). Interestingly, a variant reading of the Onkelos translation has לא אמית ("did not kill").

BOOK III, FIRST SECTION, PART 4, CHAPTER 4

Concerning the resolution of some objections which befall it:

For immense objections obtain concerning both the thing in itself and the way in which it has been posited.[1]

To begin with, concerning the possibility of the thing in itself:

. . . inasmuch as in the corruption of the compounded individual man, his simple components decompose into their elements, even if it should be demonstrated true that [in the resurrection] the components which were part of Reuben will return by the will of God, may He be blessed, still, there is no escaping that there will be a new creation, and that it will not be true of him [that is resurrected] that he is he [who had previously lived]. Now, one of the essential purposes in this miracle is supposed to be the manifestation in it of the divine justice to give reward and punishment to the very individual who served or transgressed. But if it is not true that he is he, then the reward or punishment will not be to him himself![2]

Second, granting that in the recomposition of the simple components of the compound the divine justice is manifest: if some of these components were in the convexity of the element of fire and some of them in the center of the earth or in other compounds, such that some of them even were part of the body of a lion and some of them part of an ant, will those animals decompose and become part of the individual meriting resurrection?! This is much too far-fetched to be conceivable!

Third, since it is posited that one of the essential purposes [of the resurrection] is the manifestation in it of the divine justice, how is it permissible that this miracle be for some and not for others? Yet it is as such that it was posited in Chapter 1 of this Part. Thus, the divine justice will not be manifest to those who do not merit this miracle.

Fourth, it is dubious — assuming that the resurrection is universal to the entirety of our nation, in accordance with the literal sense of the Mishnah, which says "All Israel has a portion in the world-to-come"[3] — whether they will *all* die before the time of the resurrection! For the proposition that they will arise and live after death, even if they die *after* the resurrection, is very ridiculous, for it would necessarily follow that the thing would be carried out continuously! But the text screams out, saying: "Before the great and terrible day of the Lord."[4] This would indicate that this universal miracle will take place at one time and will not be carried on continuously.

Fifth, we find in the Prophets promises to our nation as a whole, which transcend the custom of nature; like longevity, in saying, "For the youngest shall die a hundred years old, and the sinner being a hundred years old shall be accursed";[5] and like the promise of prophecy, in saying, "And your sons and your daughters shall prophesy. Your old men shall dream dreams. Your young men shall see visions."[6] Now, it might be dubious whether these promises refer to the time of the resurrection or to the days of the Messiah. Whichever the case, it is an astonishing thing! For if these promises refer to the time of the resurrection, it would seem that [the resurrected] will use their senses and will die, which is contrary to what has been posited. And if they refer to the days of the Messiah, then the dictum of Samuel is contrary to it. For he said: "There is nought between this world and the days of the Messiah, except subjugation to the kingdoms alone.[7]

These are the objections which obtain to this matter, according to what was posited, and we should say in their resolution:

As for the first and the second [objections], which concern the possibility of the thing in itself: since it has been established that the power of God, may He be blessed, is infinite; and, likewise, His knowledge extends over an infinite number of objects; and all things are in His province, and even though they be extremely improbable in nature, they are extremely probable to Him, each in the same ratio, with no difference obtaining between them; it is not improbable that at that time His Wisdom decrees that this great miracle shall take place, the components of the compound will be in such a way that they are prepared to return to recompose as they were at first, without necessitating the decomposition of other animals. But this notwithstanding, it would seem that this miracle does not require that [the components that recompose] be those [original] components themselves. For since it is evident that even if they are those components themselves, it would not be true of them that they constitute him who is he [who had previously lived]. Thus, there is no advantage in those [original] components coming together, and all the more so if it would be necessary to separate them from other animals. Nevertheless, the divine justice would be manifest in them. For if God were to create a creation of the temperament and characteristics possessed by Reuben, for example, such that "not one hair of his head fall to the ground,"[8] something which is possible in His ordinance, may He be blessed, and [Reuben's] soul, which is a substance enduring *per se* were to unite with this creation, there is no doubt that this soul and its faculties would use this body, upon its union with it, identically as it has used the body of Reuben. And since among the entirety of its faculties are memory and imagination, it will in this [new] body remember its first status just as if it had united with the simple components of the elements of which its body had been composed in the beginning. For a given pound of the element of water, for example, bears no imprint as to whether it has come from the concavity of the element or from its convexity. This is self-evident. Now, since this soul will thus use this body, it is confirmed that the divine justice will be demonstrated true in it. And why not? Indeed, consider Reuben, for example. Having been born small of size with his vegetative soul, he thereupon grows up. Now, just as the parts of his body were generated out of the food which descended through the organs of his body — and it is evident of every single part of his body that it was generated from food which had been exterior to his body — and yet his entire body is one substance; so this soul unites with this body whose characteristics are just like Reuben's body's, and although the parts of his body are from places exterior, when they unite with this soul, they become one substance with it. And inasmuch as the soul is essential form to the possessor of the soul, giving him his essence, this soul is a form to this body, and gives it its essence. And inasmuch as the soul does not change its essence, it is necessary that the body which unites with it be assimilated to it, just as food is assimilated to the consumer of the food, and is converted into his body. This may be seen from what our Rabbis of blessed memory accepted, saying: "The righteous will stand in their clothing; this is an *a fortiori* deduction from wheat."[9] (The intent of this dictum is that since the uncovering of the genitals is so very reproachful that God decreed concerning man, upon his knowing good and evil, "And He made for them garments of skin and clothed them,"[10] it is not appropriate that the righteous stand nude. Now, they made the *a fortiori* deduction from wheat to teach thereby that God, may He be blessed, brings things into existence in the most praiseworthy way; and just as wheat goes out in its clothing to guard it against injuries, so the righteous will stand in their clothing to guard them from reproach.) We have cited this dictum only to indicate that just as there is no special care taken with regard to the clothing that it be from the same components of that in which he was buried, as long as it is in its likeness, as if he were sleeping in his clothing, for in this there is some indication of the individuality of the man —, so there is no special care taken concerning the body, that the components of the elements be those which had been separated from it, as long as they be in the same relation, as we said. Yet, if there is no escape from saying that [the components of the resurrected body] are those components which had separated from the first compound, there is no harm in this. This will suffice in resolution of these two objections.

As for the third [objection], which concerns its having been posited that the miracle is for some and not for others: how is this permissible in the ordinance of divine justice? It is appropriate that we add to it what we promised in Chapter 1; namely, an exposition of the portion in which the manifestation of the divine justice is demonstrated true. Now, I say: since one cannot get away from the literal sense of the text, which indicates that the resurrection will not be universal, and since it has been demonstrated that one of the essential purposes of it is the manifestation of divine justice, it would seem that the resurrection will be for the thoroughly righteous and the thoroughly wicked. They will suffice to make manifest the divine justice: "some to everlasting life, and some to reproaches and everlasting abhorrence."[11] As for the mediocre ones, those who did not reach the degree that this great and awesome miracle be performed for them, the reward pertaining to their soul will suffice them. And if they did not achieve their corporeal requital in their lifetime, this has occurred owing to the smallness of their degree; but the Judge is faithful to weigh on the scales of His Wisdom the measure of that corporeal requital of which he is deserving, and recompense him twofold, or whatever His simple loving-kindness decrees, in the reward pertaining to the soul. Thus the divine justice will be confirmed in the weighing of the two species of requital. Indeed, it seems that the statement of the Poet refers to this: "The judgments of the Lord are true, they are righteous [or: just] together."[12] This is to say, that if the corporeal requital is not righteous concerning some men, then together, the corporeal requital and the requital pertaining to the soul will be righteous. (We[13] have seen fit to interpret this in the sense of *judgments of the Lord* that recompense man, and we did not see fit to interpret it in the sense of the *promulgation of the judgments* [i.e., the laws], for concerning the promulgation of the judgments [i.e., the laws] the terms "truth" and "falsehood" are impredicable, but rather "fine" and "bad" or "suitable" and "correct" and "unsuitable" and "incorrect.") According to this, those who merit the resurrection are those who are thoroughly righteous, for the mediocre men are not worthy of this great miracle; and the divine justice will not permit them to merit it. Thus, our saying "*All* Israel has a portion [helek] in the world-to-come,"[14] may mean one of two things. Either we may say that it means "the *majority* of Israel," on the basis of our principle, "One is not to make inferences from universal propositions, even where an exception is stated."[15] Or we may say that "All Israel has a *portion* [helek]," which is to say that it is an *inheritance*[16] [*yerushah*] to them and a promise of requital in this Law, while in previous divine laws it had never been promised, so that if all of [Israel] were righteous, they would all merit this; and [those who interpret it thus] find proof in the text which says, "Thy people also shall be all righteous, they shall inherit the land forever,"[17] that is, the land of life, and this is not the case with regard to any other people.

If we say that the "world-to-come" comprises the time of the resurrection *and* the requital of the soul which comes after death, evidence might be cited from [the Rabbis'] statement, "The pious of the nations of the world have a portion in the world-to-come,"[18] for it does not seem that they will merit the pleasantness of the resurrection.[19] Further evidence appears from the phraseology of the Blessing of the Heavenly Lights on the Sabbath, which makes reference to four periods, saying: "There is none comparable to You, O Lord our God, in this world; there is none other than You, our King, in the life of the world-to-come; there is nothing but You, our Redeemer. In the days of the Messiah; and none is similar to You, our Deliverer, in the resurrection."[20] It seems that [the Rabbis who composed this blessing] took them in order: beginning with *this world,* which is prior; after it, the *world-to-come,* which is immediately after death; after it, the *Messiah,* who is prior to the resurrection; and after him, the *resurrection,* which comprises the actual rising and the pleasantness which follows it. Now, since the other dictum [about the pious Gentiles] and dicta besides that one imply that the world-to-come means the time of the resurrection, it seems that this term [sc., "world-to-come"] comprises both [the requital of the soul immediately after death, and the resurrection]. However, should we say that it comprises only the time of the resurrection, we will have to interpret the phraseology of the blessing such, that "this world" comprises this world in life and in death, and the "world-to-come" means the pleasantness of the time of the resurrection after the actual rising — which is what is meant by "resurrection." But howsoever this term ["world-to-come"] is interpreted, once the purpose and benefits of this wonderful miracle have been demonstrated — namely, the manifestation of divine justice, to make reward and punishment fitting, to bestow faith, and to bring about the purposes of creation — it becomes evident that there is no room for the notion of the Master Guide [Maimonides][21] in the correct opinion, according to which those who merit the resurrection will not die and will not eat, but, according to the literal sense of the dictum, "the righteous sit with crowns on their heads, enjoying the radiance of the Indwelling."[22] For it is necessary that they be in their body, with their limbs and their organs, in order that the divine justice be manifested. Moreover, although it may be the case that they will not eat or drink, nor use their sense of taste or their organs of procreation, still, they will speak and hear, and serve God, and hold fast to His Law, as was the case with Elijah. Furthermore, together with this, they will impart the correct faith to others, as will be seen presently in the resolution of the fourth objection.

As for the fourth [objection], concerning the time prior to the resurrection, whether they will *all* die; for if we take the Mishnah in its literal sense, to say that "All Israel has a portion in the world-to-come" refers to the resurrection, it would seem to be necessary that they all die before the resurrection. But I say that even when we take the dictum in its literal sense as referring to the resurrection, and that the proposition is a universal one, still, the prior death of them all is not entailed. For the world-to-come comprises the actual rising and the time after the rising. Thus, with regard to that generation which will be in the time of the rising, even if they do not merit the adhesion and union, and use their sense organs and die, still, they will have a portion in the world-to-come, for it has been established in what preceded that among the benefits of this miracle is to bestow faith in the hearts of others, who thereby will come to merit what they would not have merited, were it not for this miracle. Thus it is confirmed that "All Israel has a portion in the world-to-come." And it is plausible that the dictum affirming that the pious of the nations of the world have a portion in the world-to-come is said with respect to that generation which is at the time of the resurrection, and to the generations following it, without this implying that they merit the rising [after they die].

Be that as it may, the resolution of the fifth objection is something very easy. To wit: the promises found in the words of the prophets will be realized in that generation which is in the time of the rising and in the following generations, for they will be influenced by those who arise, from the "spirit of knowledge and fear of the Lord."[23] And even if they use all their sense organs, live long, and procreate, no contradiction occurs from this.

This is what seems to be the case concerning the resolution of these objections, in accordance with the premises which are in our hands from the tradition and from what appears from conjecture and consideration. God knows, may His Name be lauded, high above all blessing and praise! Amen. Amen.

NOTES

1. *Or ha-Shem*, II, 3, 1: למה שהוא מבואר שלא יצויר מציאותו אצל השכל לא יתואר עליו ... היכלת בשום צד, כאלו תאמר קבוץ השלילה והחיוב בדבר אחד בעינו מצד אחד.
2. Cf. *Or ha-Shem*, II, 6, 1; IIIA, 3, 3; IIIA, 4, 3.
3. *Sanhedrin* 10:1.
4. Joel 3:4, Mal. 3:23.
5. Isa. 65:20.
6. Joel 3:1.
7. BT *Sanhedrin* 99a.
8. I Sam. 14:45.
9. BT *Ketubot* 111b, BT *Sanhedrin* 90b.
10. Cf. Gen. 3:21.
11. Dan. 12:2.
12. Ps. 19:10. Cf. Maimonides, *Guide*, III, 26.
13. This parenthetical aside is directed against Maimonides, *Guide*, III, 26, where the verse is interpreted in the way rejected by Crescas. Crescas' defense of his own interpretation against Maimonides' is based on remarks by Maimonides in *Guide*, I, 2.
14. *Sanhedrin* 10:1.
15. BT *'Erubin* 27a. Cf. Gersonides, *Wars*, I, 13, p. 91.
16. The Hebrew word for "portion" (helek) sometimes means "inheritance."
17. Isa. 60:21. Cf. Maimonides, *Mishneh Torah*, Teshubah 3:5.
18. *Tosephta Sanhedrin* 13:2. Maimonides, *Mishneh Torah*, 3:5 (cf. *Keseph Mishneh, ad loc.*); *'Edut* 11:10; *Melakhim* 8:11.
19. Cf. Albo, *'Ikkarim* IV, 31, p. 308.
20. Cf. Albo, *'Ikkarim* IV, 31, pp. 315–316.
21. According to Maimonides, the resurrected do eat and die. Cf. *Commentary on Mishnah*, Perek Helek; *Resurrection*. Maimonides' position is discussed critically by Nahmanides, *Torat ha-Adam*, pp. 307–311. Cf. Albo, *'Ikkarim*, IV, 35, p. 347. Crescas treats of Maimonides' position in *Or ha-Shem*, IIIA, 4, 1.
22. BT *Berakhot* 17a.
23. Isa. 11:2.

ALBO, *IKKARIM*

Translation by Isaac Husik

BOOK IV, CHAPTER 35

Belief in the resurrection of the dead is obligatory according to the tradition of our people, as we explained above.[1] Logic does not require it, but since it is something whose existence is rationally conceivable, we are obliged to believe it, as we explained in that place.[2] Particularly is this the case, since it is confirmed by experience. Elijah brought back to life the son of the widow of Zarephath,[3] while Elisha revived the son of the Shunammite woman,[4] and a thing to which experience testifies must be believed, even if it is not required by logic. For example, it is absolutely true that there is a stone which attracts iron, because experience shows it, though logic does not require it. We must therefore believe that God will revive the dead, even after they turn to dust, because it is something the mind can conceive.

To understand why this is a resurrection and not a new creation, we must bear in mind that a thing which has once received a higher influence or power and has lost it, is more prepared to receive it a second time than it was in the beginning. For example, wood which has once been kindled and has received the form of fire, which was later extinguished, is more ready to receive the form of fire a second time than in the beginning. Also a person who once received the spirit of prophecy and lost it, is more prepared to receive it a second time than he was in the beginning. The reason is because when a thing receives any higher influence or power, though it loses it later, there remains in it an impression of the influence which it once received. Hence the Rabbis say:[5] "'And I will bring your sanctuaries unto desolation'[6]—they are sacred even in their desolation." They also say: an article which was used in connection with holy things should be hidden.[7] The reason is because it retains an impression of the divine object for which it served as a seat or in some other capacity. In the same way, therefore, we say that the body, which was the seat of the soul, a higher power, retains an impression of the divine power which it received in the beginning, even after the soul leaves it at the time of death.

And the proof of this is found in the case of the man who died and was buried in the grave of Elisha. The bones of Elisha had sufficient power to bring him back to life by coming in contact with him,[8] although the soul of Elisha had long departed from the body, for he had been dead more than a year, as the Bible testifies. Nevertheless as soon as the dead man came in contact with the bones of Elisha, he rose and stood on his feet. This was due to the impression which remained in the bones of the divine object of which they were the seat. This is the reason also why in time of trouble we prostrate ourselves upon the graves of the righteous. For on account of the impression, in those bones, of the divine spirit which they lodged, they are more prepared to mediate the divine influence than others. This may be illustrated also in the rod of Moses. It was nothing but dry wood, nevertheless, since it was in the hand of Moses when the prophetic inspiration began to rest upon him, it was always used in the performance of the signs, as we read: "And thou shalt take in thy hand this rod, wherewith thou shalt do the signs."[9] And Elisha said to Gehazi: "And lay my staff upon the face of the child."[10]

The resurrection must be explained in the same way. The body of the righteous man, by reason of the impression remaining in it of the divine spirit which it lodged, is more prepared without doubt to receive the same divine spirit a second time than it was at first, as the Rabbis say:[11] "If those who never had been came to life, surely those who once had been would come to life again." In other words, a thing which was not fit to receive a higher power and yet received it once, is surely fit to receive it a second time, because it retains an impression and preparation for receiving it a second time more easily than at first.

Moreover the object which has the fitness to receive some power or influence, has the power, as it were, to compel the giver to bestow the influence or power upon it, as, for example, though fire does not by nature move downward, yet when we take a lamp which has been extinguished and is still smoking and put it under another lamp that is burning, the smoke rising from the extinguished lamp will force the fire of the burning lamp to let down its flame through the smoke to the extinguished lamp and it will burn again as before. This is the reason why the Bible compares the human soul to a lamp: "The spirit of man is the lamp of the Lord."[12] The soul of man is like the light of a burning lamp. Just as the light of a burning lamp, even after it has left the wick, will burn a second time more easily than at first because of the impression of the fire which it retains, so the light of the soul which has left the body can return to the body and dwell in it, by reason of the preparation which it retains, more easily than it came to it in the beginning. This takes place when the divine Wisdom decrees that it should. . .

As to the manner of resurrection, the Rabbis say[13] that there is a certain dew with which God will revive the dead. It seems, therefore, that the dew which God will cause to descend upon the earth will have in it the virtue of the semen of the male, which gives the form of the person, while the earth at that time, by reason of its preparation, will have the virtue of the seed of the female, which gives the matter of the newly born individual. The prophecy of Ezekiel concerning the dead which he brought back to life disagrees with this opinion, if we interpret the text literally. Be this, however, as it may, whether after the resurrection the people will eat and drink and beget children and die in the usual manner [or not], we have already explained that it is a matter of dispute among the great men of more recent times. Maimonides and a great many distinguished men who follow him say that the persons resurrected will use all their sense functions in the natural way, and then will die again and return to dust. Rabbi Meir Halevi[14] and Nahmanides are of the opinion that after resurrection, the persons in question will live as long as their natural capacity permits them, and then their bodies will be transmuted by purification and will become like the body of Elijah. And thenceforth they will continue to exist as body and soul, but will no longer use any sense functions, will not eat or drink or die and will remain forever without eating and drinking. It seems too that this latter is the opinion of some of the Rabbis of the Talmud, for they say[15] that the righteous whom God will resurrect will not return to dust.

Although this opinion seems strange, nevertheless it may be believed, since the mind can conceive it and experience testifies in its favor, for Moses lived forty days and forty nights without eating and drinking, though Moses did not exist forever in his body, since he died when his time came. They hold that the individual will exist forever, and prove their point from Elijah. The best solution in this and similar cases is the answer R. Joshua ben Hananiah gave to the Alexandrians—"When they come to life again, we will consult about the matter."[16]

An important question in connection with the resurrection is whether it embraces the whole world, as some nations think, or the whole of our nation, or only a few of them. It is a matter which is not clearly alluded to in Scripture. The expression in Daniel:[17] "And many of them that sleep in the dust of the earth shall awake," if it refers to the resurrection, indicates that not the whole world, nor the whole of our nation, nor even the majority of them, will be resurrected, but only a few. For the word "many" does not denote the majority of those that sleep in the dust, but only a few, like the expression: "And many from among the peoples of the land became Jews,"[18] which does not signify a majority of the peoples of the land, but only a few—three or five or ten or a hundred or a thousand, for example. Another similar expression is: "Many will entreat the favour of the liberal man."[19] Moreover our Rabbis say:[20] "The power of rain is for the righteous as well as the wicked, the resurrection of the dead is for the perfectly righteous only."

If we say that the entire world will be resurrected, or the whole of our people, i.e. that they will all come back to life and stand in judgment on the day announced for the judgment of the world, and that the righteous will remain forever enjoying delight, while the wicked will live forever and suffer, then the passage in Daniel does not refer to resurrection, but must be understood in the way in which some literalists interpret it, as referring to the exaltation of the lowly nation in the days of the Hasmoneans or in the days of the Messiah. At that time, they say, the lowly nation, or many of the survivors, who are like those who sleep in the dust, will awake and rise to a degree which will be permanent and from which the nation will not again descend, but which it will occupy forever; while the other nations and their wicked men will always remain low and subdued under Israel: "Some to everlasting life, and some to reproaches and everlasting abhorrence."[21]

Some of the later writers confirm the opinion of these commentators by saying that the incident of the dead being revived by Ezekiel took place in a prophetic vision, as we read: "The hand of the Lord was upon me, and the Lord carried me out in a spirit . . ."[22] The whole chapter is an allegory, typifying the misery of the Israelitish people in the Babylonian exile, where they were like dead men buried and devoid of all hope. But at the time of the second temple, in the days of the Hasmoneans, they rose again to a high degree, and rooted out the worship of idols. Then all those who came up from the Babylonian exile recognized and knew that the Lord is God. This is expressed in the biblical text in the words: "These bones are the whole house of Israel; behold, they say: Our bones are dried up, and our hope is lost; we are clean cut off."[23] And at the end he says: "Behold, I will open your graves, and cause you to come up out of your graves, O My people; and I will bring you into the land of Israel."[24] All this is an allusion to the return from captivity and settlement in the holy land, which led the Israelites to acknowledge God, as we read further: "And ye shall know that I am the Lord, when I have opened your graves, and caused you to come up out of your graves . . . and I will put My spirit in you, and ye shall live, and I will place you in your own land . . ."[25]

This is also the final opinion of the Gemara:[26] "R. Judah says: It is really (*beẹ̄met*) an allegory." It is true that there is a dispute concerning the matter in the Gemara, where some one says: "I am a descendant of those people and these are the phylacteries which my great-grandfather left me," but this is merely a hyperbole, for it is an accepted rule that the expression 'really' (*beëmet*) indicates that the statement for which it vouches is authoritative.[27] If, then, the passage in Daniel above mentioned does not refer to resurrection, then it is possible that resurrection embraces the whole world or the entire Jewish people, but there is no allusion to it in the Bible. The verse: "Awake and sing, ye that dwell in the dust,"[28] has the same meaning as: "He raiseth up the poor out of the dust,"[29] and other passages. The belief in resurrection is therefore merely traditional, and the verse: "I kill and I make alive; I have wounded, and I heal,"[30] concerning which the Rabbis say that just as the wounding and the healing concern the same person so the killing and the making alive also concern the same person,[31] is not a *promise* of resurrection, but a statement that God is able to do this thing.

But even if we say that resurrection is for the purpose of rewarding the body, which suffered pain in the service of God, and that it is appropriate, in view of God's justice, to reward the identical thing that did the service and punish the same thing that was guilty of disobedience and not something else (though this is not a good argument, because punishment is inflicted upon the transgressor and not upon the instrument—we do not punish the sword, but the homicide), at any rate it follows that the resurrection will not take place at the time of the Messiah (according to the one who says that there is no difference between the present day and the Messianic age except freedom from political subjection)[32] and that only a few persons will enjoy it at that time, like Moses and Aaron and others, who will rise up at that time miraculously to publish to the world the belief in God. The main resurrection will take place on the day of judgment and it will embrace the whole Jewish people or the greater part thereof, or the whole world or the greater part thereof, for they all deserve reward and punishment.

But this opinion is hard to accept. For if we say that the body will be resurrected in order to be rewarded for the pain it endured, and that it will enjoy pleasure forever without eating and drinking, and will not change from day to day as our bodies now change, the question is: which body will rise at the time of the resurrection? The body of man changes continually from day to day with the food that comes in from outside. There would have to rise with any individual, say Reuben, any number of bodies belonging to the different periods of his life, so that they may all enjoy the pleasure. And if we say that Reuben will rise with a matter and a temperament similar to his original temperament, in order that his soul may dwell in that matter and temperament, and that this matter, being similar to the original matter, may enjoy pleasure, as we said above in the name of R. Aaron Halevi,[33] then the divine justice which, on this theory, resurrects the dead in order to pay them for the trouble they suffered, fails, for it is not proper to reward Simeon for a service done by Reuben. We have already explained before[34] the thought that led to the idea that reward and punishment must include the body as well as the soul, and we made it clear[35] that reward and punishment are not in the same case. The nature of punishment is such that it requires the existence of a body or of something to confine the soul, so that the soul may receive its punishment therein, but there is no such necessity in reward. Hence Maimonides agrees that the main reward that God bestows upon man is conferred upon the soul and not upon the body.

It seems, therefore, that the purpose of resurrection is not in order to reward the body, but either to give the individual an opportunity to acquire greater perfection than he acquired before, prevented as he was by external hindrances, exile, poverty and the like, and not through evil choice or any condition in the individual himself; or to make known in the world the great power of God and to publish the true faith. In this case resurrection may be confined to the righteous alone, as the Rabbis say, and will take place in the Messianic age. We can find a confirmation of this view in Daniel, where we read: "But go thou thy way till the end be; and thou shalt rest, and shalt stand up to thy lot, at the end of the days."[36] The word "end" (*kez*) when used without qualification, applies to the redemption from exile. "And thou shalt rest," means that he will die before the end. "And shalt stand up," alludes to the resurrection which will take place in the Messianic age, and which will be for the perfectly righteous only. And if we say that "end" refers to death, which is "the end of all flesh,"[37] the words: "shalt stand up," would likewise denote a promise that he will live again in the resurrection. For if he were thinking of the "world to come" after death, he could not say that after he rests he will stand up to the lot at the end of the days, there being no connection between the end of days and the world to come. There is no doubt, therefore, that the text refers to the resurrection of the righteous in the Messianic age.

But there is no reference in the Bible to the general resurrection, which will take place on the day of judgment. The passage in the Bible: "I will gather all nations, and will bring them down into the valley of Jehoshaphat; and I will enter into judgment with them there for My people and for My heritage Israel,"[38] does not refer to resurrection at all, as we can see from the context. This resurrection, therefore, is believed in as a result of tradition only. This is the best interpretation of these matters that I have selected.

Those who say that at the time of the resurrection the bodies will have everlasting delight or everlasting pain, without eating and drinking, and that they will not die again after resurrection in order that they may receive eternal reward or punishment for their deeds, and that this resurrection does not embrace the whole world, nor a majority, nor the whole Jewish people, nor yet a majority of them, but is limited to a few, the perfectly righteous men, can be compared to a person who affirms and denies a thing in the same breath without knowing it. For if the resurrection is intended for a few only and not for the rest, its purpose can not be to reward the body, but either to publish to the world the belief in God by means of the wonderful miracle that can be seen by every one, or to give the righteous man an opportunity to earn happiness and a degree of existence which he was not able to attain the first time on account of the yoke of the exile and the other troubles and hindrances which prevent a man from attaining the perfection of which his nature permits.

NOTES

1. I, 23, p. 184.
2. I, 22, p. 179.
3. I Kings 17, 22.
4. II Kings 4, 35.
5. Megillah 28a.
6. Lev. 26, 31.
7. Megillah 26b.
8. II Kings 13, 20.
9. Ex. 4, 17.
10. II Kings 4, 29.
11. Sanhedrin 91a.
12. Prov. 20, 27.
13. Hagigah 12b.
14. See above, p. 298, note 4.
15. Sanhedrin 92a.
16. Niddah 70b.
17. 12, 2.
18. Esth. 8, 17.
19. Prov. 19, 6.
20. Ta'anit 7a; ed. Malter, p. 39.
21. Dan. 12, 2.

22. Ezek. 37, 1.
23. Ibid. 11.
24. Ezek. 37, 12.
25. Ibid. 13–14.
26. Sanhedrin 92b.
27. Baba Mez'ia 60a.
28. Isa. 26, 19.
29. I Sam. 2, 8.
30. Deut. 32, 39.
31. Pesahim 68a.
32. Sanhedrin 99a.
33. See IV, 30, p. 300.
34. Ibid., p. 297.
35. See IV, ch. 33, end, p. 335.
36. Dan. 12, 13.
37. Gen. 6, 13.
38. Joel 4, 2.